Essential COBOL: A First Course in Structured

Essential COBOL: A First Course in Structured COBOL (ANSI 1985)

Raymond W. Norman
Senior Lecturer in Computing
Bristol Polytechnic

McGRAW-HILL BOOK COMPANY

London · New York · St Louis · San Francisco · Auckland · Bogotá · Caracas
Hamburg · Lisbon · Madrid · Mexico · Milan · Montreal · New Delhi
Panama · Paris · San Juan · São Paulo · Singapore · Sydney · Tokyo · Toronto

Published by
McGRAW-HILL Book Company (UK) Limited
SHOPPENHANGERS ROAD · MAIDENHEAD · BERKSHIRE · ENGLAND
TEL: 0628-23432; FAX: 0628-770224

British Library Cataloguing in Publication Data
Norman, Raymond W.
　Essential COBOL: a first course in structured
　COBOL (ANSI 1985).
　1. Computer systems. Programming languages.
　COBOL language
　I. Title
　005.133
ISBN 0–07–707233–2

Library of Congress Cataloging-in-Publication Data
Norman, Raymond W.
　Essential COBOL: a first course in structured
　COBOL (ANSI 1985) / Raymond W. Norman.
　　p.　cm.
　Includes indexes.
　ISBN 0–07–707233–2
　1. COBOL (Computer program language)
　2. Structured programming.　I. Title.
QA76.73.C25N67　　1990
005.13′3—dc20

Copyright © 1991 McGraw-Hill Book Company (UK) Limited. All rights reserved. No part of this publication may be reproduced, stored in a retrieval system, or transmitted, in any form or by any means, electronic, mechanical, photocopying, recording, or otherwise, without the prior permission of McGraw-Hill Book Company (UK) Limited.

1234 CL 9321

Typeset by Paston Press, Loddon, Norfolk
and printed and bound in Great Britain by Clays Ltd, St Ives plc

For my parents
Beryl, Bob, Edith and Harry

CONTENTS

Preface — xiii

Additional teaching materials — xv

Acknowledgements — xvii

PART 1 — 1

1 Introduction — 3
   1.1 History of COBOL — 3
   1.2 International standards — 4
   1.3 Advantages and disadvantages of COBOL — 5
   1.4 Virtual environments — 7
   1.5 Terminology — 9
   1.6 Language formats — 10
   1.7 Exercises — 13

2 Basic program structure — 14
   2.1 Four divisions — 14
   2.2 **Accept** and alphanumeric strings — 20
   2.3 **Display** and alphanumeric strings — 21
   2.4 Test before loops using **perform** — 23
   2.5 Alignment of numeric strings — 30
   2.6 Figurative constants — 31
   2.7 Conditional expressions — 33
   2.8 Records and level numbers — 42
   2.9 Exercises — 47

3 Data validation — **50**
   3.1 Alphabetic strings — 50
   3.2 Classes of data — 51
   3.3 Class tests — 52
   3.4 The **evaluate** statement — 53
   3.5 Reference modification — 64
         3.5.1 Using numeric literals — 64
         3.5.2 Using numeric data items — 66
   3.6 Case study: post3 (pattern matching) — 71
   3.7 Exercises — 76

4 Inter-program communication — **80**
   4.1 Basic terms — 80
   4.2 Use of data — 83
   4.3 Sample program containing two nested programs — 87
   4.4 Scope of program-names — 90
   4.5 Information hiding — 95
   4.6 Case study: post4 (nested programs) — 98
   4.7 Exercises — 101

5 Table-handling I — **103**
   5.1 Single-level tables — 103
   5.2 **Occurs** clause — 104
   5.3 Subscripts — 105
   5.4 **Redefines** clause — 106
   5.5 Multiple-level tables — 111
   5.6 Case study: tic1 (playing tic-tac-toe) — 116
   5.7 Exercises — 137

6 Text string manipulation — **140**
   6.1 **String** — 140
   6.2 **Unstring** — 151
   6.3 **Inspect** — 160
   6.4 Justification — 166
   6.5 Edit masks — 167
        6.5.1 Simple alphanumeric masks — 167
        6.5.2 Simple numeric masks — 168
   6.6 Case study: lim1 (limericks) — 168
   6.7 Exercises — 177

7 Processing text files — **179**
   7.1 File entries — 181
   7.2 File statements — 184
   7.3 Reading and displaying text files — 187
   7.4 Accepting and writing text records — 190
   7.5 Copying text files — 192

7.6	Creating new information from existing text files	193
7.7	Rewriting and extending text files	197
7.8	Case study: renum1 (numbering text files)	199
7.9	Exercises	202

8 Issues in program design – decision tables — 209
8.1	Limited entry decision tables	209
8.2	Evaluating lists of conditions	222
8.3	Case study: the triangle problem	224
8.4	Exercises	228

PART 2 — 231

9 Information representation I — 233
9.1	Natural numbers	233
9.2	Base numbers	235
9.3	Information codes	237
9.4	Accepting unsigned numbers	242
9.5	Accepting signed numbers	251
9.6	Accepting numbers with decimal points	261
9.7	Documentation for program accept3	266
9.8	Filters and mapping functions	269
9.9	Screen management	270
9.10	Exercises	275

10 Complex program structures — 277
10.1	Separate program compilation	277
10.2	**Copy** statement	287
10.3	**Initial** and **common** program attributes	289
10.4	**Global** and **external** data attributes	293
10.5	Case study: driver2 (testing screen-handling)	297
10.6	Exercises	302

11 Information representation II — 303
11.1	Level, class and category	303
11.2	Usage clause	307
11.3	Data validation and conversion	314
11.4	Case study: stock1 (validating numeric input)	316
11.5	Exercises	320

12 Programming calculations — 323
12.1	Size error phrases	323
12.2	Rounding option	325
12.3	Compute	325
12.4	Add	329

	12.5	Subtract	330
	12.6	Multiply	330
	12.7	Divide	331
	12.8	Exercises	332

13 Table-handling II — 337
	13.1	Indexing	337
	13.2	Search	339
	13.3	Search all	342
	13.4	Variable-length tables	346
	13.5	Case study: resist1 (resistor colour codes)	349
	13.6	Exercises	355

14 Sorting and merging files — 358
	14.1	Sort	360
		14.1.1 Input procedures	363
		14.1.2 Output procedures	367
	14.2	Merge	371
		14.2.1 Output procedures	373
	14.3	Exercises	376

15 Writing reports using control breaks — 378
	15.1	Algorithm design	378
	15.2	Program design	387
	15.3	Writing printed reports	393
	15.4	Exercises	395

16 Master file update — 397
	16.1	External transactions	399
	16.2	Algorithm design	402
	16.3	Internal transactions	404
	16.4	Program design	405
	16.5	Case study exercises	419

17 Indexed files — 421
	17.1	Sequential access	422
	17.2	Random access	424
	17.3	Dynamic access	426
	17.4	Case study: indtut1 (handling indexed files)	429
	17.5	Exercises	438

18 Additional COBOL features — **440**
    18.1 Modules — 440
    18.2 Statements — 441
    18.3 Files — 443
    18.4 Other — 444
    18.5 Case study: trans1 (a string translator written in COBOL-74) — 444
    18.6 Exercises — 455

APPENDICES — **457**

A Lists of reserved words — **458**
    A.1 Full list — 458
    A.2 General list – X3.23 — 460

B Glossary — **463**

C Instruction formats — **488**
    C.1 Full formats — 488
    C.2 General formats – X3.23 — 498

D ASCII codes — **536**

E VT terminals — **538**

Index to programs and files — **539**

Index to figures — **541**

Subject index — **545**

PREFACE

My aim in writing this book is to introduce COBOL as a modern data-processing language.

Essential COBOL introduces programming in COBOL as defined by the latest ANSI standard which was published in 1985. It does not attempt to use COBOL as a vehicle for teaching business studies or the business concepts that may motivate many commercial users of the language. Instead the book emphasizes general and practical examples that should appeal to a wide range of interests and should be accessible to the experience of the majority of readers.

This book presents the material needed for an introductory programming course. It assumes that the reader has an introductory knowledge of computing concepts. (For those who are fresh to computing the Glossary contains a full set of definitions for general terms as well as those specific to COBOL.)

Each chapter contains a number of Self-Check Questions. These are intended to be read as part of the text and provide a means of reviewing the implications of new material. Each chapter also introduces a number of sample programs which incorporate key features of the COBOL language. Most chapters include a case-study program that integrates material presented in that and previous chapters. These programs are intended to expose readers to programs that will stretch their interests beyond the usual student programming exercise. Each chapter ends with a set of graded general exercises that suggest ideas for new programs and a set of exercises that suggest enhancements to the case-study program. Therefore upon completion of the book students should have a solid grasp of COBOL that is grounded in a deep understanding of the nature of the language as well as a general knowledge of many approaches to program design, documentation, enhancement and maintenance.

The COBOL language has been in use for over 20 years. The latest standard COBOL includes within it most of the features from earlier standards. This benefits industrial users in that programs written many years ago will continue to be compiled by compilers conforming to the language standard. However, this is a mixed blessing for students because the standard itself is not a useful guide to good programming practice. Not only does it incorporate old features that are marked for deletion in the next standard but it also contains options in the general formats which in practice are rarely used as alternatives by experienced programmers working within a specific environment.

Furthermore, alternatives may not be supported by some compiler implementations, some features may give rise to different results in different implementations, and some extended features may be widely used in specific implementations even though they are not part of the standard language.

Therefore this text assumes that you are approaching COBOL with a fresh interest either as a new student following an introductory programming course or as an experienced programmer who is engaged in self-study and who wants to know the best that the revised language standard has to offer. Language features that have been superseded by improved features in the new standard are not presented. In particular, the text emphasizes the writing of standard portable programs.

The first half of the book begins with an extensive coverage of character-string manipulation through the use of simple interactive programs that have line-oriented accept and display statements. At the same time key concepts in data usage and record structure are introduced so that the reader develops a solid understanding of these areas before considering the more complex problems of data conversion.

In-line conditional statements and reference modification are also introduced in Part 1 so that the reader is able to create structured programs that manipulate strings in a clear and concise fashion.

Nested programs and parameter mechanisms are introduced at about the point where the source code of the sample programs begins to be longer than a single page of computer listing output. Thus the reader is encouraged to develop modular programs with local data from the start in contrast to the massive programs with global data pools that are typical of the past.

The second half of the book contains many of the features that teachers more commonly associate with former COBOL courses. This material should be better understood and more soundly incorporated into structured programs as a result of the initial spadework undertaken in the first half.

Throughout there is an emphasis on the essentials required for programming in COBOL. Therefore although the coverage is not exhaustive it is complete in two important senses. Firstly, those who master this material will be competent junior COBOL programmers who will be more modern in their approach to COBOL programming than those who have not as yet studied the new standard. Secondly, the essential foundation provided here will enable the reader to assimilate other features and facilities with confidence.

The programs were tested on a MicroVAX 3800 computer running under VAX/VMS 5.2 and using VAX COBOL Version 4.0. It is assumed that the reader has access to a high-level *validated** COBOL compiler such as VAX COBOL.

The programs have been written to be portable. Therefore I hope that they will find their way on to a variety of systems with little or no modification.

---

* Words in italics are defined in the Glossary.

ADDITIONAL TEACHING MATERIALS

The following materials are available to lecturers directly from the author:

1. *Case-study booklets.* Each case study includes material on user requirements, system designs, and program designs as well as program listings and a variety of exercises.
    Four case studies are available at present. Each consists of an A4 booklet suitable for local reproduction as well as source programs on magnetic media.
    (a) Multi-choice: Creates multiple-choice test papers from a master file of possible test questions. It also marks the answers from test papers and tabulates results. This case emphasizes table-handling, arithmetic operations, and report production.
    (b) Docopy: Concatenates text files into a single report file. The header and footer lines as well as the files for reporting are specified at run time. Docopy emphasizes the run-time control of files through the use of declaratives.
    (c) TTT: Plays a game of tic-tac-toe as either the first or second player. The program is an extensive exercise in heuristics and the design of algorithms.
    (d) CITE: Manages a multi-key bibliography. The program emphasizes interactive dialogue design and management of indexed files.

    It is hoped that further case studies will be available in the near future.
2. *Multiple-choice questions.* This material consists of an A4 booklet of over 500 multiple choice questions as well as a master text file of the questions on magnetic media. Papers can be created and the answers marked using the multi-choice case-study program.
3. *All tables, diagrams, and programs.* These are available as a set of A4 transparency masters that are suitable for local reproduction.
4. *Abridged version of the X3.23 ANSI standard.* This version is suitable for use by students who wish to compare the COBOL standard to particular implementations or who wish to study particular features in greater depth. It includes all of the general

background material pertinent to this text but excludes other materials and modules such as the Report Writer feature. It is available in single copies of loose-leaf A4 suitable for local reproduction or in bound A5 copies suitable for distribution to students.

5. *All programs printed in the book*. These are available as ASCII text files on the following magnetic media:
   - VAX/VMS $\frac{1}{2}$ inch transport tape (1600 BPI; BACKUP format)
   - VAX/VMS TK52 tape cartridge (BACKUP format)
   - IBM-PC compatible double-sided high-density $5\frac{1}{4}$ inch floppy disk.

   In addition the files can be transferred to you via the JANET network.

   Please direct enquiries for further information, price lists, and order forms to:

Ray Norman
Computer Studies and Mathematics
Bristol Polytechnic
Coldharbour Lane
Frenchay
Bristol BS16 1QY
England.

tel: 0272 656261 ext 2765
fax: 0272 657450
JANET: RW_NORMAN@UK.AC.BRISTOL-POLY.CSMVAX

ACKNOWLEDGEMENTS

I wish to acknowledge my sincere thanks to my colleagues who helped in bringing this project to life. David Coward and Craig Duffy read early drafts at a time when it was not entirely clear what was essential. David Coward also provided invaluable assistance in the construction of the multi-choice case study and provided many useful questions and examples. Chris Goodwin kindly produced the copy for the COBOL full formats.

I must also thank my students who provided so much helpful criticism in the classroom. They deserve special thanks for coping with drafts of materials during the various stages of production. In particular, Bruce Duncan proof-read many of the chapters and found many inconsistencies in the programs.

COBOL is an industry language and is not the property of any company or group of companies, or of any organization or group of organizations.

No warranty, expressed or implied, is made by any contributor or by the CODASYL COBOL Committee as to the accuracy and functioning of the programming system and language. Moreover, no responsibility is assumed by any contributor, or by the committee, in connection herewith.

The authors and copyright holders of the copyrighted materials used herein

FLOW-MATIC (trademark of Sperry Rand Corporation), Programming for the UNIVAC(R)I and II, Data Automation Systems copyrighted 1958, 1959, by Sperry Rand Corporation; IBM Commercial Translator Form No. F 28-8013, copyrighted 1959 by IBM; FACT, DSI 27A5260, copyrighted 1960 by Minneapolis-Honeywell

have specifically authorized the use of this material in whole or in part, in the COBOL specifications. Such authorization extends to the reproduction and use of COBOL specifications in programming manuals or similar publications.

VAX and VMS are registered trademarks of Digital Electric Corporation.

Ever since his first ecstasy or vision of Christminster and its possibilities, Jude had meditated much and curiously on the probable sort of process that was involved in turning the expressions of one language into those of another. He concluded that a grammar of the required tongue would contain, primarily, a rule, prescription, or clue of the nature of a secret cipher, which, once known, would enable him, by merely applying it, to change at will all words of his own speech into those of the foreign one. . . . Thus he assumed that the words of the required language were always to be found somewhere latent in the words of the given language by those who had the art to uncover them, such art being furnished by the books aforesaid.

When, therefore, having noted that the packet bore the postmark of Christminster, he cut the string, opened the volumes, and turned to the Latin grammar, which chanced to come uppermost, he could scarcely believe his eyes.

The book was an old one – thirty years old, soiled, scribbled wantonly over with a strange name in every variety of enmity to the letterpress, and marked at random with dates twenty years earlier than his own day. But this was not the cause of Jude's amazement. He learnt for the first time that there was no law of transmutation, as in his innocence he had supposed (there was, in some degree, but the grammarian did not recognize it), but that every word in both Latin and Greek was to be individually committed to memory at the cost of years of plodding.

Jude flung down the books, lay backward along the broad trunk of the elm, and was an utterly miserable boy for the space of a quarter of an hour. . . . The charm he had supposed in store for him was really a labour like that of Israel in Egypt.

Jude the Obscure by Thomas Hardy, Chapter 4.

Part 1

1
INTRODUCTION

This chapter gives a brief history of COBOL, discusses its advantages and disadvantages as a programming language, and introduces many of the concepts relevant to COBOL programming.

1.1 HISTORY OF COBOL

In May, 1959 representatives from computer manufacturers, the United States government, industry, and education created an organization known as the COnference on DAta SYstem Languages (CODASYL).

The goal of CODASYL was to create a programming language that fulfilled the commercial data-processing requirements of government and industry alike. They decided that this new language should be:

- problem-oriented
- machine-independent
- capable of change and amendment
- written as simple English or pseudo-English
- concrete and avoiding symbolism as far as possible.

By April of the following year CODASYL had published the specification for a COmmon Business Oriented Language (COBOL) under the leadership of Commander Grace Hopper of the United States Navy.

Over the years the language has evolved through three main standards. The first standard specification was published in 1968 and is now known as 'First Standard COBOL'.

This standard was superseded in 1974 by a second standard. At present the majority of existing COBOL programs conform to this standard which is now known as 'Second Standard COBOL'.

The latest major development in the history of COBOL occurred in 1985 with the publication of the third standard. It is now this version of the language which is correctly referred to as COBOL.

This book uses the terms COBOL-68, COBOL-74, and COBOL to differentiate between these three standards.

1.2 INTERNATIONAL STANDARDS

The COBOL language is defined by the American National Standards Institute in the following publication:

ANS for Information Systems – Programming Language-COBOL (ANSI X3.23-1985)

This standard was adopted by the International Standards Organization in 1985 as ISO standard 1989.

The COBOL language definition is based on the concept of functional processing modules. The full language contains 11 modules as shown in Fig. 1.1. Of these seven are called required modules because intermediate and high conforming implementations of the language require them.

COBOL incorporates the concept of levels of functionality. There are two possible levels for nine of the modules and only one level for the other two. Level 1, which is the lower level, always has less functionality than level 2, even though it may include many of the same general features. For example, the nucleus contains the display statement which among its many uses enables a program to write data to the screen of a terminal. At level 1 the display statement only allows the writing of single lines to the screen. At level 2 a

Required modules	*Levels*
Nucleus	1 or 2
Sequential Input–Output	1 or 2
Relative Input–Output	1 or 2
Indexed Input–Output	1 or 2
Inter-Program communication	1 or 2
Sort–Merge	1 only
Source text manipulation	1 or 2

Optional modules	
Report writer	1 only
Communication	1 or 2
Debug	1 or 2
Segmentation	1 or 2

Figure 1.1 COBOL's functional modules

	Required modules							Optional modules			
	NUC	SEQ	REL	INX	IPC	SRT	STM	RPW	COM	DEB	SEG
High	2	2	2	2	2	1	2	−1	−12	−12	−12
Inter	1	1	1	1	1	1	1	−1	−12	−12	−12
Low	1	1	–	–	1	–	–	–	–	–	–

A dash (–) means that the module is not required

2 * 2 * 3 * 3 * 2 * 2 * 3 * 2 * 3 * 3 * 3 = 23 328 possibilities

Figure 1.2 Conforming COBOL implementations

portion of a line can be written with one display statement that uses the no advancing option. This statement can then be followed by a further display statement to complete the line. (The standard requires that level 2 for a module contains all of the functionality of level 1. In other words, level 1 is always a subset of level 2.)

In order for an implementation of the language to conform to the minimum standard it must include at least the nucleus, the sequential input–output, and the inter-program communication modules at level 1.

Other implementations can be created that conform to the standard by using the higher level of the three required modules or by adding any of the other modules at either level. In theory this means that it is possible to create many thousands of different implementations within the standard. (See Fig. 1.2.)

In practice most implementations can be classified as low, intermediate, or high levels of implementation. The fact that an implementation is low or intermediate does not mean that high-level features are excluded. For example, it is possible to have a compiler that includes a level 1 nucleus with a display statement that is at level 2. The module as a whole will be classed as level 1 because other level 2 features are omitted.

The coherence of many COBOL implementations can be obscured by the inclusion of system-dependent features that are not defined by COBOL. For example, the display statement may be extended to allow data to be written to the screen of a terminal using line and column coordinates. The worst case occurs when a feature that is defined at level 2 is omitted and replaced by a similar system-dependent feature. In this circumstance a supplier can advertise conformance with the COBOL standard (at level 1) even though for most purposes programmers will be forced to use system-dependent features. The moral of this tale is: conformance to the general standard is not a sufficient guarantee.

This book introduces the main features of high-level COBOL. It does not contain material on any of the optional modules. It avoids the use of system-dependent features except to show how these should be managed as part of an overall strategy for program design.

1.3 ADVANTAGES AND DISADVANTAGES OF COBOL

It is often stated that COBOL has the advantages and disadvantages which are summarized in Fig. 1.3.

Advantages

1. Syntax and reserved words based on English
2. Machine-independence which thereby promotes software portability
3. Useful features for data editing and file handling
4. Extended for database processing
5. Continually subject to update
6. Significant international investment in programs
7. Increasingly widespread microcomputer implementations

Disadvantages

1. Lengthy coding
2. Limited mathematical capabilities
3. Lack of standards for screen management
4. Standard allows too many alternative features
5. Standard does not define certain crucial areas of program behaviour, e.g. numeric input from the keyboard

Figure 1.3 Advantages and disadvantages of COBOL

Clearly one person's advantage is another's disadvantage. For example, the fact that COBOL's syntax and reserved words are based on English gives the language the appearance of being non-technical. It therefore may appear to be attractive to many who wish to program without the need to cope with the apparently more rigorous demands of languages such as FORTRAN or Pascal. Such hopes are to a large extent an illusion because in the final analysis all procedural languages must cope with the rigours of accurate specification for the same basic model of computation. Therefore if a program must be a correct logical statement, then surely it is a disadvantage to base it upon a natural language such as English which is likely to be long-winded and ambiguous?

Arguments such as these are a popular pastime among programmers, although in most cases the debate is superficial and inconclusive. The main reason for this is that the decision on whether or not one language is better than another is largely a matter of whether or not it has the features you require for the job at hand. For example, an application requiring complex data conversions and file handling might well be better suited to COBOL than Pascal. A second point is that many issues concerning language quality are best decided comparatively even if the comparison is with an abstract language. The fact that most programmers are fluent in one language only and generally biased in its favour does not lead to fruitful enquiry.

The crucial issue for COBOL is the matter of conformance to standards. Many COBOL features are truly standard. By this we mean that programs which incorporate them will produce the same functional behaviour on different computer systems provided that they have been compiled on the system using a validated compiler conforming to the COBOL standard. Thus the standard allows programmers to develop programs on one computer system and implement them on another. Maintaining the independence of source programs is crucial for those who wish to write programs for sale to the public or who wish to protect themselves from dependence on hardware and software suppliers.

Some features of COBOL are not truly standard in that compiler implementors may be free:

- to define the functional behaviour of certain statements in the running program
- to use alternative syntax in the source program.

These two loopholes work to the advantage of large suppliers of computer systems because most programmers know their particular dialect of COBOL better than they know the standard. This may be partly due to the fact that the manuals with which they are supplied by manufacturers do not take great care to highlight the peculiarities of their particular dialect. The result is that most COBOL programs that have been written to date are not fully portable and the organizations which own these programs are dependent on the particular compiler supplied with their systems.

This state of affairs also works against the particular interests of students of COBOL and those who wish to teach the language in accordance with general programming principles. A casual glance at the popular teaching texts reveals that particular dialects are being taught as though they were the common standard in some universal sense even though the programs they give rise to are not written in standard COBOL and are not portable between compilers. The approach adopted in this book is to teach the standard and to focus upon a regular and common subset of features when there are alternatives.

1.4 VIRTUAL ENVIRONMENTS

A *virtual environment* is a collection of resources that create a usable system at a particular level within the computer system. These levels are layered one on top of another. A virtual environment at any particular level uses the lower levels to create its environment.

At the core of all systems is a machine. By using the machine the operating system creates an operating environment with a specific set of related facilities and functions. A

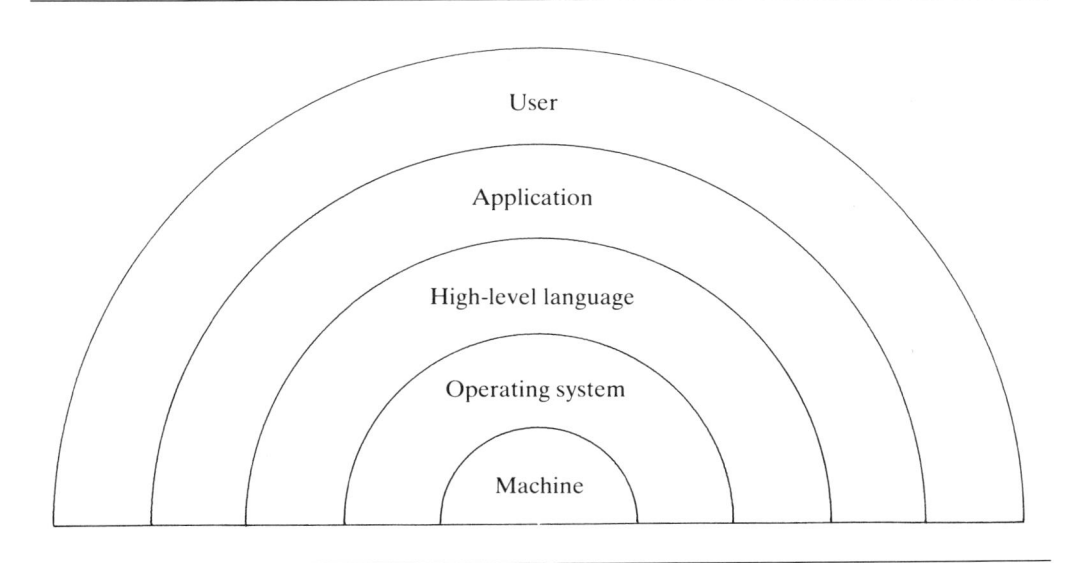

Figure 1.4 Virtual environments

virtual environment at the operating system level typically includes a command interpreter, process management, and file management.

At the next level a compiler or other form of language translator creates a virtual programming environment. It also depends on the lower levels. It is here that the programmer creates applications which are defined in high-level languages such as COBOL, Ada, or LISP. This level is implemented by the compiler writer who is referred to as the *implementor* in standard COBOL.

At the next higher level programs in a language such as COBOL create a virtual environment for the benefit of the user. This level is implemented by the application programmer.

Each level is conceptually distinct from those contained beneath it. Virtual environments at a certain level may or may not allow some access to lower levels. The long-term trend in computing is towards reducing direct access to lower levels by providing those features and facilities required by an environment in a form appropriate to its level. Thus programmers increasingly demand language translation systems that protect them from a need to know about the implementation details of underlying operating systems and users increasingly demand applications that provide a common interface that is portable from computer to computer.

Imagine a person who has decided to buy a spreadsheet program. One program may be chosen rather than another based on the features and facilities it implements as a 'spreadsheet language'. Buying the program involves a decision to try to fit the form of the virtual environment implemented by the spreadsheet program into the context of the work environment. If the right program has been chosen it will enrich the work environment.

But imagine another person who has decided to **write a spreadsheet program**. One compiler may be preferred to another, depending on its features and facilities. The context is that of writing a spreadsheet program and the form is the language features and facilities provided by the language compiler. A poor choice of language or compiler may result in the production of a poor quality program with an inadequate user interface. A failure of this sort results in the production of a poor quality virtual environment for the user of the application.

Imagine a person who has decided to write a compiler for a programming language. One operating system and computer may be chosen rather than another. The quality of the final compiler will in large part depend upon whether or not the operating system offers the features and facilities required by the language in question, and this in turn depends on whether or not these can be realized in terms of the physical computer.

In each of these cases a virtual environment is required within a context. The ultimate success of the virtual environment will depend on:

- the quality of its interface in implementing the required features and facilities at that level
- its ability to co-operate with other virtual environments at the same level towards the achievement of overall goals
- its ability to hide implementation details that are more appropriate to lower levels.

A standard COBOL compiler provides a wide range of standard features and facilities.

These enable a programmer to create application programs that can implement many different types of virtual environment.

SELF-CHECK QUESTION

Q   What would normally be included in the virtual environment used by a COBOL programmer?

A   A COBOL compiler and a text editor for producing the text of programs are the basic tools required. In addition, there is likely to be other systems software such as a linker which is a tool that can combine two or more programs into a single program. It is common practice for the programmer to have access to the command language of the operating system for tasks such as file management. (This access to the lower level is becoming less frequent with the growth in new tools that co-ordinate the whole of the program production process from a single common interface.)

1.5 TERMINOLOGY

COBOL terminology has evolved over the years in parallel with the development of computer science as a discipline. The tendency for COBOL not to remove features but nevertheless to incorporate new ones also applies to the language's terminology. In consequence the language now contains many synonyms or near synonyms that can be confusing to the beginner and expert alike.

One key area of terminology should be mentioned at the outset. COBOL now uses the newer terms variable and identifier as well as the older terms data item and data-name. In most cases the terms variable and data item are interchangeable. However, this is not the case with data-name and identifier. The term data-name refers to the name given to a piece of data when it is declared in the data division of a program. The term identifier refers to a reference to data in the procedure division of a program.* These two divisions between them constitute the bulk of a program and provide in COBOL a clear separation between the declaration of data on the one hand and the manipulation of data by program statements on the other.

There are five rules for forming user-defined words such as data-names. These are listed in Fig. 1.5. In addition, it should be noted that standard COBOL considers lower and upper case letters to be equivalent.

Appendix A contains a full list of the COBOL reserved words that are used in this book as well as the complete list from the X3.23 standard. In addition, Appendix B is a Glossary of important COBOL terms, computing terms and general concepts.

COBOL reserved words are printed in **boldface** where they first appear in the text.

---

* Data-names are not necessarily unique. When data is referenced in statements in the procedure division this is done by using an identifier. In most cases the identifier and data-name are the same. However, when a data-name does not imply a unique reference, a complex identifier is constructed using the data-name and other elements. Thus identifiers and data-names are not always necessarily the same. These issues are discussed in detail in later chapters.

1. User-defined words can be from 1 to 30 characters long.
2. Upper- and lower-case letters 'A' ... 'Z' and 'a' ... 'z', the ten digits '0' ... '9' and the hyphen '-' can be used.
3. The first character must be a letter.
4. The last character must be a letter or a digit.
5. *Reserved* words such as 'division' cannot be used.

Figure 1.5 Rules for forming user-defined words

Many of these words have entries in the glossary. Other terms and concepts are printed in *italics* when they are first introduced. They are also in the Glossary. You should refer to the Glossary regularly.

SELF-CHECK QUESTIONS

Q   Use the rules for forming user-defined words, refer to the lists of reserved words in Appendix A, and determine which of the following are not valid user-defined words:

(a)	x	(b)	space	(c)	variable
(d)	ABACUS	(e)	reader-	(f)	flag
(g)	Oboy	(h)	top-o'the-day	(i)	stop-run
(j)	22	(k)	MyVaR	(l)	i-1
(m)	THE+VAR	(n)	pic	(o)	my.text

A   Valid user-defined words: `x, variable, ABACUS, flag, stop-run, MyVar, i-1`
Reserved words: `space, pic`
Invalid words: `reader-, Oboy, top-o'the-day, 22, THE+VAR, my.text`
Note in particular that `i-1` is a single user-defined word and not the arithmetic expression i − 1. (Arithmetic operators must always be separated by spaces in COBOL.)

Q   Are the following user-defined words equivalent?

`George   george   GEORGE   GeOrGe`

A   Yes. Upper- and lower-case letters are equivalent when used to construct user-defined words.

1.6 LANGUAGE FORMATS

The *syntax* of the COBOL language is described by general formats. These are reproduced in Appendix C. These general formats have been included to save you the necessity of referring to the X3.23 publication. They will also be a help in assessing the formats that may be supplied with a particular compiler to determine how closely they conform to the standard.

The formats used in writing this book have been termed 'full formats'. They are also reproduced in Appendix C. These full formats include all of the features presented in the text and are a handy student reference. They are called full formats because they describe fully the COBOL syntax taught in this text and because they provide a full coverage of the features which they describe.

These full formats are easier to understand than the general formats for three reasons. Firstly, they omit alternative syntactical constructions in favour of those which are easy to understand and most widely used. Secondly, they omit many optional reserved words which make the syntax unnecessarily complicated. Thirdly, they use subset definitions as a way of simplifying the syntax from the general formats. You should understand a full format completely before attempting to understand its general format.

Simple formats are used within the main body of the text to present those features of the language that are under immediate discussion within a chapter. Their advantage is that they focus on the particular matter at hand by defining a commonly used form within the language. The simple formats are subsets of the full formats.

All three formats use:

- square brackets, [ ], to indicate that an option can be omitted
- braces, { }, to indicate that one of the enclosed options must be used
- ellipsis, ..., to indicate that the previous construction can be repeated
- choice indicators, {| |}, to indicate that one or more options must be selected but that each option can appear only once.

For example, the full syntax for the compute statement is:

```
 compute {identifier-1 [rounded]}... = arithmetic-expression-1
[{| size error     statement-1 |}]
 {| not size error statement-2 |}
 end-compute
```

This tells us that the reserved word compute must be followed by a list of one or more identifiers and that any of the identifiers can be followed by the reserved word rounded. The list is ended by an equals sign which is then followed by an arithmetic expression. The next three lines can be skipped entirely. It is legal to include line 2 and line 3 or line 2 only or line 3 only. In any of these three cases then line 4 must be included. (The full use of the compute statement will not be covered until much later in the book. For the moment you should concentrate on how the formats are used to specify order.)

SELF-CHECK QUESTIONS

The following questions give rules for the construction of a meal. Each contains a sentence and a format based on the COBOL format conventions. Analyse the sentence and then determine whether or not it is a true statement according to the syntax rules of the format.

(Each keyword in a format only entitles you to one serving!)

Q The meal is mandatory and the starter is always followed by the maincourse and this is always followed by dessert.

$$\{\text{starter} \quad \text{maincourse} \quad \text{dessert}\}$$

A Yes. The braces imply that everything within must be selected once from left to right.

Q Maincourse is always followed only by a single dessert.

$$[\text{maincourse} \ \{\text{dessert}\}\ldots]$$

A No. The braces imply that there must be at least one dessert but the ellipsis allows further desserts. Therefore maincourse is always followed by one or more desserts. It is also possible to skip the meal entirely because the whole format is surrounded by square brackets.

Q Maincourse can be followed immediately by two coffees.

$$[\text{maincourse} \ [\text{dessert}] \ [\text{coffee}]]$$

A No. There is no ellipsis in the diagram. Therefore if there is a maincourse it can be followed by 0 or 1 desserts and afterwards by 0 or 1 coffees.

Q Maincourse can be skipped in favour of a coffee.

$$[\text{maincourse} \ \{\text{dessert}\} \ [\text{coffee}]]$$

A No. The whole meal can be skipped but if you have the meal it must consist of a main course and a dessert and 0 or more coffees. (It is more common to leave out the braces when there is no ellipsis.)

Q Coffee and dessert can be taken in any order after the maincourse.

$$\text{maincourse} \ \begin{Bmatrix} \text{coffee} \\ \text{dessert} \end{Bmatrix} \ldots$$

A Yes. The ellipsis implies a reselection of either keyword from within the braces. At a minimum you must have either one coffee or one dessert.

Q Does the following diagram mean the same thing?

$$\text{maincourse} \ \begin{Bmatrix} \text{coffee} \ldots \\ \text{dessert} \ldots \end{Bmatrix}$$

A No. It implies that the maincourse is followed either by 1 or more coffees in succession or by 1 or more desserts in succession. It is not possible to alternate between the two.

Q Does the following diagram mean the same thing?

$$\text{maincourse} \ \left\{ \left| \begin{array}{c} \text{coffee} \\ \text{dessert} \end{array} \right| \right\}$$

A No. It implies that the maincourse is followed by a coffee and a dessert or a coffee only or a dessert only.

1.7 EXERCISES

1. What does the acronym COBOL stand for?
2. Why was COBOL created?
3. Name three advantages of COBOL and explain why these may also be considered in certain circumstances to be disadvantages.
4. Name two disadvantages of COBOL and explain why these may also be considered in certain circumstances to be advantages.
5. Is COBOL a machine-dependent language?
6. By what name is COBOL-74 now officially known?
7. Is it more correct to refer to the current COBOL standard as COBOL or as COBOL-85?

2
BASIC PROGRAM STRUCTURE

By the end of this chapter you will be able to understand and amend a program that echoes data from the keyboard to the screen of a terminal. In addition, you will have learned many basic COBOL terms, used simple forms of the **accept** and **display** statements, and constructed a *test before loop* using the **perform** statement.

2.1 FOUR DIVISIONS

Noddy1 (Fig. 2.1) is almost the shortest COBOL program that can be written. It simply displays two lines of *text* on the terminal screen. Although its purpose is minimal it provides an opportunity to look at some of the basic elements of program construction.

The first executable statement in the program is the display statement on line 11. It causes a *string* of text to be written to the screen followed by a RETURN character. (The RETURN positions the cursor to the beginning of the next line in preparation for further statements.)

The display statement on line 12 outputs a second string of text and another RETURN.

The **stop run** statement on line 13 terminates the program by returning control to the operating system.

The output from noddy1 is two lines of text:

```
Hello
I am Noddy
```

Double quotes (") are used in COBOL as text *delimiters*. Strings of characters within

```
 1 identification division.
 2 program-id. noddy1.
 3*Purpose: Display a two-line message.
 4
 5 environment division.
 6
 7 data division.
 8
 9 procedure division.
10 para1.
11     display "Hello"
12     display "I am Noddy"
13     stop run.
14
15 end program noddy1.
```

Figure 2.1 Program noddy1

delimiters such as those displayed by noddy1 are called *nonnumeric literals*. "Hello" is a nonnumeric literal.

Noddy1 will be used as a basis for creating more programs in the next few chapters. Although we need to examine the whole of the program in detail only lines 2, 11, 12 and 15 will need to be changed in order to create many other simple programs. The other lines in the program will be used as a *template*.

COBOL programs consist of four **divisions** and an **end program header**.

The **identification division** contains the name of the program in the **program-id paragraph**. Each new program must be given a name in this paragraph. The program name is a user-defined word.

The **environment division** contains information about the virtual environment external to the program. Program Noddy1 and all of the programs in the first six chapters use the default environment. Therefore there are no entries required in this division at present.

The last two divisions are the largest and most complex parts of most COBOL programs. However, in our first example the **data division** is empty because we have not defined any data.

The **procedure division** contains a program's procedures. The simplest form of procedure is the paragraph. Line 10 declares a single paragraph called para1 which contains three executable statements on lines 11 to 13. (All of the programs in Part 1 are single paragraph programs defined in this way. We will defer discussion of the paragraph feature and COBOL procedures in general until Part 2.)

A COBOL program always begins its execution with the first statement in the first procedure which in this case is the display statement at line 11. The execution of *successive* statements then proceeds until the stop run statement is encountered.

The last line in the program is the end program header. It marks the end of the program text for the compiler and is not itself an executable statement. The program name that it gives must always be the same as the name in the program-id paragraph at the top of the program.

In general the four divisions can be subdivided into *sections*, sections into *paragraphs*,

```
:                          :     :                 :                    :
Margin                  Margin Margin           Margin               Margin
L                          C     A                 B                    R
:                          :     :                 :                    :
: 1 : 2 : 3 : 4 : 5 : 6 : 7 : 8 : 9 : 10 : 11 : 12 : 13 : .... : n :
----------------------------  ---  ---------------  --------------------
      Sequence Number Area      :         Area A              Area B
                                :
                         Indicator Area
```

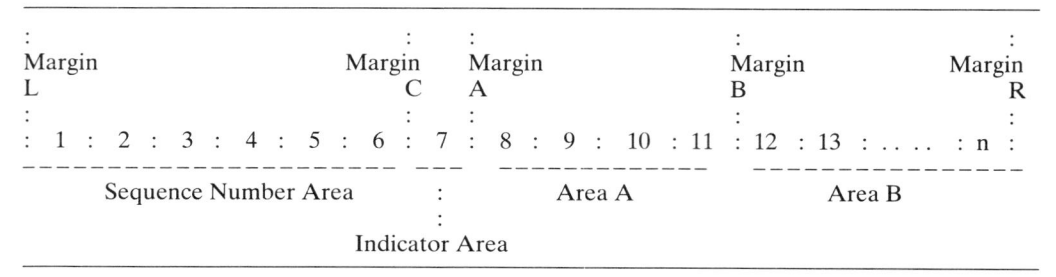

Figure 2.2 Reference format for source code lines

paragraphs into *sentences*, sentences into *statements*, statements into *phrases*, and phrases into *words* or other *elements*. However, the rules for doing this within the language are by no means fully consistent. Therefore these subdivisions and the rules which govern their use will only be introduced as they are needed.

There is a column specific layout for the lines in a COBOL program. This layout is called the *reference format* (Fig. 2.2). There are four areas to the source code line. These are bounded by five margins as shown in Fig. 2.2. The numbers represent character positions on a line. For example, *area A* begins in column 8 and ends in column 11.

The sequence number area is used to write the sequence numbers of the source lines. The sample programs in this book include sequence numbers so that lines from the programs can be identified easily.

When you write COBOL programs you can put six spaces in this area. (Some COBOL implementations such as VAX COBOL may allow you to omit the sequence number area altogether. However, this a non-standard format.)

The indicator area may contain a special character. The two most common indicators are the asterisk, '*', and the oblique '/'. The asterisk causes the rest of the line to be treated as a comment. The oblique in column 7 must not be followed by other characters on the line. It causes any listing produced by the compiler to begin on a new page from this point onwards.

Area A is reserved as the start for major elements of a program such as the four division headers.

Area B holds minor elements of a program such as individual statements. It is of a width determined by the implementation. (It will always extend up to and including column 72 but in many cases it may be longer.)

SELF-CHECK QUESTIONS

Q How many executable statements does program noddy1 contain?
A Three. These are the two display statements and the stop run statement.

Q Why is the environment division empty in noddy1?
A Because the program uses the default environment. (This default includes the displaying of display strings on the terminal screen.)

Q What are the four divisions of a COBOL program?
A Identification, environment, data and procedure.

Q Must the data division header be followed by a blank line?
A No. Blank lines are always skipped by the compiler. They are included in a program to make it easier to read.

Q Is line 15 part of para1?
A No. Only lines 11 through to 13 are part of para1. Line 15 marks the end of the text of the program.

Q Which line in noddy1 is a comment?
A Line 3. This is because it has an asterisk in column 7.

Q What is the effect of placing a '/' in column 7?
A The output listing from the COBOL compiler will start printing the program on a new page from this point. This feature is useful in long programs so that major parts of the program begin on a new page.

Q Is it possible to create comments that are more than one line long?
A Yes, but every line must contain an asterisk in column 7. (Then, in effect, the compiler treats every line as a separate comment.)

Q Is it legal to use reserved words such as display within comments?
A Yes. Any combination of printable characters can be used in a comment. Therefore it is possible to turn lines containing COBOL statements into comments by writing an asterisk in column 7.

Q Can a comment line contain a comment in columns 1 to 6?
A No. This is the sequence number area. It should contain either a sequence number or blanks.

Program echo1 in Fig. 2.3 uses *data items* and takes input from the keyboard. It begins by inviting the user to type a single character.

Lines 15 and 17 display 2 lines of text on the screen and force the cursor to the beginning of a third line.

Line 18 causes control to be transferred to the keyboard. The user may then enter a character terminated by a RETURN. When the user strikes the RETURN key, control returns to the program and the character which the user typed is made available to the program in the k1-char data item.

Line 20 moves the character value in k1-char to s2-char. Therefore immediately after the execution of the **move** statement both data items will hold the same character value.

Lines 8 to 11 show the data division with a **working-storage section**. This section is used to define any data items that must be allocated storage by the compiler and that might be referenced by statements in the procedure division.

The basic data structure in COBOL is the **record**. The simplest form of record is that for an *elementary* data item defined at the 01 level. Lines 10 and 11 above are the data entries that define these records. They define k1-char and s2-char each as one character elementary data items.

```
 1 identification division.
 2 program-id. echo1.
 3*Purpose: Accept one character from the keyboard.
 4*         Echo it to the screen.
 5
 6 environment division.
 7
 8 data division.
 9 working-storage section.
10 01  k1-char   pic x.
11 01  s2-char   pic x.
12
13 procedure division.
14 para1.
15     display "echo1 begins"
16
17     display "Input a character"
18     accept k1-char
19
20     move k1-char to s2-char
21     display s2-char
22
23     display "echo1 ends"
24     stop run.
25
26 end program echo1
```

Figure 2.3 Program echo1

Each *data entry* includes a name. These names are termed *data-names* where they are defined in the data division (e.g. line 11) but are generally termed *identifiers* when they appear in the procedure division (e.g. line 21).

The data-names are user-defined words. They have been formed by following a convention that is used throughout the book. Each data-name contains a hyphen that divides a prefix from a root. The prefix consists of a letter and a digit. The letter is an abbreviation of the name of a data source or area such as the keyboard (k) or the screen (s). The digit is the number of the record in the data division. When two data-names share the same root this indicates that they are closely related. Thus k1-char is the input character and s2-char is a version of the character for output. The reason for a convention such as this becomes more obvious when one sees large COBOL programs. It is not uncommon for COBOL programs to contain many hundreds of data-names on scores of records. Therefore most organizations consider it good practice to use conventions of this kind. (Data-names for examples that are used in the text but which are not part of working programs have prefixes beginning with 'e'.)

The **picture** *clause* defines the general characteristics of an elementary data item. A definition is restricted to certain symbol combinations. One of the most common forms uses the symbol 'x' to define character data items. When 'x' is the defining symbol the data item is termed *alphanumeric*. This simply means that it can hold any character value.

Thus k1-char and s2-char are elementary alphanumeric data items. Each of them can hold one character.

Alphanumeric data items can be of any length subject to a maximum defined by your implementation. The length is determined by counting symbols. All of the following are valid definitions for elementary data items defined as records at the 01 level:

```
01  e1-var          pic x.       ⎫
01  e2-var          pic x(1).    ⎬   1 character long
01  e3-var          pic x(01).   ⎭

01  e4-var          pic xxx.     ⎫
01  e5-var          pic x(0003). ⎬   3 characters long

01  e6-var          pic xxxx.    ⎫
01  e7-var          pic x(4).    ⎬   4 characters long
```

Each of the three sets above defines items of the same length. In the first set e1-var is one character long. E2-var and e3-var both contain an occurrence operator within brackets. The occurrence operator must be a positive integer greater than zero. It states the number of times the preceding symbol will occur.

The convention adopted in this book is one that is used by many COBOL programmers, namely, to define data items of under four characters without an occurrence operator:

```
01  e8-var          pic x.
01  e9-var          pic xx.
01  e10-var         pic xxx.
```

When four or more characters are required, then the operator is included without leading zeros. For example:

```
01  e11-var         pic x(4).
01  e12-var         pic x(20).
01  e13-varbig      pic x(113).
```

SELF-CHECK QUESTIONS

Q What are the user-defined words in program echo1?
A The user-defined names are: echo1, k1-char, s2-char, and para1.

Q What will be the effect of moving line 24 of echo1 to line 16?
A Only the first string of text will be displayed and then control will be returned to the operating system. As a result the subsequent statements in the program will be *unreachable*. As a rule the last statement of a program must always be the one that returns control.

Q Can para1 be written as 1para?
A No. It is not permitted to begin a user-defined word with any character other than a letter of the alphabet.

Q Is it legal to display k1-char directly at line 19?

A Yes. It is legal to display or accept any character item. However, it would not have been correct to display k1-char prior to line 18 because its value is undefined before the execution of the accept statement which gives it an initial value.

Generally speaking we will treat the keyboard and screen as distinct devices with separate areas of data. Therefore the program has two data items and the value of the input item is explicitly moved to the output item.

Maintaining separate data in this way will demonstrate its usefulness later when programs are larger and the structure of data becomes more complex.

Q Define an elementary alphanumeric data item that is ten characters long.

A Both of the following definitions are correct:

```
01 e1-var pic xxxxxxxxxx.
01 e2-var pic x(10).
```

The second is preferable because it is shorter and more clearly shows that the length of the data item is 10 characters.

Q Is the following definition correct? If so, how long is the data item?

```
01 e3-odd-one pic x(10)xxx(3).
```

A The definition is correct and defines a string of 15 characters. In both cases the occurrence operator binds only to the character that immediately precedes it. Therefore the second and third 'x' define the 11th and 12th character respectively. Definitions such as these are not helpful when there is only one defining symbol.

2.2 ACCEPT AND ALPHANUMERIC STRINGS

The following simple format of the **accept** statement was used in program echo1. It causes data to be transferred from the keyboard to a data item.

```
accept identifier
```

An identifier is a reference in a procedure division statement to data that is defined in the data division.

Echo1 accepted a single character as input. However, input strings may be longer, shorter, or equal in length to the accepting data item. COBOL provides a set of simple rules that govern the moving and subsequent alignment of alphanumeric data (Fig. 2.4).

---

1. The left-hand side of the input character string is aligned with the left-hand side of the accepting data item.
2. If the input string is longer than the accepting data item then the resulting string in the data item will be truncated on the right.
3. If the input string is shorter then the result will be padded to the right with spaces.
4. If the string is the same length all of the characters will be accepted.
5. The RETURN character is never accepted nor made available to the program.

Figure 2.4 Default rules governing **accept** with alphanumeric strings

Keyboard source	Result in accepted data item target is pic x(5).
AB⟨RET⟩	ABΔΔΔ
ΔAB⟨RET⟩	ΔABΔΔ
ABCDE⟨RET⟩	ABCDE
ABCDEF⟨RET⟩	ABCDE

Note: ⟨RET⟩ denotes a single depression of the RETURN key
Δ denotes a space character

Figure 2.5 Effect of **accept** on alphanumeric data items

Alignment at the left-hand side and padding with spaces or truncation at the right-hand side is called left justification. This is the default justification for alphanumeric data items.

Figure 2.5 shows the effect of accepting strings of various lengths into a data item that is five characters in length.

2.3 DISPLAY AND ALPHANUMERIC STRINGS

The **display** statement transfers data from the program to the terminal screen.

The full format for the **display** statement is:

$$\text{display} \begin{Bmatrix} \text{identifier} \\ \text{literal} \end{Bmatrix} \ldots [\text{no advancing}]$$

A single display statement can be used to output data from more than one source. For example,

```
display "OneΔ" e1-var "ΔTwoΔ" e2-var
```

interleaves literals with the values of data from the data division. (The braces in the format show that at least one identifier or literal must be included in a display statement. The ellipsis that follows the braces shows that one of the elements within the braces can be repeated any number of times.)

The no advancing phrase is optional. When it is absent the output will be followed by a single RETURN character that will cause the cursor to move to the beginning of the next line. When the no advancing phrase is present only the data from the program will be transferred and the cursor will remain at the end of the line. This feature is particularly useful when writing prompts for input:

```
display "InputΔaΔstring:Δ" no advancing
accept e3-string
```

22 ESSENTIAL COBOL: A FIRST COURSE IN STRUCTURED COBOL

The above display statement will leave the cursor on the same line so that `e3-string` will be accepted on the same line as the prompt.

If a nonnumeric literal requires an embedded double quote this can be written as two double quotes in succession. For example,

```
display "And∆he∆said∆to∆me:∆""What's∆up∆Doc?"""
```

will be written to the screen as

```
And∆he∆said∆to∆me:∆"What's∆up∆Doc?"
```

In general, it is possible to include any of the printable characters within a nonnumeric literal including the single quote or apostrophe as well as the space.

SELF-CHECK QUESTIONS

Q What is the result of the following paragraph?

```
procedure division.
para1.
    display "Hello" no advancing
    display "I∆am∆Noddy"
    stop run.
```

A The result will be:

```
HelloI∆am∆Noddy
```

A space after `"Hello"` could be included as either the last character of this string or the first character of the next string.

Q What is the result of the following paragraph where `e1-var` is a 6-character item containing `"ROBERT"`?

```
procedure division.
para1.
    display "Hello∆" e1-var ".∆How∆are∆you?∆∆" no advancing
    display "I∆am∆Noddy."
    stop run.
```

A The result will be:

```
Hello∆ROBERT.∆How∆are∆you?∆∆I∆am∆Noddy.
```

Q Will the following paragraph produce the same output as the paragraph in the previous question?

```
procedure division.
para1.
    display "Hello∆" no advancing
    display  e1-var   no advancing
    display ".∆How∆are∆you?∆∆" no advancing
    display "I∆am∆Noddy."
    stop run.
```

A Yes.

Q Is it possible to write a display statement that outputs a string that contains the double quote character? For example:

```
I will say "Bye" for now.
```

A Yes. When double quotes are required within a string they are written as a double occurrence of the character.

```
display "I∆will∆say∆""Bye""∆for∆now."
```

Q Is this statement legal?

```
display "Hello"
        "to"
        "you"
```

A Yes. It will output Hellotoyou on a single line.

Q Is this statement legal?

```
display ""
```

A Yes. It implies that an empty string is to be displayed. The output will be a single RETURN.

2.4 TEST BEFORE LOOPS USING PERFORM

The previous programs have followed a simple pattern of execution in that each statement was executed only once and in the order in which it appeared in the program text. This relationship within a set of statements is known as a sequence.

However, one of the most powerful features of computing systems is their ability to execute sets of statements more than once or iteratively. The most common statement used in COBOL for controlling *iteration* is the **perform** statement.

This control statement can take many different forms and has a variety of uses which are considered in later chapters. For the present we will consider an amendment to the program to incorporate a simple use of **perform** to cause a set of statements to be executed zero or more times.

In echo2 (Fig. 2.6) the control of the **perform** statement begins with the word **perform** at line 23 and ends with the word **end-perform** at line 28. Therefore all of the statements on lines 24 to 27 are under the control of the perform statement, that is, they are within its *scope of control*.

A simple format for the perform statement is:

```
perform test before until condition
    {statement}...
end-perform
```

This form of the **perform** statement states that a *conditional test* takes place prior to the execution of the statements contained within the perform. If the condition is false then the

```
1 identification division.
2 program-id. echo2.
3*Purpose: Echo a string of up to 5 characters.
4*         Demonstrate iteration with test-before
5*         for an alphanumeric literal.
6
7 environment division.
8
9 data division.
10 working-storage section.
11 01   k1-string   pic x(5).
12 01   s2-string   pic x(5).
13
14 procedure division.
15 para1.
16     display "echo2 begins"
17
18     display "Type 'Q' to quit"
19     display "Up to five characters will be echoed"
20
21     accept k1-string
22
23     perform test before until k1-string = "Q    "
24        move k1-string to s2-string
25        display s2-string
26        display "Type another string or 'Q' to quit"
27        accept k1-string
28     end-perform
29
30     display "echo2 ends"
31     stop run.
32
33 end program echo2
```

Figure 2.6 Program echo2

statements within its scope will be executed and the condition will be tested again. However, if the condition is true then control will pass to the next statement immediately following the end-perform.

The effect of this upon the *flow of control* is to create a test before loop, that is, a loop where the contained statements are executed zero or more times depending on the result of a test that immediately precedes each execution. The *flowchart* in Fig. 2.7 illustrates the flow of control within echo2.

Loops raise a number of questions concerning program construction. A key point pertinent to all loops is that the programmer must manage the data in such a way that the condition which will terminate the loop will occur during the run of the program. Therefore the design of a program with a loop must take into account the state of the data both before and after the execution of a loop as well as the actions within the loop that will ensure its successful termination.

In echo2 the condition is a test on k1-string. This item is input immediately prior to

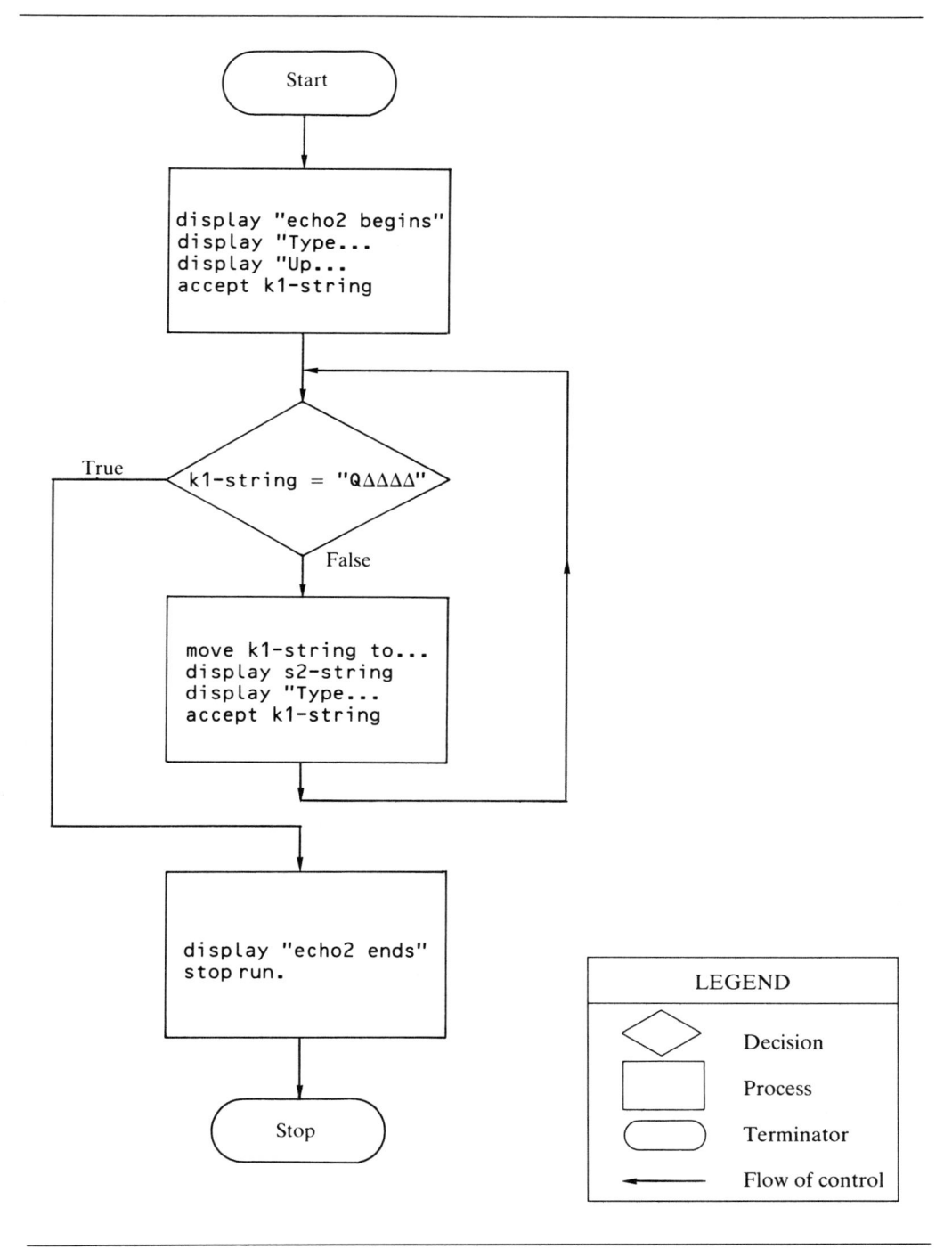

Figure 2.7 Flowchart of program echo2

```
 1 identification division.
 2 program-id. draw1.
 3*Purpose: Display a column of 10 asterisks down the
 4*         left-hand side of the screen.
 5
 6 environment division.
 7
 8 data division.
 9 working-storage section.
10 01   w1-ctr   pic 99.
11
12 procedure division.
13 para1.
14     display "draw1 begins"
15
16     move 1 to w1-ctr
17
18     perform test before until w1-ctr > 10
19       display "*"
20       compute w1-ctr = w1-ctr + 1
21     end-perform
22
23     display "draw1 ends"
24     stop run.
25
26 end program draw1
```

Figure 2.8 Program draw1

the commencement of the loop (line 21) and re-input as the last statement within the loop (line 27). Therefore the loop can be seen to be under the full control of the user who can decide whether or not to continue executing the statements within the loop.

If a "Q" is input in response to either of the accept statements, the test condition will become true and control will pass to line 30. In response to any other input the loop will continue with the execution of the statements on lines 24 to 27.

Flowcharts are useful diagrams to assist in explaining how certain statements behave. In fact, although the COBOL standard is mostly written in English, it uses flowcharts from time to time in order to avoid ambiguity. We will also use flowcharts to assist in defining the execution behaviour of certain statements.

However, flowcharts are poor tools for designing application programs in high-level languages such as COBOL because they reduce structured statements such as the **perform** statement to a less abstract and more mechanical level.

Loops can be used to create iterative behaviours in programs that are independent of input. For example, program draw1 in Fig. 2.8 will write a column of ten asterisks down the left-hand side of the screen. It uses a counter to determine how many times to iterate the statements within the test before loop.

In this example the '9' symbol has been used in the picture clause to define w1-ctr as a **numeric** data item (line 10). The symbol is used twice. Therefore w1-ctr has two digits and can hold numeric character values in the range of 00 to 99 inclusive. (The 'w' prefix stands for working-storage and 'ctr' is an abbreviation of counter.)

Lines 16, 18 and 20 use numbers in the program text to initialize the counter, to state the conditional test and to increment the counter. Numbers used in this way are called numeric literals. They are never enclosed in quotation marks and leading zeros are optional.

Prior to the execution of the loop the counter is initialized to 1 by the **move** statement at line 16. This creates an initial value for the conditional test used by the loop.

The conditional test at line 18 is `w1-ctr > 10`. This determines whether or not the counter is greater than 10. If the condition when tested is found to be false then the body of the loop will be executed. If it is found to be true then the execution of the program will proceed with the next statement after the loop at line 23.

Within the body of the loop there are two statements. The first of these is a **display** statement that outputs an asterisk followed by a RETURN. (It is this **display** statement which creates the column of asterisks.)

The second statement in the loop is a **compute** statement which increases the counter by 1 each time it is executed. This statement will also be executed 10 times, thereby causing the counter to move from its initial value of 1 through to a final value of 11 by increments of 1.

Thus after 10 executions of the body of the loop, the counter will have a value which causes the test condition to become true and the loop will terminate.

Values in the range of 00 to 10 would return **false** for the test on line 18 and values in the range of 11 to 99 would return **true**. However, the program has been constructed in such a way that `w1-ctr` can only take the values of 1 through 11 in their counting order. Thus `w1-ctr` is truly a counter and has been constrained to take a limited number of

Line number	Program action
14	Display.
16	`W1-ctr` becomes 1.
18	Greater than 10? No. Perform control continues.
19	Display.
20	`W1-ctr` becomes 2.
18	Greater than 10? No. Perform control continues.
19	Display.
20	`W1-ctr` becomes 3.
etc.	etc.
18	Greater than 10? No. Perform control continues.
19	Display.
20	`W1-ctr` becomes 10.
18	Greater than 10? No. Perform control continues.
19	Display.
20	`W1-ctr` becomes 11.
18	Greater than 10? Yes. Perform control ends.
23	Display.
24	Return control to operating system.

Figure 2.9 Order of statement execution in program draw1

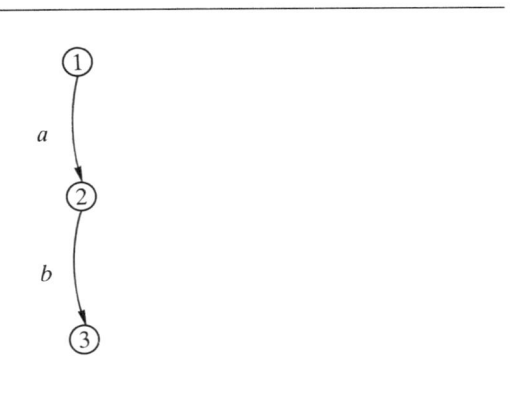

Figure 2.10 A simple flowgraph

successive values so that the iterative behaviour of the program is strictly controlled and predictable.

We can follow the order of statement execution in draw1 and write this as a list of line numbers (Fig. 2.9).

The line numbers show three possible patterns which can occur when the program executes. The first and last patterns always occur once and in the same order. If we label them as pattern *a* (lines 14,16) and pattern *b* (lines 23,24) we can visualize their relationship as a simple diagram called a *flowgraph* (Fig. 2.10).

Point 1 is the start of the program and point 3 is its termination. We can see that line pattern *a* links point 1 to point 2 which is the test at the top of the loop. If the test returns true, then we can go directly from point 2 to point 3 because they are linked by the *b* pattern. However, if the test is false we need to execute pattern *c* (lines 18,19,20) and return to point 2. This information can be added to the flowgraph as a link from point 2 to itself (Fig. 2.11).

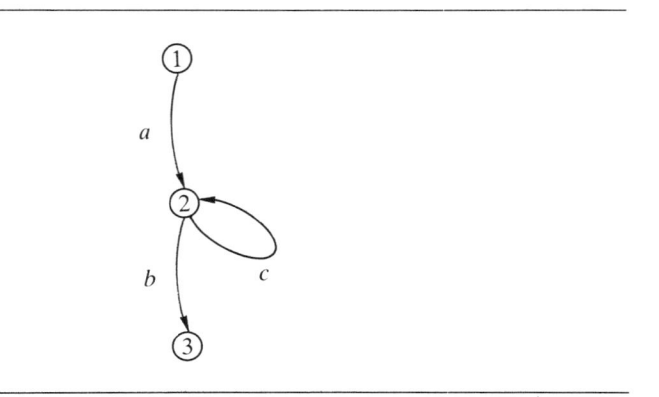

Figure 2.11 Flowgraph with a return link

Flowgraphs of this type are very closely related to flowcharts. They have a much wider range of application than flowcharts but for the moment we will simply use them to visualize the order of execution of statements. As we read from the top to the bottom the flowgraph clearly shows the following:

1. There are three sequences of statements in the program.
2. *a* is the first sequence (statements on lines 14,16).
3. *b* is the last sequence (statements on lines 23,24).
4. *c* is a sequence that may be iterated zero or more times because it is in a loop (statements on lines 18,19,20).

It is possible to create loops within loops with extraordinarily complex test conditions. For the present we will only use test before loops for two clearly defined circumstances:

1. Under user control for input termination as in echo2.
2. To force a set of statements to execute a counted number of times as in draw1.

In the first case we will always accept the test data item directly. In the second case we will test a counter that is changed with one of the following compute statements:

```
compute identifier = identifier + 1

compute identifier = identifier - 1
```

When a compute statement is executed the expression to the right of the equal sign is evaluated to produce a value. This value is then assigned to the identifier shown to the left of the equal sign. Thus these simple forms can be used to increment or decrement a counter.

By adhering to these restrictions we will be able to create many useful programs that embody many powerful features without needing to introduce unnecessary complexity into the flow of control of our programs.

Test before loops conform to a general design which is expressed by the following pseudo-code:

```
initialize_test_item
perform test before until test_condition_true
   do_statements
   change_test_item
end-perform
```

Prior to entering the loop the item that controls the loop must be initialized to a value. A loop constructed in this way will execute zero times if the initialization has caused the test condition to become true. The test takes place at the top of the loop and the test item is changed by a statement within the loop which is usually at the bottom. The change to the test item must be a change that will lead toward the termination of the loop. We will use this pseudo-code as a template for writing further test before loops.

1. Numeric data items are aligned on the assumed decimal point.
2. When the source data item is longer than the target data item then the result in the target will be truncated and leading digits will be lost.
3. When the source data item is shorter, then the result will be padded with as many leading zeros as are required.
4. When the items are the same length then all of the digits will be moved.

Figure 2.12 Default rules governing the use of **move** with numeric data items

2.5 ALIGNMENT OF NUMERIC STRINGS

The numeric strings used in Part 1 are unsigned whole numbers. The lowest value they may contain is zero. The highest value they may contain depends on the number of '9' symbols used in the picture clause. (The COBOL maximum is 18 digits.) For these numeric strings COBOL assumes a decimal point to the right of the least significant digit.

```
01   e1-var           pic 9(4).
```

Therefore e1-var may take any numeric value in the range of zero to nine thousand, nine hundred and ninety-nine.

Source numeric strings may be longer, shorter, or equal in length to the target data item.

COBOL provides a set of simple rules that govern the alignment of numeric strings when they are moved. These are given in Fig. 2.12. Examples of the result of move statements where the source data item is numeric are given in Fig. 2.13.

Literal to data item		
Source	Result	
literal	picture	value
5	pic 9.	"5"
05	pic 9.	"5"
52	pic 9.	"2"
12345	pic 999.	"345"

Data item to data item			
Source		Result	
picture	value	picture	value
pic 9.	"5"	pic 9.	"5"
pic 99.	"02"	pic 99.	"02"
pic 99.	"05"	pic 9.	"5"
pic 99.	"45"	pic 999.	"045"

Figure 2.13 Effect of moving data to numeric data items

The **move** statement transfers data to one or more data items. It has the following full syntax:

$$\text{move} \begin{Bmatrix} \text{identifier-1} \\ \text{literal} \end{Bmatrix} \text{to} \{\text{identifier-2}\}\ldots$$

In all of the examples given in this chapter the source and target have always been either both numeric or both alphanumeric. COBOL has features that assist in conversion between numeric and alphanumeric strings as well as conversion to other forms of numeric representation. However, these features are complex and contain many pitfalls for the new programmer. Therefore they will not be covered until Chapter 9, where they are presented in full.

For the present we will only move numeric literals to numeric items and not attempt conversion between numeric and alphanumeric strings. By doing so we will be able to maintain a consistent and correct representation of data in terms that are easily comprehended.

SELF-CHECK QUESTION

Q Consider the following three data entries:

```
01   e1-ctr      pic 9(5).
01   e2-string   pic xxx.
01   e3-string   pic x(6).
```

Are all of the following moves valid?

```
1.   move         5  to e1-ctr
2.   move     12345  to e1-ctr
3.   move    123456  to e1-ctr

4.   move "123456" to e3-string
5.   move "123456" to e2-string e3-string
```

A Yes. After the first move `e1-ctr` will hold the character "5" with four leading zeros. The leading 1 will be lost due to truncation in the third move. The fifth move takes advantage of the fact that a move can have more than one target. However, as a result of the move the characters "456" will be lost to `e2-string` owing to truncation.

2.6 FIGURATIVE CONSTANTS

Figurative constants are special literal values generated by the compiler. They assist in initializing and testing data items without the need to write literals directly. The two most common figurative constants are **space** and **zero**.

Space can be used in conjunction with alphanumeric items of any length. Zero can be used with alphanumeric and numeric items of any length.

Consider the following four records:

```
data division.
working-storage section.
01 e1-var pic x.
01 e2-var pic x(12).
01 e3-var pic 9.
01 e4-var pic 9(8).
```

All of these statements are valid:

```
move space to e1-var
move space to e2-var

move space to e1-var e2-var

move zero  to e1-var e2-var

move zero  to e1-var

move zero  to e3-var e4-var

move 10 to e4-var
perform test before until e4-var = zero
  display "Hello"
  compute e4-var = e4-var - 1
end-perform
```

In each of these examples the figurative constant stands in the place of the appropriate literal. For example, `move space to e1-var` causes one space to be moved but `move space to e2-var` causes 12 spaces to be moved.

In every case the meaning of the figurative constant is dependent on the definition of the target item. This context dependency is true for all figurative constants. It allows them to be used for data initialization and testing without needing to calculate the specific size of the target beforehand.

SELF-CHECK QUESTIONS

Q Define a counter that can be used to iterate a set of statements in a test before loop a total of five times.

A `01 e1-ctr pic 9.`

Q Write a test before loop with a correct initialization to display five columns of the string "HELLO".

A The following statements will display "HELLO" five times:

```
move 1 to e1-ctr
perform test before until e1-ctr > 5
  display "HELLO"
  compute e1-ctr = e1-ctr + 1
end-perform
```

These statements will also display "HELLO" five times:

```
    move 0 to e1-ctr
    perform test before until e1-ctr = 5
      display "HELLO"
      compute e1-ctr = e1-ctr + 1
    end-perform
```

In both cases the final value minus the initial value of the counter is equal to five. There are many ways to write a loop to do something a specific number of times. Try to write two loops similar to those above but which decrement w1-ctr with the following statement:

```
    compute e1-ctr = e1-ctr = 1
```

Q Which of the above lines can be rewritten using figurative constants?
A The line:

```
    move 0 to e1-ctr
```

can be rewritten as:

```
    move zero to e1-ctr
```

Q Write another test before loop to display the string "BACKWARDS" four times. Use the following conditional test to control the perform:

```
    until e1-ctr = zero
```

A The following statements will display "BACKWARDS" four times:

```
    move 4 to e1-ctr
    perform test before until e1-ctr = zero
      display "BACKWARDS"
      compute e1-ctr = e1-ctr - 1
    end-perform
```

2.7 CONDITIONAL EXPRESSIONS

In COBOL simple conditional expressions can be formed by using two *operands* and a *relational operator*. The operands can be an identifier and a literal or two identifiers. For example, all of the following are simple *conditional expressions* using the equals operator:

```
    e1-var = "quit"
    e2-var = 25
    e3-var = e4-var
```

In the first two expressions the first operand is an identifier and the second operand is a literal. E1-var must be defined by a picture clause using the 'x' symbol because it is tested against a nonnumeric literal. Similarly e2-var must be defined by a picture clause using the '9' symbol because it is tested against a numeric literal. In the third expression both operands must be either numeric or alphanumeric.

Simple conditional expressions of this type are called *relation conditions* because they

$$\begin{Bmatrix} \text{identifier-1} \\ \text{literal-1} \end{Bmatrix} \begin{Bmatrix} [\text{not}] > \\ [\text{not}] < \\ [\text{not}] = \\ >= \\ <= \end{Bmatrix} \begin{Bmatrix} \text{identifier-2} \\ \text{literal-2} \end{Bmatrix}$$

Relational operator	Meaning
=	equal to
>	greater than
<	less than
>=	greater than or equal to
<=	less than or equal to
not >	not greater than
not <	not less than
not =	not equal to

Figure 2.14 Relational operators

express a relationship between two operands by means of a relational operator. The operands must always be *compatible*. When the expression is evaluated at run time it will evaluate to a value of true or false. This truth value can then be used to change the flow of control in the program.

A simple format for the relation condition is given in Fig. 2.14 together with a listing of the eight relational operators that the format implies.

SELF-CHECK QUESTIONS

Q Use a different relational operator to express the same relationship:

1. e1-var not > e2-var
2. e3-var not < e4-var

A The following expresssions are equivalent to those above:

1. e1-var <= e2-var
2. e3-var >= e4-var

Q How many times will the following test before loop execute?
```
move 1 to e5-var
perform test before until e5-var not < 7
  display "looping"
  compute e5-var = e5-var + 1
end-perform
```

A The display statement will be executed seven times. It would be simpler to use the expression 'e5-var > 7', which would produce the same number of iterations.

In addition, COBOL provides *condition-name* conditions as a way of specifying simple conditions. These require *condition entries* in the data division.

A condition entry is defined by using the special level number 88 followed by a condition-name, the reserved word **value**, and a list of one or more values to be used for the test. The condition entry must immediately follow the data entry it references. For example:

```
data division.
working-storage section.
01   e1-var        pic xx.
01   e2-var        pic x.
     88  e2-var-ok value "y".
01   e3-var        pic xxx.
     88  e3-var-ok value "abc" "def" "xyz".
```

This data division contains three data items for a total of six characters. E2-var is immediately followed by a condition entry that defines the meaning of the condition-name e2-var-ok.

When the compiler encounters a condition-name during its analysis of the data division it notes the condition for later reference. In this case e2-var-ok is noted as an equality test against the data item e2-var.

When the compiler later finds the condition-name in the procedure division it will substitute in its place the required test of equality. Therefore the following two phrases will produce exactly the same result from the compiler for the given entries:

```
perform test before until e2-var-ok

perform test before until e2-var = "y"
```

E3-var is followed by a condition entry that lists more than one test after the keyword value. When the compiler discovers the condition-name in the procedure division it will substitute in its place the necessary logic to ensure the following:

1. Starting at the beginning of the list each test for equality is made in turn.
2. When one of the tests results in true then the condition-name condition is considered to be true and the testing terminates.
3. When one of the tests results in false then the next test in the list is tested.

Therefore the condition-name condition will be true when the result of any one of the tests specified on the list is true and false when all of the tests on the list are found to be false.

The following statements could appear in a program as a way of trapping an incorrect input:

```
accept e3-var
perform test before until e3-var-ok
    display "Variable invalid - must be in {abc,def,xyz}"
    display "Please re-enter:Δ" no advancing
    accept e3-var
end-perform
```

The first accept statement gives e3-var an initial value. Provided that it is either "abc", or "def", or "xyz" the loop will not execute, However, when e3-var is any other value the

```
 1 identification division.
 2 program-id. echo3.
 3*Purpose: This program is identical to echo2 except that it
 4*          uses a condition-name for the test.
 5
 6 environment division.
 7
 8 data division.
 9 working-storage section.
10 01   k1-string        pic x(5).
11      88   k1-eok   value "Q    "
12                         "q    ".
13 01   s2-string        pic x(5).
14
15 procedure division.
16 para1.
17      display "echo3 begins"
18
19      display "Type 'Q' to quit"
20      display "Up to 5 characters will be echoed"
21
22      accept k1-string
23
24      perform test before until k1-eok
25         move k1-string to s2-string
26         display s2-string
27         display "Type another string or 'Q' to quit"
28         accept k1-string
29      end-perform
30
31      display "echo3 ends"
32      stop run.
33
34 end program echo3
```

Figure 2.15 Program echo3

loop will be entered and the user will be trapped within it until a valid value is entered at the keyboard.

Program echo3 uses a similar condition-name. The condition entry is defined on lines 11 and 12. The condition-name is then used in the procedure division on line 24.

It is also possible to use the reserved word **thru** to specify an inclusive range for a test. For example,

```
data division.
working-storage section.
01   e4-var       pic 9.
     88   e4-var-ok value 1 thru 4.
01   e5-var       pic x.
     88   e5-var-ok value "a" thru "d"
                         "k"∆"q"∆"v"
                         "x" thru "z"
```

E4-var-ok will be true if var4 has the value 1, 2, 3, or 4 at the time the test is made.
E5-var-ok will be true if var5 has the value "a", "b", "c", "d", "k", "q", "v", "x", "y" or "z".

The simple syntax for the value clause when it is used in creating a condition list is as follows:

```
value {literal-2 [thru literal-3] }...
```

Using condition-name conditions has a number of advantages for the programmer:

1. Increased program clarity that contributes to documentation.
2. Test requirements defined only once and next to the data.
3. Alternative conditions expressed as a list of simple tests.

SELF-CHECK QUESTIONS

Q Write a data entry and condition entry for a two character item that will be tested to determine whether or not it is any of the following: "TO" or "to" or "Fo".
A The condition-name condition will be true if e1-var is any of "TO", "to", or "Fo":

```
01  e1-var          pic xx.
    88  it-does value "TO"Δ"to"Δ"Fo".
```

Q Is the order of the entries in the list of conditions important?
A Yes. The order of evaluation is always from the first to the last condition in the list. Therefore a program will run more efficiently if the most frequently tested entries are at the beginning of the list.

Q Can the entries in the condition list be separated by commas?
A Yes. The comma as well as the semi-colon is treated as if it were a space. The entries in the list must be separated by at least one of these three characters.

COBOL also provides the three *logical operators*: **and**, **or**, **not**. These can be used to form complex conditions from simple conditions.

The **and** operator can be used to join two conditions into a complex condition:

```
e1-var = "quit" and e2-var = "last"
```

In the above example two relation conditions are combined into a single complex condition. When e1-var is equal to "quit" and e2-var is equal to "last" then the entire expression evaluates to true. In all other cases it is false.

We can see that the effect of the **and** operator is that the complex condition will be true only when both conditions are true. This can be summarized in the *truth table* shown in Fig. 2.16.

The logical operator **or** is less restrictive than **and**:

```
e1-var = "quit" or e2-var =Δ"last"
```

condition-1 and condition-2 → value
true and true → true
true and false → false
false and true → false
false and false → false

Figure 2.16 Truth table for the logical operator **and**

When either `e1-var` is equal to `"quit"` or `e2-var` is equal to `"last"` then the entire expression evaluates to true. The only time this expression will be false is when `e1-var` is not `"quit"` and `e2-var` is not `"last"`.

Thus the effect of the **or** operator is that the complex condition will be true if either condition is true. This can also be summarized in a truth table (Fig. 2.17).

We can see that condition entries often provide a simpler means for specifying complex conditions when the simple conditions are connected by the **or** operator. For example the loop condition in program echo2 can be specified in either of the following forms:

```
perform test before until k1-eok
perform test before until k1-string = "qΔΔΔΔ" or k1-string = "QΔΔΔΔ"
```

The last logical operator, **not**, is used to reverse the truth value of a conditional expression (Fig. 2.18).

The three logical operators are in a hierarchy of *precedence* that affects their *order of evaluation*. **Not** has the highest precedence, **and** is in the middle, and **or** has the lowest precedence.

not c1 and c2

not c3 or c4

In both of the above complex expressions the **not** binds to the first condition only. Parentheses can be used to clarify the meaning of expressions. Thus

(not c1) and c2

(not c3) or c4

condition-1 or condition-2 → value
true or true → true
true or false → true
false or true → true
false or false → false

Figure 2.17 Truth table for the logical operator **or**

condition-1 → value		
not	true	→ false
not	false	→ true

Figure 2.18 Truth table for the logical operator **not**

mean exactly the same thing. Parentheses can also be used to change the order of evaluation. For example,

   not (c1 and c2)

   not (c3 or c4)

These clearly do mean something different from the previous expressions because now the truth value of the complex expression in parentheses is to be reversed and not merely the first term. We can demonstrate that these expressions are not logically equivalent by using truth tables.

As an example we will attempt to discover whether the following two expressions are logically the same:

   expression-1:   (not c1) and c2

   expression-2:   not (c1 and c2)

Each of c1 and c2 may be either true or false when evaluated. Therefore there are four possible combinations of values for the two simple conditions (Fig. 2.19).

We can add a third column to this table (Fig. 2.20) to show the result of applying the **not** operator to c1 in column 1. (These values are taken from the **not** truth table.) We can now apply the **and** operator to the values in columns 2 and 3 in order to solve the first expression. (The results are written in the fourth column of Fig. 2.21.)

By extending this process we can work out the meaning of the second expression (Fig. 2.22). The fifth column is the result of applying the **and** operator to columns 1 and 2. The sixth column is the result of applying **not** to the fifth column. We can see that the fourth and sixth columns do not contain the same results. Therefore the two expressions exp-1 and exp-2 are not logically equivalent. Multi-column truth tables such as this are often very helpful aids in understanding complex logical expressions.

c1	c2
true	true
true	false
false	true
false	false

Figure 2.19 Truth value combinations for two conditions

40 ESSENTIAL COBOL: A FIRST COURSE IN STRUCTURED COBOL

c1	c2	not c1
true	true	false
true	false	false
false	true	true
false	false	true

Figure 2.20 Result of applying the logical operator **not**

c1	c2	not c1	expression-1
true	true	false	false
true	false	false	false
false	true	true	true
false	false	true	false

expression-1 = (not c1) and c2

Figure 2.21 Result of expression-1

c1	c2	not c1	expression-1	c1 and c2	expression-2
true	true	false	false	true	false
true	false	false	false	false	true
false	true	true	true	false	true
false	false	true	false	false	true

expression-1 = (not c1) and c2
expression-2 = not (c1 and c2)

Figure 2.22 Truth table proving that expression-1 and expression-2 are unequal

SELF-CHECK QUESTIONS

Q The **or** operator cannot differentiate between a single operand that is true and two operands that are true. It is often called an inclusive or operator to differentiate it from the exclusive or operator (**xor**) which is the same except that it returns false when both operands are true. Write a truth table for the **xor** operator.

A The truth table in Fig. 2.23 defines the **xor** operator.

c1 xor c2	→ value
true xor true	→ false
true xor false	→ true
false xor true	→ true
false xor false	→ false

Figure 2.23 Truth table for proving logical operator **xor**

Q COBOL does not include an **xor** operator. Assume that c1 and c2 are condition-names. Use the defined operators (and,or,not) to write an expression in COBOL that specifies the **xor** operator.

A (c1 and not c2) or (c2 and not c1).

Q Write a multi-column truth table to demonstrate that:

(not c1) and (not c2) = not (c1 or c2)

A In Fig. 2.24, the fifth column holds the results for the left-hand expression. The seventh column holds the results for the right-hand expression.

The relationship between these two expressions is one of De Morgan's Laws, named after the famous nineteenth century logician. De Morgan's other law states that:

(not c1) or (not c2) = not (c1 and c2)

The distributive laws state that:

(c1 and c2) or c3 = (c1 or c3) and (c2 or c3)

(c1 or c2) and c3 = (c1 and c3) or (c2 and c3)

These three laws can also be proved by using multi-column truth tables.

Q What is the point in proving these laws?
A Firstly, it is good practice in learning to decode logical expressions. It is not uncommon to be given two logical expressions that are thought to mean the same thing but for which a practical proof is required. It is usually easier to construct a proof using tables than it is to write and test a program to do the same thing.

c1	c2	not c1	not c2	not c1 and not c2	c1 or c2	not (c1 or c2)
true	true	false	false	false	true	false
true	false	false	true	false	true	false
false	true	true	false	false	true	false
false	false	true	true	true	false	true

Figure 2.24 Truth table proving one of De Morgan's rules

Secondly, the relationships expressed in these laws are often misunderstood by programmers. For instance, an incorrect translation of the first of De Morgan's laws is a very common programmer error. Thirdly, the ability to recognize these laws assists in rewriting expressions into equivalent forms which may be more convenient to use in a particular program.

2.8 RECORDS AND LEVEL NUMBERS

In the previous sections all of the data items we created were elementary data-items using the symbols 'x' and '9' in picture clauses.

Until now the elementary items we have used have also been records. However, COBOL allows us to associate groups of elementary items within records. This is done by using level numbers to create a hierarchy of association. Level numbers in the range of 01 to 49 can be used to design a hierarchy of data within a record.

In order to illustrate a simple example in data structure we can consider one possible format for British postal codes:

```
01   k1-postcode.
     03   k1-leadalpha            pic xx.
     03   k1-leadnumber           pic xx.
     03   k1-postspacer           pic x.
     03   k1-trailnumber          pic x.
     03   k1-trailalpha           pic xx.
```

The above record defines an eight character data structure with the name of k1-postcode. It has five elementary items. The item at the 01 level is a *group item* because it has no picture clause of its own and because it contains other items within it. Any reference to the group item k1-postcode is a reference to all eight characters whereas, for example, a reference to k1-leadnumber only refers to the third and fourth characters.

A more complex structure could be created:

```
01   k1-postcode.
     03   k1-firsthalf.
          05   k1-firstalpha      pic xx.
          05   k1-firstnumber     pic xx.
     03   k1-postspacer           pic x.
     03   k1-secondhalf.
          05   k1-secondnumber    pic x.
          05   k1-secondalpha     pic xx.
```

This record provides an alternative structure for the same characters. Any of the eight data items in the record can be referenced by accept, display, or move statements.

Figure 2.25 gives a sequence of possible move statements as well as the outcome after each move for data in this record.

The following record introduces the reserved word **filler** as well as another form of the value clause which is used for data initialization.

k1-postcode *before execution*	*statement*	k1-postcode *after execution*
unknown	move space to k1-postcode	△△△△△△△△
△△△△△△△	move "SW" to k1-postcode	SW△△△△△△
SW△△△△△△	move "15" to k1-firstnumber	SW15△△△△
SW15△△△△	move "2PW" to k1-secondhalf	SW15△2PW
SW15△2PW	move k1-firsthalf to k1-secondhalf	SW15△SW1
SW15△SW1	move k1-secondhalf to k1-firsthalf	SW1△△SW1
SW1△△SW1	move "9" to k1-secondnumber	SW1△△9W1

Figure 2.25 Effect of **move** on group items

```
01    s2-postcode.
      03   filler        value space   pic xx.
      03   s2-string     value "BS16"  pic x(4).
      03   filler        value " - "   pic xxx.
      03   s2-message                  pic x(4).
```

The reserved word **filler** is used for data items which are required as part of a record definition but which are never referenced directly by the program. In this example the fillers define data items which will be used to improve the formatting of a line of output. (In later chapters we will see that the concept of filler is very useful when programs share data from the same files but only have an interest in a subset of the data.)

In general, filler data items help to improve the readability of a program. The programmer knows from reading the data division that data items exist as part of the data definition even though they are never referenced directly by statements such as **move**.

The value clause when used with a data item causes the compiler to assign an initial value to the data item when the program is initialized at run time. In the above example the two fillers and `s2-string` are initialized. However, `s2-message` has not been given a value clause. Therefore it must be initialized by the programmer before it is referenced in any way. Figure 2.26 shows the value in `s2-postcode` before and after the execution of selected move statements.

In summary, when a value clause is used with level numbers 01 to 49 it causes initial values to be assigned to data items in the working storage. However, when a value clause is used with level 88 in a condition entry it specifies one or more values to be used in conditional tests.

s2-postcode *before execution*	*statement*	s2-postcode *after execution*
△△BS16△-△????	move space to s2-message	△△BS16△-△△△△△
△△BS16△-△△△△△	move "AB" to s2-postcode	AB△△△△△△△△△△△
AB△△△△△△△△△△△	move "RHS" to s2-message	AB△△△△△△△RHS△

? = unknown value

Figure 2.26 Effect of **value** clause and **filler** items

Thus the value clause has two formats that are used for entirely different purposes.

Format-1:   `value literal-1`   for data initialization

Format-2:   `value {literal-2 [thru literal-3] }...`   for condition lists

SELF-CHECK QUESTION

Q   Why is the thru option not available in format 1?
A   This format is used to initialize data. It is not possible for any item of data to have more than one value at the same time.

The program in Fig. 2.27 invites the user to input 8 character postcodes and to terminate input with a single "Q" or "q". It splits each postcode in half and displays each half with a message.

Prior to the execution of the first statement at line 27 the data specified at lines 20 and 22 will be initialized. (Note that line 12 specifies a conditional test. It does not imply any form of initialization.)

The loop body is contained in lines 34 to 46. It is designed in accordance with our previous pseudo-code template. It shows a test item initialization at line 31 and a change to the same test item at the bottom of the loop at line 46. Thus the loop will iterate zero or more times depending on when the user decides to input a "q" or "Q".

Line 36 moves the first four characters from the `k1-postcode` record to character positions 3 to 6 of the `s2-postcode` record.

Line 37 moves a 17-character literal to the 18 character `s2-message`. (As a result of this move `s2-message` will be padded with a space in the 18th position.)

Lines 38 and 42 display the two parts of the original postcode in turn. The display string is defined by `s2-postcode` and consists of:

- 2 leading spaces followed by
- 4 characters from either `k1-firsthalf` or `k1-secondhalf` followed by
- a separator of "Δ-Δ" followed by
- a message of 18 characters.

Program post1 appears to work for postcodes such as "SW15Δ2PW" but appears to be in error for "BS7Δ3JR". The reason for this is that the program assumes that two digits will always follow the first two letters. This would work for "BS07Δ3JR". Unfortunately British postcodes do not show leading zeros for the embedded numbers. We will defer this problem until a later version of the postcode program.

```cobol
 1 identification division.
 2 program-id. post1.
 3*Purpose: Divide an 8 character postcode into 2 parts.
 4
 5 environment division.
 6
 7 data division.
 8 working-storage section.
 9 01  k1-postcode.
10     03   k1-firsthalf.
11          05   k1-firstalpha         pic xx.
12              88   k1-eok value "Q " "q ".
13          05   k1-firstnumber        pic xx.
14     03   k1-postspacer              pic x.
15     03   k1-secondhalf.
16          05   k1-secondnumber       pic x.
17          05   k1-secondalpha        pic xx.
18
19 01  s2-postcode.
20     03   filler         value space pic xx.
21     03   s2-string                  pic x(4).
22     03   filler         value " - " pic xxx.
23     03   s2-message                 pic x(18).
24
25 procedure division.
26 para1.
27     display "post1 begins"
28
29     display space
30     display "Input a postcode or 'Q' to quit"
31     accept k1-postcode
32
33     perform test before until k1-eok
34       display "This postcode consists of two parts:"
35
36       move k1-firsthalf  to s2-string
37       move "is the first part" to s2-message
38       display s2-postcode
39
40       move k1-secondhalf to s2-string
41       move "is the second part" to s2-message
42       display s2-postcode
43
44       display space
45       display "Input another postcode or 'Q' to quit"
46       accept k1-postcode
47     end-perform
48
49     display "post1 ends"
50     stop run.
51
52 end program post1
```

Figure 2.27 Program post1

SELF-CHECK QUESTIONS

Q What will happen when a program containing the following record initializes at run time?

```
01  e1-vars.
    03  e1-var1    value "---"   pic x(3).
    03  e1-var2    value "52"    pic xx.
    03  e1-var3    value space   pic x(80).
```

A The record of 85 characters will be initialized to three dashes, followed by the characters "5" and "2" followed by 80 spaces.

Q How many characters of data are there in the following record and what will happen when the program initializes?

```
01  e2-vars.
    03  e2-var1    value "ab"   pic x(4).
    03  e2-var2                 pic x.
```

A There are five characters but only the first four are defined with values.

The size of a record is determined by taking the sum of its picture clauses. During initialization e2-var1 will be initialized to "ab∆∆" because initialization is always done according to the rules governing the **move** statement. The value of e2-var2 is undefined and therefore may contain garbage.

Q Is the following definition valid?

```
01  e3-vars.
    03  e3-var7    value "ab"   pic x(5).
        88  e3-var7ok           value space.
```

A Yes. E3-var7 will be initialized to "ab∆∆∆". The figurative constant space is always context dependent. In the case of condition-names the context is defined by the picture clause of the item being tested. Therefore this conditional test is equivalent to a test for "∆∆∆∆∆".

Q Is the following definition valid?

```
01  e4-vars.
    03  e4-var8    value "ab"   pic x(5).
        88  e4-var8ok           value "cd".
```

A Yes. Although the condition implies a test between items of unequal length the shorter operand will be padded with spaces for the purpose of testing. Thus the condition e4-var8ok will be true if e4-var8 has the value "cd∆∆∆".

Q What will occur when a program containing the following record initializes? What tests could be made in a program?

```
01  e5-vars.
    03  e5-var9    value 23     pic 99.
        88  e5-var9ok           value 92 55 22.
    03  e5-var10   value "qu"   pic xx.
        88  var10ok             value "ab" "77".
```

A   The record will be initialized to the four characters "23qu".
   The condition e5-var9ok will be true if e5-var9 is ever equal to 92, 55, or 22. The condition e5-var10ok will be true if e5-var10 is ever equal to "ab" or "77".

Q   Is the following definition valid?

        01   e6-vars.
             88   e6-varok   value "abcd".
             03   e6-var11   pic xx.
             03   e6-var12   pic xx.

A   No. Condition-names can only be defined for elementary items. Methods for creating alternative data structures for the same data will be covered later when we look at the redefines clause.

Q   Consider the following data-entries:

        01   e7-string.
             03   filler   pic xx.
             03   e7-tail   pic 99.

   Which of the following moves is valid?

        1.   move   12   to e7-string
        2.   move   "12"   to e7-string
        3.   move   "3456" to e7-string
        4.   move   "6789" to e7-tail

A   The first move is invalid because the source is a numeric literal and the target is a group item. (Remember that a group item is always treated as an alphanumeric.)
   The second move is legal but results in e7-tail being filled with spaces. Therefore any subsequent reference to e7-tail will be faulty because it does not contain a number.
   The third move is valid and e7-tail will take the value 56.
   The fourth move is valid. No characters will be moved to the filler item because it is not part of the target. E7-tail will take the value 89 because of the alignment on the assumed decimal point.

2.9 EXERCISES

1 Compile, link and run programs noddy1 and echo1.
2 Discover the following characteristics for your compiler:
   (a) Is the environment division header required?
   (b) Is the configuration section required?
   (c) Can the sequence number area be omitted from the program source?
   (d) Does area B extend beyond column 72?
   (e) What is the largest picture size allowed for an alphanumeric elementary data-item?

3   Discover the error messages your compiler gives for the following errors:

   (a) group item with a picture clause:
   ```
   01   e1-group    pic x.
        03   e1-elem pic x.
   ```

   (b) missing period:
   ```
   01   e2-group
        03   e2-elem pic x.
   ```

   (c) elementary item missing a picture clause:
   ```
   01   e3-group.
        03   e3-elem1.
        01   e3-elem2              pic x.
   ```

4   Use noddy1 as a basis for writing noddy2 which can display the following 18 characters on two lines:

   "Hello",
   I'mΔNoddy.

5   Write a program called reverse1 to accept three strings of different lengths and to display them in the opposite order to that in which they were accepted.

6   Write noddy3 to ask the name of the program user and then to engage in a short dialogue. You might ask a few simple questions and then produce simple replies that incorporate the answers you have been given. For example:

HowΔtallΔareΔyou?	program
5'Δ2"⟨RET⟩	user
WhatΔisΔtheΔcolourΔofΔyourΔeyes?	program
blue⟨RET⟩	user
DoΔyouΔlikeΔbeingΔ5'Δ2"ΔwithΔeyesΔofΔblue?	program

7   Rewrite echo1 as echo4 so that all user-defined words are single characters such as a, or b, or c. Amend it further so that all strings of spaces between user-words are reduced to a single space or a RETURN. Comment on the result.

8   Draw a flowchart for program draw1. Write full statements or pseudo-code in the flowchart instead of line numbers.

9   Write program odd1 to accept a string of seven characters in length and to display a string of all the even-numbered characters.

```
 -------------              XX        XX
 I   I   I   I              XX        XX
 -------------               XX XX
 I   I   I   I                XXX
 -------------               XX XX
 I   I   I   I              XX        XX
 -------------              XX        XX
```

Figure 2.28   **Figure 2.29**

10 (a) Without using a loop write program draw2 to display the pattern of hyphens and upper-case character "I" shown in Fig. 2.28.
    (b) Analyse the program for statements that are repeated. Redesign the program to use a test before loop with a numeric counter to control the repeated statements.
    (c) Draw a flowgraph of both the old and new versions of this program.
11 Write program draw3 to display a large initial such as that shown in Fig. 2.29.

3
DATA VALIDATION

By the end of this chapter you will understand data *classes*, simple character validation by data class, reference modification, and the use of pattern matching as a technique for data validation.

In addition, you will have learned forms of the **evaluate** statement using simple conditions.

3.1 ALPHABETIC STRINGS

In the previous chapter we created alphanumeric data items by using the symbol 'x' and numeric data items by using the symbol '9' in the picture clause. It is also possible to define **alphabetic** data items with the symbol 'a'.

We could rewrite the previous postcode record to reflect the fact that characters embedded within the postcode are expected to be either alphanumeric, numeric or alphabetic characters:

```
01   k1-postcode.
     03   k1-firsthalf.
          05   k1-firstalpha          pic aa.
               88   k1-eok            value "QΔ"Δ"qΔ".
          05   k1-firstnumber         pic 99.
     03   k1-postspacer               pic x.
     03   k1-secondhalf.
          05   k1-secondnumber        pic 9.
          05   k1-secondalpha         pic aa.
```

The above record still describes eight characters of data. The first and second as well as the seventh and eighth characters are described as alphabetic. The third, fourth and sixth are numeric, and the fifth is alphanumeric.

In practice a record that is being used to store input prior to validation is likely to be described only as alphanumeric. However, once validation is completed it is not uncommon to use record descriptions that use the classes of numeric and alphabetic. This can clearly show that the characters contained in certain substrings belong to narrower classes than the class alphanumeric which includes all characters.

3.2 CLASSES OF DATA

The *Venn diagram* in Fig. 3.1 shows the relationship between COBOL data classes.
There are five data classes.* The full COBOL character set is alphanumeric. It

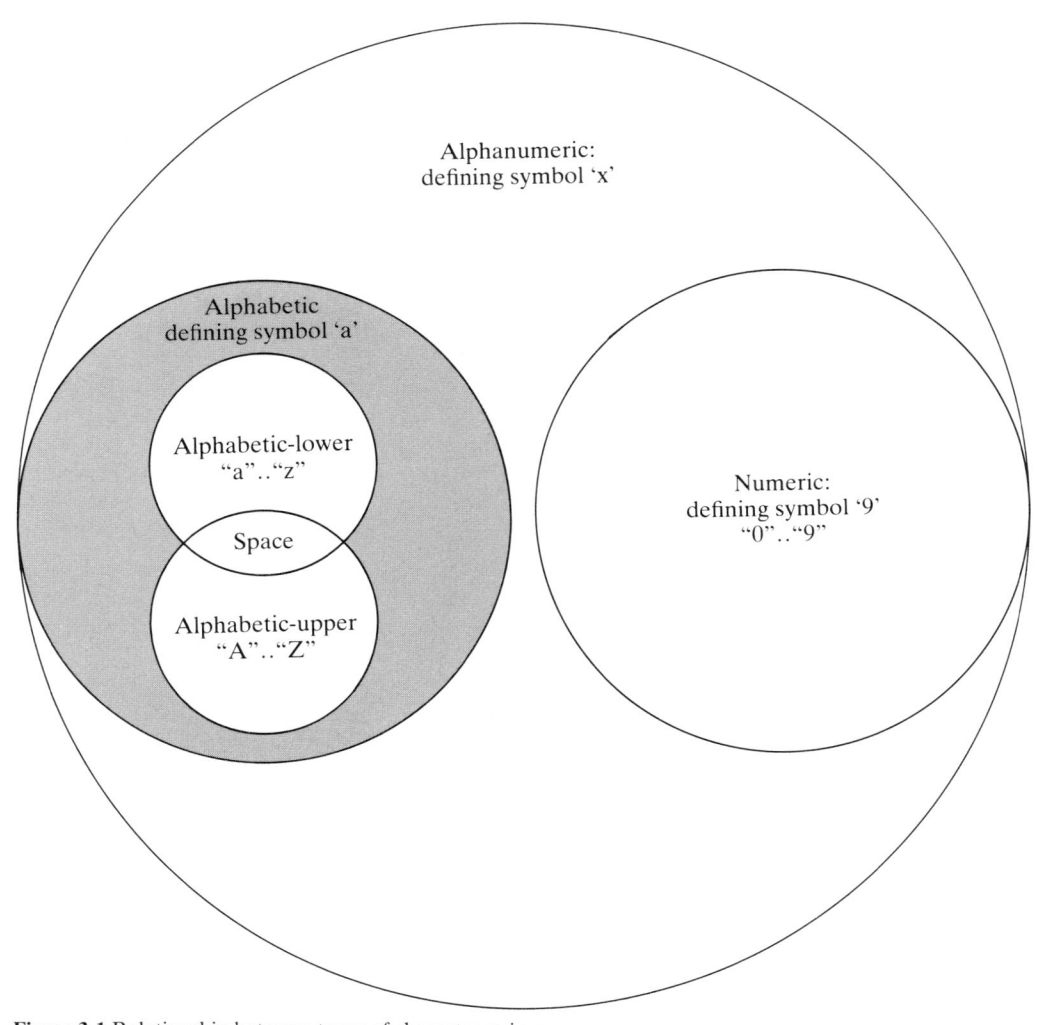

Figure 3.1 Relationship between types of character strings

---

* The shaded portion in Fig. 3.1 contains no characters.

Level of item	Class
Elementary	Alphanumeric or numeric or alphabetic
Group	Always alphanumeric

Figure 3.2 Item levels and data classes

contains all printable characters including punctuation as well as many unprintable characters such as RETURN. (The non-printable characters are covered in Chapter 9.)

The alphabetic and numeric subsets contain no characters in common. The alphabetic subset includes both the upper- and lower-case alphabets as well as the space character. The alphabetic-lower and alphabetic-upper share the space character.

The maximum length of alphanumeric and alphabetic strings is defined by the implementor and is generally a very high number. The maximum length of a numeric string is 18 digits as defined by the COBOL language. (There is also a provision for indicating a sign for numeric strings. This is covered in Chapter 12.)

A group item can be constructed from elementary items of different classes. Therefore it is always treated as an alphanumeric item. (For example, the statement `accept k1-postcode` in program post1 is an alphanumeric move.)

3.3 CLASS TESTS

COBOL provides *class tests* in order to determine the class to which a string of characters belongs. This facility is invaluable in helping to determine the correctness of character input.

1. Class tests may be made on either group or elementary items.
2. Numeric tests cannot be made against a group that contains or an elementary item that uses the symbol "a" in its picture clause.
3. Alphabetic tests cannot be made against a group that contains or an elementary item that uses the symbol "9" in its picture clause.
4. The tests will be true if the strings contain only the following characters:

Class test	String contents
numeric	"0" to "9"
alphabetic-lower	space, and "a" to "z"
alphabetic-upper	space, and "A" to "Z"
alphabetic	space, and "a" to "z", and "A" to "Z"

5. The class-name feature allows the programmer to define additional classes of characters for class tests.

Figure 3.3 Basic rules for making class condition tests

The general format of the class condition is:

$$\text{identifier [not]} \begin{Bmatrix} \text{numeric} \\ \text{alphabetic} \\ \text{alphabetic-lower} \\ \text{alphabetic-upper} \\ \text{class-name} \end{Bmatrix}$$

We can see that the word **not** can be used to reverse the truth value of a test. Figure 3.3 gives the basic rules for making class condition tests. They show that there is a relationship between the defining symbol used in a picture clause and certain restrictions on the use of class tests. Alphanumeric items can be the subject of any class test.

SELF-CHECK QUESTION

Q The following record contains five data items. To which class does each item belong? Which class tests can be made against which items?

```
01  e1-group.
    03  e1-first.
        05  e1-second      pic 999.
        05  e1-third       pic xxx.
    03  e1-fourth.
        05  e1-fifth       pic 999.
        05  e1-sixth       pic aaa.
    03  e1-seventh.
        05  e1-eighth      pic aaa.
        05  e1-ninth       pic aaa.
    03  e1-tenth.
        05  e1-eleventh    pic 999.
        05  e1-twelfth     pic 999.
    03  e1-thirteenth.
        05  e1-fourteenth  pic xxx.
        05  e1-fifteenth   pic xxx.
```

A E1-group, e1-first, and e1-fourth are all of the class alphanumeric. They should not be tested for class because they contain mixed picture clauses. E1-third, e1-thirteenth, e1-fourteenth and e1-fifteenth are also class alphanumeric and can be tested for any class because they contain only 'x' picture clauses.

The elementary items are easier to remember. For example, e1-twelfth can be tested for numeric, e1-sixth can be tested for the alphabetic classes, and e1-fourteenth can be tested for either the alphabetic classes or the numeric class.

3.4 THE EVALUATE STATEMENT

The ability to test an item to determine whether or not its contents are within a particular class of character data is an essential part of data validation. However, a useful program must not only be able to determine the class but also take appropriate actions dependent on the result of a class test.

The **evaluate** statement can be used to select alternative paths. One of the most useful forms of the evaluate statement has the following simple format:

```
evaluate condition
   when    true
      statement-1
   when    false
      statement-2
end-evaluate
```

The condition can be any condition that upon evaluation results in a truth value. The reserved word **when** opens the scope for a test against the condition. The test is immediately followed by a statement. For example,

```
evaluate firstalpha alphabetic
   when    true
      display "first alpha valid"
   when    false
      display "first alpha invalid"
end-evaluate
```

will output only one of the possible messages depending on the value of firstalpha at the time the test is made.

COBOL uses the term 'when phrase' to refer to the combination of the reserved word **when**, its particular test, and the particular statement associated with it. We will refer to these three things in combination as a *rule*.

The rules can be written in the reverse order:

```
evaluate firstalpha alphabetic
   when    false
      display "first alpha invalid"
   when    true
      display "first alpha valid"
end-evaluate
```

In both cases the first rule is the first to be evaluated and the second rule will be evaluated only if the first one fails.

Similarly the following statement will test firstnumber to determine whether or not it is numeric and output an appropriate message:

```
evaluate firstnumber numeric
   when    true
      display "first number valid"
   when    false
      display "first number invalid"
end-evaluate
```

As well as the fact that the rules can be written in any order, one of them can be omitted:

```
evaluate firstnumber numeric
   when    false
      display "first number invalid"
end-evaluate
```

In the above example there is no rule for true. Therefore when `firstnumber numeric` is true no action will be taken and control will pass to the next statement in the program, that is, the statement following the end-evaluate.

Program post2 incorporates three separate evaluate statements to validate the correctness of the first four characters within a postcode. (Like post1 it cannot manage "BS7△3JR".)

Lines 10 to 18 declare the postcode record that is accepted from the keyboard. The terminating condition for the program is `k1-eok`, which is a test of the first two characters in the accepted string. It is described at line 13 and tested at line 39.

Lines 39 to 76 are the main program loop. Lines 37 and 75 accept a string from the keyboard, thereby ensuring that a new string value is available for testing before entering the loop and after each iteration of the loop.

Provided that `k1-eok` is not true the body of the loop will be executed. Immediately upon entering the loop the string may or may not contain a string in which the first four characters are valid. At line 41 the assumption is made that the string is correct and `w3-valid` is set to true using the set statement which has the following simple format:

```
         set condition-name to true
```

Line 28 states that `w3-valid` is true when `w3-result` equals "y". The result of the set statement is that the value "y" is moved to `w3-result`. Therefore the following two statements can be seen to have the same effect on the data:

```
set w3-valid to true
move "y" to w3-result
```

A set statement is used in preference to a move statement because it clearly shows that an initial condition is set for subsequent testing.

Lines 43 to 49 contain the first evaluate statement which attempts to disprove the assumption that the postcode is valid. When the result of the alphabetic class test is true, namely that the first two characters are letters or spaces, the first rule will be followed. When the result is false the statements controlled by the second rule will be executed thereby causing the display of a message and the setting of `w3-invalid` to true.

Both `w3-valid` and `w3-invalid` are mutually exclusive tests against the data item `w3-result`. When `w3-invalid` is true then `w3-valid` must be false. Thus the purpose of this evaluate statement is to attempt to disprove our original assumption concerning the validity of the postcode and to output an appropriate message.

Lines 51 to 57 contain a second evaluate statement that tests the third and fourth characters for numerics. This statement also attempts to disprove the original assumption.

```
 1  identification division.
 2  program-id. post2.
 3* Purpose: Divide an 8 character postcode into 2 parts.
 4*          Check that the first part is in the form "aa99".
 5
 6  environment division.
 7
 8  data division.
 9  working-storage section.
10  01 k1-postcode.
11     03 k1-firsthalf.
12        05 k1-firstalpha          pic aa.
13           88 k1-eok value "Q " "q ".
14        05 k1-firstnumber         pic 99.
15     03 k1-postspacer             pic x.
16     03 k1-secondhalf.
17        05 k1-secondnumber        pic 9.
18        05 k1-secondalpha         pic aa.
19
20  01 s2-postcode.
21     03 filler        value space pic xx.
22     03 s2-string                 pic x(4).
23     03 filler        value " - " pic xxx.
24     03 s2-message               pic x(18).
25
26  01 w3-coderesult.
27     03 w3-result                 pic x.
28        88 w3-valid    value "y".
29        88 w3-invalid  value "n".
30/
31  procedure division.
32  para1.
33      display "post2 begins"
34
35      display space
36      display "Input a postcode or 'Q' to quit"
37      accept k1-postcode
```

DATA VALIDATION 57

```
38    perform test before until k1-eok
39    set w3-valid to true
40
41
42
43    evaluate k1-firstalpha alphabetic
44        when    true
45            display "first alpha valid"
46        when    false
47            display "first alpha invalid"
48            set w3-invalid to true
49    end-evaluate
50
51    evaluate k1-firstnumber numeric
52        when    true
53            display "first number valid"
54        when    false
55            display "first number invalid"
56            set w3-invalid to true
57    end-evaluate
58
59    evaluate w3-valid
60        when    true
61            display "postcode is:"
62            move k1-firsthalf    to s2-string
63            move "is the first part" to s2-message
64            display s2-postcode
65
66            move k1-secondhalf to s2-string
67            move "is the second part" to s2-message
68            display s2-postcode
69        when    false
70            display "invalid postcode"
71    end-evaluate
72
73    display space
74    display "Input another postcode or 'Q' to quit"
75    accept k1-postcode
76    end-perform
77
78    display "post2 ends"
79    stop run.
80
81 end program post2.
```

Figure 3.4 Program post2

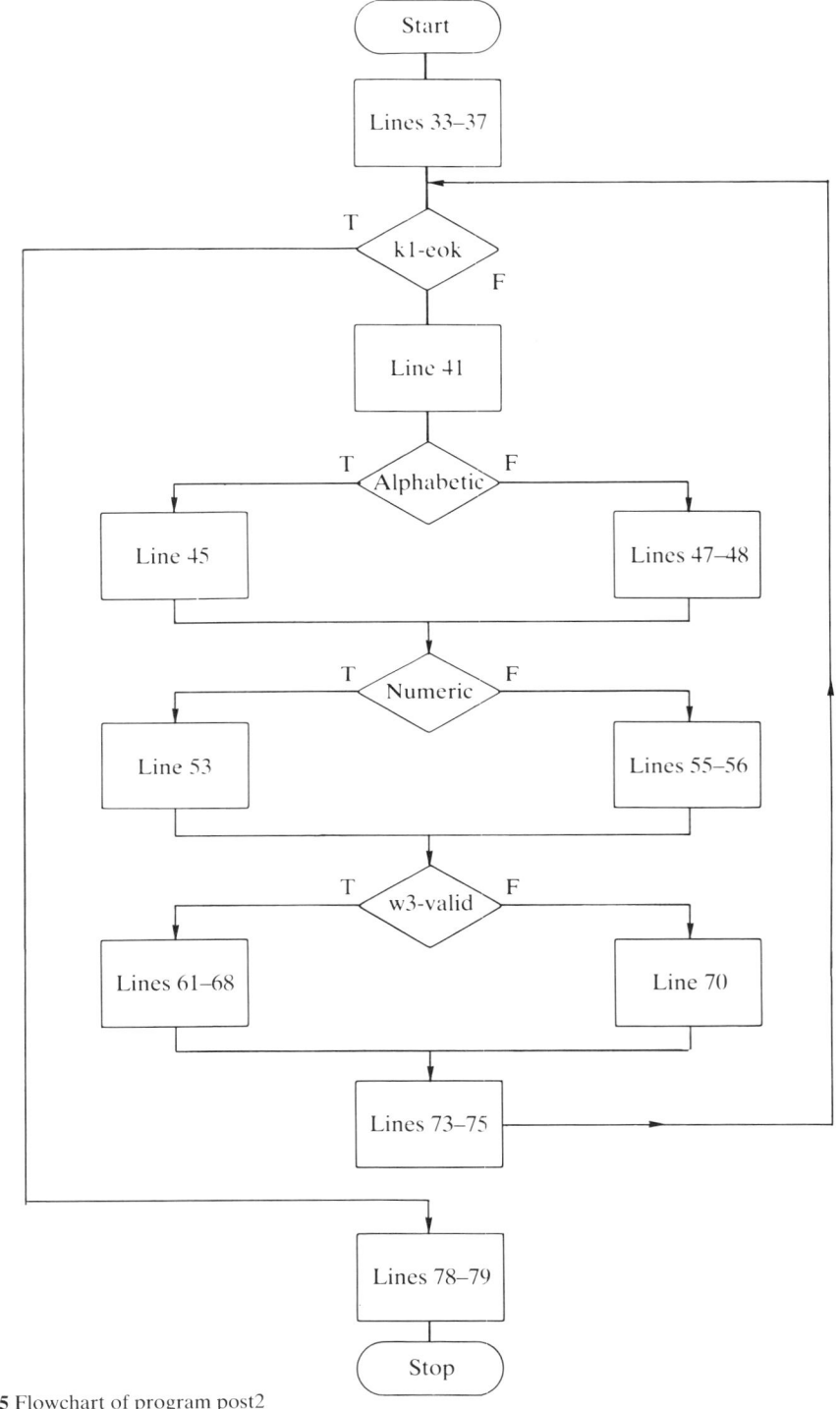

58 ESSENTIAL COBOL: A FIRST COURSE IN STRUCTURED COBOL

Figure 3.5 Flowchart of program post2

DATA VALIDATION 59

Lines 59 to 71 contain the final evaluate statement. It tests to see whether or not the original assumption is still true. When it is still true it displays the postcode and when it is false it displays an appropriate message.

Figure 3.5 illustrates the flow of control within post2 as a flowchart.

Thus the evaluate statements in post2 follow a simple pattern of selection which can be represented by the pseudo-code and flowchart shown in Fig. 3.6.

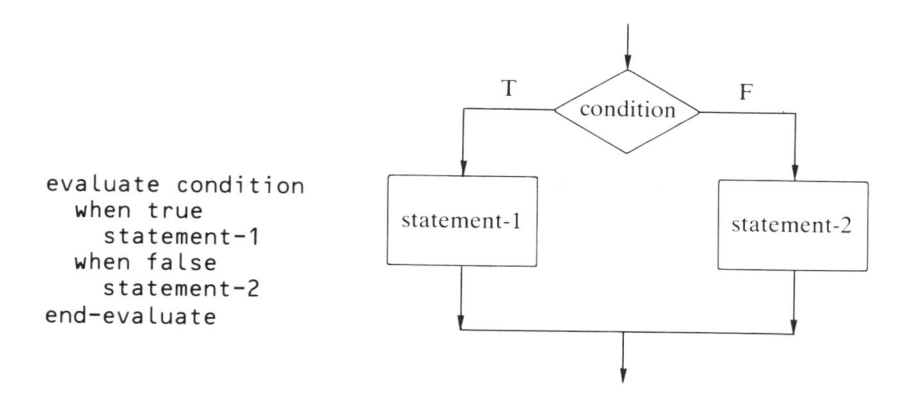

```
evaluate condition
   when true
      statement-1
   when false
      statement-2
end-evaluate
```

Figure 3.6 Pseudo-code and flowchart for selection

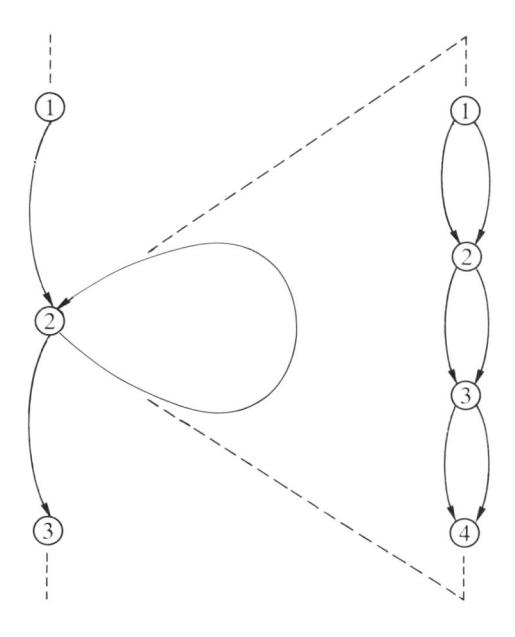

Figure 3.7 Flowgraph expansion showing statement nesting

Program post2 can also be described using a main flowgraph and a nested flowgraph (Fig. 3.7).

We can see that the outer level (nesting level 1) is similar to previous programs. The inner level (nesting level 2) is a decomposition of the link from point 2 to itself. With practice you will discover that you can visualize these simple patterns as you read programs and that these patterns will occur frequently.

SELF-CHECK QUESTIONS

Q   Is "Q∆15∆∆∆∆" a valid postcode in program post2?
A   No. The two leading characters will cause `k1-eok` to be true and the body of the loop will not execute.

Q   What amendment could be made to post2 so that "Q∆15∆∆∆∆" will be found to be a valid code?
A   The test condition for the main loop must be changed. For example, we might test for 8 spaces or for "Q∆∆∆∆∆∆∆".

Q   Is "∆Q12∆∆∆∆" a valid postcode in program post2?
A   Yes. The first characters are alphabetic.

Q   Is "A∆∆1∆∆∆∆" a valid postcode in program post2?
A   No. The third character must be numeric.

Q   Is "∆∆12∆∆∆∆" a valid postcode in program post2?
A   Yes. The first two characters are alphabetic.

Q   Redraw the flowgraphs for post2 and label the links with the appropriate line numbers.

The **evaluate** statement is a powerful and flexible feature for selecting between alternative paths. Another simple format for it is:

```
evaluate  {true }
          {false}
   {when       condition   statement-1}...
   [when       other       statement-2]
   end-evaluate
```

As before the order of evaluation is still always from the first to the last rule. When the first true rule is found the statement associated with it will be executed and control will pass to the next statement after the end-evaluate terminator. The other rule is by definition always true and will be executed if it is ever reached. (The other rule must always be the last rule.)

```
evaluate true
   when    e2-var = "jenny△"
      display "Hello△Jenny△"
   when    e2-var = "tom△△△"
      display "Hello△Thomas"
   when    e2-var = "liz△△△"
      display "Hello△Elizabeth"
   when    e2-var = "harry△"
      display "Hello△Henry"
   when    other
      display "Hello△whoever△you△are"
end-evaluate
```

In the above example one of the rules will always be executed because the other rule will always be true if it is ever reached.

The condition stated after the reserved word evaluate is called the selection subject and the condition stated in each rule is a selection object.

selection subject	–	selection object	= result
true	–	false	= false
false	–	true	= false
true	–	true	= true
false	–	false	= true
true	–	other	= true
false	–	other	= true

Figure 3.8 Truth table for the **evaluate** statement

As each rule is evaluated the object is reduced to true or false. (If the keyword **true** or **false** is used then no reduction is required.) The subject and object are then evaluated according to the truth table shown in Fig. 3.8. If the result is true, then the rule is true and the associated statement will be executed. We can see that a result is true only when the subject and object evaluate to the same truth value or when **other** is used. (The effect of **other** is to force a true result.)

Program post2 introduced the **set** verb as a way of causing a condition to become true. Its simple format is:

```
set condition-name to true
```

It has the effect of moving the value listed against the condition-name to the associated data item.

Consider the following data item and condition-name:

```
01   e3-var              pic x.
     88   e3-c1          value "Y".
```

The statement set e3-c1 to true will cause a "Y" to be moved to e3-var.

Although COBOL allows condition-names to be tested for a truth value of true or false, the set statement can only be used to assign a value of true. If COBOL allowed `e3-c1` to be set to false it is entirely arbitrary what value should be assigned to `e3-var`. Therefore setting condition-names to false is not allowed.

In cases where a *switch* with only two possible settings representing true and false is needed two condition-names should be used. For example:

```
01   e4-var      pic x.
     88   e4-off    value "N".
     88   e4-on     value "Y".
```

The switch can be used in the program with either of the following statements:

```
set e4-off to true
set e4-on  to true
```

In cases where the condition-name has a list of conditional values the set statement will always assign the first possible value to the data item. For example:

```
01   e5-var      pic x.
     88   e5-off    value "N" "n".
     88   e5-on     value "Y" "y".
```

The result of setting `e5-off` to true is that `e5-var` becomes "N".

In cases where the conditions are meant to be exclusive, it is important that the lists never contain the same values. Consider the following example where this is the case:

```
01   e6-var      pic x.
     88   e6-c1    value "1" "5".
     88   e6-c2    value "3" "2" "1".
```

If `e6-c1` is set to true then `e6-var` becomes "1". In any subsequent program tests both conditions will be true because the value "1" appears in each of the condition lists. Such a use of condition-names is valid and sometimes useful. However, it should be avoided when mutually exclusive condition-names are required.

SELF-CHECK QUESTIONS

Q Write an evaluate statement to display "Yes" when the condition `c1` is true and "No" in all other cases.

A These two statements are correct:

```
evaluate c1
   when    true
      display "Yes"
   when    false
      display "No"
end-evaluate
```

```
evaluate true
  when   c1
    display "Yes"
  when   other
    display "No"
end-evaluate
```

The first statement is clearer and therefore preferable.

Q Is the following statement equivalent to those written above?

```
evaluate true
  when   c1
    display "Yes"
  when   false
    display "No"
end-evaluate
```

A No. The subject and the object for the second rule are true and false respectively. True **and** false is false. Therefore the statement in the second rule is unreachable. If an action is to be undertaken only when a condition is true and in no other circumstances the correct form for the statement is:

```
evaluate true
  when   c1
    display "Yes"
end-evaluate
```

Q What is the effect of the following statement?

```
evaluate true
  when   true
    display "Yes"
  when   c1
    display "No"
end-evaluate
```

A True **and** true is always true. Therefore the first statement will always be executed and the second statement is unreachable. The whole statement has the same effect as a single display "Yes".

Q Does COBOL protect the programmer from writing unreachable statements?

A No. The COBOL standard does not define whether or not a compiler should identify unreachable statements. However, many good compilers will do so with simple errors such as those above.

Q In logic the following relationship is known as *equivalence*:

(c1 and c2) or (not c1 and not c2)

What relationship does this have to the evaluate statement?

A   The evaluate statement implements an equivalence relationship between the subject and its object. Therefore true **and** true are considered a subject and object match as are false **and** false.

The evaluate statement goes further than this by using the keyword **other** which will match with any subject. Thus:

(subject and object) or (not subject and not object)

more closely expresses the way that equivalence is used in the evaluate statement. (We have to remember that the keyword **other** is always equivalent to any truth value for the subject.)

3.5 REFERENCE MODIFICATION

Our previous data definition gave us a data structure that allowed us to define the layout of an eight-character postcode and to access various sub-elements in its character string. COBOL provides *reference modification* as an alternative technique for writing identifiers that can reference substrings.

In reference modification a complex identifier is constructed by supplementing a simple identifier with information that specifies which characters in the string are to be referenced. Its full format is

```
simple-identifier(left-position: [length])
```

The left-position indicates the position at which the substring starts and the length indicates the length of the substring.

3.5.1 Using numeric literals

Let us recall the definition of postcode in program post2:

```
01  k1-postcode.
    03  k1-firsthalf.
        05  k1-firstalpha          pic aa.
        05  k1-firstnumber         pic 99.
    03  k1-postspacer              pic x.
    03  k1-secondhalf.
        05  k1-secondnumber        pic 9.
        05  k1-secondalpha         pic aa.
```

All of the reference modifications shown in Fig. 3.9 are legal and could be used in program statements. In each case the characters referenced are considered to be alphanumeric because `k1-postcode` is alphanumeric.

The rules in Fig. 3.10 summarize the correct use of reference modification and should be studied carefully.

Using reference modification	Using simple identifiers
k1-postcode(1:2)	k1-firstalpha
k1-postcode(3:2)	k1-firstnumber
k1-postcode(5:1)	k1-postspacer
k1-postcode(6:1)	k1-secondnumber
k1-postcode(7:2)	k1-secondalpha
k1-postcode(1:4)	k1-firsthalf
k1-postcode(6:3)	k1-secondhalf

Figure 3.9 Valid references using reference modification

1. The identifier must reference a character string.
2. Both left-position and length must be greater than zero.
3. A left-position or length that attempts to reference a character beyond the end of the string is not allowed.
4. The length can be omitted in which case the reference will default to the maximum length from the given left-position.

Figure 3.10 Rules for using reference modification.

SELF-CHECK QUESTIONS

Q Is k1-postcode(1:) a legal identifier?
A Yes. It is constructed using rule 4. It references the same data as k1-postcode without reference modification.

Q Is k1-postcode(2:) a legal identifier?
A Yes. It references the second to the last character.

Q Are k1-postcode(0:2) or k1-postcode(8:2) legal identifiers?
A No. Both attempt to reference outside the string.

Q Is k1-postcode(8:1) a legal identifier?
A Yes. It references the last character.

Q Is k1-firstnumber(2:1) a legal identifier?
A Yes. It references the second digit of k1-firstnumber. (Remember that the defining symbols 'x', 'a', and '9' are used to define character strings and the class tests are used to ensure that these strings hold only those characters that are consistent with their pictures.)

Thus we have two ways to construct identifiers:

1. By using data-names as identifiers as in post2.
2. By using data-names that are reference modified with literals as outlined above.

Both of these ways provide a *static* reference to the data. By static we mean that the unique identifier for the data is determined when the program is written and cannot be changed during program execution. Therefore if a different string or substring must be referenced the program must be rewritten and recompiled.

Most references to data are static. However, the question arises as to which of these two methods of static reference is preferable. Unfortunately there is no simple and definitive answer to such a question.

Using simple identifiers forces the reader to check the data division in order to determine which characters are being referenced. Reference modification using literals allows the programmer to use a simpler data structure. However, this simplicity is offset by the greater complexity of the data references in the procedure division.

The final decision as to which of these two forms to use in a commercial programming environment is likely to depend upon external factors such as the way in which pre-existing record definitions have been written and the nature of the application being programmed.

In general, it is preferable to design programs in such a way that data complexity is presented within the data description and not the procedural code. Therefore it is unlikely that most programmers will ever wish to use reference modification with literals only.

3.5.2 Using numeric data items

The left-position and length in a modified reference can be variables, thereby allowing us to change the left-position and length under program control.

As a first problem let us suppose that we wish to write a program that determines the length of a character string. The string will have a length in the range of 1 to 10 characters. It has neither leading nor embedded spaces but may have trailing spaces. A string of spaces should cause the program to terminate. (Figure 3.11 shows six test cases for this problem.)

The following data definitions provide a description for the data needed to accept and check the contents of an input string of 10 characters:

Possible input	Expected result
⟨RET⟩	termination
T⟨RET⟩	01; continuation
AB⟨RET⟩	02; continuation
hijklmnop⟨RET⟩	09; continuation
abcdefghij⟨RET⟩	10; continuation

Figure 3.11 Test data for program refmod1

DATA VALIDATION 67

```
01  k1-string          pic x(10).
01  w2-reference.
    03  w2-ref         pic 99.
        88  w2-min     value 01.
        88  w2-max     value 11.
    03  w2-result      pic 99.
```

We know that `k1-string(1:1)` refers to the first character in the string and that `k1-string(10:1)` refers to the last character. A reference to any character in the string could be expressed as `k1-string(w2-ref:1)` provided that `w2-ref` held a value in the range of 1 through to 10. (`W2-result` will be used to display the string length.)

The following statements enable us to increment `w2-ref` from an initial value of 1 through to a final value of 11 for a total of 10 possible iterations.

```
set w2-min to true
perform test before until w2-max
   compute w2-ref = w2-ref + 1
end-perform
```

Upon first entering the loop `w2-ref` will have a value of 1. Eventually the compute statement will cause `w2-ref` to reach a value of 11, the test condition for the loop will become true and the loop will stop executing. The compute statement itself will be executed 10 times.

The loop we have constructed will always execute 10 times. However, the problem requires us to take one of two alternative actions:

1. When the character is a space calculate the `w2-result` as 1 less than the current value of `w2-ref` and terminate the loop.
2. When the character is not a space add 1 to `w2-ref` in preparation for a check on the next character.

Therefore the next task is to construct an **evaluate** statement to include these alternatives:

```
evaluate k1-string(w2-ref:1) = space
   when     true
     compute w2-result = w2-ref - 1
     set w2-max to true
   when false
     compute w2-ref = w2-ref + 1
end-evaluate
```

The above **evaluate** statement will yield a result in all cases where a trailing space exists. However, when the string contains no spaces the false rule will be executed 10 times and `w2-max` will become true thereby terminating the loop without giving a value to `w2-result`.

Therefore we can see that an initial hypothesis, namely that the string contains 10 non-space characters is needed, and that the evaluate statement can be used within the loop to disprove this.

```
*       Reference the start of the string
        set w2-min to true
*       Assume that the string is 10 characters long
        move 10 to w2-result
*       CHECK until the end of the string or the first space
        perform test before until w2-max
          evaluate k1-string(w1-ref:1) = space
            when    true
*             Concede that it is less that 10 characters long
              compute w2-result = w2-ref - 1
              set w2-max to true
            when    false
              compute w2-ref = w2-ref + 1
          end-evaluate
        end-perform
*       END-CHECK
```

Program refmod1 incorporates these statements to check strings and to terminate execution when the first string of spaces is found.

Line 25 accepts an initial value for k1-string. If the user types a single RETURN or spaces followed by a single RETURN, the condition k1-eok will become true. In all other cases the condition will be false.

The main loop of the program begins at line 27 and ends at line 45. Provided that k1-eok is true the main loop will execute. The last statement within the loop is another **accept** statement at line 44 and it establishes a new value for the k1-eok test. Thus the main loop will be executed zero or more times and the statements within the loop are reached only if k1-eok is true upon entering the loop.

The set statement at line 28 establishes an initial value for w2-ref. Line 29 sets w2-result to 10 as an initial hypothesis.

The inner loop of the program begins at line 30 and ends at line 38. The evaluation of the string begins with the first character. Provided that w2-max is not true the **evaluate** statement within the loop will continue to be executed. Line 33 disproves that the string contains no spaces. At this point we have found a space and therefore the string length must be one character less than the current value of w2-ref.

The first time the **evaluate** is executed w2-ref will have a value of 1. If the first character is a space character the first rule will be executed, the result will be calculated to be zero and w2-max will be set to true, thereby terminating the loop. However, if the first character is not a space the second rule will be executed and the loop will proceed.

Thus the loop will continue to execute until a space is found or until w2-ref takes the value of 10 thereby causing w2-max to become true.

Most of the difficulties associated with writing loops are *semantic* rather than syntactic. In other words, it is easy to write statements that are correct, compilable statements but which nevertheless produce incorrect output when they are executed in the running program.

Rigorous testing is one approach to uncovering semantic errors. However, in order to create rigorous test data the problem being solved must be well understood. Even though a

```
 1 identification division.
 2 program-id. refmod1.
 3*Purpose: Count the number of characters in a string.
 4
 5 environment division.
 6
 7 data division.
 8 working-storage section.
 9 01   k1-string            pic x(10).
10      88   k1-eok          value space.
11
12 01   w2-reference.
13      03   w2-ref          pic 99.
14           88 w2-min       value 01.
15           88 w2-max       value 11.
16      03   w2-result       pic 99.
17
18 procedure division.
19 para1.
20      display "refmod1 begins"
21
22      display space
23      display "Type a string of up to 10 characters or"
24      display "a single RETURN to quit"
25      accept k1-string
26
27      perform test before until k1-eok
28        set w2-min to true
29        move 10 to w2-result
30        perform test before until w2-max
31          evaluate k1-string(w2-ref:1) = space
32            when    true
33              compute w2-result = w2-ref - 1
34              set w2-max to true
35            when    false
36              compute w2-ref     = w2-ref + 1
37          end-evaluate
38        end-perform
39
40        display "The string was " w2-result " characters long."
41
42        display space
43        display "Type another string or a RETURN to quit"
44        accept k1-string
45      end-perform
46
47      display "refmod1 ends"
48      stop run.
49
50 end program refmod1.
```

Figure 3.12 Program refmod1

test may uncover an error it may not always point to a solution. Furthermore, as a program increases in size it becomes more and more difficult to specify effective tests.

Formal program verification is another approach to increasing confidence in the correctness of programs. However, formal methods usually require a correct specification of the problem being solved and this specification often approaches the complexity of the program. As with testing, formal methods may uncover an error but not the solution. They also tend to be most useful on small-scale problems.

Trace execution is a third approach to testing. It is specifically aimed at demonstrating the order of statement execution in the running program. In order to trace a program it is important to create a set of data that will:

- test at least every statement in the program once
- check the boundary conditions that are implied by all conditional statements.

Figure 3.13 shows eight test cases for two test runs together with the expected outcomes for each run. It is useful when writing a loop to construct such a table and to determine by checking the program at your desk that it will behave in the way in which you intended. The boundary condition for the outer loop is an input of spaces. This must be tested as both the first and the last input thereby requiring at least two runs of the program. The second run tests the inner loop to ensure that the boundary length of 10 is correctly processed. Strings of 9 and 11 characters are included to ensure that the program works correctly for values that lie immediately to either side of the upper boundary.

We can see that when the input is more than ten characters long the program cannot identify this problem and gives a length of 10. This difficulty is caused by the fact that standard COBOL moves the input string from the keyboard *buffer* to the variable according to the rules of the alphanumeric move and truncates strings that are longer than the program expects. In later programs we will define the input as slightly longer than expected so that we can check to see whether or not non-space characters occur in the excess length. However, even if we had defined the input field as `pic x(11)` we would still have calculated `"abcdefghij∆∆k"` as a length of 10 although `"abcdefghijk"` could have

	Possible input	*Expected result*
RUN1:		
	⟨RET⟩	termination
RUN2:		
	T⟨RET⟩	01; continuation
	AB⟨RET⟩	02; continuation
	AB ggg⟨RET⟩	02; continuation
	hijklmnop⟨RET⟩	09; continuation
	abcdefghij⟨RET⟩	10; continuation
	abcdefghijk⟨RET⟩	10; termination
	⟨RET⟩	termination

Figure 3.13 Test cases for two runs of program refmod1

been detected as invalid. (COBOL does not provide a way to determine the actual number of characters typed into the keyboard buffer.)

The test data show another fault in the solution. This is that forward checking from the first to the last character causes the program to assume that the string ends at the first embedded space. Later programs will overcome the limitation in this approach by checking backwards for spaces from the last to the first character and then ensuring afterwards that the string does not contain embedded spaces.

SELF-CHECK QUESTIONS

Q Is `e1-postcode(e1-ref + 2:e1-len - 1)` a legal identifier?
A Yes. Both the left position and the length can be arithmetic expressions using the plus or minus sign. The values to which such expressions evaluate at run time must be legal references within the string.

Q Redraft Fig. 3.13 to list against each test case the line numbers that it will cause to be executed.

Q Program refmod1 has three nesting levels. Draw three flowgraphs similar to those drawn for program post2 in order to show the decomposition of the program clearly.

3.6 CASE STUDY: POST3 (PATTERN MATCHING)

Postcodes are increasingly becoming a necessary feature of modern communications. In many countries companies and other large users of postal services are required to use postcodes when sending large amounts of mail.

Unfortunately for programmers there is no internationally agreed standard for postcodes. Figure 3.14 shows some of the different rules that exist in three different countries.

1. The original USA zip code is a single five digit character string.
2. The latest British postcode is in two parts separated by a space.
   The first part can take one of three forms:

   (a) two alphabetics and two numerics;
   (b) two alphabetics and one numeric;
   (c) one alphabetic, one numeric and one alphabetic.

   The second part is always one numeric followed by two alphabetics.
3. The Canadian postcode is in two parts which are separated by a space.
   The first part is always one alphabetic followed by one numeric and one alphabetic.
   The second part is always one numeric followed by one alphabetic and one numeric.

Figure 3.14 Rules for constructing certain international postcodes

72 ESSENTIAL COBOL: A FIRST COURSE IN STRUCTURED COBOL

10249	rule 1
SW15 2PW	rule 2a
BS16 1QR	rule 2a
BA1 7TT	rule 2b
W1N 2XA	rule 2c
M4Y 1N6	rule 3

Figure 3.15 Some valid postcodes

These rules explicitly state the encoding for five different kinds of correct postcode. Figure 3.15 gives a few examples of the very large number of postcodes that are correct according to these rules.

The problem we shall solve is to determine whether or not a string of characters contains a correct postcode according to one of the above rules. An essential clue to solving the problem is to see that the rules as stated are closely related to the concept of data class.

The maximum string length for any code is 8 characters. If we define the input as a string of 9 characters we can check to make sure that the last character is a space, i.e. that the input string was not longer than 8 characters.

Therefore what patterns are allowable within the nine characters to be validated? Figure 3.16 summarizes all of the valid patterns which might exist. These patterns can be shown as test conditions against a 9 character string of data:

```
01  w3-postcode    pic x(9).
    88  w3-rule1   value "99999    ".
    88  w3-rule2a  value "aa99 9aa ".
    88  w3-rule2b  value "aa9 9aa  ".
    88  w3-rule2c  value "a9a 9aa  ".
    88  w3-rule3   value "a9a 9a9  ".
```

	Character position								
Rule	:	1	2	3	4	5	6	7	8	9
1	:	9	9	9	9	9	Δ	Δ	Δ	Δ
2a	:	a	a	9	9	Δ	9	a	a	Δ
2b	:	a	a	9	Δ	9	a	a	Δ	Δ
2c	:	a	9	a	Δ	9	a	a	Δ	Δ
3	:	a	9	a	Δ	9	a	9	Δ	Δ

Where a denotes alphabetic
       9 denotes numeric
       Δ denotes space

Figure 3.16 Postcode patterns

Our next problem is to find a way of reducing the variety of characters that exist in a postcode string to the three characters shown above. A test for space as well as the class tests can be used to construct the following three tests:

```
w3-postcode(w2-ref:1) = space
w3-postcode(w2-ref:1) alphabetic
w3-postcode(w2-ref:1) numeric
```

Note that the alphabetic class includes the space character. Therefore we must test for space first and if this is found to be true then no further testing is required.

As we have seen the evaluate statement tests conditions and executes statements according to the priority in which the rules are written.

```
evaluate true
  when    w3-postcode(w2-ref:1) = space
    continue
  when    w3-postcode(w2-ref:1) alphabetic
    move "a" to w3-postcode(w2-ref:1)
  when    w3-postcode(w2-ref:1) numeric
    move "9" to w3-postcode(w2-ref:1)
end-evaluate
```

The first rule in the above evaluate statement will do nothing to a space because the **continue** statement is defined as an empty statement. When it is encountered no action will be taken. Therefore its effect in the above **evaluate** statement is to leave a space character unchanged. The continue statement is COBOL's null statement. It may be used wherever a format requires a statement to be specified.

The second rule replaces an alphabetic by the character "a". It does not include space even though the space character is alphabetic because this was covered by the first rule.

The third rule replaces a numeric character by a "9".

We can now use reference modification within a while loop to check each character in the string in turn and change non-spaces to one of the three possible characters that will be used in subsequent testing.

```
*       Reference the start of the string
        set w2-min to true

*       CONVERT the whole string to a pattern of space, "a" and "9"
        perform test before until w2-max
          evaluate true
            when w3-postcode(w2-ref:1) = space
              continue
            when w3-postcode(w2-ref:1) alphabetic
              move "a" to w3-postcode(w2-ref:1)
            when w3-postcode(w2-ref:1) numeric
              move "9" to w3-postcode(w2-ref:1)
          end-evaluate
          compute w2-ref = w2-ref + 1
*       end-perform
        END-CONVERT
```

```
 1  identification division.
 2  program-id. post3.
 3 *Purpose: Determine whether or not an 8 character postcode is valid.
 4
 5  environment division.
 6
 7  data division.
 8  working-storage section.
 9  01  k1-postcode      pic x(9).
10      88  k1-eok       value "Q            ".
11                              "q            ".
12
13  01  w2-reference.
14      03  w2-ref       pic 99.
15          88  w2-min   value 01.
16          88  w2-max   value 10.
17
18  01  w3-postcode      pic x(9).
19      88  w3-rule1     value "99999    ".
20      88  w3-rule2a    value "aa99 9aa ".
21      88  w3-rule2b    value "aa9 9aa  ".
22      88  w3-rule2c    value "a9a 9aa  ".
23      88  w3-rule3     value "a9a 9a9  ".
24
25  procedure division.
26  para1.
27      display "post3 begins"
28
```

```
29      display space
30      display "Input a postcode or 'Q' to quit"
31      accept k1-postcode
32
33      perform test before until k1-eok
34          move k1-postcode to w3-postcode
35          set w2-min to true
36          perform test before until w2-max
37              evaluate true
38                  when w3-postcode(w2-ref:1) = space
39                      continue
40                  when w3-postcode(w2-ref:1) alphabetic
41                      move "a"  to w3-postcode(w2-ref:1)
42                  when w3-postcode(w2-ref:1) numeric
43                      move "9"  to w3-postcode(w2-ref:1)
44              end-evaluate
45              compute w2-ref = w2-ref + 1
46          end-perform
47
48          evaluate true
49              when w3-rule1
50                  display "rule1"
51              when w3-rule2a
52                  display "rule2a"
53              when w3-rule2b
54                  display "rule2b"
55              when w3-rule2c
56                  display "rule2c"
57              when w3-rule3
58                  display "rule3"
59              when other
60                  display "invalid"
61          end-evaluate
62
63          display space
64          display "Input another postcode or 'Q' to quit"
65          accept k1-postcode
66      end-perform
67
68      display "post3 ends"
69      stop run.
70
71  end program post3.
```

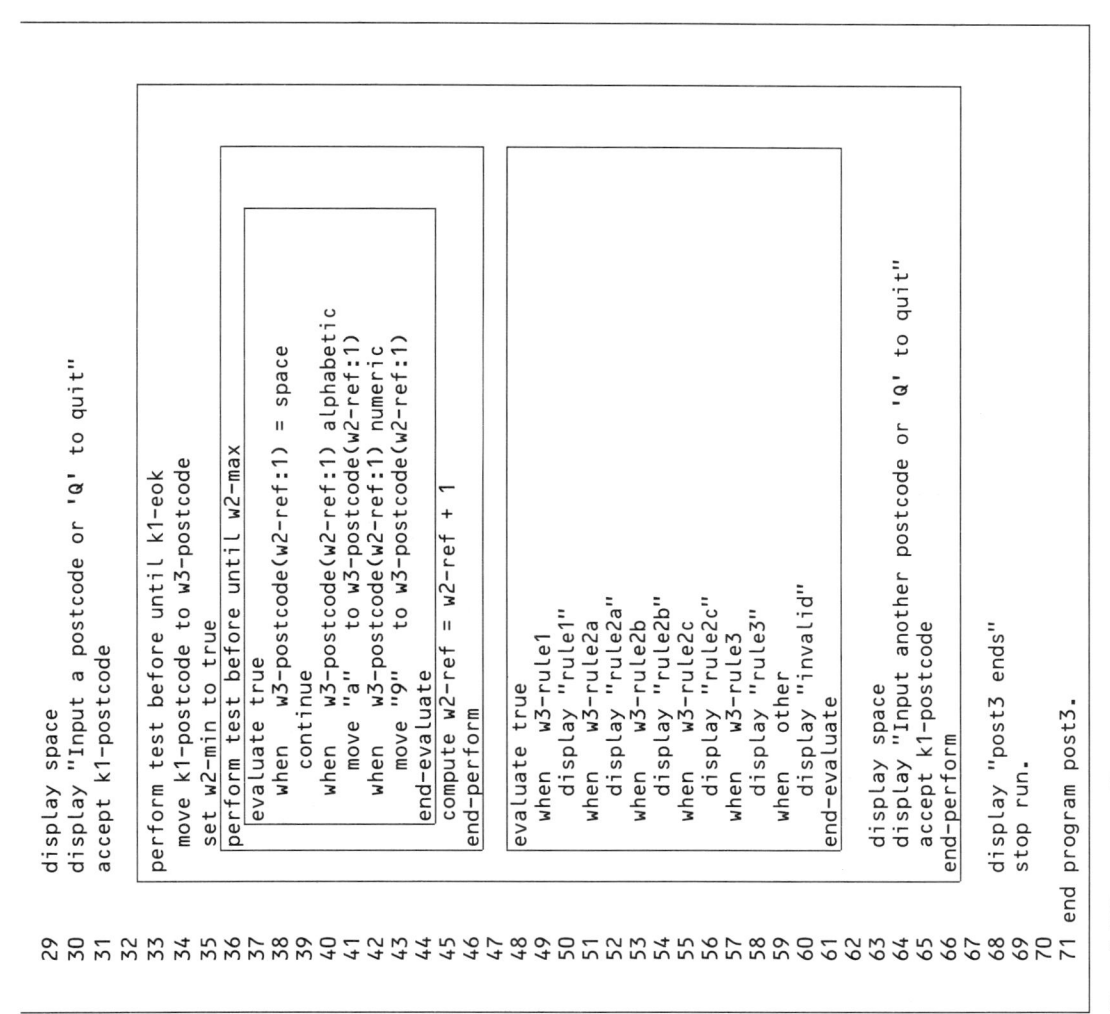

Figure 3.17 Program post3

Once the variety in the character string has been reduced to the three test characters a single **evaluate** statement can be used to determine which, if any, of the rules has been satisfied:

```
evaluate true
  when    w3-rule1
    display "rule1"
  when    w3-rule2a
    display "rule2a"
  when    w3-rule2b
    display "rule2b"
  when    w3-rule2c
    display "rule2c"
  when    w3-rule3
    display "rule3"
  when    other
    display "invalid"
end-evaluate
```

We can see that the total solution has been designed with only nine rules. The three rules in the first evaluate statement reduced the variety of valid characters from 37 to 3 and the six rules in the second evaluate statement selected the appropriate action.

Program post3 in Fig. 3.17 implements the postcode validation.

Lines 34 to 46 convert the string prior to the pattern matching and lines 48 to 61 match the pattern. These are contained within an outer loop which is driven by the user (lines 33 to 66).

If we had not converted the data to a simpler form before testing we would not have been able to find valid postcodes except by testing each character in turn to ensure that it fell within an acceptable range.

Figure 3.18 shows the full set of tests that would have to be made to determine the validity of a postcode if the character variety were not reduced.

The boxes give a visual indication of the nesting of rules that would have resulted from following such a strategy. Thus rule 2a would require tests 4–10.

In conclusion we can see that by first reducing the character variety in a pattern-matching problem the necessary tests for pattern correctness are reduced and simplified. The greatest difficulty in designing solutions for problems of this kind is in recognizing in the first place that there is a need for managing and matching patterns.

3.7 EXERCISES

3.7.1 General

1 Write program refmod2 to count the number of non-space characters in a 10 character string that has been entered at the keyboard in a right-justified form with no embedded spaces. (By right-justified we mean that the string may have leading spaces but no trailing spaces. Embedded spaces have at least one non-space character to either side. Therefore "Joe∆" is left justified, "∆Joe" is right-justified and "J∆oe" has embedded spaces.)

DATA VALIDATION 77

Rule	Test	Number
1	postcode(7:1) = space	1
	postcode(1:5) numeric	2
	postcode(6:4) = space	3
2	postcode(7:1) alphabetic	4
2a + 2b	postcode(7:3) numeric	5
2a	postcode(7:4) numeric	6
	postcode(1:2) alphabetic	7
	postcode(5:1) = space	8
	postcode(8:1) alphabetic	9
	postcode(9:1) = space	10
2b	postcode(7:4) = space	11
	postcode(1:2) alphabetic	12
	postcode(5:1) numeric	13
	postcode(8:2) = space	14
2c	postcode(7:3) alphabetic	15
	postcode(1:1) alphabetic	16
	postcode(2:1) numeric	17
	postcode(5:1) numeric	18
	postcode(8:2) = space	19
3	postcode(7:1) numeric	20
	postcode(1:1) alphabetic	21
	postcode(2:1) numeric	22
	postcode(3:1) alphabetic	23
	postcode(4:1) = space	24
	postcode(5:1) numeric	25
	postcode(6:1) alphabetic	26
	postcode(8:2) = space	27

Figure 3.18 Full set of tests for postcodes in original form

2 Write program refmod3 to make the following three counts for an 18 character string:

(a) total number of leading spaces;
(b) total number of trailing spaces;
(c) total number of embedded spaces.

3 Write program refmod4 to take two strings of any length of up to 10 characters each and display them as a single string with no embedded spaces. Assume that if the two inputs have any spaces they will only be trailing spaces, that is, that the inputs are left justified with no embedded spaces.

4 Write program refmod5 to take a string of up to 25 characters in which there may be a single asterisk "*" that is used as a separator character. The program should split the original string at the separator and display the resulting two substrings without the separator. Enhance Refmod5 so that it displays the lengths of the two substrings.

5 Local telephone numbers in North America have three digits followed by a separator followed by four digits. They can also have an area code prefix consisting of three digits and a separator. For example,

```
772-7675            local number
214-772-7675        local number prefixed by an area code
```

Write program telnum1 to check whether or not a string holds a valid telephone number.

6 Bumpf International specializes in a particular range of disposable paper products. These products are stored in its warehouse by inventory codes that have the following fixed patterns of alphabetic and numeric characters:

```
BR-123
DEF-3456
912-AB-621
```

Write program bumpf1 which when given a string of characters will determine whether the string conforms to a correct pattern.

7 A college uses the following degree abbreviations:

```
BA  = Bachelor of Arts
BS  = Bachelor of Science
MA  = Master of Arts
MS  = Master of Science
PhD = Doctorate
```

Write a program that can determine whether or not a string contains a valid course code according to the following rules:

(a) a course code consists of a degree abbreviation followed by a space followed by a year followed by a space followed by a code followed by any number of spaces. For example,

```
BA∆4∆326
```

(b) The bachelor years must be 1, 2, 3, or 4. Other degrees must be 1 or 2.

(c) The bachelor codes are three digit, the master codes are two digit, and the doctorate codes are one digit.

All of the following are valid course codes and can be used as test cases for the program:

BA△4△326
BS△1△120
MA△2△97
PhD△1△7
PhD△2△0

Before writing the program make sure that you have developed a good set of test cases for both valid and invalid data.

(*Hint:* Note that positions 4 through 8 in all cases hold either spaces or numeric characters. "BA△4△326" could be reduced to "BA△n△nnn" provided that the first three characters are "BA△", the fourth character is in the range of "1" to "4" and the final three characters are numeric.)

8 Crossword puzzles often include anagrams. These are words for which the letters can be rearranged to form different words. Thus the letters of the word stop can be arranged to form the words tops and spot. When trying to solve anagrams people often try to discover all of the ways in which a set of letters can be rearranged. Work out by hand the number of permutations that can be made of words with 1 to 3 letters. Write program permut1 to take a word of up to 3 different letters and list all of its permutations on the screen.

9 A palindrome is a word such as kayak which is spelt the same forwards and backwards. Write program pal1 to detect whether or not a word is a palindrome.

3.7.2 Case study

10 Program post3 incorporates three main sets of functional statements. Insert documentation to draw the eye of the reader to these three sets.
11 Draw a flowgraph of post3. Use the flowgraph to determine the depth of nesting within the program.
12 Use the information in Fig. 3.18 to draft an outline in pseudo-code for a program that solves the same problem as post3 but without the first step of variety reduction. Determine the depth of nesting that would result in this program. Consider the impact upon both post3 and the draft program of adding further postcodes with the following rules:

  Rule 4. Old British Codes
    (a) one alphabetic followed by one numeric
    (b) one alphabetic followed by two numerics
    (c) two alphabetics followed by one numeric
    (d) two alphabetics followed by two numerics

13 Rewrite post3 as post3a to include the old British postcodes.
14 The latest zip code consists of five numerics followed by a hyphen and a further four numerics. Rewrite post3a to include this latest form of zip code.

4
INTER-PROGRAM COMMUNICATION

COBOL provides facilities by which a program can communicate with one or more other programs. In this chapter we shall concentrate on the key mechanisms used in constructing a program with *nested* programs. In Chapter 10 we shall examine other program communication facilities.

Nested programs provide the programmer with a means for splitting large and complicated programming tasks into smaller ones. In general the program will co-ordinate the overall task and nested programs will provide solutions to subtasks that have been isolated within the general design.

In its simplest form inter-program communication allows a program to call a program that is nested within its source text. (For example, program main1 in Fig. 4.2 contains a nested program.) Thus a program and its nested program are part of the same *compilation unit*. The program can transfer execution control and can pass data as *parameters* to the nested program by means of the **call** statement.

Post4 is a case study program and it appears at the end of this chapter. It is a small example of a program that contains a nested program. It solves the same problem as post3 from the previous chapter. You should spend a few moments reviewing post3 and comparing it with post4 before reading the rest of the chapter.

4.1 BASIC TERMS

The relationship between a program and its nested program can be visualized using a *structure chart* (Fig. 4.1). In this example the *calling* program is named main1 and the *called* nested program is nest1. The highest level is always level 1. Nest1 is nested at level 2.

Structure charts are an example of a general structure in computing that is called a

```
        ┌─────────┐
        │  main1  │                    Level 1
        └────┬────┘
             │
        ┌────┴────┐
        │  nest1  │                    Level 2
        └─────────┘
```

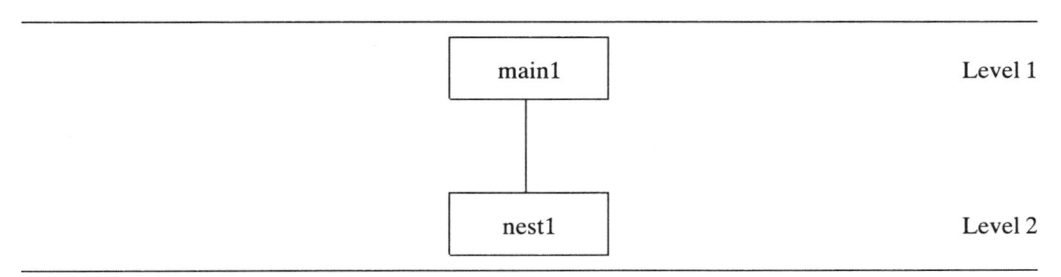

Figure 4.1 Structure chart for program main1

tree. The program at the top is the root of the tree. The children of the root are shown at level 2. In this example main1 is the root and nest1 is its only child. (Main1 is also the parent of nest1 because the path to nest1 is direct.)

It is the case that a tree may contain many parents and children but that it will only have one *root*. The root will always be at level 1 and the first statement of the root program will be the point at which execution of the program always begins. (In all of our examples up to Chapter 10 the root will always be the first program in the text file. As a result it will be the first program in the *object* file that is produced by the compiler and thus the first program to be encountered by the linker. The linker assumes that the first program it finds in the object file is the root.)

The *control line* connecting the root program to a nested program indicates that it is under the control of the root. In this example main1 can transfer control into nest1 at will. The statement in main1 which can cause this transfer of control into nest1 is

```
call "nest1"
```

When this statement is encountered in main1, control immediately passes into nest1. The first statement to be executed will be the first statement in the procedure division of nest1. Control will remain within nest1 until it has finished executing and returns control.

We have seen in previous chapters that a program will stop executing and return control to the operating system upon reaching the **stop run** statement. (This will continue to be the method by which control will return from the root program.) A called program will in a similar manner return control to the calling program when it reaches the **exit program** statement. Thus the control line on the structure chart marks a path into a called program and back into the program which called it.

This is the only means by which a program can cause the execution of another program. Thus the statements within each program are hidden from the other program. This strict separation between the programs supports the division of tasks between programs. Thus a program can be called to do something without the calling program needing to know or even being allowed to know which particular statements the called program uses in performing its task.

The terms *called program* and *calling program* are used to identify the relationship between the program that has the call statement in its text and the program that it calls. This is the relationship visualized with the control line. The term nested program describes the fact that the source text of one program is physically nested within the text of another.

```
 1 identification division.
 2 program-id. main1.
 3*Purpose: Show the structure of a program with a nested program.
 4/
 5 environment division.
 6
 7 data division.
 8
 9 procedure division.
10 para1.
11     display "main1 begins"
12
13     call "nest1"
14
15     display "main1 ends"
16     stop run.
17
18 identification division.
19 program-id. nest1.
20
21 environment division.
22
23 data division.
24
25 procedure division.
26 para1.
27     display "   nest1 begins"
28
29     display "     Hello from nest1"
30
31     display "   nest1 ends"
32     exit program.
33
34 end program nest1.
35 end program main1.
```

Figure 4.2 Program main1 containing nested program nest1

(In the discussion so far these terms would seem to be synonymous. However, by the end of this chapter we will have discovered that not all nested programs can be called and by the end of Chapter 10 we will see that a called program in certain circumstances might not be nested.)

The root program in Fig. 4.2 is main1. It calls nest1, which displays a message. When the program runs execution begins with the statement at line 11. The call statement transfers execution control to the statement at line 27, which is the first executable statement in the nested program. The exit program at line 32 returns control to the root, where execution resumes with the display statement at line 15. Control is returned to the operating system by the stop run statement at line 16. Therefore the output from the program will be the following five lines of text:

```
main1∆begins
∆∆nest1∆begins
∆∆∆∆Hello∆from∆nest1
∆∆nest1∆ends
main1∆ends
```

A *level* of program nesting is opened with an identification division header and closed with an end program header. In this example nest1 is opened while main1 is still open, thereby causing it to be nested within main1. Nest1 is then closed on line 34 and main1 is closed at line 35. (One of the main purposes of a structure chart is to help us to visualize the program nesting that is brought about by the use of these statements.)

4.2 USE OF DATA

The four divisions in each program are physically separate from each other and by default they are local in *scope*. In other words, no statement in one program can access data in another program directly. For this reason identical data-names and identifiers could be used in the two programs even though the purposes for which they are intended might not be related.

COBOL provides a number of features that allow a calling program to make specific records available to a called program. The most common way to make data available is through the use of parameters.

Parameters are records defined in a calling program at the 01 level. The called program must also have a description of the parameter record and this is written in a new section of the data division called the linkage section. Every parameter that is to be passed from a calling program to a called program must be defined as a record in the linkage section of the called program.

There are two parameter mechanisms available in COBOL: *reference* and *content*. Passing a parameter by reference makes the parameter record from the calling program directly available to the called program. Any change made to the data by the called program will persist in the calling program after control is returned to it.

Passing a parameter by content causes only a copy of the parameter record to be made available to the called program. It can then use the copy as its own data but when control is returned to the calling program the copy is destroyed, thereby guaranteeing that any changes made to the copy will not persist in the calling program. Thus the content parameter mechanism creates for the called program a local record that only exists while the called program is executing. The initial value of this local record is taken from the record that is passed by the calling program. Its successive values are determined by the execution of the called program.

The parameters to be passed to a called program are shown on a using list that is appended to the call statement. For example,

```
call "nest1" using reference e1-parm
                   content   e2-parm
```

passes two records to nest1. Any change to `e1-parm` within nest1 will persist after the

```
 1 identification division.
 2 program-id. main2.
 3*Purpose: Show a calling program and called program with parameters.
 4/
 5 environment division.
 6
 7 data division.
 8 working-storage section.
 9 01   w1-string  pic x(5).
10 01   w2-string  pic x(5).
11
12 procedure division.
13 para1.
14     display "main2 begins"
15
16     move "James" to w1-string
17     move "Brown" to w2-string
18     call "nest2" using content w1-string
19                         content w2-string
20
21     display "main2 ends"
22     stop run.
23
24 identification division.
25 program-id. nest2.
26
27 environment division.
28
29 data division.
30 linkage section.
31 01   l1-string  pic x(5).
32 01   l2-string  pic x(5).
33
34 procedure division using l1-string
35                          l2-string.
36 para1.
37     display "The parameters are " l1-string "and "
38                                   l2-string
39     exit program.
40
41 end program nest2.
42 end program main2.
```

Figure 4.3 Programs main2 and nest2 with two parameters

return to the calling program as a side effect of having called nest1. But `e2-parm` is a content parameter. At the time the call is made nest1 will be given a copy of the data for its use and when control is returned to the calling program the copy will be destroyed. Thus the `e2-parm` record in the calling program will be exactly as it was immediately prior to the call to nest1.

The called program also must have a using list. This is appended to the procedure division header in the called program. For example,

```
procedure division using e1-parm
                        e2-parm.
```

The parameters are also described in the called program as records at the 01 level in the linkage section.

Execution begins in program main2 at line 14 with a display statement and the initialization of its two records in working-storage. At line 18 main2 transfers control to nest2 and passes it two content parameters which are copied from `w1-string` and `w2-string` into `l1-string` and `l2-string` respectively.

Execution continues at line 37 where the values of the copied records are displayed. Nest2 returns control at line 39 and the copies are destroyed by the time that the display statement at line 21 executes. Thus the program begins execution with two data items, has four data items during the time that the called program is executing, and then reverts to having two data items.

When a call is made the parameter lists in the calling program and the called program are matched item by item from left to right without regard to the names. In the program main2 different names were used in the calling program and the called program.

However, the called program could have defined and listed the parameters as `w1-string` and `w2-string`. It could also have listed the parameters as `w2-string` and `w1-string`, in which case the data from main2 which was associated with `w1-string` would have appeared to the called program as `w2-string` and `w2-string` would have appeared as `w1-string`. Therefore it is important to use naming conventions that assist in understanding the relationship between data in calling and called programs.

SELF-CHECK QUESTIONS

Q List the line numbers for all statements in main2 and nest2 in their order of execution.
A Lines 14, 16, 17, 18, 37, 39, 21, 22.

Q Can a structure chart show a program to have more than one root?
A No. The root is always a unique program. It is always the first program written in the source text. When the program executes, execution always begins with the first statement in the procedure division of the root program.

Q What is the difference between statement nesting and program nesting?
A Statement nesting considers the nesting relationship between statements in a single program which may be either a calling program or a called program. Program nesting considers the relationship between the root program and the programs that are nested or within it.

```
                    ┌─────────┐
                    │    P    │
                    └────┬────┘
                         │
                    ┌────┴────┐
                    │    Q    │
                    └────┬────┘
                    ┌────┴────┐
              ┌─────┴───┐ ┌───┴─────┐
              │    R    │ │    S    │
              └─────────┘ └─────────┘
```

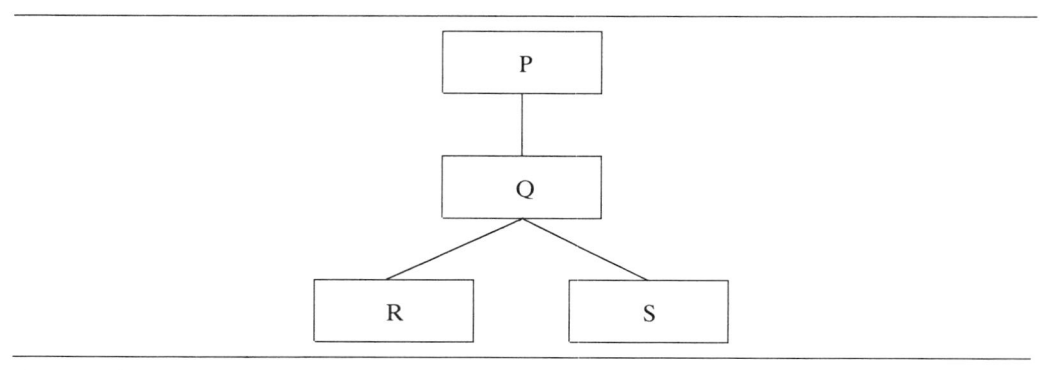

Figure 4.4 Structure chart for program P

Q Consider the structure chart shown in Fig. 4.4 as both a tree and as a structural representation of a program. What terms can be used to describe P, Q, R and S as well as the relationships between them?

A If we think of this as a tree then P is the root as well as being the parent of Q; Q is the parent of R and S as well as being the child of P; R and S are the children of Q.

If we think of this as a COBOL program then P, Q, R and S are all programs. P is the root program and Q, R and S are nested programs. P calls Q, thus Q is called by P; Q calls R and S, thus R and S are called by P. Other relationships can be described. For example, although S is nested *directly* within Q and therefore *indirectly* within P, it can only be called by Q. Programs R and S are nested at level 3 within Q.

Parameters passed to called programs can be listed on the structure chart as is shown in Fig. 4.5.

The parameters are listed to the right-hand side of the control line. Each parameter shows the mechanism (reference or content) used in the call as well as the name of the parameter in the calling program. Diagrams such as these show essential information concerning the construction of a program. Not only are they a useful form of documentation for completed programs but they are also a useful means of visualizing relationships between programs during early program design.

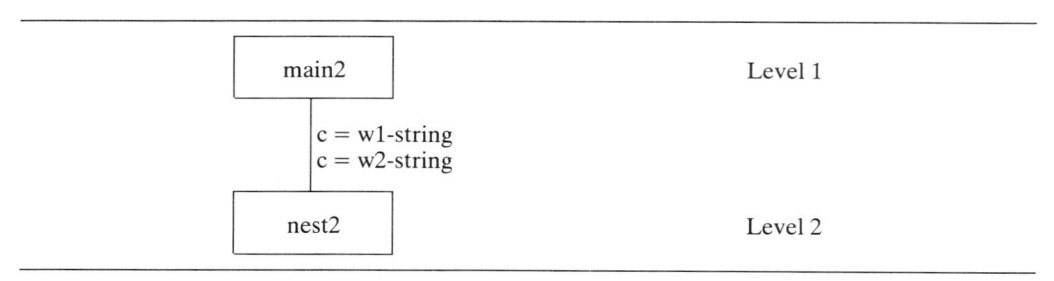

```
              ┌─────────┐
              │  main2  │                          Level 1
              └────┬────┘
                   │ c = w1-string
                   │ c = w2-string
              ┌────┴────┐
              │  nest2  │                          Level 2
              └─────────┘
```

Figure 4.5 Structure chart for program main2

INTER-PROGRAM COMMUNICATION 87

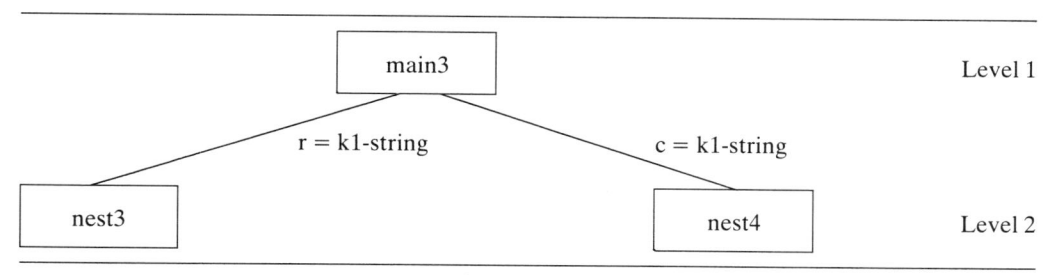

```
                    ┌─────────┐
                    │  main3  │                            Level 1
                    └─────────┘
            r = k1-string    c = k1-string
    ┌─────────┐                    ┌─────────┐
    │  nest3  │                    │  nest4  │             Level 2
    └─────────┘                    └─────────┘
```

Figure 4.6 Structure chart for program main3

4.3 SAMPLE PROGRAM CONTAINING TWO NESTED PROGRAMS

The structure chart in Fig. 4.6 shows that program main3 contains two programs at program nesting level 2. Its purpose is to demonstrate clearly the difference between the reference and content parameter mechanisms. (To assist in doing this programs nest3 and nest4 are identical.) The complete program is listed in Fig. 4.7.

When nest3 is called it reverses the order of the characters in the reference parameter k1-string which appears to it as l1-string. Because the parameter mechanism is reference the subsequent display of k1-string in main3 shows that it has been arranged in reverse order.

When nest4 is called it executes identical statements. However, the result of its reversal is not passed back to the main program because the mechanism used for the call is content. The subsequent display of the string in main3 shows that its string is unaffected.

Thus with a keyboard input of "abc" followed by "QΔΔ", the program will respond as follows:

```
main3 begins
Type a string of 3 characters or 'Q' to quit
abc⟨RET⟩
cba
cba
Type a string of 3 characters or 'Q' to quit
Q
main3 ends
```

The string "cba" shows that the first call causes the string to be reversed. However, the next output listed is "cba" which clearly demonstrates that the reversal in the second called program is not returned to the calling program.

The program also demonstrates the independence that exists between the statements in programs. Thus the nested programs know nothing of the loop that is used in main3. Main3 for its part knows nothing of the methods used in the nested programs for reversing the string. However, main3 does know that it will not get a result back from nest4 because the call at line 24 clearly states that the parameter mechanism is content.

```
 1  identification division.
 2  program-id. main3.
 3 *Purpose: Demonstrate the difference between:
 4 *          reference and content parameters.
 5
 6  environment division.
 7
 8  data division.
 9  working-storage section.
10  01  k1-string  pic xxx.
11      88  k1-eok  value "Q "
12                        "q ".
13  procedure division.
14  para1.
15      display "main3 begins"
16
17      display "Type a string of 3 characters or 'Q' to quit"
18      accept k1-string
19      perform test before until k1-eok
20          call "nest3" using reference k1-string
21          display "result of first call is:"
22          display k1-string
23
24          call "nest4" using content k1-string
25          display "result of next call is:"
26          display k1-string
27
28          display "Type a string of 3 characters or 'Q' to quit"
29          accept k1-string
30      end-perform
31
```

```
32      display "main3 ends"
33      stop run.
34*
35  identification division.
36  program-id. nest3.
37
38  data division.
39  working-storage section.
40  01 w1-string pic xxx.
41
42  linkage section.
43  01 l1-string pic xxx.
44
45  procedure division using l1-string.
46  para1.
47      move l1-string(1:1) to w1-string(3:1)
48      move l1-string(2:1) to w1-string(2:1)
49      move l1-string(3:1) to w1-string(1:1)
50      move w1-string     to l1-string
51      exit program.
52
53  end program nest3.
54/
55  identification division.
56  program-id. nest4.
57
58  data division.
59  working-storage section.
60  01 w1-string pic xxx.
61
62  linkage section.
63  01 l1-string pic xxx.
64
65  procedure division using l1-string.
66  para1.
67      move l1-string(1:1) to w1-string(3:1)
68      move l1-string(2:1) to w1-string(2:1)
69      move l1-string(3:1) to w1-string(1:1)
70      move w1-string     to l1-string
71      exit program.
72
73  end program nest4.
74  end program main3.
```

Figure 4.7 Program main3

SELF-CHECK QUESTIONS

Q Program main3 uses two nested programs that are identical in all respects except that they have different program-names. Would the same result have occurred if both calls had been to the same program, that is, either to nest3 or nest4?

A Yes. The two programs are identical. The specification of the reference and content mechanisms is made in the calling program. Called programs contain no indication of the mechanism that is used in a call. Therefore because nest3 and nest4 are functionally identical, they are interchangeable.

Q Could nest3 use a loop and reference modification to accomplish the string reversal instead of the move statements?

A Yes. Any statements can be included in a called program. The means by which a called program achieves its result is hidden from the calling program.

Q Can a called program be thought to have a goal or function?

A Yes. Usually the goal of any program is to map one or more of its inputs to one or more of its outputs in a specific way. For example, the goal of nest3 is to map L1-string as input into L1-string as output but in reverse order. In this loose sense its goal, function, and objective are one and the same thing. There may of course be other goals and objectives such as run-time efficiency. These other general issues are not included in the term *function*, which is usually reserved for a statement of the relationship between input and output.

4.4 SCOPE OF PROGRAM-NAMES

In larger programs nesting can often occur to many levels with nested programs themselves containing further programs.

Figure 4.8 describes main4, which is nested in a particular way. In this example main4 is the root. It is also the parent of B and D. Of course, they are parents in their own right. All of their children have only one parent. We can redraw this structure chart as a tree, a flowgraph or a Venn diagram as has been done in Fig. 4.9.

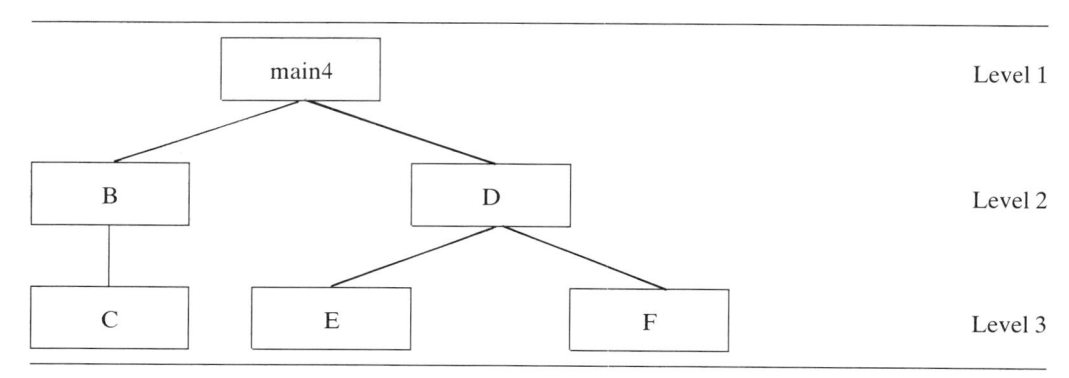

Figure 4.8 Structure chart for program main4

(a) Tree

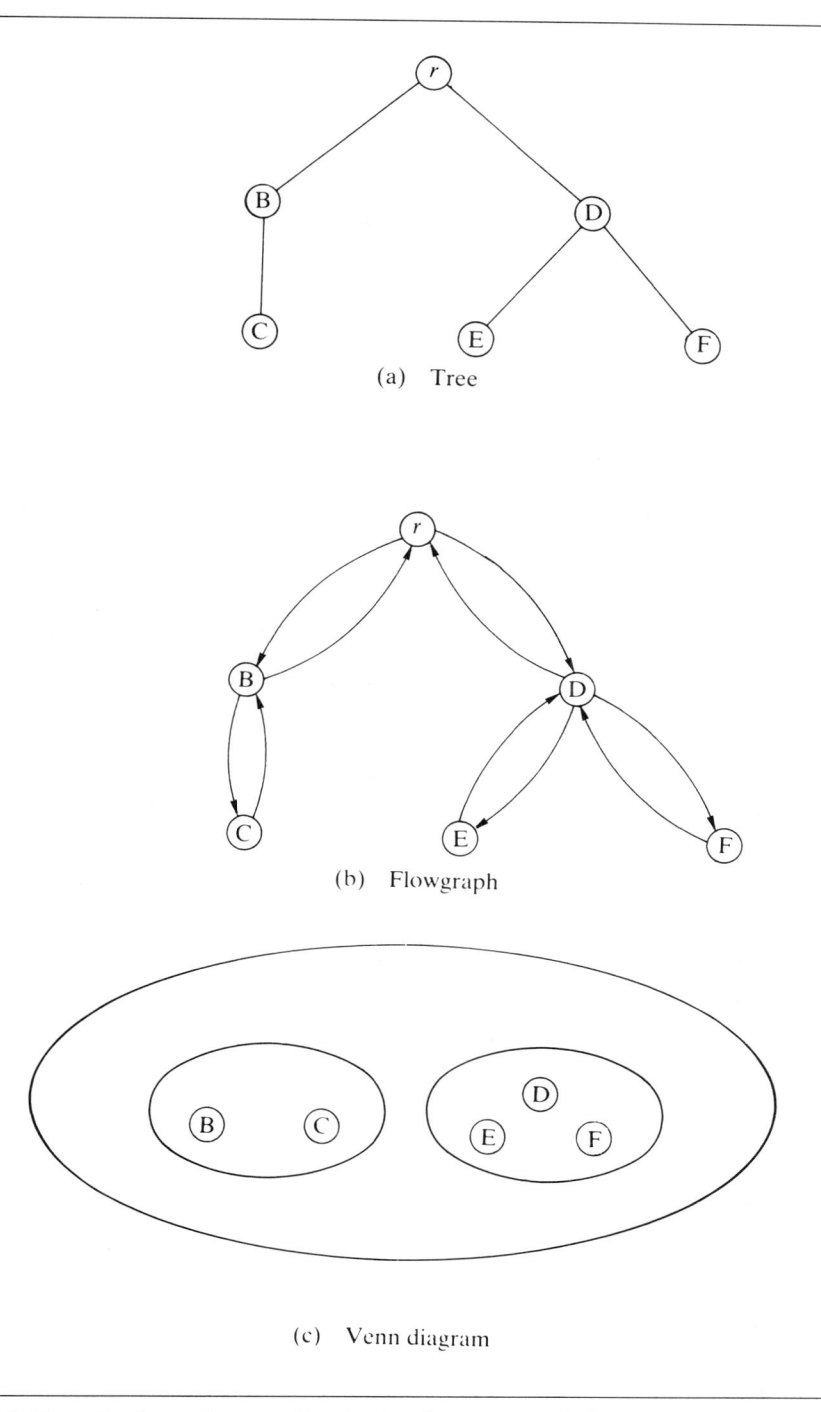

(b) Flowgraph

(c) Venn diagram

Figure 4.9 Alternative forms of representing structure for program main4

```
identification division.
program-id. Main4.
data division.
...
procedure division.
...
    stop run.

identification division.
program-id. B.
data division.
...
procedure division.
...
    exit program.

identification division.
program-id. C.
data division.
...
procedure division.
...
    exit program.
end program C.

end program B.

identification division.
program-id. D.
data division.
...
procedure division.
...
    exit program.

 identification division.
program-id. E.
data division.
...
procedure division.
...
    exit program.
end program E.

identification division.
program-id. F.
data division.
...
procedure division.
...
    exit program.
end program F.

end program D.

end program Main4.
```

Box Diagram

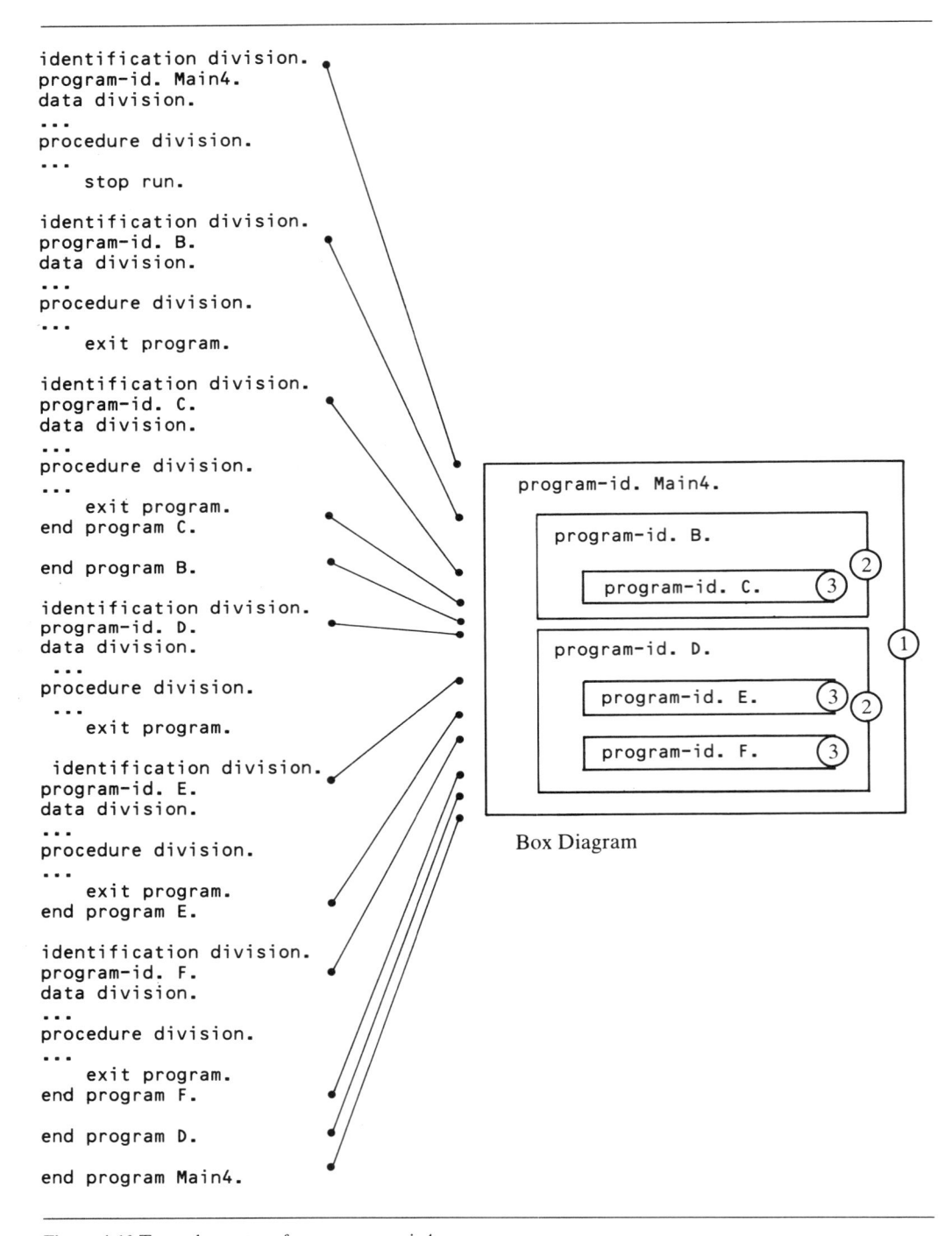

Figure 4.10 Textual structure for program main4

Relation	Calling scope	Is call allowed?
main4 to B	directly contained	Yes
main4 to D	directly contained	Yes
main4 to C	indirectly contained	No
main4 to E	indirectly contained	No
main4 to F	indirectly contained	No
B to E	no calling relationship	No
B to F	no calling relationship	No

Figure 4.11 Nested calling scope for program main4

Each of these diagrams is a different way of representing the same structure and may be useful in certain circumstances. As we have seen the tree is closely related to the structure chart and shows the top-down nature of execution control quite clearly. The Venn diagram for its part is closely related to the box diagrams which we have been drawing around programs and nested programs. These diagrams clearly show that some programs are contained within other programs. (In fact, COBOL uses the terms *nested* and *contained* as interchangeable terms.)

The flowgraph form of representing structure clearly shows the execution path of the whole program. It is possible to delete each point in the flowgraph and replace it with the flowgraph of each individual program. The result will be one large flowgraph that gives information about the overall complexity of the program in terms of points and links. Structures such as these can be represented mathematically and are the basis of many techniques for measuring software quality characteristics.

These are issues that will concern us more at a later stage. For the moment the important point to notice is that all of these diagrams provide slightly different ways of representing the same basic structures.

Program main4 directly contains programs B and D (Fig. 4.10). Therefore program main4 can call either program. Similarly, program B directly contains program C and can therefore call it. However, program main4 indirectly contains C because program B exists at an intervening level. As a result program main4 cannot call program C. The full set of possible nested calling relations for program main4 are listed in Fig. 4.11.

In summary, we can see that by default a program has the name of a nested program within its calling scope only when it directly contains that program. (The box diagram in Fig. 4.10 and the structure chart in 4.8 clearly illustrate these relationships.)

One further relationship we have not considered is that which exists between programs at the same level, for example, B and D. The COBOL standard states that if a program is separately compiled it may reference the names of other programs that are separately compiled. The standard goes on to define a *separately compiled program* as follows:

A program which, together with its contained programs, is separately compiled from all other programs.

According to this definition program B is not separately compiled from main4. The same applies to program D. Therefore B and D cannot call each other because they cannot be compiled separately from the program in which they are nested.

One final point is that COBOL does have additional inter-program communication features that allow other relationships to be created between calling and called programs. These will be covered in Chapter 10 once the fundamentals of nested program structures have been explored fully.

SELF-CHECK QUESTIONS

Consider the box diagram for a program shown in Fig. 4.12.

Q Can program A call either program E or F?
A No. They are contained indirectly.

Q Can program C call either program E or F?
A No. They are contained indirectly in other programs.

Q Can program B call program C?
A No. Neither program directly contains the other. Neither program is separately compiled because they are both compiled as part of program A.

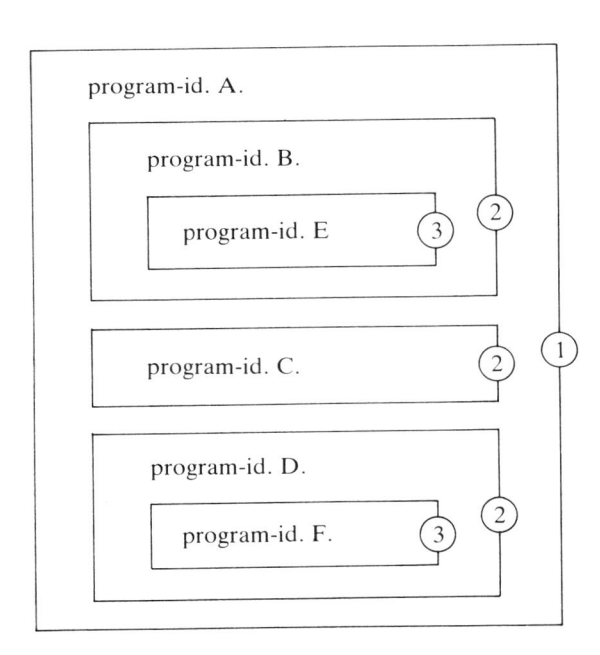

Figure 4.12 Box diagram for program A

4.5 INFORMATION HIDING

Let us imagine that we have discovered a need for a called program that can take a number of input strings delimited by trailing spaces, *concatenate* them into a single string, and output the result. Each input string will be presented to the called program in turn as it is accepted by a root program. When the user inputs only spaces the result of the concatenation will be displayed by the root program and the program will stop running. (For the time being we will assume that no input strings have either leading or embedded spaces.)

The structure chart (Fig. 4.13) illustrates a general design approach for program string1 in which the called program concat1 will be passed two parameters. The first is k1-string, which is the string to be concatenated. It is shown as a content parameter because concat1 needs only a copy of it in order to process it. The parameter s2-string is shown as a reference parameter because concat1 will give this data item new values which must be made available to string1 for display.

String1 is similar to previous programs and is listed in Fig. 4.15. In writing it we have made the additional assumptions that:

1. The input strings will be a maximum of five characters in length. (The design of k1-string guarantees that all strings will have at least one trailing space to mark the end of the string.)
2. The maximum length of a concatenated string will be 20 characters.
3. The general design of the parameter interface between string1 and concat1 is correct.

The last assumption is of necessity provisional until we have designed and written concat1.
The function of concat1 must now be stated more clearly:

Take a new string to be concatenated and append it to the end of the old string which is the result of previous concatenations. (We assume that at least one space marks the end of a string.)

The test data in Fig. 4.14 show the results we would expect from concatenating a new string to an old string.

We can see that we will have to keep track of the position at which each character from new is to be appended to old. Furthermore, we will need to decide a sensible means of

New	Old	Result
a△△△△△	spaces	a
motor△	a	amotor
car△△△	amotor	amotorcar

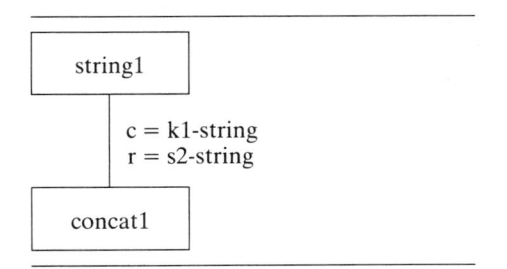

Figure 4.13 Structure chart for program string1

Figure 4.14 Sample test data for concatenation

```
1  identification division.
2  program-id. string1.
3 *Purpose: Accept successive strings. Display a concatenated result.
4
5  environment division.
6
7  data division.
8  working-storage section.
9  01 k1-string.
10    03 k1-input         pic x(5).
11    88 k1-eok           value space.
12    03 filler value space pic x.
13
14 01 s2-string           pic x(20).
15    88 s2-empty         value space.
16
17 procedure division.
18 para1.
19    display "string1 begins"
20
21    set s2-empty to true
22    display "Enter a string: "          " no advancing
23    accept k1-input
24
25    perform test before until k1-eok
26       call "concat1" using content k1-string
27                            reference s2-string
28
29          display "Result of concatenation: " s2-string
30
31          display "Enter a string: "       " no advancing
32          accept k1-input
33    end-perform
34
35    display "string1 ends"
36    stop run.
```

```
37/
38 identification division.
39 program-id. concat1.
40*Purpose: Concatenate a new string to an old string.
41
42 environment division.
43
44 data division.
45 working-storage section.
46 01 w1-ref         pic 9.
47    88 w1-min      value 1.
48
49 01 w2-ref         pic 99.
50    88 w2-min      value 01.
51
52 linkage section.
53 01 l1-new         pic x(6).
54
55 01 l2-old         pic x(20).
56    88 l2-empty    value spaces.
57
58 procedure division using l1-new
59                                l2-old.
60 para1.
61     evaluate l2-empty
62        when  true
63           set w2-min to true
64     end-evaluate
65
66     set w1-min to true
67
68     perform test before until (l1-new(w1-ref:1) = space
69        move (l1-new(w1-ref:1) to l2-old(w2-ref:1)
70        compute w1-ref = w1-ref + 1
71        compute w2-ref = w2-ref + 1
72     end-perform
73
74     exit program.
75
76 end program concat1.
77 end program string1.
```

Figure 4.15 Program string1

determining when we have transferred all of the characters from new. This is easily done because we know that the occurrence of a space character marks the end of character transfer from old.

A further inspection of the test data shows that the following patterns emerge in the character positions being transferred:

New	Old
1	1
1,2,3,4,5	2,3,4,5,6
1,2,3	7,8,9

We can use reference modification to effect the character transfers provided that the left-position for new is initialized to 1 as each new string is processed and the left-position for old is allowed to increment from an initial value of 1 through to a final value that represents the total number of transferred characters. We will assume that when the old string is spaces we are about to process the first new string.

In conclusion we can see that concat1 hides from string1 the method that it uses for concatenation as well as the working-storage items that it uses to assist in the concatenation. Furthermore, string1 knows that k1-string cannot be corrupted in any way by the behaviour of concat1 because the parameter mechanism is content. Thus we can see that string1 is for the most part dedicated to managing the keyboard and screen for the user and that the concatenation subtask is abstracted out of this main task. Therefore if we wished to change the user interface we would define changes for string1 but if we wished to change the method of concatenation we would change concat1. Both programs can be defined as functions that transform input to output. In the case of string1 its input is accepted from the keyboard and its output is displayed to the screen. In the case of concat1 both its input and output items are parameters. In total there are two interfaces. The first is between the user and string1 and the second is between string1 and concat1.

4.6 CASE STUDY: POST4 (NESTED PROGRAMS)

Information hiding is a concept that is useful in designing programs. Central to this concept is the idea that a program should incorporate and hide a single design decision. Usually this decision relates to the hiding of a major data structure, a complex algorithm, or an input–output device.

As well as hiding information, a program can use parameters to define the operations that it is able to carry out for the benefit of a calling program.

Program post4 (Fig. 4.16) is a rewritten version of post3 in which the nested program check1 determines whether or not the postcode is valid.

As a result the structure of the root program is now more clearly seen as a user-driven loop that accepts postcodes for testing. It hides within it all of the design decisions relating to how data is to be accepted from and displayed to the user. We can see that its program structure is similar to earlier programs that were driven from the keyboard.

Check1 hides within it the method for determining whether or not a given string contains a valid postcode.

The call to check1 passes two parameters for the argument k1-postcode and the result s2-result. The first is a content parameter because check1 does not need to change the postcode for the root program. The second is a reference parameter so that the result of the check can be passed back.

4.7 EXERCISES

4.7.1 General

1. Rewrite program main3 as main5 but with only one nested program. Amend the program so that the nested program can count the number of times it is called and the root can display this total at the end of the run.
2. Rewrite main5 above so that the nested program uses a loop to effect the character transfer.
3. Write a nested program square within program draw4. Program draw4 should accept a character from the keyboard and pass it to square which will use it to draw a square made up of that character.
4. Add program triangle to draw4 so that the root program can call for either a square or triangle to be drawn on the terminal screen.
5. Write nested program TV to take an input string and determine whether or not it is the call letters for a television channel. If the call letters are known, e.g. "ITV", return the channel number, e.g. "channel 4". If the call letters are unknown return an appropriate message.
6. The first three verses of a popular Christmas carol are as follows:

    On the first day of Christmas my true love sent to me
    A partridge in a pear tree.

    On the second day of Christmas my true love sent to me
    Two turtle doves and
    A partridge in a pear tree.

    On the third day of Christmas my true love sent to me
    Three french hens
    Two turtle doves and
    A partridge in a pear tree.

    Write program carol to generate these three verses in the given order by using calls to nested programs.
7. Program string1 cannot concatenate more than 20 characters without producing unpredictable results. Rewrite string1 as string2 so that it outputs an appropriate message when the user attempts to concatenate more than 20 characters.
8. Write string3 to allow strings to have leading or embedded spaces. (Use trailing spaces to determine the end of a new string.)

```
 1  identification division.
 2  program-id. post4.
 3 *Purpose: Demonstrate post3 rewritten with a subprogram.
 4
 5  environment division.
 6
 7  data division.
 8  working-storage section.
 9  01  k1-postcode   pic x(9).
10      88  k1-eok    value "Q"
11                          "q".
12  01  s2-result     pic x(7).
13
14  procedure division.
15  para1.
16      display "post4 begins"
17
18      display space
19      display "Input a postcode or 'Q' to quit"
20      accept k1-postcode
21
22      perform test before until k1-eok
23          call "check1" using content k1-postcode
24                              reference s2-result
25
26          display s2-result
27          display space
28          display "Input another postcode or 'Q' to quit"
29          accept k1-postcode
30      end-perform
31
32      display "post4 ends"
33      stop run.
34 *
35  identification division.
36  program-id. check1.
37
38  data division.
39  working-storage section.
40
41  01  w1-reference.
42      03  w1-ref    pic 99.
43          88  w1-min value 01.
44          88  w1-max value 10.
45
```

```
46  linkage section.
47  01  l1-postcode              pic x(9).
48      88  l1-rule1             value "99999   ".
49      88  l1-rule2a            value "aa99 9aa".
50      88  l1-rule2b            value "aa9 9aa ".
51      88  l1-rule2c            value "a9a 9aa ".
52      88  l1-rule3             value "a9a 9a9 ".
53
54  01  l2-result                pic x(7).
55
56  procedure division using l1-postcode
57                                 l2-result.
58  para1.
59      set w1-min to true
60      perform until w1-max
61          evaluate true
62              when l1-postcode(w1-ref:1) = space
63                  move space to l1-postcode(w1-ref:1)
64              when l1-postcode(w1-ref:1) alphabetic
65                  move "a" to l1-postcode(w1-ref:1)
66              when l1-postcode(w1-ref:1) numeric
67                  move "9" to l1-postcode(w1-ref:1)
68          end-evaluate
69          compute w1-ref = w1-ref + 1
70      end-perform
71
72      evaluate true
73          when l1-rule1
74              move "rule1"   to l2-result
75          when l1-rule2a
76              move "rule2a"  to l2-result
77          when l1-rule2b
78              move "rule2b"  to l2-result
79          when l1-rule2c
80              move "rule2c"  to l2-result
81          when l1-rule3
82              move "rule3"   to l2-result
83          when other
84              move "invalid" to l2-result
85      end-evaluate
86
87      exit program.
88
89  end program check1.
90  end program post4.
```

Figure 4.16 Program post4

9   Write nested program numbers which when passed a parameter outputs one of the following depending on the setting of the parameter:

- every number in the range of 1 to 20 inclusive
- all even numbers in this range
- all odd numbers in this range.

10   Write program vowels to count all the vowels in successive lines of text. Result should be displayed after every line by one nested program and at the end of run by another nested program. (*Hint:* Remove each character in turn from the line and put it in a single character data item that can be tested using condition-names.)

4.7.2 Case study

11   Write a structure chart for program post5. Ensure that it clearly shows parameters and parameter mechanisms.

12   Write a flowgraph for each program in post5 as a way of identifying the statement nesting that exists in both programs.

13   Write a brief description of program check1 so that it could be used by a calling program without any need to examine the text within the program. Your description should focus on the parameter interface in order to define what the result for any possible input will be.

14   Question 10 at the end of Chapter 3 suggested adding a fourth rule for old British postcodes. Which program in post4 is affected and why? Rewrite post4 as post4a to include the fourth rule.

15   Rewrite either post4 or post4a as post5 so that the output message strings are held in the root program. The result parameter should be changed to an alphanumeric item that is set to a value in the following set:

$$\{1\Delta, 2a, 2b, 2c, 3\Delta, 4a, 4b, 4c, 4d\}$$

16   Document post5 with the following:
  (a)   structure chart showing all parameters;
  (b)   short narrative description for each program;
  (c)   short description of program interfaces.

5
TABLE-HANDLING I

By the end of this chapter you will have learned to construct one and two dimensional *tables*, to initialize them with the value clause, and to **redefine** them as table elements that can be accessed by *subscripts*. In addition, you will have been introduced to a case study program of over 400 lines.

5.1 SINGLE-LEVEL TABLES

In previous chapters we constructed records that allowed us to access particular characters within a text string. We also used reference modification to extract characters from strings.

However, some problems require us to be able to access one or more of a set of data items that have different values. These kinds of problems in their simplest forms can be solved using tables.

Most of us use tables or manipulate information that can be arranged in tables almost every day of our lives without necessarily thinking of the procedures we use to do this.

In each case the value known beforehand is called the argument. This is checked

Argument	*Table*	*Result*
name	telephone book	telephone number
diary date	diary	diary entry
index entry	this book	page number
city	postal directory	postcode

Figure 5.1 Common examples of table problems

104   ESSENTIAL COBOL: A FIRST COURSE IN STRUCTURED COBOL

American expression	*British expression*
apartment	flat
baby carriage	pram
broil	grill
candy	sweets
cookie	biscuit
hood	bonnet
intermission	interval
trunk	boot

Figure 5.2 Some American expressions and their British counterparts

against the entries in the table and if a match is found with an entry in the table we can extract the result entry (Fig. 5.1).

In 1919 H. L. Mencken listed many of the specific differences between American and British English. The list has evolved over the years but nevertheless many culturally specific synonyms still persist. Figure 5.2 lists eight of these paired expressions as a table. Such a table can be used within a COBOL program to find a British expression when given an American expression.

5.2 OCCURS CLAUSE

Firstly, let us consider the requirements for a single pair of expressions from Fig. 5.2. For example, a suitable data entry for "candy" and "sweets" might be:

```
05   w1-entry.
     07   w1-entry-US           pic x(5).
     07   w1-entry-GB           pic x(6).
```

This could be initialized by moving "candy" to `w1-entry-US` and "sweets" to `w1-entry-GB`.

However, Fig. 5.2 contains eight pairs of similar expressions. By adding the **occurs** clause we can specify that items are to be repeated a specified number of times.

```
05   w1-entry    occurs 8.
     07   w1-entry-US           pic x(13).
     07   w1-entry-GB           pic x(8).
```

`w1-entry` is now a COBOL table of eight *elements* because it uses the **occurs** clause in its data entry.

All elements within a table must be defined identically. Therefore the level 07 items have been increased in size to allow for the largest entries which are `"baby carriage"` and `"interval"`. Each element occupies 21 characters. In total the table occupies 8 times 21, that is, 168 characters.

The string lengths of thirteen and eight are based on the values in Fig. 5.2. However, the pairs in this table by no means represent an exhaustive set of test data. For example, the pair `'windshield-windscreen'` are not included. This pair is of immediate interest because 'windscreen' is longer than eight characters and therefore could not be included in the program without redesigning the table. In practice, it is good defensive programming style to aim for consistency and to be generous in determining maximum lengths wherever practicable. We will leave this table as it is for the moment so that it closely resembles the particular test data which we have to hand. As a later exercise you will be asked to make both entries the same length (consistency) and to allow for expressions of 32 characters (generosity).

5.3 SUBSCRIPTS

Although the table now contains eight identical elements the data-names w1-entry, w1-entry-US, and w1-entry-GB are no longer unique. For example, consider the following statement:

```
move "broil" to w1-entry-US
```

This statement is illegal because it does not specify which of the eight occurrences of w1-entry-US is intended as the target of the move. Therefore COBOL provides subscripting as a means for uniquely identifying particular elements within tables.

A *subscript* can be a numeric literal or a numeric data item. It must never be less than one. The maximum value for a subscript is the value given in the **occurs** cause. Therefore the valid range for a subscript in this example is 1 to 8 inclusive.

A subscript is written within parentheses after the data-name thereby forming a unique identifier. Thus the following statement is legal:

```
move "broil" to w1-entry-US(3)
```

In this example the numeric literal 3 in combination with the data-name forms a unique identifier for a table element.

It is common to use a data item as a subscript so that its value can be changed under program control.

```
01  w1-synonyms.
    03  w1-sub                    pic 9.
    03  w1-entries.
        05  w1-entry    occurs 8.
            07  w1-entry-US       pic x(13).
            07  w1-entry-GB       pic x(8).
```

In the above example a subscript, w1-sub, and the table are defined within the same record. (The subscript can be defined anywhere in the data division. However, it has been included next to the table as a matter of design to show that this subscript and this table are closely associated. It is generally good practice to design records so that closely associated data items appear together.)

The following statement is legal provided that w1-sub holds a value in the range of 1 to 8 at the time the statement is executed:

```
move "broil" to w1-entry-US(w1-sub)
```

Statement	Effect	
move space to w1-entries	w1-entries	becomes spaces
move "candy△△△△△△△△sweets" to w1-entry(4)	w1-entry-US(4) w1-entry-GB(4)	becomes "candy△△△△△△△△" becomes "sweets△△"
move "apartment" to w1-entry-US(1) move w1-entry-US(4) to w1-entry-GB(1) move space to w1-entry(1)	w1-entry-US(1) w1-entry-GB(1) w1-entry(1)	becomes "apartment△△△△" becomes "candy△△△" becomes 21 spaces
move 4 to w1-sub display w1-entry(w1-sub) display w1-entry-GB(w1-sub)	w1-sub "candy△△△△△△△△sweets△△" "sweets△△"	becomes 4 displayed displayed

Figure 5.3 Some valid statements using tables

Figure 5.3 shows the results of successive statements on the table and its subscript. In particular, note that w1-entry, w1-entry-US and w1-entry-GB are all items that must be subscripted because they are all table elements or items that are described within table elements.

5.4 REDEFINES CLAUSE

We can initialize the contents of a table by using move statements similar to those in Fig. 5.3.

However, in cases where the set of table element values is a permanent feature of the program it is possible to define data items with appropriate values and then to redefine the same area as a table.

```
01  w1-synonyms.
    03  w1-sub                                          pic 9.
        88  w1-min                                      value 1.
        88  w1-max                                      value 9.

    03  w1-values.
        05  filler value "apartment△△△△flat".           pic x(21).
        05  filler value "baby△carriagepram".           pic x(21).
        05  filler value "broil△△△△△△△△grill".          pic x(21).
        05  filler value "candy△△△△△△△△sweets".         pic x(21).
        05  filler value "cookie△△△△△△△biscuit".        pic x(21).
        05  filler value "hood△△△△△△△△△bonnet".         pic x(21).
        05  filler value "intermission△interval".       pic x(21).
        05  filler value "trunk△△△△△△△△boot".           pic x(21).

    03  w1-entries redefines w1-values.
        05  w1-entry    occurs 8.
            07  w1-entry-US                             pic x(13).
            07  w1-entry-GB                             pic x(8).
```

1. Multiple redefinitions are allowed.
2. The subject that is redefined must be followed immediately by its redefinitions.
3. The subject and its redefining entries must have the same level number.
4. The redefining entry cannot also contain the reserved word **occurs** at the same level. (The word **occurs** must be used at a lower level within it.)
5. The redefining entry cannot contain value clauses that initialize data values. (It can contain value clauses that are used to specify condition-names within level 88 entries.)
6. Provided that a redefining data-name is not referenced in the program a filler data item can be used.
7. For level numbers 02 to 49 the redefining entries must be the same length or less than the subject.
8. For level number 01 the redefining entries can be of any length.

Figure 5.4 Main rules governing the use of the **redefines** clause

The record now holds a one-character numeric subscript followed by 168 specific characters of data within w1-values. W1-entries then redefines w1-values as a table of 8 occurrences of w1-entry. In total the record still holds only 169 characters of data, the contents of characters 2 through 169 are defined by the value clauses in w1-values, w1-entries redefines these values, and the table elements allow access to the values as a table.

Figure 5.4 presents the main rules that govern the use of the redefines clause.

SELF-CHECK QUESTIONS

Q Why was filler used to define the entries in w1-values?
A These text strings are not referenced as part of the subject but from within the table. Therefore they do not need to be given data-names.

Q Why is "apartment∆∆∆∆flat" only 17 characters long when the picture clause in the entry is x(21)?
A The initialization of variables with the value clause follows the same rules as those for the move statement. Therefore the variable is initialized to "apartment∆∆∆∆flat∆∆∆∆". This feature saves the programmer from having to write long strings of trailing spaces.

Q Do the filler entries within w1-values have rules governing their length?
A There are no rules governing the length of these entries but there are rules governing the overall length of w1-values. It is good practice in nearly all cases to force the subject and any entries which redefine it to be the same length.

Q Can occurs and redefines be used in the same data entry?
A No.

Q Does the subscript have to be in the same record as the table?
A No. Provided that it is correctly defined as a numeric item it could appear anywhere within the data division.

```
 1  identification division.
 2  program-id. look-up1.
 3 *Purpose: This program drives subprogram mencken1.
 4
 5  environment division.
 6
 7  data division.
 8  working-storage section.
 9  01  w1-entry.
10      03  w1-entry-US        pic x(13).
11          88  w1-quit        value space.
12      03  w1-entry-GB        pic x(8).
13
14  procedure division.
15  para1.
16      display "Look-up1 begins"
17
18      display "Enter a word or RETURN to quit: " no advancing
19      accept w1-entry-US
20      perform test before until w1-quit
21          call "mencken1" using reference w1-entry
22          evaluate w1-entry-GB = spaces
23              when true
24                  display "No matching GB word in table"
25              when false
26                  display "The matching GB word is:    " w1-entry-GB
27          end-evaluate
28          display "Enter a word or RETURN to quit: " no advancing
29          accept w1-entry-US
30      end-perform
31
32      display "Look-up1 ends"
33      stop run.
```

```
34
35  identification division.
36  program-id. mencken1.
37 *Purpose: Returns a British expression to match
38 *         a given United States expression.
39
40  environment division.
41
42  data division.
43  working-storage section.
44  01  w1-synonyms.
45      03  w1-sub                           pic 9.
46          88  w1-min                       value 1.
47          88  w1-max                       value 9.
48
49      03  w1-values.
50          05  filler value "apartment      flat"        pic x(21).
51          05  filler value "baby carriagepram"          pic x(21).
52          05  filler value "broil          grill"       pic x(21).
53          05  filler value "candy          sweets"      pic x(21).
54          05  filler value "cookie         biscuit"     pic x(21).
55          05  filler value "hood           bonnet"      pic x(21).
56          05  filler value "intermission   interval"    pic x(21).
57          05  filler value "trunk          boot"        pic x(21).
58
59      03  w1-entries redefines w1-values.
60          05  w1-entry  occurs 8.
61              07  w1-entry-US              pic x(13).
62              07  w1-entry-GB              pic x(8).
63
64  linkage section.
65  01  l1-entry.
66      03  l1-entry-US                      pic x(13).
67      03  l1-entry-GB                      pic x(8).
68
69  procedure division using l1-entry.
70  para1.
71      move spaces to l1-entry-GB
72      set w1-min to true
73
74      perform test before until w1-max
75
76          evaluate true
77              when (l1-entry-US = w1-entry-US(w1-sub))
78                  move w1-entry-GB(w1-sub) to l1-entry-GB
79                  set w1-max to true
80              when other
81                  compute w1-sub = w1-sub + 1
82          end-evaluate
83
84      end-perform
85
86      exit program.
87
88  end program mencken1.
89  end program look-up1
```

Figure 5.5 Program look-up1 containing the nested program mencken1

110　ESSENTIAL COBOL: A FIRST COURSE IN STRUCTURED COBOL

Q Could the subscript have a picture clause that defines a potentially larger number, e.g. 'pic 999', even though there are only eight occurrences in the table?

A Yes. However, the programmer is always responsible for ensuring that the subscript is always within the correct range. In this example the range is 001 to 008 inclusive.

Q Can a filler data item be redefined?

A No. This would be an attempt to reference a data-name of filler. The name filler can never be referenced.

Program mencken1 in Fig. 5.5 can be used to check the contents of the table. In response to a US argument mencken1 returns as a result either:

- a GB entry when a matching entry is found, or
- spaces when no matching entry exists.

The root program look-up1 has been written as a means of demonstrating and testing mencken1 at a terminal. Programs that fulfil this testing function are called drivers. This driver contains a loop within which there are successive calls to mencken1 followed by a display of the result. In general we can see that look-up1 'manages' the user and mencken1 'manages' the table. (This separation of function is similar to that which was achieved in program post4.) Such separations are useful because they not only help to divide large tasks into smaller ones but also help to localize the effects of required modifications. For example, program look-up1 does not need to know anything concerning the internal organization of mencken1. Therefore a programmer could redesign the input and output formats for the user with the confident expectation that these changes would not affect mencken1. Similarly, another programmer could add new entries to the table without needing to worry about the internal design of look-up1. The only case where both programs would need to be carefully reviewed is when it is necessary to change the parameter record which links them. Separation of function becomes increasingly important as the size of programs increases.

By common agreement between the root program and the called program a result of spaces is taken to mean that there is no match in the table. Therefore line 71 in mencken1 can be understood as establishing an initial hypothesis that no match will be found in the table. Line 72 sets the subscript to 1 in preparation for the loop.

The loop and its evaluate statement attempt to disprove the original hypothesis. When a match is found the result is moved from the table and the loop is terminated. Otherwise the search continues and will terminate when all of the occurrences in the table have been checked.

In order to find a GB entry mencken1 must search from the first to the last entry in the table. If we assume that on average a request for one colour is as likely as a request for any other, then the average number of table entries that mencken1 will have to check is

$$\frac{1+2+3+4+5+6+7+8}{8} = 4.5 = \frac{8+1}{2}$$

In general, the sum of the number of entries divided by the occurrence value gives us the average number of times the table will have to be accessed. This average value is always one-half of the number of entries in the table plus 1.

SELF-CHECK QUESTIONS

Q What is the average number of times table elements will have to be accessed when there are 10 entries that are equally likely to be accessed?

A 5.5 times. In a table with an equal number of entries the mid-point lies mid-way between the two middle entries.

Q What would be the effect of testing mencken1 with a set of input data that had the following characteristics:

- 8 US arguments matched entries in the table
- 4 new US arguments did not match (e.g. "running shoe").

Imagine that the test took place over a very long period of time and that all 12 inputs were equally represented.

A Each of the additional four arguments would cause mencken1 to check the whole of the table.

As a result the average number of checks would be

$$\frac{1+2+3+4+5+6+7+5*8}{8+4} = \frac{68}{12} = 5.6$$

We can see that each nonexistent entry requires a search of the whole table and therefore the amount of time spent in table searching increases. This can be an important factor in very large tables where it is possible that many arguments may not match. (In such cases it may be more practical to sort the entries in the table or to use indexed files with keys. Both of these topics are covered later in the book.)

5.5 MULTIPLE-LEVEL TABLES

COBOL allows up to seven levels of occurs nesting and subscripting. For example, consider Fig. 5.6, where some American entries are shown to have a second matching British entry.

The record in Fig. 5.7 contains a COBOL table that can store this data as a two-level table. It also has subscripts for accessing both the first and the second level.

American	British 1	British 2
apartment	flat	
baby carriage	pram	perambulator
broil	grill	
candy	sweets	
cookie	biscuit	bun (Scotland)
hood	bonnet	villain
intermission	interval	
trunk	boot	

Figure 5.6 More American expressions and their British counterparts

```
01  w1-synonyms.
    03  w1-sub1                                        pic 9.
        88  w1-min1                                    value 1.
        88  w1-max1                                    value 9.
    03  w1-sub2                                        pic 9.
        88  w1-min2                                    value 1.
        88  w1-max2                                    value 3.

    03  w1-values.
        05  filler value "apartment      flat"         pic x(39).

        05  filler value "baby carriagepram"           pic x(26).
        05  filler value                "perambulator" pic x(13).

        05  filler value "broil          grill"        pic x(39).

        05  filler value "candy          sweets"       pic x(39).

        05  filler value "cookie         biscuit"      pic x(26).
        05  filler value                "bun(Scotland)" pic x(13).

        05  filler value "hood           bonnet"       pic x(26).
        05  filler value                "villain"      pic x(13).

        05  filler value "intermission interval"       pic x(39).

        05  filler value "trunk          boot"         pic x(39).

    03  w1-entries redefines w1-values.
        05  w1-entry    occurs 8.
            07  w1-entry-US                            pic x(13).
            07  w1-entry-GB occurs 2                   pic x(13).
```

Figure 5.7 Record containing a two-level table

The table holds eight occurrences of w1-entry. Each consists of a `w1-entry-US` and a double occurrence of `w1-entry-GB`. In total the table occupies:

1st occurs * (w1-entry-US length + (2nd occurs * w1-entry-GB length))

or

8 * (13 + (2 * 13))

which is equal to 312 characters of data.

When using multiple subscripts the first subscript refers to first level and each following subscript refers to the next following level in the table. For example,

```
display w1-entry-GB(6,2)
```

will display "villain∆∆∆∆∆∆" because this is the second GB item (level 2) within the sixth occurrence of `w1-entry` (level 1).

For this table the identifier w1-entry-GB(2,6) is invalid. Although the first subscript is valid the second one is invalid because there are not 6 occurrences at the second level within the table. Identifiers such as this will cause a compilation error because the compiler can check the value of the subscripts against the appropriate **occurs** clauses.

However, the following statements will compile correctly even though they will subsequently cause a run-time error:

```
move 2 to e1-sub1
move 6 to e1-sub2
display w1-entry-GB(e1-sub1,e1-sub2)
```

In this example we have a semantic error. All three statements are syntactically correct but the effect of the second move is to cause the subscript used by the display statement to be out of bounds.

SELF-CHECK QUESTIONS

Q Which of the following statements is valid? What will be the effect of each statement?

1. `display w1-entry(1)`
2. `display w1-entry-US(1)`
3. `display w1-entry-GB(2,1)`
4. `move space to w1-entries`
5. `move zero to w1-entries`

A All of these statements are valid and have the following effects.
1. The first occurrence of w1-entry is displayed:
   "apartmentΔΔΔΔflatΔΔΔΔΔΔΔΔΔΔΔΔΔΔΔΔΔΔΔΔΔΔ"
2. The first occurrence of w1-entry-US is displayed:
   "apartmentΔΔΔΔ"
3. The first occurrence of w1-entry-GB within the second occurrence of w1-entry is displayed:
   "pramΔΔΔΔΔΔΔΔΔ"
4. All 312 characters within w1-entries become the space character.
5. All 312 characters within w1-entries become the zero character.

Q There are 10 countries in which a certain health organization provides information on a variety of diseases. Code a two-level table that can be used to store a maximum of five diseases. The names of countries are 20 characters long and the names of diseases are 15 characters long.

A
```
01  e1-health.
    03  e1-countries            occurs 10.
        05  e1-country                      pic x(20).
        05  e1-diseases.
            07  e1-disease      occurs 5    pic x(15).
```

Q How many characters are stored in the above table?
A $10 * (20 + 5 * 15) = 950$

114 ESSENTIAL COBOL: A FIRST COURSE IN STRUCTURED COBOL

The way in which we design a table depends on the use which we intend to make of it within a program. The following two examples are both valid redefinitions of the 312 characters of w1-values and could be used in a program instead of or in conjunction with the original redefinition.

```
03  w1-entries2 redefines w1-values.
    05  w1-entry2 occurs 8.
        07  w1-entry-exp occurs 3          pic x(13).
03  w1-entries3 redefines w1-values.
    05  w1-entry3 occurs 24                pic x(13).
```

The first example does not differentiate between American expressions and British expressions. Thus `w1-entry-exp(3,1)` refers to "broil△△△△△△△△".

The second example has redefined the table as 24 occurrences at the first level. The string "broil△△△△△△△△" is now referred to as `w1-entry3(7)`.

The choice of a structure for a table ultimately depends on the use to which it will be put within a program. These questions of design choice will be explored more fully in Chapter 13. For the moment we can see that the use of the redefinition clause allows us to have more than one description of the same data area.

SELF-CHECK QUESTIONS

Q The health organization discussed previously has expanded to cover 95 countries and 200 diseases world-wide. The name of any disease on which information is available in a country will be entered into an occurrence of disease. Rewrite the previous two-level table to reflect these changes.

A
```
01  e2-health.
    03  e2-countries        occurs 95.
        05  e2-country              pic x(20).
        05  e2-diseases.
            07  e2-disease occurs 200 pic x(15).
```

Q How many characters are stored in the above table?

A $95 * (20 + 200 * 15) = 286\,900$ characters.

Q It has been realized that although there are 200 possible diseases no more than 20 are covered in any one country. Furthermore, they have become so numerous that they are now referred to by number: the first disease ever covered has been given number 1 and each new disease is given the next available number. Rewrite the design to allow two tables. The first table will be similar to the one above but with a disease maximum of 20 occurrences. It will hold disease numbers. The second table will be a single level table of disease names.

A The values accessed by identifiers in the form `e3-disease(sub1,sub2)` can be used as subscripts to the names table.

```
    01  e3-health.
        03  e3-countries occurs 95.
            05  e3-country                    pic x(20).
            05  e3-diseases-covered.
                07  e3-disease occurs 20      pic 999.
    01  e4-disease-table.
        03  e4-disease-names.
            05  e4-disease-name occurs 200 pic x(15).
```

Q How many characters are stored in the two new tables?

A $(95 * (20 + 20 * 3)) + (200 * 15) = 10\,600$ characters.

This is less than 4 per cent of the storage requirements for the previous solution. When designing tables it is always sensible to ask whether or not it is always necessary to store redundant information such as spaces.

Q Is it possible to access data in tables using reference modification?

A Yes. Group items containing tables can be reference modified. Subscripted data items can also be reference modified. For example,

```
w1-entry-GB(w1-sub1,w1-sub2)(1:5)
```

is an identifier for the first five characters of an item at the second level of occurrence within a table. Although there may be occasions when a complicated reference such as this cannot be avoided, it is usually best to move the item from the table to an elementary work item and then to reference the work item.

For example,

```
move w1-entry-GB(w1-sub1,w1-sub2) to e5-work-GB
display e5-work-GB(1:5)
```

The first statement clearly moves the item from the table. The second statement then displays the first five characters. In programs where there are multiple references there will be a saving in execution time.

Q A life insurance company wishes to produce a table of rates where the rate can be stored as a numeric character string with a picture of 9(6). The rates are for men or women between ages 18 and 65 for three products: whole life, level term, and 20-year endowment. Design a table to hold this information.

A The lowest age is 18. This can be stored in the first occurrence of age, thereby saving 17 redundant occurrences. The last occurrence will be $65 - 17$, or 48.

```
    01  e6-rates.
        03  e6-sex                occurs 2.
            05  e6-age            occurs 48.
                07  e6-product occurs 3.
                    09  e6-rate           pic 9(6).
```

Q How many characters are there in the above table?

A $2 * 48 * 3 *$ a length of $6 = 1728$ characters

Q Add a new group item at the 03 level to the above record. Include within it three appropriate subscripts and condition-names.

```
A   03  e6-subscripts.
        05  e6-subs             pic 9.
            88  e6-valid-sex    value 1, 2.
            88  e6-female       value 1.
            88  e6-male         value 2.
        05  e6-suba             pic 99.
            88  e6-valid-age    value 18 thru 65.
        05  e6-subp             pic 9.
            88  e6-valid-product value 1 thru 3.
            88  e6-whole-life   value 1.
            88  e6-level-term   value 2.
            88  e6-endow20      value 3.
```

Note that when **valid-age** is true the base must be adjusted prior to using the table by subtracting 17 from the age subscript.

5.6 CASE STUDY: TIC1 (PLAYING TIC-TAC-TOE)

Tic-tac-toe, or noughts and crosses as it is called in Britain, is a game with which most readers are likely to be familiar. The game uses vertical and horizontal lines to create a board of nine squares. Each player in turn puts a mark in an empty square and the first player to achieve a horizontal, vertical, or diagonal line of marks is declared the winner.

Usually a board is marked out on a sheet of paper. To play the game at a terminal we need to invent a board that can be displayed from the characters commonly available on the keyboard, as shown in Fig. 5.8.

This layout for a board, although aesthetically uninteresting, provides a simple design that is easily programmed. The hyphen character "-" frames the top and bottom of the board and divides the rows of squares from one another. The upper-case "I" provides vertical lines and the question marks show where either an "x" or an "o" can be placed within the board.

The details of writing the board to the screen will be discussed later. For the present we can see that the only changeable information within the board relates to the nine squares. The following record description incorporates this information:

```
01  w1-board.
    03  w1-row occurs 3.
        05  w1-square occurs 3 pic x.
```

```
-------------
I ? I ? I ? I
-------------
I ? I ? I ? I
-------------
I ? I ? I ? I
-------------
```

Figure 5.8 Playing board for tic1

Thus `w1-square(1,1)` refers to the top left-hand square, `w1-square(3,3)` refers to the bottom right-hand square, and `w1-row(1)` refers to the top row.

Tic-tac-toe, in common with other games, incorporates within its rules a great deal of information about the order in which operations can be undertaken by the players. The rules and the order in which events take place within a game provide important clues as to the structure of any program that is capable of managing that game.

A game begins with all squares empty and each player plays in turn. A check is made on the state of the game after each play. The game is over when one of the following happens:

1. A player halts the game.
2. A player has made three plays that form a horizontal, vertical, or diagonal line.
3. All the squares are full and no player has made a line.

The pseudo-code in Fig. 5.9 incorporates much of the information concerning the order of execution of the rules of the game.

This pseudo-code provides a loop which continues to be performed until the game is over. We know from the rules of the game that the behaviour of the two players is similar. Furthermore we have made explicit two important facts, namely, that a player cannot make a play without seeing the board and that after a play is made the board must be studied to see whether or not the game is over. Finally the pseudo-code makes the order of these operations explicit.

Let us next consider the problem of ending the game. This is an important problem because we have said that the main loop through the game will continue until the game is over but none of the operations within the loop show how this will be brought about. Upon analysis it appears that a game might end for any of the following reasons:

1. A player decides to halt the game.
2. A player wins outright.
3. The game is a stalemate.

Clearly the first possibility is decided by a player but the other two are an outcome of studying the state of the game. The important observation this leads us towards is the fact

```
empty_the_board

perform test before until game_over
   show-board
   first_player_plays
   study-game

   show-board
   second_player_plays
   study-game
end-perform
```

Figure 5.9 Initial pseudo-code for program tic1

that certain actions are undertaken by a player but other actions are automatically a result of following the rules of the game. Let us examine a bit more closely the other things that a user might do. The most obvious of these is to mark correctly one of the available squares. However, although all nine squares are available at the beginning of the game there are fewer available as the game proceeds. What should be done if a player tries to mark a square that is already played? What should be done if the user decides to place a mark outside of the board? Clearly, both of these situations are covered implicitly by the rules of tic-tac-toe. Therefore if a program is to be able to manage the game it must also be capable of dealing with these possibilities.

The following outline shows that there are four possibilities for the player and three for the program. We will find that these possibilities must be incorporated into the program's data structures so that the player and the program can keep track of the state of the game and communicate their decisions to one another:

```
Player:
  Valid:
    Chooses an unmarked square.
    Decides to halt the game.
  Invalid:
    Tries to mark a square that is no longer available.
    Strays outside the board boundaries.
End-Player

Program:
  First player wins outright.
  Second player wins outright.
  The game is a stalemate.
End-Program
```

The constraints attached to a player can be easily accommodated. Firstly, the dimensions of the board are static. Therefore it should be a straightforward matter to make sure that a player does not try to play outside the bounds of the board by making sure that no square with subscripts less than 1 or greater than 3 are ever allowed. Secondly, provided that the contents of the board can be checked it is possible to determine that a play is against an available square.

Let us therefore imagine the existence of a program called enter-play that can 'manage' a player provided that it is passed the following parameters:

```
linkage section.
01  l1-board.
    03  l1-row          occurs 3.
        05  l1-square   occurs 3   pic x.
01  l2-result.
    03  filler                     pic 9.
        88  l2-playok              value .
        88  l2-playhalt            value .
01  l3-play.
    03  l3-row                     pic 9.
    03  l3-col                     pic 9.
```

Enter-play can be used in turn for each of the players because the input from each player is identical. (The program will always know which player can play next because the game states that each player plays in turn and that the first player always plays with the "x" marker. What is essentially important is not the marker value but the square on which the player wishes to place the marker.)

The first parameter record is the board which can be a content parameter. The second parameter gives enter-play an item in which to record the outcome of a play. (The values for the conditions will not be assigned until we have checked through the whole of the problem and resolved any relations or conflicts that may exist across the whole of the program.) The third parameter will contain the row and column subscripts for the play that is being requested against the board.

Provided that enter-play is allowed to check the contents of the board it can trap the user into either making a valid play or halting the game. If the player makes a valid play it can return the two subscript values that identify the square the user wants to play.

Let us now turn our attention to the other programs that might be created to 'manage' the game of tic-tac-toe. Showing the board occurs at two different places in our initial pseudo-code. We can imagine the existence of a program that when passed the contents of the board is capable of displaying it upon the screen. Therefore we will assume that it can be written. The other important possible program is 'study-game' which when allowed to see the contents of the board can determine the correct game outcome according to the rules for checking the board. Let us imagine that it exists as well and that it can have the following parameters passed to it:

```
linkage section.
01    l1-board.
      03   l1-row              occurs 3.
           05   l1-square      occurs 3    pic x.
01    l2-result.
      03   filler                          pic 9.
           88   l2-winner1                 value ?.
           88   l2-winner2                 value ?.
           88   l2-stalemate               value ?.
```

Once again the board is a content parameter because study-game does not have to change the values on the board. However, the result must be a reference parameter so that the decision taken by the program can be passed back. The above data design does not show a value that means that the game is not over. Therefore we are implying that the function of study-game is only to set the winner and stalemate values when the game is found to be over for these reasons but to do nothing to the result in other cases.

Based on the above outline sketch we can now suggest a structure. Figure 5.10 shows the relationship that could exist between a root program based on the original pseudo-code and the three called programs that can implement the three main functional requirements for the management of the game.

The structure chart also shows that the player is a source of data for the program in two different places. Firstly, program enter-play accepts either a valid play for one of the nine squares or a request to halt the game. However, the root program also accepts an input from the user to determine whether or not the user wishes to quit the program. This

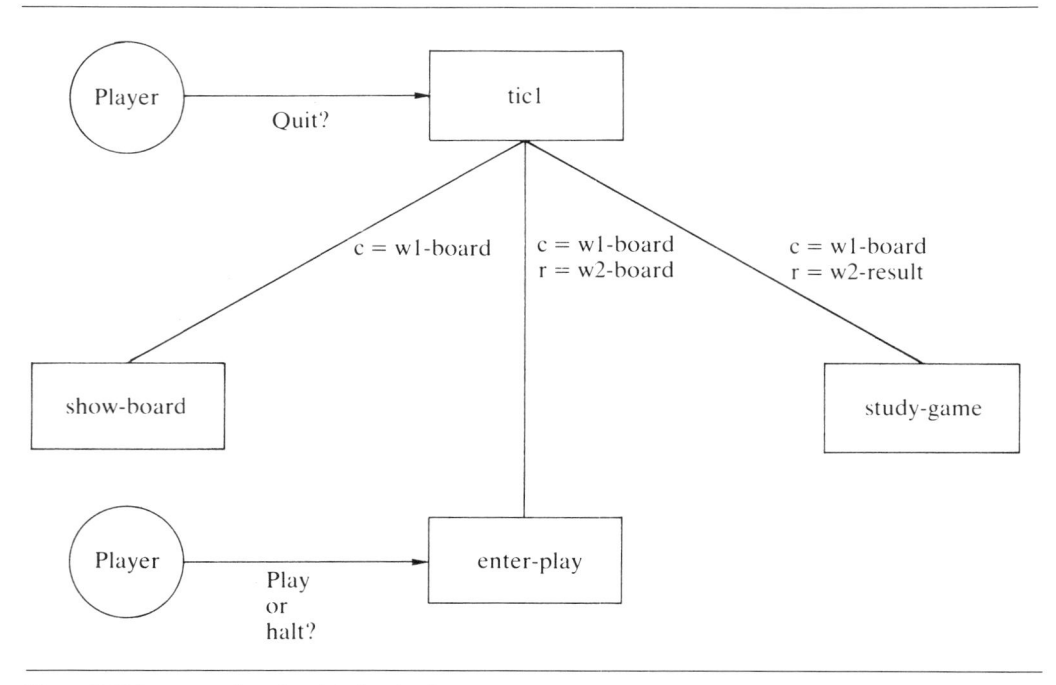

Figure 5.10 Structure chart for tic1 showing input streams

has been added at this point by the realization that if the program can manage a single game, then it is reasonable to allow it to manage subsequent games should this be required. In effect, we have smuggled into the design of the program a data item to drive the main loop of the program. The root will now play any number of games until the players quit.

This now suggests that the halt input should mean that the game and not the program is to be halted. The root program will then halt the game and ask the players whether they wish to continue with a new game or to stop the program running.

We are now in a position to write the data divisions for the programs. Figure 5.11 contains the data for the root program in tic1.

The first record holds the board as discussed earlier. The second record is more complicated because it represents the state of the game at any time during its course. Tic1 can begin a game by setting w2-startgame to true. Enter-play can then change the state of the game by setting either w2-playok or w2-playhalt to true. (The first value is set when a player enters a valid play while the second is set when the player asks to have the game halted. No other values are allowed from enter-play because all other possible user inputs are filtered out by it.)

Study-game can set w2-winner1, w2-winner2 or w2-stalemate to true, thereby telling the root program that the game is over. The condition w2-gameover acts as a convenient way to test for the four reasons to end a game. One of these is supplied by enter-play while the other three are supplied by study-game. Once a game is over the root program can start a new game by moving spaces to the board and setting w2-startgame to true.

```
data division.
working-storage section.
01  w1-board.
    03  w1-row          occurs 3.
        05  w1-square  occurs 3 pic x.

01  w2-result.
    03  filler                  pic 9.
        88  w2-startgame        value 0.
        88  w2-playok           value 1.

        88  w2-gameover         value 2 thru 5.
        88  w2-playhalt         value 2.
        88  w2-winner1          value 3.
        88  w2-winner2          value 4.
        88  w2-stalemate        value 5.

01  w3-play.
    03  w3-row                  pic 9.
    03  w3-col                  pic 9.

01  k4-request                  pic x.
    88  k4-quit                 value "q", "Q".
```

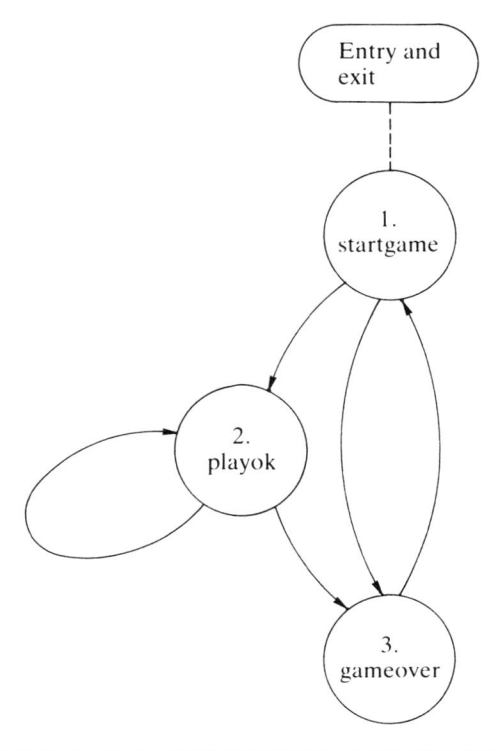

Figure 5.11 Data for root program tic1; flowgraph model of `w2-result`

```
empty_the_board

PLAY a game
perform test before until gameover

   FIRST player plays
   call show-board
   call enter-play
   evaluate true
     when    playok
       mark_square_with_x
       study-game
   end-evaluate
   END-FIRST

   SECOND player plays
   evaluate gameover
     when    false
       call show-board
       call enter-play
       evaluate true
         when    playok
           mark_square_with_o
           study-game
       end-evaluate
   end-evaluate
   END-SECOND

   CHECK state of game
   evaluate gameover
     when    true
       call show-board
       accept keyboard_request
       evaluate quit
         when    false
           empty_the_board
           set startgame to true
       end-evaluate
   end-evaluate
   END-CHECK

end-perform
END-PLAY
```

Figure 5.12 Final pseudo-code for program tic1

The successive values that `w2-result` can take over the course of a game are modelled by the flowgraph which is included in Fig. 5.11. We can see that to play tic-tac-toe we must start a game. From this point we might make a valid play or immediately call a halt to the game. When we make a valid play we can then continue making valid plays or move forward to gameover for any of the four reasons discussed above. Once we have reached gameover we can move forward out of the program or we can return to startgame.

TABLE-HANDLING I

The third record holds the subscript values for each play as they are passed back from enter-play. (The root program knows whether it is the first or the second player that is playing and therefore can move an "x" or "o" into the board as appropriate.)

The last record holds a data-item that allows the players to tell the root that they wish to quit playing altogether.

Figure 5.12 shows the final pseudo-code for the root program. The evaluate statement at the bottom of the main loop has been added so that additional games can be played within a single run of the program. When a game is over the keyboard is interrogated to see whether or not another game is needed. When the players want to quit nothing is done, gameover remains true, and control passes out of the loop. However, when the players want another game then the board is emptied and startgame is set to true so that for the next iteration of loop, the data state of the program is the same as it was prior to the very first iteration.

Recovering the main loop in this way yields a simpler program than would have been the case if we had used a nested loop of the following construction:

```
...
perform test before until user-quits
   ...
   perform test before until user-quits or gameover
      ...
   end-perform
   ...
end-perform
...
```

The second key feature to note is that the management of the first and second players is not entirely identical. If the first player has halted the game then not only is there no need to study the game but there is no play required from the second player. However, if the first player has played she may have won the game in which case there is also no need to ask the second player for a play.

SELF-CHECK QUESTION

```
evaluate gameover
  when    false
    call show-board
    call enter-play
    evaluate true
      when    playok
        mark_square_with_o
        study-game
    end-evaluate

  when    true
    call show-board
    accept keyboard_request
    evaluate quit
      when    false
        empty_the_board
        set startgame to true
    end-evaluate
end-evaluate
```

Q The last two evaluate statements in Fig. 5.12 both test gameover. The first one tests it for false whereas the second one tests it for true. Why therefore is the above pseudo-code incorrect?

A This pseudo-code is incorrect because the game may become over as a result of either calling enter-play for the first player or studying the game for the first player. If this happens then the statements shown on the true rule will not be executed. (Remember that only one **when** rule is ever executed.) If you are in any doubt concerning this try drawing flowgraphs as a way of visualizing the differences in logical structure.

Unfortunately, there is no simple and mechanical way to design a correct processing algorithm for this or any other problem that you have not encountered before. The most common source of error in writing programs is to attempt to write and debug a program for which the processing algorithms are only partially understood. The result is that during testing the programmer then gropes in the dark towards an algorithm. The program may finally work but it is likely to be patched over and stuck together with bits of data and statements that are created on the spot to overcome immediate difficulties. It may be so complex and riddled with so many errors in design that it is beyond human comprehension and therefore beyond further useful development.

1. Analyse the problem by trying to work out the order in which events must occur.
2. Look for regularities in the input patterns and in the operations that must be applied to data.
3. Try to discover the data structures that are central to the problem and write these as data records.
4. Draft the outline of a processing algorithm in pseudo-code:
   (a) Omit sequences that you think can be grouped together by using a pseudo-statement such as show_board. Such a pseudo-statement may ultimately be replaced by any number of statements which may include calls to programs, but at this stage of the analysis it has been identified as a likely sequence of operations.
   (b) Try to incorporate all loops and evaluations of alternatives at the outer level of the algorithm. If this is difficult try at least to write notes concerning their properties.
   (c) Use upper-case words to block out major features, especially those which will need to be decomposed into more deeply nested levels of control.
5. Check pseudo-statements to see whether or not they are likely candidates as programs. The crucial questions to ask concerning a possible program are:
   (a) Does it have a function that can be clearly summarized?
   (b) Will it be used more than once?
   (c) Would it remove complex detail from the main algorithm?
   (d) Can it do its work with only part of the data from the calling program?
      (i) Which items does it need to reference?
      (ii) For which items does it merely need to know the content?
6. Draft a structure chart.
7. Check for any parameters that are passed to more than one program and justify to yourself that this is useful. If the parameter is a reference parameter make certain that there is no conflict between what one program will do with it relative to another and that the behaviour of the parameter is well understood at the calling level.
8. Draft the data divisions for all programs.
9. Redraft the pseudo-code for the main algorithm but insert calls to programs as required.
10. Draft the pseudo-code for the programs.

Figure 5.13 Guidelines for writing programs

```
working-storage section.
01  k3-play.
    03  k3-alpha        pic x.
        88  k3-valid    value "1" thru "3", "h", "H".
        88  k3-playhalt value                "h", "H".
    03  filler          pic x.
        88  k3-blank    value space.

01  w2-result           pic 9.
    88  w2-playdone     value 1, 2.
    88  w2-playok       value 1.
    88  w2-playhalt     value 2.
    88  w2-playduff     value 3.

linkage section.
01  l1-board.
    03  l1-row          occurs 3.
        05  l1-square occurs 3 pic x.

01  l2-result.
    03  filler          pic 9.
        88  l2-playok   value 1.
        88  l2-playhalt value 2.

01  l3-play.
    03  l3-row          pic 9.
    03  l3-col          pic 9.

pseudo-code.
    Assume an invalid input

    perform test before until w2-playdone
      ROW or halt is entered
        accept   k3-play
        Trap invalid input with a perform loop
      END-ROW

        COLUMN or halt is entered when play is not halted
          Save the row
          accept   k3-play
          Trap invalid input with a perform loop
          Save the column if the game is not halted
        END-COLUMN

        CHECK the result
          when it is halted leave loop
          when it is a play on an empty square leave loop
          when it is a play on a full square it is duff
               therefore continue the loop
        END-CHECK
    end-perform

    At this point either a good play exists or a halt has been
    requested
    move w2-result to l2-result
```

Figure 5.14 Outline for program enter-play

```
working-storage section.
01  s1-board.
    03  s1-separator.
        05  filler      value "-------------" pic x(13).

    03  s1-linecontents.
        05  s1-rsub                            pic 9.
            88  s1-rowmin                      value 1.
            88  s1-rowmax                      value 4.
        05  w1-csub                            pic 9.
            88  s1-colmin                      value 1.
            88  s1-colmax                      value 4.

        05  s1-lineliterals.
            07  filler value "I   I   I   I" pic x(13).

        05  s1-ticline redefines s1-lineliterals.
            07  filler                         pic x.
            07  filler occurs 3.
                09  filler                     pic x.
                09  s1-square                  pic x.
                09  filler                     pic x.
                09  filler                     pic x.
linkage section.
01  l1-board.
    03  l1-row        occurs 3.
        05  l1-square occurs 3               pic x.
pseudo-code.
    Display the top line

    THREE pairs of row and line separator
    perform test before until ?
      Display a tic-tac-toe line
      Display a separator line
    end-perform
    END-THREE
```

Figure 5.15 Outline for program show-board

Therefore our goal is not merely to write a program that is correct but to write one that exhibits minimum complexity and maximum design quality. A detailed discussion of these issues is beyond the scope of this text but from a practical point of view many of the key issues are summarized in Fig. 5.13.

By following these guidelines it should be possible to clarify a programming problem and to draft a solution that contains the essential structural features of the final product.

Figures 5.14 to 5.16 outline the data divisions and the pseudo-code for the three called programs. They contain enough detail to demonstrate that the main order of operations that we have proposed is feasible and correct and that the data requirements for each program can be met.

```
working-storage section.
01  w1-subscripts.
    03  w1-rsub                 pic 9.
        88  w1-rowmin           value 1.
        88  w1-rowmax           value 4.
    03  w1-csub                 pic 9.
        88  w1-colmin           value 1.
        88  w1-colmax           value 4.
    03  w1-ssub                 pic 99.
        88  w1-squaremin        value 01.
        88  w1-squaremax        value 10 11.
        88  w1-stalemate        value 10.
        88  w1-squaresempty     value 11.

01  w5-testcolumn.
    03  w5-square1              pic x.
    03  w5-square2              pic x.
    03  w5-square3              pic x.

linkage section.
01  l1-board.
    03  l1-row         occurs 3.
        05  l1-square  occurs 3 pic x.

01  l2-result.
    03  filler                  pic 9.
        88  l2-winner1          value 3.
        88  l2-winner2          value 4.
        88  l2-stalemate        value 5.

pseudo-code.
    STALEMATE check for all squares full
        when at least one square set empty squaresempty to true
        when all full set stalemate to true
    END-STALEMATE

    CHECK-ROWS for a winner

    CHECK-COLUMNS for a winner

    CHECK-DIAGONALS for a winner
```

Figure 5.16 Outline for program study-game

Having reached a stage where all four programs have been outlined in sufficient detail to demonstrate that the solution is well structured and feasible it is necessary to form a plan for further work. At this point we could write all four programs and then try to test the set of programs at once. This approach is the least desirable because it means that four programs may be in error at once and they may generate errors into each other through their parameters.

If we write the root program first then it will be difficult to test because it will not have

1. Write and test a root program that:
   (a) contains the complete data division;
   (b) initializes the board to spaces;
   (c) loops until the user asks it to quit.
2. (a) Write program show-board.
   (b) Amend the root program so that it calls show-board from within the loop.
   (c) Test the root program and show-board so that you can display a board on screen.
3. (a) Write program enter-play to accept inputs but without the validation.
   (b) Amend the root program so that it calls enter-play and inserts the play into board prior to the call to show-board.
   (c) Test the program with valid input to ensure that the squares appear in the board correctly.
4. (a) Write enter-play in its entirety.
   (b) Amend the root so that it displays the result that is passed back from enter-play.
   (c) Test the program to ensure that enter-play functions correctly in its ability to filter out invalid inputs and that the result that it passes back to the root program is correct.
   (d) Remove the display of the result from the root program.
5. (a) Amend the root program so that it:
      (i) calls the two players in order;
      (ii) displays appropriate messages to the players;
      (iii) inserts the markers in the board correctly;
      (iv) loops until the user terminates with "h" or "H" from enter-play. (The acceptance of the "Q or "q" should be commented out for the time being.)
   (b) Test the program. This should demonstrate that the two players can place their marks on empty squares only and that the program can be terminated by entering "h" or "H" instead of valid coordinates.
6. (a) Amend the root to bring back the statements that were commented out in step 5. Make any changes necessary to allow for more than one game.
   (b) Test the program to demonstrate that when a game is halted by enter-play, the root can continue with a new game or proceed to end of run.
7. (a) Write study-game so that it can check for a winner by seeing whether or not the same mark appears in all three squares of any of the three rows.
   (b) Write the whole of the root so that it calls study-game after each player plays a square. Insert display statements after each call to ascertain that the result passed by from study-game is correct.
   (c) Test the program to ensure that study-game can identify winners in any of the three rows and that the root program responds correctly.
8. Complete study-game in one or more steps and test.

Figure 5.17 Implementation sequence for program tic1

its nested programs to call to provide it with the information that is crucial to its operation. If we write the nested programs first then they cannot be tested because of the absence of a root program. This dilemma can be resolved either by writing the root program and using three skeleton programs that merely pass back a set of valid values or by writing a skeleton root that calls the other completed programs. The first approach is called a top-down strategy while the second is bottom-up.

There is a great deal of debate among professionals concerning which of these two approaches is the more desirable. When we designed the programs we found it necessary to move back and forth between the nested programs and the root program in order to ensure that the total design was coherent. In a similar manner we will continue to bring the solution into being by writing and testing from both the bottom and the top.

In doing so the goal we shall follow is to try to find the path through the problem which provides us with the most correct program at any given time. In other words, we shall use a combined strategy that carefully limits the introduction of new and untested components. The implementation sequence for tic1 is given in Fig. 5.17, and the complete program is listed in Fig. 5.18.

Program tic1 is the most complex program we have examined so far. As with any complex program it is not possible to understand it without comprehending its behaviour as a whole. The easiest way to do this is to run it. As you do so make some rough notes of the order in which messages are displayed and inputs are requested.

Once you have a fairly clear idea of the kind of game that tic1 creates for the players you should then use your rough notes as a guide to the order in which the text of the programs should be read. Begin by reading the root program and by playing a game at the same time. This will give you an indication of those aspects of the program's overall behaviour that are part of the root program and those aspects that are hidden away in called programs. When you have a fairly clear indication of how the root behaves you should then study each of the called programs in turn. When doing so pay particular attention to the parameter interfaces because it is by these means that the programs communicate with each other. (By definition any data that is parametized is local to a program and therefore part of the local task.)

Most of the statements within tic1 will be familiar to you. What is novel about the program is its size and the complexity of the inter-relationships between program, data and statements. However, there are two lines within enter-play that are singled out for particular attention. These are lines 180 and 194 where the subscript values from the keyboard are moved into the subscripts that are used against the table:

```
...
121 working-storage section.
122 01   k3-play.
123      03   k3-alpha              pic x.
124           88   k3-valid         value "1" thru "3" ∆ "h" "H".
125           88   k3-playhalt      value              "h" ∆ "H".
126      03   filler                pic x.
127           88   k3-blank         value space.
...
135 linkage section.
...
145 01   l3-play.
146      03   l3-row                pic 9.
147      03   l3-col                pic 9.
...
180              move k3-alpha    to l3-row
...
194              move k3-alpha    to l3-col
...
```

Each of the move statements moves an alphanumeric item to a numeric item. In both cases the item k3-alpha has been subject to a **validation trap** using k3-valid as well as checked to ensure that k3-playhalt is false. The result of passing these two tests is that by the time the moves take place it is known that k3-alpha must contain a character in the range of "1".."3".

```
 1 identification division.
 2 program-id. tic1.
 3*Purpose: Maintain and display a game of tic-tac-toe for two players.
 4*         Monitor the game and declare the winner or a stalemate.
 5
 6/environment division.
 7
 8 data division.
 9 working-storage section.
10 01  w1-board.
11     03  w1-row         occurs 3.
12         05 w1-square occurs 3 pic x.
13
14 01  w2-result.
15     03  filler              pic 9.
16         88  w2-startgame    value 0.
17         88  w2-playok       value 1.
18
19         88  w2-gameover     value 2 thru 5.
20         88  w2-playhalt     value 2.
21         88  w2-winner1      value 3.
22         88  w2-winner2      value 4.
23         88  w2-stalemate    value 5.
24
25 01  w3-play.
26     03  w3-row              pic 9.
27     03  w3-col              pic 9.
28
29 01  k4-request              pic x.
30     88  k4-quit             value "q" "Q".
31/
32 procedure division.
33 para1.
34     display "tic1 begins"
35
36*    Initialize the first game
37     move space to w1-board
38     set w2-startgame to true
39
40*    PLAY a game
41     perform test before until w2-gameover
42
43*      FIRST player plays
44       call "show-board" using content w1-board
45       display "Player 1 now playing"
46       call "enter-play" using content   w1-board
47                                 reference w2-result
48                                 reference w3-play
49
50       evaluate true
51         when   w2-playok
52           move "x" to w1-square(w3-row,w3-col)
53           call "study-game" using content   w1-board
54                                     reference w2-result
55       end-evaluate
56*      END-FIRST
57
```

```
 58*        SECOND player plays when game is not over
 59         evaluate w2-gameover
 60           when    false
 61             call "show-board" using content w1-board
 62             display "Player 2 now playing"
 63             call "enter-play" using content   w1-board
 64                                     reference w2-result
 65                                     reference w3-play
 66         end-evaluate
 67
 68         evaluate true
 69           when   w2-playok
 70             move "o" to w1-square(w3-row,w3-col)
 71             call "study-game" using content   w1-board
 72                                     reference w2-result
 73         end-evaluate
 74*        END-SECOND
 75/
 76*        CHECK state of game for all possible terminations
 77         evaluate w2-gameover
 78           when   true
 79             call "show-board" using content w1-board
 80
 81             evaluate true
 82               when    w2-winner1
 83                 display "Player 1 wins this game"
 84               when    w2-winner2
 85                 display "Player 2 wins this game"
 86               when    w2-stalemate
 87                 display "This game is a stalemate"
 88               when    w2-playhalt
 89                 display "This game halted"
 90             end-evaluate
 91
 92*          Start a new game if asked to continue
 93           display space
 94           display "Do you want to play another game?"
 95           display "Type RETURN to continue or 'Q' to quit: " no advancing
 96           accept k4-request
 97           evaluate k4-quit
 98             when    false
 99               move space to w1-board
100               set w2-startgame to true
101           end-evaluate
102           display space
103
104         end-evaluate
105*        END-CHECK
106
107     end-perform
108*    END-PLAY
109
110     display space
111     display "tic1 ends"
112     stop run.
113/
114 identification division.
115 program-id. enter-play.
116*Purpose: Get valid plays including a request to halt the game.
117
```

```
118 environment division.
119
120 data division.
121 working-storage section.
122 01  k3-play.
123     03  k3-alpha            pic x.
124         88  k3-valid        value "1" thru "3" "h" "H".
125         88  k3-playhalt     value              "h" "H".
126     03  filler              pic x.
127         88  k3-blank        value space.
128
129 01  w2-result               pic 9.
130     88  w2-playdone         value 1 2.
131     88  w2-playok           value 1.
132     88  w2-playhalt         value 2.
133     88  w2-playduff         value 3.
134
135 linkage section.
136 01  l1-board.
137     03  l1-row      occurs 3.
138         05 l1-square occurs 3 pic x.
139
140 01  l2-result.
141     03  filler              pic 9.
142         88  l2-playok       value 1.
143         88  l2-playhalt     value 2.
144
145 01  l3-play.
146     03  l3-row              pic 9.
147     03  l3-col              pic 9.
148
149 procedure division using l1-board
150                           l2-result
151                           l3-play.
152 para1.
153*    Assume an invalid input
154     set w2-playduff to true
155
156*    GET-PLAY
157     perform test before until w2-playdone
158*      Sign-on the player
159       display space
160       display "Enter plays as row and column values."
161       display "Both values must be in the range of 1 to 3."
162       display "An ""H"" or ""h"" at any time will halt the game."
163       display space
164
165*      ROW or halt is entered
166       display " row: " no advancing
167       accept  k3-play
168
169*      Trap invalid input
170       perform test before until k3-valid and k3-blank
171          display "Invalid row. Try again"
172          display " row: " no advancing
173          accept k3-play
174       end-perform
175*      END-ROW
176/
```

```
177*        COLUMN or halt is entered if play is not halted
178         evaluate k3-playhalt
179           when    false
180             move k3-alpha    to l3-row
181             display " col: " no advancing
182             accept   k3-play
183
184*            Trap invalid input
185             perform test before until k3-valid and k3-blank
186               display "Invalid col. Try again"
187               display " col: " no advancing
188               accept k3-play
189             end-perform
190
191*            Save the column if the game is not halted
192             evaluate k3-playhalt
193               when    false
194                 move k3-alpha    to l3-col
195             end-evaluate
196         end-evaluate
197*        END-COLUMN
198
199*        CHECK the result
200         evaluate k3-playhalt
201           when    true
202             set w2-playhalt to true
203           when    false
204             evaluate l1-square(l3-row,l3-col) = space
205               when    true
206                 set w2-playok to true
207               when    false
208                 display "This square is occupied."
209                 display "Try again."
210                 set w2-playduff to true
211             end-evaluate
212         end-evaluate
213*        END-CHECK
214       end-perform
215*      END-GET-PLAY
216
217*      At this point either a good play exists or a halt has been requested
218      move w2-result to l2-result
219
220      exit program.
221
222 end program enter-play.
223/
224 identification division.
225 program-id. show-board.
226*Purpose: Display the board and its plays.
227
228 environment division.
229
230 data division.
231 working-storage section.
232 01  s1-board.
233     03  s1-separator.
234         05  filler    value "-------------" pic x(13).
235
```

```
236        03  s1-linecontents.
237            05  s1-rsub                          pic 9.
238                88  s1-rowmin                    value 1.
239                88  s1-rowmax                    value 4.
240            05  s1-csub                          pic 9.
241                88  s1-colmin                    value 1.
242                88  s1-colmax                    value 4.
243
244            05  s1-lineliterals.
245                07  filler value "I   I   I   I" pic x(13).
246
247            05  s1-ticline redefines s1-lineliterals.
248                07  filler                       pic x.
249                07  filler occurs 3.
250                    09  filler                   pic x.
251                    09  s1-square                pic x.
252                    09  filler                   pic x.
253                    09  filler                   pic x.
254
255 linkage section.
256 01  l1-board.
257        03  l1-row      occurs 3.
258            05 l1-square occurs 3               pic x.
259/
260 procedure division using l1-board.
261 para1.
262        display space
263
264*       Display the top line
265        display s1-separator
266
267*       THREE pairs of row and line separator
268        set s1-rowmin to true
269        perform test before until s1-rowmax
270
271*         Display a tic-tac-toe line
272          set s1-colmin to true
273          perform test before until s1-colmax
274            move l1-square(s1-rsub,s1-csub) to
275                 s1-square(s1-csub)
276            compute s1-csub = s1-csub + 1
277          end-perform
278          display s1-ticline
279
280*         Blank the line just displayed
281          set s1-colmin to true
282          perform test before until s1-colmax
283            move space to s1-square(s1-csub)
284            compute s1-csub = s1-csub + 1
285          end-perform
286
287          display s1-separator
288
289          compute s1-rsub = s1-rsub + 1
290        end-perform
291*       END-THREE
292
293        display "Player 1 is x; player 2 is o"
294        display space
295
296        exit program.
297
```

```cobol
298 end program show-board.
299/
300 identification division.
301 program-id. study-game.
302*Purpose: Study the game after each play and determine whether it
303*         should end with a winner or in a stalemate.
304
305 environment division.
306
307 data division.
308 working-storage section.
309 01  w1-subscripts.
310     03  w1-rsub                 pic 9.
311         88  w1-rowmin           value 1.
312         88  w1-rowmax           value 4.
313     03  w1-csub                 pic 9.
314         88  w1-colmin           value 1.
315         88  w1-colmax           value 4.
316     03  w1-ssub                 pic 99.
317         88  w1-squaremin        value 01.
318         88  w1-squaremax        value 10 11.
319         88  w1-stalemate        value 10.
320         88  w1-squaresempty     value 11.
321
322 01  w5-testcolumn.
323     03  w5-square1              pic x.
324     03  w5-square2              pic x.
325     03  w5-square3              pic x.
326
327 linkage section.
328 01  l1-board.
329     03  l1-row        occurs 3.
330         05  l1-square occurs 3 pic x.
331
332 01  l2-result.
333     03  filler                  pic 9.
334         88  l2-winner1          value 3.
335         88  l2-winner2          value 4.
336         88  l2-stalemate        value 5.
337
338 procedure division using l1-board
339                           l2-result.
340 para1.
341*    STALEMATE check for all squares full
342     set w1-squaremin to true
343     perform test before until w1-squaremax
344       evaluate l1-board(w1-ssub:1) = space
345         when  true
346           set w1-squaresempty to true
347         when  false
348           compute w1-ssub = w1-ssub + 1
349       end-evaluate
350     end-perform
351
352     evaluate w1-stalemate
353       when  true
354         set l2-stalemate to true
355     end-evaluate
356*    END-STALEMATE
```

```
357/
358*    CHECK-ROWS for a winner
359     set w1-rowmin to true
360     perform test before until w1-rowmax
361       evaluate l1-row(w1-rsub)
362         when    "xxx"
363           set l2-winner1 to true
364         when    "ooo"
365           set l2-winner2 to true
366       end-evaluate
367       compute w1-rsub = w1-rsub + 1
368     end-perform
369*    END-CHECK-ROWS
370
371*    CHECK-COLUMNS for a winner
372     set w1-colmin to true
373     perform test before until w1-colmax
374       move l1-square(1,w1-csub) to w5-square1
375       move l1-square(2,w1-csub) to w5-square2
376       move l1-square(3,w1-csub) to w5-square3
377       evaluate w5-testcolumn
378         when    "xxx"
379           set l2-winner1 to true
380         when    "ooo"
381           set l2-winner2 to true
382       end-evaluate
383       compute w1-csub = w1-csub + 1
384     end-perform
385*    END-CHECK-COLUMNS
386
387*    CHECK-DIAGONALS for a winner
388*    Check one
389     move l1-square(1,1) to w5-square1
390     move l1-square(2,2) to w5-square2
391     move l1-square(3,3) to w5-square3
392     evaluate w5-testcolumn
393       when    "xxx"
394         set l2-winner1 to true
395       when    "ooo"
396         set l2-winner2 to true
397     end-evaluate
398
399*    and then other
400     move l1-square(1,3) to w5-square1
401*    (2,2) moved in the previous diagonal check
402     move l1-square(3,1) to w5-square3
403     evaluate w5-testcolumn
404       when    "xxx"
405         set l2-winner1 to true
406       when    "ooo"
407         set l2-winner2 to true
408     end-evaluate
409*    END-CHECK-DIAGONALS
410
411     exit program.
412
413 end program study-game.
414 end program tic1
```

Figure 5.18 Program tic1

In COBOL it is legal to move an alphanumeric item to a numeric item provided that the alphanumeric item contains only digit characters. Therefore these moves are correct and after the moves the subscripts can be used with confidence as numbers. However, if k3-alpha had not contained digits then the result of the move would be unpredictable. On some systems it might cause a run time error at the time of the move and on others it might cause the subscripts to take unpredictable values that thereby cause run time errors later in the program execution when the subscripts are used. In any case in COBOL it is always the **responsibility of the programmer to ensure that only alphanumeric items containing digits are moved to numeric items**.

There are many questions concerning data representation and validation that are closely related to the issue of inputting numeric data into programs. These will be fully covered in Chapters 9 and 11.

5.7 EXERCISES

5.7.1 General

1. Rewrite look-up1 as look-up1a so that it includes the pair 'trash' and 'rubbish' within the table.
2. Rewrite look-up1 as look-up1b so that it accepts a British argument and produces an American result.
3. Rewrite look-up1 as look-up1c so that it incorporates the table with multiple British entries as shown in Fig. 5.6.
4. Rewrite look-up1 as look-up1d so that it accepts an argument and checks it against first the British entries and when not matched then the American entries. When a match is made look-up1b should display a message to say whether the match was found in the British or American part of the table.
5. Rewrite the call letters program (4.7.1, no. 5) so that it uses a table of call letters as arguments and channel numbers as results.
6. Rewrite the Christmas carol program (4.7.1, no. 6) so that it uses a table to hold the lines of the carol. The lines for the twelve days of Christmas are:

   Twelve lords a-leaping
   Eleven ladies dancing
   Ten pipers piping
   Nine maids a-milking
   Eight drummers drumming
   Seven swans a-swimming
   Six geese a-laying
   Five gold rings
   Four calling birds
   Three French hens
   Two turtle doves and
   A partridge in a pear tree.

138 ESSENTIAL COBOL: A FIRST COURSE IN STRUCTURED COBOL

7 (a) Write a program that contains a table of synonyms. When given an argument it should check the table and list the original argument and its synonyms.
  (b) Write a second version of the program which will load the contents of the table from the keyboard by using a program that is called during the root program initialization. (Test your program carefully to ensure that the upper limit on the number of table entries available and used works correctly.)

8 A disorganized cook always has ingredients such as eggs, cheese and potatoes on hand in the kitchen but can never think of what to cook.
  (a) Write a program which when given an ingredient will suggest a number of dishes which might be made with that ingredient.
  (b) Write a second version of the program which when given two ingredients will list only those dishes that contain those two ingredients.

5.7.2 Case study

9 If a player enters a position which is already taken, the player will be prompted to choose another square. However, the display will continue to scroll and will eventually move off the screen if the player keeps on entering incorrect values. Rewrite tic1 as tic2 so that the board is re-displayed after a player chooses an occupied square.

10 Rewrite tic1 as tic3 so that it incorporates each of the following amendments. You should test each amendment in turn before attempting the next one:
  (a) Draw the tic-tac-toe board using different literals.
  (b) Count the number of games that the user plays. Display the total at the end of the run.
  (c) Accept the play input as a two digit item which has the following definition. Prompt the players accordingly:

```
...
03  k3-alpha      pic xx.
    88  k5-valid  value "11"∆"12"∆"13"
                        "21"∆"22"∆"23"
                        "31"∆"32"∆"33".
    88  k5-halt         "H∆"∆"h∆".
03  filler redefines k3-alpha.
    05  k3-row    pic 9.
    05  k3-col    pic 9.
...
```

  (d) Study-game at present continues to make subsequent checks even after a game is found to be over. Amend the program so that it does not make subsequent checks once the game is found to be over.

11 Draw the flowgraph of the root program and compare it to the flowgraph which we drew in Fig. 5.11. In which essential respects is it different?

12 Figure 5.11 shows that an evaluate statement was chosen as the means for recovering the main loop so that subsequent games could be played but in the discussion that followed it was suggested that this could also have been done with a doubly nested perform loop. Rewrite tic1 as tic4 to accomplish this. (Be sure to write out the pseudo-

code for doing this before writing the program. The outer loop should test for the end of run and the inner loop should test for end of run or end of game.)

13 Imagine that program tic1 does not exist.
   (a) Write a narrative description of the requirements for a program which can play tic-tac-toe. You should clearly state the rules of the game including all of the information concerning the order in which events take place. However, do not make any assumptions concerning the use of COBOL or any particular program structure.
   (b) Discuss your narrative with another programmer who has not seen tic1. Make notes of any criticisms made of your narrative and, in particular, of any aspects of the narrative that may be incomplete or ambiguous. Try to assess whether or not the other programmer's approach to solving the problem is different from the one used in tic1.

14 Write the requirements for tic1 as an exercise in specification. You should include:
   - Layout of the screen displays used by the program. (A short narrative describing the viewpoint of the players. The narrative should clearly describe the order in which the screen displays will be presented, the inputs that a player may enter, and the result that will occur for each of the inputs.)
   - Structure chart including all input sources.
   - Brief narrative for each program to describe its function. For at least one program, for example study-game, try to include in the narrative a specification of the program in a pseudo-code. (Try writing the pseudo-code without looking at the program. Afterwards try cheating by writing the pseudo-code from the program text.)
   - List of every parameter used in tic1. (The list should be in prefix order within root name order.) Each root should have a general definition and each prefix should state any information that is relevant to the use of the parameter within a particular program. For example, board would need to have at a minimum the four entries shown in Fig. 5.19 with descriptive information stated against each entry.

A two-dimensional table of nine characters that models the squares of a tic-tac-toe board. It is initialized as spaces and then is filled with alternating 'x' and 'o' characters until a game is over.

Prefix	Program	Comment
l1-	enter-play	A content parameter so that a play against a particular square can be validated to ensure that the square is indeed empty.
l1-	study-game	A content parameter from which the state of the game is determined.
s1-	show-board	A content parameter holding the values to be displayed on the screen.
w1-	tic1	Working-storage. The program uses the subscript values in the play record to mark squares in the board.

Figure 5.19 Parameters used for board

6
TEXT STRING MANIPULATION

This chapter introduces the **string**, **unstring** and **inspect** statements. These three statements provide high-level features that are invaluable to the programmer when checking and manipulating strings of text. They are examples of statements that create a high level of procedural abstraction.

Before reading this chapter spend a few minutes examining the full formats of these three statements in Appendix C.

6.1 STRING

The **string** statement can be used to concatenate all or parts of a set of text strings into a single string. Source data is scanned from left to right and as the *scan* proceeds characters are transferred one by one into a target item. Only those characters that are explicitly transferred to the target item will alter the contents of the target. In other words, unlike the move statement there is no space filling in the target.

A simple format for the string statement is:

```
string identifier-1 delimited size into identifier-3
```

The first statement in Fig. 6.1 transfers five characters from the source to the target. In the second statement the target is longer and as a result only the first five characters are transferred to the target item. Therefore the last five characters in the target will remain as they were. In all three examples the number of characters that are transferred is **delimited** by the size of the source item.

The third statement attempts to transfer a large source into a small target. The first

```
                 Data
01   e1-source            pic x(5).
01   e2-target.
     03   e2-t1           pic x(5).
     03   e2-t2           pic x(10).
     03   e2-t3           pic xxx.
             Statements
string e1-source delimited size into e2-t1
string e1-source delimited size into e2-t2
string e1-source delimited size into e2-t3
```

Figure 6.1 Three simple **string** statements

three characters will be transferred successfully but on attempting to transfer the fourth character a condition called **overflow** will occur.

Overflow occurs when a target is not large enough to hold the full number of characters that are available for transfer from the source. In this example, after the transfer of three characters execution control will pass to the next statement in the program without causing a run-time error even though overflow has occurred.

Overflow is not necessarily an error although it is usually the case that a program needs to take appropriate action when it occurs. The syntax of the string statement allows this to be done as the following expanded simple format shows:

```
string identifier-1 delimited size into identifier-3
  ⎡⎧⎪ overflow       statement-1 ⎪⎫⎤
  ⎢⎨⎪ not overflow   statement-2 ⎬⎪⎥
  ⎣end-string                       ⎦
```

The inclusion of either or both of the overflow phrases causes the string statement to be conditional. Therefore when either or both of these phrases are used the **end-string** scope delimiter must also be used.

The following statement rewrites the stringing of e1-source into e2-t3 with an overflow phrase added:

```
string e1-source delimited size into e2-t3
  overflow
    display "Target too small for this input"
end-string
```

We can see from the data that e1-source must always be larger than e2-t3. Therefore this string statement will always cause an overflow condition. If we were to find such a statement in a program we might well ask why it was that the programmer did not realize that five characters cannot be transferred into a three character item! The answer in this peculiar case is that the programmer has indeed made a semantic error because the program will always display 'Target too small for this input' when the string statement is executed. If the original intention had been to truncate the string by the two low-order characters then the original string statement without overflow is preferable. (However, a move statement will put the truncated result into e2-t3 with the greatest efficiency and clarity.)

Why then do the overflow phrases exist? The answer to this becomes clearer when we look at another simple format for the string statement:

```
string {identifier-1 ... delimited literal-2}... into identifier-3
  [{| overflow      statement-1 |}]
  [{| not overflow  statement-2 |}]
  end-string
```

In this syntax we can see that the ellipses imply that lists of items can be used as the source. Furthermore, the transfer of characters from these lists of source items can be delimited by the occurrence of a literal within each source item. For example,

```
string e1-source delimited "Δ" into e2-t3
  overflow
    display "Target too small for this input"
end-string
```

If e1-source holds "abcΔΔ" then three characters will be transferred and the overflow condition will not occur because the first occurrence of a space has been specified as the delimiter. However, if e1-source holds "abcdΔ" then the target will be full before the space is encountered and the overflow condition will occur. If the source holds "abcde", then "abc" will still be transferred and the overflow will still occur in spite of the fact that the source did not hold a space. This happens because a source item is ultimately delimited by its size regardless of whether or not the delimiting literal occurs within it. A delimiter itself is never transferred into a target.

Therefore we can see that this string statement could be used to transfer strings of one, two or three characters that are delimited by a space in the source and to identify undelimited strings that are longer than three characters.

In the above example we have used the literal "Δ" to delimit the source. It is also legal to use figurative constants such as **space** as delimiters. When figurative constants such as **space** or **zero** are used only one character is implied as a delimiter.

SELF-CHECK QUESTIONS

For the following data:

```
01   e3-sources.
     03   e3-s1   value "abcΔd"      pic x(5).
     03   e3-s2   value "qrstuvw-x"  pic x(9).
     03   e3-s3   value "/mnoΔΔp"    pic x(7).
01   e4-target                       pic x(20).
```

Q What will be the result of the following statement?

```
string e3-s1
       e3-s2
       e3-s3  delimited space into e4-target
    overflow
      display
    not overflow
      display "no overflow"
end-string
```

A The characters "abc", "qrstuvw-x", and "/mno" will be transferred into target for a total of 16 characters. The last four characters of target will be unchanged by the action of the string statement. The message "no overflow" will be displayed.

Q What will be the result of the following statement?

```
string e3-s1
       e3-s2
       e3-s3 delimited size into e4-target
    overflow
      display "overflow"
    not overflow
      display "no overflow"
end-string
```

A The characters "abc∆d", "qrstuvw-x", and "/mno∆∆" will be transferred into target for a total of 20 characters. The final "p" of e3-s3 will not be transferred. The message "overflow" will be displayed.

Q What will be the result of the following statement?

```
string e3-s1  delimited space
       e3-s2  delimited "-"
       e3-s3  delimited "∆∆" into e4-target
    overflow
      display "overflow"
    not overflow
      display "no overflow"
end-string
```

A The characters "abc", "qrstuvw", and "/mno" will be transferred into target for a total of 14 characters. The final six characters of target will remain unaltered. The message "no overflow" will be displayed.

Q What will be the result of the following statement?

```
string e3-s1  delimited spaces
       e3-s2
       e3-s3  delimited "∆∆" into e4-target
    overflow
      display "overflow"
    not overflow
      display "no overflow"
end-string
```

A The delimiter for e3-s2 is the same as for e3-s3 because e3-s2 and e3-s3 form a list appearing before the delimiter phrase. The figurative constant **spaces** is the same as space. Therefore the delimiter for e3-s1 is a single space only. Therefore the characters "abc", "qrstuvw-x", and "/mno" will be transferred. There will be no overflow.

Q Will this statement have the same effect as the one in the previous question?

```
string e3-s1
       e3-s2
       e3-s3  delimited spaces into e4-target
   overflow
      display "overflow"
   not overflow
      display "no overflow"
end-string
```

A The delimiter in this case is always a single space. It will have the same effect for these particular data items. (The two string statements could produce different results for another set of data.)

Q Suggest a new set of values for e3-sources for which these last two string statements will give different outcomes.

A The following data will produce the outcomes given below for a target that has been initialized to spaces:

```
01  e3-sources.
    03  e3-s1   value "aΔcde"       pic x(5).
    03  e3-s2   value "qrΔtuΔΔxy"   pic x(9).
    03  e3-s3   value "jΔlmnop"     pic x(7).

    second last string:   "aqrΔtujΔlmnopΔΔΔΔΔΔΔ"
    last string:          "aqrjΔΔΔΔΔΔΔΔΔΔΔΔΔΔΔΔΔ"
```

Upon a closer examination of the string statement it becomes clear that at a lower level, hidden from the programmer, counters of some sort must be controlling the transfer of characters from the source items to the target item.

One of these counters, the counter that points to the current character in the target item, can be made visible in the program by using the **pointer** phrase. By using this phrase we can initialize the pointer to a value of our choice and check its value after the transfer of characters is complete.

```
    string {identifier-1 ... delimited literal-2}... into identifier-3
⎡  [pointer identifier-4]                            ⎤
⎢  ⎧⎰ overflow statement-1     ⎫                     ⎥
⎢  ⎨   not overflow statement-2 ⎬                    ⎥
⎣  end-string                                        ⎦
```

The item used as a pointer is similar in concept to both the left position indicator used with reference modification and the subscript used with tables. It must be a numeric item and during character transfer it must be within a valid range (1 through to the length of the target). When a pointer is used in a string statement the programmer must ensure that it contains a value that is in range prior to the execution of the string statement.

This pointer might be made visible by the programmer for two reasons. Firstly, there may be a need to start a transfer of characters to a position other than the first character of the target. Secondly, there may be a need to count the number of characters that have been transferred. For example, consider the following statements where `e4-source` contains "abcΔd", `e4-ptr1` is defined as a two-digit numeric item, and `e4-target` is a 10-character item:

```
move 2 to e4-ptr1
string    e4-source delimited "Δ" into e4-target
  pointer e4-ptr1
  overflow
    display "overflow"
  not overflow
    display "no overflow"
end-string
```

```
       03  e4-ptr2            pic 9.
       03  filler             pic x.
           88 finished        value "Y".
           88 not-finished    value "N".

move 2 to e4-ptr1
move 1 to e4-ptr2
set not-finished to true

perform test before until finished
  evaluate e4-ptr1 numeric and e4-ptr1 > 0 and e4-ptr1 < 11
    when false
      evaluate e4-source(e4-ptr2:1) = "Δ"
        when    true
          set finished to true
          display "no overflow"
        when    false
          move e4-source(e4-ptr2:1) to e4-target(e4-ptr1:1)
      end-evaluate
      evaluate e4-ptr2 = 5
        when    true
          set finished to true
          display "no overflow"
        when false
          compute e4-ptr2 = e4-ptr2 + 1
      end-evaluate
      compute e4-ptr1 = e4-ptr1 + 1

    when    true
      set finished to true
      display "overflow"
  end-evaluate
end-perform
```

Figure 6.2 Simulation outline for a **string** statement

The pointer initially points to the character position in the target at which the transfer will begin. After a stringing operation the pointer value is one greater than the number of characters that have been transferred. In this example, characters 1 to 3 of the source will be transferred to positions 2 to 4 of the target. The pointer will hold a value of 5 after the transfer.

The semantic behaviour of the above move and string statements can be simulated with other statements and additional data as outlined in Fig. 6.2.

In effect using the string statement has saved the programmer from having to define a switch(finished/not-finished), define an additional pointer for the source item (e4-ptr2), increment the pointers directly, and evaluate the state of the source and the target for each iteration of a loop in which the character transfer is effected. Thus the string statement gives the programmer a higher and more abstract statement structure in which to state the processing requirements for the intended stringing operation.

The clear advantage is that the programmer is saved the task of writing a lower level set of statements to effect transfers. However, there is a possible disadvantage in that the programmer must understand the semantic behaviour that is implied by the syntax of the string statement.

The programmer who understands how to use statements such as these is able to write programs that quickly and clearly manipulate data but this is possible only if prior to writing a program the implied semantics are well understood. Thus there is a trade-off between the time taken to learn more complicated statements and the time taken to write

$$\text{string} \left\{ \begin{Bmatrix} \text{identifier-1} \\ \text{literal-1} \end{Bmatrix} \ldots \text{delimited} \begin{Bmatrix} \text{identifier-2} \\ \text{literal-2} \\ \text{size} \end{Bmatrix} \right\} \ldots$$

```
    into           identifier-3
    [pointer       identifier-4]
    [{  overflow       statement-1  }]
    [{  not overflow   statement-2  }]
    [end-string]
```

1. When a figurative constant is used as either a source item or a delimiter its size is always one character.
2. The string statement obeys the rules for alphanumeric moves except that the target is not filled with trailing spaces.
3. Data transfer ends when one of these conditions is found to be true:
   (a) All of the characters from the source have been moved to the target.
   (b) The end of the target has been reached.
4. When the pointer phrase is used it must be initialized to a value in the range of 1 through to the maximum number of characters in the target. This must be done prior to the execution of the string statement.
5. After a string operation that has not caused overflow the pointer will be one greater than the position of the last character that was transferred into the target.
6. Overflow occurs if the pointer becomes out of range. This occurs when the target is full and there are still more characters available for transfer. Pointers that are less than one also cause overflow.
7. A delimiter can be the size of a source item, or a pattern appearing in a source item that matches either a literal or the contents of another item. If the delimiter phrase is omitted then the default delimiter is size.

Figure 6.3 Full format and rules governing the **string** statement

programs. In every case the time taken to learn statements such as these is well rewarded. Always the goal is to learn how to use such statements easily with the help of a text or manual. It is not to memorize their syntax.

Now that the major features of string have been introduced we can consider the full format for the string statement and the general rules which govern its use (Fig. 6.3).

We can see that the source can be a mixture of data items and literals. For example,

```
string e5-surname      delimited space
       ",Δ"            delimited size
       e5-forename     delimited space
    into e5-fullname
```

might be used in preparing a name such as "Horner,ΔJack".

SELF-CHECK QUESTIONS

For the following data:

```
01  e6-line             pic x(20).
01  e7-ptr1             pic 99.
01  e8-Canada.
    03  e8-province     pic xxx.
    03  e8-postcode.
        05  e8-part1    pic xxx.
        05  e8-part2    pic xxx.
```

Q If e8-Canada holds "ONTM4Y1N6" what is the effect of the following statements:

```
move spaces to e6-line
string e8-province  ".ΔΔ"  e8-part1  "Δ"  e8-part2
   into e6-line
```

A The move ensures that e6-line will be initialized to spaces. After execution of the string statement e6-line will contain:

"ONT.ΔΔM4YΔ1N6ΔΔΔΔΔΔΔ"

Overflow will not occur because the five source items are delimited by size. Their total size (13 characters) is less than the size of the target (20 characters).

Q What would the result have been if the following moves and string had been executed:

```
move spaces to e6-line
move 3 to e7-ptr1
string     e8-province  ".ΔΔ"  e8-part1  "Δ"  e8-part2
   into    e6-line
   pointer e8-ptr1
```

A After execution of the string statement the print line will contain:

"ΔΔONT.ΔΔM4YΔ1N6ΔΔΔΔΔ"

Overflow will not occur because there is no attempt to transfer into the target beyond the 20th character.

For the following data:

```
01   e1-sentence        pic x(25).
01   e2-source.
     03   e2-word1      pic x(6).
     03   e2-word2      pic x(6).
     03   e2-word3      pic x(6).
     03   e2-word4      pic x(6).
     03   e2-word5      pic x(6).
     03   e2-word6      pic x(6).
```

Q What would be the result upon e1-sentence of the following statements:

```
move space to e1-sentence
move "MaryΔΔhadΔΔΔaΔΔΔΔΔlittlelamb"   to e2-source

string e2-word1 delimited space   "-"
       e2-word2 delimited space   "-"
       e2-word3 delimited space   "-"
       e2-word4 delimited space   "-"
       e2-word5 delimited space   "-"
       e2-word6 delimited space
   into e1-sentence
   overflow
      display "sentence too long"
   not overflow
      display "sentence ok"
end-string
```

A The first move statement will initialize the six items in e2-source. Note that e2-word6 becomes spaces. After the execution of the string statement e1-sentence will hold:

   "Mary-had-a-little-lamb-ΔΔ"

22 characters will be transferred, for although the delimiter for a "-" string is space there is no space within it. Therefore the default of size applies and the whole of the string, that is, the single character is moved. The following has the same effect and is easier to read:

```
string e2-word1 "-"
       e2-word2 "-"
       e2-word3 "-"
       e2-word4 "-"
       e2-word5 "-"
       e2-word6 delimited space
   into e1-sentence
   overflow
      display "sentence too long"
   not overflow
      display "sentence ok"
end-string
```

Q What would be the effect of the above string statement if e2-source is initialized to:

   "ItsΔΔΔfleecewasΔΔΔwhiteΔasΔΔΔsnow"

A The number of characters available for transfer into e1-sentence is 28. Therefore the overflow condition will be raised.

For the following data:

```
01  e3-sentence-rec.
    03  e3-ptr              pic 99.
        88  e3-start        value 2.
    03  e3-sentence         pic x(25).
01  e4-source.
    03  e4-words.
        05  e4-word occurs 6 pic x(6).
```

Q Assume the `e4-source` holds "Mary△△had△△△a△△△△△littlelamb" and that `e3-sentence` has been initialized to spaces. Use a string statement and the pointer `e3-ptr` to transfer the contents of `e4-word(1)`, followed by a single hyphen into the second and subsequent character positions of `e3-sentence`.

A These statements will move "Mary-" to `e3-sentence` in positions 2 to 6. At the end of the string operation the pointer will hold a value of 7.

```
set e3-start to true
string    e4-word(1) delimited space, "-"
  into    e3-sentence
  pointer e3-ptr
```

Q Rewrite `e4-source` as a table of words preceded by a two digit subscript.

A
```
01  e4-source.
    03  e4-sub              pic 99.
        88  e4-start        value 1.
        88  e4-end          value 7.
    03  e4-words.
        05  e4-word occurs 6 pic x(6).
```

Q Use the above table and write a test before loop that contains a string statement to transfer each word in turn into `e3-sentence`. The loop should terminate if overflow occurs and each word in `e3-sentence` should be followed by a "-". Start the transfer into `e3-sentence` beginning at its second character.

A The following statements will string "Mary-had-a-little-lamb-" into the target.

```
set  e3-start to true
move space to e3-sentence

set  e4-start   to true
move "Mary△△had△△△a△△△△littlelamb"  to e4-source

perform test before until e4-end
  string    e4-word(e4-sub) delimited space "-"
    into    e3-sentence
    pointer e3-ptr
    overflow
      display "sentence△too△long"
      set e4-end to true
    not overflow
      compute e4-sub = e4-sub + 1
  end-string
end-perform
```

150   ESSENTIAL COBOL: A FIRST COURSE IN STRUCTURED COBOL

Q The above question places a trailing "-" into the target. Redesign the statements so that this does not occur.

A This can be done in three ways. The easiest is to leave the main body of the statements as they are. Provided that there was no overflow, after the loop the pointer can be decremented by 1 and a space moved to this position.

The other two ways are very similar and depend on recognizing that the words and hyphens can be seen in pairs in either of two ways. If the first word leads on its own then the balance of the string can be visualized as

-word2-word3-word4-word5-word6

where there are five pairs of a pattern. These five pairs can be processed within a single loop. However, if you see the string as beginning with the pattern

word-

then there are five of these followed by a single word. In both cases the loop must count five rather than six times. Depending on which approach you use a single **string** statement must appear just before or just after the loop for the first or last word. Note that the list of items for the **string** statement within the loop is in a different order each time.

Q Consider the following records:

```
01   e5-screen.
     03   e5-ptr              pic 999.
          88 e5-start         value 001.
     03   e5-line             pic x(120).
01   e6-customer.
     03   e6-name.
          05   e6-title       pic x(5).
          05   e6-forename1   pic x(20).
          05   e6-forename2   pic x(20).
          05   e6-surname     pic x(20).
```

It is known that there are no embedded or leading spaces in e6-customer although the forenames may be completely blank. The title holds abbreviations such as "Mr△△" with no period. Write statements to fill e5-line with a string of the following form:

    Mr. B. D. Drummond
    Mr. Drummond
    Mr. B. Drummond

The different versions result due to the presence or absence of forenames. Note that when the first forename is present the first initial portion occupies three characters. There is no need to check for overflow. Why?

A There is no need to check for overflow because the e5-line is long enough to accommodate any possible result:

```
         set e5-start to true
         move spaces to e5-line

         string    e6-title ".Δ" delimited size
            into      e5-line
            pointer e5-ptr

         evaluate e6-forename1 not = space
           when    true
             string    e6-forename1(1:1) ".Δ" delimited size
                into      e5-line
                pointer e5-ptr
         end-evaluate
         evaluate e6-forename2 not = space
           when    true
             string    e6-forename2(1:1) ".Δ" delimited size
                into      e5-line
                pointer e5-ptr
         end-evaluate
         string    e6-surname delimited space
            into      e5-line
            pointer e5-ptr
```

Q The processing requirement has now been respecified to require the removal of spaces between initials in cases where a second initial is needed. The result is that the surname is preceded by a space when there are initials but otherwise not. (The title still always ends with a space.)

   Mr.ΔB.D.ΔDrummond
   Mr.ΔDrummond
   Mr.ΔB.ΔDrummond

Rewrite the string statements to produce the correct results as shown above.

A All of the statements will remain the same except for those which control the transfer of the second forename. In this case the string statement is preceded by a compute statement that decrements the pointer by 1:

```
         evaluate e6-forename2 not = space
           when    true
             compute   e5-ptr = e5-ptr - 1
             string    e6-forename2(1:1) ".Δ" delimited size
                into      e5-line
                pointer e5-ptr
         end-evaluate
```

6.2 UNSTRING

The **unstring** statement is in many ways the opposite of the string statement. It can be used to transfer characters from a source string into one or more target substrings.

   A simple format for the unstring statement is:

```
unstring identifier-1 into identifier-2
```

$$\begin{bmatrix} \left\{ \begin{vmatrix} \text{overflow} & \text{statement-1} \\ \text{not overflow} & \text{statement-2} \end{vmatrix} \right\} \\ \text{end-unstring} \end{bmatrix}$$

Characters will be transferred one by one from the source to the target. If the target is not large enough to hold all of the characters from the source overflow will occur. By default the source is delimited by its size. As with the string statement, no space filling occurs in the target item.

In such a simple form the statement is of limited usefulness. It might be used to move a short string to a long string without space filling. In such a case there would never be overflow. Therefore such a statement could be written in the simple form:

```
unstring e1-var into e2-var
```

The power of the unstring statement becomes clearer when we consider that the target can be a list of data items and that the transfer of characters can be diverted to the next item in the list when a specific delimiter is found. The *limit-test* is used to specify delimiters:

```
unstring identifier-1 [delimited limit-test] into {identifier-2}...
```

$$\begin{bmatrix} \left\{ \begin{vmatrix} \text{overflow} & \text{statement-1} \\ \text{not overflow} & \text{statement-2} \end{vmatrix} \right\} \\ \text{end-unstring} \end{bmatrix}$$

Consider the following example where a source date in the American form of month followed by day and year (mm/dd/yy). This is transferred into a target date in the European form of ddmmyy:

```
01  e1-date   value "02/29/92" pic x(8).
01  e2-date.
    03  e2-day                  pic xx.
    03  e2-month                pic xx.
    03  e2-year                 pic xx.
    unstring e1-date delimited "/"
       into   e2-month
              e2-day
              e2-year
```

In this example the limit-test is the literal "/" which is expected to occur in the source. The target is a list of three items.

As a result of executing this statement `e2-date` will hold the six numeric characters from the source in their new order. The delimiters themselves are not transferred but serve to cause the scanner to stop transferring to the current item in the target list and to begin transferring to the next item.

The limit-test can specify a list of alternative test items. When this is done the alternates in the list are separated by the keyword **or**.

```
unstring e1-date delimited "*" or "-" or space
    into  e2-month
          e2-day
          e2-year
```

In this example the delimiters of "/", "-", and a single space are treated as alternates. Thus source date such as "02/29/92", "02-29△92", "02△29/92" will produce the same result in e2-date.

Overflow will occur if target items are filled and the source still contains characters to be transferred.

Consider the following example with the same data:

```
unstring e1-date delimited "/" or "-" or space
    into  e2-month
          e2-day
    overflow
        display "bad△move"
    not overflow
        display "good△move"
end-string
```

In this case overflow will occur because a complete scan of the source item cannot take place. There are six characters in the source item to be transferred but only four characters in the two target items.

When the source contains none of the specified delimiters overflow will not necessarily occur. For example, when the source contains no delimiters the result will be that the first two characters will be transferred into e2-month and the next six characters will be lost. Thus the truncated result will be the same as that produced by an alphanumeric move statement.

Other forms of the limit-test will be presented later in the chapter. For the moment we will use literals for limit-tests.

SELF-CHECK QUESTIONS

Q If e1-date has been initialized to "017/3/48" and e2-date to spaces what is the effect of:

```
unstring e1-date delimited "/" or "-" or space
    into e2-month
         e2-day
         e2-year
    overflow
        display "bad△move"
    not overflow
        display "good△move"
end-string
```

A The character before the first delimiter is lost, only one character is transferred into the first position of `e2-day`, and the year is transferred successfully. Thus `e2-date` now holds "3∆0148".

The unstring statement also includes **delimiter**, **count**, and **tallying** phrases to assist the programmer in checking the contents of items.

```
unstring identifier-1  [delimited limit-test [or limit-test]...]
   into  {identifier-2 [delimiter identifier-3] [count identifier-4]}...
   [tallying identifier-6]
   [{overflow     statement-1}]
   [{not overflow statement-2}]
   [end-unstring]
```

A delimiter phrase can be specified for each target item. When the transfer to a target item has been completed the unstring statement will transfer the delimiter found in the source into the item given in the delimiter phrase. For example,

```
unstring e1-date  delimited "/" or "∆"
   into  e2-month delimiter e2-mlim
```

can transfer the two characters of the month into `e2-month` and the delimiter into `e2-mlim`.

If the whole of the source is scanned then it will be treated as though it had been delimited by a space and a space will be placed in the appropriate delimiter. The fact that in this case the string statement places a space in a delimiter item could create semantic difficulties in a program. If the programmer had initialized the delimiter item to space prior to the execution of the unstring it would not be possible to know afterwards whether an item had a value of space due to initialization or due to the action of the unstring statement. For this reason it is wise to initialize delimiter items to values other than spaces or expected delimiter characters.

A count phrase can also be specified for each target item. If a count has been specified the value of the number of characters checked during transfer from the source will be moved to the item given in the count phrase.

```
unstring e1-date  delimited "/" or "∆"
   into  e2-month count e2-mctr
```

If `e1-date` held a valid date prior to this string statement, then after its execution the item `e2-month` will hold the two numeric characters that have been transferred and `e2-ctr` will hold a value of 2. However, if the `e1-date` had been initialized to "123/45/8", then `e2-month` would contain "12" and `e2-mctr` would contain 3 as a result of the unstring statement.

A single tallying item keeps track of the number of target items that have received characters during the transfer. Although the delimiter and count phrases apply to separate items in the target list the tallying phrase applies to the target as a whole.

```
unstring e1-date  delimited "/" or "△"
   into    e2-month e2-day e2-year
   tallying e3-tally
```

E3-tally will be incremented by one for each item in the target list that has received characters. Therefore for a valid date the e3-tally will be 3 greater than it was prior to the execution of the unstring. Note that if e1-date had contained the string "12345678", then the tally would only be incremented by 1. (If there had been a count specified for e2-month then this would have been given a value of 8.)

SELF-CHECK QUESTIONS

Consider the following data and statements:

```
01  e1-date              pic x(8).
01  e2-date.
    03  e2-day           pic xx.
    03  e2-month         pic xx.
    03  e2-year          pic xx.
01  e3-workers.
    03  e3-tally         pic 9.
    03  e3-counts.
        05  e3-dctr      pic 9.
        05  e3-mctr      pic 9.
        05  e3-yctr      pic 9.
    03  e3-delimiters.
        05  e3-dlim      pic x.
        05  e3-mlim      pic x.
        05  e3-ylim      pic x.
    move spaces to e2-date
    move "???" to e3-delimiters
    unstring    e1-date  delimited "/" or "-" or space
       into     e2-month delimiter e3-mlim count e3-mctr
                e2-day   delimiter e3-dlim count e3-dctr
                e2-year  delimiter e3-ylim count e3-yctr
    tallying e3-tally
       overflow
          display "Not△all△characters△scanned"
       not overflow
          display "Source△completely△scanned"
    end-string
```

Q If e1-date is initialized to "02/29/92" what is the effect of the above statements?

A After the unstring statement e2-date will hold "290292". The three counts will each have a value of 2. E3-mlim and e3-dlim will each have a value of "/". The not overflow phrase will be executed.

E3-ylim will hold a space because the ultimate delimiter for the third substring in the source is by default its length. Therefore the unstring will place a space in the third delimited item. E3-tally will be 3.

Q If e1-date is initialized to "011/3/48" what is the effect of the above statements?
A After the unstring statement e2-date will hold "3△0148". E3-mctr will be 3 because there were three characters found before the delimiter. E3-dctr will be 1 and e3-yctr will be 2. E3-mlim and e3-dlim will each be "/" and e3-ylim will be a space. E3-tally will be 3. The not overflow phrase will be executed.

Q If e1-date is initialized to "012348△△" what is the effect of the above statements?
A After the unstring statement e2-date will hold "△△01△△". E3-mctr will be six because there were six characters found before the delimiter which by default is the size of the source. E3-dctr and e3-yctr will be zero. E3-mlim, e3-dlim and e3-ylim will all be spaces. E3-tally will be one. The not overflow phrase will be executed.

Q If e1-date is initialized to "01////△△" what is the effect of the above statements?
A After the unstring statement e2-date will hold "△△01△△". E3-mctr will be two. E3-dctr and e3-yctr will be zero. E3-mlim, e3-dlim and e3-ylim will all be "/". E3-tally will be 1. The overflow phrase will be executed because there are characters in the source which were not scanned.

In the following example e4-sentence has been initialized to "Mary△had△a△little△lamb". We wish to transfer each word to a separate target. The count phrase and tally phrase allow us to count characters in each word and the total number of words respectively.

```
01  e4-sentence-rec.
    03  e4-sentence            pic x(25).
01  e5-word-rec.
    03  e5-tally               pic 99.
    03  e5-tables.
        05  e5-delimiters.
            07  e5-lim  occurs 6 pic x.
        05  e5-counts.
            07  e5-ctr  occurs 6 pic 99.
        05  e5-words.
            07  e5-word occurs 6 pic x(6).
    move zero    to e5-tally
    move all "?" to e5-delimiters
    move zero    to e5-counts
    move space   to e5-words

    move "Mary△had△a△little△lamb"  to e4-sentence
```

```
          unstring    e4-sentence delimited space
             into     e5-word(1)  delimiter e5-lim(1)  count e5-ctr(1)
                      e5-word(2)  delimiter e5-lim(2)  count e5-ctr(2)
                      e5-word(3)  delimiter e5-lim(3)  count e5-ctr(3)
                      e5-word(4)  delimiter e5-lim(4)  count e5-ctr(4)
                      e5-word(5)  delimiter e5-lim(5)  count e5-ctr(5)
          tallying e5-tally
```

After the execution of the above unstring statement the counts will hold the values 4, 3, 1, 6 and 4 and the tally will hold the value 5.

In this example the reserved word **all** has been used before the literal "?" in the second move statement. **All** causes the literal which follows it to be treated as if it were a figurative constant. Thus **all** "?" causes the target to be filled with six question mark characters. (By initializing the delimiter items to a character that is known not to be in the source it is possible to check afterwards to see exactly how many delimiters were found and what values they have. This would not have been possible if we had initialized the area to spaces.)

SELF-CHECK QUESTIONS

Q What would happen if in the previous example `e4-sentence` had been initialized to "Its∆fleece∆was∆white∆as∆snow"?

A Overflow would have occurred because there were still characters in the source that were not transferred. Because no overflow phrase was specified program execution would have continued with the next statement after the unstring statement.

Q Why is the statement `move zero to e5-counts` legal but the statement `move 0 to e5-counts` illegal?

A Zero is a figurative constant and the target is an alphanumeric group item of 12 characters. After this legal move statement each count will be initialized to two zero characters. `Move 0 to e5-counts` is illegal because 0 is a numeric literal but the group item is not numeric.

Both of these statements are legal:

```
move 0 to e5-ctr(1)
move zero to e5-ctr(1)
```

This is because the figurative constant zero can be used for either an alphanumeric or a numeric target.

In addition, the unstring statement includes a **pointer** phrase that allows transfer to start from a position other than the first character in the source. When an unstring statement begins execution the pointer must be within range. If all of the characters have been transferred successfully then the pointer will be one greater than the length of the source item. Prior to the execution of each unstring statement the pointer must point to the required starting character. Overflow will occur if the pointer is outside the range of 1 to the maximum for the source.

Consider the following statements:

```
01  e4-sentence-rec.
    03  e4-sentence              pic x(25).
01  e5-word-rec.
    03  e5-ptr                   pic 99.
    03  e5-tables.
        05  e5-delimiters.
            07  e5-lim occurs 6 pic x.
        05  e5-counts.
            07  e5-ctr  occurs 6 pic 99.
        05  e5-words.
            07  e5-word occurs 6 pic x(6).
    move "And∆everywhere∆that" to e4-sentence
    move      1 to e5-ptr
    move space to e5-word(1)
    move    "?" to e5-lim(1)
    move      0 to e5-ctr(1)
    unstring   e4-sentence delimited space
      into     e5-word(1)  delimiter e5-lim(1)  count e5-ctr(1)
      pointer  e5-ptr
      overflow
        display "Not∆all∆characters∆scanned"
      not overflow
        display "Source∆completely∆scanned"
    end-unstring
```

After this unstring statement e5-word(1) will become "And∆∆∆" and e5-lim(1) will become a space. In addition, e5-ctr(1) will become 3 because this is the number of characters that have been transferred into e5-word(1), and e5-ptr will become 5 so that it points to the next available character for transfer in the source. The overflow phrase will be executed because the scan of all 20 characters has not been completed.

If the pointer had originally been initialized to a value of five, then after the unstring e5-word(1) will become "everyw", e5-lim(1) will become a space, e5-ctr(1) will become 10 and e5-ptr will become 16 which points to the beginning of the third word. We can see that by changing the pointer and by checking the various items associated with the string operations, it is possible to discover most of the information that is important concerning the structure of the source and its transfer into a set of target items. Once a programmer has analysed a problem and knows what is required it is a relatively easy task to fulfil the requirement with the necessary statements provided that the programmer understands the semantics of the statements.

The full format for the unstring verb is:

```
unstring identifier-1
   [delimited limit-test [or limit-test]...]
   into     {identifier-2 [delimiter identifier-3] [count identifier-4]}...
   [pointer  identifier-5]
   [tallying identifier-6]
   [[{overflow     statement-1}]
    [{not overflow statement-2}]]
   end-unstring
```

The end-unstring scope delimiter is only used when an overflow phrase is used. The format for the limit-test is:

$$[\text{all}] \begin{Bmatrix} \text{identifier-7} \\ \text{literal-1} \end{Bmatrix}$$

and either the identifier or literal can be greater than one character.

SELF-CHECK QUESTIONS

Q Which of the following items must a programmmer initialize to a value prior to the execution of an unstring statement:

> pointer
> count
> delimiter
> tallying

A All of these items except the count should be initialized to a known value. This is crucial for items such as the pointer to ensure that it is in the correct range. It is advisable for the delimiter so that the item can be checked afterwards to see whether or not it has been changed. The count does not need to be initialized because the unstring statement moves a value to it.

It is in some ways helpful to think of the pointer and the tallying items as running totals on the source and the target list respectively.

Q What is the difference between a pointer in a string statement and a pointer in an unstring statement?

A For a string statement the pointer points to the next available position for transfer into the target. It must always be in the range of 1 to the length of the target immediately prior to the string operation.

For an unstring statement the pointer points to the next available character in the source. It must always be in the range of 1 to the length of the source immediately prior to the unstring operation.

Q What is the difference in the meaning of overflow between the string and unstring statements?

A For both string and unstring an overflow condition exists when the target or targets are full but the source or sources still contain characters available for transfer.

In both cases the overflow condition is set when the pointer goes out of range during statement execution. (Note that this includes a pointer becoming less than 1 for any reason.)

Q Respecify the unstring statement from the previous self-check question that used `e5-word-rec`. It should be placed within a loop so that zero to six words can be transferred successfully. (Attempts to transfer more than six words should be detected.)

A Note that the subscript is displayed within the loop to identify which word is the cause of a message.

```
01  e6-sentence-rec.
    03  e6-ptr                      pic 99.
        88  e6-min value 01.
        88  e6-max value 26.
    03  e6-sentence                 pic x(25).

01  e7-word-rec.
    03  e7-tally                    pic 99.
    03  e7-table.
        05  e7-sub                  pic 9.
            88  e7-min value 1.
            88  e7-max value 7.
        05  e7-counts.
            07  e7-ctr occurs 6 pic 99.
        05  e7-words.
            07  e7-word     occurs 6 pic x(6).

    move zero    to e7-tally
    move zero    to e7-counts
    move space   to e7-words

    set  e6-min to true
    move "Mary∆had∆a∆little∆lamb"  to e6-sentence

    set e7-min to true
    perform test before until e6-max or e7-max
      unstring   e6-sentence delimited space
         into    e7-word(e7-sub) count e7-ctr(e7-sub)
         tallying e7-tally
         pointer e6-ptr
         overflow
            display "this∆word∆is∆" e7-sub
         not overflow
            display "last∆word∆is∆" e7-sub
      end-unstring
      compute e7-sub = e7-sub + 1
    end-perform
```

6.3 INSPECT

The **inspect** statement provides a powerful high-level mechanism for counting and replacing characters within a text string.

The full format for the **inspect** verb is:

```
inspect identifier-1
```
$$\begin{Bmatrix} \text{tallying} & \{\text{identifier-4 for tally-list}\}\dots \\ \text{replacing} & \{\text{replace-list}\}\dots \\ \text{tallying} & \{\text{identifier-4 for tally-list}\}\dots \text{ replacing } \{\text{replace-list}\}\dots \\ \text{converting} & \begin{Bmatrix}\text{identifier-2}\\ \text{literal-1}\end{Bmatrix} \text{ to } \begin{Bmatrix}\text{identifier-3}\\ \text{literal-2}\end{Bmatrix} \text{ [delimiter-list]}\dots \end{Bmatrix}$$

The first point to notice is that there are four main paths through the syntax of the statement. The tallying phrase provides the means to count character patterns in a string and the replacing phrase provides the means to replace one pattern with another.

The third path simply allows both tallying and replacing to occur in a single inspect statement. As it happens these options operate entirely independently of one another. Therefore an inspect statement in this form has exactly the same effect as an inspect statement with the counting phrase immediately followed by an inspect statement with the replacing phrase.

The fourth path shows the converting option. It provides a simpler and more convenient way to change one set of characters in a string into another set.

The format shows there are tally, replace, and delimiter lists. Furthermore the syntax for the tally and replace lists incorporates delimiter lists. The easiest way to understand the effect of the inspect statement is to review examples of it in use. Therefore before turning to Appendix C where the general and full formats for the inspect statements are included, take a few moments to consider the examples on the next few pages.

Our first example uses the tally phrase with a tally-list:

```
move zero to e1-ctr
inspect e1-string
   tallying e1-ctr for leading space
```

In this example the **inspect** statement is used to count the number of leading spaces in a string. If e1-string holds "ΔAB", then e1-ctr will become 1. If the whole of the string is spaces, then e1-ctr will become a value equal to the length of the string. If the string holds "ΔAΔ", then e1-ctr will still become 1 because there is only one leading space.

The **inspect** statement does not initialize the tallying counters. This gives the programmer the freedom to use counters for summing the effects of a number of successive statements. It also allows the programmer to initialize to a different base value if this is required. For example, imagine that you wished to unstring characters beginning at the first non-space character in a string that contained leading spaces. The following statements would position the pointer correctly in preparation for the unstring:

```
move 1 to e1-ptr
inspect e1-string
   tallying e1-ptr for leading space
```

We can see that after this inspect `e1-ptr` has a value that is 1 greater than the number of leading spaces. For strings with no leading spaces the pointer will still be pointing to the first character.

It is also possible that the string might consist entirely of spaces, in which case `e1-ptr` will finish with a value that is one greater than the length of the string.

A form of the **inspect** statement which is useful in number conversion uses a replace-list:

```
inspect e1-string
  replacing leading space by zero
```

Thus a string of "ΔΔΔ12" is changed to "00012". We can see that this is not the same as:

```
inspect e1-string
  replacing all space by zero
```

which not only changes "ΔΔ120" to "00120" but also changes "ΔΔ12Δ" to "00120".

It is possible to include more than one entry on a tally-list and more than one tally-list after the tallying phrase. When this is done each list is processed in turn as a separate scan of the string. Characters that are counted in one scan are not counted in subsequent scans. For example:

```
move zero to e1-ctr1 e1-ctr2 e1-ctr3
inspect e1-string
  tallying e1-ctr1 for all "a" "e" "i" "o" "u"
           e1-ctr2 for all "y"
           e1-ctr3 for characters
```

As a result of these statements `e1-ctr1` will hold the total number of vowels found in the string, `e1-ctr2` the number of "y" characters, and `e1-ctr3` the total number of other characters.

As a result of the following statements a string containing "recieve" will be changed to "receive" and `e1-ctr1` will be incremented to 1.

```
move zero to e1-ctr1
inspect e1-string
  tallying  e1-ctr1 for all "ie" after "c"
  replacing leading "ie" after "c" by "ei"
```

A string containing "client" will remain unchanged and untallied because "lie" does not match the rule specified by either the tally-list or the replace-list.

The above two rules are not exactly the same. The statement will also change "recieiexx" to "receieixx" because the pattern "ie" leads the balance of the string after the "c". In this case the count will be 2. However, "reciexxie" also contains two "ie" patterns. It will be changed to "receixxie" because there is only one leading pattern after the "c". The tally will hold a value of 2 because it is being used to count all of the occurrences of the pattern in the string.

A common requirement is to substitute one set of characters for another. For example,

```
inspect e1-string
   replacing all "a" by "A"
             all "e" by "E"
             all "i" by "I"
             all "o" by "O"
             all "u" by "U"
```

The convert phrase provides an economical way to specify the same requirement. The two strings supplied by the converting phrase maps one set of characters into another:

```
inspect e1-string converting "aeiou" to "AEIOU"
```

In this example a list of lower-case vowels is matched to a list of upper-case vowels. Its effect is to convert all the lower-case vowels in e1-string to upper case. Therefore a string containing "The Letter" becomes "ThE LEttEr". The convenience of this feature is further improved by the use of identifiers.

```
inspect e1-string converting e1-list to e2-list
```

SELF-CHECK QUESTIONS

Q Define any necessary data and write an inspect statement to convert a sentence of 80 characters from upper to lower case.

A The following data and inspect statement will accomplish the conversion. (Note that the values of e3-old and e4-new can be changed at run time if this is required.)

```
01  e2-sentence                                       pic x(80).
01  e3-old  value "ABCDEFGHIJKLMNOPQRSTUVWXYZ"        pic x(26).
01  e4-new  value "abcdefghijklmnopqrstuvwxyz"        pic x(26).

inspect e2-sentence converting e3-old to e4-new
```

Q What will happen when e2-sentence already contains some lower-case letters or other characters that are not in either e3-old or e4-new?

A These characters will not be changed by the inspect statement.

The following three examples provide a more detailed picture of how successive scans affect the tallying counters and the string. The first example does five tally scans:

```
move zero to e2-ctr0 e2-ctr1 e2-ctr2 e2-ctr3 e2-ctr4
inspect e2-string
   tallying e2-ctr0 for all "AB" all "D"
            e2-ctr1 for all "BC"
            e2-ctr2 for leading "EF"
            e2-ctr3 for leading "B"
            e2-ctr4 for characters
```

As a result of this inspect the five scans will count characters as shown by the dashes beneath the example string. (Characters that have been counted in a scan do not participate in a later scan.)

```
"EFABDBCGABEFGG"   example string before the inspect
 ---     --        scan 1: e2-ctr0 becomes 3
       --          scan 2: e2-ctr1 becomes 1
 --                scan 3: e2-ctr2 becomes 1
                   scan 4: e2-ctr3 becomes 0
         -  ----   scan 5: e2-ctr4 becomes 5
```

Notice that the third scan is for leading "EF". Although the string contains "EF" in two different spots only the first "EF" in positions 1 and 2 is leading.

The second example does seven replacing scans:

```
inspect e2-string
    replacing      all "AB" by "XY"  "D" by "X"
                   all "BC" by "VW"
                   leading "EF" by "TU"
                   leading "B" by "S"
                   first "G" by "R"
                   first "G" by "P"
                   characters by "Z"
```

As a result of this inspect the 7 scans will replace characters as marked beneath the original string. Characters that are changed in one scan are never available to subsequent scans. However, the whole string is always checked for delimiters and other boundary conditions. Thus scan 5 finds the first "G" at position 8 and changes it to an "R" but scan 6 uses the altered string and finds the first "G" at position 13.

```
"EFABDBCGABEFGG"   example string before the inspect
   XYX    XY       scan 1: → "EFXYXBCGXYEFGG"
         VW        scan 2: → "EFXYXVWGXYEFGG"
  TU               scan 3: → "TUXYXVWGXYEFGG"
                   scan 4: →  no change
            R      scan 5: → "TUXYXVWRXYEFGG"
               P   scan 6: → "TUXYXVWRXYEFPG"
              ZZ Z scan 7: → "TUXYXVWRXYZZPZ"
```

The third example combines the two previous inspect statements into one:

```
move zero to e2-ctr0 e2-ctr1 e2-ctr2 e2-ctr3 e2-ctr4
inspect e2-string
   tallying    e2-ctr0 for all "AB" all "D"
               e2-ctr1 for all "BC"
               e2-ctr2 for leading "EF"
               e2-ctr3 for leading "B"
               e2-ctr4 for characters
   replacing   all "AB" by "XY" "D" by "X"
               all "BC" by "VW"
               leading "EF" by "TU"
               leading "B" by "S"
               first "G" by "R"
               first "G" by "P"
               characters by "Z"
```

TEXT STRING MANIPULATION   **165**

This inspect statement will have exactly the same effect as the original two statements. The source string will be scanned 12 times in all. The tallying scans take place first and have no effect on the replacing scans that follow.

SELF-CHECK QUESTIONS

Q   If e2-string held the value "BABABC", what would be the effect of the previous move and inspect statements on the counters and on the value of e2-string?

A   The counters would become 2, 0, 0, 1, 1 respectively.
E2-string would become "SXYXYZ".

Q   Similarly, what would happen if e2-string contained "BBBC"?

A   The counters would become 0, 1, 0, 2, 0 respectively.
E2-string would become "SSVW".

Q   What would be the effect of the following statements when e3-string holds "ABA"?

```
move zero to e3-ctr0 e3-ctr1
inspect e3-string
   tallying   e3-ctr0 for characters
              e3-ctr1 for all "A"
   replacing  characters by "Z"
              all "A" by "X"
```

A   The first tallying cycle counts three characters. Therefore there are no further characters to be counted in the second cycle and e3-ctr1 remains at zero.
   The first replacing cycle changes the string to "ZZZ". Therefore there are no characters to be replaced by the second cycle.

Q   What would be the effect of the following statements when e3-string holds the value "BBEABDABABBCABEE"?

```
move zero to e3-ctr0 e3-ctr1 e3-ctr2
inspect e3-string
   tallying   e3-ctr0 for all "AB" before "BC"
              e3-ctr1 for leading "B" after "D"
              e3-ctr2 for characters after "A" before "C"
   replacing  all "AB" by "XY" before "BC"
              leading "B" by "W"  after "D"
              first "E" by "V"    after "D"
              characters by "Z"   after "A" before "C"
```

A   The tallying cycles will change the counters as follows:

```
         1
1234567890123456

BBEABDABABBCABEE
   --  ----           e3-ctr0 becomes 3
                      e3-ctr1 stays at zero
        -   -         e3-ctr2 becomes 2
```

The replacing cycles will change the string as follows:

```
                 1
        1234567890123456
        ────────────────
        BBEABDABABBCABEE
           XY XYXY            all "AB" by "XY" before "BC"
                              leading "B" by "W" after "D"
                  V           first "E" by "V" after "D"
                              characters by "Z" after "A" before "C"

        BBEXYDXYXYBCABVE      is the result
```

Q What would have happened if e3-string had contained "ADDDDA"?

A The first two counters would remain at zero but the third counter would become 5. This is because 5 characters were encountered after "A" but prior to "C". In other words the absence of the "C" delimiter caused the rest of the string to be counted. Similarly the last replacing cycle will change the string to "AZZZZZ".

Q What is the effect of the following statement when e4-string holds the value "ac∆aebdfbcd-ab∆d"?

```
inspect e4-string
   converting "abcd" to "xyzx" after space before "-"
```

A As a result of the inspect e4-string will be converted to "ac∆xeyxfyzx-ab∆d".

6.4 JUSTIFICATION

In previous chapters we have seen that alphanumeric moves are left justified by default. COBOL provides a feature to allow *right justification* when this is needed.

```
01    e1-old          pic x(10).
01    e1-new          pic x(10) just right.
```

Imagine that e1-old contains the string "BEANO∆∆∆∆∆" and we wish to put "∆∆∆∆∆BEANO" into e1-new.

```
move e1-old(1:5) to e1-new
move "BEANO" to e1-new
```

Either of the above move statements will force a right aligned move between the source and the target.

SELF-CHECK QUESTION

Q What is the effect of:

```
01..e1-old value "12345"        pic x(5).
01   e1-new value "∆∆∆∆∆BEANO"  pic x(10) just right.

move e1-new to e1-old
```

A After the move e1-old will be spaces. This is because the justification is always determined by the target field which in this case is left justified.

6.5 EDIT MASKS

Edit masks allow the programmer to create edited versions of character strings. The main use for these edited versions is as output to the terminal screen or to printed reports. An edit mask is constructed by putting special editing characters into what would otherwise have been the definition of an alphanumeric or numeric item. The resulting items thereby become alphanumeric-edited or numeric-edited items.

It is possible to create a wide variety of edit masks. For the present we will consider only simple edit masks that can be used for character strings.

6.5.1 Simple alphanumeric masks

The least complicated form of editing for alphanumeric fields is simple insertion editing to insert blanks. When the source is moved to the target item spaces will be inserted into the target wherever a "b" appears in its picture clause (see Fig. 6.4). In all other respects the rules for moving data apply, namely, left justification, truncation and padding.

Two other editing characters are available and can be used in the same way. These are the oblique or solidus "/" and the zero "0" which cause the insertions of these characters. The "b", "/" and "0" editing characters can be used in any combination (see Fig. 6.5).

	Source		Target		
	picture	value	picture	value	length
(a)	pic x(4).	ABCD	pic xxbxx.	AB△CD	5
(b)	pic x(5).	QRSTZ	pic xxbxxbx.	QR△ST△Z	7
(c)	pic x(5).	45678	pic b(3)x(3)bxx.	△△△456△78	9
(d)	pic x(7).	QR23ZWS	pic b(3)x(3)bxx.	△△△QR2△3Z	9
(e)	pic x(3).	QRS	pic b(3)x(3)bxx.	△△△QRS△△△	9

Figure 6.4 Using alphanumeric edit masks – space character insertions

	Source		Target		
	picture	value	picture	value	length
(a)	pic x(4).	ABCD	pic xx/xx.	AB/CD	5
(b)	pic x(5).	QRSTZ	pic xx0xx/x.	QROST/Z	7
(c)	pic x(5).	QRSTZ	pic 0(3)x(3)/xx.	000QRS/TZ	9
(d)	pic x(7).	QRSTZWS	pic b(3)x(3)bxx.	△△△QRS△TZ	9
(e)	pic x(3).	QRS	pic /(3)x(3)/xx.	///QRS/△△	9
(f)	pic x(6).	010191	pic xx/xx/xx.	01/01/91	8

Figure 6.5 Using alphanumeric edit masks – other character insertions

168 ESSENTIAL COBOL: A FIRST COURSE IN STRUCTURED COBOL

	Source		Target		
	picture	value	picture	value	length
(a)	pic 9(4).	0000	pic z(4).	ΔΔΔΔ	4
(b)	pic 9(3).	000	pic z(4).	ΔΔΔΔ	4
(c)	pic 9(5).	12345	pic z(4).	2345	4
(d)	pic 9(4).	0001	pic z(4).	ΔΔΔ1	4
(e)	pic 9(4).	0204	pic z(4).	Δ204	4
(f)	pic 9(4).	0000	pic z(3)9.	ΔΔΔ0	4

Figure 6.6 Using numeric edit masks – space character insertions

6.5.2 Simple numeric masks

The simplest form of numeric edit mask uses the "z" character to create zero suppression editing for leading zeros (Fig. 6.6).

As is the case with other numeric moves the source and target are aligned at the decimal point and the target is either truncated at the left or filled with leading zeros as required. The editing then causes any leading zero that is defined by a "z" in the target to be replaced by blanks.

6.6 CASE STUDY: LIM1 (LIMERICKS)

Limericks are five-line poems with a simple rhyme structure in which the first and second lines rhyme with the fifth line and the third line rhymes with the fourth line:

A neophyte programmer tried
Within a called program to hide,
A structural tension
So beyond comprehension
That the root program suddenly died.

In this case study we will develop program lim1 to accept a limerick from the keyboard, to do a simple analysis, and to write a short report to the screen.

	1 2 3 1234567890123456789012345678 90123...
Columns	
inital prompt	Input a 5 line limerick
5 lines in turn where *n* is the line number currently being input	n:

Figure 6.7 Input layout for lim1

```
                                   1         2         3
Columns                   123456789012345678901234567890123...

l is the line number   1. -line:l empty
w is the word number   2. -line:l word:w too long
                       3. -line:l >w words
```

Figure 6.8 Layout for error messages for lim1

The input format required by lim1 will consist of an initial prompt for a limerick followed by a prompt for five lines of text which can be up to 78 characters long (Fig. 6.7).

Once the limerick is input it will be validated to ensure that:

1. All lines contain some text i.e. no empty lines.
2. No words are longer than the character maximum set by lim.
3. No lines contain more words than the word maximum set by lim.

These errors will be written to the screen as the first report (Fig. 6.8).

When the limerick contains an empty line the analysis will stop but in other cases analysis will continue with long words truncated to the maximum number of characters and long lines reduced to the maximum number of words. The results will be written to the screen, as shown in Fig. 6.9.

When we compare the input to the output a number of correspondences become apparent:

1. The report of word counts could be produced on a line-by-line basis without any need to store previous lines.
2. This could also be done with the report of the total words per line.
3. The last word in each line could be saved to construct the extracted rhymes at the end of the program.

```
                                   1         2         3
Columns                   123456789012345678901234567890123...

header                    Line       Wordcount
                          1          4
                          2          5
five word counts          3          3
                          4          3
                          5          6

footer with total         There are 21 words in total

extracted rhymes          "tried" rhymes with "hide" and "died"
                          "tension" rhymes with "comprehension"
```

Figure 6.9 Output layout for lim1

Therefore a program could be written that only stored each line in turn and saved any information for reporting at the end. However, if this is done it means that the full limerick will not exist as a data structure within the program but only as individual lines and a current counter. Furthermore, a data structure will allow us to separate input statements from output statements more clearly. The cost of storing the full limerick is reasonably small, five lines instead of one line. Therefore we will use a table to store the limerick.

```
01   w1-lim.
     03   w1-lsub                  pic 9.
     03   w1-lines.
          05   w1-line occurs 5 pic x(78).
```

The use of this data structure will allow us to fill the table by using a called program for input. Other programs can then analyse its contents and produce reports without concerning themselves with line constraints within the limerick. It also means that inter-line processing such as swapping rhyming lines could be included at a later date without needing to rewrite the program completely.

The processing implied for a single limerick is as follows:

```
get_limerick
produce_report_1
evaluate empty_line_error_found
  when true
    continue
  when false
    produce_report_2
end-evaluate
```

This is easily designed into a loop that will allow us to process any number of limericks until asked to stop:

```
get_limerick

perform test before until asked_to_stop
  produce_report_1
  evaluate empty_line_error_found
    when true
      continue
    when false
      produce_report_2
  end-evaluate
  get_limerick
end-perform

stop run.
```

Get_limerick is a process within the main algorithm which could be put into a called program. The only other input specified is the request to stop processing. Although this could be contained within the root program it would mean that input is being processed from two different programs. Therefore we will design all input requests into get_limerick and redesign the main data structure into which it will put its input to reflect this:

```
01    w1-lim.
      03   filler                  pic x.
           88 w1-lvalid value "v".
           88 w1-lquit  value "q".
      03   w1-lsub                 pic 9.
      03   w1-lines.
           05   w1-line occurs 5 pic x(78).
```

The root program can pass w1-lim to the program and it can be returned with either a valid limerick or a request to stop processing. The details of how this is done is thereby hidden from the root program.

The two stages of analysis on the limerick proceed one after the other and result from processing the data in the main data structure. These could be left within the root program, or put into either one or two called programs. If they are put into two programs the fact that the second report is to be suppressed as the result of errors found in the first report will have to be communicated to the second program via the root program. If the processing is left in the root program it will mean that the root program is managing output as well as driving the main process. This could lead to a high level of complexity in later enhancements if either the main process or the output process expanded.

Therefore we will place the analysis in a single called program that will also display its results to the screen.

This leads us to conclude that the structure chart for the program will be as shown in Fig. 6.10.

This structure gives us a high degree of task separation with only one main data structure. We are now in a position to write the root program and begin to specify the called programs more clearly (see Fig. 6.11).

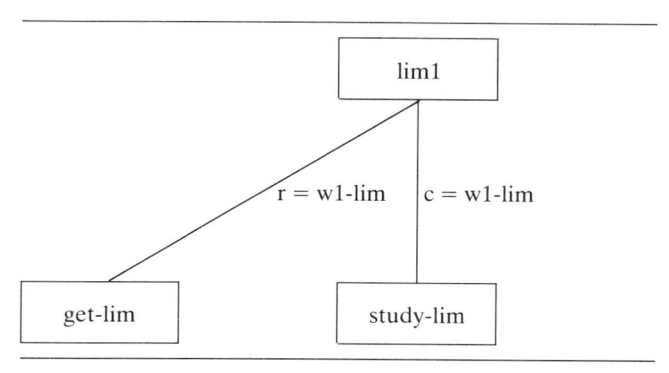

Figure 6.10 Structure chart for lim1

```
 1 identification division.
 2 program-id. lim1.
 3*Purpose:  Accept a 5-line limerick and display a short report which
 4*          gives rhymes and word counts.
 5
 6 environment division.
 7
 8 data division.
 9 working-storage section.
10 01  w1-lim.
11     03  filler value space      pic x.
12         88  w1-eok              value "q".
13     03  w1-sub                  pic 9.
14     03  w1-lines.
15         05  w1-line occurs 5 pic x(78).
16
17 procedure division.
18 para1.
19     display "lim1 begins"
20
21     call "get-lim"   using reference w1-lim
22     perform test before until w1-eok
23       call "study-lim" using content   w1-lim
24       call "get-lim"   using reference w1-lim
25     end-perform
26
27     display "lim1 ends"
28     stop run.
29/
30 identification division.
31 program-id. get-lim.
32*Purpose:  Accept 5 lines of text.
33
34 environment division.
35
36 data division.
37 working-storage section.
38 linkage section.
39 01  l1-lim.
40     03  l1-request              pic x.
41         88  l1-unknown          value "u".
42         88  l1-ok               value "q", space.
43         88  l1-valid            value space.
44         88  l1-quit             value "q".
45     03  l1-sub                  pic 9.
46         88  l1-linemin          value 1.
47         88  l1-linemax          value 6.
48     03  l1-lines.
49         05  l1-line occurs 5 pic x(78).
50
51 procedure division using l1-lim.
52 para1.
53     display space
54
55     set l1-unknown to true
56     display "Type RETURN to continue or 'Q' to quit: "
57       no advancing
58     accept  l1-request
59     inspect l1-request converting "Q" to "q"
60
```

```cobol
 61        perform test before until l1-ok
 62          display "Type RETURN to continue or 'Q' to quit: "
 63            no advancing
 64          accept   l1-request
 65          inspect l1-request converting "Q" to "q"
 66        end-perform
 67
 68        evaluate l1-valid
 69          when    true
 70            set l1-linemin to true
 71            display space
 72            display "Type in a 5 line limerick"
 73            display space
 74
 75            perform test before until l1-linemax
 76              display l1-sub ":" no advancing
 77              accept l1-line(l1-sub)
 78              compute l1-sub = l1-sub + 1
 79            end-perform
 80        end-evaluate
 81
 82        exit program.
 83
 84 end program get-lim.
 85/
 86 identification division.
 87 program-id. study-lim.
 88*Purpose: Study the text and display a report.
 89
 90 environment division.
 91
 92 data division.
 93 working-storage section.
 94 01  w1-string-workers.
 95*         pointer to characters in l1-line(l1-sub)
 96      03  w1-ptr                    pic 99.
 97          88  w1-ptrmin             value 01.
 98          88  w1-ptrmax             value 79.
 99
100*         count of number of words in l1-line(l1-sub)
101      03  w1-wordtally              pic 99.
102          88  w1-tallymin           value 00.
103          88  w1-tallymax           value 10.
104
105*         count of number of characters in a word in l1-line(l1-sub)
106      03  w1-charctr                pic 99.
107          88  w1-charmin            value 00.
108          88  w1-charmax            value 11 thru 99.
109
110 01  w2-lim.
111      03  w2-lsub                   pic 9.
112          88  w2-linemin            value 01.
113          88  w2-linemax            value 06.
114
115      03  w2-lines.
116          05  w2-line occurs 5.
117              07  w2-wsub           pic 99.
118                  88  w2-wordmin    value 01.
119              07  w2-words.
120                  09  w2-word occurs 10 pic x(10).
121
```

```
122        03  w2-wordtot                        pic 99.
123
124*           Switch to control reporting
125        03  filler                            pic x.
126            88  w2-missingwords               value "y".
127            88  w2-nomissingwords             value "n".
128*           Switch to control reasons for overflow
129        03  filler                            pic x.
130            88  w2-nooverflow                 value "n".
131            88  w2-longword                   value "w".
132            88  w2-longline                   value "l".
133            88  w2-emptyline                  value "e".
134
135 01 s3-screen.
136        03  s3-line                           pic x(78).
137        03  s3tot                             pic z9.
138
139 linkage section.
140 01 l1-lim.
141        03  filler                            pic x.
142        03  l1-sub                            pic 9.
143        03  l1-lines.
144            05  l1-line occurs 5              pic x(78).
145/
146 procedure division using l1-lim.
147 para1.
148        display space
149
150*       Convert all punctuation to spaces
151        inspect l1-lines
152            replacing all "." by space
153                      all "," by space
154                      all ";" by space
155                      all ":" by space
156
157*       ANALYSE the 5 lines of a limerick
158        set w2-nooverflow to true
159        move space to w2-lines
160        set w2-linemin to true
161        perform test before until w2-linemax
162
163           set w2-wordmin(w2-lsub) to true
164           set w1-charmin          to true
165           set w1-tallymin         to true
166           set w1-ptrmin           to true
167
168*          Scan up to the first non-space character
169           inspect l1-line(w2-lsub)
170             tallying w1-ptr for leading space
171
172*          Check for an empty line
173           evaluate w1-ptrmax
174             when true
175               display "-line:" w2-lsub " empty"
176               set w2-emptyline to true
177           end-evaluate
178
```

```
179*        EMPTY a line into the table
180         perform test before until w1-ptrmax
181*          DO a word
182           unstring l1-line(w2-lsub)
183             delimited   all space
184             into        w2-word(w2-lsub,w2-wsub(w2-lsub))
185             count       w1-charctr
186             pointer     w1-ptr
187             tallying    w1-wordtally
188             overflow
189               evaluate w1-tallymax and not w1-ptrmax
190                 when    true
191                   display "-line:" w2-lsub " has more than "
192                     w1-wordtally " words"
193                   set w1-ptrmax to true
194                   set w2-longline to true
195                 when    false
196                   compute w2-wsub(w2-lsub) = w2-wsub(w2-lsub) + 1
197               end-evaluate
198           end-unstring
199*          END-DO
200
201           evaluate true
202             when    w1-charmax
203               display "-line:" w2-lsub
204                   " word:" w1-wordtally " too long"
205               set w2-longword to true
206           end-evaluate
207         end-perform
208*        END-EMPTY
209
210         move w1-wordtally to w2-wsub(w2-lsub)
211         compute w2-lsub = w2-lsub + 1
212       end-perform
213/    END-ANALYSE
214
215*    REPORT the word counts
216       display space
217       display "Line       Wordcount"
218
219       move zero to w2-wordtot
220       set w2-linemin to true
221       perform test before until w2-linemax
222         move w2-wsub(w2-lsub) to s3tot
223         display w2-lsub "          " s3tot
224         compute w2-wordtot = w2-wordtot + w2-wsub(w2-lsub)
225         compute w2-lsub = w2-lsub + 1
226       end-perform
227
228       display space
229       move w2-wordtot to s3tot
230       display "There are " s3tot " words in total"
231*    END-REPORT
232
```

176 ESSENTIAL COBOL: A FIRST COURSE IN STRUCTURED COBOL

```
233*    CHECK for failure
234     set w2-nomissingwords to true
235     evaluate true
236       when    w2-longline
237         set w2-missingwords to true
238       when    w2-longword
239         set w2-missingwords to true
240       when    w2-emptyline
241         set w2-missingwords to true
242       when    w2-word(1,w2-wsub(1)) = space
243         set w2-missingwords to true
244       when    w2-word(2,w2-wsub(2)) = space
245         set w2-missingwords to true
246       when    w2-word(5,w2-wsub(5)) = space
247         set w2-missingwords to true
248       when    w2-word(3,w2-wsub(3)) = space
249         set w2-missingwords to true
250       when    w2-word(4,w2-wsub(4)) = space
251         set w2-missingwords to true
252     end-evaluate
253*    END-CHECK
254
255*    GOOD limerick report
256     evaluate w2-missingwords
257       when    true
258         display "This input cannot be a limerick"
259       when    false
260         display space
261         move spaces to s3-line
262         string """"""              delimited size
263                w2-word(1,w2-wsub(1))   delimited space
264                """" rhymes with """"   delimited size
265                w2-word(2,w2-wsub(2))   delimited space
266                """" and """"           delimited size
267                w2-word(5,w2-wsub(5))   delimited space
268                """"""                  delimited size
269            into s3-line
270         display s3-line
271
272         move spaces to s3-line
273         string """"""              delimited size
274                w2-word(3,w2-wsub(3))   delimited space
275                """" rhymes with """"   delimited size
276                w2-word(4,w2-wsub(4))   delimited space
277                """"""                  delimited size
278            into s3-line
279         display s3-line
280     end-evaluate
281*    END-GOOD
282
283     exit program.
284
285 end program study-lim.
286 end program lim1
```

Figure 6.11 Program lim1

6.7 EXERCISES

6.7.1 General

1 Write program reverse1 to accept strings of text from the keyboard that are all either upper or lower case. Use the inspect statement to convert from one case to the other and display the result.

2 Write separate inspect statements to convert:

    (a)   ΔΔ99   to   0099
    (b)   99Δ9   to   9909
    (c)   Δ9Δ9   to   09x9

3 Rewrite program post4 as post5 by using the inspect statement with the convert phrase.

4 An earlier self-check question outlined three ways to ensure that a table of words using the separator "-" could be concatenated by a string statement within a loop to ensure that the target did not contain a trailing "-". Write programs string2, string3, and string4 to demonstrate these three approaches.

5 A parameter string has been designed so that any of these five characters as well as the comma is a valid separator: (*,:,/,:,-). The parameter string can contain up to five fields and any field can be zero to ten characters long. Intermediate fields can be omitted such that one to five fields can be input. For example:

```
i = in1,,o = tp2,run
```

is a valid parameter string for fields 1, 2 and 4 with fields 3 and 5 blank. Write program parm1 which can take as input a parameter string and display to the screen the values of the five fields in the form:

```
fld1 i = in1
fld2
fld3 o = tp2
fld4 run
fld5
```

6 (a) Write an unstring statement to place the following text string without punctuation into the given record which has first been initialized to spaces:

```
Doe/John/22 The High Street/Bathavon/BATH/BA9 6PU
    01  name-and-address.
        03   fullname.
             05   surname         pic x(20).
             05   forenames       pic x(20).
        03   address.
             05  line1            pic x(20).
             05  line2            pic x(20).
             05  line3            pic x(20).
             05  line4            pic x(20).
             05  line5            pic x(20).
             05  line6            pic x(20).
```

(b) Redefine the address area as a table of lines. Add a new data item named `postcode` at the 03 level.
(c) Find the line in the address table that contains a valid postcode, put this into `postcode`, and fill the line where it was found in the address table with spaces.
(d) Write statements to produce an address label in the following form:

```
John Doe,
22 The High Street,
Bathavon,
BATH         BA9 6PU
```

7 Write program reverse2 to convert a string of mixed upper- and lower-case characters so that each character has its case reversed. This problem is considerably more difficult than the one which was posed for reverse1. Try using two copies of the string. In one copy remove all of the lower case with a convert statement and in the other remove all of the upper case. You can then do further processing on each of these strings separately. The final remaining problem will be to integrate them into a single string again.

8 Write program reverse3 to take a sentence of text as input and display it in reversed order on the screen. (Each word should still be in its original word order within the sentence.)

6.7.2 Case study

9 Lim1 outputs the following message when there is only one word:

```
There are 1 words in total
```

Rewrite lim1 as lim2 so that when there is only one word it displays the message:

```
There is only one word
```

10 (a) Rewrite lim1 as lim3 so that it accepts up to 10 lines of text instead of 5. (You should remove the call to `study-lim` by turning it into a comment.)
(b) Replace `study-lim` in lim3 with a new program to count the number of lines of text and the number of words in total.
(c) Change the report to include the number of words per line.

7
PROCESSING TEXT FILES

Files exist independently from programs. They are part of the operating environment and are managed under the control of the operating system. The COBOL source files that you have created with text editors are examples of text files. Both text editors and compilers are programs that manipulate text files. Whereas a text editor will allow you to put any text of your choice within a file without particular regard to its contents, a COBOL compiler will only be happy reading text files that contain correct COBOL.

The fact that very different kinds of programs can use similar products suggests that the concept of a file is separate from the meaning of its contents in much the same way that the concept of a data item is separate from the value that it may take at a particular time. We have also seen in previous chapters that all data items are restricted in the operations that can be performed upon them as well as in values that they may assume. For example, three of the following statements are illegal for alphanumeric data items:

```
view e1-alpha
read e1-alpha
move 2 to e1-alpha
move "2" to e1-alpha
```

The first statement is not an operation that is known by COBOL. The second statement is more difficult. We will discover in this chapter that COBOL does have a read statement but as it happens the read statement requires the name of a file upon which to operate. It is illegal to attempt to read a data item, even though other languages such as Pascal have operations that are very similar to this. The third statement is a known operation for data items. Unfortunately the integer 2 is not within the valid range of e1-alpha which can only take character data. The final statement is valid because the character "2" is compatible with an alphanumeric data item. And we know that there are further rules that determine exactly how the move will be done.

File processing is the term that COBOL uses for operations on files. There are many rules that govern file processing. A few of these such as those concerned with valid file names are constrained by the rules associated with particular operating systems. Therefore COBOL allows within its standard a certain degree of flexibility to compiler implementors, so that COBOL programs can interface easily with the file management systems that are provided as part of the operating environment. Most of the rules concerned with file processing are defined within the COBOL language. However, files have an existence of their own. One advantage of this arrangement is that files can be used by different programs provided they adhere to the general rules governing that type of file. Once again, a text editor and a COBOL compiler provide a good example of this. It is possible that the writers of the text editor and compiler that you are using have never met one another. Nevertheless it is possible for you to use these different software products in your program development because they both adhere to the same rules for using text files.

However, there is a learning disadvantage for the programmer to this aspect of language independence. This is that terms used in different languages and operating environments may mean the same thing, may mean almost the same thing, or may mean something entirely different.

One example of a term that creates this difficulty is *text file*. Firstly, this is a general term for files such as those which are created under the control of a text editor. However, this term is not universally used in the same way. For example, Pascal defines the term text file to mean a certain type of character file consisting of lines and characters upon which only certain operations are valid.

For its part, COBOL does not use the term text file at all even though it is perfectly capable of processing these same files. Instead a text file is considered to be a *sequential file* with *variable-length records*. Furthermore, those operations that are valid in COBOL do not exactly match those of Pascal on a one-to-one basis even though it is easy to write a COBOL program that manages a text file in exactly the same way as any Pascal program.

The moral of the story is that if you know another language make sure that you understand the similarities and differences that exist between it and COBOL. Secondly, do not assume that you cannot do something in any language simply because it does not contain the terminology you expect to find.

The COBOL language is well known for its extensive file-processing facilities. These include support for *relative* and *indexed* files. Many COBOL dialects have now been extended to allow database processing. Later in the text we will consider simple forms of indexed files. But we begin our discussion in this chapter by looking at COBOL sequential files and in particular at sequential files containing variable-length records as a way of processing text files.

COBOL views all files as collections of records. The most common form of file is the sequential file where the records are in a specific order. A file might exist prior to the running of a particular program. In this case the order of its records is pre-established and records must be read into the program in the order in which they were originally created in the file.

A file might not exist prior to the running of a program. In this case the program might create records and then write them into a file. By doing so it establishes the order of the records within the file by the order in which they are written.

As a general rule we can say that the order of records within a sequential file is always defined by the program that creates a file and that this order is the order in which it wrote the records to that file.

For COBOL, a text file is merely a special type of sequential file with variable-length records in which each line of text exists as a single record. Although a text editor allows you to rearrange characters within lines and lines within a file, a COBOL program processing a text file requires you to read the file in its specific record order. These records can then be manipulated in memory and written out to a new file in the same or a different order as required.

Text files are widely used in data processing. It is possible to build sophisticated systems in which both text editors and COBOL programs use text files as a means of creating, storing, and communicating information in order to achieve some higher data processing goal as determined by the designers of the system. For example, a text editor might be used to prepare a text file holding name and address lines and COBOL programs then might validate the lines and write a report such as a telephone directory into a file.

Alternatively, a COBOL program might be used to assist the user to enter valid name and address lines into a text file prior to further processing by other programs. In so doing the creators of an application create a virtual environment for the user.

7.1 FILE ENTRIES

When processing any kind of file a program must establish a link between itself and the operating environment where the file exists. This is done with file-control entries within the **file-control** paragraph. This paragraph is part of the **input–output** section of the environment division.

$$\left[\begin{array}{l} \texttt{environment division.} \\ \left[\begin{array}{l}\texttt{input-output section.} \\ \left[\begin{array}{l}\texttt{file-control.} \\ \quad \{\texttt{file-control-entry}\}\ldots\end{array}\right]\end{array}\right]\end{array}\right]$$

Within the file-control paragraph there must be at least one file-control entry. There must be one entry for each file that the program uses.

A simple format for the file-control entry for a sequential file is

```
select file-name-1  assign  data-name-1.
```

File-name-1 is the internal name by which the file is known within the program. Data-name-1 is the external name by which the file is known within the operating environment. Thus the **select** statement serves to establish the link between the program and the operating system. The value referenced by the data-name-1 must be a string of characters that is a valid name for a file according to the rules of the operating environment.

The rules for constructing a valid name will differ from system to system. Throughout this and later chapters we will use a style of name that is widely accepted. It is in the form "myfile.dat" in which the string before the period is a root name and the string after the period is an extension name.

Our format for the data division is now as follows:

$$\begin{bmatrix} \text{data division.} \\ \begin{bmatrix} \text{file section.} \\ \begin{bmatrix} \text{file-description-entry} \\ \{\text{record-description-entry}\}\dots \end{bmatrix} \dots \end{bmatrix} \\ \begin{bmatrix} \text{working-storage section.} \\ [\text{record-description-entry}]\dots \end{bmatrix} \\ \begin{bmatrix} \text{linkage section.} \\ [\text{record-description-entry}]\dots \end{bmatrix} \end{bmatrix}$$

The file section must always be included when files are used. Within the section there must be one file-description-entry for each file that is used by the program.

```
fd   file-name-1
     [record varying integer-1 to integer-2]
     [depending      data-name-1]
     [value of id    data-name-2].
   {record-description-entry}...
```

The reserved word **fd** is an abbreviation for file description. It is immediately followed by a file-name that is identical to the file-name used in a prior select statement. The use of file-name-1 in the fd associates this internal description within the program with the external file name that is referred to by the select statement.

The next clause is the **record** clause,* which is used to specify the minimum and maximum character length for records in the file.

The existence of the **record** clause identifies a file as a variable-length record file. The integer values must be in the range of 1 to the maximum character length allowed by the operating environment. (The sample programs in this and later chapters will use variable length records that have 1 to 255 characters in each record.)

The **depending** clause is used with variable-length record files to name an item that holds the number of characters in each record. As a file is being read this item will take on

---

* The format shows that the **record** clause is optional. When it is omitted the file is assumed to have fixed length records, that is, all its records are exactly the same length. This is commonly done in commercial applications for files with fixed length records. These files will not be examined further for three reasons.

Firstly, not all operating environments provide an easy means to create sequential files with *fixed-length records* except by using COBOL programs to write them in the first place or by using special utilities. Secondly, text editors and text files are widely used and available. Therefore these files with which the bulk of students are already familiar are the preferred choice. Thirdly, it is easy to understand the concept of a fixed-length record file once variable-length record files are well understood. However, the converse is not true.

successive values that give the length in characters of each record in the file. Thus if the file held the following three lines:

```
I
Love
EcclesΔCakes
```

then three records would be read from the file and the item referenced by data-name-1 would take the successive values of 1, 4 and 12 as the result of each successive read. The depending clause is optional for input files. Its use allows us to know the number of characters in a record without the need to calculate this by some other means within the program.

The depending clause is also used for output text files. In this case it should always be defined. Prior to each write the data item should be initialized to a value that is equal to the number of characters in the record. If this is not done the output results will be unpredictable.

The **value of id** clause also associates the internal file description with its external name. The exact syntax of this statement can vary from compiler to compiler and some may allow you to omit it entirely. (This clause is marked to be made obsolete in the next COBOL standard.)

The final entry in the fd is the record-description-entry. This is defined as a record, that is, at the 01 level. It must be large enough to hold the longest record in the file. The main restriction on this record is that it cannot contain value clauses that attempt to initialize data items. The reason for this is that the action of reading input records or writing output records establishes the values of the data. To use value clauses would be in contradiction with this other method of establishing data values through file operations.

As a general rule we should note that although the record description defines an area of memory, this area is intimately associated with the operating environment and its physical implementation of the file. In general we will only refer to this area via read and write statements and not by any other means. As a principle we will provide the minimum definition of data in the fd that is consistent with file processing and continue to do the bulk of our data processing in either working-storage or linkage records.

SELF-CHECK QUESTIONS

Q Why does COBOL not provide a standard for naming files?

A Files are a resource associated with the operating environment and not with any particular program or programming language. For this reason the external name of a file is governed by rules outside COBOL.

Q Is the following data division valid?

```
data division.
file section.
working-storage section.
linkage section.
```

A Yes. The format supports a completely empty data division. It is possible that a program skeleton might look like this early in its development. A finished program that still contained no data could omit the data division entirely as was the case with program noddy1 in Chapter 1.

Q What is the purpose of the record varying clause?
A To describe the minimum and maximum size of variable-length records. The minimum is always one. The maximum is defined by the implementation.

Q What is the purpose of the depending clause?
A To make the value of the record length available to the program.

Q When are these two clauses not required?
A When processing files of fixed-length records. For files of variable length records such as text files it is usually a good idea to use both clauses even though in certain limited circumstances the depending clause is not necessary.

Q Which two data-names from the fd appear in the select statement and what is their purpose?
A File-name-1 and data-name-2 appear in the select statement. The first gives an internal name to the file which can be used in file operation statements in the procedure division. The second refers to a data item that can be initialized at run time with the external name by which the operating environment knows the file.

Q Why are there two names instead of one?
A This method allows the programmer to use the external file-name as data. For example, you can prompt the user for a file-name at run time and then open the file. (COBOL has a less flexible feature for specifying file-names but this causes the external name to be compiled into the program as a literal. We will not consider this feature because it provides no advantage.)

7.2 FILE STATEMENTS

Two of the statements which can be used to manipulate files are **open** and **close**.

The **open** statement initiates the processing of a file in a particular *mode*. The most common modes are input and output where input readies a file for reading and output readies a file for writing (Fig. 7.1).

```
open    {input   {file-name-1}...}
        {output  {file-name-2}...} ...
```

As the above format implies, a single open statement can be used to make all files ready for processing although it is perfectly legal to use a separate open statement to open each file in turn.

Once a file is opened its mode is established until the file is closed with a close statement.

```
open input e1-file
close e1-file
```

Statements		Meaning
1. `open input  e1-file`		ready e1-file as input
2. `open output e1-file`		ready e1-file as output
3. `open input  e1-file`		ready e1-file as input and
`     output e2-file`		e2-file as output
4. `open input  e1-file e2-file`		ready 2 files as input and
`     output e3-file e3-file`		3 files as output
`            e5-file`		
5. `open input  e1-file e2-file`		ready 3 files as input and
`     output e3-file`		4 files as output
`     input  e4-file`		
`     output e5-file e6-file e7-file`		

Figure 7.1 Legal open statements

The above two statements are in a correct sequence. Between them can be placed any read statements that are required. However, the following statements are incorrect:

```
        open input e1-file
*       process as input here
        open output e1-file
*       process as output here
        close e1-file
```

The second open statement attempts to open a file in output mode that is already open in input mode. The two statements are in conflict and will result in a run-time error when the second open is attempted. The following fragment correctly changes the mode from input to output by closing the file and then opening it with a new mode:

```
        open input e1-file
*       process as input here
        close e1-file

        open output e1-file

*       process as output here
        close e1-file
```

The full format of the close statement allows more than one file to be closed with one statement:

$$\text{close } \{\text{file-name}\}...$$

Once the mode of a file has been established by an open statement only certain file statements can be used before the file is closed. When the file is open in input mode only read statements can be used and when the file is open in output mode only write statements can be used. The order of statements that this implies can be visualized as a flowgraph (Fig. 7.2).

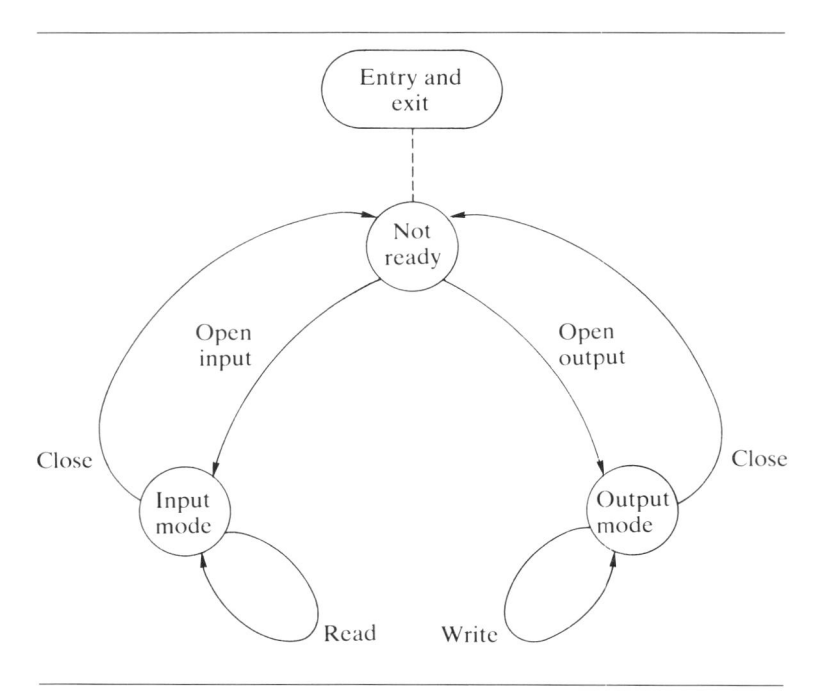

186 ESSENTIAL COBOL: A FIRST COURSE IN STRUCTURED COBOL

Figure 7.2 Order of execution of file operations

This ordering applies to each file independently. Thus one file may not be open, another may be open in input mode, while other may be open for output. Thus when writing a program it is important to ensure that the order of operations for each file conforms to this flowgraph model.

In addition, it is always good practice to ensure that all files are closed by explicit close statements prior to the execution of the stop run even though in some operating environments the file may be closed automatically for you.

The information that is used to ensure that the file operations are being carried out in the correct sequence is held in a special storage area called a *file connector*. Each file used by a program has a file connector associated with it that holds all of the necessary information to associate an internal file description with its external and physical realization within the operating system environment. (The file connector is not directly visible to the program even though it is influenced by details in the program such as the file-name, the record length and the order of file operations.)

The **read** statement makes available the next *logical record* from a file. Identifier-1 references a record in the working-storage section or linkage section of the program.

```
read file-name-1 into identifier-1
   end     statement-1
  [not end statement-2]
end-read
```

Provided that the file is not empty, after the execution of the first read statement the record in the program which is referenced by identifier-1 will contain the first record from the file.

For text files this will be the first line of text, its characters will be left justified, and short lines will be padded out with spaces as if it had been moved by the move statement.

As long as records are being read into the program the **not end** condition will be true and the statement associated with it will be executed.

Any text file can have zero or more lines of text within it. This raises the possibility that the first or a subsequent read might not be able to make a record available because the end of the file has been discovered. When this occurs the **end** condition will become true and the statement associated with it will be executed. When the end condition is true the following are also always true:

1. The contents of the record which is referenced by identifer-1 are undefined. Therefore they should not be processed in any way.
2. No further read statements can be executed. The only legal file operation at this point is to close the file.

Thus every read causes either the end or the not end condition to become true. The syntax of the read provides for statements to handle each of these logical possibilities.

In certain special circumstances one or other of the end phrases can be omitted. However, for the moment we will use both the end and not end phrases. When either or both of these phrases is used the end-read delimiter is required.

The **write** statement releases a record to an output file.

```
write record-name from identifier-1
```

The read and write statements in COBOL are not fully complementary in their construction. We have seen that a read uses the name of a file whereas the write uses the name of a record within the fd of a file.

The following sections present a number of sample programs that are models for writing certain types of file processing programs. You should study these carefully in order to understand the ways in which file operations relate one to the other.

7.3 READING AND DISPLAYING TEXT FILES

Program read1 in Fig. 7.3 opens a text file as input, reads lines from the file, and displays them on the screen.

The file-control paragraph contains a select statement (line 10) for a file with the internal name of i1-file. This is assigned a value by a data item that is defined at line 23. Its data entry does not contain a value clause to initialize the item. Therefore when the program is ready to begin executing the file will not have a defined name. (This is supplied by the accept statement at line 33 which is prior to the open statement.)

The file section (line 13) contains a file-description for the file. Line 15 specifies that each record in the file can contain 1 to 255 characters and the depending clause (line 16) names the item that will hold a count of the number of characters in each record (line 22).

```
 1 identification division.
 2 program-id. read1.
 3*Purpose: Read a variable-length record file and display each record
 4*          as a line of text on the screen.
 5
 6 environment division.
 7
 8 input-output section.
 9 file-control.
10     select i1-file assign w1-filename.
11
12 data division.
13 file section.
14 fd  i1-file
15     record varying 1 to 255
16     depending      w1-ctr
17     value of id    w1-filename.
18 01  filler                         pic x(255).
19
20 working-storage section.
21 01  w1-file.
22     03  w1-ctr binary              pic 999.
23     03  w1-filename                pic x(20).
24     03  w1-data                    pic x(255).
25     03  filler value "n"           pic x.
26         88  w1-eof                 value "y".
27
28 procedure division.
29 para1.
30     display "read1 begins"
31
32     display "Enter name of input file: " no advancing
33     accept w1-filename
34
35     open input i1-file
36
37     perform test before until w1-eof
38       read i1-file into w1-data
39         end
40            set w1-eof to true
41         not end
42            display w1-data(1:w1-ctr)
43       end-read
44     end-perform
45
46     close i1-file
47     display "read1 ends"
48     stop run.
49
50 end program read1
```

Figure 7.3 Program read1

The fd record is defined at line 18. It is given the name filler because it is never referenced by the program. Its picture clause allows it to contain 255 characters, which is the maximum size of each record as stated in the record varying clause.

The data entry for the counter at line 22 uses the keyword **binary**. This keyword causes the compiler to implement the counter as a binary item for reasons of efficiency.

The use of binary items is fully covered in Chapters 9 and 11. For the present we need to know that the item is not a character item. Therefore it cannot be displayed at the terminal screen and cannot be used according to the rules that we have learned in previous chapters. Each use of a file counter in this chapter is valid and will be discussed briefly in the notes as it is used. (You would be wise not to attempt any other form of use with binary items until you have studied Chapters 9 and 10.)

At line 33 the name of the file is initialized. This is immediately followed by the opening of the file. In cases where the file does not exist at the time the open statement is executed the program will cause a run-time error. Lines 37 to 44 contain a perform loop that uses the condition `w1-eof`. This condition has an initial value of false (lines 25–26). Eof is an abbreviation for end-of-file. Therefore the program begins with an initial assertion that end-of-file is not true. In other words the assertion that we make prior to executing the statements within the loop is that the file contains more records.

Therefore we can see that the loop will execute once in any case. Line 38 shows the read statement that is executed at least once. At the first read the file may be either empty or have one or more records in it. When it is empty the read will cause the end condition to become true. As a result the end-of-file condition will be set (line 40), and the loop will terminate.

However, if the file is not empty then the read will transfer the input record into `w1-data`, initialize `w1-ctr` to a value that is equal to the number of characters in the record, and execute the statement under the control of the not end phrase (line 42). In this case it is a display that uses reference modification and the `w1-ctr` so that the portion of data that is displayed is exactly the number of characters that were found in the record.

When the read statement moves data into `w1-data` it takes account of the value of `w1-ctr` when doing so. It moves the number of characters specified by `w1-ctr` and then follows them with enough trailing spaces to pad out the balance of the item. Therefore

```
display w1-data
```

would be a legal statement at line 42 but it would always display 255 characters regardless of how long the text record was in the file. Therefore using reference modification in conjunction with the counter allows us to display only the data that was physically stored in the file's record.

The action of the read statement with the into phrase can be thought of as a read combined with an alphanumeric move. In other words when the record from the file is shorter than the target then the target is padded with spaces. For the VAX it is also true that when the target is too short then the data will be truncated in the target. Regardless of whether or not the target is padded or truncated the counter will always show the true number of characters that existed in the physical record.

The minimum and maximum shown within the file description (lines 15 and 18) are more problematical. The depending on clause must always be shown as being in the range of 1 to *n*. The minimum of 1 is a problem because it assumes that a record always contains at least one character but this is not always true. Some systems such as the VAX store blank lines as lines with zero characters and in this case it is perfectly valid to read a record with a length of zero characters.

However, some systems may use a base value of 2 or 4. For example, a blank line might have a value of 2 and a line of 23 characters would then have a count of 25. The explanation for this lies outside the scope of this chapter except to say that the discrepancy in length is caused by the strategy a particular operating system adopts for storing records. In any case the record in the target, in this example w1-data, will always be the correct number of characters.

SELF-CHECK QUESTIONS

Q What will happen in program read1 if the statements at lines 33 and 35 are reversed?
A The program will compile correctly but will fail with a run-time error because the file-name will be undefined at the time the open is executed.

Q How many times are the statements controlled by the end condition of a read statement executed?
A Only once when the end of the file is detected.

Q What is the value of the record named by the into phrase after the end of the file is detected?
A Its value is undefined.

Q Imagine a file of four lines of text. How many reads will it take to process the file in program read1?
A It will take five reads. The first four reads will each move a line of text into w1-data and give a value to w1-ctr. The fifth read will cause w1-data and w1-ctr to become undefined and will pass control to the statement written within the end phrase.

Q What whould happen if a sixth read were attempted on the four-line file?
A It would cause a run-time error.

Q At present program read1 displays the whole of a file. This could be most annoying to the viewer. What should be done so that the program pauses after displaying each line and waits for the user to type a carriage return?
A An accept statement should be inserted just after the display at line 42 but before the end-read at line 43. This will cause both the display and accept to be treated as a single statement. A single data item such as w2-pause will also need to be added at line 27 so that the program has something to accept even though it provides no useful data to the program.

7.4 ACCEPTING AND WRITING TEXT RECORDS

Program write1 in Fig. 7.4 opens a text file as output, accepts lines of text from the keyboard, calculates the length of each line, and writes the lines to the file. Each line of text that is typed at the keyboard is ended with a RETURN. As a result of the accept statement these lines will be left-justified with trailing spaces. Write1 takes each line in turn and checks from the last to the first for the first non-space character. It does this by redefining the line as a table of characters and using the counter associated with the line as a subscript. When it finds the first non-space character then w1-ctr contains a value which is the length

```
 1 identification division.
 2 program-id. write1.
 3*Purpose: Accept lines of text from the keyboard and write them to a
 4*          variable-length record file.
 5
 6 environment division.
 7
 8 input-output section.
 9 file-control.
10     select o1-file assign w1-filename.
11
12 data division.
13 file section.
14 fd  o1-file
15     record varying 1 to 255
16     depending     w1-ctr
17     value of id   w1-filename.
18 01  o1-rec                          pic x(255).
19
20 working-storage section.
21 01  w1-file.
22     03  w1-ctr     binary           pic 999.
23         88  w1-max   value 255.
24     03  w1-filename                 pic x(20).
25     03  w1-data.
26         05  filler                  pic x(10).
27             88  w1-eok      value space.
28         05  filler                  pic x(245).
29     03  filler redefines w1-data.
30         05  w1-char occurs 255      pic x.
31
32 procedure division.
33 para1.
34     display "write1 begins"
35     display "Enter the output file name: " no advancing
36     accept w1-filename
37     display "Enter lines of text for the file"
38
39     open output o1-file
40
41     accept w1-data
42     perform test before until w1-eok
43       set w1-max to true
44       perform test before until w1-char(w1-ctr) not = space
45         compute w1-ctr = w1-ctr - 1
46       end-perform
47       write o1-rec from w1-data
48       accept w1-data
49     end-perform
50
51     close o1-file
52     display "write1 ends"
53     stop run.
54
55 end program write1
```

Figure 7.4 Program write1

192 ESSENTIAL COBOL: A FIRST COURSE IN STRUCTURED COBOL

of the line. The main loop in write1 stops processing when a line with 10 leading spaces is found.

7.5 COPYING TEXT FILES

Program copy1 in Fig. 7.5 prompts the user for the names of input and output files and then copies the input file to the output file. As each read statement at line 51 is executed either the end phrase will be executed or the not end phrase will be executed. If the not end phrase is executed, then the read must have been successful and not only will the contents of w1-data have been updated but also the counter, w1-ctr, will have been given the correct value for the length of the input record.

```
1 identification division.
2 program-id. copy1.
3*Purpose: Copy an existing variable-length record file to a new one.
4
5 environment division.
6
7 input-output section.
8 file-control.
9     select i1-file   assign w1-filename.
10    select o2-file   assign w2-filename.
11
12 data division.
13 file section.
14 fd  i1-file
15     record varying 1 to 255
16     depending     w1-ctr
17     value of id   w1-filename.
18 01  filler                        pic x(255).
19
20 fd  o2-file
21     record varying 1 to 255
22     depending     w2-ctr
23     value of id   w2-filename.
24 01  o2-rec                        pic x(255).
25
26 working-storage section.
27 01  w1-file.
28     03  w1-ctr binary             pic 999.
29     03  w1-filename               pic x(20).
30     03  filler     value    "n"   pic x.
31         88 w1-eof                 value    "y".
32     03  w1-data                   pic x(255).
33
34 01  w2-file.
35     03  w2-ctr binary             pic 999.
36     03  w2-filename               pic x(20).
37
38 procedure division.
39 para1.
40     display "copy1 begins"
41
```

```
42      display "Enter name of  input file: " no advancing
43      accept w1-filename
44      display "Enter name of output file: " no advancing
45      accept w2-filename
46
47      open input   i1-file
48           output  o2-file
49
50      perform test before until w1-eof
51        read i1-file into w1-data
52          end
53            set w1-eof to true
54            display "copy successful"
55          not end
56            evaluate w1-ctr = zero
57              when true
58                move 1 to w2-ctr
59              when false
60                move w1-ctr to w2-ctr
61            end-evaluate
62            write o2-rec from w1-data
63        end-read
64      end-perform
65
66      close i1-file
67            o2-file
68      display "copy1 ends"
69      stop run.
70
71 end program copy1
```

Figure 7.5 Program copy1

The COBOL definition for variable-length records does not take into account the possibility of blank lines in a file as can be seen by the record varying clause which requires a minimum length of one character. Nevertheless blank lines can exist in text files and this therefore raises the question of how we should deal with this non-standard problem.

Many systems such as the VAX allow record lengths of zero as a way of indicating blank lines. Therefore the evaluate statement at line 56 finds blank lines on input by checking the counter for the value zero. However, all COBOL systems require that when variable-length records are written to a file the counter must be within the range specified by the record-varying clause for that file. Therefore when copy1 finds a blank line on input it moves 1 to the counter for the output file (line 58). When the VAX operating system writes this record to the file it will see that it is a record composed of spaces and convert it to a record containing no characters but with a length of zero. Therefore a record of spaces and a length of 1 on output will appear on later input as a length of zero. (Other operating systems may store records as a single space. They may also have a base value other than zero as was mentioned previously.)

7.6 CREATING NEW INFORMATION FROM EXISTING TEXT FILES

The main loop that specified the copying process in program copy1 is essentially as follows:

```
perform test before until w1-eof
  read i1-file into w1-data
    end
      set w1-eof to true
      display "copy successful"
    not end
      move w1-ctr to w2-ctr
      write o2-rec from w1-data
  end-read
end-perform
```

During the execution of the loop a record from the input is transferred into w1-data by the **read into** statement and immediately afterwards the **write from** statement transfers the record to output. Thus every record from the input file passes through w1-data on its way to the output file.

All of the statements with the exception of the write statement are concerned with managing the input file. The write statement writes each record in turn into the output file.

Figure 7.6 shows the relationship that exists between the files and the loop. We can transform the data as it moves from input to output provided that we insert statements to do this immediately after the read but prior to the write statement. In fact the transforming statements as well as the write statement and the file entries for the output can be hidden within a nested program thereby giving the structure chart shown in Fig. 7.7.

Program copy2 in Fig. 7.8 specifies this new relationship clearly. The parameter passed to the file handler is w2-file. This record not only contains the file-name and data but also a single character item (line 30) to indicate the output file operation that is required. Only the process and close operations are required because program ohandle can itself determine that its output file is not open when it is first called.

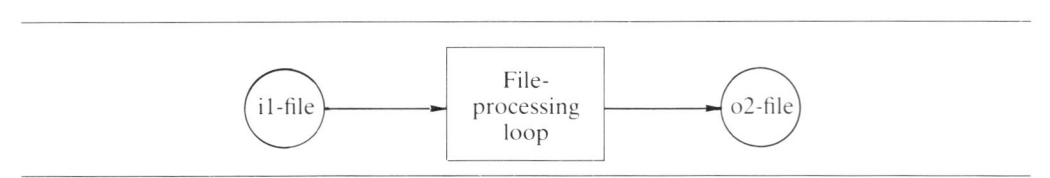

Figure 7.6 Relationship between loop and files in program copy1

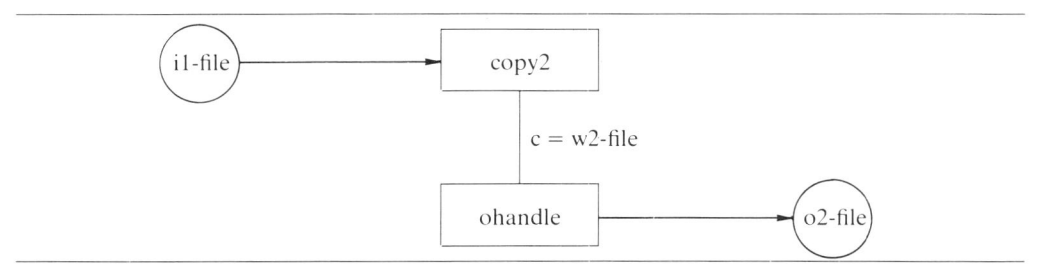

Figure 7.7 Structure chart for copy2

This approach to file handling has a number of advantages. Firstly, it hides away all complexity associated with the file. It offers up the file to the calling program as a data structure with a set of operations that can be applied to it. Secondly, the design of a file handler and most of its statements can be reused in other programs where a similar file-processing requirement exists. Thirdly, non-standard aspects of file handling can be isolated within programs that are dedicated to the task of file handling. Within very large applications this will help to isolate non-standard features within the one program, thereby improving the maintainability and portability of the application.

```
1  identification division.
2  program-id. copy2.
3 *Purpose: Copy an existing variable length record file to a new one
4 *         using the output handling program "ohandle".
5
6  environment division.
7
8  input-output section.
9  file-control.
10     select i1-file   assign w1-filename.
11
12 data division.
13 file section.
14 fd  i1-file
15     record varying 1 to 255
16     depending       w1-ctr
17     value of id     w1-filename.
18 01  filler              pic x(255).
19
20 working-storage section.
21 01  w1-file.
22     03  w1-ctr binary pic 999.
23     03  w1-filename   pic x(20).
24     03  filler        pic x.
25         88  w1-noteof value "n".
26         88  w1-eof    value "y".
27
28 01  w2-file.
29     03  w2-filename   pic x(20).
30     03  filler        pic x.
31         88  w2-process value "p".
32         88  w2-close   value "c".
33     03  w2-data       pic x(255).
34
35 procedure division.
36 para1.
37     display "copy2 begins"
38
39     display "Enter name of  input file: " no advancing
40     accept w1-filename
41     display "Enter name of output file: " no advancing
42     accept w2-filename
43
44     open input  i1-file
45
46     set w1-noteof  to true
47     set w2-process to true
48
```

```
 49      perform test before until w1-eof
 50         read i1-file into w2-data
 51            end
 52               set w1-eof to true
 53            not end
 54               call "ohandle" using content w2-file
 55         end-read
 56      end-perform
 57
 58      close i1-file
 59      set w2-close to true
 60      call "ohandle" using content w2-file
 61
 62      display "copy2 ends"
 63      stop run.
 64/
 65 identification division.
 66 program-id. ohandle.
 67*Purpose: Write a stream of records to a variable-length record file.
 68
 69 environment division.
 70 input-output section.
 71 file-control.
 72    select o1-file   assign w1-filename.
 73
 74 data division.
 75 file section.
 76 fd  o1-file
 77     record varying 1 to 255
 78     depending      w1-ctr
 79     value of id    w1-filename.
 80 01  o1-rec                     pic x(255).
 81
 82 working-storage section.
 83 01  w1-file.
 84     03  w1-ctr binary          pic 999.
 85         88  w1-max             value 256.
 86     03  w1-filename            pic x(20).
 87     03  filler value "c"       pic x.
 88         88  w1-open            value "o".
 89         88  w1-closed          value "c".
 90     03  filler                 pic x.
 91         88  w1-done    value "y".
 92         88  w1-notdone value "n".
 93
 94 linkage section.
 95 01  l1-rec.
 96     03  l1-filename            pic x(20).
 97     03  filler                 pic x.
 98         88  l1-process         value "p".
 99         88  l1-close           value "c".
100     03  l1-data.
101         05  l1-char occurs 255  pic x.
102
103 procedure division using l1-rec.
104 para1.
105     evaluate true
106        when    w1-closed
107           move l1-filename to w1-filename
108           open output o1-file
109           set  w1-open to true
110     end-evaluate
111
```

```
112        evaluate true
113          when l1-process
114            set w1-max to true
115            set w1-notdone to true
116            perform test before until w1-done
117              compute w1-ctr = w1-ctr - 1
118              evaluate true
119                when    l1-char(w1-ctr) not = space
120                  set w1-done to true
121                when    w1-ctr = 1
122                  set w1-done to true
123              end-evaluate
124            end-perform
125            write o1-rec from l1-data
126
127          when l1-close
128            close o1-file
129            set w1-closed to true
130        end-evaluate
131
132        exit program.
133
134    end program ohandle.
135  end program copy2
```

Figure 7.8 Program copy2

In program copy2 it is now clear that the root program manages the input file and that program ohandle manages the output file under the direction of the root. Copy2 can be used as a model for many application programs that transform an input file into an output file. The statements particular to an application can be inserted either immediately before the call at line 54 or as the first statements in ohandle where it processes each record (between lines 113 and 114). The first possibility is preferable because it maintains the integrity of ohandle as an output handler. The transforming statements could be contained within another called program thereby further separating the application from both the input and output processing.

7.7 REWRITING AND EXTENDING TEXT FILES

The open statement has two other options. The **i-o** option allows a file to be open for input and output at the same time. This allows single records in a sequential file to be rewritten within the file without changing the contents of other records. The **extend** option allows new records to be added to the end of an existing file.

$$\text{open} \begin{Bmatrix} \text{input} & \{\text{file-name-1}\}... \\ \text{output} & \{\text{file-name-2}\}... \\ \text{i-o} & \{\text{file-name-3}\}... \\ \text{extend} & \{\text{file-name-4}\}... \end{Bmatrix}...$$

When a file is open in i–o mode it can be read sequentially like any file that is open in input

198 ESSENTIAL COBOL: A FIRST COURSE IN STRUCTURED COBOL

mode. Prior to reaching the end of the file a record that has just been read can be rewritten with the rewrite statement:

```
rewrite record-name-1 from identifier-1
```

Program rewrite1 in Fig. 7.9 gives an example of how lines in a file can be modified without reading in the entire input file and writing it to a new output file.

Its read statement reads in the whole of the file from the first to the last record and as each record is read it is echoed to the screen. The program then accepts a new line from the keyboard into `s2-data`. The evaluate checks this line to determine whether or not the contents of the line from the file are to be changed. If the user has typed "DEL" then the line from the file is rewritten as spaces. If the user has replied by typing characters, then this new line is rewritten to the file. (A single RETURN from the keyboard causes the line to be all blanks and therefore no action is taken by the program.)

```
1 identification division.
2 program-id. rewrite1.
3*Purpose: Display each record in a variable-length record file.
4*         Rewrite new versions of records to the file.
5
6 environment division.
7
8 input-output section.
9 file-control.
10     select i1-file assign w1-filename.
11
12 data division.
13 file section.
14 fd  i1-file
15     record varying 1 to 255
16     depending      w1-ctr
17     value of id    w1-filename.
18 01  i1-rec                          pic x(255).
19
20 working-storage section.
21 01  w1-file.
22     03  w1-ctr binary               pic 999.
23     03  w1-filename                 pic x(20).
24     03  w1-data                     pic x(255).
25     03  filler value "n"            pic x.
26         88  w1-eof                  value "y".
27
28 01  s2-screen.
29     03  s2-data.
30         05  filler                  pic xxx.
31             88  s2-delete           value "DEL".
32         05  filler                  pic x(252).
33
34 procedure division.
35 para1.
36     display "rewrite1 begins"
37
38     display "Enter input-output filename: " no advancing
39     accept w1-filename
40
```

```
41      open i-o i1-file
42
43      perform test before until w1-eof
44        read i1-file into w1-data
45          end
46            set w1-eof to true
47          not end
48            display w1-data(1:w1-ctr)
49            accept   s2-data
50            evaluate true
51              when    s2-delete
52                move spaces to w1-data
53                rewrite i1-rec from w1-data
54              when    s2-data not = spaces
55                move s2-data to w1-data
56                rewrite i1-rec from w1-data
57            end-evaluate
58        end-read
59      end-perform
60
61      close i1-file
62      display "rewrite1 ends"
63      stop run.
64
65 end program rewrite1
```

Figure 7.9 Program rewrite1

Therefore by hitting the RETURN key repeatedly it is possible to browse through the lines in a file. At any time a line can be deleted by typing "DEL" or replaced with a new line by typing some other set of characters.

The number of lines in a file and the length of each line are always determined when a file is created. Therefore it is not possible to use the rewrite statement to insert a new line between two existing lines. Similarly it is illegal to try to change the counter associated with each line. Therefore rewrite1 cannot delete lines physically from the file but changes them to a string of spaces that is the same length. (Lines from the keyboard that are longer than the original will be truncated and lines that are shorter will be padded with spaces.)

The main use for this option is to allow minor corrections to large files.

Program copy3 in Fig. 7.10 demonstrates the use of the extend option. When this is used an existing file is opened and new lines are written at the end of the file without causing any change to records that were originally in the file. This option is particularly useful when data is to be collected over a period of time prior to processing. For example, a bank clerk might wish to enter loan transactions over a working day but interrupt this work for coffee-breaks and lunch. By the end of the day the file may have been extended any number of times.

7.8 CASE STUDY: RENUM1 (NUMBERING TEXT FILES)

Not all COBOL compilers require the sequence area in COBOL columns 1 to 6 to be present in a program's source code. This case study presents program renum1, which is capable of translating the source text of programs from one format on input into another on output.

```cobol
 1 identification division.
 2 program-id. copy3.
 3*Purpose: Accept lines from the keyboard and add them as records
 4*         to the end of an existing variable-length record file.
 5
 6 environment division.
 7
 8 input-output section.
 9 file-control.
10     select o1-file assign w1-filename.
11
12 data division.
13 file section.
14
15 fd  o1-file
16     record varying 1 to 255
17     depending       w1-ctr
18     value of id     w1-filename.
19 01  o1-rec                          pic x(255).
20
21 working-storage section.
22 01  w1-file.
23     03  w1-ctr binary               pic 999.
24         88  w1-max                  value 256.
25     03  w1-filename                 pic x(20).
26     03  filler                      pic x.
27         88  w1-done     value "y".
28         88  w1-notdone  value "n".
29     03  w1-data.
30         05  filler                  pic x(10).
31             88  w1-eok              value space.
32         05  filler                  pic x(245).
33     03  filler redefines w1-data.
34         05  w1-char occurs 255      pic x.
35
36 procedure division.
37 para1.
38     display "copy3 begins"
39
40     display "Enter the name of the file to be extended: "
41       no advancing
42     accept w1-filename
43
44     open extend o1-file
45     display "Type new lines."
46     display "Terminate with a single RETURN"
47
48     accept w1-data
49     perform test before until w1-eok
50       set w1-max to true
51       set w1-notdone to true
52
53       perform test before until w1-done
54         compute w1-ctr = w1-ctr - 1
55         evaluate true
56           when w1-char(w1-ctr) not = space
57             set w1-done to true
58           when w1-ctr = 1
59             set w1-done to true
60         end-evaluate
61       end-perform
62
```

```
63         write o1-rec from w1-data
64         accept w1-data
65      end-perform
66
67      close o1-file
68
69      display "copy3 ends"
70      stop run.
71
72 end program copy3
```

Figure 7.10 Program copy3

The decision tree in Fig. 7.11 more clearly shows that the six sequence characters will be either added, replaced, deleted or left unchanged, depending on the output requirement and on the state of the input.

It is often the case that many program texts need to be converted from one form to another at the same time and it is not always true that all programs in a set will be in exactly the same format at the time the conversion is required. For example, some might have old sequence numbers and others may have no sequence area at all, but the output requirement might be to give all of the texts new sequence numbers.

Therefore the input to renum1 will be a set of file names for the programs that require conversion. These names themselves will be contained in a text file (i1-file). The requirement will be that all of these programs should be converted to the required output format regardless of the format of the input.

The structure chart in Fig. 7.12 shows a root program with three nested programs. The root reads in the stream of file names for the programs that are to be converted. As each name is read it is passed as a parameter to copy4 which then calls ihandle2 to read the file of program text line by line. Copy4 does any necessary conversion to each line, after which it calls ohandle2 to write the line to the output file.

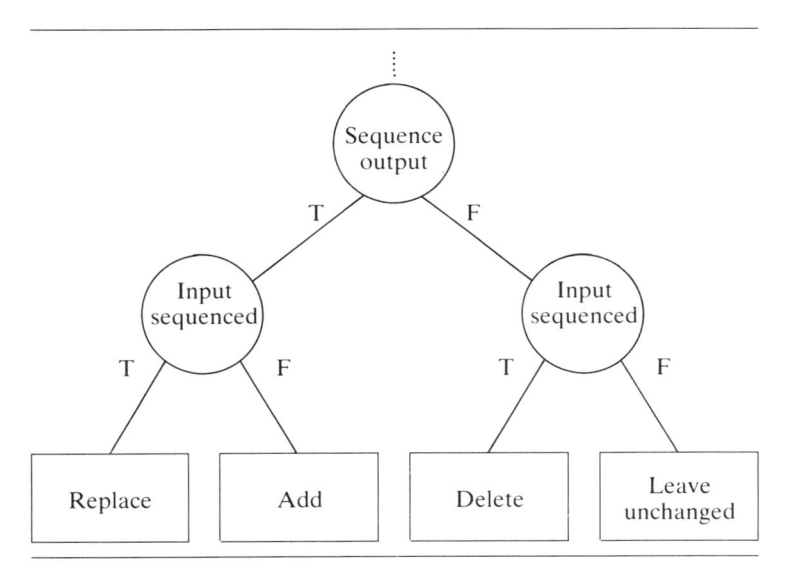

Figure 7.11 Decision tree for program renum1

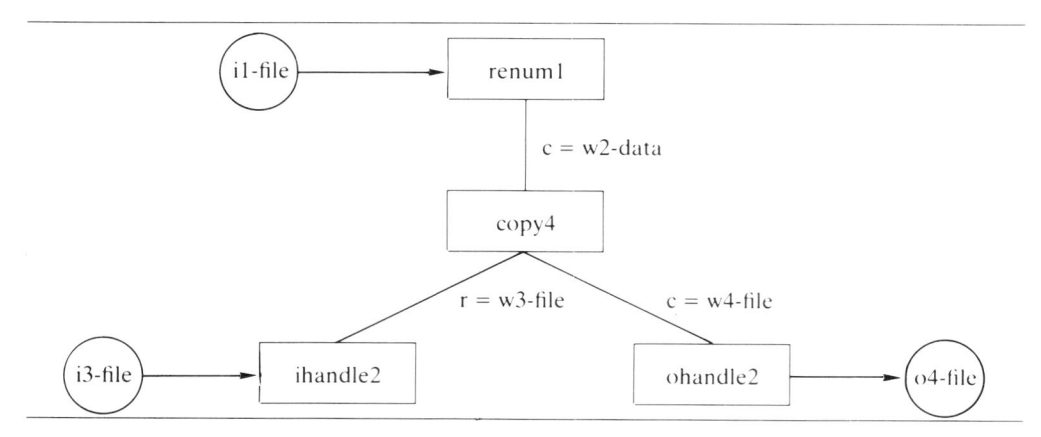

202 ESSENTIAL COBOL: A FIRST COURSE IN STRUCTURED COBOL

Figure 7.12 Structure chart for renum1

In a general sense, the root program manages the run. Not only must it read each line from i1-file so that the programs that require conversion are known but it must also determine what conversion is required for output. For its part copy4 manages each program that must be converted.

Copy4 and its use of an input and output handler presents yet another model of a program design that is common in data processing. In this case the transformation takes place within copy4 that has control of both input and output. Copy4 and its two nested programs should be compared carefully to copy2 so that you are certain of the close relationship that each bears to the other. (The fact that copy4 is called successively to transform different files does not enter into the comparison. We could just as easily imagine copy2 called successively to undertake a series of copying operations.)

```
1 identification division.
2 program-id. renum1.
3*Purpose: Copy COBOL text files with or without
4*         the sequence area (cols 1-6) into output text files.
5
6 environment division.
7 input-output section.
8 file-control.
9     select i1-file assign w1-filename.
10
11 data division.
12 file section.
13 fd  i1-file
14     record varying 1 to 41
15     depending on w1-ctr
16     value of id w1-filename.
17 01  filler              pic x(41).
18
19 working-storage section.
20 01  w1-file.
21     03  w1-ctr binary   pic 999.
22     03  w1-filename     pic x(20).
23     03  filler          pic x.
24         88  w1-noteof   value "n".
25         88  w1-eof      value "e".
26
```

```
27 01  w2-data.
28     03  w2-indicator      pic x.
29         88  w2-unknown    value space.
30         88  w2-valid      value "Y" "y" "N" "n".
31     03  w2-copynames      pic x(41).
32/
33 procedure division.
34 para1.
35     display "renum1 begins"
36
37     display "Enter name of  control file: " no advancing
38     accept w1-filename
39     open input i1-file
40
41     set w2-unknown to true
42     perform test before until w2-valid
43       display "Sequence the output? Type 'Y' or 'N': " no advancing
44       accept w2-indicator
45     end-perform
46
47*    PROCESS the control file
48     set w1-noteof to true
49     perform until w1-eof
50       read i1-file into w2-copynames
51         end
52           set w1-eof to true
53         not end
54           display "copying: " w2-copynames
55           call "copy4" using content w2-data
56       end-read
57     end-perform
58*    END-PROCESS
59
60     close i1-file
61     display "renum1 ends"
62     stop run.
63/
64 identification division.
65 program-id. copy4.
66*Purpose: Copy a single file having first adjusted the
67*         sequence area on each line in the file
68
69 environment division.
70
71 data division.
72 working-storage section.
73 01  w3-file.
74     03  w3-ctr binary         pic 999.
75     03  w3-filename           pic x(20).
76     03  filler                pic x.
77         88  w3-read           value "r".
78         88  w3-eof            value "e".
79     03  w3-line.
80         05  w3-sequence       pic x(6).
81             88  w3-ansispace  value space.
82             88  w3-ansinum1   value "000001".
83             88  w3-ansinum2   value "     1".
84         05  w3-body           pic x(249).
85
```

```
86  01  w4-file.
87      03  w4-ctr binary           pic 999.
88      03  w4-filename             pic x(20).
89      03  filler                  pic x.
90          88  w4-write            value "w".
91          88  w4-close            value "c".
92      03  w4-line.
93          05  w4-sequence         pic z(5)9.
94          05  w4-body             pic x(249).
95
96  01  w5-temp.
97      03  filler                  pic x.
98          88  w5-ansi             value "A".
99          88  w5-notansi          value "N".
100     03  w5-sequence             pic 9(6).
101
102 linkage section.
103 01  l2-data.
104     03  filler                  pic x.
105         88  l2-ansi             value "Y" "y".
106         88  l2-notansi          value "N" "n".
107     03  l2-copynames            pic x(41).
108/
109 procedure division using l2-data.
110 para1.
111*    SET up the names for the input and the output
112     move spaces to w3-filename w4-filename
113     unstring l2-copynames delimited all space
114       into w3-filename w4-filename
115
116     evaluate true
117       when  w4-filename = space
118         move w3-filename to w4-filename
119     end-evaluate
120*    END-SET
121
122*    GET the first line from the file and check its structure
123     set w3-read  to true
124     set w4-write to true
125
126     call "ihandle2"   using reference w3-file
127
128     evaluate w3-ansispace or w3-ansinum1 or w3-ansinum2
129       when   true
130         set w5-ansi to true
131       when   false
132         set w5-notansi to true
133     end-evaluate
134*    END-GET
135
136*    PROCESS the lines in the file
137     move zero to w5-sequence
138     perform until w3-eof
139       compute  w5-sequence = w5-sequence + 1
140*      Check the first line of the input against the output required
141       evaluate true
142         when   w5-ansi and l2-ansi
143*          Input sequenced and output sequenced
144           move w3-ctr  to w4-ctr
145           move w5-sequence to w4-sequence
146           move w3-body to w4-body
```

```
147        when    w5-ansi and l2-notansi
148*          Input sequenced but output unsequenced
149           compute w4-ctr = w3-ctr - 6
150           move w3-body to w4-line
151        when    w5-notansi and l2-ansi
152*          Input unsequenced but output sequenced
153           compute w4-ctr = w3-ctr + 6
154           move w5-sequence to w4-sequence
155           move w3-line to w4-body
156        when    w5-notansi and l2-notansi
157*          Input unsequenced and output unsequenced
158           move w3-ctr   to w4-ctr
159           move w3-line to w4-line
160        end-evaluate
161
162        call "ohandle2" using content   w4-file
163        call "ihandle2" using reference w3-file
164     end-perform
165*    END-PROCESS
166
167     set w4-close to true
168     call "ohandle2" using content w4-file
169
170     exit program.
171/
172 identification division.
173 program-id. ihandle2.
174*Purpose: Read lines of input from the old COBOL text files
175
176 environment division.
177 input-output section.
178 file-control.
179     select i3-file   assign w3-filename.
180
181 data division.
182 file section.
183 fd  i3-file
184     record varying 1 to 255
185     depending on   w3-ctr
186     value of id    w3-filename.
187 01  filler                        pic x(255).
188
189 working-storage section.
190 01  w3-file.
191     03  w3-ctr binary             pic 999.
192     03  w3-filename               pic x(20).
193     03  filler value "c"          pic x.
194         88  w3-closed             value "c".
195         88  w3-open               value "o".
196     03  w3-data                   pic x(255).
197
198 linkage section.
199 01  l3-file.
200     03  l3-ctr binary             pic 999.
201     03  l3-filename               pic x(20).
202     03  filler                    pic x.
203         88  l3-read               value "r".
204         88  l3-eof                value "e".
205     03  l3-data                   pic x(255).
206
```

```
207 procedure division using l3-file.
208 para1.
209     evaluate true
210       when    w3-closed
211         move l3-filename to w3-filename
212         open input i3-file
213         set w3-open to true
214     end-evaluate
215
216     evaluate true
217       when    w3-open
218         read i3-file into l3-data
219           end
220             set l3-eof to true
221             move zero to l3-ctr
222             move spaces to l3-data
223             close i3-file
224             set w3-closed to true
225           not end
226             move w3-ctr to l3-ctr
227         end-read
228     end-evaluate
229
230     exit program.
231
232 end program ihandle2.
233/
234 identification division.
235 program-id. ohandle2.
236*Purpose: Write lines of output to the new COBOL text files
237
238 environment division.
239 input-output section.
240 file-control.
241     select o4-file   assign w4-filename.
242
243 data division.
244 file section.
245 fd  o4-file
246     record varying 1 to 255
247     depending on   w4-ctr
248     value of id    w4-filename.
249 01  o4-rec                          pic x(255).
250
251 working-storage section.
252 01  w4-file.
253     03  w4-ctr binary               pic 999.
254     03  w4-filename                 pic x(20).
255     03  filler value "c"            pic x.
256         88  w4-open                 value "o".
257         88  w4-closed               value "c".
258
259 linkage section.
260 01  l4-file.
261     03  l4-ctr binary               pic 999.
262         88  l4-empty-line           value zero.
263     03  l4-filename                 pic x(20).
264     03  filler                      pic x.
265         88  l4-write                value "w".
266         88  l4-close                value "c".
267     03  l4-line                     pic x(255).
268
```

```
269 procedure division using l4-file.
270 para1.
271     evaluate w4-closed
272       when    true
273         move l4-filename to w4-filename
274         open output o4-file
275         set  w4-open to true
276     end-evaluate
277
278     evaluate true
279       when    l4-write
280         evaluate l4-empty-line
281           when    true
282             move 1 to w4-ctr
283           when    false
284             move l4-ctr to w4-ctr
285         end-evaluate
286         write o4-rec from l4-line
287
288       when    l4-close
289         close o4-file
290         set w4-closed to true
291     end-evaluate
292
293     exit program.
294
295 end program ohandle2.
296 end program copy4.
297 end program renum1.
```

Figure 7.13 Program renum1

7.9 EXERCISES

7.9.1 General

1. This exercise is especially for those readers who are using a non-VAX/VMS system. Create a small text file with a known number of lines where each line has a known number of characters. Rewrite read1 as read2 in which the display statement at line 42 is replaced by a new statement:

    ```
    display w1-data(1:w1-ctr) "**"
    ```

    Display the file and you will find two asterisks at the end of each line. There should be no spaces immediately prior to the asterisks. If there are then the number of spaces shown on each line will be a constant value. This value is the adjustment that you should make to the line counter prior to using a record. It should be subtracted from the counter for every record that is read into a program and added to the line counter for every record immediately before it is written.

2. Rewrite read1 as read3, in which each line is displayed with a line number.
3. Rewrite read1 or read3 as read4, in which the file is displayed in groups of 20 lines and the user is invited to display more lines or terminate the program.
4. Program write1 terminates when it finds a line with 10 leading spaces. This is not necessarily the best test for the end of input from the keyboard in that the following

line would cause the main loop to terminate:

△△△△△△△△△△This line has 10 leading spaces

Rewrite program write1 as write2, in which the main loop terminates for lines that are all spaces. These should be discovered when the counter is decremented to zero.

5. Rewrite either program write1 or write2 as program write3, in which reference modification is used rather than a table with a subscript.
6. Write program write4 to allow blank lines. (You will need a new means for detecting the end of the input, for example, **EOF in columns 1–5.)
7. The i–o and extend modes impose restrictions on file operations. Redraw the flowgraph from Fig. 7.2 to include these two additional modes and their associated operations.
8. Program rewrite1 would be more useful if it displayed a line number as well as the text from the file on every line. Write program rewrite2 to do this.
9. Write program rewrite3, which warns the user when a line is too long to be rewritten. The program should allow the option of writing the truncated line to the file or typing in a new line.
10. Write program chop1 to copy an input file to output but delete the leading five characters from every line. (Use copy1 as a model.)

7.9.2 Case study

11. The root program determines the output requirement and copy4 determines the input format. Find the statements in both programs within renum1 where these determinations are made. Write pseudo-code descriptions for both programs.
12. The control file (i1-file) for program renum1 contains lines of text. Each line is a record that determines the name of both an input file and the output file that is associated with it. Examine the record layout for w2-data and consider the statements at lines 111 to 119. Write a brief description for the benefit of a user to explain how records should be written into i1-file. Include examples of both correct and incorrect records and explain how the program will react when it encounters each of these records.
13. The control file (i1-file) for renum1 cannot contain empty lines.
    (a) Rewrite renum1 as renum2 in which the control file can contain empty lines that are skipped on input.
    (b) Amend renum2 so that the control file can contain comment lines that are also skipped on input. (You might define a comment line as one in which the first character is an asterisk. These might be used to assist a user of the program in remembering why records were placed in the file.)
14. Rewrite either renum1 or renum2 as renum3 so that it gives the option of using either i1-file as the source for the input or the keyboard.
15. Rewrite renum3 as renum4 which displays a short report for each text file that is converted. Each report should state the number of blank lines or page throw lines (a "/" in COBOL column 7), the number of comment lines, and the number of other lines that are found in each input file.

8
ISSUES IN PROGRAM DESIGN – DECISION TABLES

Decision tables are a means of specifying sets of actions to be undertaken in response to given conditions. There are two main types of decision table: limited entry and extended entry. Limited entry tables use conditions that are limited to being true or false whereas extended entry tables use conditions that are multi-way such as a test against a particular variable for different values.

8.1 LIMITED ENTRY DECISION TABLES

A limited entry decision table is divided into four areas or quadrants (Fig. 8.1). The stubs on the left-hand side list the conditions and the actions that can be taken. The entries on the right-hand side are expressed in columns where a column shows a possible condition state and its associated set of actions. Thus a complete column is a rule. For example, the decision table in Fig. 8.2 shows a condition, the actions which are to be undertaken, and the two rules.

The condition stub shows a limited condition, that is, a binary condition that can be either true or false. The condition entry shows the two possible states for the condition. The actions which must be undertaken for each condition state are shown by the 'X' underneath in the action entry. (A dash in the action entry means that the action is not part of the rule.)

Condition stub	Condition entry
Action stub	Action entry

Figure 8.1 Four quadrants of a decision table

210 ESSENTIAL COBOL: A FIRST COURSE IN STRUCTURED COBOL

Condition stub	Condition entry
height > 6	T F
Action stub	*Action entry*
display "tall"	X -
display "short"	- X

Figure 8.2 Decision table with one condition – two rules

Tables of this kind are referred to as being complete because they completely cover all possible condition states. (In this simple example the single condition is covered by one rule for true and another for false.)

We can see that the decision table as a form of specification is closely related to the evaluate statement:

```
evaluate height > 6
  when    true
    display "tall"
  when    false
    display "short"
end-evaluate
```

Decision tables can contain more than one condition. The decision table in Fig. 8.3 is also complete. It contains a second condition and this has caused the number of possible condition states and therefore the number of rules to increase to 4.

This number is the result of multiplying together the possibilities for each condition from the condition stub:

(true or false) * (true or false) → 2 * 2 → 4

This relationship is more conveniently expressed with powers of 2:

$2^{number\_of\_conditions}$ = number_of_rules

Condition stub	Condition entry
height > 6	T T F F
hair = "black"	T F T F
Action stub	*Action entry*
display "tall"	X X - -
display "dark"	X - X -
display "short"	- - X X
display "fair"	- X - X

Figure 8.3 Decision table with two conditions – four rules

Each of the four columns expresses a rule that associates a possible condition state with an ordered set of actions. (By ordered we mean that the actions must be undertaken in the order in which they are marked with Xs in the action entry.) Therefore the appropriate response to a height of 7 and hair that is "black" is to display "tall" followed by "dark".

The evaluate statement has been designed so that specifications expressed as decision tables can be easily written in COBOL. The following example directly translates the logic of the table in Fig. 8.3 into a single evaluate statement:

```
evaluate height > 6
              also hair = "black"
  when    true  also true
    display "tall"
    display "dark"

  when    true  also false
    display "tall"
    display "fair"

  when    false also true
    display "short"
    display "dark"

  when    false also false
    display "short"
    display "fair"
end-evaluate
```

The keyword **also** is used as a separator. It allows us to write the conditions as a list which is called the *subject*. Each rule then states an *object list* taken from the condition entry together with the appropriate actions taken from those that are marked in the action entry. A rule is satisfied when each element in the object list matches with each element in the *subject list*. For example, a height of 5 and hair that is "brown" causes the subject list to be evaluated to false **also** false. Therefore the evaluated subject matches the last rule and the result will be to display "short" followed by "fair".

The evaluate statement provides a valuable tool for writing complex conditional logic. However, it is often easy to miss crucial rules when specifying complex problems. Furthermore, it is often useful to specify conditional logic prior to programming so that analysts and users alike can check its validity for a particular application. The decision table is a design tool that meets these requirements.

Figure 8.4 shows a complete decision table for assessing policy loadings for automobile insurance premiums. In this case 2^3 confirms that there are eight rules required to construct a complete decision table for the three conditions. We can see that the table lists all of these rules and is complete because each possibility of true or false for each condition is represented.

We can also see that a particular pattern is emerging in the condition entry:

c1	TT	TT	FF	FF
c2	TT	FF	TT	FF
c3	TF	TF	TF	TF

212 ESSENTIAL COBOL: A FIRST COURSE IN STRUCTURED COBOL

Condition stub	Condition entry
age > 21	TTTTFFFF
engine > 2000	TTFFTTFF
convictions > 2	TFTFTFTF

Action stub	Action entry
policy loading = 45 percent	X - - - - - - -
policy loading = 15 percent	- X - - - - - -
policy loading = 30 percent	- - X - - - - -
no loading	- - - X - - - -
no policy to be issued	- - - - X - - -
policy loading = 60 percent	- - - - - X - -
policy loading = 50 percent	- - - - - - X -
policy loading = 10 percent	- - - - - - - X

Figure 8.3 Decision table with three conditions – eight rules

As we read from left to right the third condition changes from true to false with each rule. However, the second condition changes one-half as quickly and so two true values are followed by two false values. The first condition also changes one-half as quickly again so that four true values are followed by four false values. Thus a pattern of 2, 4, 8, ... emerges to describe the rate of change in the truth values as we move from bottom to top. We will see in later tables that this doubling continues in limited entry decision tables because each of the conditions is binary. The pattern is more conveniently expressed as:

$$2^1, \quad 2^2, \quad 2^3, \quad 2^4, \quad 2^5, \quad 2^6, \quad 2^7, \quad \ldots$$

where the base represents the binary nature of each condition and the power represents the number of conditions in the condition stub. In general we can express this fact as:

$$v^c$$

where v is the variety in the conditions and c is the number of conditions. This allows us to calculate the number of rules for any decision table simply by knowing the number of conditions. For example, a table of eight conditions will require 2^8 or 256 rules to make it complete.

Program risk1 in Fig. 8.5 incorporates an evaluate statement that implements the decision table in Fig. 8.4. This evaluate statement is also complete. When it is executed it will always cause one of the eight rules to be satisfied provided that l1-data holds numeric data.

It is often the case that certain conditions are of overriding importance. Let us imagine that based on previous claims experience it has been decided that insurance will not be issued to young people who drive large cars. In this case the outcome of two of the previous rules will be the same. The decision table in Fig. 8.6 shows a dash against the third condition in rule 5 to show that this condition does not need to be tested.

```
 1 identification division.
 2 program-id. risk1.
 3
 4 environment division.
 5
 6 data division.
 7
 8 linkage section.
 9 01   l1-data.
10      03   l1-age          pic 99.
11      03   l1-engine       pic 9(4).
12      03   l1-convictions  pic 99.
13
14 procedure division using l1-data.
15 para1.
16      evaluate l1-age > 21 also
17                           l1-engine > 2000 also
18                                            l1-convictions > 2
19      when    true   also true   also true
20         display "policy loading = 45 percent"
21
22      when    true   also true   also false
23         display "policy loading = 15 percent"
24
25      when    true   also false  also true
26         display "policy loading = 30 percent"
27
28      when    true   also false  also false
29         display "no loading"
30
31      when    false  also true   also true
32         display "no policy to be issued"
33
34      when    false  also true   also false
35         display "policy loading = 60 percent"
36
37      when    false  also false  also true
38         display "policy loading = 50 percent"
39
40      when    false  also false  also false
41         display "policy loading = 10 percent"
42      end-evaluate
43
44      exit program.
45
46 end program risk1
```

Figure 8.5 Program risk1

For rule 5 the same action will be taken regardless of whether the third condition is true or false. In other words 'FT-' now stands in the place of both 'FTT' and 'FTF'. Rules containing dashes are called abbreviated rules whereas those without dashes are full rules. It is quite common to find that tables contain abbreviated rules.

Condition stub	Condition entry
age > 21	T T T T F F F
engine > 2000	T T F F T F F
convictions > 2	T F T F - T F

Action stub	Action entry
policy loading = 45 percent	X - - - - - -
policy loading = 15 percent	- X - - - - -
policy loading = 30 percent	- - X - - - -
no loading	- - - X - - -
no policy to be issued	- - - - X - -
policy loading = 50 percent	- - - - - X -
policy loading = 10 percent	- - - - - - X

Figure 8.6 Decision table for three risk conditions – seven rules

The question now arises as to whether or not this decision table is still complete. Each dash means that two rules have been combined into one. Therefore a rule with d dashes is replacing 2^d full rules.

There is a simple calculation formula which can be applied to demonstrate completeness for limited entry tables. It requires us to take the number of dashes in each rule as a power of 2 and then to sum these values for all rules. The sum should be the same as 2 raised to the number of conditions:

$$2^c = \sum 2^d_r$$

Therefore the completeness test result for this table is:

$$2^3 = 2^0 + 2^0 + 2^0 + 2^0 + 2^1 + 2^0 + 2^0$$
$$= 1 + 1 + 1 + 1 + 2 + 1 + 1$$
$$8 = 8$$

We see that six of the rules have zero dashes and therefore each contributes 1 to the final result. However, the fifth rule has a single dash and therefore contributes 2.

Often a number of abbreviated rules relating to different conditions are required. For example, see Fig. 8.7. We can see that the table is complete: $(4 + 1 + 1 + 2 = 8)$. The following evaluate statement implements the table and is also complete:

```
evaluate age < 21
          also engine > 2000
                    also convictions > 2
    when    true  also any   also any   display "action-1"
    when    false also true  also true  display "action-1"
    when    false also true  also false display "action-2"
    when    false also false also any   display "action-3"
end-evaluate
```

ISSUES IN PROGRAM DESIGN – DECISION TABLES **215**

```
age < 21              T F F F
engine > 2000         - T T F
convictions > 2       - T F -

action-1              X X - -
action-2              - - X -
action-3              - - - X
```

Figure 8.7 Decision table using abbreviated rules

In this example the keyword **any** is used to force a match. It is used in exactly the same way as a dash in the condition entry. Therefore the first rule from the decision table shows 'T - -' and this is translated into the first object list of "true also any also any". This abbreviated rule covers four complete rules in both the decision table and the evaluate statement.

SELF-CHECK QUESTIONS

Q Is it permissible to write the following evaluate statement which uses the keyword **other**?

```
evaluate age < 21
         also engine > 2000
                        also convictions > 2
   when    true  also any   also any    display "action-1"
   when    false also true  also true   display "action-1"
   when    false also true  also false  display "action-2"
   when    false also false also any    display "action-3"
   when    other                        display "hello"
end-evaluate
```

A Yes. This is a correct COBOL evaluate statement. However, we know that the first four rules encode a complete decision table that covers all eight full rules. Therefore the other rule will never be reached. Other rules similar to this might be useful when testing a program to ensure that tables are indeed complete. For example, if through faulty reasoning we had omitted one of the first four rules, then the other rule could be used to detect the incompleteness of the preceding rules. Of course, such a 'safety net' is never a substitute for designing a logically correct table in the first place.

Q Is it permissible to write the following evaluate statement which uses the **other** rule instead of "false also false also false"?

```
evaluate age < 21
         also engine > 2000
                        also convictions > 2
   when    true  also any   also any    display "action-1"
   when    false also true  also true   display "action-1"
   when    false also true  also false  display "action-2"
   when    other                        display "action-3"
end-evaluate
```

A Yes. This is a correct COBOL statement because the inclusion of the other rule will cause any decision table to be complete. (Any condition states not covered by preceding rules will in any case be covered by the other rule.)

216 ESSENTIAL COBOL: A FIRST COURSE IN STRUCTURED COBOL

```
                    c1      TFFFFF
                    c2      -TFFFF
                    c3      --TFFF
                    c4      ---TFF
                    c5      ----TF
                    c6      -----T
evaluate c1    also c2    also c3    also c4    also c5    also c6
  when   true  also any   also any   also any   also any   also any   ...
  when   false also true  also any   also any   also any   also any   ...
  when   false also false also true  also any   also any   also any   ...
  when   false also false also false also true  also any   also any   ...
  when   false also false also false also false also true  also any   ...
  when   false also false also false also false also false also true  ...
  when   false also false also false also false also false also false ...
end-evaluate
```

Figure 8.8 Mutually exclusive rules for six conditions

A common pattern arises in decision tables where only one condition is true to the exclusion of others.

In Fig. 8.8 we see that when c1 is true there is no need to test the other conditions but when it is false c2 must be tested.

An important property of all decision tables is that the rules can be rotated. Thus the outline table and evaluate statement in Fig. 8.9 are logically equivalent to those in Fig. 8.8 even though the rules have been rotated in a deliberate attempt to make them difficult to follow.

Usually it is good practice to order the rules from left to right and from top to bottom so that truth values move down and across the table as in Fig. 8.8. This orderly practice makes the rules easier to read even though the rotation does not affect the logical outcome. It also has the beneficial effect of placing closely related rules in adjacent columns and this makes it much easier to discover missing or incorrect rules.

```
                    c1      FFFFFFT
                    c2      TFFFFF-
                    c3      -TFFFF-
                    c4      --FTFF-
                    c5      --F-TF-
                    c6      --T--F-
evaluate c1    also c2    also c3    also c4    also c5    also c6
  when   false also false also false also true  also any   also any   ...
  when   false also false also false also false also true  also any   ...
  when   true  also any   also any   also any   also any   also any   ...
  when   false also true  also any   also any   also any   also any   ...
  when   false also false also false also false also false also true  ...
  when   false also false also false also false also false also false ...
  when   false also false also true  also any   also any   also any   ...
end-evaluate
```

Figure 8.9 Version of Fig. 8.8 but with rules rotated

ISSUES IN PROGRAM DESIGN – DECISION TABLES **217**

```
              end-of-file        TFFFFFF
              end-of-sentence    -TFFFFF
              end-of-phrase      --TFFFF
              end-of-word        ---TFFF
              end-of-syllable    ----TFF
              letter-is-vowel    -----TF
```
```
evaluate end-of-file
          also end-of-sentence
                  also end-of-phrase
                          also end-of-word
                                  also end-of-syllable
                                          also letter-is-vowel
    when   true  also any   also any   also any   also any   also any   ...
    when   false also true  also any   also any   also any   also any   ...
    when   false also false also true  also any   also any   also any   ...
    when   false also false also false also true  also any   also any   ...
    when   false also false also false also false also true  also any   ...
    when   false also false also false also false also false also true  ...
    when   false also false also false also false also false also false ...
end-evaluate
```

Figure 8.10 Possible priority conditions for a text file

This type of pattern also arises in circumstances where there is a known priority of conditions as in Fig. 8.10.

Let us imagine that this priority of conditions exists within a text analysis program that analyses the use of vowels within syllables that it extracts. Clearly, when end-of-file is true no other testing can take place because there are no further sentences, phrases, words, syllables, or vowels left to analyse. (This priority holds for each condition in the condition stub in that all previous conditions must be false before a condition is allowed to be tested.)

The evaluate statement shown in Fig. 8.10 is correct. However, the program will run very inefficiently because the last rule which covers all consonants in the whole of the file will be the last one to be tested.

This inefficiency is considerably reduced by completely rotating the order of the rules so that the last is the first and so on. However, the program will still be inefficient. For example, when end-of-file is true, six rules will have to be evaluated fully before the seventh rule containing the end-of-file actions is reached. (In any case every consonant will still require six tests returning false before the action can be taken.)

Therefore it is common practice to write a table where there is such a clear priority of conditions in the following way:

```
evaluate  true
    when      end-of-file        ...
    when      end-of-sentence    ...
    when      end-of-phrase      ...
    when      end-of-word        ...
    when      letter_is_vowel    ...
    when      other              ...
end-evaluate
```

The important point to note is that in such an evaluate statement it is not possible to

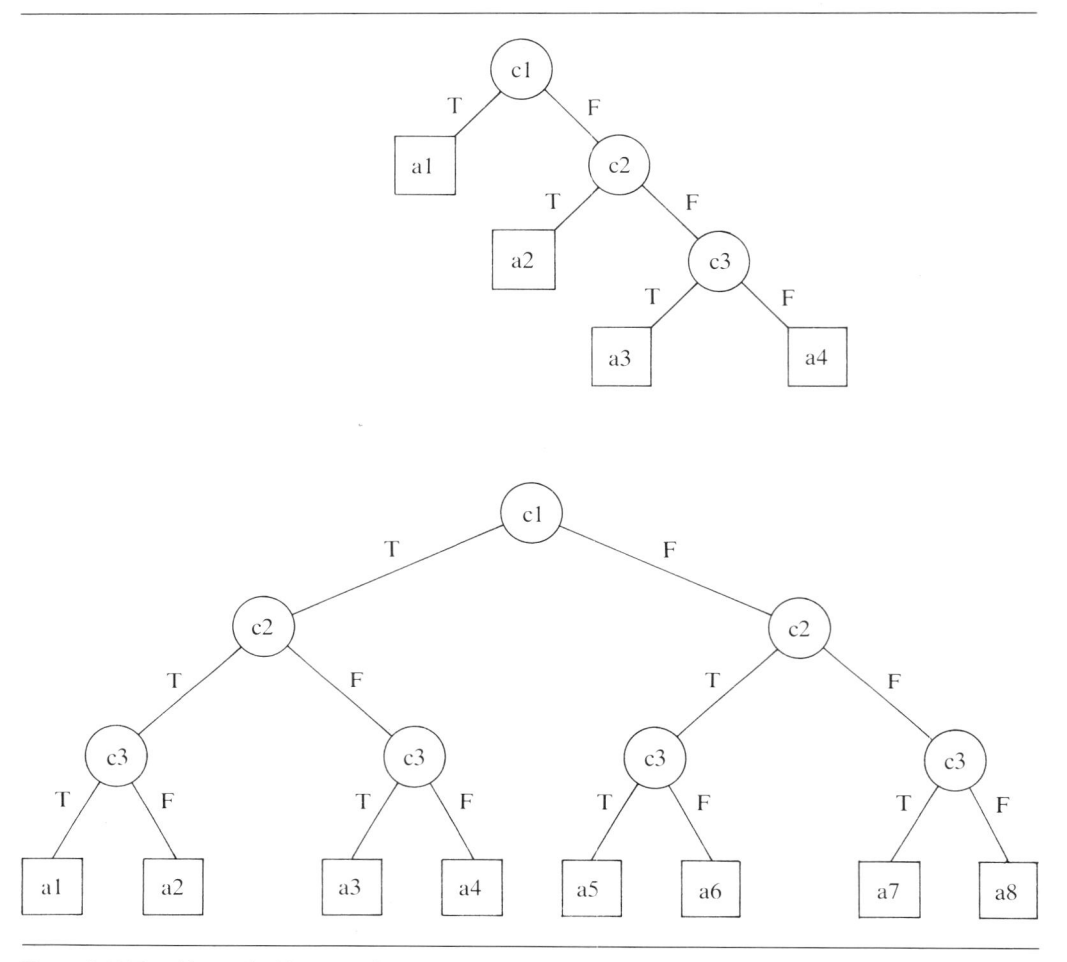

Figure 8.11 Two binary decision trees for three conditions

rotate the rules. Therefore it is not the logical equivalent to the original decision table because now each rule depends upon the previous rule having been false. The difference between these two evaluate statements is easily visualized by drawing their binary decision trees in the form shown for three conditions in Fig. 8.11.

In general, when working from specifications that are written as decision tables, one should avoid decision tables where the rules cannot be rotated. They should only be used when:

1. The priority of conditions is consistent and unbroken from the first to the last condition in the table.
2. There are clear indications that the efficiency of the final program will be compromised by including a complete evaluate statement.

ISSUES IN PROGRAM DESIGN – DECISION TABLES 219

3. The originator of the decision table agrees that the optimization should be undertaken.

In any case both the original decision table and the resulting evaluate statement should be documented to indicate that conditional priorities have been exploited in writing the program.

SELF-CHECK QUESTIONS

Q A problem has six conditions having only yes or no answers and seven possible actions. How many full rules would a limited entry decision table require to cater for this problem?

A 2 raised to the power of 6 is 64. Therefore the number full of rules is 64. (The number of actions does not affect the number of rules.)

Q Analyse the following limited entry decision table and determine whether or not it is complete.

```
c1          T   T   F   F   F
c2          T   F   T   F   F
c3          -   -   F   T   F
c4          -   -   -   F   F
           ─────────────────────
action-1    -   X   X   -   X
action-2    X   -   -   X   -
```

A The table is incomplete because it is missing four full rules.

$$2^2 + 2^2 + 2^1 + 2^0 + 2^0 = 4 + 4 + 2 + 1 + 1 = 12$$

However, $2^4 = 16$.

The four missing rules are:

```
F   F   F   F
T   T   F   F
T   T   T   F
T   F   T   T
```

Q Could the above four rules be replaced by a smaller set of rules?

A Yes. The first two rules could be replaced by an abbreviated rule:

```
F   F   F
T   F   F
T   T   F
-   T   T
```

This could be done in a table if the actions for the first two full rules were the same.

220 ESSENTIAL COBOL: A FIRST COURSE IN STRUCTURED COBOL

```
c1            - T
c2            F -
c3            T -
c4            T T

action-1      - X
action-2      X -
```

Figure 8.12 Decision table with ambiguous rules

Decision tables may contain rules that are ambiguous. Consider the above table shown in Fig. 8.12 where two rules show different actions. If we expand the abbreviated rules into the full rules for which they stand we find the following:

		1 2				3 4 5 6
-		TF	T			TTTT
F		FF	-			TTFF
T	becomes →	TT	and	-	becomes →	TFTF
T		TT	T			TTTT

Rules 1 and 5 in the full rules are the same. Therefore there is an ambiguous overlap between the original two rules. In cases where c1 is true, c2 is false, c3 is true, and c4 is true

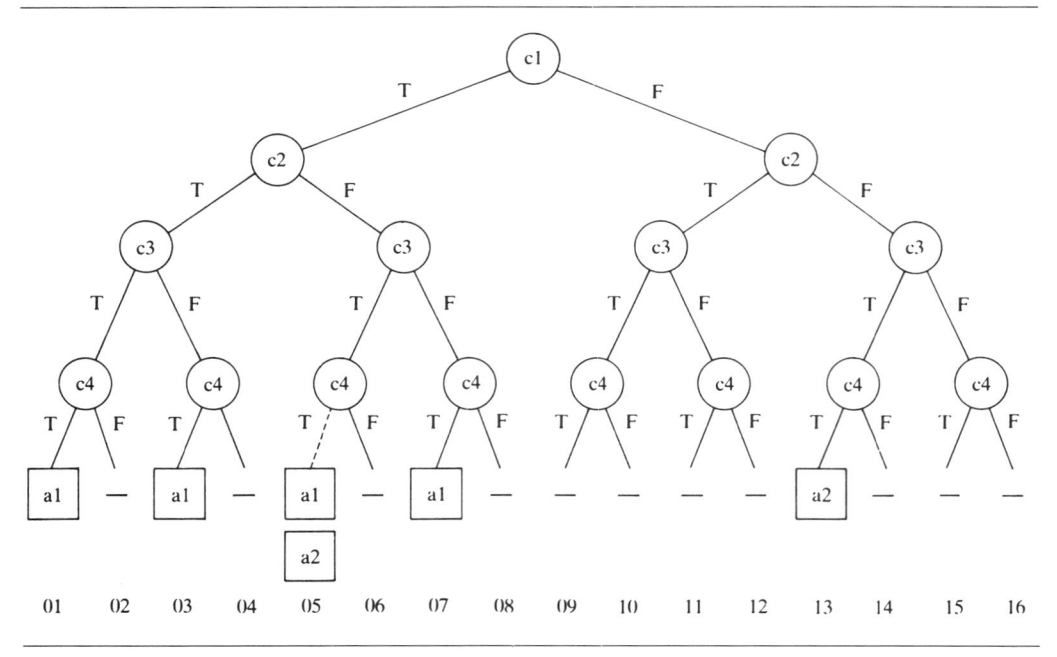

Figure 8.13 Binary decision tree demonstrating ambiguity

both of the abbreviated rules are satisfied even though they show different actions. It is important to see that even if the action had been the same the ambiguity would still exist because of the overlap in the abbreviated rules even though the problem might not lead to errors in a running program. The binary decision tree in Fig. 8.13 illustrates the problem of ambiguity by showing the paths for the 16 full rules.

We can see that the fifth full rule shows two different actions owing to the ambiguity of the original abbreviated rules. When checking a table for ambiguity it is usually advisable to sketch a table of full rules or a decision tree beforehand. Then as you check your table the expansion of each rule can be marked against this second table or the tree.

SELF-CHECK QUESTION

Q Analyse the decision table in Fig. 8.14 for completeness and ambiguity.

	1	2	3	4	5
c1	T	F	F	F	F
c2	T	T	F	F	F
c3	-	F	-	T	F
c4	-	-	-	F	F
action-1	X	-	X	X	-
action-2	-	X	-	-	X

Figure 8.14 Incomplete and ambiguous decision table

A The table should have 2^4, that is, 16 full rules because there are four binary conditions. However, the columns add up to 12. Therefore four rules appear to be missing.

Rules 3, 4 and 5 show false and false for the first two conditions, but rule 3 has a dash for conditions c3 and c4. Therefore rule 3 has aleady catered for rules 4 and 5. Rule 4 has the same action entries as rule 3 and therefore is a duplication. Rule 5 poses a greater problem because its action entries are different from rule 3. Therefore rules 3 to 5 are ambiguous.

One way to correct this error is to expand rule 3 only for those full rules that are not covered by rules 4 and 5. This will produce the following result shown in Fig. 8.15.

	1	2	3	4	5
c1	T	F	F	F	F
c2	T	T	F	F	F
c3	-	F	-	T	F
c4	-	-	T	F	F
action-1	X	-	?	X	-
action-2	-	X	?	-	X

Figure 8.15 Incomplete decision table without ambiguity

This table of five rules has no ambiguity but covers only 10 full rules. The six missing rules can be covered by the following two abbreviated rules:

```
T  F
F  T
-  T
-  -
```

As the above example shows there is no necessary relationship between completeness and ambiguity.

8.2 EVALUATING LISTS OF CONDITIONS

The full format for the evaluate statement is given in Fig. 8.16. We can see that the target of an evaluation can be a list of subjects in which the subjects are separated by the keyword **also**. Similarly object lists can be constructed in which the objects are separated by **also**.

Subject and object lists can be constructed in a variety of ways. However, it is always the case that each subject in the subject list must be compatible with each object in an object list. The evaluation of the lists is always done from left to right and the number of subjects must be the same as the number of objects. (The concept is similar to that which we encountered previously with lists of parameters.)

```
evaluate subject [also subject]...
  {when    object [also object]...   statement-1}
  [when    other                     statement-2]  ...
end-evaluate
```

Notes:

1. A subject has the following format:

$$\begin{Bmatrix} \text{identifier-1} \\ \text{literal-1} \\ \text{expression-1} \\ \text{true} \\ \text{false} \end{Bmatrix}$$

2. An object has the following format:

$$\begin{Bmatrix} \text{any} \\ \text{condition-1} \\ \text{true} \\ \text{false} \\ \text{test} \end{Bmatrix}$$

3. A test has the following format:

$$[\text{not}] \begin{Bmatrix} \text{identifier-3} \\ \text{literal-3} \\ \text{arithmetic-expression-3} \end{Bmatrix} \text{thru} \begin{Bmatrix} \text{identifier-4} \\ \text{literal-4} \\ \text{arithmetic-expression-4} \end{Bmatrix}$$

Figure 8.16 Full format – **evaluate** statement

Example 1. Testing an alphanumeric subject for specific values
```
evaluate e1
  when    "b"              ...
  when    "c" thru "m"     ...
  when    "p" thru "q"     ...
  when    other            ...
end-evaluate
```

Example 2. Testing a subject list with four subjects; using the keyword **any** to match a subject
```
evaluate e2        also e3            also e4    also e5
  when    "y"      also 16 thru 92    also any   also "n"   ...
  when    "y"      also 93 thru 94    also "n"   also "n"   ...
  when    "n"      also 97            also any   also "y"   ...
  when    "n"      also any           also any   also any   ...
  when    other                                             ...
end-evaluate
```

Example 3. Testing for matching expressions
```
evaluate e6 > 6 and e6 < 30    also e7 - 8
  when    e8 > 12              also e9                 ...
  when    true                 also e8 - 2             ...
  when    false                also not 5 thru 11      ...
  when    other                                        ...
end-evaluate
```

Figure 8.17 Evaluate – compatible subject and object lists

The rules governing compatibility are designed to ensure that a subject and object together can be evaluated to values that can be compared to give a result that is either true or false. Figure 8.17 gives a set of examples that illustrates the main rules for *compatibility matching*.

The first example shows a subject that is an alphanumeric data item. The first rule has an object that is a valid alphanumeric value. Therefore the subject and object are compatible and the rule will be true when e1 has a value of "b", that is, when the value of the subject and the value of the object match. The second rule tests for an inclusive range using the **thru** operator. When e1 is within this range the subject and object match. The third rule uses the keyword **other** which will always match with any subject list.

The second example uses lists with four subjects and four objects. The first rule uses the keyword **any** as the third object. An object of **any** will always match as true with its corresponding subject. (We can also deduce that e3 must be a numeric item because its corresponding object uses numeric literals in a range test.)

In the third example the subject list contains two subjects each of which are expressions. The first subject is a Boolean expression that can be evaluated to a value of true or false while the second subject is an arithmetic expression that can be evaluated to an integer value. The first rule contains a Boolean expression as the first object and a data item as the second object.

Consider the following test data: e6 = 15; e7 = 11; e8 = 14; e9 = 5. By substitution we can reduce the expressions in the table to the following:

```
evaluate 15 > 6 and 15 < 30  also  11 - 8
    when    14 > 12           also  5
    when    true              also  14 - 2
    when    false             also  not (5 thru 11)
    when other
end-evaluate
```

BECOMES

```
        evaluate true   also 3
            when true   also 5
            when true   also 12
            when false  also not (5 - 11)
            when other
        end-evaluate
```

The first two rules will not be followed for this test data because the subject and object lists do not match. In the third rule the second object matches the second subject but this rule will not be followed because the first subject and the first object do not match. Therefore the other rule will be followed because **other** always matches.

These three examples show that the evaluate statement can be used to construct much more complex logical structures than those which we examined with limited entry decision tables. There are forms of decision table that correspond to any possible evaluate statement but a greater examination of these lies well outside the limits of a text on COBOL. As a general rule you should try to use limited entry decision tables and their corresponding evaluate statements in preference to more complex forms. Multi-way selections based on lists of data items as shown in Examples 1 and 2 in Fig. 8.17 are also useful ways to express common branching problems. The third example which uses expressions in both the subject and object lists is difficult to follow. Statements of this kind should be avoided wherever possible and then should only be used if you are certain that one of the other forms of representation is even more complex for the problem at hand.

8.3 CASE STUDY: THE TRIANGLE PROBLEM

In this case study we will concentrate on the analysis of a simple problem so that its required solution can be stated clearly and concisely. Our goal will be not to write a program as such but to complete all of the preliminary and necessary work prior to programming so that a competent programmer could prepare a program that fully implemented the required solution. In order to do this we will pay particular attention to the specification of input and output as well as to the central function that can transform input to output.

The problem we will analyse concerns triangles. Given three integer values that represent three lengths is it possible for them to form the sides of a triangle? If they can form a triangle how can it be classified? (We will only concern ourselves with triangles in two-dimensional space. These are the triangles that can be drawn on paper with a pencil and a straight edge.)

Pause for a moment and try to write down those sets of values that in your view would make a good test for a program that could make such decisions for sets of three numbers. (One set of values might be 3, 3, and 3 which could represent an equilateral triangle, that is, one which has sides of equal length.)

1. Scalene triangle, e.g. 7,8,5
2. Equilateral triangle, e.g. 4,4,4
3. Isosceles triangle, e.g. 5,5,2
4. Three permutations for 3 above, e.g. 5,5,2; 5,2,5; 2,5,5
5. One side zero, e.g. 3,0,4
6. One side negative, e.g. -2,3,4
7. Sum of two sides is equal to the third, e.g. 1,2,3
8. Three permutations for 7 above, e.g. 1,2,3; 3,2,1; 3,1,2
9. Sum of two sides is less than the third, e.g. 2,3,7
10. Three permutations of 9 above, e.g. 2,3,7; 7,3,2; 3,2,7
11. Three sides zero, i.e. 0,0,0
12. Non-numeric set, e.g. a,7,8
13. Fewer than three values, e.g. 2,5
14. Correct specification of expected output for 1 to 13 above

Figure 8.18 Myers' checklist for test data for the 'triangle problem'

Glenford J. Myers* poses a simple version of this problem. He reports that even professional programmers, on average, score only 7.8 out of a possible 14 for their design of test cases for this problem. Try scoring test data against Myers' checklist (Fig. 8.18). Award yourself one mark for each point that is included in your test cases.

If you are like most people you will have scored fairly low on this informal test. Presumably the reason for this is that most of us assume that we understand a problem with which we have some familiarity. This is more likely to be the case if we acquired expertise in the past which is now generally not needed. Perhaps the triangle problem exposes a general human failing which in analysis and programming often causes us to begin to write programs for problems which are imperfectly understood. Therefore before considering a program let us take a few minutes to marshall some facts.

The following three general rules govern triangles and are relevant to the solution of this problem:

1. A triangle is a 3-sided polygon, that is, the corners meet to enclose a space. If the total length of any two sides is less than the length of the third side then it is not possible to form a triangle because the corners will not meet.
2. In a right-angled triangle the square of the longest side is equal to the sum of the squares of the other two sides. In obtuse triangles the square of the longest side is less than the sum of the squares of the other two sides but in acute triangles it is more.
3. Triangles can be classified in two main ways:
    (a) by angle:
    - ACUTE — All interior angles are less than 90°.
    - OBTUSE — One interior angle is greater than 90°.
    - RIGHT-ANGLED — One interior angle is equal to 90°.
    (b) by side:
    - SCALENE — All sides are of unequal length.
    - ISOSCELES — Two sides are of equal length.
    - EQUILATERAL — All sides are of equal length.

---

* Glenford J. Myers, *The Art of Software Testing*, Wiley, 1979.

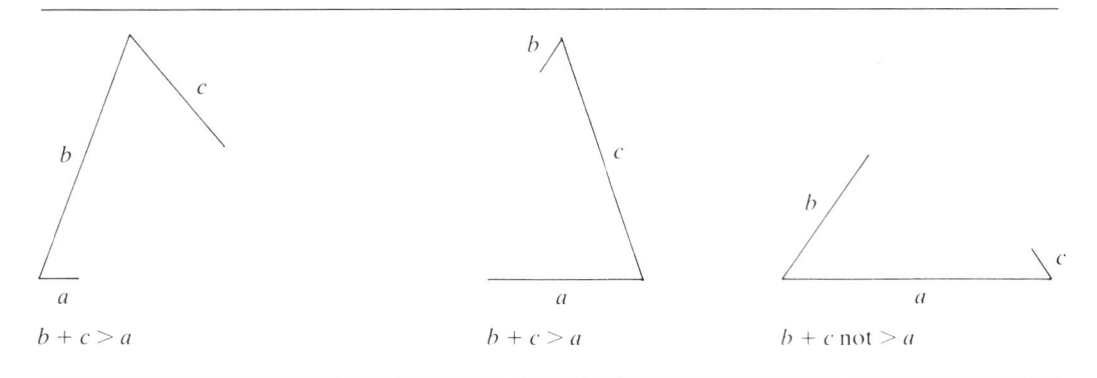

226 ESSENTIAL COBOL: A FIRST COURSE IN STRUCTURED COBOL

$b + c > a$ $\quad\quad\quad$ $b + c > a$ $\quad\quad\quad$ $b + c \text{ not} > a$

Figure 8.19 Comparing the length of the three sides

As we analyse these rules more closely we can see that the first rule has a higher priority than the other two. For example, the values 1, 7, and 2 according to first rule cannot form a triangle. Therefore it would be incorrect to use the third rule to say that these values were for a scalene triangle. Therefore the first rule is a necessary precondition for proceeding to the next two rules. If we visualize the form these lines might take we can see that the longest side is of critical importance (Fig. 8.19).

Clearly, the first two figures pass the test but the third figure does not. Therefore it is important for this test to know which of the sides is the longest and then to check its length against the sum of the other two sides if we are to avoid two redundant tests.

The second general rule also requires us to be able to identify the longest side because the arithmetic we will do on this side is not the same as for the other two sides. This rule is also of interest because it provides information that is relevant to the classification for the third general rule. Consider the right-angled triangle in Fig. 8.20.

It has triangles within and outside it that share the same base. The triangle that appears within it clearly has two sides that are shorter than those in the right-angled triangle and its apex is wider than the right-angled triangle. The outside triangle has longer

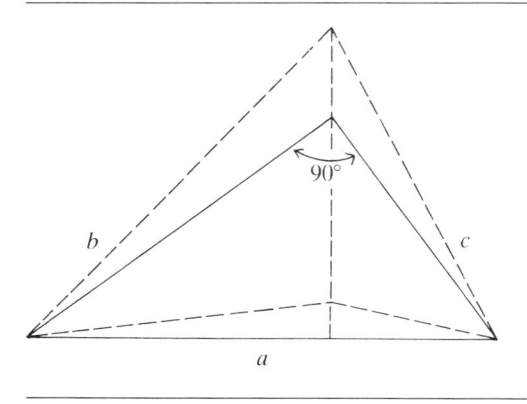

Figure 8.20 Right-angled triangle

sides but as the sides grow longer the apex of the triangle becomes smaller. This outside triangle is an acute triangle because all of its angles are less than 90°. The inside triangle is obtuse because its apex is greater than 90°. What we have found is that the second rule can be expanded to the following provided that the first rule is true:

- When $a^2 = b^2 + c^2$ then the triangle is right-angled.
- When $a^2 > b^2 + c^2$ then the triangle is obtuse.
- When $a^2 < b^2 + c^2$ then the triangle is acute.

Furthermore, we can see by inspection that if two of the above are false then the third must be true. (Any two values must either be equal or one of them must be greater.)

When we examine the third rule more closely we can see that the two methods of classification are not independent. For example, an equilateral triangle must be acute because n^2 is always less than $n^2 + n^2$. Can an isosceles triangle be right-angled, acute, or obtuse?

After carefully examining all of the relevant facts we can reduce the requirement for the input–output transformation to the steps and the decision table given in Fig. 8.21.

In conclusion, we can see that even an apparently simple problem requires considerable analysis before any programming should be undertaken. Unless you have a clear understanding of the central transformation that a program must implement it is unwise to start writing statements that are likely in the the long run to be incorrect. At a minimum it is necessary to have a clear description of the steps that must be undertaken to solve the given problem. These can then be expanded later to include additional information concerning the layouts for input and output as well as the conditions for terminating the program or the checking of a particular set of inputs. In any case programming should be delayed until all of these aspects of the required program are well understood.

---

1. Get the three values referred to below as a, b and c.
2. Shuffle the values about so that neither b nor c is greater than a. From this point on a is used as the base for a possible triangle.
3. Test for the first general rule, $(b + c) > a$, to ensure that b and c meet at an apex above the base line.
4. Provided that step three is successful then use the following decision table:

	1 2 3 4 5 6 7
$(a * a) = (b * b + c * c)$	T T F F F F F
$(a * a) > (b * b + c * c)$	- - T T F F F
$a = b = c$	- - - - T F F
$(a = b)$ or $(a = c)$ or $(b = c)$	T F T F - T F
right-angled	X X - - - - -
obtuse	- - X X - - -
scalene	- X - - - X X
equilateral	- - - - X - -
isosceles	X - X - - X -

Figure 8.21 Steps in solving the triangle problem

8.4 EXERCISES

8.4.1 General

1. Construct decision tables for the following three problems:
   (a) When it is cold and raining you should wear a heavy raincoat but when it is raining and not cold you should wear a light raincoat. However, when it is not raining and not cold then wear a jacket but when it is cold but not raining then wear a warm overcoat.
   (b) If it rains then Bill will go to town. If the sun is shining then Bill will go swimming. But if it is over 20° Celsius then Bill will go to town in any case because the shopping centre is air conditioned and he can avoid the heat by doing some window shopping. (Assume that sun showers are an impossibility.)
   (c) People wish to use a certain credit card to make purchases. When they have special credit any purchase can be processed. When the credit limit is exceeded the purchase should not be allowed except when the person has a card bearing a special symbol and then the case should be sent to the manager. Expired cards should always be rejected and those who have already made four purchases today should be referred to the manager. Other purchases should be processed.
2. Write a COBOL program called credit1 to implement the table from 1c above. The program should ask a set of questions requiring single-word replies and then state what action should be undertaken.
3. A casting company is seeking to hire leads for the musical 'Jane Eyre meets Godzilla'. They need only people between the ages of 18 and 25. If male, they want the actor to be over 7 ft in height, more than 450 lb in weight, and not bald. If female, the actor is to be less than 5 ft 4 in in height and less than 100 lb in weight and is to have shoulder length hair.
   (a) How many conditions in total are there?
   (b) How many rules in total are there?
   (c) Can the conditions be grouped?
   (d) Design 1 or more tables to define the selection criteria.
4. Write a COBOL program called cast1 to implement the solution from 3 above. (Ask each question so that it can be answered by either a 'yes' or a 'no' that is typed at the keyboard.)

8.4.2 Case study

5. Write program angle1 to implement a solution to the triangle problem:
   (a) Use the structure chart shown in Fig. 8.22 to design a root program with a nested program called Euclid that undertakes the main transformation.
   (b) I1-file should contain lines of text where each line is a set of three values followed by a comment. For example,

   20,10,10△Two△straight△lines

   is a valid record for the file. Assume that all of the records are valid and that positions 1-2, 4-5, and 7-8 always hold valid two digit numbers.

```
┌─────────────────────────────────────────┐
│                                         │
│  ( i1-file )────▶┌─────────┐            │
│                  │ angle1  │            │
│                  └────┬────┘            │
│                       │                 │
│                  ┌────┴────┐            │
│                  │  Euclid │            │
│                  └─────────┘            │
└─────────────────────────────────────────┘
```

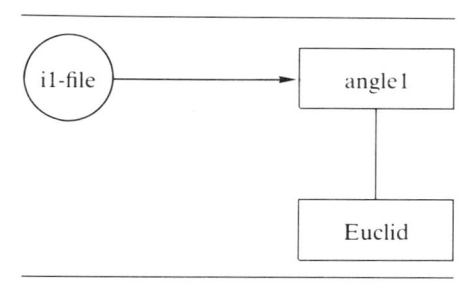

Figure 8.22 Structure chart for angle1

> As a first version write angle1 so that it simply copies the input to the screen but without calling Euclid.

(c) Design a parameter record to pass to Euclid. The record should contain the set of three side lengths as well as items to hold the decisions that Euclid will make concerning whether or not the sides form a triangle and if so how it can be classified.

(d) Use the steps in Fig. 8.21 and write Euclid.

> The multiplication required by the decision table has not as yet been covered. However, the asterisk is the multiplication operator in COBOL. Therefore statements such as:
>
> ```
> compute a1 = a * a
> ```
>
> will multiply a and put the result in a1. (Be sure that a1 is defined with a picture clause that is large enough to hold any square of a.) As an alternative you might try to use arithmetic or complex relational expressions within evaluate statements similar to those in Fig. 8.17.

(e) Rewrite angle1 as angle2 so that it calls Euclid and displays appropriate messages concerning the results that Euclid has passed back.

Part 2

9

INFORMATION REPRESENTATION I

This chapter discusses information representation in COBOL and in particular considers the ways in which numbers are represented in the language. The sample programs introduced in the chapter are studied in themselves to demonstrate the problems associated with validating numeric input from the keyboard and writing non-printable characters as output to the screen. In Chapter 10 they are tested and considered for use in different application contexts.

The number validation and screen programs are more complex than those we have considered in the past mainly because the inputs to both programs are more complex. Therefore the *escape* structure is considered as a means of moving forward in a program when no further processing can be done. Due to the fact that COBOL does not define this control structure it will be implemented by using **go to** statements. Detailed system specifications will also be examined as a means of documenting programs such as those that clearly exist to provide functions for the programs that call them.

9.1 NATURAL NUMBERS

Throughout recorded history people have been devising ways to record numbers. For example, the Romans used strings of upper-case alphabetic characters such as MCMLXXXIX. This is the Roman numeral for 1989.

When decoding a Roman numeral the characters are processed from left to right. If a character value is not found to be less than the next character value then it is added into the result. Thus LXXX is eighty. If a character value is found to be less than the next character value then it is subtracted from the result. Thus CM is nine hundred (Fig. 9.1).

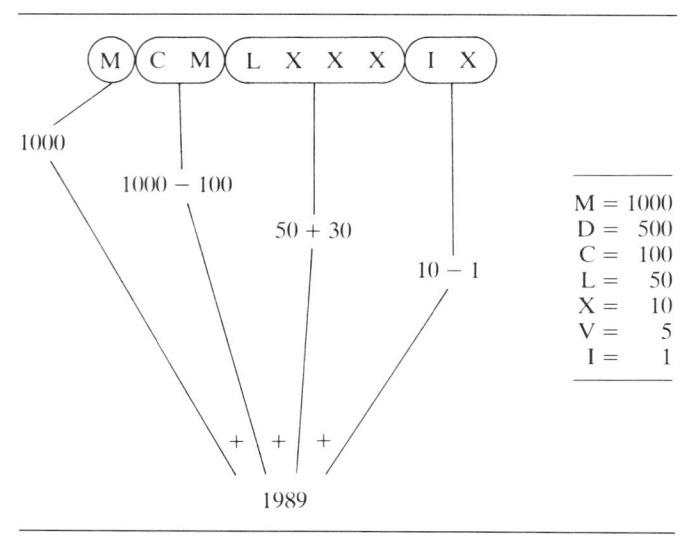

234 ESSENTIAL COBOL: A FIRST COURSE IN STRUCTURED COBOL

```
    M   C M   L X X X   I X

1000
     1000 - 100
              50 + 30                M = 1000
                        10 - 1       D =  500
                                     C =  100
                                     L =   50
                                     X =   10
                                     V =    5
                                     I =    1
         +   +  +
              1989
```

Figure 9.1 Decoding a roman numeral into modern denary notation

The rules for writing Roman numerals state that subtraction numerals can occur only as single characters in the string. Thus VIII and not IIX is the correct notation for the numeral eight.

Natural numbers recorded in this way are still sometimes seen on buildings or in film titles. But although they may be evocative of antiquity, Roman numerals are extremely difficult to use for other purposes such as arithmetic. If you are in doubt, try to add up these identical sets of numbers:

```
         V             5
       XVII           17
        IV            4
        IX            9
         I            1
       ———          ———
         ?            ?
```

Nowadays we record natural numbers in a simpler way that among other improvements clearly uses zero as a countable number. The next ten numbers after nine are written by placing the digit 1 in the tens position and by repeating the full sequence of digits from 0 to 9 in the units position. This newer notation is called denary because it uses 10 distinct

```
0   1   2   3   4   5   6   7   8   9 ...
|...|...|...|...|...|...|...|...|...|...|...|
```

Figure 9.2 Number line in denary

digits {0..9}. It enables us to make many complex calculations that are impracticable with Roman numerals.

9.2 BASE NUMBERS

The numbers we use are base 10 because they have 10 digits. We will refer to numbers in this notation as denary numbers. The numbers used by computers are binary numbers (base 2) and have the digits 0 and 1. A base 2 digit is called a bit (short for binary digit), a group of eight bits is called a byte, and one-half of a byte is a nibble.

Binary numbers are difficult for people to use directly. Therefore hexadecimal notation (base 16) is used by people as a shorthand for binary notation. In hexadecimal the additional digits needed beyond 9 are written using A to F.

Find the number 15 denary in Fig. 9.3. The same number in hexadecimal is 0Fh. (We use a leading zero before A to F to show that we mean a number in this context and not the characters "A" to "F". The lower case 'h' denotes the hexadecimal notation.)

At the sixteenth number (0Fh) we have run out of distinct digits in hexadecimal. Therefore the next number 10h is written by putting 1h in the next column to the left and putting 0h in the units column. The binary numbers are generated in the same way. Here we see that we have run out of digits after writing the second number (1b). Therefore the third number is 10b.

Denary – base 10	Hexadecimal – base 16	Binary – base 2	Ordinal position
0	0	0	first
1	1	1	second
2	2	10	third
3	3	11	fourth
4	4	100	fifth
5	5	101	sixth
6	6	110	seventh
7	7	111	eighth
8	8	1000	ninth
9	9	1001	tenth
10	0A	1010	eleventh
11	0B	1011	twelfth
12	0C	1100	thirteenth
13	0D	1101	fourteenth
14	0E	1110	fifteenth
15	0F	1111	sixteenth
16	10	10000	seventeenth
17	11	10001	eighteenth
⋮	⋮	⋮	⋮
255	0FF	11111111	two hundred and fifty-sixth
256	0F00	100000000	two hundred and fifty-seventh

Figure 9.3 Denary, hexadecimal and binary compared

236 ESSENTIAL COBOL: A FIRST COURSE IN STRUCTURED COBOL

The number 10h is not only the point at which hexadecimal carries but also one of the points where binary carries. A similar carry occurs again at 256d. Examine the first sixteen numbers closely and you will see that prior to the single carry in hexadecimal there have been four carries in binary. In other words binary reuses digits at four times the rate of hexadecimal in order to represent the same natural numbers.

Binary and hexadecimal are closely related notations due to the following relationship:

$$2^4 = 16^1 = 16$$

We see that:

1. The powers of 4 and 1 show the four to one relationship noted as the number of digit places needed to record the same information in each base system. In other words 4 bits can hold as much information as one digit of hexadecimal.
2. The bases of 2 and 16 show the number of digits for each notation.
3. The number 16 is both a power of 2 and a power of 16. This means that the two systems will carry at the same time. Therefore conversions between the two base systems can easily be accomplished using

   powers of 2 ($2^3 = 8$, $2^2 = 4$, $2^1 = 2$, $2^0 = 1$)

Conversions between hexadecimal and binary are fairly easy to do with a bit of practice (Fig. 9.4). Starting at the right-hand side we take each nibble in turn and convert it into a single hexadecimal digit. (The last nibble furthest to the left has less than 4 bits. We can add as many leading zeros as we need to bring in up to 4 bits.)

The method requires us to find and add up the powers of 2 represented by the place positions of each of the four bits (Fig. 9.5).

If a place contains 0 then it contributes nothing to the final result. If a place contains a 1 then it contributes its place value to the final result. The place values are easy to remember because each is double that of the previous. The final step is done by memory work. (You have to remember that 10d to 15d are represented as 0Ah to 0Fh.)

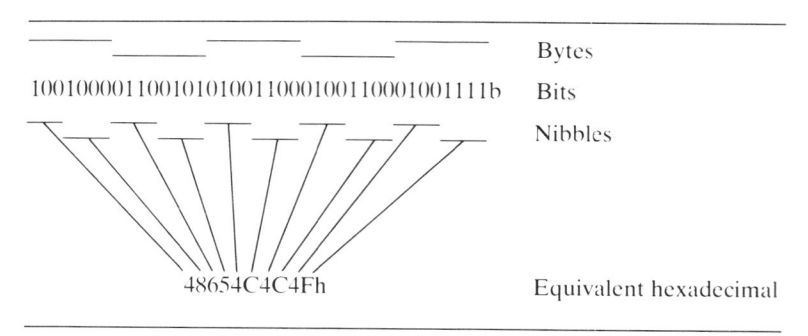

```
                                                      Bytes
1001000011001010100110001001100010011111b             Bits
                                                      Nibbles

              48654C4C4Fh                             Equivalent hexadecimal
```

Figure 9.4 Comparing binary to hexadecimal

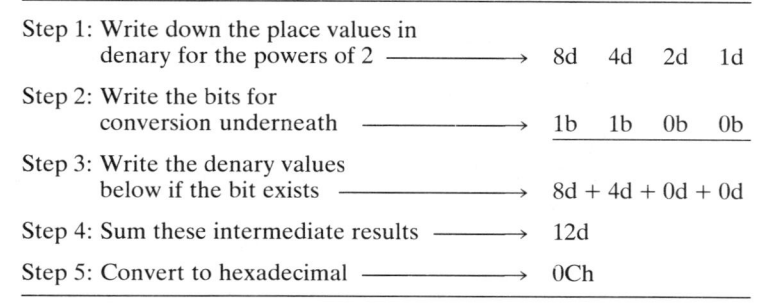

Step 1: Write down the place values in denary for the powers of 2	→	8d	4d	2d	1d
Step 2: Write the bits for conversion underneath	→	1b	1b	0b	0b
Step 3: Write the denary values below if the bit exists	→	8d + 4d + 0d + 0d			
Step 4: Sum these intermediate results	→	12d			
Step 5: Convert to hexadecimal	→	0Ch			

Figure 9.5 Converting a nibble from binary to hexadecimal by adding powers of 2

Conversion from hexadecimal to binary is similar except that it is based on subtracting out the powers of 2 rather than adding them. If the power is found it is subtracted out and 1b is written in the appropriate position in the result. If the power is not found 0b is written instead (Fig. 9.6).

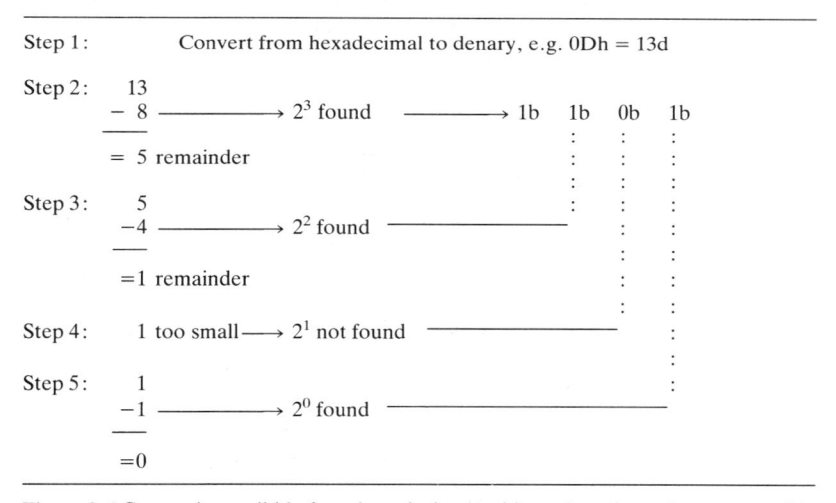

Step 1:   Convert from hexadecimal to denary, e.g. 0Dh = 13d

Step 2:   13
          $-$ 8   → 2^3 found   → 1b   1b   0b   1b
          $=$ 5 remainder

Step 3:   5
          $-$4   → 2^2 found
          $=$1 remainder

Step 4:   1 too small → 2^1 not found

Step 5:   1
          $-$1   → 2^0 found
          $=$0

Figure 9.6 Converting a nibble from hexadecimal to binary by subtracting powers of 2

9.3 INFORMATION CODES

As needs have changed throughout history the methods and symbols used for encoding information have tended to change. In our everyday life the following sets of characters are adequate for most purposes:

Characters	Description
a to z	lower-case letters
A to Z	upper-case letters
0 to 9	digits
. , ; : - ! ? '	some punctuation marks

Sample text	Meaning of symbol
Re–occurrence	Hyphen in English
x = 7 – 5	Subtraction operator in mathematics
y = 2 * –6	Negative sign in mathematics
0–60 mph in 8 seconds	Range in English meaning 'to'
T–TFF	Both true and false in a decision table
X–XX–	Skip an action in a decision table

Figure 9.7 Different contexts for the "–" character

Speakers of languages other than English may not agree that these characters are adequate. The French, for example, would at a minimum require the inclusion of accent characters such as the circumflex "^". Specialist languages such as mathematics require additional characters. And in all languages different characters may mean different things depending on the context in which they are used (see Fig. 9.7).

Thus the term 'character' refers to a written representation and the term 'symbol' refers to the meaning we attach to a character or a string of characters within a particular context. Thus 10 and ten are both symbols constructed from characters. The symbol 10 may mean the number ten in denary or the number two in binary.

Although there are many schemes available for encoding characters within a computer system they all share one characteristic in common. This is that they must be easily represented and manipulated in binary by a computer.

One of the most widely used encoding schemes is known as ASCII (pronounced AS-key). This is an acronym for the American Standard Code for Information Interchange. It was first introduced in 1963 and encodes 128 different characters as numbers in the range of zero to 127 denary.

Figure 9.8 shows the 128 ASCII characters in their counting order and provides additional information to assist in representing them as denary, binary and hexadecimal numbers.

The unit of character storage in the majority of computer systems nowadays is the byte, which is a group of 8 bits. Thus each byte is able to store a character of information. (A byte can in fact hold 2^8 or 256 different binary numbers. Computer systems do not use the leading binary digit when encoding 7-bit ASCII codes. Therefore this bit is usually set to 0b.)

The first 32 ASCII patterns (0d to 31d) are dedicated to special non-printable characters. For example, the eighth number (7d, 7h, 0000111b) is shown in the table as the BEL character. When a byte containing this special character is sent to a terminal it will make an audible sound. (BEL is short for bell. Many early terminals were fitted with a bell but nowadays buzzers and electronic whistles of one kind or another are more common.) Other characters in this group may cause visible behaviour at the terminal. For example, the fourteenth character (13d, 0Dh, 001101b) is defined as the carriage return character (CR) and causes the cursor to move to the beginning of the next line.

				HIGH NIBBLE							
	DEN			0	16	32	48	64	80	96	112
		HEX		0	1	2	3	4	5	6	7
			BIN	000	001	010	011	100	101	110	111
	00	00	0000	NUL	DLE	Δ	0	@	P	`	p
	01	01	0001	SOH	DC1	!	1	A	Q	a	q
	02	02	0010	STX	DC2	"	2	B	R	b	r
L	03	03	0011	EXT	DC3	#	3	C	S	c	s
O	04	04	0100	EOT	DC4	$	4	D	T	d	t
W	05	05	0101	ENQ	NAK	%	5	E	U	e	u
	06	06	0110	ACK	SYN	&	6	F	V	f	v
N	07	07	0111	BEL	ETB	'	7	G	W	g	w
I	08	08	1000	BS	CAN	(	8	H	X	h	x
B	09	09	1001	HT	EM	)	9	I	Y	i	y
B	10	0A	1010	LF	SUB	*	:	J	Z	j	z
L	11	0B	1011	VT	ESC	+	;	K	[	k	{
E	12	0C	1100	FF	FS	,	<	L	\	l	|
	13	0D	1101	CR	GS	-	=	M	]	m	}
	14	0E	1110	SO	RS	.	>	N	^	n	~
	15	0F	1111	SI	US	/	?	O	_	o	DEL

Note: The binary and hexadecimal nibble values can be read directly from the table.
To find a denary value for a byte read a value from the top and then add the value to the left.

Figure 9.8 7-bit ASCII codes and characters

The meaning of these special characters is always dependent on the context created by the virtual environment in which they are used and not necessarily on the standard ASCII definition. For example, the ASCII BEL character can be generated by holding down the control key and then pressing the key for the character "G". Whether or not there will be an audible sound will depend on the software you are using at the time. If you are communicating directly with the operating system you may get a different result depending on the context given by the operating system for ⟨CTRL⟩G.

If you are communicating with a program such as a text editor you are likely to get a different result depending on the meaning attached to ⟨CTRL⟩G by the text editor. (One well-known text editing program uses ⟨CTRL⟩G to mean 'delete this character'.) As we will discover later in this chapter it is possible for a COBOL program to use special characters. For the moment we will concentrate on the printable characters.

The printable characters begin at 32d and continue through to 126d. When we type these characters at the keyboard the terminal translates keystrokes into bytes containing the correct binary pattern. These are then re-translated back to the terminal screen as visible character images.

The purpose of text editing and word-processing programs is to assist in creating files of characters. These files contain bytes that represent the printable characters we have typed as well as other information that represents other textual requirements such as the carriage return. Therefore in order to have a better understanding of what is contained in files we need to understand how character information is encoded in bits, nibbles and bytes.

240 ESSENTIAL COBOL: A FIRST COURSE IN STRUCTURED COBOL

The following self-check questions will give you practice converting between number bases so that you can determine the byte patterns that correspond to keystroke combinations. The optional self-check exercise will help you to apply these concepts to considering how information is physically stored in files. It is shown as an optional exercise because the explanation of how data are stored is specific to the VAX operating system and not strictly required in order for you to be able to follow the rest of the text. However, many other systems are the same or very similar and you should be able to work through the strategy used by systems other than the VAX by following the approach outlined in the exercise. If you spend a few minutes now to understand how data are stored in files you will find that future topics such as how COBOL stores data in memory will be more clearly and more deeply understood.

SELF-CHECK QUESTIONS

Q   Convert the following numbers from one base to another:

	From	To
(a)	72h	binary
	0B2h	binary
	3Fh	denary
	20h	denary
(b)	10101010b	hexadecimal
	10011001b	hexadecimal
	01010101b	denary
	1110111b	denary
(c)	124d	hexadecimal
	132d	hexadecimal
	100d	binary
	92d	binary

A (a) 01110010b; 10110010b; 63d; 32d
   (b) 0A0Ah; 99h; 85d; 119d
   (c) 7Ch; 84h; 1100100b; 1011100b

Q   What is the bit difference between the ASCII code for "G" and "g"?
A   Bit 6 is set to 0 for "G" and to 1 for "g". The other bits are the same.

Q   Can you deduce the likely function of the control key by knowing that both CTL-G and CTL-g produce the BEL character?
A   The character "g" has the byte pattern 01100111b and the character "G" has the byte pattern 01000111b. The byte pattern for both CTL-G and CTL-g is 00000111b. In all cases the low nibble is the same and represents the seventh letter of the alphabet. Pressing either the SHIFT key or the CTL key changes the pattern of the high nibble. Therefore the function of the CTL key is to generate a high nibble of 0000b.

Q   What is the difference between the characters "A" and "1"?

A The character "1" has a high nibble of 0010b and the character "A" has a high nibble of 0100b. Both characters have the same low nibble.

Q Does the ESC key behave in the same way as the CTL and SHIFT keys?

A No. ESC is a special unprintable character with the value 00011011b. The ESC character is generated by pressing the ESC key on its own while the CTL and SHIFT keys are used in conjunction with other keys as a way of changing the binary value of the high nibble.

OPTIONAL SELF-CHECK EXERCISE

Use your text editor to create a text file containing the four lines shown in Fig. 9.9 where lines 1 and 3 contain characters and lines 2 and 4 are blank.

Text	Comments
1234	line 1 5 keystrokes
	line 2 1 keystroke
abcd	line 3 5 keystrokes
	line 4 0 keystrokes
	11 keystrokes

Figure 9.9 Creating a text file to dump

The terminal screen should contain eight visible characters ("1234","abcd") plus the effect of three depressions of the RETURN key, that is, 11 keystrokes in all.

Save the file.

Use the DUMP program supplied with your operating system to find out what byte values the file contains.

Can you find bytes for the characters "1234" and "abcd"?

Can you find bytes for the RETURN key? Some systems may represent the end of a non-blank line as 0D0Ah and the end of a blank line as 0Ah. Other systems may represent a line with two leading bytes that have a hexadecimal value that is the number of characters following for that line.

Is the last RETURN represented by a byte pattern?

Can you determine how the end of data is represented?

Is the file longer than you expected? If so, is the size of the file a number of bytes that is a power of 2, e.g. 128, 256, or 512?

The VAX/VMS DUMP Utility displays the contents of the file in hexadecimal as shown in Fig. 9.10.

The dump of the file consists of 32 lines of text. Each line is divided into three main sections. The first section shows four groups each of four bytes and is read from right to left. Thus 32310004h is the value for the first four bytes in this file and 04h is the first byte. Note that each line shows the value of 16 bytes.

Virtual block number 1 (00000001), 512 (0200) bytes

```
00006463 62610004 00003433 32310004  ..1234....abcd..  000000
00000000 00000000 00000000 0000FFFF  ................  000010
00000000 00000000 00000000 00000000  ................  000020
{25 identical lines of binary zeros have been omitted.}
00000000 00000000 00000000 00000000  ................  0001C0
00000000 00000000 00000000 00000000  ................  0001D0
00000000 00000000 00000000 00000000  ................  0001E0
00000000 00000000 00000000 00000000  ................  0001F0
```

Figure 9.10 Dump of a text file

The next section is to the right and shows the textual representation of the 16 bytes. It is read from left to right and bytes that have no textual representation are shown as the "." character.

The final section is three bytes long and is a counter in hexadecimal. It is used to calculate displacements into the file. For example, the last byte in the file before the binary zeros begin has a value of 0FFh. It is the 18th byte in the file because the counter for that line shows a value of 10h which is 16d and the byte is at position 2d in the line. In small files such as this one the counter is not crucial but in larger files it provides a handy way to calculate the exact position of bytes that lie well into the file.

The counter for the last line shows 1F0h as the displacement up to the beginning of that line and the line itself contains a further 16d (10h) bytes to the end of the file. If we add the values 1F0h and 10h we get the value 200h which is 512 in denary. Thus we can see that even though we only typed 11 characters into the file the VAX system has stored a file of 512 bytes. (The end of data has been marked in the file by 0FFFFh at byte positions 17d and 18d.)

When we examine the way in which the lines have been represented in the file we see that not all of our keystrokes have been written into the file. The first line we typed was "1234" followed by a carriage return. This is represented in the file as the first six bytes:

```
343332310004
```

The first two bytes are 0004h which is the length in bytes of the line to follow. After the next four bytes we find 0000h which is the length of the second line. This is immediately followed by another line length and the data for that line. Thus we can see that each line is represented not by a string followed by a carriage return but by a two-byte line length followed by a string. Blank lines are therefore represented by a line length of zero.

9.4 ACCEPTING UNSIGNED NUMBERS

The accept statement is the means by which character data is input from the terminal keyboard in COBOL. When the target is defined as an alphanumeric data item an accept transfers characters in accordance with the rules for an alphanumeric move.

```
 1 identification division.
 2 program-id. getnum1.
 3
 4 environment division.
 5
 6 data division.
 7 working-storage section.
 8 01    e1-number   pic 9(3).
 9
10 procedure division.
11 para1.
12     accept e1-number
13     stop run.
14
15 end program getnum1
```

Figure 9.11 Program getnum1

When accepting data the RETURN typed at the keyboard never appears in the target although COBOL responds to its presence by returning control to the COBOL program.

This basic alphanumeric facility is standard to COBOL and must be part of any valid implementation of the language. It simply transfers a string of bytes from the source keyboard to the target data item. The target will be aligned on the left and either padded with spaces or truncated if the source and target are unequal in length.

However, standard COBOL does not define a common standard for accepting numeric data items.

Consider the apparently trivial program getnum1 shown in Fig. 9.11. Getnum1 appears to accept a number from the keyboard. In order to test this program we could use the eleven test cases shown in Fig. 9.12.

Cases 1 to 7 all hold valid numbers but case 7 is too long. Cases 8 and 9 do not hold numbers. Although in some applications we might interpret the absence of a number to be zero, in many others we would wish to see the absence of a number as either an error or a missing input. Case 10 contains 2 numbers and is therefore in error. Case 11 is in error because it contains alphabetic characters.

 1. 000⟨RET⟩
 2. 1⟨RET⟩
 3. 23⟨RET⟩
 4. 312⟨RET⟩
 5. Δ54⟨RET⟩
 6. 67Δ⟨RET⟩
 7. 4567⟨RET⟩
 8. ⟨RET⟩
 9. ΔΔΔ⟨RET⟩
10. 6Δ7⟨RET⟩
11. ABC⟨RET⟩

Figure 9.12 Test cases for program getnum1

In standard COBOL only cases 1, 4 and 5 will always appear to this program as correct data. What will appear in the working-storage of the program for the other cases depends on how the compiler implementor chooses to interpret these words from the language standard:

> Any conversion of data required between the hardware device and the data item . . . is defined by the implementor.

In other words, the standard for the language contains what amounts to a loophole. Therefore although getnum1 nominally conforms to the language standard the results that a program may produce when compiled by different compilers is far from standard in terms of practical consequences!

Figure 9.13 shows the possible results in the target item that could result from different implementor strategies.

Therefore any programmer who wishes to write a fully portable program must only accept strings of data which do not imply conversion. If program getnum1 had defined e1-number as pic xxx then unconverted byte values would have been made available in the working-storage according to the rules of the alphanumeric move. Case 7 would still have been truncated but this could be managed by accepting a string longer than expected and then checking that it contained only trailing spaces beyond the maximum length.

Program getnum2 in all cases captures the string as typed at the keyboard although it still cannot discriminate an empty string (case 8) from a string of one or more spaces (case 9). The difference between these two inputs in most practical cases is not of any consequence.

	Working-storage for:		
Keyboard source	compiler A NO CONVERSION	compiler B ALPHANUMERIC TO NUMERIC • right justified • leading spaces become zero • no other conversion	compiler C ALPHANUMERIC TO NUMERIC • left justified • all spaces become zero • high nibble ignored
1. 000⟨RET⟩	303030h	303030h	303030h
2. 1⟨RET⟩	312020h	303031h	313030h
3. 23⟨RET⟩	323320h	303233h	323330h
4. 312⟨RET⟩	333132h	333132h	333132h
5. Δ54⟨RET⟩	203534h	303534h	303534h
6. 67Δ⟨RET⟩	363720h	363720h	363730h
7. 4567⟨RET⟩	343536h	353637h	343536h
8. ⟨RET⟩	202020h	303030h	303030h
9. ΔΔΔ⟨RET⟩	202020h	303030h	303030h
10. 6Δ7⟨RET⟩	362037h	362037h	363037h
11. ABC⟨RET⟩	414243h	414243h	313233h

Figure 9.13 Some different COBOL compiler implementations for accepting numbers

```
 1 identification division.
 2 program-id. getnum2.
 3
 4 environment division.
 5
 6 data division.
 7 working-storage section.
 8 01  e1-number  pic x(4).
 9
10 procedure division.
11 para1.
12     accept e1-number
13     stop run.
14
15 end program getnum2
```

Figure 9.14 Program getnum2

Both getnum1 and getnum2 are standard COBOL but only getnum2 (Fig. 9.14) is truly portable in that it will cause the same behaviour (compiler A) in all COBOL environments. What now remains is to convert valid alphanumeric strings into valid numeric strings.

The lack of COBOL standards for numeric input is best managed by hiding input definitions and their necessary conversions within programs especially designed for this purpose. Therefore a calling program could request a numeric input and the called program could accept a string, check its contents, decide whether or not it is a number, and do any necessary conversion before passing the results back to the calling program.

Figure 9.15 shows such a calling program. (As with the previous getnum programs it is only intended to demonstrate a method and does not constitute a useful application in its

```
 1 identification division.
 2 program-id. getnum3.
 3
 4 environment division.
 5
 6 data division.
 7 working-storage section.
 8 01  w1-rec.
 9     03  w1-string    pic x(21).
10     03  w1-number    pic s9(18).
11     03  w1-length    pic 99.
12     03  w1-scale     pic 99.
13     03  w1-decision  pic 99.
14
15 procedure division.
16 para1.
17     call "accept1a" using reference w1-rec
18     stop run.
19
20 end program getnum3
```

Figure 9.15 Program getnum3

246 ESSENTIAL COBOL: A FIRST COURSE IN STRUCTURED COBOL

own right.) Instead of accepting a number directly getnum3 calls accept1a, the program with which we are mainly concerned, and passes it a parameter record. The items within the record allow accept1a to return:

w1-string	the original string that was input;
w1-number	any valid number that was found in the string;
w1-length	the number of digits in the number that was input excluding leading zeros;
w1-scale	any scaling factor that needs to be used owing to a decimal point that existed in the original string;
w1-decision	the decision that w1-string takes on the state of the original string and thus an indication as to whether or not the number, length, and scale items are valid.

This record has been designed so that it can be used for any possible valid number. As such it includes a picture clause for w1-number that shows a sign. (This is denoted by writing the character "s" prior to the 9s.) It also includes a scale so that numbers with a decimal point can be reported back. We will consider these additional features later in the chapter and for the moment restrict the problem to the one with which we began, namely, the input of unsigned whole numbers such as 42 or 521.

Accept1a must therefore have a strategy for accepting strings of alphanumeric data and determining if they contain valid numbers. Accept1a is shown in Fig. 9.17. It realizes a simple but generalized strategy (Fig. 9.16) for accepting numbers of up to 18 digits which is the maximum number size allowed in COBOL. (The last step is shown as 5 because we will be inserting two steps before it later when we include the decimal point and the sign.)

Although the strategy used by accept1a is fairly straightforward the COBOL needed to solve this particular validation problem is reasonably complex and will require careful reading.

The first step accepts the input into the alphanumeric item w1-string and initializes the other items in the parameter record. In particular note that we start with the initial

---

1. Accept an input that is longer than the largest COBOL number, that is, more than 18 characters. (21 is used as a maximum because a sign and decimal point will be allowed in later versions thereby bringing the maximum up to 20. The 21st position is used to check whether or not a string longer than the allowed maximum has been input.)
2. Reject a string of spaces as an empty string.
5. (a) Align to the right-hand side.
   (b) Reject a string without enough leading space as too long.
   (c) Transform leading spaces to zeros.
   (d) Reject a string that does not pass the numeric class test as bad numeric.
   (e) Any string that has survived this far contains a number and can be moved to the target. Find the number of leading zeros now in the number part of the string. The significant part of the number will be:

   18 minus the leading zeros now in the string

   Set the decision to success.

Figure 9.16 Strategy for unsigned numbers

assumption that the string will hold a valid number and then will attempt to disprove this assumption.

The second step checks for an empty input and if this is not the case then checks to see whether or not the 21st character is a space. (Remember that the string is left-justified. Therefore the string is too long if there is a non-space character in the 21st position.)

Step 5 is controlled by the **other** rule for the evaluate statement of step 2. Therefore step 5 will not be reached if the input is not valid up to this point. Part (a) uses a perform loop to check the string backwards from the 21st character for the first non-space. When it finds the first non-space it has found the length of the non-space substring and therefore moves it to the target `w1-realigned`. This target has been described as right justified at

```
 1 identification division.
 2 program-id. accept1a.
 3*Purpose: Determine whether or not a string contains a valid
 4*         unsigned whole number.
 5 environment division.
 6
 7 data division.
 8 working-storage section.
 9 01   w1-rec.
10      03  w1-string              pic x(21).
11      03  w1-ref                 pic 99.
12          88  w1-max             value 21.
13          88  w1-min             value 00.
14      03  w1-leadzeroes          pic 99.
15      03  w1-realigned           pic x(21) just right.
16
17 linkage section.
18 01   l1-rec.
19      03  l1-string              pic x(21).
20      03  l1-number              pic s9(18).
21      03  l1-length              pic 99.
22      03  l1-scale               pic 99.
23      03  l1-decision            pic 99.
24          88  l1-success         value 00.
25          88  l1-empty-input     value 01.
26          88  l1-too-long        value 10.
27          88  l1-bad-numeric     value 11.
28          88  l1-bad-sign        value 12.
29          88  l1-bad-scale       value 13.
30
31 procedure division using l1-rec.
32 para1.
33*Step 1
34      accept w1-string
35      move w1-string to l1-string
36      move   zero to l1-number
37                     l1-length
38                     l1-scale
39      set l1-success to true
40
```

```
41*Step 2
42     evaluate true
43        when    w1-string = space
44           set l1-empty-input to true
45        when    w1-string(21:1) not = space
46           set l1-too-long to true
47        when    other
48
49*Step 5a
50           move space to w1-realigned
51           set w1-max to true
52           perform test before until w1-min
53              evaluate w1-string(w1-ref:1) not = space
54                 when    true
55                    move w1-string(1:w1-ref) to w1-realigned
56                    set w1-min to true
57                 when    false
58                    compute w1-ref = w1-ref - 1
59              end-evaluate
60           end-perform
61
62*Step 5b
63           evaluate w1-realigned(1:3) not = space
64              when    true
65                 set l1-too-long to true
66              when    false
67
68*Step 5c
69                 inspect  w1-realigned(4:)
70                    replacing leading space by zero
71                 move zero to w1-leadzeroes
72                 inspect  w1-realigned(4:)
73                    tallying w1-leadzeroes for leading zero
74
75*Step 5d
76                 evaluate w1-realigned(4:) not numeric
77                    when    true
78                       set l1-bad-numeric to true
79                    when    false
80
81*Step 5e
82                       move w1-realigned(4:) to l1-number
83                       compute l1-length = 18 - w1-leadzeroes
84                 end-evaluate
85           end-evaluate
86     end-evaluate
87
88     exit program.
89
90 end program accept1a
```

Figure 9.17 Program accept1a

line 15. Therefore the effect of the move is to force the original string which was left justified to be right justified in w1-realigned.

Part (b) of step 5 now checks to make sure that there are three leading spaces in w1-realigned. If there are not then the input must have been greater than 18 characters and therefore could not possibly be a valid unsigned whole number.

Provided that the string has survived part (b) then part (c) is done. Here the 18-character portion of the string which should hold the number is inspected and any leading spaces are replaced by zeros. Thus if the input is "1", then 17 leading zeros will be put before it but if the input is "1Δ1", then only 15 leading zeros will be put before it and the embedded space will remain. At line 72 a second inspect statement counts the number of leading zeros. This count will include not only the leading zeros that were put in the string by the previous inspect statement but also any leading zeros that were part of the original string. (An input of "01" will have been given 16 leading zeros and then counted as having 17 leading zeros in total.)

Part (d) then checks the 18 characters to see if they are numeric. If the string now contains any characters other than "0" . . "9", then this test will fail. (An original input of "1Δ1" will fail at this stage because of the embedded space.) Part (e) is only reached for valid numbers. At this point the last 18 characters of w1-realigned are moved to l1-number and the length of the number excluding leading zeros is calculated. We now know that l1-number holds a valid number because the 18 characters from w1-realigned passed the numeric test and therefore were moved to l1-number reliably.

The requirement in program accept1a that subsequent steps should not be undertaken if previous steps have failed has resulted in a program in which the evaluate statements are nested to a depth of 3. (See Fig. 9.18(a).) The program is well structured but nevertheless can be difficult to read especially because some of the actions contained within the evaluate statements are also nested. In previous programs we have often controlled nesting by, for example, putting a nested perform into a called program so that the calling program showed a functional call rather than the loop itself. This approach could be tried to simplify accept1a but would be unsuccessful for two reasons. Firstly, the original evaluate structure would have to remain in the calling program. Therefore the called programs would only hide away the actions and the increase in complexity by having many called programs would hardly offset the advantage of removing the actions from the calling program. Secondly, the called programs would all require the same parameter record and the task of one program would be *coupled* to the task of the next by the evaluate structure and the w1-decision item. In other words, the calling program and the called programs could still only be comprehended by reading them together in an attempt to understand how they affect one another.

However, another solution is available which uses the go to statement in COBOL. The structure for this solution is outlined in Fig. 9.18(b) and takes advantage of the fact that the steps are organized in such a way that a failure to pass a test at one step means that no futher action needs to be undertaken and the program can therefore reach its exit program statement immediately.

The go to statement requires a paragraph as its target. When the go to statement is executed, control is immediately transferred to the target paragraph and execution continues. In the technique demonstrated here a new paragraph is added immediately above the exit program statement so that any go to that transfers control to this point

(a) Outline of nesting in program accept1a

```
action1
evaluate condition1
   when   true
          action2
   when   false
          action3
          evaluate condition2
             when   true
                    action4
             when   false
                    action5
                    evaluate condition3
                       when   true
                              action6
                       when   false
                              action7
                    end-evaluate
          end-evaluate
end-evaluate
exit program.
```

(b) Outline of nesting in program accept1b

```
action1
evaluate condition1
   when   true
          action2
          go to para-exit
end-evaluate

action3

evaluate condition2
   when   true
          action4
          go to para-exit
end-evaluate

action5

evaluate condition3
   when   true
          action6
          go to para-exit
end-evaluate

action7.
para-exit.
   exit program.
```

Figure 9.18 Comparative outlines for programs accept1a and accept1b

causes the program to return control to its calling program immediately. As a result the second and third evaluate statements do not have to be nested because they will not be reached if a go to is executed beforehand.

The go to statement generally has a bad reputation for a number of reasons. The main reason is that it is possible to scatter paragraphs and go tos willy-nilly about a program and then to transfer control forwards and backwards across the program in such a way that it is almost impossible to follow the flow of control of the program as a whole. Such programs are known as 'spaghetti bowls' and are very difficult if not impossible to test.

However, the fact that a particular statement can be abused is not necessarily a reason to ban it altogether. Instead it should be a call for better programmer education, for the advancing of agreed rules governing the use of such statements, and for the improvement of programming languages so that the beneficial uses of such statements can be incorporated within new control structures.

Let us imagine that COBOL has a new control statement for 'escaping forward' in the text of a program and that it is called *escape*. Its delimiter will be *end-escape* and the keyword *forward* will be used to escape forward to the next statement after the end-escape. Such a statement would have the following syntax:

```
escape
   {{statement-1}...forward}
end-escape
```

As with other statements the escape could be preceded and followed by any other COBOL statements and statement-1 could be more than one statement. Such a new control statement describes concisely the use of the go to that is being recommended. There is one entry at the top (escape corresponding to the start of action1) and one exit at the bottom (end-escape corresponding to para-exit). Within any statement a forward could be included that would automatically transfer control to the end-escape. (Thus all of the `go to para-exit` statements would simply be replaced by the keyword *forward*.)

It is this controlled use of the go to which is being recommended as a way of avoiding deeply nested structures. You might consider adding escape and end-escape to your programs as comments so that it is clear to the reader that you are using the go to statement in a particular and controlled way. Other uses of the go to should without exception be avoided. (Figure 9.19 shows the program rewritten as accept1b using this approach.)

```
1 identification division.
2 program-id. accept1b.
3*Purpose: Determine whether or not a string contains a valid
4*         unsigned whole number.
5
6 environment division.
7
8 data division.
```

```
 9 working-storage section.
10 01  w1-rec.
11     03  w1-string              pic x(21).
12     03  w1-ref                 pic 99.
13         88  w1-max             value 21.
14         88  w1-min             value 00.
15     03  w1-leadzeroes          pic 99.
16     03  w1-realigned           pic x(21) just right.
17
18 linkage section.
19 01  l1-rec.
20     03  l1-string              pic x(21).
21     03  l1-number              pic s9(18).
22     03  l1-length              pic 99.
23     03  l1-scale               pic 99.
24     03  l1-decision            pic 99.
25         88  l1-success         value 00.
26         88  l1-empty-input     value 01.
27         88  l1-too-long        value 10.
28         88  l1-bad-numeric     value 11.
29         88  l1-bad-sign        value 12.
30         88  l1-bad-scale       value 13.
31
32 procedure division using l1-rec.
33 para1.
34*Step 1
35     accept w1-string
36     move w1-string to l1-string
37     move zero to l1-number
38                   l1-length
39                   l1-scale
40     set l1-success to true
41
42*Step 2
43     evaluate true
44       when   w1-string = space
45         set l1-empty-input to true
46         go to para-exit
47       when   w1-string(21:1) not = space
48         set l1-too-long to true
49         go to para-exit
50     end-evaluate
51
52*Step 5a
53     move space to w1-realigned
54     set w1-max to true
55     perform test before until w1-min
56       evaluate w1-string(w1-ref:1) not = space
57         when   true
58           move w1-string(1:w1-ref) to w1-realigned
59           set w1-min to true
60         when   false
61           compute w1-ref = w1-ref - 1
62       end-evaluate
63     end-perform
64
```

```
65*Step 5b
66      evaluate w1-realigned(1:3) not = space
67        when    true
68          set l1-too-long to true
69          go to para-exit
70      end-evaluate
71
72*Step 5c
73      inspect  w1-realigned(4:)
74        replacing leading space by zero
75      move zero to w1-leadzeroes
76      inspect  w1-realigned(4:)
77        tallying w1-leadzeroes for leading zero
78
79*Step 5d
80      evaluate w1-realigned(4:) not numeric
81        when    true
82          set l1-bad-numeric to true
83          go to para-exit
84      end-evaluate
85
86*Step 5e
87      move w1-realigned(4:) to l1-number
88      compute l1-length = 18 - w1-leadzeroes.
89
90 para-exit.
91      exit program.
92
93 end program accept1b
```

Figure 9.19 Program accept1b

9.5 ACCEPTING SIGNED NUMBERS

The numbers we have considered so far have been character strings using only the numeric characters 0 to 9. COBOL allows signed numeric character strings in two ways:

1. The sign can be written as either the character + or -. Thus a signed number will be one character longer than an unsigned number. The sign can be either the first or the last character in the string.
2. The sign can be incorporated into the bit pattern of the high nibble of either the first or the last character. Signed numbers in this form are not one character longer. (This approach is used by l1-number in the parameter record. It will be covered fully in Chapter 11.)

The first approach uses picture clauses with the sign symbol 's' and the **sign** clause. For example:

```
01  e1-adjustments.
    03  e1-realigned        pic x(21).
    03  filler redefines e1-realigned.
        05  filler          pic xx.
        05  e1-signleads    pic s9(18) sign leading separate.
    03  filler redefines e1-realigned.
        05  filler          pic xx.
        05  e1-signtrails   pic s9(18) sign trailing separate.
```

In the above record e1-signleads is defined as a 19-character numeric string with a single + or - in the first position to denote sign. E1-signtrails holds the sign character in the last position.

Both data items will pass the numeric test if they contain only digits and a correctly positioned sign character.

Imagine that e1-realigned held either of the first two test cases from Fig. 9.20. E1-realigned would not pass the numeric test because an alphanumeric item must contain only 0 to 9 in order to pass this test. However, e1-signleads would pass the numeric test for case 1 and e1-signtrails would pass the numeric test for case 2. Therefore the new problem we face is that of manipulating input strings so that valid sign characters that are input always end up in either the 3rd or 21st character position.

Consider the test cases 3 to 12 for an input of minus one. All of these cases must be recognized as minus 1 by any comprehensive strategy for signed numbers. (A further 10 test cases for correct positive numbers could be constructed by replacing the - with a +.)

Clearly our strategy must not only take these numbers into account but also work for all signed numbers with 1 to 18 digits. This is given in Fig. 9.21 and the corresponding program is in Fig. 9.22.

Program accept2 adds step 4 to determine whether or not a single sign exists. If there is more than one sign then the string is rejected and if there is no sign then step 5 is followed as before. If there is a single sign in the string then step 6 is followed.

Step 6 knows that a valid sign must be either leading or trailing the number. It therefore splits the string at the sign and expects to find one of the substrings to be only spaces. If one of the substrings is not empty then the input is rejected, otherwise either step 7 or step 8 is followed.

---

1. ΔΔΔ-12345678901234567⟨RET⟩
2. ΔΔΔ12345678901234567+⟨RET⟩
3. -1⟨RET⟩
4. ΔΔΔ-1⟨RET⟩
5. ΔΔΔΔΔΔΔΔΔΔΔΔΔΔΔΔΔ-1⟨RET⟩
6. ΔΔ-1ΔΔΔΔ⟨RET⟩
7. ΔΔ-0001ΔΔ⟨RET⟩
8. 1-⟨RET⟩
9. ΔΔ1-⟨RET⟩
10. ΔΔΔΔΔΔΔΔΔΔΔΔΔΔΔΔΔ1-ΔΔ⟨RET⟩
11. ΔΔ1-ΔΔΔΔ⟨RET⟩
12. ΔΔ0001-ΔΔ⟨RET⟩

Figure 9.20 Valid test cases for signed number input

Thus the order of steps which will be followed overall is as follows:

input of spaces	1, 2
too many signs	1, 2, 4
no sign	1, 2, 4, 5
one sign	1, 2, 4, 6
one sign trailing	1, 2, 4, 6, 7
one sign leading	1, 2, 4, 6, 8

As we read down the list we see the tests that the input must satisfy if it is to survive. As we read across we see the steps that will have been followed to that test. All valid numbers will go through steps 1, 2 and 4. The evaluate statement at line 86 guarantees that only unsigned inputs will enter step 5 and once entered the go to at line 121 guarantees that the exit will be reached.

---

*1. Accept an input that is longer than the largest COBOL signed number, that is, more than 19 characters.
*2. Reject a string of spaces as an empty string.
4. Check the string for sign characters and reject a string with more than one sign.
*5. When a string contains no sign treat as before:
   (a) Align to the right-hand side.
   (b) Reject a string without enough leading space as too long.
   (c) Transform leading spaces to zeros.
   (d) Reject a string that does not pass the numeric class test as a bad numeric.
   (e) Success!
6. When the string contains only one sign character:
   (a) Split the string into two strings at the sign character and store the sign for later use.
   (b) One of the strings must be only spaces otherwise the sign must have been embedded within other characters e.g. Δ2-2 and the string must be rejected.
7. When the first string is not spaces the sign was trailing.
   (a) The string should be right-aligned otherwise the sign was incorrectly detached, e.g. Δ1Δ-Δ and the string must be rejected.
   (b) Move the first string to the target aligned on the second last position and put the sign in the last position.
   (c) Reject a string without enough leading space as too long.
   (d) Transform leading spaces to zeros.
   (e) Reject a string that does not pass the numeric class test for strings with trailing signs.
   (f) Success!
8. When the second string is not spaces the sign was leading.
   (a) The string should be left-aligned otherwise the sign was incorrectly detached, e.g. Δ-Δ23Δ and the string must be rejected.
   (b) Align it to the right in the target.
   (c) Reject a string without enough leading space as too long.
   (d) Put the sign in position 4 and any leading zeros needed beyond this point.
   (e) Reject a string that does not pass the numeric class test for strings with leading signs.
   (f) Success!

* = Step brought forward from the strategy for unsigned numbers

---

Figure 9.21 Strategy for signed numbers

```
 1 identification division.
 2 program-id. accept2.
 3*Purpose: Determine whether or not a string contains a valid
 4*         signed whole number.
 5
 6 environment division.
 7
 8 data division.
 9 working-storage section.
10 01  w1-rec.
11     03  w1-string              pic x(21).
12     03  w1-ref                 pic 99.
13         88  w1-max             value 21.
14         88  w1-min             value 00.
15     03  w1-leadzeroes          pic 99.
16
17     03  w1-variations.
18         05  w1-trails          pic x(21) just right.
19         05  filler redefines w1-trails.
20             07  filler         pic x.
21             07  w1-trailsleft  pic x(20).
22         05  w1-leads           pic x(21).
23
24     03  w1-signs.
25         05  w1-sign            pic x.
26         05  w1-signctr         pic 99.
27             88  w1-no-sign     value 00.
28             88  w1-one-sign    value 01.
29             88  w1-bad-sign    value 02 thru 22.
30
31     03  w1-realigned           pic x(21) just right.
32
33     03  filler redefines w1-realigned.
34         05  filler             pic xx.
35         05  w1-signleads       pic s9(18) sign leading  separate.
36
37     03  w1-trailaligned redefines w1-realigned.
38         05  filler             pic xx.
39         05  w1-signtrails      pic s9(18) sign trailing separate.
40
41 linkage section.
42 01  l1-rec.
43     03  l1-string              pic x(21).
44     03  l1-number              pic s9(18).
45     03  l1-length              pic 99.
46     03  l1-scale               pic 99.
47     03  l1-decision            pic 99.
48         88  l1-success         value 00.
49         88  l1-empty-input     value 01.
50         88  l1-too-long        value 10.
51         88  l1-bad-numeric     value 11.
52         88  l1-bad-sign        value 12.
53         88  l1-bad-scale       value 13.
54
```

```
55 procedure division using l1-rec.
56 para1.
57*Step 1
58     accept w1-string
59     move w1-string to l1-string
60     move zero to l1-number
61                  l1-length
62                  l1-scale
63     set l1-success to true
64
65*Step 2
66     evaluate true
67       when   w1-string = space
68         set l1-empty-input to true
69         go to para-exit
70       when   w1-string(21:1) not = space
71         set l1-too-long to true
72         go to para-exit
73     end-evaluate
74
75*Step 4
76     set w1-no-sign to true
77     inspect w1-string
78       tallying w1-signctr for all "+" all"-"
79     evaluate true
80       when   w1-bad-sign
81         set l1-bad-sign to true
82         go to para-exit
83     end-evaluate
84
85*Step 5
86     evaluate true
87       when   w1-no-sign
88         move space to w1-realigned
89         set w1-max to true
90         perform test before until w1-min
91           evaluate w1-string(w1-ref:1) not = space
92             when   true
93               move w1-string(1:w1-ref) to w1-realigned
94               set w1-min to true
95             when   false
96               compute w1-ref = w1-ref - 1
97           end-evaluate
98         end-perform
99
100        evaluate w1-realigned(1:3) not = space
101          when   true
102            set l1-too-long to true
103            go to para-exit
104        end-evaluate
105
106        inspect  w1-realigned(4:)
107          replacing leading space by zero
108        move zero to w1-leadzeroes
109        inspect  w1-realigned(4:)
110          tallying w1-leadzeroes for leading zero
111
```

```
112       evaluate w1-realigned(4:) not numeric
113          when    true
114             set l1-bad-numeric to true
115             go to para-exit
116          end-evaluate
117
118          move w1-realigned(4:) to l1-number
119          compute l1-length = 18 - w1-leadzeroes
120*         unsigned input ok
121          go to para-exit
122       end-evaluate
123
124*Step 6 - only single signs have survived to this step
125       move spaces to w1-trails
126                     w1-leads
127                     w1-sign
128       unstring w1-string
129         delimited "+" or "-"
130         into      w1-trails delimiter w1-sign
131                   w1-leads
132
133*Step 7
134       evaluate true
135         when    w1-trails not = spaces and w1-leads not = spaces
136           set l1-bad-sign to true
137           go to para-exit
138         when    w1-trails = spaces and w1-leads = spaces
139           set l1-bad-sign to true
140           go to para-exit
141         when    w1-trails not = spaces
142           evaluate w1-trails(21:1) = space
143             when    true
144               set l1-bad-sign to true
145               go to para-exit
146           end-evaluate
147
148           move w1-trailsleft to w1-trailaligned
149
150           evaluate w1-realigned(1:2) not = space
151             when    true
152               set l1-too-long to true
153               go to para-exit
154           end-evaluate
155
156           inspect w1-realigned(3:18)
157             replacing leading space by zero
158           move zero to w1-leadzeroes
159           inspect w1-realigned(3:18)
160             tallying w1-leadzeroes for leading zero
161
162           evaluate w1-realigned(3:18) not numeric
163             when    true
164               set l1-bad-numeric to true
165               go to para-exit
166           end-evaluate
167
```

```
168            move w1-sign to w1-realigned(21:1)
169            move w1-signtrails to l1-number
170            compute l1-length = 18 - w1-leadzeroes
171*           trailing sign input ok
172
173*Step 8
174       when   w1-leads not = spaces
175            evaluate w1-leads(1:1) = space
176               when   true
177                  set l1-bad-sign to true
178                  go to para-exit
179            end-evaluate
180
181            move space to w1-realigned
182            set w1-max to true
183            perform test before until w1-min
184               evaluate    w1-leads(w1-ref:1) not = space
185                  when   true
186                     move w1-leads(1:w1-ref) to w1-realigned
187                     set w1-min to true
188                  when    false
189                     compute w1-ref = w1-ref - 1
190               end-evaluate
191            end-perform
192
193            evaluate w1-realigned(1:3) not = space
194               when   true
195                  set l1-too-long to true
196                  go to para-exit
197            end-evaluate
198
199            inspect w1-realigned(4:)
200               replacing leading space by zero
201            move zero to w1-leadzeroes
202            inspect w1-realigned(4:)
203               tallying w1-leadzeroes for leading zero
204
205            evaluate w1-realigned(4:) not numeric
206               when   true
207                  set l1-bad-numeric to true
208                  go to para-exit
209            end-evaluate
210
211            move w1-sign to w1-realigned(3:1)
212            compute l1-length = 18 - w1-leadzeroes
213            move w1-signleads to l1-number
214*           leading sign input ok
215       end-evaluate.
216
217 para-exit.
218       exit program.
219
220 end program accept2
```

Figure 9.22 Program accept2

260   ESSENTIAL COBOL: A FIRST COURSE IN STRUCTURED COBOL

Step 6 is followed for all signed numbers and the evaluate at line 134 guarantees that either step 7 or step 8 will be followed. (Steps 7 and 8 do not have go tos as their last statements because the evaluate ensures that the next statement to be reached after it is the exit.)

We can note in passing that the moves to l1-number at lines 169 and 213 automatically convert the data from a 19-character numeric item with the sign as a separate character into an 18-character numeric item with the sign stored within the string. (This is covered in greater detail in Chapter 11.)

---

*1. Accept an input that is longer than the largest COBOL number, that is, more than 20 characters.
*2. Reject a string of spaces as an empty string.
 3. Check the string for a decimal point and reject a string with more than one decimal point.
    (a) When there is no decimal point set the scale to one.
    (b) When there is a decimal point count the number of non-space characters after the decimal point until a space or the end of the string is found. This count will be the scale provided the string passes all other tests successfully.
    (c) Remove the decimal point from the string by closing up substrings surrounding it.
*4. Check the string for sign characters and reject a string with more than one sign.
*5. When a string contains no sign treat as before:
    (a) Align to the right-hand side.
    (b) Reject a string without enough leading space as too long.
    (c) Transform leading spaces to zeros.
    (d) Reject a string that does not pass the numeric class test as a bad numeric.
    (e) Success!
*6. When the string contains only one sign character:
    (a) Split the string into two strings at the sign character and store the sign for later use.
    (b) One of the strings must be only spaces otherwise the sign must have been embedded within other characters e.g. Δ2-2 and the string must be rejected.
*7. When the first string is not spaces the sign was trailing:
    (a) The string should be right-aligned otherwise the sign was incorrectly detached e.g. Δ1Δ-Δ, and the string must be rejected.
    (b) Move the first string to the target aligned on the second last position and put the sign in the last position.
    (c) Reject a string without enough leading space as too long.
    (d) Transform leading spaces to zeros.
    (e) Reject a string that does not pass the numeric class test for strings with trailing signs.
    (f) Success!
*8. When the second string is not spaces the sign was leading.
    (a) The string should be left-aligned otherwise the sign was incorrectly detached, e.g. Δ-Δ23Δ, and the string must be rejected.
    (b) Align it to the right in the target.
    (c) Reject a string without enough leading space as too long.
    (d) Put the sign in position 4 and any leading zeros needed beyond this point.
    (e) Reject a string that does not pass the numeric class test for strings with leading signs.
    (f) Success!

* = Steps brought forward from the strategy for signed numbers

---

Figure 9.23 Strategy for signed numbers with decimal points

SELF-CHECK QUESTION

Q What would be the nesting effect of writing program accept2 without using the go to statement? Try to draft an outline similar to Fig. 9.15(a) and having done so try to draw a flowgraph of both accept2 and the outline. Which has the least complex flowgraph? Why?

9.6 ACCEPTING NUMBERS WITH DECIMAL POINTS

The problem of allowing for decimal points is more straightforward than was that for allowing signs. The strategy is given in Fig. 9.23 and shows that only a further step needs to be added (step 3) and that this can be done prior to checking for the signs. The overall task is simplified by removing the decimal point from the string altogether and setting w1-scale to the scaling factor. (This factor will be correct provided that the string passes all of the other tests.) Numbers with no decimal point will have a scale factor of zero and for each shift to the left the factor is increased by one. Thus 10 has a scale factor of zero but 12.230 has a scale factor of 3. (The scale factor is thus the power of 10 by which the whole number input must be divided in order to arrive at the scaled number.)

The final program is accept3 which is listed in Fig. 9.24. It uses nearly every statement and feature that we have examined so far in COBOL and therefore is well worth a careful reading.

```
 1 identification division.
 2 program-id. accept3.
 3*Purpose: Determine whether or not a string contains a valid
 4*         signed number.
 5
 6 environment division.
 7
 8 data division.
 9 working-storage section.
10 01  w1-rec.
11     03   w1-string              pic x(21).
12     03   w1-ref                 pic 99.
13          88   w1-max            value 21.
14          88   w1-min            value 00.
15     03   w1-leadzeroes          pic 99.
16
17     03   w1-variations.
18          05   w1-trails         pic x(21) just right.
19          05   filler redefines w1-trails.
20               07   filler      pic x.
21               07   w1-trailsleft  pic x(20).
22          05   w1-leads          pic x(21).
23
24     03   w1-signs.
25          05   w1-sign           pic x.
26          05   w1-signctr        pic 99.
27               88   w1-no-sign   value 00.
28               88   w1-one-sign  value 01.
29               88   w1-bad-sign  value 02 thru 22.
30
```

```cobol
31      03  w1-decimals.
32          05  w1-scalectr         pic 99.
33              88  w1-unscaled     value 00.
34              88  w1-scaled       value 01.
35              88  w1-bad-scale    value 02 thru 22.
36          05  w1-posttotal        pic 99.
37          05  w1-postspace        pic 99.
38          05  w1-decworker        pic x(21).
39          05  w1-predec           pic 99.
40          05  w1-postdec          pic 99.
41
42      03  w1-realigned            pic x(21) just right.
43
44      03  filler redefines w1-realigned.
45          05  filler              pic xx.
46          05  w1-signleads        pic s9(18) sign leading  separate.
47
48      03  w1-trailaligned redefines w1-realigned.
49          05  filler              pic xx.
50          05  w1-signtrails       pic s9(18) sign trailing separate.
51
52 linkage section.
53 01  l1-rec.
54      03  l1-string               pic x(21).
55      03  l1-number               pic s9(18).
56      03  l1-length               pic 99.
57      03  l1-scale                pic 99.
58      03  l1-decision             pic 99.
59          88  l1-success          value 00.
60          88  l1-empty-input      value 01.
61          88  l1-too-long         value 10.
62          88  l1-bad-numeric      value 11.
63          88  l1-bad-sign         value 12.
64          88  l1-bad-scale        value 13.
65
66 procedure division using l1-rec.
67 para1.
68*Step 1
69     accept w1-string
70     move w1-string to l1-string
71     move zero to l1-number
72                   l1-length
73                   l1-scale
74     set l1-success to true
75
76*Step 2
77     evaluate true
78       when   w1-string = space
79         set l1-empty-input to true
80         go to para-exit
81       when   w1-string(21:1) not = space
82         set l1-too-long to true
83         go to para-exit
84     end-evaluate
85
```

```
 86*Step 3
 87      move zero to w1-posttotal
 88                   w1-postspace
 89                   w1-scalectr
 90      inspect w1-string
 91        tallying w1-scalectr for all "."
 92      evaluate true
 93        when  w1-bad-scale
 94          set l1-bad-scale to true
 95          go to para-exit
 96        when  w1-scaled
 97          inspect w1-string
 98            tallying w1-posttotal for characters after initial "."
 99
100          move zero to w1-signctr
101          inspect w1-string
102            tallying w1-signctr for all "+" after initial "."
103                                all "-" after initial "."
104          evaluate true
105            when  w1-bad-sign
106              set l1-bad-sign to true
107              go to para-exit
108          end-evaluate
109
110          inspect w1-string
111            tallying w1-postspace for all space after initial "."
112
113          compute l1-scale = w1-posttotal - w1-postspace - w1-signctr
114
115          compute w1-predec  = 21 - (w1-posttotal + 1)
116          evaluate true
117            when  w1-string(w1-predec:1) numeric
118              move w1-string(1:w1-predec) to w1-decworker
119            when  other
120              set l1-bad-numeric to true
121              go to para-exit
122          end-evaluate
123
124          compute w1-postdec = w1-predec + 2
125          compute w1-predec  = w1-predec + 1
126
127          evaluate true
128            when  w1-string(w1-postdec:1) numeric
129              move w1-string(w1-postdec:) to w1-decworker(w1-predec:)
130            when  other
131              set l1-bad-numeric to true
132              go to para-exit
133          end-evaluate
134          move w1-decworker to w1-string
135*         The string may still not be numeric or have faulty signs
136      end-evaluate
137
```

```
138*Step 4
139     set w1-no-sign to true
140     inspect w1-string
141       tallying w1-signctr for all "+" all"-"
142     evaluate true
143       when   w1-bad-sign
144         set l1-bad-sign to true
145         go to para-exit
146     end-evaluate
147
148*Step 5
149     evaluate true
150       when   w1-no-sign
151         move space to w1-realigned
152         set w1-max to true
153         perform test before until w1-min
154           evaluate w1-string(w1-ref:1) not = space
155             when   true
156               move w1-string(1:w1-ref) to w1-realigned
157               set w1-min to true
158             when   false
159               compute w1-ref = w1-ref - 1
160           end-evaluate
161         end-perform
162
163         evaluate w1-realigned(1:3) not = space
164           when   true
165             set l1-too-long to true
166             go to para-exit
167         end-evaluate
168
169         inspect  w1-realigned(4:)
170           replacing leading space by zero
171         move zero to w1-leadzeroes
172         inspect  w1-realigned(4:)
173           tallying w1-leadzeroes for leading zero
174
175         evaluate w1-realigned(4:) not numeric
176           when   true
177             set l1-bad-numeric to true
178             go to para-exit
179         end-evaluate
180
181         move w1-realigned(4:) to l1-number
182         compute l1-length = 18 - w1-leadzeroes
183*        unsigned input ok
184         go to para-exit
185     end-evaluate
186
187*Step 6 - only single signs have survived to this step
188     move spaces to w1-trails
189                   w1-leads
190                   w1-sign
191     unstring w1-string
192       delimited "+" or "-"
193       into    w1-trails delimiter w1-sign
194               w1-leads
195
```

```
196*Step 7
197      evaluate true
198         when   w1-trails not = spaces and w1-leads not = spaces
199            set l1-bad-sign to true
200            go to para-exit
201         when   w1-trails = spaces and w1-leads = spaces
202            set l1-bad-sign to true
203            go to para-exit
204         when   w1-trails not = spaces
205            evaluate w1-trails(21:1) = space
206               when   true
207                  set l1-bad-sign to true
208                  go to para-exit
209            end-evaluate
210
211            move w1-trailsleft to w1-trailaligned
212
213            evaluate w1-realigned(1:2) not = space
214               when   true
215                  set l1-too-long to true
216                  go to para-exit
217            end-evaluate
218
219            inspect w1-realigned(3:18)
220               replacing leading space by zero
221            move zero to w1-leadzeroes
222            inspect w1-realigned(3:18)
223               tallying w1-leadzeroes for leading zero
224
225            evaluate w1-realigned(3:18) not numeric
226               when   true
227                  set l1-bad-numeric to true
228                  go to para-exit
229            end-evaluate
230
231            move w1-sign to w1-realigned(21:1)
232            move w1-signtrails to l1-number
233            compute l1-length = 18 - w1-leadzeroes
234*           trailing sign input ok
235
236*Step 8
237         when   w1-leads not = spaces
238            evaluate w1-leads(1:1) = space
239               when   true
240                  set l1-bad-sign to true
241                  go to para-exit
242            end-evaluate
243
244            move space to w1-realigned
245            set w1-max to true
246            perform test before until w1-min
247               evaluate    w1-leads(w1-ref:1) not = space
248                  when      true
249                     move w1-leads(1:w1-ref) to w1-realigned
250                     set w1-min to true
251                  when      false
252                     compute w1-ref = w1-ref - 1
253               end-evaluate
254            end-perform
255
```

```
256            evaluate w1-realigned(1:3) not = space
257               when    true
258                  set l1-too-long to true
259                  go to para-exit
260            end-evaluate
261
262            inspect w1-realigned(4:)
263               replacing leading space by zero
264            move zero to w1-leadzeroes
265            inspect w1-realigned(4:)
266               tallying w1-leadzeroes for leading zero
267
268            evaluate w1-realigned(4:) not numeric
269               when    true
270                  set l1-bad-numeric to true
271                  go to para-exit
272            end-evaluate
273
274            move w1-sign to w1-realigned(3:1)
275            compute l1-length = 18 - w1-leadzeroes
276            move w1-signleads to l1-number
277*           leading sign input ok
278       end-evaluate.
279
280 para-exit.
281      exit program.
282
283 end program accept3
```

Figure 9.24 Program accept3

9.7 DOCUMENTATION FOR PROGRAM ACCEPT3

In previous chapters we have documented programs as a way of trying to understand them. This has included pseudo-code, flowcharts, flowgraphs, structure charts, and record layouts as well as program narratives written in English and, most importantly, the programs themselves. Program accept3 could benefit from any or all of these forms of documentation provided that they supplied a useful addition to a direct reading of the program and saved readers the task of having to write draft documentation themselves as a way of understanding what the program is intended to do. For example, a short narrative including a pseudo-code outline of the program which included the escape structure discussed previously would be useful and might ease the mind of many readers who would be frightened by seeing the first go to in the program.

In general, most of the documentation we have considered so far has been aimed at other COBOL programmers who are assumed to have the same level of technical competence as the average programmer. They in a sense are users of a program if they have to read it or maintain it at some future date.

However, there is another class of user that requires documentation. This is the person who may wish to use a program without ever reading its contents. These users are divided into two main groups, the first of which is external users who require documentation at the system level and who cannot be assumed to have any degree of computing expertise. Programmers are notoriously bad at writing this form of documentation, as anyone who has tried to use a text editor or a similarly complex piece of software that has been documented by a programmer will testify. This is best left to a technical documentation expert if one can be found to do the task. At a minimum you should attempt a study of this topic in itself before undertaking a documentation task of any complexity.

The second group consists of programmers and other systems personnel who may wish to incorporate your program into another system. To do so they need a detailed statement of how the program maps its inputs to its outputs. Documents that accomplish this go by many names. We will refer to this form of documentation as a *detailed system specification*. It is detailed in that it must provide a description of all inputs and outputs as well as the rules that govern how they are transformed. It is at the system level because it does not disclose to the reader any of the means that the program uses internally to achieve its goals. Ideally it should be as independent from the language in which the program is written as is feasible. And it is a specification in that if the user prepares an input as described, then the program should produce the output that is specified for that input.

Figure 9.25 gives a detailed system specification for program accept3. It is for the most part derived from an analysis of the purpose of the parameter. By reading this document another programmer should be able to use the program to get numeric input without needing to read the program. Typically specifications of this type are produced while systems of programs are being designed so that all of the personnel associated with a project can work on parts of the system with a degree of independence. As the system is developed they are improved so that at the end of development they stand as a permanent feature of the overall system's documentation. It is also common for functional programs to be documented in a similar way when they are used across whole sets of systems or are issued in libraries to subscribing users. Therefore whether you are writing a few programs that you intend to reuse yourself in the future or whether you are writing programs to be used by a wider audience you should practise writing documents in this style.

Detailed system specification

NAME:	Accept3	VERSION: 1.0
DATE:	April 1, 1990	
AUTHOR:	Raymond W. Norman	
IMPLEMENTATION:	Standard COBOL	
COMPILER DEPENDENCIES:	None	
MACHINE DEPENDENCIES:	None	

General purpose

Accept3 uses the COBOL ACCEPT statement to get a string of up to 21 characters from the keyboard. It then determines whether or not the string holds a valid number.

Definition of numbers

(a) An unsigned number is assumed to be positive and may have:
- up to eighteen digits on input including leading zeros
- an optional single decimal point (".") as an indicator of scale embedded within the digits. Thus 0.25 is a valid number but .25 is not.

(b) A signed number is an unsigned number as defined above with a single sign ("+" or "−") either immediately leading the number or immediately trailing it.
(c) Minus zero is an invalid signed number.

The following table gives some examples of valid numbers:

```
          1         2
123456789012345678901

+0.2
0.1-
                  -5
100000000000000000-
 999999999999999999+
  777777777777777777
  88888888.8888888888+
12.96
```

Requirements:
(a) Accept3 must be passed a single REFERENCE parameter of 45 characters that conforms to the following COBOL record description:

```
01   l1-record.
     03   l1-string         pic x(21).
     03   l1-number         pic s9(18).
     03   l1-length         pic 99.
     03   l1-scale          pic 99.
     03   l1-decision       pic 99.
          88  l1-success        value 00.
          88  l1-empty-input    value 01.
          88  l1-too-long       value 10.
          88  l1-bad-numeric    value 11.
          88  l1-bad-sign       value 12.
          88  l1-bad-scale      value 13.
```

The string that was input by the user is always returned in l1-string.

(b) When control is returned to the calling program with success:

l1-number: Holds a signed 18-digit numeric value. (It will contain as many leading zeros as are required to make up the full 18-digit length.)

l1-length: Holds a length in the range of 0 to 18. This is the length of the number excluding leading zeros.

l1-scale: Holds the scale factor in the range of 1 to 18. It represents the power of 10 by which the number should be divided in order to be scaled correctly. Thus a scale factor of 0 means that the number should be divided by 1 and a scale factor of 2 means that it should be divided by 100. (Another way of understanding the scale factor is to think of it as the number of positions from the right that the decimal point needs to be shifted into l1-number.)

(c) When control is returned with any other decision l1-number, l1-length and l1-scale are undefined. The decision taken will be one of the following:

```
empty-input:  spaces found
long-number:  number probably bigger than 18 digits
bad-numeric:  unable to decode input
bad-sign:     faulty sign detected (too many or detached)
bad-scale:    faulty scale detected (too many or misplaced)
```

Figure 9.25 Detailed system specification for program accept3

9.8 FILTERS AND MAPPING FUNCTIONS

Program accept3 takes any string of up to 21 alphanumeric characters and correctly maps it into its parameter record. By this we mean that immediately after the return of control to any program that calls accept3, the contents of the parameter record correctly describe what was found on input.

We will not attempt a formal proof of the mapping function it implements but merely note that all programs must be able to supply a correct output for every possible input. In other words, there should be no input for which there is not a defined output. (The correct output might of course be the decision **bad-numeric** with no defined values for the other items.) A program written in this way can be called with confidence because the calling program can rely on its behaviour according to its specification in much the same way that we can use statements in COBOL such as **perform** or **evaluate** by relying on their specification within the language. To the extent that we can write correct, functional programs that always produce a predictable result we have extended the original programming language by increasing its functionality. Thus program accept3 provides a means for inputting numbers from the keyboard and as such can be considered as an extension to the accept statement.

Programs such as these are often referred to as filters when they are used in a stream of data because they separate undesirable from desirable inputs. (See Fig. 9.26.)

All systems need filters of one type or another to ensure that the data which enters the system conforms to a specification of correct processable data. It is usual practice to validate input at the point it enters the system so that other parts of the system which may wish to use the data at a later stage are protected from bad input. Therefore filters are commonly used as part of input validation. However, they can also be used on output to filter a report out of a stream of data. In general we can think of a filter as a program that converts a data stream from one known form into another for the benefit of some process that will use the data further downstream. Thus the idea of a filter is closely linked to the idea of data flowing through programs and from one program to another.

Using filters and functional programs has a number of clear advantages:

1. Closely related tasks are dealt with in the one program constructed on general principles according to a specific strategy.
2. The program when written in conformity with language standards allows portability between compilers and therefore between environments.
3. In a case where a deliberate choice is made to include non-portable features, these features can be hidden within a program, thereby ensuring that the main application does not incorporate non-portable code. Thus the bulk of the application will remain portable even if certain programs need to be rewritten.

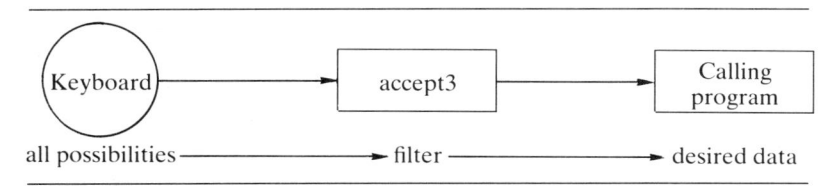

Figure 9.26 Program accept3 viewed as a filter

4. The filter or function can be tested independently from any application that may require it.
5. The program is reusable in other applications.
6. The function of the program can be defined clearly in terms of the state of the data in its parameter record immediately prior to its being called and immediately after its return of control. This assists not only in testing the program but also in documenting it for use by other programmers.
7. The program can be used as a model for creating new programs that may have a different but related mapping function. For example, with reference to accept3:
   (a) If a new filter includes the mapping function of the original it may replace the original in subsequent applications. For example, it would be possible to enhance accept3 to allow commas as optional separators (e.g. 2,143,456.78). In this case the new filter is more general than the original and can replace it in applications.
   (b) If a new filter restricts the mapping function of the original it may be useful for other purposes. For example, it would be possible to write a new program in part based on accept3 to allow dates as six digit numbers with optional separators between pairs of digits and with specified range checking on each pair (e.g. 12/12/90).

9.9 SCREEN MANAGEMENT

The final topic in this chapter departs from numeric input and considers the problem of screen management. This involves sending special characters to the terminal screen such as the escape character.

Many applications manage the terminal screen and cursor directly so that the whole of the screen can be used as a single stable area by a program. Most dialects of COBOL have been extended to provide screen management features even though there is no standard agreement on how these should be introduced into the language. In many versions the display and accept statements have been extended with additional clauses that provide features such as *cursor control* and *screen protection*. However, in other implementations of COBOL similar features have been included by extending the data division entries with screen related information.

It may be some years before screen management features are incorporated into standard COBOL. However, even when this is done it is likely that many different mutually exclusive alternatives will be included in order that leading competing dialects can claim consistency with the standard. In other words, even with the advent of screen management standards it is likely that COBOL programs that use these features may not be portable between compilers adhering to the published standard.

Therefore this section presents a strategy for isolating screen management features within programs that can be reused by other programs as a way of implementing screen management functions for a calling program.

As discussed in earlier chapters, the display statement can be used to write alphanumeric strings to the keyboard. Until now we have only been concerned with writing printable characters to the screen. However, any string of bytes is by definition alphanumeric and therefore can be written to the screen.

Function	Control characters
Erase complete screen	⟨ESC⟩[2J
Move cursor to *lin, col*	⟨ESC⟩[*lin;col*H
Show cursor	⟨ESC⟩[?25h
Hide cursor	⟨ESC⟩[?25l

Figure 9.27 Some examples of VT control codes

When terminals receive printable characters they display these on the screen in a way that is consistent with the current screen state. However, the screen and its cursor can be altered prior to the displaying of printable characters by sending the terminal a string of control characters that changes the current screen state.

There is no international standard for terminal control characters. Therefore the example shown in Fig. 9.26 uses the widely available VT standard.

Figure 9.27 shows four control codes that when written to a VT terminal will cause it to change its screen state. In all cases the first character is the escape character from the ASCII table. (It is shown in angle brackets as ⟨ESC⟩ to denote that it cannot be printed.) When a VT terminal receives this character it checks subsequent characters to determine which function is required and then performs the required function.

For example, the escape character followed by the three printable characters "[2J" will cause the terminal to erase the screen. However, the cursor will still be in the same position that it held prior to erasing the screen. To move the cursor to the first column of the first line the terminal must receive the escape character followed by "[1;1H". (The numbers for lines and columns are 1 to 3 digits without leading zeros. For example the eight characters "⟨ESC⟩[12;15H" will move the cursor to line 12, column 15.)

In order to represent a non-printable character we write a list of symbols and a matching list of values within the special-names paragraph of the environment division:

```
environment division.
configuration section.
special-names.
   [symbolic   symbolic-character-list is integer-value-list.]
```

The symbolic-character-list gives a list of one or more symbols that will be used within the program. The integer-value-list gives the ordinal positions of the required values within the underlying collating sequence.

Program screen1 in Fig. 9.25 only requires the escape character. Therefore the list contains only the one entry:

```
symbolic ESC is 28.
```

Symbols in the list can be any user-defined words. (The above list uses ESC because this is a common abbreviation for this character but ESCAPE, escape, char27 or c27 would all have been equally valid.) The integer value is 28 because this character occupies the 28th position in the ASCII collating sequence.

Once a symbol is defined in this way it can be used within the program as a figurative constant. All of the entries and statements in Fig. 9.28 are legal COBOL.

272 ESSENTIAL COBOL: A FIRST COURSE IN STRUCTURED COBOL

Entry or statement	Comment
01 e1 pic x value ESC. 01 e2 pic x(5) value ESC. 01 e3 pic xxx.	one escape character five escape characters
move ESC to e3 move all ESC to e3 display e1 no advancing display ESC no advancing	e3 becomes ⟨ESC⟩ followed by two spaces e3 becomes three ⟨ESC⟩ characters one ⟨ESC⟩ displayed one ⟨ESC⟩ displayed
move "2J" to e3 display ESC e3 no advancing	e3 given a value and . . . . . . screen erased
display ESC "[1;1H" no advancing display "HELLO" no advancing	cursor moved to line 1, column 1 five characters displayed in the top left-hand corner
display ESC "[10;2H" no advancing display "BYE" no advancing	three characters displayed on line 10 beginning at column 2
display ESC "[2J" no advancing	screen erased

Figure 9.28 Effect of using a symbolic character within a COBOL program

```
 1 identification division.
 2 program-id. screen1.
 3
 4 environment division.
 5 configuration section.
 6 special-names.
 7    symbolic ESC is 28.
 8
 9 data division.
10 working-storage section.
11 01  w1-coordinate-lengths.
12     03  w1-refline                    pic 9.
13         88  w1-line-valid             value 0 thru 2.
14     03  w1-refcol                     pic 9.
15         88  w1-col-valid              value 0 thru 2.
16
17 linkage section.
18 01  l1-rec.
19     03  l1-argument                   pic 99.
20         88  l1-erase-screen           value 01.
21         88  l1-new-cursor             value 02.
22         88  l1-hide-cursor            value 03.
23         88  l1-show-cursor            value 04.
24     03  l1-cursor-coordinates.
25         05  l1-line                   pic 999.
26             88  l1-line-valid         value 001 thru 024.
27         05  l1-col                    pic 999.
28             88  l1-col-valid          value 001 thru 080.
29     03  l1-result                     pic 99.
30         88  l1-success                value 01.
31         88  l1-bad-cursor             value 02.
32         88  l1-unknown                value 99.
33
```

```cobol
34 procedure division using l1-rec.
35 para1.
36     set l1-success to true
37
38     evaluate true
39       when    l1-erase-screen
40         display ESC "[2J" no advancing
41
42       when    l1-new-cursor
43         evaluate l1-line numeric and l1-col numeric
44           when    false
45             set l1-bad-cursor to true
46             go to para-exit
47         end-evaluate
48
49         evaluate l1-line-valid and l1-col-valid
50           when    false
51             set l1-bad-cursor to true
52             go to para-exit
53         end-evaluate
54
55         move zero to w1-refline
56         inspect l1-line
57           tallying w1-refline for
58             leading zeroes
59         evaluate w1-line-valid
60           when    false
61             set l1-bad-cursor to true
62             go to para-exit
63         end-evaluate
64
65         move zero to w1-refcol
66         inspect l1-col
67           tallying w1-refcol for
68             leading zeroes
69         evaluate w1-col-valid
70           when    false
71             set l1-bad-cursor to true
72             go to para-exit
73         end-evaluate
74
75         compute w1-refline = w1-refline + 1
76         compute w1-refcol  = w1-refcol  + 1
77         display ESC "["
78           l1-line(w1-refline:) ";" l1-col(w1-refcol:) "H" no advancing
79
80       when    l1-hide-cursor
81         display ESC "[?25l" no advancing
82
83       when    l1-show-cursor
84         display ESC "[?25h" no advancing
85       when    other
86         set l1-unknown to true
87     end-evaluate.
88
89 para-exit.
90     exit program.
91
92 end program screen1
```

Figure 9.29 Program screen1

274 ESSENTIAL COBOL: A FIRST COURSE IN STRUCTURED COBOL

The purpose of program screen1 (Fig. 9.29) is to implement the four functions for the benefit of a calling program so that it need not contain statements such as those in Fig. 9.28. To do this program screen1 uses a single parameter record (line 18) that requires the calling program to set the argument to one of the four required functions. *New-cursor* is the only function that requires cursor coordinates. These must always be supplied for a new cursor and must be within range (lines 26 and 28).

A calling program will continue to display text and accept inputs but prior to doing so it can call screen1 to change the state of the terminal screen. For example, if a calling program defines the parameter record used by screen1 (line 18) it could make the following call to move the cursor to the 12th column of line 10:

```
set l1-new-cursor to true
move 10 to l1-line
move 12 to l1-col
call "screen1" using reference l1-rec
```

The initialization and call could also be accomplished in two statements instead of 4:

```
move "021012" to l1-rec
call "screen1" using reference l1-rec
```

Program screen1 is not a complicated program and should present few problems. It also uses go to statements as a means of implementing the escape structure. The forward reference to the para-exit paragraph is used only when the input that is passed to the program is found to be defective.

For example, the evaluate statement at line 43 checks to see that the line and column coordinates are numeric when a move to a new cursor position has been requested. If they are not the go to causes a transfer of control to the end of the program because no further processing can be done. However, if they are numeric then the evaluate statement at line 47 checks to ensure that they are in range. (Note that the data must have passed the numeric test before it can be used as numeric data at line 49. The result of using an item as numeric data when it has not passed the numeric test is always undefined.)

The main area of complication in screen1 is the representation of the cursor coordinates. The VT standard says that the cursor value must be 1 to 3 digits but without leading zeros. (It is possible to reset the screen so that it has more than 24 lines and 80 columns. This is why 3 digits are allowed.) Therefore the program checks a 3-digit numeric string for leading zeros and uses reference modification to avoid writing the zeros to the screen.

The evaluate at line 49 guarantees that the line and column are in range. Thus at lines 55 and 65 the coordinates are treated as numbers in the range of 001 to 999 and the number of leading zeros is determined in each case. The two compute statements increment the reference modifiers so that they point to the the start of the number excluding the leading zeros. The display statement at line 77 uses the reference modifiers to write the new cursor position to the terminal.

Screen1 is written as a model of a functional program that can be called by programs that need to manage the screen. In a sense it sits above the functions of the terminal as a means of offering up the functionality of the terminal in a more general and machine independent form. As such it aids portability because lines such as line 40 which are specific to the VT standard need only appear in this one program.

9.10 EXERCISES

1. Rewrite program getnum3 as getnum4 which contains a loop that can be terminated from the keyboard. Getnum4 should successively call program accept1a and display the results of inputs at the screen. Thus you can use it to test accept1a. (You should display a prompt for input in getnum4 immediately before the call to accept1a because it does not display any prompts itself.)
2. Write a detailed system specification for screen1.
3. Write pseudo-code and a flowgraph for step 3 of program accept3.
4. Program accept3 could be enhanced to allow commas as separators between groups of three digits in the whole number portion of an input. Commas are allowed only in the whole number portion, therefore any validation for commas should occur before any decimal point is removed. Write pseudo-code for a new step that can check for legal commas and remove them from the string prior to further validation. (Delay writing and testing this program until the end of the next chapter.)
5. Write program date1 to accept eight character date strings with separators between the day, month, and year digit pairs. Rewrite getnum4 as getnum5 in order to test date1. Write a detailed system specification for date1 prior to writing the program. Amend the specification after you have finished and then compare the amended version to the original in order to determine those aspects of the problem you omitted from the original.
6. Write busy1 to call screen1 and draw a set of boxes with decreasing sides on the screen (Fig. 9.30).

    Your program should start at the top left-hand corner and work around the outside towards the centre. It might help you in testing if you draw each side with a

```
XXXXXXXXXXXXXXXXXXXXXXXXX
                         X
XXXXXXXXXXXXXXXXXXXXXX   X
X                    X   X
X   XXXXXXXXXXXXXXX  X   X
X   X             X  X   X
X   X   XXXXXXXX  X  X   X
X   X   X      X  X  X   X
X   X   X  XXX X  X  X   X
X   X   X  X   X  X  X   X
X   X   X  XXXXXX X  X   X
X   X   X         X  X   X
X   X   XXXXXXXXXXX  X   X
X   X                X   X
X   XXXXXXXXXXXXXXXXXX   X
X                        X
XXXXXXXXXXXXXXXXXXXXXXXXXX
```

Figure 9.30 Screen image for program busy1

different digit or letter. Try drawing the shape on a piece of squared paper beforehand so that you know the correct coordinates for the shape before you start.

7   Write busy2 in which the coordinates are contained in a table. The program can then take successive sets of coordinates from the table and call screen1 from within a loop.

8   Write form1 to draw a simple form on the screen asking for inputs such as name and address. Then go back to the appropriate locations on the screen and accept the inputs.

9   Rewrite form1 as form2 in which the form coordinates are held in a table. The table should also contain the strings of texts and their lengths so that the whole of the form can be written by a single loop that uses successive entries in the table. (A text string can be output using the length as a reference modifier.)

10
COMPLEX PROGRAM STRUCTURES

COBOL is widely used in industry to develop application software for large data processing systems. In most of these systems there is a requirement for programs to share other generally useful programs and common source text. By the end of this chapter you will understand how to share the object code of compiled programs between different object programs as well as how to share source text between different source programs. In addition, you will have been introduced to the **initial** and **common** attributes for programs as well as the **global** and **external** data attributes for records and files.

10.1 SEPARATE PROGRAM COMPILATION

Until now we have copied the source text from one file to another when we have wanted a particular program to be included in different programs. This approach has a number of practical problems associated with it. Firstly, the source text will be reproduced within all the programs which use it. Thus the text files of programs will be unnecessarily enlarged by the inclusion of duplicated programs. Secondly, the proliferation of program texts will create problems should a particular program need to be changed. Not only will all text copies of a program need to be amended but also each containing program will need to be recompiled in the process. The compile time overheads alone that are required to recompile all programs within a large application consisting of many programs will be a particular disadvantage. Thirdly, the object code will exist within the object version of each program. Thus not only will the source text contain duplication but also this duplication will be mirrored within the object code versions of the programs.

Therefore COBOL supports separate compilation for called programs as a way of managing these overheads and of supporting separate program development. Programs

Root
- First program encountered by the linker
- Exists at nesting level 1
- Can contain nested programs

Nested
- Directly or indirectly contained
- Exists at level n where $n > 1$
- Can contain nested programs

Internal separately compiled
- Internal to the text file of the root
- Appended after the end program header of the root
- Exists at nesting level 1
- Can contain nested programs

External separately compiled
- External to the text file of the root
- Has its own object file
- Behaves as if at nesting level 1
- Can contain nested programs

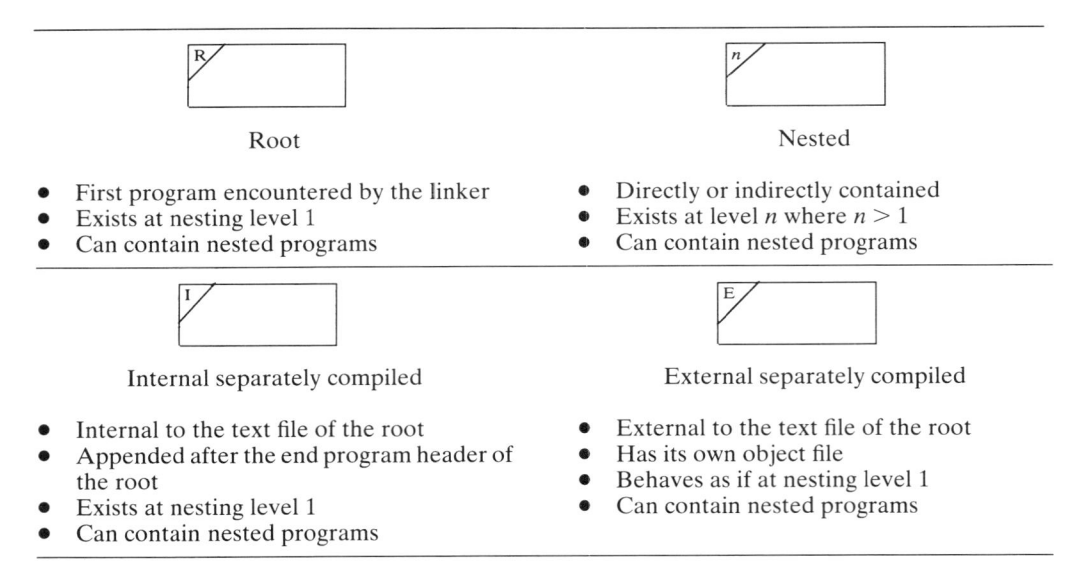

Figure 10.1 Program classification – four main ways

such as the number validation programs and the screen handler from the previous chapter were developed to solve general problems. By adjusting our methods to use this feature these programs can be stored in reusable forms so that they can be easily incorporated into new applications as required.

We need to distinguish between a called program that is nested within the source text of its calling program and a called program that is separately compiled and therefore not part of the compilation unit of the calling program. To do this we will use the terms *nested* and *separately compiled*. In addition, we will see that a separately compiled and called program may be within the same text file as its calling program or within a different text file. We will use the terms *internal* and *external** to distinguish this relationship.

As a result of these new terms we can see that COBOL programs can be classified in the four main ways outlined in Fig. 10.1.

The root is always a special case. It and its nested programs are always compiled together but separately from other programs. Therefore the terms 'internal separately compiled' and 'external separately compiled' describe possible relationships between the root and other programs that are not nested within it. (By definition nested programs always have a nesting level that is greater than 1 and separately compiled programs including the root always have a nesting level equal to 1.)

To begin with we will consider external, separately compiled programs. These programs have no nesting relationship with those programs that call them. Figure 10.2 shows a structure chart where root program K calls external program L. Program K also directly contains program M at nesting level 2. The 'E' in the top left-hand corner reminds us that program L is an external, separately compiled program which is not nested within any other program.

---

* The concepts of external program and external data attribute are not related.

COMPLEX PROGRAM STRUCTURES 279

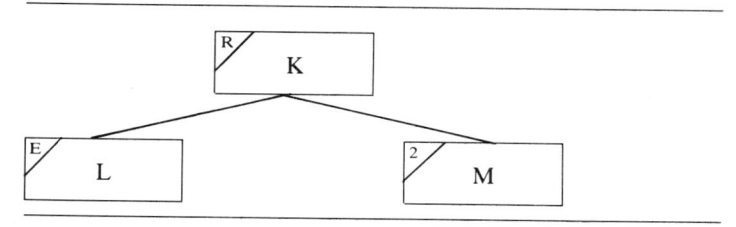

Figure 10.2 Relationship between separately compiled and nested programs

Both L and M could contain nested programs and program K could contain additional children at level 2. Further children such as these would be added in the usual way and annotated with the appropriate level number.

We will start by considering the number validation programs from the previous chapter as examples of programs that can be separately compiled as external programs.

As with other programs a separately compiled program must be tested. In cases where the calling program is not written or not available it is usual to write a driver program. We first encountered a driver program in Chapter 5 when lookup1 was written merely as a means to demonstrate that mencken1 functioned correctly. Drivers are often written by programmers for testing purposes and then thrown away. As such they are not part of a delivered application program even though their writing and testing in themselves create overheads. Fortunately most drivers look much the same and with a bit of practice it is usually possible to write a new driver based on the source text of a previous one.

Figure 10.3 lists a driver for the accept programs. Its purpose is to test that any one of the programs meets its intended specification independent of any particular application.

```
1  identification division.
2  program-id. driver1.
3 *Purpose: This program is a test driver for the accept programs.
4
5  environment division.
6
7  data division.
8  working-storage section.
9  01  k1-string              pic x.
10     88  k1-eok              value "Q" "q".
11
12 01  w2-rec.
13     03  w2-string           pic x(21).
14     03  w2-number           pic s9(18).
15     03  w2-length           pic 99.
16     03  w2-scale            pic 99.
17     03  w2-decision         pic 99.
18         88  w2-success          value 00.
19         88  w2-empty-input      value 01.
20         88  w2-too-long         value 10.
21         88  w2-bad-numeric      value 11.
22         88  w2-bad-sign         value 12.
23         88  w2-bad-scale        value 13.
24
```

```
25 01   w3-progname                  pic x(10).
26
27 01   s4-number                    pic s9(18) sign leading separate.
28
29 procedure division.
30 para1.
31     display "driver1 begins"
32     display "Type RET or 'Q' to quit: " no advancing
33     accept k1-string
34
35     evaluate k1-eok
36       when    false
37         display "program name: " no advancing
38         accept w3-progname
39     end-evaluate
40
41     perform test before until k1-eok
42       display "********** test case **********"
43       display "                    1         2"
44       display "           123456789012345678901"
45       display "string:    " no advancing
46       call w3-progname using reference w2-rec
47
48       evaluate true
49         when    w2-success
50           display "success"
51         when    w2-empty-input
52           display "empty-input"
53         when    w2-too-long
54           display "too-long"
55         when    w2-bad-numeric
56           display "bad-numeric"
57         when    w2-bad-sign
58           display "bad-sign"
59         when    w2-bad-scale
60           display "bad-scale"
61       end-evaluate
62
63       display "w2-number: " w2-number
64       move w2-number to s4-number
65       display "s4-number:"  s4-number
66       display "length:    " w2-length
67       display "input:     " w2-string
68       display "scale:     " w2-scale
69       display "Type RET or 'Q' to quit: " no advancing
70       accept k1-string
71     end-perform
72
73     display "*******************************"
74     display "driver1 ends"
75     stop run.
76
77 end program driver1
```

Figure 10.3 Program driver1 – a driver to test program accept3

The reason that driver1 can be used to test any of these programs is mainly due to the fact that all of the accept programs have a common parameter interface. We will begin by considering a test for program accept3.

At line 42 driver1 displays a visual typing guide for a test case. The call statement at line 46 calls an accept program to provide an input as well as its decision concerning that input.

Lines 48 to 68 then display at the screen the data from the parameter record and messages to give clues concerning the behaviour of the called program. Thus driver1 does not provide test data directly but it provides a means of harnessing the called program to the keyboard and screen so that it can be tested.

The call at line 46 is of particular interest in that it uses the identifier option instead of the literal option as in previous programs. Prior to the execution of the call statement the data item w3-progname must be initialized to the name of a valid program. (In this example the valid name will be 'accept3'.)

The initialization of w3-progname will be done by the accept statement at line 38. We will respond to the prompt by typing "accept3", so that the item holds a correct value at the time the call is made.

There are two consequences of this calling feature which are of immediate interest. Firstly, the calling program does not define the name of a program as a literal. This means that this program can be used over and over without the need to recompile it. Therefore using a call with the name specified as an identifier produces a program that can be used to call any program that happens to use the same parameter list. Secondly, if the user types the name of the called program incorrectly in response to the accept statement at line 38, the program will generate a run-time error when it reaches the call statement at line 46. The exact nature of this problem will become clearer when we examine the relevant steps in the development cycle.

Figure 10.4 illustrates the steps that should be followed in order to use program accept3 as an external separately compiled program in conjunction with driver1.

Steps 1 and 2 separately compile the source text for the two programs into separate object code files. These steps can occur at any time and in any order provided that both steps are successfully completed prior to Step 3. Because the first two steps are entirely independent it is impossible for the compiler to check the two programs against each other. Once these two steps are complete there will be two object programs in separate files to match the two original source programs.

Step 3 uses the linker to combine the object code from the two files into a single executable program. By default the file containing the executable program will take the name of the main program. (The root program must always be the first name given as a parameter to the linker because the linker expects to find the first executable statement in this program.)

Even once Step 3 is complete the name of the program that will be called has not been supplied. (Remember: This is supplied at run time by the value that w3-progname holds immediately prior to the call.) Therefore the linker cannot check the validity of the parameters because it does not know the name of the program that will be called.

Although the detection of a possible error has been delayed beyond compile time, separate compilation provides great flexibility for allowing programs to be reused. From a practical point of view it supports the division of work between programmers at the same boundaries as those that exist between programs. In addition, the fact that two programs are compiled at separate times means that they can be written at separate times perhaps by different people who have never met and may work for different organizations.

282 ESSENTIAL COBOL: A FIRST COURSE IN STRUCTURED COBOL

Step 1: successfully compile accept1a. (VAX command: $ cobol accept3⟨RET⟩)

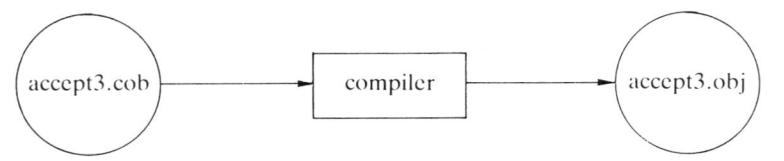

accept3.cob → compiler → accept3.obj

Step 2: successfully compile driver1. (VAX command: $ cobol driver1⟨RET⟩)

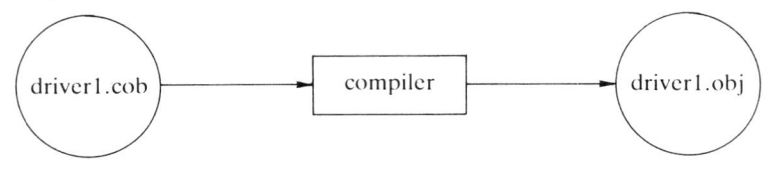

driver1.cob → compiler → driver1.obj

Step 3: link the object code of accept1a into driver1 to form an executable verson of the program. (VAX command: $ link driver1,accept3⟨RET⟩)

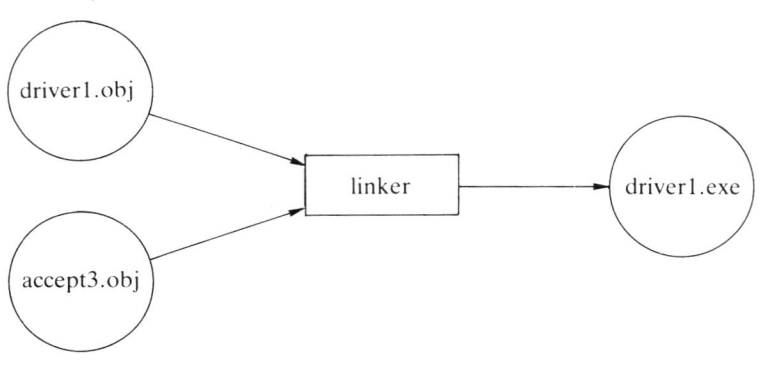

driver1.obj, accept3.obj → linker → driver1.exe

Figure 10.4 Developing a main program and an external called program

This separation highlights how important it is to have well-defined programs with well-defined interfaces. With a high level of correct functional specification it is possible to use a program written at another time or by someone else with a high degree of confidence.

The full format for the call statement includes an exception phrase which can detect that a called program cannot be made available at run time:

$$\text{call} \begin{Bmatrix} \text{literal-1} \\ \text{identifier-1} \end{Bmatrix} \left[\text{using} \begin{Bmatrix} \begin{bmatrix} \text{reference} \\ \text{content} \end{bmatrix} & \text{identifier-1} \end{Bmatrix} \dots \right]$$

$$\begin{bmatrix} \text{exception} \quad \text{statement-1} \\ [\text{not exception} \quad \text{statement-2}] \\ \text{end-call} \end{bmatrix}$$

When the exception phrase is used the not exception phrase can be added as well. If the exception phrases are used then the end-call delimiter should be used because these phrases make the call statement conditional.

Neither of the exception phrases should be used when calling with a literal program-name. The reasons for this become clear when we think about the compile, link, and run operations. If a program is nested and called using a literal it is possible to check the reference at compile time to ensure that it is resolved. If a program is separately compiled and called using a literal it is possible to check the reference at link time to ensure that it is resolved. Therefore literal references can always be checked prior to running the program.

However, when the identifier option is used the name of the program is not available for checking until run time. It is possible that at the time the call is attempted the data item may have a value that cannot be resolved to the name of a program available within the run unit. Therefore the exception phrases assist us in managing this possibility at run time.

For example, the statements at lines 46 to 68 in program driver1 could be changed to:

```
call w3-progname using reference w2-rec
  exception
    display "unknown program name"
    display "Please re-enter: " no advancing
    accept w3-progname
  not exception
    evaluate...
    display...
    move...
    display...
    display...
    display...
    display...
end-call
```

Such a change would enable the program to recover execution in the event that the user entered an incorrect program-name at run time.

SELF-CHECK QUESTIONS

Q Is it possible to call a nested program with the call identifier option?
A Yes.

Q Is it possible for the linker to detect an error in the name of a called nested program prior to run time if the call identifier option is used?
A No. Whether the program is separately compiled and then supplied to the linker or nested it is not possible to detect an error earlier than run time. This is because in both cases the name will not be supplied until run time.

Q Could the compiler or linker detect an error of the above type if the value of the program-name had been given in the working-storage section with a value clause?
A No. To do so would imply a semantic analysis of the program. Therefore checking is still delayed until run time when the call is made. This will be after the values in the working-storage are initialized.

Q Is there any case where the linker can detect possible errors in call statements?

A Most linkers should detect a case where a separately compiled program is called with the call literal option. An error cannot be detected at compile time because the programs are separately compiled. However, the name of the program is known at link time and the linker should be able to determine whether or not a required called program is available.

Q What is the technical term for matching calls with the names of called programs at compile, link, or run time?

A *Resolution*. Thus a nested call with the literal option is resolved at compile time, a call with the literal option to a separately compiled program can be resolved at link time, and a call with the identifer option is resolved at run time.

Q Is it legal to compile accept1a, accept2 and accept3 into separate object versions and then to link all three of them with driver1 into a single executable program?

A This is perfectly legal. The current version of driver1 is written in such a way that you could only test one program in a single run. However, it would be a simple task to amend the main loop of driver1 so that after testing one program it is possible to input the name of another program and test it rather than quit.

You should be aware that the object code for all of the accept programs would be in the executable program at level 1. The structure chart of this program would be as shown in Fig. 10.5.

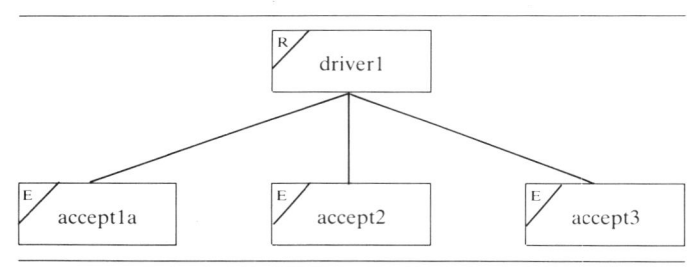

Figure 10.5 Program driver1 linked to three programs

Q What would be the effect of copying the text of the accept programs one after the other into a single text file after the text for driver1?

A The functional result would be the same as that discussed in the previous question and answer, that is, all of the programs would be separately compiled.

Q What would be the difference in the structure chart if the text of programs accept1a, accept2 and accept3 had been copied into the source text of driver3 at nesting level 2?

A The structure charts would be identical except that a nesting level of 2 would be shown in the top left-hand corner.

As we have seen, the run unit produced by the linker can include a number of programs. It is also the case that the unit can include programs with the same program-name. When any two programs have the same name one of them must be directly or indirectly contained within another separately compiled program.

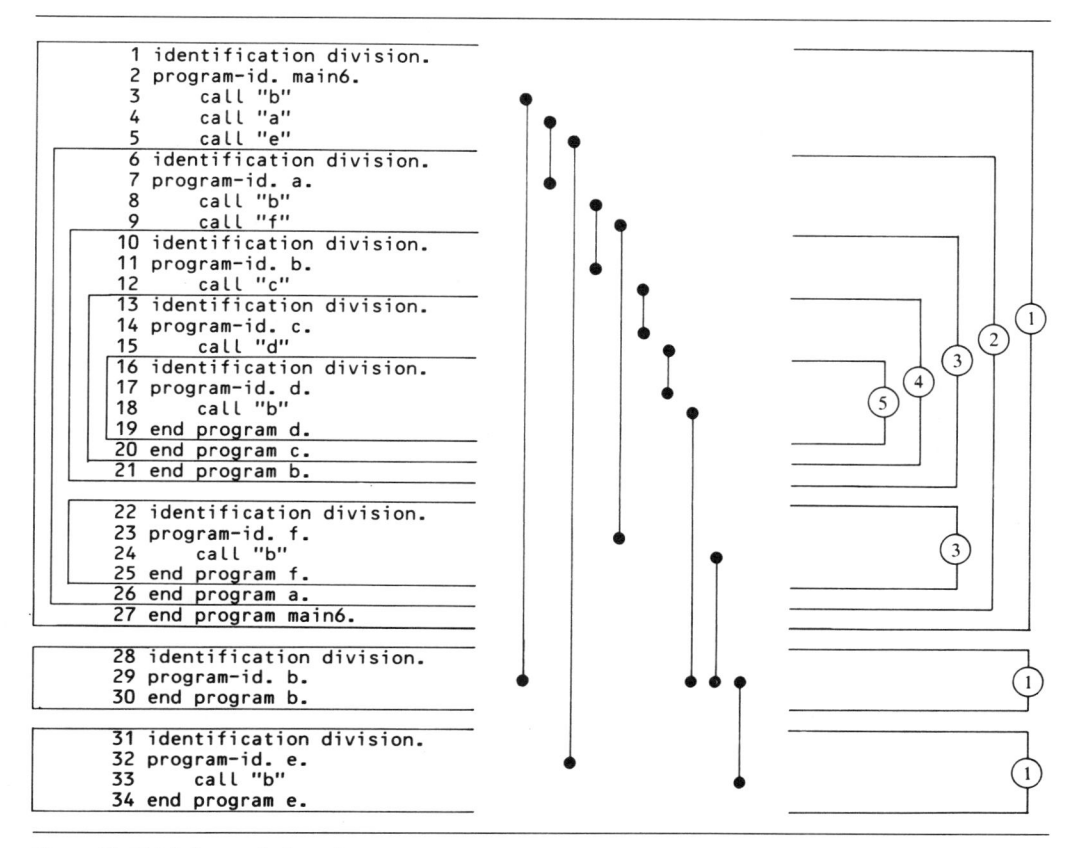

```
 1 identification division.
 2 program-id. main6.
 3     call "b"
 4     call "a"
 5     call "e"
 6 identification division.
 7 program-id. a.
 8     call "b"
 9     call "f"
10 identification division.
11 program-id. b.
12     call "c"
13 identification division.
14 program-id. c.
15     call "d"
16 identification division.
17 program-id. d.
18     call "b"
19 end program d.
20 end program c.
21 end program b.
22 identification division.
23 program-id. f.
24     call "b"
25 end program f.
26 end program a.
27 end program main6.
28 identification division.
29 program-id. b.
30 end program b.
31 identification division.
32 program-id. e.
33     call "b"
34 end program e.
```

Figure 10.6 Main6 – resolution of program-names

Furthermore, within a run unit a separately compiled program can reference any other separately compiled program provided that the calls are not recursive. Figure 10.6 demonstrates these possibilities for the skeleton program main6. It has three programs at level 1. Main6 is the root because it is the first program. Program B (line 28) and program E (line 31) are internal programs at nesting level 1 in the same text file. (They could have been external programs and supplied to the linker. In either case the relationship between them and main6 is the same because they are both separately compiled.)

The vertical lines in the figure show the resolutions for all of the possible calls that are possible within the program structure. The call at line 3 is a call to the separately compiled program B. This is because the program B at line 10 is indirectly contained and therefore not available to main6. However, program A can call program B at line 10 because it is directly contained.

The call in program F is resolved as a call to the separately compiled program. This also happens with program D. This is because neither of these programs directly contain a program B.

SELF-CHECK QUESTIONS

Q Can program B at line 10 call program B?
A Yes. Such a call will be resolved by the separately compiled program B at line 28.

Q If program B at line 28 were removed could program B at line 10 still call program B?
A No. This violates two important rules. Firstly, B is not nested within itself. The call therefore violates the rule which says that in the absence of separately compiled programs a called program must be directly contained. Secondly, even if the call were allowed it would be recursive. COBOL does not allow programs to call themselves.

Q Can program E call program A?
A No. It does not contain program A. A program can only be called if it is directly contained or if it is separately compiled.

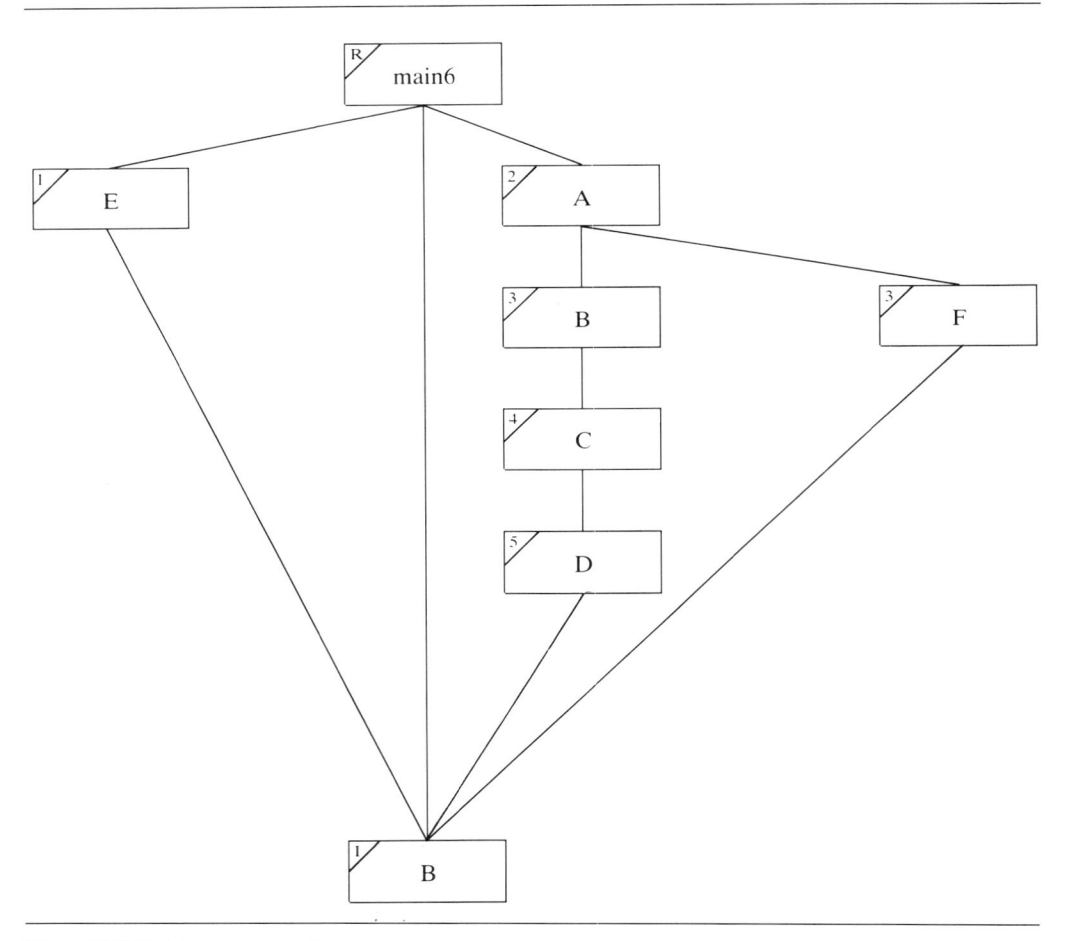

Figure 10.7 Main6 – structure chart

The structure chart for main6 is shown in Fig. 10.7. The chart demonstrates two structural characteristics that are common in many data-processing applications. These are known as *fan-out* and *fan-in*. As we move down from the root (main6), we can see that there is a tendency for the scope of control to fan out to include more than one program. Thus main6 calls two programs as does program A.

At the bottom of the chart the scope of control fans in such that program B is called by four other programs. Fan-out at the top is usually the result of the decomposition of a main task into subtasks. Fan-in at the bottom results from a requirement for the same program at different points in the overall solution.

We know that main6 is the root because it is at the top of the chart and has an 'R' in the top left-hand corner. Program E as well as the program B at the bottom are both internal programs and this is indicated by the 'I' in the top left-hand corner. All three programs are separately compiled and therefore are at nesting level 1.

The root contains five nested programs down to a nesting level of 5. These are all contained programs and are therefore compiled within the root.

Although program main6 does not exist beyond this brief example we might imagine that it is the structure for a file-processing program. Program E might in this scenario be a file-handling program under the control of the root. The core of the record processing might be held in program A which itself is decomposed into programs B and F. Program B is then further decomposed into programs C and then D.

The separately compiled program B might be something such as a program to convert dates from one form to another. The structure shows that this program is required in four different places in the overall design. Although the problem we have outlined is entirely hypothetical it shows that important features concerning the structure of a solution can be captured by a structure chart. Further work on designing parameter interfaces and algorithms could be undertaken to establish even greater structure for a proposed solution well before the writing of the final programs.

10.2 COPY STATEMENT

The **copy** statement allows the incorporation of existing source text into a COBOL program at compile time. This feature is particularly invaluable when common record definitions need to be used by many programs.

Programs driver1 and accept3 have a parameter record in common. This source text could be created in a separate file. Then at the point in the program where the source text is required the copy statement would be written as shown by the following simple syntax:

```
copy file-name-1
```

File-name-1 is the name of the file that contains the text to be copied. When the program is being compiled, the compiler will process text from the program up to the copy statement. At this point it will switch to the file that is named by the copy statement and process all of the text in that file. The compiler will then revert to processing the rest of the program source text. Thus the stream of text that is compiled by the compiler will be the same as if the copied text had existed in the program in the first place.

288 ESSENTIAL COBOL: A FIRST COURSE IN STRUCTURED COBOL

Step 1: Put Source Text into a File, for example, rec001.cop

```
01   l1-rec.
     03   l1-string           pic x(21).
     03   l1-length           pic 99.
     03   l1-number           pic s9(18).
     03   l1-length           pic 99.
     03   l1-scale            pic 99.
     03   l1-decision         pic 99.
          88  l1-success        value 00.
          88  l1-empty-input    value 01.
          88  l1-too-long       value 10.
          88  l1-bad-numeric    value 11.
          88  l1-bad-sign       value 12.
          88  l1-bad-scale      value 13.
```
} rec001.cop

Step 2: Put the copy statement into the program source text in place of the record.

    copy "rec001.cop".

Rename the variables in the program to conform with the record. Rename the program.

Step 3: Compile the program. (VAX Command: $ cobol driver1⟨RET⟩)

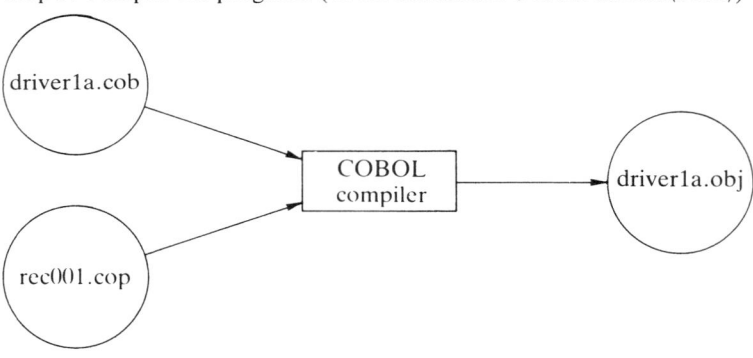

Fig. 10.8 Using the **copy** statement

Figure 10.8 gives the steps that need to be followed to use the copy statement for the parameter record in program driver1.

SELF-CHECK QUESTIONS

Q Suggest two possible benefits from using the copy statement in programs.
A Firstly, source text that is used in more than one program only needs to be written in one place. This has the effect of reducing the amount of source text overall for a particular application. Secondly, the fact that only one version of a text exists helps in managing programs during their initial development as well as during their future enhancement. For example, it is common practice in many organizations for systems analysts to have responsibility for record definitions that are used across applications

and in external programs. The management of these definitions is made easier by the existence of master copies of the text.

Q Does the use of the copy statement in programs reduce the size of the object code files?
A No. The copy statement only removes duplication in the source texts.
Q Can only record definitions be place in files for copying?
A No. Any program text can be copied into a program. This includes statements from the procedure division.

10.3 INITIAL AND COMMON PROGRAM ATTRIBUTES

COBOL provides two useful program attributes that allow you to over-ride certain language default mechanisms for programs.

The simplest of these is the **initial** attribute. By default a called program is only in its initial data state the first time it is called within a run. On subsequent calls the program is in the data state that existed when it returned control to its calling program. When the initial attribute is used a called program will be in its initial data state every time it is called. As a result data items that specify value clauses will be re-initialized even though the value of an item may have been changed in a prior execution of the program. (This also implies that if an item did not specify a value clause it is undefined upon each and every entry to the program.)

Other aspects of the program's data state are also re-initialized. For example, files that were opened during a previous execution are automatically closed and control mechanisms associated with perform statements are reset. (In practice, neither of these last two points will be of interest to programmers who close their files and who refrain from using unstructured performs and go to statements.)

The **common** attribute allows you to over-ride the default restriction against calling indirectly contained programs. A program with the common attribute can be called by any program that is contained by the program that directly contains it but with one exception. It cannot be called by any program that is contained within itself.

This relationship is best understood by using a simple example. Imagine that program X directly contains program Y, which has the common attribute. Program X can still call program Y as would have been the case without the common attribute. However, all of the programs within X can now call Y as well. The sole exception to this is those programs that are nested in Y.

The box diagram in Fig. 10.9 shows the relaxation in the calling rules that results by using the common attribute. We can see that in addition to X, programs Z and Q can also call Y. Program R cannot call Y because it is contained within it. Program W cannot call Y because Y is indirectly contained in W. The tree in Fig. 10.9 provides a slightly different representation of the same structure. From this we can see that a program with the common attribute enables siblings and their children to call it.

The box diagram in Fig. 10.10 gives a more complex example to show the relationship between a contained program with the common attribute and a separately compiled program with the same name. Contained program B at line 10 is a common program within

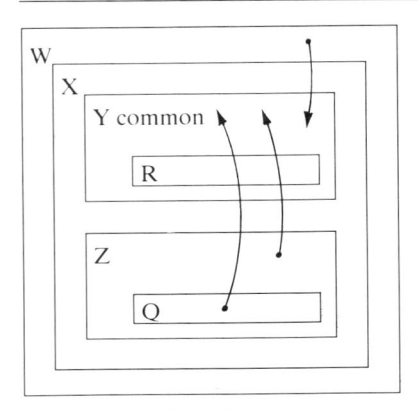

290 ESSENTIAL COBOL: A FIRST COURSE IN STRUCTURED COBOL

(a) Box diagram

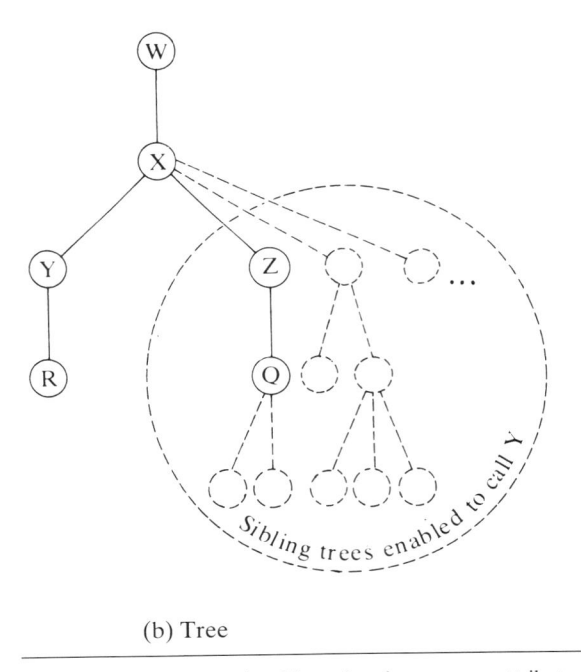

(b) Tree

Figure 10.9 Calling relationships using the **common** attribute

program A. A second program B at line 33 is separately compiled. We can see that program A, the siblings of A and the children of siblings all have their calls to B resolved to the common program. All other calls to B are resolved to the separately compiled program.

The structure chart in Fig. 10.11 provides a clear way of visualizing the calling relationships in main7. We can see that programs F and B are at nesting level 3 of main7 and are directly contained within program A. Therefore program F is a sibling of B and program G is a child of F. Both of these programs can call B. (The dotted control lines

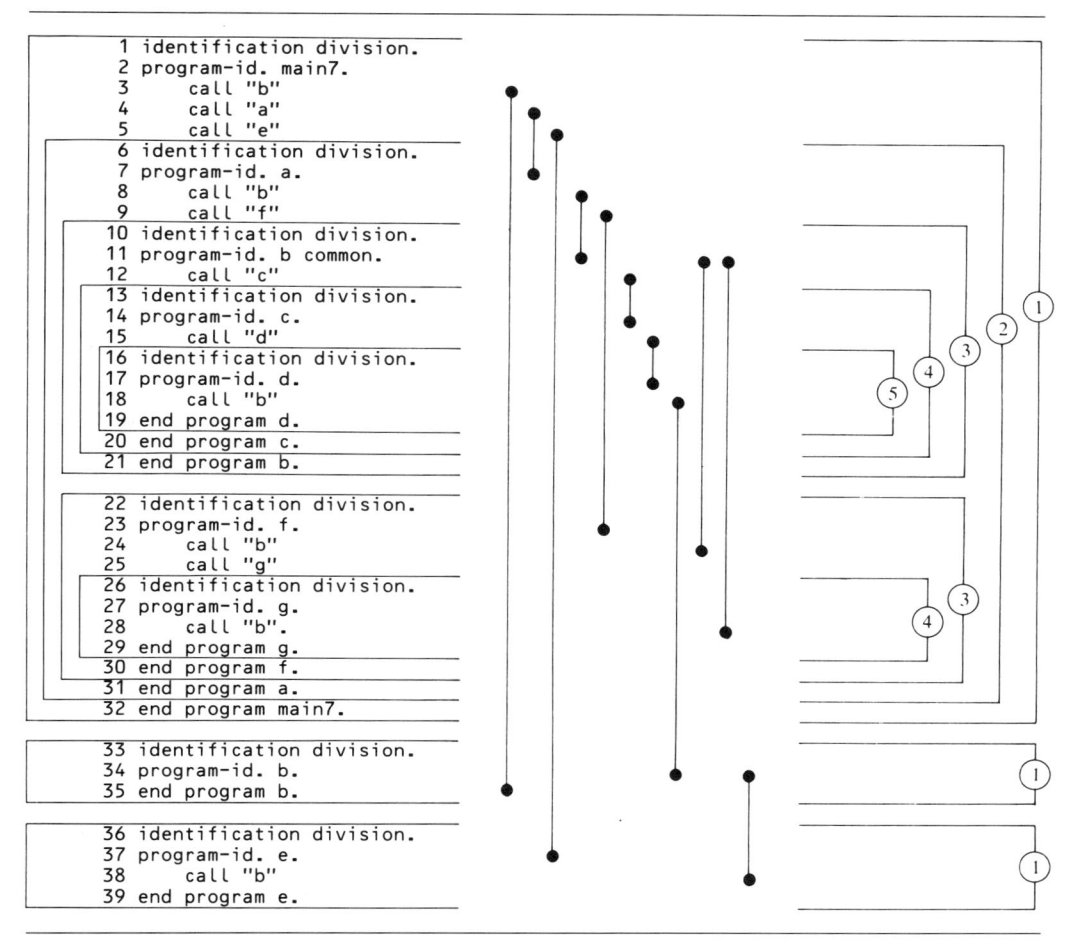

```
 1 identification division.
 2 program-id. main7.
 3      call "b"
 4      call "a"
 5      call "e"
 6 identification division.
 7 program-id. a.
 8      call "b"
 9      call "f"
10 identification division.
11 program-id. b common.
12      call "c"
13 identification division.
14 program-id. c.
15      call "d"
16 identification division.
17 program-id. d.
18      call "b"
19 end program d.
20 end program c.
21 end program b.
22 identification division.
23 program-id. f.
24      call "b"
25      call "g"
26 identification division.
27 program-id. g.
28      call "b".
29 end program g.
30 end program f.
31 end program a.
32 end program main7.
33 identification division.
34 program-id. b.
35 end program b.
36 identification division.
37 program-id. e.
38      call "b"
39 end program e.
```

Figure 10.10 Outline for program main7 with a **common** program

show that these programs are calling a common program. The 'C' in the lower left-hand corner of the program box denotes that program B is common.)

The initial and common clauses have the following full format:

    program-id. program-name [common] [initial].

The common attribute can only be specified for a contained program. The initial attribute can be specified for any program.

SELF-CHECK QUESTIONS

Q   Would you use the initial attribute with a file handler?

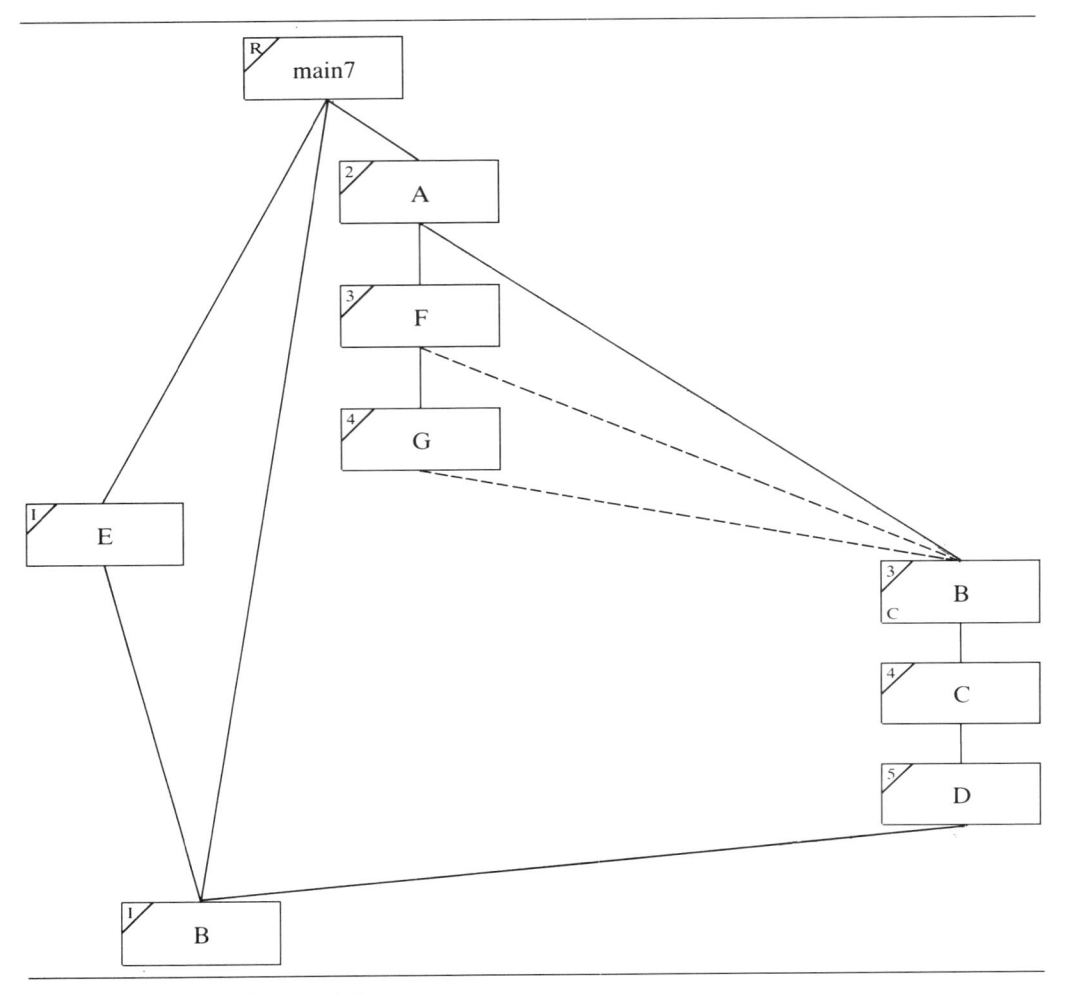

Figure 10.11 Structure chart – main7

A While there are always exceptions to a rule it is likely to be the case that a file handler would not have the initial attribute. The reason for this is that most file handlers have a data item that they use as a switch in order to remember whether or not the file they are handling is open. If the initial attribute were used then the program would initialize the value of such a switch every time it was called.

Q What is the similarity between separate compilation and the common attribute?

A Both separate compilation and the common attribute enable similar calling relationships at their nesting level. For example, consider the alternative box diagram shown in Fig. 10.12 for the programs given in Fig. 10.9.

In this diagram there are three separately compiled programs. We see that program Z and its children can call Y. However, Y can also call Z and this was not

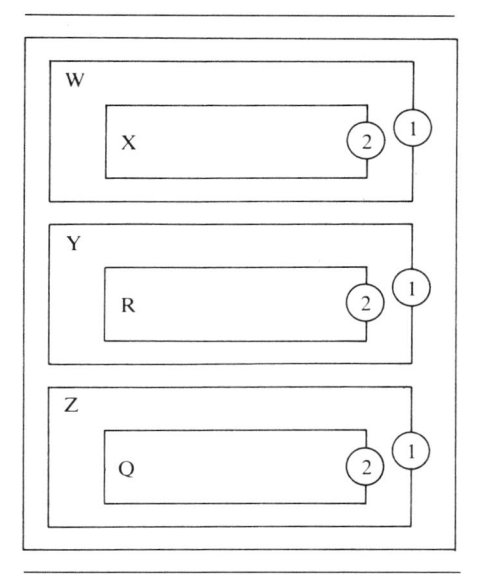

Figure 10.12 Alternative structure for Fig. 10.9

supported by Fig. 10.9. Therefore the common attribute gives us a finer degree of control. (In no case can a program call itself or be called by a program that it is currently calling. Such calls are recursive.)

10.4 GLOBAL AND EXTERNAL DATA ATTRIBUTES

In COBOL the scope of all data is local by default. However, in previous chapters we have seen that a reference parameter can be used to give a called program access to a record within the calling program while a content parameter can be used to copy a record into the called program as local data.

The **global** attribute provides a means for making data available to contained programs without the need to pass the data as a parameter. In effect this attribute removes the default local scope and gives the data a global scope.

This attribute can be given to any record that is in a file description entry or the working-storage section of a program. The attribute also causes all of the data-names and condition-names that are used within the record to be available to the contained programs.

The global attribute can also be given to a file-name. When this is done the file-connector for the file becomes available to all of the contained programs. For example, as a consequence of giving a file-name the global attribute, it is possible for one program to open and close a file but for another to read it. The record-names and any data-names and condition-names associated with the file also become available.

When a contained program declares a name that is the same as a name that is already global to the contained program, then references in the contained program are resolved to the new name and not to the global name. In other words local names take precedence over global names. (The new local names may of course be global in which case they will be global to other programs that are contained at a deeper level of nesting.)

An important difference between COBOL and some other languages is that global names are only available to contained programs and not to containing programs. They are not available to separately compiled programs.

Figure 10.13 gives an outline for program main8 in which the vertical lines show how the names are resolved. Once again these relationships are more easily visualized with a structure chart as has been done in Fig. 10.13.

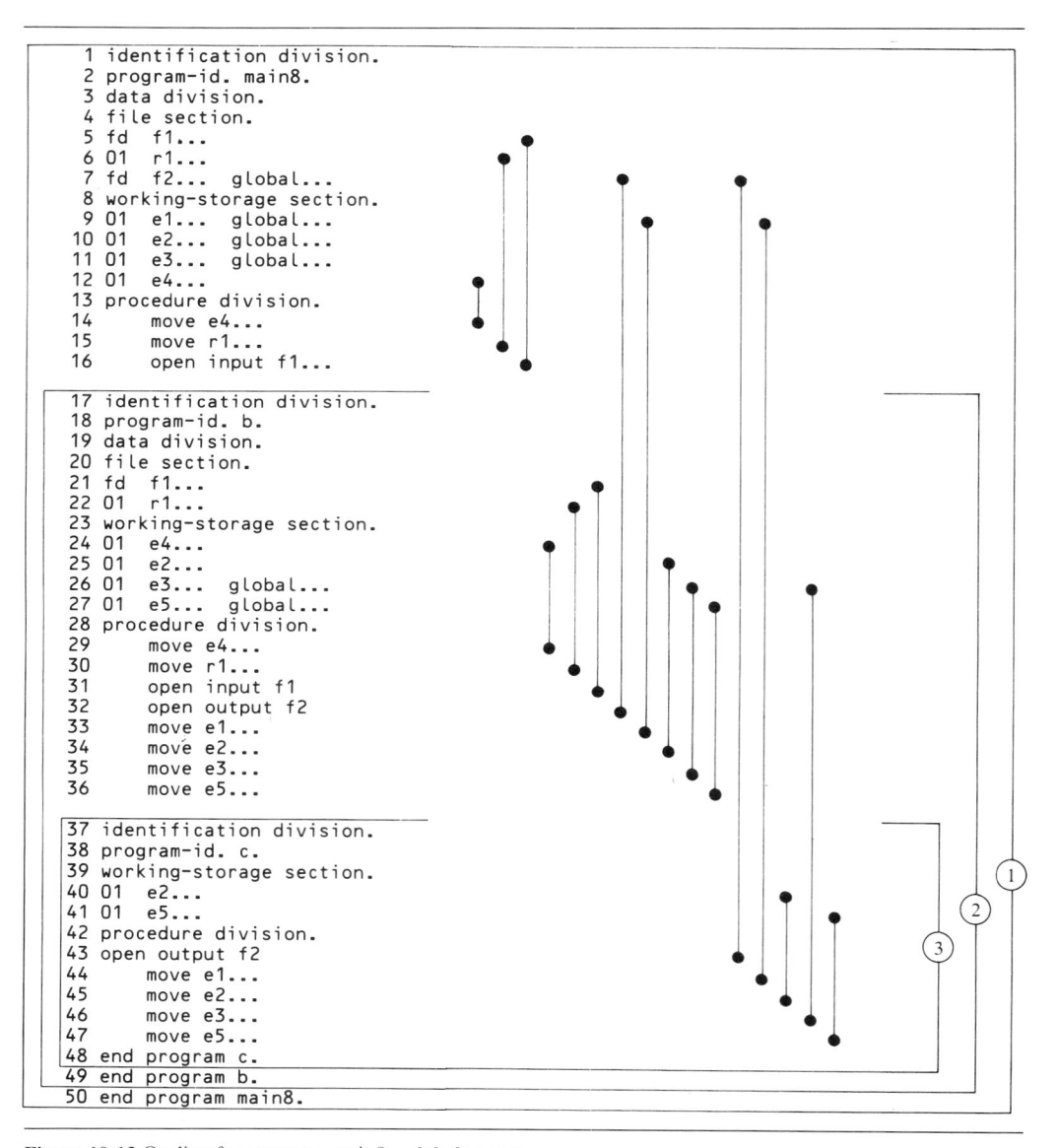

```
 1 identification division.
 2 program-id. main8.
 3 data division.
 4 file section.
 5 fd   f1...
 6 01   r1...
 7 fd   f2...    global...
 8 working-storage section.
 9 01   e1...    global...
10 01   e2...    global...
11 01   e3...    global...
12 01   e4...
13 procedure division.
14      move e4...
15      move r1...
16      open input f1...
17 identification division.
18 program-id. b.
19 data division.
20 file section.
21 fd   f1...
22 01   r1...
23 working-storage section.
24 01   e4...
25 01   e2...
26 01   e3...    global...
27 01   e5...    global...
28 procedure division.
29      move e4...
30      move r1...
31      open input f1
32      open output f2
33      move e1...
34      move e2...
35      move e3...
36      move e5...
37 identification division.
38 program-id. c.
39 working-storage section.
40 01   e2...
41 01   e5...
42 procedure division.
43      open output f2
44      move e1...
45      move e2...
46      move e3...
47      move e5...
48 end program c.
49 end program b.
50 end program main8.
```

Figure 10.13 Outline for program main8 – **global** names

COMPLEX PROGRAM STRUCTURES   295

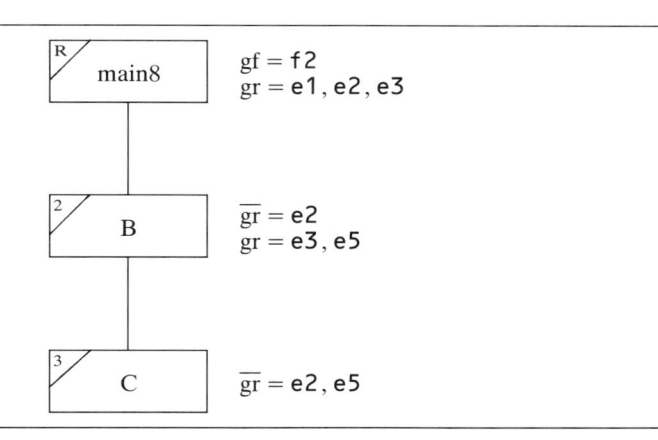

```
  R                          gf = f2
        main8                gr = e1, e2, e3


  2                           ___
                              gr = e2
         B                    gr = e3, e5


  3                           ___
                              gr = e2, e5
         C
```

Figure 10.14 Main8 – structure chart notation for **global** data

The terms gf and gr are used to the right-hand side of a program box to denote global files and global records respectively. A bar over a term shows that the name is locally declared at a lower level.

Thus f2 and e1 are available to all three programs. Although e2 is given the global attribute in main8, local names take precedence in both programs B and C. The global declaration for e3 in program B replaces the global declaration from main6 for program B and its nested programs. Therefore program C has available to it the e3 from program B and not from main8.

In general we can see that global data requires as careful and consistent a notation as parameters do in order that the structure chart can continue to document the data relations that exist between programs.

In addition, the **external** attribute may be given to record-names or file-names. The name then becomes external to the program in which it is defined and becomes associated with the run unit in preference to any particular program. As a result any program in the run unit can use the record or file provided it describes it correctly.

This feature is intended to assist in creating common pools of data between separately compiled programs. Thus two or more programs could use the same file connector provided that each program described the file with the same name, used the external attribute, and described the file as having the same characteristics including the same record-names. Similarly, a set of programs could share a temporary record if each declared the record in its working-storage section as having the external attribute and the same name. All subordinate items must also have the same names and be the same size.

An external record cannot have a redefines clause within it or a value clause that is used to initialize data values. However, it is possible to follow the description of an external record with a further record that completely redefines it. For example,

```
    01   e7-rec external.
         03   e7-num1       pic 99.
              88   e7-ok    value 20.
         03   e7-num2       pic 9.
    01   e8-rec redefines e7-rec.
         03   e7-chars      pic x(3).
```

In this case the first record must be included in this form in the working-storage of any program that wishes to use e7-rec. These three characters of data will only exist once in the whole of the run unit. The redefinition is optional. It can be omitted or written in any form that is consistent with the rules for using the redefines clause. Not only can different programs have different redefinitions but any program can have multiple redefinitions.

Although the feature is intended to support data sharing between separately compiled programs, the external name does not need to be declared by the program at nesting level 1. It can be declared within any contained program. The sole restriction is that it must appear in only one program within each separately compiled program.

The simple formats for the global and external clauses are as follows:

01   data-name-1 [external] [global]

The fact that a record or a file can be either global or external means that our approach to annotating our structure charts must be extended to incorporate these possibilities. Any of the following can be considered to be a valid notation:

$$\begin{array}{ll} gf & \overline{gf} \\ gr & \overline{gr} \\ ef & \overline{ef} \\ er & \overline{er} \\ egf & \overline{egf} \\ egr & \overline{egr} \end{array}$$

SELF-CHECK QUESTIONS

Q A program declares a global record. Is this record available to programs that call this program?

A No. Global data is only available to contained programs and not to containing programs.

Q A record is defined as global at program nesting level 2. Can a program at nesting level 3 use the same data-name for a new record without the global attribute?

A Yes. The new record is now available to the program at nesting level and takes precedence over the original record. In effect the record is local to the program at nesting level 3 although it could be used as a parameter in calls to other programs.

Q Could the same record from the previous question have been defined using the global attribute?

A Yes. In this case the record would be available as a global record to any programs that are contained at level 4 or deeper.

10.5 CASE STUDY: DRIVER2 (TESTING SCREEN-HANDLING)

Driver2 is a testing program to test the correctness of the screen handling program from the previous chapter. The parameter record has been placed in a text file called `rec002.cop` which contains the text shown in Fig. 10.15. The screen program has been rewritten as screen2 to use the copy statement.

Whereas the last driver program (driver1) accepted test cases from the keyboard and displayed the results on the screen, driver2 supplies successive parameters to change the state of the screen by reading a file. Therefore the test cases have been placed in a file so that the screen can be used more easily to show the results of the tests. Each case is read in succession and driver2 uses the test data to supply parameters for a call to screen2. After each call driver2 checks the case to see if it includes a string of text to be displayed. After displaying any text that is required it then accepts a single character from the keyboard. Figure 10.16 gives a structure chart for the program and Fig. 10.17 lists the contents of the test case file. The programs are listed in Figs 10.18 and 10.19.

```
 1  01    l1-rec.
 2     03    l1-argument              pic 99.
 3        88    l1-erase-screen       value 01.
 4        88    l1-new-cursor         value 02.
 5        88    l1-hide-cursor        value 03.
 6        88    l1-show-cursor        value 04.
 7     03    l1-cursor-coordinates.
 8        05    l1-line               pic 999.
 9           88    l1-line-valid      value 001 thru 024.
10        05    l1-col                pic 999.
11           88    l1-col-valid       value 001 thru 080.
12     03    l1-result                pic 99.
13        88    l1-success            value 01.
14        88    l1-bad-cursor         value 02.
15        88    l1-unknown            value 99.
```

Figure 10.15 Parameter record in text file `rec002.cop`

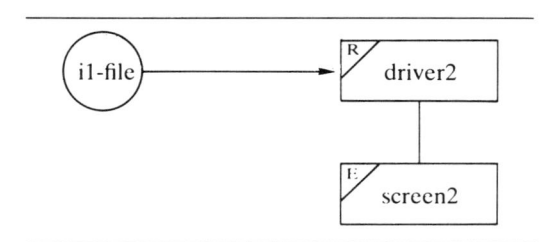

Figure 10.16 Structure chart for driver2 calling screen2

```
         1         2         3         4         5         6
123456789012345678901234567890123456789012345678901234567890
 Lines that begin with a space are comment lines.
 Other lines contain a test case record.

 *** GROUP 1 *** Two strings and one input item.
 case  1 - erase screen
01
 case  2 - new cursor
02 001 001 --------LINE-1--------
 case  3 - new cursor
02 003 001 field1=
 case  4 - new cursor
02 003 010

 *** GROUP 2 *** Four strings and two input items. Hide and Show
 case  5 - hide cursor
03
 case  6 - erase screen
01
 case  7 - new cursor
02 001 001 ---------TOP----------
 case  8 - new cursor
02 024 001 -------BOTTOM---------
 case  9 - new cursor
02 004 001 field2=
 case 10 - show cursor
04
 case 11 - new cursor
02 004 010
 case 12 - new cursor
02 004 025 field3=
 case 13 - new cursor
02 004 035

 *** GROUP 3 *** Bad Parameters
 case 14 - new cursor
02 000 000
 case 15 - new cursor
02 000 001
 case 16 - new cursor
02 001 000
 case 17 - new cursor
02 aaa 000
 case 18 - new cursor
02 000 zzz
 case 19 - new cursor
02 bbb yyy
 case 20 - new cursor
02  10 00
 case 21 - new cursor
02
 case 22 - new cursor
02 00 00
         1         2         3         4         5         6
123456789012345678901234567890123456789012345678901234567890
```

Figure 10.17 File idriver2.dat – test cases for program driver2

```
 1 identification division.
 2 program-id. driver2.
 3*Purpose: This program is a test driver for screen2.
 4
 5 environment division.
 6 input-output section.
 7 file-control.
 8    select i1-file assign w1-filename.
 9
10 data division.
11 file section.
12 fd   i1-file
13      record varying 1 to 255
14      depending      w1-ctr
15      value of id    w1-filename.
16 01   filler              pic x(255).
17
18 working-storage section.
19 01   w1-file.
20      03   w1-ctr binary    pic 999.
21      03   w1-filename      pic x(20).
22      03   filler value "n" pic x.
23           88 w1-eof        value "y".
24      03   w1-rec.
25           05   w1-argument    pic 99.
26           05   filler redefines w1-argument.
27                07   filler     pic x.
28                     88   w1-skip value space.
29                07   filler     pic x.
30           05   filler         pic x.
31           05   w1-line        pic 999.
32           05   filler         pic x.
33           05   w1-col         pic 999.
34           05   filler         pic x.
35           05   w1-message     pic x(67).
36
37 01   s2-screen.
38      03   s2-pauser        pic x.
39      03   s2-len           pic 999.
40
41 copy "rec002.cop".
42
43 procedure division.
44 para1.
45      display "driver2 begins"
46
47      display "Enter name of test file for the screen: " no advancing
48      accept w1-filename
49      open input i1-file
50
```

300 ESSENTIAL COBOL: A FIRST COURSE IN STRUCTURED COBOL

```
51      perform test before until w1-eof
52        read i1-file into w1-rec
53        end
54          set w1-eof to true
55        not end
56          evaluate w1-skip
57            when    false
58              move w1-argument to l1-argument
59              move w1-line     to l1-line
60              move w1-col      to l1-col
61              call "screen2" using reference l1-rec
62              evaluate true
63                when    not l1-success
64                  continue
65                when    l1-new-cursor and w1-message = spaces
66                  accept s2-pauser
67                when    l1-new-cursor and w1-message not = spaces
68                  move zero to s2-len
69                  inspect w1-message tallying s2-len
70                    for characters before initial " "
71                  display w1-message(1:s2-len) no advancing
72              end-evaluate
73          end-evaluate
74        end-read
75
76      end-perform
77      display "display driver2 ends"
78      stop run.
79
80 end program driver2
```

Figure 10.18 Program driver2

```
 1 identification division.
 2 program-id. screen2.
 3
 4 environment division.
 5 configuration section.
 6 special-names.
 7     symbolic ESC is 28.
 8
 9 data division.
10 working-storage section.
11 01  w1-coordinate-lengths.
12     03  w1-refline               pic 9.
13         88  w1-line-valid        value 0 thru 2.
14     03  w1-refcol                pic 9.
15         88  w1-col-valid         value 0 thru 2.
16
17 linkage section.
18 copy "rec002.cop".
19
20 procedure division using l1-rec.
21 para1.
22     set l1-success to true
23
```

```cobol
24      evaluate true
25        when    l1-erase-screen
26          display ESC "[2J" no advancing
27
28        when    l1-new-cursor
29          evaluate l1-line numeric and l1-col numeric
30            when    false
31              set l1-bad-cursor to true
32              go to para-exit
33          end-evaluate
34
35          evaluate l1-line-valid and l1-col-valid
36            when    false
37              set l1-bad-cursor to true
38              go to para-exit
39          end-evaluate
40
41          move zero to w1-refline
42          inspect l1-line
43            tallying w1-refline for
44              leading zeroes
45          evaluate w1-line-valid
46            when    false
47              set l1-bad-cursor to true
48              go to para-exit
49          end-evaluate
50
51          move zero to w1-refcol
52          inspect l1-col
53            tallying w1-refcol for
54              leading zeroes
55          evaluate w1-col-valid
56            when    false
57              set l1-bad-cursor to true
58              go to para-exit
59          end-evaluate
60
61          compute w1-refline = w1-refline + 1
62          compute w1-refcol  = w1-refcol  + 1
63          display ESC "["
64            l1-line(w1-refline:) ";" l1-col(w1-refcol:) "H" no advancing
65
66        when    l1-hide-cursor
67          display ESC "[?25l" no advancing
68
69        when    l1-show-cursor
70          display ESC "[?25h" no advancing
71
72        when    other
73          set l1-unknown to true
74      end-evaluate.
75
76 para-exit.
77     exit program.
78
79 end program screen2
```

Figure 10.19 Program screen2

10.6 EXERCISES

10.6.1 General

1. Compile accept3 and driver1 separately. Link accept3 into driver1. Run driver1 to ensure that you understand the relationship between the driver and the called program. Force the program to fail with a run-time error by giving it an incorrect program name. Make a note of the error that your operating environment generates.
2. Rewrite driver1 as driver3 with a call statement that uses the exception phrases to recover execution of the program. Test this with accept3.
3. Rewrite driver1 or driver3 so that the name of the called program can be changed after any test case. Link all of the accept programs into driver3. Test the program to ensure that all of the called programs can be tested in a single run of the program.
4. Reconsider question 4 from the previous chapter and write accept4 to accept numbers that contain commas. Test the program using driver1 or driver3.
5. Rewrite busy1 from question 6 in the previous chapter as busy3. The new program should take its input stream from a file. Once you have demonstrated that busy3 can draw the same figure, design a new file that will allow busy3 to draw another figure.
6. Write stream1 that calls accept3. Stream1 should write all valid strings to one file and all invalid strings to another file, thereby creating a permanent record of a test session. (Each line in the files should contain only the 21 characters from w1-string.)
7. Rewrite stream2 from stream1. The new program should allow you to insert a one-line comment from the keyboard into the file with each test case.

10.6.2 Case study

8. Compile driver2 and screen2 separately. Link screen2 into driver2. Run driver2 to ensure that you understand the relationships between the driver, the input file and the called program. Add a few new test cases to the input file and re-run the program.
9. Rewrite the programs as driver4 and screen4 so that they use an external record rather than the parameter record. This will enable you to remove the linkage section and the use of parameters.
10. Rewrite the programs as driver5 and screen5 with new functions added such as ringing the bell. (See Appendix E for an indication of some other VT functions. You might also try to find a manual for the particular terminal that you are using and incorporate functions that are documented within it.)
11. Write a detailed system specification for screen5.

11
INFORMATION REPRESENTATION II

In computing the concept of data type is used to define the set of values that a variable may assume. If a data type is well defined it is possible to define operations upon that type that are also well defined. This may include operations for converting from one type to another.

The COBOL language was created before many of the concepts underlying data typing were clearly understood by language designers. Instead COBOL has the concepts of *level*, **class**, *category* and **usage** which govern the sets of values that a variable may legally assume as well as the results of conversion operations on these variables. These concepts are not generally consistent and incorporate many special rules concerning the attributes of data. In addition, features such as redefinition allow the programmer to define an area of data with one set of attributes and then to redefine the same area with other attributes that may be different from the original definition.

Consequently COBOL allows operations on data that in many other languages are forbidden. For example, in Chapter 9 we discovered that it is possible to accept the contents of an alphanumeric string into a numeric data item with unpredictable results. Similar difficulties can occur with the move statement.

The many features that support the conversion of data from one form to another can be an advantage in that an experienced programmer is able to do powerful data manipulations easily and efficiently. However, this can be a disadvantage in that an inexperienced programmmer can write statements in programs that may be unpredictable in certain circumstances, that are not portable between compilers, and that are difficult to debug.

11.1 LEVEL, CLASS AND CATEGORY

COBOL uses the term category to formalize the rules for the construction of pictures. The category of an item depends upon the symbols that are used in its picture.

Category	Some characters for constructing pictures
Alphabetic	a
Numeric	9 s v
Numeric edited	9 z . ,
Alphanumeric edited	x b / 0
Alphanumeric	x

Figure 11.1 Categories and pictures

Figure 11.1 shows some of the characters that are commonly used in constructing picture clauses. In Chapter 6 we briefly looked at edit masks and found that edit characters could be included in specific ways within pictures. We said that items which used these edit characters were alphanumeric edited or numeric edited items. Figure 11.1 shows that the 's' and 'v' can also be used in constucting numeric picture clauses. The 's' is used to represent the sign of a number while the 'v' represents its scale. We discovered in Chapter 9 that a numeric item with a sign may or may not represent this as a separate character. The 'v' when used for scaling is never represented as data. It merely serves as information to the compiler as to how a numeric item is to be scaled. For this reason is it called an *implied decimal point*.

```
01 e1-scaled-item      pic s9(16)v99.
```

The picture clause for the above item defines 18 digits. Because the sign separate clause has not been used the sign will be hidden within the character representation of either the first or the last digit depending on the strategy used by your compiler. (Where and how it is hidden should in most cases not concern you. The important point is to know that the sign is not stored as a separate character.) The implied decimal point tells the compiler how decimal alignment should take place during moves and calculations. The test study program at the end of this chapter provides working examples of how these numeric items are used in practice.

We can see that items in different categories can have pictures constructed in different ways and that this has some bearing on the way that data is stored and on the rules for moving data from one item to another. Previously we considered the ideas of class and the class test. What then is the relationship between class, the class test, and category?

An item might have a picture that causes it to be of the category alphabetic. This item could then be tested with the alphabetic test to see whether or not it did indeed contain only letters of the alphabet and spaces. Thus the concept of category is closely related to the description of an item whereas the class test is related to the value that an item might contain.

A similar logic applies to the numeric class and category. Consider the following record:

```
01   e1-rec.
   03   e1-var1         pic 999.
```

We know that `e1-var1` is category numeric. If it passes the numeric class test then we know that the data it contains is of the numeric class and that therefore it can be used as a number.

However, it is legal in COBOL to move spaces to `e1-rec`. As a result of this move `e1-var1` would still be considered to be within the category numeric but it would now hold data inappropriate to its class and therefore could not be used as a number within a program.

Conceptual difficulties occur when we wish to test an item of the alphanumeric category to see whether or not its contents belong to the numeric class. If the contents of the item pass the numeric class test then we know that the contents of the item can be used as a numeric item provided it is described as belonging to the numeric category. Usually this is achieved by moving the alphanumeric category item to a numeric category item. Thus, for example, the following data descriptions and statements would always guarantee that `e2-var2` which belongs to the numeric category always held data that was of the class numeric:

```
01  e2-rec.
    03  e2-var1         pic x.
    03  e2-var2         pic 999.
evaluate e2-var1 numeric
  when    true
    move e2-var1 to e2-var2
    display "variable e2-var2 now in range 000 to 009"
  when    false
    move zero to e2-var2
    display "variable e2-var2 forced to be 000"
end-evaluate
```

In fact, it is not necessary to move the data in order to use it. In the next example, three characters are redefined by an item that is category numeric:

```
01  e3-rec.
    03  e3-var1                         pic xxx.
    03  e3-var2 redefines e3-var1       pic 999.
    03  e3-var3    value 12345          pic 9(5).
evaluate e3-var1 numeric
  when    true
    compute e3-var3 = e3-var3 + e3-var2
  when    false
    display "variable e3-var1 was not numeric"
end-evaluate
```

We can see that even after the execution of the evaluate statement it is still possible for `e3-var2` to contain data that is of the wrong class. In other words, the contents of a data item as determined by class can be inconsistent with its category as determined by its picture.

Therefore it is a general rule that no data item should be used unless it is known by previous actions that the contents of the item are of the correct class for its category. These actions may have occurred just prior to the use of the data. In many cases they may have

306 ESSENTIAL COBOL: A FIRST COURSE IN STRUCTURED COBOL

Level type	Class	Category	Symbols
Elementary	① Alphabetic	Alphabetic	a
	② Numeric	Numeric	9 s v
	③ Alphanumeric	Numeric edited Alphanumeric edited Alphanumeric	9 z , . x / b 0 x
Group	④ Alphanumeric	Alphabetic Numeric Numeric edited Alphanumeric edited Alphanumeric	a 9 9 z , . x b / 0 x

Correct class tests:

① Alphabetic test.

② Numeric test; sign allowed.

③ Numeric test; no sign allowed; category must be alphanumeric.
   Alphabetic test but the category must be alphanumeric.

④ Numeric test against the group provided that each item in the group is either category alphanumeric or category numeric without a sign.
   Alphabetic test against the group provided that each item in the group is either category alphabetic or category alphanumeric.

Figure 11.2 Relationship between level type, class and category

occurred some time before as would be the case when data is validated upon entry to an application system but then stored in files for long periods of time.

Figure 11.2 shows the relationships between levels, classes and categories.

In summary we can make the following observations by combining information from this table with our previous knowledge of levels and classes:

1. The alphabetic class contains only the alphabetic category and the numeric class contains only the numeric category.
2. Elementary items that are of the class alphanumeric can be of three different categories but only those that are of the category alphanumeric can be the subject of a class test.
3. A group item is always alphanumeric and can contain items of any category.
4. An alphabetic class test against a group item can be understood as a test against each elementary item in the group in succession. Each elementary item must have a picture clause with either 'a's or 'x's only.
5. A numeric class test against a group item can be understood as a test against each elementary item in the group in succession. Each elementary item must have a picture clause with either '9's or 'x's only.

11.2 USAGE CLAUSE

The usage clause specifies the format of a data item in the computer's storage. COBOL provides a number of forms of data usage so that the programmer can control the storage format of data.

The default usage is display which specifies character strings. Therefore all of the data we have considered in previous chapters where usage has not been explicitly stated has been **display** by default.

The three records shown in Fig. 11.3 show different ways of defining four characters of display data. In the first example the usage is display by default. In the second example the usage is explicitly defined at the group level. When this is done the usage applies to all elementary items. In the third example two elementary items are given an explicit display usage. (E6-var2 in the third example is display by default.)

When defining display data, COBOL programmers tend to use the default form shown in the first record because it is brief and therefore convenient. However, whether the word display is written explicitly or only implied the resulting data will still be treated as character strings.

Many modern computer systems that are used for data processing address memory at the level of hardware in units of 32 bits. These units are called *words*. (Therefore a word is made up of four 8-bit bytes and can hold four characters.)

The system will also allocate physical memory for records at word boundaries even though a program may not use or have access to all of the physical memory that is thereby allocated. COBOL does not require records to be contiguous within memory but items within a record must be contiguous and in the order described. Consider program usage1 in Fig. 11.4, which has three records, each of which will begin on a word boundary.

The first and second records will each require a word. The third record will require two contiguous words because the items in the record describe a total of seven characters. Therefore the amount of physical storage that will be allocated for the program's working-storage will be four words in total.

```
01  e4-rec.
    03   e4-var1              pic 9.
    03   e4-var2              pic 9.
    03   e4-var3              pic 99.
01  e5-rec display.
    03   e5-var1              pic 9.
    03   e5-var2              pic 9.
    03   e5-var3              pic 99.
01  e6-rec.
    03   e6-var1 display      pic 9.
    03   e6-var2              pic 9.
    03   e6-var3 display      pic 99.
```

Figure 11.3 Three different ways to define display usage

```
 1 identification division.
 2 program-id. usage1.
 3*Purpose: Illustrate allocation of memory
 4
 5 environment division.
 6
 7 data division.
 8 working-storage section.
 9 01 w1-rec.
10     03   w1-var1     pic 9.
11
12 01 w2-rec.
13     03   w2-var2     pic 9.
14     03   w2-var3     pic 9.
15
16 01 w3-rec.
17     03   w3-var4     pic 9.
18     03   w3-var5     pic 9(5).
19     03   w3-var6     pic 9.
20
21 procedure division.
22 para1.
23     display "usage1 begins"
24
25     move 1 to w1-var1
26     move "3" to w3-rec
27     compute w3-var5 = w1-var1 + w3-var4
28     display "The answer is " w3-var5
29
30     display "usage1 ends"
31     stop run.
32
33 end program usage1
```

Figure 11.4 Program usage1

The first move statement in the program will require access to the first byte of a word while the second move statement will require access to four bytes of one word and the first three bytes of the next adjacent word. Out of the 16 bytes that have been physically allocated only ten of them are available as defined by the program's records.

Questions associated with storage strategies could be avoided entirely if all data could always be treated as strings of characters as we have done up until now. However, it is the case that numbers defined as strings of characters are not always efficient in use. Consider the compute statement in program usage1. It is likely that the compiler will have generated additional instructions to convert the numeric values of w1-var1 and w3-var4, added them together in a temporary location, and then converted the result back into w3-var5 as a string of characters. Therefore COBOL supplies other forms of usage for numeric items so that numbers can be defined in ways that are more efficient in the context of the underlying system.

The first of these is the usage **binary**. A binary item is a number that is stored as a string of bits with a base of 2. For example, in Chapter 7 we described the record length counter for a file with the usage binary because the system required a representation of binary and not display.

The amount of storage space occupied by a number with a usage of binary depends on the number of digits specified in its picture description as well as the overall storage strategy used by a particular system. Most systems that use 32-bit words provide for the efficient use of binary numbers that are stored in 16, 32 or 64 bits on boundaries that are *halfword*, *word* or *doubleword* boundaries. One bit is used to represent the sign. Therefore the bits available to store the number will be 15, 31 or 63 bits.

Figure 11.5 lists picture descriptions for binary items in the range of 1 to 10 digits and shows the amount of storage that is required for numbers with these pictures. (The COBOL maximum is 18 digits plus a sign. Signed numbers of 10 to 18 digits can be stored in a doubleword.)

In order to support efficient computation, binary numbers should be aligned to appropriate boundaries. Thus binary items of 1 to 4 digits should be on a byte boundary divisible by 2 (halfword), 5 to 9 digits on a byte boundary divisible by 4 (word), and 10 to 18 digits on a boundary divisible by 8 (doubleword).

Figure 11.6 shows six records that correctly define four numeric data items. The items in each record can be used with varying degrees of computational efficiency.

The first record defines character data. Computations with this data may be inefficient because the strings may need to be converted. The second record defines the data as binary but without any regard to boundary alignment. This data is likely to be more efficient in use because the conversion step will not be needed. However, it is still likely that efficiency will be reduced for items that are not properly aligned.

COBOL picture	Largest denary number	Storage allocation Bytes	Generic term	VAX term	IBM term	Largest number stored
pic s9	9	2	halfword	word	halfword	32 767
pic s99	99	2	halfword	word	halfword	32 767
pic s999	999	2	halfword	word	halfword	32 767
pic s9(4)	9 999	2	halfword	word	halfword	32 767
pic s9(5)	99 999	4	word	longword	fullword	2 147 483 644
pic s9(6)	999 999	4	word	longword	fullword	2 147 483 644
pic s9(7)	9 999 999	4	word	longword	fullword	2 147 483 644
pic s9(8)	99 999 999	4	word	longword	fullword	2 147 483 644
pic s9(9)	999 999 999	4	word	longword	fullword	2 147 483 644
pic s9(10)	9 999 999 999	8	doubleword	doubleword	doubleword	$>9.2 * 10^{18}$

Note: Binary ranges are assumed to be -2^{n-1} to $+2^{n-1} - 1$ where n is the number of bits in the allocated storage. One is subtracted from the power to allow for the bit that is needed to represent the sign. One is subtracted from the largest number to allow for zero which is assumed positive. For example, 16 bits stores 2^{16} values in the range -2^{15} to $+2^{15} - 1$.

Figure 11.5 Typical storage strategy for binary numbers

Record definitions			Byte allocation	Boundary aligned?	Comment
01 e1-rec.					1. character data
03 e1-var1		pic 9.	1	n/a	2. total of 5 words
03 e1-var2		pic 9(5).	5	n/a	3. last 2 bytes unused
03 e1-var3		pic 9.	1	n/a	
03 e1-var4		pic 9(11).	11	n/a	
01 e2-rec.					1. binary data
03 e2-var1	binary	pic 9.	2	yes	2. total of 4 words
03 e2-var2	binary	pic 9(5).	4	no	3. no unused bytes
03 e2-var3	binary	pic 9.	2	yes	
03 e2-var4	binary	pic 9(11).	8	yes	
01 e3-rec.					1. binary data
03 e3-var1	binary	pic 9.	2	yes	2. total of 6 words
03 filler		pic xx.	2	n/a	3. 8 filler bytes
03 e3-var2	binary	pic 9(5).	4	yes	
03 e3-var3	binary	pic 9.	2	yes	
03 filler		pic x(6)	6	n/a	
03 e3-var4	binary	pic 9(11).	8	yes	
01 e4-rec.					1. binary data
03 e4-var4	binary	pic 9(11).	8	yes	2. total of 4 words
03 e4-var2	binary	pic 9(5).	4	yes	3. no unused bytes
03 e4-var1	binary	pic 9.	2	yes	
03 e4-var3	binary	pic 9.	2	yes	
01 e5-rec.					1. binary data
03 e5-var4	binary	pic s9(11).	8	yes	2. total of 4 words
03 e5-var2	binary	pic s9(5).	4	yes	3. no unused bytes
03 e5-var1	binary	pic s9.	2	yes	4. all items signed
03 e5-var3	binary	pic s9.	2	yes	
01 e6-rec.					1. binary data
03 e6-var1	binary sync	pic s9.	2	yes	2. total of 6 words
03 e6-var2	binary sync	pic s9(5).	4 + 2	yes	3. 8 slack bytes
03 e6-var3	binary sync	pic s9.	2	yes	4. all items signed
03 e6-var4	binary sync	pic s9(11).	8 + 6	yes	

Figure 11.6 Six valid record definitions to illustrate the usage **binary**

The third record uses filler items to force the binary items into correct alignment. For example, we can see that e3-var4 is preceded by a total of 16 bytes. Therefore e3-var4 is aligned on the third doubleword boundary within the record. All of the binary items in this record can be used efficiently but eight filler bytes have been inserted to accomplish this.

The fourth record shows a better solution. In this example the items have been rearranged so that larger items come first and smaller items are grouped together. The record is now eight bytes shorter.

The fifth record shows the best solution. The reason for this is that all items have been given a sign. It is the case that most binary items will be signed in memory even though the picture clause may specify the number as unsigned. The consequence is that if items are defined without a sign the compiler will have to generate additional instructions to mask the sign from the running program. Therefore it is preferable to show a sign for a numeric item when this is possible. There are two exceptions to this. Firstly, the compiler implementation may specify that an item should be unsigned as is the case with the character counter for a file. Secondly, using an unsigned item as a target for a numeric move provides a convenient way to extract an absolute value in cases where this is explicitly required by an application.

The sixth record shows a different solution. In this example the **synchronized** clause has been used. This clause will cause the compiler to force word alignment automatically. It has a similar effect to that which was achieved explicitly in the third record. Its marginal advantage is that word alignment for a particular system will occur without the programmer needing to know the system's word size or alignment strategy. The severe disadvantage is that because not all systems may align data in the same way its use may have adverse consequences on program and data file portability.

Often the term slack byte is used to describe the bytes that are inserted into a record to force correct alignment. It is preferable for a programmer to insert slack bytes explicitly if they are needed and not resort to the implicit insertion of slack bytes as occurs with the synchronized clause. Therefore we will not consider this clause further.

A second important usage is **packed-decimal**. COBOL specifies that in this usage a number is stored as a base 10 number in which each digit of the number occupies the minimum amount of storage space. The main use for packed-decimal numbers is for numeric items in large files of records. Their use reduces the record size and often results in computations that are more efficient than those using numbers in character strings.

In practice, most systems will store each digit as a nibble and allocate a further nibble for the sign. Thus the number +345 will occupy four nibbles which is two bytes. A number such as −12 only requires three nibbles but this will be rounded up to a full number of bytes by treating the number as −012.

We can see from Fig. 11.7 that a packed-decimal number never takes up more space than a display number. For larger numbers this usage requires less space. Their use may

COBOL picture	Largest denary number	Storage required in bytes
pic s9	+9	1
pic s99	+99	2
pic s999	+999	2
pic s9(4)	+9999	3
pic s9(5)	+99999	3
...	...	...
pic s9(18)	18 digits plus a sign	10

Note: The storage requirement can be calculated as:

$$\text{bytes} = (n + 1)/2 \text{ rounded up}$$

where n is the number of digits in the picture clause. Thus for a sixteen digit number:

$$(16 + 1)/2 = 8.5 \text{ which is 9 bytes.}$$

Packed-decimal items are byte aligned.

Figure 11.7 Typical storage strategy for the usage **packed-decimal**

make a significant contribution to reduced execution times for programs that do large amounts of calculating.

Both binary and packed-decimal are forms of *internal data representation*. However, standard COBOL only supports the accepting and displaying of items that have a usage of display. Therefore in order to display a binary or packed-decimal item it should first be moved to a display item. The move will automatically convert the item from its internal representation and the display item can then be output as characters.

Conversion between the display numeric representation and the internal numeric representations is a possible overhead on processing. If a numeric item is used only once in a computation it is not reasonable to convert the item to a more efficient representation by explicit moves because the compiler will automatically generate any necessary conversions and use temporary variables at run time as required. However, if a variable is used a repeated number of times, then there may be significant savings achieved by explicitly converting it once to an appropriate internal representation. Furthermore, if an item is never required in a display representation then it is more efficient to define it with an appropriate internal representation.

In any case when numeric data first enters a system it must always be carefully validated to ensure that its contents are indeed numeric before it is converted to any form of numeric representation. Furthermore, some compilers do not fully support moves of data directly from alphanumeric to numeric items with usage of binary and packed-decimal. Therefore it is advisable to move valid data via numeric display items and from there to an appropriate binary or packed-decimal target.

	Category of target		
Category of source	Alphabetic	Alphanumeric edited Alphanumeric	Numeric integer Numeric noninteger Numeric edited
Alphabetic	1	1,2	—
Alphanumeric	1	1,2	4
Alphanumeric edited	1	1,2	—
Numeric integer	—	1,2,3	5
Numeric noninteger	—	—	5
Numeric edited	—	1	5

1. Left-justified; padded to right with spaces or truncated as required. (No conversion unless step 2 included.)
2. Automatic usage conversion when source and target are not the same usage.
3. Any sign in source ignored.
4. Only 'x' in picture; character contents in "0" .. "9"
5. Justified on decimal point; zero filling or replacement with edit characters as required by the receiving item.
   (When both source and target are signed then the sign is moved.
    When only source is signed then the absolute value is moved.
    When only target is signed then a positive sign is put into the target.)

Figure 11.8 Effect of **move** statement by category of source and target

Requirement	Numeric usage
Record lengths for variable length records	Unsigned binary
Subscript used repeatedly in a loop	Signed binary (sign included for efficiency)
Subscript accepted, validated and used once to access a table element	Unsigned display
Search verb indexes	Index (sign is illegal)
Financial amounts in files of records	Signed packed-decimal

Figure 11.9 Data requirements and choice of representation

Binary:	• Numbers represented in binary as bit strings	
	• Picture	• only the characters 9, s, v and p
	• Class	• always numeric
		• may not be the subject of a class test
	• Size	• 1 to 18 digits plus a sign
	• Storage	• as determined by the implementor, e.g. 2, 4 or 8 bytes
Computational: (also Comp)	• Numbers represented in a form determined by the compiler implementor (In most cases this is likely to be a synonym for binary.)	
Display:	• Strings represented in the standard data format of the computer, e.g. ASCII byte strings	
	• Picture	• any valid combination
	• Category	• depends on the characters in its picture clause
		• may be subject of a class test
	• Size	• for non-numeric strings from 1 to a maximum determined by the implementor, e.g. 65 535
		• for numeric strings 1 to 18 digits plus a sign
	• Storage	• as determined by the implementor, e.g. 1 character per byte but for numeric strings the sign may be either a separate character or embedded within the string
Packed-decimal:	• Numbers represented in denary in such a way that each digit occupies the minimum amount of space	
	• Picture	• only the characters 9, s, v and p
	• Category	• always numeric
		• may not be the subject of a class test
	• Size	• 1 to 18 digits
	• Storage	• as determined by the implementor, e.g. one nibble for the sign plus one nibble per digit rounded up to an even number of nibbles
Index:	• Numbers used to reference elements in a table. The exact representation is determined by the compiler implementor	
	• Picture	• none
	• Class	• always numeric
		• may not be the subject of a class test
	• Size	• not applicable

Figure 11.10 Usage in COBOL

314   ESSENTIAL COBOL: A FIRST COURSE IN STRUCTURED COBOL

The final usage provided by standard COBOL is **index**. This particular usage will be covered fully in Chapter 13, where it is used in table handling. For the present we can note that an index is a special item that is used when accessing table elements under the control of the search statement. Items with a usage of index do not have picture clauses and there are certain restrictions associated with their use.

Figure 11.9 gives a few examples of how data requirements can influence the choice of representation. Subsequent sample programs will use binary, packed-decimal, and index items where these are appropriate. Their uses will be explained within the context of the particular programs in which they are required.

Figure 11.10 gives the most important forms of usage in standard COBOL. Note that **computational** is also a usage in COBOL. This should be avoided because the standard does not specify how this will be implemented.

11.3 DATA VALIDATION AND CONVERSION

The extensive features that COBOL has for data representation and conversion between different representations are important in making the language an important one for data processing. Typically data begins its life as character strings that are input at terminals. Once the data is captured it is then often converted to internal representations that are suitable for long-term use within a system. Thereafter from time to time it may need to be reported back at terminals or on printed reports so that it can be examined and perhaps changed by users of the system. The case study program at the end of this chapter shows how program stock1 uses program accept3 to create a record of data using different forms of representation. In this section we will simply consider a single data item and imagine the processes through which it might pass from input at a terminal to a final report.

The item we will use is called amount. Let us imagine that it is a piece of data in a financial application and enters the application at a terminal. In this application we will assume that amount must be less than 5000 pounds or dollars and that the user can optionally type in a pence or cents fraction to the amount. Thus all of the following values are valid character strings that the user may wish to type in response to a prompt for an amount:

    5000
    5000.00
    4999.99
    4999.98
    1246.25
    1246
    0000.01
    0000.00

We can call accept3 to get a number for us and when it returns control we can check to see what sort of number the user has typed. (Clearly if accept3 reports an error then we need check no further but should display an appropriate error message to the user and call accept3 again.) The number that accept3 returns to the calling program should be either 0 to 4 digits long with a scale factor of 0 or 0 to 6 digits long with a scale factor of 2. If it is not we should call accept3 again to get a number that is within range. However, if it is in range then we can move l1-number to a more appropriate representation.

```
01   e1-rec.
     03   e1-amount1                              pic s9(4)v99.
     03   e1-amount2 redefines e1-amount1 pic s9(6).
```

If the scale factor is 2 then l1-number should be moved to e1-amount2 so that the 0 to 6 digits in the number are correctly aligned as pence/cents. If the scale factor is 0 then l1-number should be moved to e1-amount1 so that the pounds/dollars are properly aligned. COBOL always aligns on the decimal point and then either fills with zeros or truncates to either side of the decimal point as necessary. Therefore by moving l1-number to e1-amount1 the pence/cents part of the number will be initialized to two zeros.

Whether the move was to e1-amount1 or to e1-amount2 it is now the case that e1-amount1 holds a valid numeric amount with the implied decimal point in the correct position. It is six characters long and has a sign stored within it. However, the value within it is within the range of −9999.99 to +9999.99. Therefore a condition-name condition could be used to make certain that the item is within the range specified by the application:

```
01   e1-rec.
     03   e1-amount1                              pic s9(4)v99.
          88   e1-valid value 0000.00 thru +5000.00
     03   e1-amount2 redefines e1-amount1 pic s9(6).
```

The plus sign on the condition is optional because in the absence of the sign the item is assumed to be positive. (A minus value could also have been used provided that range is in ascending order. For example, −5000.00 to +5000.00.) Provided that e1-amount1 passes the range test we can proceed to use the item but if it fails the test we should output an appropriate error message and call accept3 for another input.

Once e1-amount is valid within the terms of the financial application we can then convert it to an internal form if this is required. Imagine that amount is one of 200 items on a master record and that the system holds over a million master records. It might be the case that all numeric financial items are stored as packed-decimal.

```
03   e2-amount packed-decimal pic s9(5)v99.
```

In this case e1-amount could be moved directly to e2-amount in the master record and would be automatically converted to the correct form of representation. E2-amount has been shown as one digit longer that e1-amount1. The reason for this is that the sign and each of the digits in a packed-decimal item take up a nibble. Therefore the item will still only take four bytes to store and allows for inflationary expansion of the amount at no cost in storage. (It is common practice to show packed-decimal amounts as uneven numbers of digits in this way.)

At some future time it may be necessary to report e2-amount. Because it is stored in an internal representation it cannot be displayed by standard COBOL. Therefore prior to being displayed it should be moved to an appropriate numeric edited item which will convert it back to a character string.

```
       03   e3-amount           pic 9(5).99.           01234.56
       03   e4-amount           pic z(4)9.99.          △1234.56
       03   e5-amount           pic z(4)9.            △1234
       03   e6-amount           pic $(5).99.          $1234.56
```

The four simple edit masks above are examples of appropriate numeric edited targets to which e2-amount might be moved for reporting purposes. The strings to the right-hand side show the character string that would result if e2-amount held a value of +0123456 at the time the move was made to a target. Many other edit characters are available in COBOL. These are to be found in the published standard and in the language reference manuals supplied by various suppliers.

11.4 CASE STUDY: STOCK1 (VALIDATING NUMERIC INPUT)

Program stock1 in Fig. 11.11 is a short validation program that demonstrates how to manage numeric input from the keyboard. The application is entirely hypothetical. In practice, most stock control records would contain considerably more data than this. However, the study is realistic in the sense that it covers the data validation problems that are usually encountered with numbers. Thus a live application would contain more data but not necessarily more unique validation problems. The other reason that stock1 is not truly an application is that the data it captures from the keyboard is not permanently stored. This has been done intentionally so that other issues do not conceal the central problem of data validation. (Storing the data in files is outlined in the case study exercises.)

```
 1 identification division.
 2 program-id. stock1.
 3*Purpose: To build valid stock records from keyboard input.
 4
 5 environment division.
 6
 7 data division.
 8 working-storage section.
 9 copy "rec001.cop".
10
11 01  k2-infield            pic x.
12     88  k2-eok value "Q" "q".
13
14 01  k3-stock-rec.
15     03  k3-code                     pic 9(4).
16         88  k3-code-valid           value 1000 thru 6521.
17     03  k3-desc                     pic x(20).
18     03  k3-cost packed-decimal      pic s9(9)v99.
19         88  k3-cost-valid           value 00000001.00 thru 10000000.00.
20     03  k3-disc                     pic sv999.
21         88  k3-disc-valid           value .050 thru .990.
22     03  k3-supplier-list.
23         05  k3-sub                  pic 99.
24         05  k3-suppliers occurs 10.
25             07  k3-supplier         pic 999.
26
```

```
27 01  w4-stock-workers.
28     03   filler packed-decimal.
29          05   w4-cost              pic s9(8)v99.
30          05   w4-cost-unscaled     redefines
31               w4-cost              pic s9(10).
32     03   filler.
33          05   w4-disc              pic sv999.
34          05   w4-disc-unscaled     redefines
35               w4-disc              pic s999.
36     03   w4-end-suppliers          pic x.
37          88   w4-not-end           value space.
38          88   w4-end               value "N" "n".
39
40 procedure division.
41 para1.
42     display "stock1 begins"
43
44     display "Type 'Q' to quit"
45     accept k2-infield
46
47*    MAIN-LOOP
48     perform test before until k2-eok
49        display "Input a stock record"
50
51*       CODE
52        display "Code: " no advancing
53        call "accept3" using l1-rec
54        move l1-number to k3-code
55        perform test before until l1-success and
56                                 l1-length < 5 and
57                                 l1-scale = 0 and
58                                 k3-code-valid
59           display "bad input"
60           display "CODE: " no advancing
61           call "accept3" using l1-rec
62           move l1-number to k3-code
63        end-perform
64*       END-CODE
65
66*       DESCRIPTION
67        display "Description :" no advancing
68        accept k3-desc
69*       COST
70        display "Cost: " no advancing
71        call "accept3" using l1-rec
72        move l1-number to w4-cost-unscaled
73        move w4-cost to k3-cost
74        perform test before until l1-success and
75                                 l1-length < 11 and
76                                 l1-scale = 2 and
77                                 k3-cost-valid
78           display "bad input"
79           display "Cost: " no advancing
80           call "accept3" using l1-rec
81           move l1-number to w4-cost-unscaled
82           move w4-cost to k3-cost
83        end-perform
84*       END-COST
85
```

```
 86*        DISCOUNT
 87         display "Discount: " no advancing
 88         call "accept3" using l1-rec
 89         move l1-number to w4-disc-unscaled
 90         move w4-disc to k3-disc
 91         perform test before until l1-success and
 92                                   l1-length < 4 and
 93                                   l1-scale = 3 and
 94                                   k3-disc-valid
 95           display "bad input"
 96           display "Discount: " no advancing
 97           call "accept3" using l1-rec
 98           move l1-number to w4-disc-unscaled
 99           move w4-disc to k3-disc
100         end-perform
101*        END-DISCOUNT
102
103*        SUPPLIERS
104         move 1 to k3-sub
105         display "Input suppliers? Y/N: " no advancing
106         accept w4-end-suppliers
107         perform test before until w4-end
108           display "Supplier: " no advancing
109           call "accept3" using l1-rec
110           move l1-number to k3-supplier(k3-sub)
111           perform test before until l1-success and
112                                     l1-length < 4 and
113                                     l1-scale = 0
114             display "bad input"
115             display "Supplier: " no advancing
116             call "accept3" using l1-rec
117             move l1-number to k3-supplier(k3-sub)
118           end-perform
119           display "Input another? Y/N: " no advancing
120           accept w4-end-suppliers
121           compute k3-sub = k3-sub + 1
122           evaluate true
123             when    k3-sub = 11
124               set w4-end to true
125           end-evaluate
126         end-perform
127*        END-SUPPLIERS
128
129         display "Type 'Q' to quit"
130         accept k2-infield
131       end-perform
132*    END-MAIN-LOOP
133
134     display "stock1 ends"
135     stop run.
136
137 end program stock1
```

Figure 11.11 Program stock1

The program takes five input data items and after validation moves them to a stock record (line 14). The main loop (lines 48 to 131) prompts the user for each item in turn and then calls accept3 using a copy of its parameter record (line 9).

As each item is accepted it is validated by a validation trap. For example, line 53 of the program calls accept3 for a code which must be four digits long and in the range of 1000 to 6521 (line 15). The number resulting from the call is moved to k3-code and then the validation trap (lines 55 to 63) ensures that the value in k3-code is valid. The tests for the trap are in the following priority and are connected by the **and** operator:

1. l1-success
2. l1-length < 5
3. l1-scale = 0
4. k3-code-valid

The first test ensures that accept3 has returned a number. If this first test fails then COBOL's *short circuit evaluation* guarantees that the other conditions will not be tested because regardless of their result the overall value of the complex condition will be false and therefore the contents of the loop must be executed. However, if the first test is true then the second condition will be tested and so on down to the fourth test. Thus the loop will be executed if any one of the tests fails and not executed only if all of them succeed in being true.

The first test has the highest priority because none of the other items to be tested has a defined value if accept3 does not return with a number. The second and third tests have the same priority but both of these have a higher priority than the fourth test. For example, if the user had typed 12345.67 at the keyboard, accept3 would have returned success with a number of 1234567, a length of 7 and a scale of 2. The move to k3-code would result in it holding a value of 4567 due to the alignment on the decimal point. Thus k3-code-valid would be true even though the number returned by accept3 was out of range.

In this particular example the priority of the tests can be swapped about without any change to the overall result. However, it is wise always to write tests that have an implied priority in their correct sequence for the following reasons:

1. If the tests contained intermediate statements between them then the results may be unreliable. This would occur, for example, if the control structure were written as four nested perform loops with additional statements in each loop.
2. The running program will be more efficient because the test with the highest priority is tested first and therefore subsequent tests can be skipped if the first one fails.
3. It is easier to read when the tests are correctly prioritized. In this example the control of the perform loop can be translated into the following narrative:

   'Skip this loop provided that accept3 returns a number, that this number is less than five digits, that it is unscaled, and that it falls in the range of 1000 to 6521.'

The second item that the program takes as input is a description of a 20-character alphanumeric string (line 68). This is not validated. The third item is a cost which is defined at line 18 as a signed packed-decimal item of 11 digits plus a sign. (This will be stored in six bytes.) K3-cost-valid shows that the valid range is from 1 to 10 million pounds/dollars (eight digits) and that the item is scaled for pence/cents (two digits). The picture clause uses the 'v' symbol to show where the implied decimal point exists within the digits for any moves or calculations. (Note that the picture clause defines 11 digits but that the range is up to only 10 digits. Remember that 10 and 11 digits both take up the same number of bytes with packed-decimal items.)

The number that is returned from accept3 is moved to a signed 10 digit number at line 72. The filler at line 28 shows that both w4-cost and w4-cost-unscaled are packed-decimal items. Therefore as a result of the move the number will have been converted into packed-decimal and properly aligned. At line 74 a redefined version of the same number is moved to k3-cost. Both w4-cost and k3-cost share the same scaling factor so the result in k3-cost is that the number is correctly aligned on the implied decimal point.

However, the original number that was returned by accept3 may have been garbage and if this was the case then k3-cost now also holds garbage. Therefore the validation trap at line 74 ensures that the number was correct, that it had a correct length, that it had a scale of 2, and that the result in k3-cost is in range.

The fourth item, discount, is handled in a similar manner. It has been included to show that the implied decimal point can appear at the beginning of the string. (However, accept3 requires numbers to have a leading digit. Therefore the user must type numbers such as 0.057 even though COBOL allows the implied decimal point at the beginning of the digit string.)

The final item is a table of suppliers that is at the end of the stock record. The outer loop (line 107) builds up a table of suppliers' numbers and the inner loop (line 111) provides a validation trap for each number.

11.5 EXERCISES

11.5.1 General

1 Write a program called usage2 which contains a large record with numeric items that have picture clauses similar to those in Fig. 11.5. You might sub-divide the record into groups that have the same picture clauses but different usages. Use a series of paired statements to give different values to each item and to write a record to a file.

   Dump the file and compare the contents of the file with the record definition in the program. First find the correct alignments for each data item and then decode the hexadecimal values from the dump to ensure that you understand how each item is stored.

2 Write program usage3 which displays the contents of the record at the screen. Items with an internal representation should be moved to an appropriate edited item prior to display.

3 Write program usage4 which uses screen2 to display each item at a set of predetermined coordinates so that the display is represented as columns of data that are decimal point aligned on the screen.

4 Write program bench1 to discover the relative execution efficiency of display, packed-decimal and binary items. The basic test element might be a statement to add two

numbers followed by a statement to multiply two numbers. These should be contained within separate loops which are executed a very large number of times for each of the three usages. Your program will have to accept the time from the system immediately before and after the execution of each loop. (See general formats as well as the COBOL manual for your installation for specific information concerning how time is represented by your system.) The total time taken to execute each loop can then be calculated and the different times can be represented as ratios. (A further variation would be to execute the test for pairs of numbers from one to 18 digits that are either signed or unsigned.)

If you are using your own microcomputer then the results will be reliable. However, if you are working in a multi-user environment then the elapsed times will depend on many additional factors that are beyond your immediate control, such as the number of other people that are using the system at the time your program executes. Therefore you should consider writing a benchmark program of this type as a group exercise with the help of your instructor. In any case, your intention to run the program should be discussed with a representative from your computer centre so that arrangements can be made to run it during the middle of the night or at some other time when there are no other users on the system.

11.5.2 Case study

5   Compile stock1 and link accept3 into it. Run stock1 until you are confident of the user behaviour it prompts and until you can follow the progress of the program as it moves through its various loops.

6   The stock record is not initialized to any values prior to putting values into the record. This does not cause problems with the first four items because the program is written in such a way each item is given a value in the main loop. However, the table of suppliers can contain 0 to 10 numbers and if the table is not filled with a full 10 valid numbers then those that follow the last input from the keyboard will be undefined. Therefore rewrite stock1 as stock2 in which the record is either initialized to spaces at the top of the main loop or the table of suppliers is initialized to spaces prior to entering in the first supplier. This will guarantee that the record is always filled with trailing spaces.

7   The item k3-sub is used to enter items in the table. However, after the items have been entered k3-sub is one greater than the number of items in the table. Rewrite stock2 as stock3 so that after completing the table of of suppliers, k3-sub holds a value that is the exact number of suppliers in the table. (This value should be in the range of 1 to 10.)

8   Rewrite stock3 as stock4 in which the program calculates the record length of the stock record at the bottom of the main loop and then writes the record with this length to a file called stock.dat.

9   Design a set of test cases for input to stock4. Run stock4. Dump stock.dat to ensure that you understand the storage strategy that the system has used in writing the stock records to the file.

10 Rewrite stock4 as stock5 in which the record has been changed. For example, you might change the discount item to packed-decimal. Run stock5 with the same test

cases from the previous question, dump the file and compare the two file dumps for the differences that your change has made. (If you want to make more than one change to the record you should do a dump and comparison after each change so that you are certain of the effects you are producing.)

11 Rewrite either stock4 or stock5 as stock6 in which the program uses calls to screen2 to present a stable screen to the user.

12 Rewrite stock6 as stock7 so that the program displays a count of the number of records that the user has input. It might also allow the user to decide at the bottom of the main loop whether or not to write the record to the file.

12
PROGRAMMING CALCULATIONS

COBOL has five arithmetic verbs: **compute**, **add**, **subtract**, **multiply** and **divide**. With the exception of modular division, the compute statement can be used to do all arithmetic calculations. Nevertheless the other four verbs have been included for completeness.

By the end of this chapter you will be able to do accurate arithmetic with these verbs, understand the importance of signed numbers for most arithmetic operations, determine the existence of intermediate results, and use the size error and rounded phrases.

12.1 SIZE ERROR PHRASES

In previous chapters we have taken care to ensure that computed values always fall within a known range. This may not always be possible. Firstly, calculations may have to be done on data that is supplied from outside the program. Secondly, an application may evolve over time under the pressure of factors such as inflation and corporate growth which might cause data values to increase in size beyond their initial specification. COBOL provides two size error phrases that assist in managing these problems.

Consider the following statement when e1-var is described as a one-digit unsigned number:

```
compute e1-var = e1-var + 1
```

What will happen when e1-var holds the value 9 immediately prior to the execution of the compute statement? COBOL states that the value of e1-var will remain unchanged when the size of the result is in error relative to the picture clause of the target. However, if e1-var had initially been in the range of 0 to 8 then the compute statement would have

323

incremented the target by 1. Therefore a target data item will or will not hold a new value depending on whether or not a computation is successful.

COBOL provides **size error** phrases to assist in managing this issue:

```
compute e1-var = e1-var + 1
  size error display "e1-var - overflow in compute statement"
end-compute
```

The rules for the size error phrase state that if a size error occurs then control will be transferred to the size error phrase and the target of the computation will not be affected. Thus the phrase provides us with the ability to take some form of corrective or evasive action should a problem arise. There is also a **not size error** phrase:

```
compute e1-var = e1-var + 1
    size error     display "e1-var - overflow in compute statement"
not size error display "compute was successful"
end-compute
```

In the above example the size error phrases each contain display statements for purposes of illustration only. In financial applications it is not uncommon for size error phrases to control substantial sets of statements that do calculations or write error reports.

There are three possibilities that may cause an arithmetic statement to produce a size error:

1. The result is too large to be stored in the target item. This example is similar to the one above but uses the multiplication operator. The result of multiplying 99 times 99 is 9801. Therefore the result is too large for the target.

   ```
   01   e2-var   value 99   pic s99.
   01   e3-var   value 99   pic s99.
   01   e4-var              pic s999.

       compute e4-var = e2-var * e3-var
           size error display "e4-var is overflowing"
       end-compute
   ```

2. Division by zero. The parentheses force e5-var and e6-var to be summed prior to the division. This gives an intermediate result of zero. Division by zero is always illegal no matter how it arises.

   ```
   01   e5-var   value +8   pic s9.
   01   e6-var   value -8   pic s9.
   01   e7-var   value 23   pic s99.

       compute e7-var = e7-var / (e5-var + e6-var)
           size error display "attempted division by zero"
       end-compute
   ```

3. Violation of the rules of exponentiation. The double asterisk (**)is the exponentiation operator. It can be used to raise a number to a power. It is illegal to raise zero to the power of zero and this will therefore result in a size error.

```
01  e8-var   value +0  pic s9.
01  e9-var   value +0  pic s9.
01  e10-var            pic s9(18).

    compute e10-var = e9-var ** e8-var
      size error display "faulty exponentiation"
    end-compute
```

The above examples are contrived. This is because the values used in these expressions are initialized by value clauses. Therefore by a simple inspection of the data we can see that each statement will result in a size error. In practice the source of the data is likely to be external to the program and then the size error phrases should be used because it is not easy to know prior to running the program whether or not size errors might occur.

12.2 ROUNDING OPTION

Calculations often yield fractional results. For example,

```
01  e11-var  value 2  pic s9.
01  e12-var  value 3  pic s9.
01  e13-var           pic s9v99.

    compute e13-var = e11-var / e12-var
```

Dividing 2 by 3 will give a result of 0.6 repeating. COBOL by default will truncate fractional results. Therefore this compute statement will put a result of 0.66 in the target. However, the following statement will put 0.67 in the target:

```
    compute e13-var rounded = e11-var / e12-var
```

Rounding up occurs when the fraction is 0.5 or more. Lesser values such as 0.49 repeating are rounded down. As with the size error phrases, this option is also available for all of the arithmetic verbs.

12.3 COMPUTE

The compute statement enables us to assign the value of an arithmetic expression to one or more numeric data items. Its full syntax is as follows:

```
compute {identifier-1 [rounded]}... = arithmetic-expression-1

 [{| size error       statement-1 |}]
 [{| not size error   statement-2 |}]
 [ end-compute                       ]
```

Operator	Meaning
+	addition
−	subtraction
*	multiplication
/	division
**	exponentiation

Order of evaluation of arithmetic expressions

1. Sign of number
2. Exponentiation
3. Multiplication and division
4. Addition and subtraction

Exponentiation rules

1. A value of zero raised to the exponent zero results in a size error.
2. If both a positive and a negative result are possible, a positive result is returned.
3. If no *real number* results then a size error exists.

Figure 12.1 Arithmetic rules and operators

If neither of the size error phrases is used then the compute statement is unconditional and the end-compute is not used. If either or both of the size error phrases is used then the statement becomes conditional and the end-compute scope delimiter is required.

The target or targets of a compute statement can be numeric or numeric edited items. However, the arithmetic expression cannot include numeric edited items. It must be constructed from elementary numeric items, numeric literals, and the five *arithmetic operators*. Parentheses can be used to over-ride the default order of evaluation. The arithmetic operators and rules governing their use are shown in Fig. 12.1.

The arithmetic operators in common with the logical and relational operators must be preceded and followed by at least one space. For example,

```
compute e1-var = e1-var - 8 * e1-var + 5 / e1-var
```

Even when the order of evaluation is correct it is good practice to use parentheses to improve the readability of a statement:

```
compute e1-var = e1-var - (8 * e1-var) + (5 / e1-var)
```

The exponentiation operator is used to calculate values to a power. For example,

```
compute e1-var = e1-var ** 3
```

gives the cube of e1-var whereas

```
compute e1-var = e1-var ** 0.5
```

gives the square root of e1-var.

The right-hand side of a compute statement is simply defined by COBOL as an arithmetic expression. For most purposes this allows us considerable flexibility in designing statements. However, this raises an issue of which the programmer must be aware. This is that the evaluation of an arithmetic expression may require intermediate results. Compare the following examples:

```
01   e1-var1  value 3   pic 9.
01   e1-var2  value 6   pic 9.
     compute e1-var1 = e1-var1 - e1-var2
     compute e1-var1 = e1-var1 - 1
```

The first statement will yield a result of 3 because the operands are not signed. Therefore the second statement will yield a final result of 2. However, consider the effect of the following compute statement for the same data:

```
compute e1-var1 = (e1-var1 - e1-var2) - 1
```

The sub-expression in parentheses calculates an intermediate result which is then to be decremented by 1. If the intermediate result were unsigned, then the final result would be 2 as in the previous example. However, intermediate results are signed. Therefore 3 minus 6 is -3 and 1 subtracted from -3 gives a result of -4. Due to the fact that e1-var1 is unsigned, the final result will be 4 and not 2.

COBOL allows the targets of arithmetic statements to be either numeric or numeric edited and either signed or unsigned. However, the use of numeric edited targets or unsigned targets causes a compiler to generate additional code and intermediate results. When we consider this together with the semantic problem of getting different results with unsigned operands, it becomes clear that numbers in COBOL should be signed and unedited wherever possible.

The size of intermediate results is not specified in the COBOL standard. However, a validated compiler will support 18 digit numbers for most purposes. For example, VAX COBOL uses signed intermediate results of up to 26 digits.

COBOL allows arithmetic to be done with numeric items that are stored in any usage. However, expressions that have numeric items with incompatible usages will force the compiler to generate conversion code. This may be critical in some applications where high volumes of data are being processed.

Therefore it is good practice to try to do arithmetic with signed numbers of the same usage and of a maximum picture size relative to the required storage allocation. (See Chapter 11.) Thus the previous example might have been written using signed numbers as follows:

```
01   e1-var1  binary value 3   pic s9(5).
01   e1-var2  binary value 6   pic s9(5).
     compute e1-var1 = (e1-var1 - e1-var2) - 1
```

Data may be the subject of many computations during its lifetime. Therefore it is sensible to convert data to suitable internal forms when it is first input and validated in an application. In industry it is common for companies to have a policy concerning number specification that includes the sign, picture size, and usage for different styles of number.

SELF-CHECK QUESTIONS

Q What is the output from the following?

```
01  e1-vars.
    03  e1-var1  value  1   pic 9.
    03  e1-var2  value  2   pic 9.
    03  e1-var3  value 30   pic 99.

    compute e1-var3 = e1-var3 + 1
    display e1-var3
    compute e1-var3 = e1-var2 * e1-var1
    display e1-var3 " " e1-var2 " " e1-var1
    compute e1-var3 = (e1-var2 + 2) * 5
    display e1-var3 " " e1-var2
    compute e1-var3 = ((e1-var2 + 2) * 5) / (e1-var1 + 1)
    display e1-var3 " " e1-var2 " " e1-var1
```

A The output is:

```
31
02 2 1
20 2
10 2 1
```

Q What is the output from the following?

```
01  e2-vars.
    03  e2-var1  value 09   pic 99.
    03  e2-var2  value 20   pic 99.
    03  e2-var3  value 30   pic 99.

    compute e2-var3 e2-var2 = e2-var1 * e2-var1
    display e2-var3 " " e2-var2 " " e2-var1
    compute e2-var3 = ((e2-var2 - 80) * 2) * (e2-var1 - 6)
    display e2-var3 " " e2-var2 " " e2-var1
```

A The output is:

```
81 81 09
06 81 09
```

Q What is wrong with each of the following compute statements?

```
linkage section.
01  e3-vars.
    03  e3-var1  pic s9.
    03  e3-var2  pic s9.
    03  e3-var3  pic s99.

procedure division using e3-vars.
para1.
    compute e3-var3 = e3-var1 + 1000
    compute e3-var3 = (e3-var3 + 2) * 5
    compute e3-var3 = e3-var2 * e3-var1 / e3-var1
    compute e3-var3 = ((e3-var2 + 2) * 5)/ (e3-var1 - 1)
```

A The first statement will always produce a result that is too large for the target. The second statement may produce a result that is too large. The last two examples may result in an attempt to divide by zero.

12.4 ADD

The full format for the add statement provides two main options:

$$\text{add} \begin{Bmatrix} \text{identifier-1} \\ \text{literal-1} \end{Bmatrix} \dots \text{to} \begin{Bmatrix} \{\text{identifier-2 [rounded]}\}\dots \\ \begin{Bmatrix} \text{identifier-3} \\ \text{literal-2} \end{Bmatrix} \text{giving } \{\text{identifier-4 [rounded]}\}\dots \end{Bmatrix}$$

$$\begin{bmatrix} \begin{Bmatrix} \text{size error} & \text{statement-1} \\ \text{not size error} & \text{statement-2} \end{Bmatrix} \\ \text{end-add} \end{bmatrix}$$

The first option allows a data item or a literal to be added to an existing value. For example,

```
add 1 to e1-ctr
```

will increment e1-ctr by 1. It is often used in preference to

```
compute e1-ctr = e1-ctr + 1
```

simply because it is briefer.*

The second option which uses the giving phrase is a useful way of adding two numbers together when the result is to be placed into a list of one or more target items.

```
add 1 to e1-var1 giving e1-var2
compute e1-var2 = e1-var1 + 1
add 1 to e1-var1 giving e1-var2 e1-var3 e1-var4
compute e1-var2 e1-var3 e1-var4 = e1-var1 + 1
```

The statements in each of the above pairs produce the same results. The first pair puts the result into a target list consisting of one item while the second pair puts the result into three items. None of these four statements changes the value of e1-var1.

---

* In past decades many COBOL compilers used to generate inefficient or incorrect code for compute statements. This caused the statement to be banned in many organizations in its early years. Nowadays, the compute statement is well implemented and questions of relative efficiency or correctness should not influence your choice between it and any of the other arithmetic verbs.

12.5 SUBTRACT

The full format for the subtract statement provides two main options:

$$\text{subtract} \begin{Bmatrix} \text{identifier-1} \\ \text{literal-1} \end{Bmatrix} \ldots \text{from} \begin{Bmatrix} \{\text{identifier-2 [rounded]}\}\ldots \\ \begin{Bmatrix} \text{identifier-3} \\ \text{literal-2} \end{Bmatrix} \text{giving} \{\text{identifier-4 [rounded]}\}\ldots \end{Bmatrix}$$

$$\begin{bmatrix} \begin{Bmatrix} \text{size error} & \text{statement-1} \\ \text{not size error} & \text{statement-2} \end{Bmatrix} \\ \text{end-subtract} \end{bmatrix}$$

The first option allows a data item or a literal to be subtracted from an existing value. It is very similar to the add statement in its use as the following examples show:

```
subtract 1 from e1-ctr
compute e1-ctr = e1-ctr - 1
```

The above paired subtract and compute statements have the same effect.

The second option which uses the giving phrase is a useful way of subtracting one number from another when the result is to be placed into a list of one or more target items.

```
subtract 1 from e1-var1 giving e1-var2
compute e1-var2 = e1-var1 - 1
subtract 1 from e1-var1 giving e1-var2 e1-var3 e1-var4
compute e1-var2 e1-var3 e1-var4 = e1-var1 - 1
```

The statements in each of the above pairs produce the same results. The first pair puts the result into a target list consisting of one item while the second pair puts the result into three items. None of these four statements changes the value of e1-var1.

12.6 MULTIPLY

The full format for the multiply statement provides two main options:

$$\text{multiply} \begin{Bmatrix} \text{identifier-1} \\ \text{literal-1} \end{Bmatrix} \ldots \text{by} \begin{Bmatrix} \{\text{identifier-2 [rounded]}\}\ldots \\ \begin{Bmatrix} \text{identifier-3} \\ \text{literal-2} \end{Bmatrix} \text{giving} \{\text{identifier-4 [rounded]}\}\ldots \end{Bmatrix}$$

$$\begin{bmatrix} \begin{Bmatrix} \text{size error} & \text{statement-1} \\ \text{not size error} & \text{statement-2} \end{Bmatrix} \\ \text{end-multiply} \end{bmatrix}$$

The first option allows a data item or a literal to be multiplied with an existing value. It is very similar to the add statement in its use as the following examples show:

```
multiply 2 by e1-ctr
compute e1-ctr = e1-ctr * 2
```

The above paired multiply and compute statements have the same effect.

The second option which uses the giving phrase is a useful way of multiplying one number with another when the result is to be placed into a list of one or more target items.

```
multiply 2 by e1-var1 giving e1-var2
compute e1-var2 = e1-var1 * 2

multiply 2 by e1-var1 giving e1-var2 e1-var3 e1-var4
compute e1-var2 e1-var3 e1-var4 = e1-var1 * 2
```

The statements in each of the above pairs produce the same results. The first pair puts the result into a target list consisting of one item while the second pair puts the result into three items. None of these four statements changes the value of e1-var1.

12.7 DIVIDE

The full format for the divide statement provides a number of options:

```
divide
    {identifier-1} into {identifier-2 [rounded]} ...
    {literal-1  }
    {identifier-1} into {identifier-2}  giving {identifier-3 [rounded]} ...
    {literal-1  } by   {literal-2  }          {identifier-4 [rounded] [remainder identifier-4]}
    [{ size error     statement-1 }]
    [{ not size error statement-2 }]
    [end-divide]
```

The first option allows one number to be divided into a list of one or more numbers. The results are stored into the items in the list.

```
divide 2 into e1-ctr
compute e1-ctr = e1-ctr / 2

divide 2 into e1-var1 e1-var2 e1-var3 e1-var4
```

The above paired divide and compute statements have the same effect. The second divide statement has no functionally equivalent compute statement.

The second main option uses the **giving** phrase and allows the operands to be reversed with the keywords into and by. For example:

```
divide 3 into e1-var1 giving e1-var2
divide e1-var1 by 3 giving e1-var2
compute e1-var2 = e1-var1 / 3

divide 3 into e1-var1 giving e1-var2 e1-var3 e1-var4
divide e1-var1 by 3 giving e1-var2 e1-var3 e1-var4
compute e1-var2 e1-var3 e1-var4 = e1-var1 / 3

divide 3 into 5 giving e1-var2 e1-var3 e1-var4
divide 5 by 3 giving e1-var2 e1-var3 e1-var4
compute e1-var2 e1-var3 e1-var4 = 5 / 3
```

The statements within each of the above three triplets produce the same result. The first triplet put the result into a target list consisting of one item while the second triplet puts the results into three items. None of these six statements changes the value of e1-var1. The statements in the last triplet all divide two literals and put the result into the items in the target list.

In all of the above examples a fractional result will be truncated although the rounded option can be used to produce rounded results. Therefore 5 divided by 3 might result in either 1.66 or 1.67 for a target with a two-digit fractional portion, depending on whether truncation or rounding is specified.

However, it is also the case that 5 divided by 3 can produce whole number results. In this case the result will be 1 with a remainder of 2. The remainder phrase allows us to specify modular arithmetic of this type:

```
divide 3 into e1-var1 giving e1-var2 remainder e1-rem
divide e1-var1 by 4 giving e1-var2 remainder e1-rem

divide 5 by 3 giving e1-var2 remainder e1-rem
divide 3 into 5 giving e1-var2 remainder e1-rem
```

The statements in each pair will have the same result. There are no equivalent compute statements.

12.8 EXERCISES

There is no case study for this chapter. Instead extra exercises have been included. For every exercise you should ensure that the numeric data you use is valid numeric data prior to doing any calculations.

1   A leap year is a calendar year of 366 days in which February 29 (leap day) is the additional day. Its purpose is to make up the difference between the calendar year (365 days) and the solar year (365.2422 days). However, an additional day every four

years is slightly more than the time required to make up the difference. Therefore in those century years that are not divisible by 400 there is no February 29th in order to bring the calendar back into line with the solar year. As a result the year 1900 was not a leap year but the year 2000 will be.

Write program leap1 that when called will determine whether or not a given year is a leap year.

2 On his fifth birthday Uncle Scrooge had the financial wisdom to invest 100 dollars in a savings account. If interest remained constant at 15 percent and was compounded annually, how much was in his account on his 10th birthday? Write program scrooge1 to solve this problem.

3 Rewrite scrooge1 as scrooge2 so that it can make a similar calculation based on the inputs: present age in years, age in years at withdrawal, required rate of annual interest.

4 Some years later Uncle Scrooge decided to become a millionaire. He discovered that a required sum of money could be realized by an initial sum at a fixed annual rate of interest. For example, 100 dollars can be realized by investing 86.96 dollars for one year at 15 percent as a result of the following formula where n is the amount of the initial investment:

$$\frac{15 * n}{100} + n = 100$$

Write program scrooge3 that by working backwards can determine how many years it will take to become a millionaire for a given initial investment and a given rate of interest.

5 A piggy bank contains a sum of money in pennies, nickels, and dimes. Write program piggy1 that when given the sum of money in the piggy bank as well as the number of pennies and dimes it contains will calculate the number of nickels. (1 dollar = 10 dimes = 20 nickels = 100 pennies.)

6 The brightness of light from a source decreases by the inverse square of the distance from it. Write program light1 that will calculate brightness for a given distance from the source.

7 Write program expiry1 to decode a product expiry date. For example, Obfuscator Co. Inc. codes months as even letters, each digit of the day as 'Z' to 'Q', and the year as the ordinal position of 'A' to 'Z' from a base year of 1985. Thus 5 February 1990 is encoded as D-V-E.

8 John Bull is about to become a sales representative for a window replacement company. He must choose between three different payment arrangements:
  (a) a wage of 200 pounds per week with no commission;
  (b) a wage of 2 pounds per hour for a maximum 40 hour week with 18 per cent commission on sales;
  (c) a straight commission of 25 per cent plus 1.50 for every window sold.

Write program window1 that when given a range of hours and a range of expected sales will generate an earnings forecast for John.

9 A square root can be calculated by raising a number to the power of 0.5. Use the

exponentiation operator and write program root1 to produce a table for the numbers 1 to 20 that gives the number, its square, and its square root.

10 A useful computing formula for standard deviation is:

$$S = \sqrt{\frac{\sum X_i^2 - ((\sum X_i)^2/N)}{N}}$$

After an interview with a statistician you have learned that N is the number of observations, X is the value of each observation and i means that the operation should be done for each value of X. Furthermore your notes show that the formula can be operationalized into the following steps:

1. Square each X value.
2. Find the sum of the squares.
3. Take the sum of the X values and square the sum.
4. Divide the squared sum by N, subtract it from the sum of the squares, divide by N, and finally take the square root.

It is known that the standard deviation for the following set of 16 values is 6.01:

15,12,26,9,10,12,13,11,31,19,8,14,12,12,14,10

(a) Use the formula and operational steps to design variables and an algorithm for the calculation of standard deviation.
(b) Hand check the algorithm to ensure that it works correctly for the above test data.
(c) Write program stdev1 which when given a list of values at the keyboard will correctly calculate a standard deviation.
(d) Review the program and determine the limits for N and X within which it can successfully operate. Ensure that the program does not calculate spurious standard deviations for empty lists, non-numeric input, or values of X that are larger than expected.

11 Write program magic1 to investigate the result of following these steps:

1. Choose any four digits.
2. Rearrange them to form the largest and smallest number.
3. Subtract the smaller from the larger to get a new four-digit number.
4. Use this new number to repeat steps 2 and 3

How many subtractions can be done before nothing new happens?

12 Write program product1 to find three consecutive odd numbers which when multiplied together give the result 357 627.

13 Write program sum1 to find two consecutive square numbers which when summed give the result 1405.

14 A palindromic number is one which reads the same forwards and backwards. A prime number is a whole number which is only divisible by 1 or itself. The number 131 is both prime and palindromic. Write program pal1 to find the other four prime and palindromic numbers between 100 and 200.

15 Blaise Pascal, the French mathematician, philosopher, and religious zealot, for whom the Pascal programming language is named, is also known for discovering the following triangle:

```
              1
            1   1
          1   2   1
        1   3   3   1
      1   4   6   4   1
    1   5  10  10   5   1
```

Pascal's triangle has many interesting properties. One of these is that the numbers within the frame of 1s are formed by adding pairs of adjacent numbers from the line above.

(a) Write program zealot1 to display a Pascal triangle of 10 lines on the screen.

(b) Find other interesting properties in the triangle by hand. Write program zealot2 to demonstrate these same properties by computation.

16 Nim is a game for two people. The game starts with any number of counters arranged in any number of piles. Players take turns to remove counters. When making a play, each player can only remove counters from one pile and must take at least one counter. The winner is the player who takes the last counter from the last pile.

In Nim every position can be considered as safe or unsafe. From a safe position any play will create an unsafe position. But from an unsafe position a play may create either a safe position or an unsafe position. Therefore the player who can determine safe from unsafe positions can usually win a game over someone who is new to the game.

One strategy for playing Nim uses the following steps to decide how to make the next play:

1. Take the value of the number of counters in each pile and convert it to a binary number expressed as a string of 0 and 1 characters. For example, four piles with 7, 6, 9, and 12 counters will convert as follows:

Piles	Binary string
$A = 7$	111
$B = 6$	110
$C = 9$	1001
$D = 12$	1100

2. Sum each column from the binary strings but without carrying. As a result each column will add up to a number in the range of 0 to 9. In this example the sum string is 2322.

3. It is the case that all unsafe positions have one or more odd digits in the sum string. Therefore a move from unsafe to safe must remove counters in such a way that columns that add up to an odd number convert to an even number. For this example there are many safe moves. The following table gives three of them.

Piles	Unsafe	Safe	Safe	Safe
$A = 7$	111	111	111	11
$B = 6$	110	110	10	110
$C = 9$	1001	1001	1001	1001
$D = 12$	1100	1000	1100	1100
	2322	2222	2222	2222

Thus removing 4 from pile *D*, or 2 from pile *B*, or 2 from pile *A* will make the position safe.

Write program nim1 to play a game of Nim. It should ask a player to start the game by stating a number of piles and the number of counters in each pile. The program should then make the first move and continue playing with the player until one of them wins. Your program is likely to win most of the time.

(A player cannot win if the first position is unsafe and the opponent moves to a safe position on every subsequent move. When faced with a safe position the best bet is to remove one counter and hope that the opponent will move to an unsafe position.)

13
TABLE-HANDLING II

The ability to handle tables of data is a common requirement in data processing systems. COBOL provides the **search** statement so that tables held in memory can be searched easily and efficiently by specifying the main criteria to be used in the searching operation. By the end of this chapter you will be able to search any table of data *serially* and ordered tables of data by a *binary search* technique.

13.1 INDEXING

We have seen in Chapter 5 that any numeric item can be used as a subscript to access an element in a table. COBOL also provides indexing as a means to access table elements.

An index is a special data item with the following characteristics:

1. Internal representation. The exact method of representation is chosen by the implementor. (It is likely to be in a binary halfword or word similar to the usage binary. The location in memory of the index is not visible to the program.)
2. No picture clause. Because the implementor is free to represent the index by any means, there is no need for the programmer to supply a picture clause.
3. The **set** statement is used to change the value of an index.

Indexes must be used with tables that are searched with the search verb. For other purposes subscripts and indexes can be used as alternatives. The usual advantage given for using an index is that it is likely to be more efficiently implemented by the compiler although a signed subscript with a usage of binary will be in most cases equally as efficient. Subscripts at times have a clear advantage in that any numeric item can be used as a

338 ESSENTIAL COBOL: A FIRST COURSE IN STRUCTURED COBOL

subscript and the compiler will generate any necessary conversion code. However, subscripting with items that are not binary should generally be avoided except where the execution of statements using subscripted items occurs only a few times during a program run. (In this case the run-time conversion does not represent a serious overhead.)

Program bike1 in Fig. 13.1 includes a table of 10 bicycle parts and costs. In response to an input the program checks its table to determine whether or not the part exists in the table. When it is found bike1 outputs the associated cost. When it is not found it displays an appropriate message.

Bike1 defines its index for the table on line 24. The program uses the index in a similar way to a subscript except that it changes the value of the index with the set statement. A simple syntax for the set statement when it is used to change the value of an index is as follows:

$$\text{set index-name-1} \begin{Bmatrix} \text{to} \\ \text{up by} \\ \text{down by} \end{Bmatrix} \text{integer-1}$$

```
1 identification division.
2 program-id. bike1.
3*Purpose: To demonstrate an indexed search using PERFORM
4
5 environment division.
6
7 data division.
8 working-storage section.
9 01   w1-bikeparts.
10     03   w1-values.
11          05   filler value "lamp       1022"  pic x(14).
12          05   filler value "bars       0924"  pic x(14).
13          05   filler value "pedal      0512"  pic x(14).
14          05   filler value "frame      4576"  pic x(14).
15          05   filler value "grips      0210"  pic x(14).
16          05   filler value "streamers 0075"  pic x(14).
17          05   filler value "reflector 0058"  pic x(14).
18          05   filler value "saddle bag0724"  pic x(14).
19          05   filler value "spoke      0012"  pic x(14).
20          05   filler value "inner tube0298"  pic x(14).
21
22     03   w1-entries redefines w1-values.
23          05   w1-entry occurs   10
24                    indexed w1-ind.
25               07   w1-part              pic x(10).
26               07   w1-cost              pic 99v99.
27
28 01   w2-bikepart.
29     03   filler value "part="           pic x(5).
30     03   w2-part                        pic x(10).
31          88   w2-eok                    value space.
32     03   filler value "; cost="         pic x(7).
33     03   w2-cost                        pic 99.99.
34/
35 procedure division.
36 para1.
37     display "bike1 begins"
38
```

```
39      display "Enter the name of a part or RET to quit: "
40         no advancing
41      accept w2-part
42
43      perform test before until w2-eok
44         set w1-ind to 1
45         perform until w1-ind > 11
46            evaluate true
47               when    w1-ind = 11
48                  display "not found"
49               when    w1-part(w1-ind) = w2-part
50                  move w1-cost(w1-ind) to w2-cost
51                  display w2-bikepart
52                  set w1-ind to 11
53            end-evaluate
54            set w1-ind up by 1
55         end-perform
56
57         display "Enter the name of another part or RET to quit: "
58            no advancing
59         accept w2-part
60      end-perform
61
62      display "bike1 ends"
63      stop run.
64
65 end program bike1
```

Figure 13.1 Program bike1

The **to** option allows an index to be initialized to any unsigned value The **up by** and **down by** options are used to increment and decrement an index by a value greater than zero.

In program bike1 the index is incremented by 1 at line 54 so that as a consequence of executing the loop the elements in the table are systematically examined from the first to the last or until a match is found between the part argument and a part item in the table.

13.2 SEARCH

The search verb has two main forms: **search** and **search all**. The search form is used for searching successive elements in a table. It has the following full format:

```
search identifier-1

   [end                     statement-1]
   {when condition-1 statement-2}...
   end-search
```

Identifier-1 must always refer to a data item that has an occurs clause and an index associated with it. Immediately prior to the execution of the search statement the index must be given a value that is within the range of the table as defined by the occurs clause.

Searching will then begin with the item that is indexed by the initial value of the index. When the condition specified by the **when** phrase becomes true the statement associated with the when phrase will be executed and the search will terminate. If the last element in the table has been checked and the condition is still not true then the statement associated with the **end** phrase will be executed and the search will terminate.

The underlying algorithm operates by incrementing the index after each element is checked. Therefore when an index is initialized to a value that is greater than the number of elements in the table the end condition will become true at the commencement of the search. (If the index is initialized to less than 1 then the search will cause a run-time error.)

Program bike2 in Fig. 13.2 is functionally equivalent to bike1 but uses the search statement to check the table of bicycle parts.

At line 44 the index is set to 1 so that the search will start at the first element in the table. As a result of the search either the statement at line 47 will be executed once (no element matches) or the two statements at lines 49–50 will be executed once (match found).

When a match is found the index will remain set to the same value after the termination of the search. However, if no match is found the value of the index is undefined. Therefore although the end phrase is optional it should always be used to control the termination of a sequential search. (Never rely on the index having a value that is one greater than the number of occurrences in the table.)

Program bike1 starts its sequential search at the first item. However, it is legal to start at a higher item. This gives flexibility to support the searching of only part of a table.

The sequential search allows more than one when phrase to be used. The reason for this is to allow matching to be specified on any condition that may relate an argument to table elements. For example, imagine a case where a table of names and telephone numbers is in ascending order by name and the requirement is to find the telephone

```
 1 identification division.
 2 program-id. bike2.
 3*Purpose: To demonstrate SEARCH
 4
 5 environment division.
 6
 7 data division.
 8 working-storage section.
 9 01   w1-bikeparts.
10      03    w1-values.
11            05    filler value "lamp       1022" pic x(14).
12            05    filler value "bars       0924" pic x(14).
13            05    filler value "pedal      0512" pic x(14).
14            05    filler value "frame      4576" pic x(14).
15            05    filler value "grips      0210" pic x(14).
16            05    filler value "streamers 0075" pic x(14).
17            05    filler value "reflector 0058" pic x(14).
18            05    filler value "saddle bag0724" pic x(14).
19            05    filler value "spoke      0012" pic x(14).
20            05    filler value "inner tube0298" pic x(14).
21
22      03    w1-entries redefines w1-values.
23            05    w1-entry occurs   10
24                        indexed w1-ind.
25                  07    w1-part            pic x(10).
26                  07    w1-cost            pic 99v99.
27
```

```
28 01  w2-bikepart.
29     03  filler value "part="          pic x(5).
30     03  w2-part                       pic x(10).
31         88  w2-eok                    value space.
32     03  filler value "; cost="        pic x(7).
33     03  w2-cost                       pic 99.99.
34/
35 procedure division.
36 para1.
37     display "bike2 begins"
38
39     display "Enter the name of a part or RET to quit: "
40        no advancing
41     accept w2-part
42
43     perform test before until w2-eok
44       set w1-ind to 1
45       search w1-entry
46         end
47           display "not found"
48         when w1-part(w1-ind) = w2-part
49           move w1-cost(w1-ind) to w2-cost
50           display w2-bikepart
51       end-search
52
53       display "Enter the name of another part or RET to quit: "
54          no advancing
55       accept w2-part
56     end-perform
57
58     display "bike2 ends"
59     stop run.
60
61 end program bike2
```

Figure 13.2 Program bike2

number for a given name. Clearly for an argument such as "Smith" there is no need to look beyond the Smiths in order to determine that there is no matching telephone number in the table.

```
set e1-ind to 1
search e1-entry
  end
    display "not found"
  when e1-name(e1-ind) = k2-name
    display "The number is " e1-number(e1-ind)
  when e1-name(e1-ind) > k2-name
    display "not found"
end-search
```

The above search statement specifies that the search may end for any of three reasons. Firstly, the end of the table may be reached with no match found. Secondly, the name argument may match a name in the table (first when). Thirdly, a name in the table may be found that is greater than the name argument.

In a way that is similar to the evaluate statement the end and when phrases are considered in a top-down priority. Firstly, the index value is checked to see if it is outside the range of the table. If it is then the search will terminate. If it is not then the first when phrase will be checked. If its condition is true then the search will terminate. If it is not then the next when phrase will be checked. This process continues until all of the when phrases have been checked and then the index will be automatically incremented in preparation for the next pass through the search.

The condition specified in a when phrase can be any conditional expression.

13.3 SEARCH ALL

The **search all** form allows a table to be searched by a binary rather than by a sequential search. The underlying searching algorithm for a binary search depends on the fact that the elements of a table are in order by some item in the table elements that is considered to be a key, that is, a data item that has the same position and description in every element. Each key value must be unique and the keys in the table must be in either ascending or descending order.

The bicycle parts table has been reordered in Fig. 13.4 (lines 11 to 20) to meet this requirement. The elements are now in ascending order by part so that 'bars' is the first key in the table and 'streamers' is the last.

The standard somewhat obscurely states that 'a non-serial type of search operation may take place'. In practice COBOL implementations use what is commonly called a *binary* or logarithmic search. This approach to searching requires the search space to be divided in half each time a match is not found. Although search all is very efficient for large tables there is a computational overhead involved in calculating values for the index. Therefore it is likely that for very small tables it will be more efficient to use a sequential search.

An algorithm for a binary search specifies that the middle key in the table will be the first key to be examined. If a match is found then the search terminates. If the argument is lower then only the lower half of the table is searched next but if the argument is higher then only the upper half is searched next. The search space is constantly halved in this way until either a match on the key is found or it is determined that the key is not in the table.

For example, imagine a table that contains 64 numbers in the range of zero to 5000. We know that the numbers are in order in the table from the lowest to the highest. Our problem will be to check the table the minimum number of times to determine whether or not a given number appears within it. At the beginning the search space is all of the 64 elements in the table. The first element we will check is element 32.* If this is the number

---

* Although the number 64 can be divided in half there is no middle element in the range 1 to 64. Therefore let us assume that when there are an even number of elements, the middle element will always be the highest element in the bottom half. When there are an odd number of elements let us assume that the middle element will be number of elements to search divided in half and rounded up.

Thus for a table of 64 elements the middle element is 64/2 or 32 but for a table of 65 elements the middle element is 65/2 which when rounded up is 33.

we are looking for then the search can terminate. Let us suppose that the number we are looking for is lower than the value found at 32. In this case we want to enter at the midpoint in the bottom half of the table. This point will be 32/2 or 16. Once again the number we are looking for may be in this element, or a higher or lower element. If it is higher then we need to consider elements 17 to 31 as the next search space.

For our hypothetical table of 64 elements we can see that a pattern emerges as the size of the search space is reduced (Fig. 13.3).

Expressed as power of 2	2^6	2^5	2^4	2^3	2^2	2^1	2^0
Expressed as integer value	64	32	16	8	4	2	1

Figure 13.3 Search space reductions for a table of 64 elements

The pattern shows us that the time taken to find an element in the table increases slowly relative to the increase in elements. This relationship is logarithmic and can be expressed as:

$$T = \log_2 N$$

which expresses the fact that time (T) in terms of the number of elements to be examined only doubles as the number of elements in the search space (N) is squared. For example, a table of 1000 entries takes 10 attempts to find a match in a binary search while a table of 1 000 000 entries only takes 20 attempts. Clearly, such a simple strategy for searching has many useful applications and COBOL provides the **search all** form of the search statement in order to give the programmer the benefit of the binary search at a high level of procedural abstraction.

A simple format for the search all is as follows:

```
search all identifier-1

    [end             statement-1]
     when test-1 statement-2
end-search
```

As with the sequential search identifier-1 must always refer to a data item that has an occurs clause and an index associated with it.

Program bike3 in Fig. 13.4 is a rewritten version of bike2. Note that the table elements at lines 11 to 20 are in ascending order by bicycle part. (A binary search will give unpredictable results if the data in the table is not correctly ordered.)

At line 24 the bicycle part is specified as the **ascending** key for the search. It is also legal to use the word **descending** for a table with keys in a descending order. Of course, any one table can be in only one order and therefore the ascending and descending options are mutually exclusive.

```cobol
 1 identification division.
 2 program-id. bike3.
 3*Purpose: To demonstrate SEARCH ALL
 4
 5 environment division.
 6
 7 data division.
 8 working-storage section.
 9 01   w1-bikeparts.
10      03  w1-values.
11          05  filler value "bars       0924" pic x(14).
12          05  filler value "frame      4576" pic x(14).
13          05  filler value "grips      0210" pic x(14).
14          05  filler value "inner tube0298" pic x(14).
15          05  filler value "lamp       1022" pic x(14).
16          05  filler value "pedal      0512" pic x(14).
17          05  filler value "reflector 0058" pic x(14).
18          05  filler value "saddle bag0724" pic x(14).
19          05  filler value "spoke      0012" pic x(14).
20          05  filler value "streamers 0075" pic x(14).
21
22      03  w1-entries redefines w1-values.
23          05  w1-entry occurs    10
24                  ascending  w1-part
25                  indexed    w1-ind.
26              07  w1-part             pic x(10).
27              07  w1-cost             pic 99v99.
28
29 01   w2-bikepart.
30      03  filler value "part="         pic x(5).
31      03  w2-part                      pic x(10).
32          88  w2-eok                   value space.
33      03  filler value "; cost="       pic x(7).
34      03  w2-cost                      pic 99.99.
35/
36 procedure division.
37 para1.
38     display "bike3 begins"
39
40     display "Enter the name of a part or RET to quit: "
41       no advancing
42     accept w2-part
43
44     perform test before until w2-eok
45       search all w1-entry
46         end
47           display "not found"
48         when w1-part(w1-ind) = w2-part
49           move w1-cost(w1-ind) to w2-cost
50           display w2-bikepart
51       end-search
52
53       display "Enter the name of another part or RET to quit: "
54         no advancing
55       accept w2-part
56     end-perform
57
58     display "bike3 ends"
59     stop run.
60
61 end program bike3
```

Figure 13.4 Program bike3

The search statement is at line 45. Note that the index is not initialized prior to the start of the search. This is because the underlying algorithm has its own definition of how the middle of a table is to be found. (In any case this middle value is variable because it also depends on the number of elements in the table.)

When the test specified by the when phrase is true the statement associated with the when phrase will be executed and the search will terminate. If the table has been fully checked and the when test is still not true, then the statement associated with the end phrase will be executed and the search will terminate. The tests that are allowed on when phrases for the binary search are more restricted than for the sequential search.

A test has the following format:

$$\text{identifier-2} = \begin{Bmatrix} \text{identifier-3} \\ \text{literal-1} \\ \text{arith-exp-1} \end{Bmatrix}$$

It is always the case that identifier-2 must be an indexed item that is a key to the table. Furthermore, the only tests that are allowed are for equality and only one when phrase is allowed. The reason for this is that the table is ordered by key and only one key can be a correct match for a search argument that is a key value.

However, it is possible to have ordered tables that require more than one key. In these cases a number of indexes must be checked to ensure that the arguments have been correctly matched across all of the keys in the table. Therefore a single when phrase can be extended with the and operator to specify these additional tests:

```
search all identifier-1

  [end                            statement-1]
    when test-1 [and test-2]...statement-2
  end-search
```

Once again the example of a table of names and telephone numbers provides a simple example to present this concept. Imagine a table in ascending order by both surname and forename within surname. Lines of data for such a table might appear as follows:

```
...
BorowskiΔΔPeterΔΔΔΔΔ9367219
SinghΔΔΔΔΔPrabhatΔΔΔ2216532
SmithΔΔΔΔΔΔElizabethΔ2345133
SmithΔΔΔΔΔΔJohnΔΔΔΔΔΔ6562612
SmytheΔΔΔΔElizaΔΔΔΔΔΔ2018294
TdziakΔΔΔΔΔJillΔΔΔΔΔΔΔ3410234
WongΔΔΔΔΔΔJenniferΔΔ2098167
...
```

It is clear that the data must be ordered by surname, but when two elements have the same surname then they are ordered by forename. Thus John Smith is expected to come after Elizabeth Smith and not before.

```
working-storage section.
01  e3-phonetable.
    03  e3-phoneline  occurs      nn
                      ascending e3-surname
                      ascending e3-forename
                      indexed    e3-ind.
        05  e3-surname  pic x(10).
        05  e3-forename pic x(10).
        05  e3-phone    pic x(7).
```

Provided that the table has been correctly filled with data and the arguments have been initialized (perhaps by accept statements) then the following binary search will take account of both of the keys that are used in the table:

```
search all e3-phoneline
  end
    display "not in my book"
  when e3-surname(e3-ind)  = k4-surname and
       e3-forename(w3-ind) = k4-forename
    display "The number is " e3-phone(e3-ind)
end-search
```

13.4 VARIABLE-LENGTH TABLES

A final feature of interest is the ability to use tables in which the number of elements depends on the value of a data item. This is especially useful when the data that is to be loaded into a table is stored in a file and the number of potential elements for the table is not known until run time.

As an example let us reconsider the table look-up problem from Chapter 5 where the mencken program was used to match expressions. The contents of the original table are now to be stored in a file called imencken.dat (Fig. 13.5) and the mencken program is to load the contents of the file into a table.

Program look-up2 is the same as look-up1 except that it has been rewritten as a separately compiled program (see Fig. 13.6).

Program mencken2 (Fig. 13.7) has been rewritten so that it defines a table that can contain 0 to 80 elements (line 31) depending on the value of a variable (line 32). (The variable, `w1-limit`, is defined at line 29 as a numeric item.)

```
apartment∆∆∆∆flat
baby∆carriagepram
broil∆∆∆∆∆∆∆∆grill
candy∆∆∆∆∆∆∆∆sweets
cookie∆∆∆∆∆∆∆biscuit
hood∆∆∆∆∆∆∆∆∆bonnet
intermission∆interval
trunk∆∆∆∆∆∆∆∆boot
```

Figure 13.5 File imencken.dat containing data for a table

```
1 identification division.
2 program-id. look-up2.
3*Purpose: This program drives subprogram mencken2.
4
5 environment division.
6
7 data division.
8 working-storage section.
9 01  w1-entry.
10     03  w1-entry-US                    pic x(13).
11         88  w1-quit                    value space.
12     03  w1-entry-GB                    pic x(8).
13
14 procedure division.
15 para1.
16     display "look-up2 begins"
17
18     display "Enter a word or RETURN to quit: " no advancing
19     accept w1-entry-US
20     perform test before until w1-quit
21       call "mencken2" using reference w1-entry
22       evaluate w1-entry-GB = spaces
23         when    true
24           display "No matching GB word in table"
25         when    false
26           display "The matching GB word is:         " w1-entry-GB
27       end-evaluate
28       display "Enter a word or RETURN to quit: " no advancing
29       accept w1-entry-US
30     end-perform
31
32     display "look-up2 ends"
33     stop run.
34
35 end program look-up2
```

Figure 13.6 Program look-up2

```
1 identification division.
2 program-id. mencken2.
3*Purpose: This subprogram produces a British expression to match
4*         a given United States expression.
5
6 environment division.
7 input-output section.
8 file-control.
9    select i1-file assign w1-filename.
10
11 data division.
12 file section.
13 fd  i1-file
14     record varying 1 to 255
15     value of id    w1-filename.
16 01  filler                          pic x(255).
17
```

```
18 working-storage section.
19 01  w1-synonyms.
20     03  w1-filename value "imencken.dat" pic x(12).
21     03  filler       value "n"            pic x.
22         88  eof                           value "y".
23
24     03  filler       value "e"            pic x.
25         88  w1-full                       value "f".
26         88  w1-empty                      value "e".
27
28     03  w1-entries.
29         05  w1-limit                      pic 99.
30             88  w1-max                    value 80.
31         05  w1-entry    occurs    0 to 80
32                         depending    w1-limit
33                         ascending key w1-entry-US
34                         indexed      w1-ind.
35             07  w1-entry-US               pic x(13).
36             07  w1-entry-GB               pic x(8).
37
38 linkage section.
39 01  l1-entry.
40     03  l1-entry-US                       pic x(13).
41     03  l1-entry-GB                       pic x(8).
42
43 procedure division using l1-entry.
44 para1.
45     evaluate true
46       when   w1-empty
47         move 1 to w1-limit
48         set w1-ind to 1
49         open input i1-file
50         perform test before until w1-full
51           read i1-file into w1-entry(w1-ind)
52             end
53               compute w1-limit = w1-limit - 1
54               set w1-full to true
55               close i1-file
56             not end
57               evaluate w1-max
58                  when   true
59                    set w1-full to true
60                  when   false
61                    set w1-ind up by 1
62                    compute w1-limit = w1-limit + 1
63               end-evaluate
64           end-read
65         end-perform
66         display "There are " w1-limit " entries in the table"
67     end-evaluate
68
69     move spaces to l1-entry-GB
70     search all w1-entry
71       when w1-entry-US(w1-ind) = l1-entry-US
72         move w1-entry-GB(w1-ind) to l1-entry-GB
73     end-search
74
75     exit program.
76
77 end program mencken2
```

Figure 13.7 Program mencken2

Mencken2 begins its execution with no data in the table. The evaluate statement at line 45 is used to determine whether the table is initially empty or has been filled with data from the file. When the program is first called the table will be empty and therefore the contents of the file will be read so that each line from the file is translated into one element in the table. After processing the file the variable w1-limit will contain a value that is equal to the number of lines read from the file which is also the number of elements that have been put into the table. (This includes zero lines for an empty input file.)

At line 70 a binary search takes place. The search uses the value of w1-limit as the size of the table. Thus if the table holds zero elements the end condition will become immediately true. If the table contains elements then the binary search will be undertaken subject to the upper limit shown in w1-limit. The only restriction on using this method is that the maximum size of the table is a value that is compiled into the program (line 31) and this upper limit cannot be exceeded by the table index at any time.

13.5 CASE STUDY: RESIST1 (RESISTOR COLOUR CODES)

In electronics a resistor is an electrical component that introduces a known amount of resistance into a circuit. Resistance can be measured and the unit of measurement in which this is expressed is *ohms*.

Resistors come in various shapes and sizes. Most resistors are a tubular shape with at least three colour bands. The resistor colour code is a means of identifying a resistor's value as well as its tolerance as a percentage rating.

The first and second band are closest to one end and represent a numeric value. The third band gives a factor by which this value must be multiplied to get the resistance value in ohms.

The fourth band if present gives the tolerance of the resistor. If the fourth band is absent the resistor is assumed to have a tolerance of 20 per cent.

Figure 13.8 gives the 12 possible bands and the meaning of a colour when it is used for

Colour	1st digit	2nd digit	Multiplier	Percentage tolerance
Black	0	0	1	—
Brown	1	1	10	1
Red	2	2	100	2
Orange	3	3	1 000	3
Yellow	4	4	10 000	4
Green	5	5	100 000	—
Blue	6	6	1 000 000	—
Violet	7	7	10 000 000	—
Grey	8	8	100 000 000	—
White	9	9	—	—
Gold	—	—	0.1	5
Silver	—	—	0.01	10
No colour	—	—	—	20

Figure 13.8 Resistor colour codes

350 ESSENTIAL COBOL: A FIRST COURSE IN STRUCTURED COBOL

one of the four bands. The absence of a fourth band by default means that the resistor has a tolerance of 20 per cent. This is represented by the thirteenth entry in the table.

Program resist1 (Fig. 13.9) uses program get-input to take in a string of colours separated by a space or comma (line 88). These are placed in a table in linkage called l1-colours (line 80) which is passed back to the root program. Get-input uses a validation trap but because it only knows about lengths of strings and string separators it cannot trap all input errors. For example, the colour "pink" will be accepted by get-input because a colour substring of four characters is accepted by its limited validation criteria.

Once the root program has a table containing three or four possible colours it calls calc-resist to calculate the resistance. To do this it has a table (line 149) that contains all of the information from the table in Fig. 13.8. Zero is a valid value in the resistance calculations. Therefore the table is defined as alphanumerics and an entry of space indicates that a value does not exist. Each search is for a separate colour band. The search statements look up the colour in the table and provided that the entry is numeric, a value is extracted and moved to a numeric field where it is used for calculation. If the table entry is not numeric then an error from a table of errors (line 182) is moved to a table of errors (line 202) that is returned to the root for the particular colour string that it passed as an argument. The calculation at line 281 takes place only if the resistor is valid (line 282). The test for validity is against the error table.

```
 1 identification division.
 2 program-id. resist1.
 3*Purpose: To give the values for resistors from their colour bands
 4
 5 environment division.
 6
 7 data division.
 8 working-storage section.
 9 01    w1-colours                     pic x(24).
10       88   w1-eok                    value spaces.
11
12 01    w2-result.
13       03   w2-resistance             pic s9(10)v99.
14       03   w2-tolerance              pic sv99.
15       03   w2-errors.
16            05   w2-sub               pic 9.
17                 88 w2-valid-resistor value 0.
18            05   filler.
19                 07   w2-error occurs 4 pic x(16).
20
21 01    s2-result.
22       03   s2-resistance             pic z(10).99.
23       03   s2-tolerance              pic z(10).99.
24
25 procedure division.
26 para1.
27       display "resist1 begins"
28
29       call "get-input" using reference w1-colours
30
```

```
31*     MAIN loop
32      perform test before until w1-eok
33        display "The colours used are: " w1-colours
34        call "calc-resist" using content   w1-colours
35                                 reference w2-result
36        evaluate w2-valid-resistor
37          when    true
38            move w2-resistance to s2-resistance
39            move w2-tolerance  to s2-tolerance
40            display "Resistance in ohms is:         " s2-resistance
41            display "  with a percent tolerance of: " s2-tolerance
42          when    false
43            display "Colour coding errors as follows:"
44            perform test before until w2-sub = 0
45              display "  " w2-error(w2-sub)
46              compute w2-sub = w2-sub - 1
47            end-perform
48        end-evaluate
49
50        call "get-input"   using reference w1-colours
51      end-perform
52*     END-MAIN loop
53
54      display "resist1 ends"
55      stop run.
56/
57 identification division.
58 program-id. get-input.
59*Purpose: To get a string of three or four colours
60
61 environment division.
62
63 data division.
64 working-storage section.
65 01   k1-colours                    pic x(80).
66      88  k1-eok                    value "Q" "q".
67
68 01   w1-string-work.
69      03  w1-counters.
70          05  w1-ctr    occurs 4  binary pic s9(5).
71              88  w1-ctrval             value 3 thru 6.
72      03  w1-tally              binary pic s9(5).
73          88  w1-tallyval               value 3, 4.
74      03  w1-ptr                binary pic s9(5).
75      03  filler                       pic x.
76          88  w1-valid                  value "V".
77          88  w1-invalid                value "I".
78
79 linkage section.
80 01   l1-colours.
81      03  l1-colour occurs 4           pic x(6).
82
83 procedure division using l1-colours.
84 para1.
85      display space
86      display "Input 3 or 4 colours followed by a RETURN or 'Q' to quit"
87      display "Separate the colours by a space or comma"
88      accept k1-colours
89      move space to l1-colours
90
```

```
 91*    MAIN loop
 92     perform test before until k1-eok
 93*      Assume that the input will be valid
 94       set w1-valid to true
 95*      Start unstringing from the first character
 96       move 1 to w1-ptr
 97*      Assume no colours to start with
 98       move 0 to w1-tally
 99*      GET the four colours
100       unstring k1-colours delimited space or ","
101         into l1-colour(1) count w1-ctr(1)
102              l1-colour(2) count w1-ctr(2)
103              l1-colour(3) count w1-ctr(3)
104              l1-colour(4) count w1-ctr(4)
105         pointer  w1-ptr
106         tallying w1-tally
107         overflow
108           evaluate true
109             when   w1-ctrval(1) and w1-ctrval(2) and w1-ctrval(3) and
110                    w1-ctr(4) < 7 and w1-tallyval
111               set k1-eok to true
112             when   k1-colours(w1-ptr:) not = space
113               display "Input has wrong or too many colours"
114               set w1-invalid to true
115             when   other
116               display "Input has wrong or too few colours"
117               set w1-invalid to true
118           end-evaluate
119       end-unstring
120*      END-GET
121
122*      RECOVER for bad input
123       evaluate w1-invalid
124         when   true
125           display "Input 3 or 4 colours followed by a RETURN or 'Q' to quit"
126           display "Separate the colours by a space or comma"
127           accept k1-colours
128           move space to l1-colours
129       end-evaluate
130*      END-RECOVER
131
132     end-perform
133*    END-MAIN loop
134
135     exit program.
136
137 end program get-input.
138/
139 identification division.
140 program-id. calc-resist.
141*Purpose: To map colour bands to resistance and tolerance for a
142*         given resistor
143
144 environment division.
145
```

```
146 data division.
147 working-storage section.
148 01  w1-resistor-table.
149     03  w1-colour-entries.
150         05  filler value "black 0000000000100 -"  pic x(21).
151         05  filler value "brown 110000000100001"  pic x(21).
152         05  filler value "red   220000001000002"  pic x(21).
153         05  filler value "orange330000010000003"  pic x(21).
154         05  filler value "yellow440000100000004"  pic x(21).
155         05  filler value "green 5500010000000 -"  pic x(21).
156         05  filler value "blue  6600100000000 -"  pic x(21).
157         05  filler value "violet7701000000000 -"  pic x(21).
158         05  filler value "gray  8810000000000 -"  pic x(21).
159         05  filler value "white 99            - -"  pic x(21).
160         05  filler value "gold  --0000000001005"  pic x(21).
161         05  filler value "silver--0000000000110"  pic x(21).
162         05  filler value "      --          -20"  pic x(21).
163     03  filler redefines w1-colour-entries.
164         05  w1-colours occurs 13 indexed w1-ind.
165             07  w1-colour     pic x(6).
166             07  w1-digit1     pic x.
167             07  w1-digit2     pic x.
168             07  w1-multiplier pic x(11).
169             07  w1-tolerance  pic xx.
170
171 01  w2-calculators.
172     03  w2-alphas.
173         05  w2-digit1          pic 9.
174         05  w2-digit2          pic 9.
175         05  w2-dmultiplier     pic 9(11).
176         05  w2-dtolerance      pic 99.
177     03  w2-numerics redefines w2-alphas.
178         05  w2-value           pic 99.
179         05  w2-multiplier      pic 9(9)v99.
180         05  w2-tolerance       pic v99.
181
182 01  w3-error-table.
183     03  w3-errors.
184         05  filler value "colour 1 unknown"  pic x(16).
185         05  filler value "colour 2 unknown"  pic x(16).
186         05  filler value "colour 3 unknown"  pic x(16).
187         05  filler value "colour 4 unknown"  pic x(16).
188         05  filler value "colour 1 invalid"  pic x(16).
189         05  filler value "colour 2 invalid"  pic x(16).
190         05  filler value "colour 3 invalid"  pic x(16).
191         05  filler value "colour 4 invalid"  pic x(16).
192     03  filler redefines w3-errors.
193         05  w3-error occurs 8               pic x(16).
194
195 linkage section.
196 01  l1-colours.
197     03  l1-colour   occurs 4    pic x(6).
198
199 01  l2-result.
200     03  l2-resistance           pic s9(10)v99.
201     03  l2-tolerance            pic sv99.
202     03  l2-errors.
203         05  l2-sub              pic 9.
204             88  l2-valid-resistor value 0.
205         05  filler.
206             07  l2-error occurs 4  pic x(16).
207
```

```cobol
208 procedure division using l1-colours l2-result.
209 para1.
210*    Assume no errors in the colour bands
211     set l2-valid-resistor to true
212
213*    BAND1
214     set w1-ind to 1
215     search w1-colours
216       end
217         compute l2-sub = l2-sub + 1
218         move w3-error(1) to l2-error(l2-sub)
219       when w1-colour(w1-ind ) = l1-colour(1)
220         evaluate w1-digit1(w1-ind) numeric
221           when    true
222             move w1-digit1(w1-ind) to w2-digit1
223           when    false
224             compute l2-sub = l2-sub + 1
225             move w3-error(5) to l2-error(l2-sub)
226         end-evaluate
227     end-search
228*    END-BAND1
229
230*    BAND2
231     set w1-ind  to 1
232     search w1-colours
233       end
234         compute l2-sub = l2-sub + 1
235         move w3-error(2) to l2-error(l2-sub)
236       when w1-colour(w1-ind) = l1-colour(2)
237         evaluate w1-digit2(w1-ind) numeric
238           when    true
239             move w1-digit2(w1-ind) to w2-digit2
240           when    false
241             compute l2-sub = l2-sub + 1
242             move w3-error(6) to l2-error(l2-sub)
243         end-evaluate
244     end-search
245*    END-BAND2
246
247*    BAND3
248     set  w1-ind  to 1
249     search w1-colours
250       end
251         compute l2-sub = l2-sub + 1
252         move w3-error(3) to l2-error(l2-sub)
253       when w1-colour(w1-ind) = l1-colour(3)
254         evaluate w1-multiplier(w1-ind) numeric
255           when    true
256             move w1-multiplier(w1-ind) to w2-dmultiplier
257           when    false
258             compute l2-sub = l2-sub + 1
259             move w3-error(7) to l2-error(l2-sub)
260         end-evaluate
261     end-search
262*    END-BAND3
263
```

```
264*      BAND4
265       set  w1-ind  to 1
266       search w1-colours
267         end
268           compute l2-sub = l2-sub + 1
269           move w3-error(4) to l2-error(l2-sub)
270         when w1-colour(w1-ind) = l1-colour(4)
271           evaluate w1-tolerance(w1-ind) numeric
272             when    true
273               move w1-tolerance(w1-ind) to w2-dtolerance
274             when    false
275               compute l2-sub = l2-sub + 1
276               move w3-error(8) to l2-error(l2-sub)
277           end-evaluate
278       end-search
279*      END-BAND4
280
281*      Calculate resistance for valid colour bands
282       evaluate l2-valid-resistor
283         when    true
284           compute l2-resistance =  w2-value * w2-multiplier
285           compute l2-tolerance  =  w2-tolerance
286         when    false
287           move 0 to l2-resistance
288           move 0 to l2-tolerance
289       end-evaluate
290
291       exit program.
292
293   end program calc-resist.
294 end program resist1.
```

Figure 13.9 Program resist1

13.6 EXERCISES

13.6.1 General

1 Write program hex1 which when given an input in hexadecimal such as '313236' does a table look-up and translates this to '126' on output. (Translate only numbers for the moment so that the size of the table is small.)
2 Rewrite hex1 as hex2 so that it can translate in both directions using the table.
3 Write program hex3 that when given any input as a hexadecimal string translates it into either a printable character representation such as "ΔΔA" or an abbreviation such as "NUL" or "ΔFF". (Each pair of hex inputs should be matched by three character outputs. It would assist in testing if the input string were redisplayed with space between each pair of hex inputs and the matching output were displayed directly beneath.)

The secret to solving this exercise is to find an efficient way to convert from hexadecimal to pure binary numbers.

```
01  e1-rec.
    03  e1-var1 binary pic 999.
    03  filler redefines e1-var1.
        05  e1-lobyte  pic x.
        05  e1-hibyte  pic x.
```

The above record shows that the two bytes that will be allocated for a binary number can be redefined to allow the bytes to be manipulated separately. (*Note:* Some systems may express the high and low bytes in the reverse order.) A table such as this can be used to prepare the sixteen binary values in the order of 0 to 15 by moving 0 to `e1-var1` and then incrementing it. These values for `e1-lobyte` will be unsigned binary values expressed as a byte. These sixteen new values can be moved to a table of sixteen characters. A matching table of sixteen characters can then be prepared with the values "0" to "9" and "A" to "F". A single inspect statement with the convert option can then be used to convert the input from characters into a string of bytes in which the low nibble of each byte holds a binary value in the range of 0 to 0Fh.

Further statements are then needed to translate pairs of bytes with their low nibbles into a single binary number with the correct high and and low nibble in the low byte. (You can use a compute statement to shift a low nibble into a high nibble. To do this first put the byte back into a binary number. A second compute can be used to sum two binary numbers with the correct high and low nibbles.) Once this is done you will have a binary number in the range of 0 to 255d (0 to 0FFh) which can be used in a table look-up. (*Note:* If the number falls within a printable range then there is no need to store that value in the table. The byte can be extracted directly and printed with two leading spaces.)

4 Write program tele1 which displays a set of names and telephone numbers that are maintained as text in a file called tele.dat. The program should read in the contents of tele.dat at the beginning of each run and put an entry for each person in a table. The user should then be allowed to look up the number of a person whose name has been supplied.

5 Rewrite tele1 as tele2 in which the user can add new people to the end of the table, remove existing entries by changing them to spaces, and change the telephone number for an existing entry. At the end of the run tele2 should write a new version of the table to a new file. In doing so it should skip blank entries because these have been deleted. (You should use a switch which is set to true the first time a user adds, changes or deletes an entry and then use this switch to decide at the end of run whether or not to write the table to the file. Otherwise a casual browse through the file will cause the program to write a new file even though the table has not been changed.)

13.6.2 Case study

6 Rewrite resist1 as resist2 so that it allows separators with trailing spaces between the colours and both upper- and lower-case input.

7 Resist1 displays the colours of the resistor at line 33. Rewrite resist1 as resist3 so that it displays the colours with the same separator that was used on input at the keyboard.

8   Rewrite resist1 as resist4 so that the get-input program gives a diagnostic message to show which colour is at fault when an input colour is too short.
9   Rewrite resist1 as resist5 so that the main program manages the error messages and program calc-resist only establishes a message number.
10 Rewrite resist4 as resist6 so that the program loads its messages from a text file that can be amended separately from the program. (You should consider adding a new program called get-table to do this. It should also validate that the number of messages and their lengths are valid.)
11 Rewrite resist1 or resist6 as resist7 so that the searching activity is contained within a new program called by calc-resist. (Consider using only a single search statement in this new program.)

14

SORTING AND MERGING FILES

The **sort** and **merge** statements enable the programmer to sort one or more files of records into the same order or to merge two or more files of records which are already in the same sorted order.

Consider the 10 records each containing 11 characters as shown in Fig. 14.1.

A key is a field that has the same start position and length in every record. For example, if we consider the full 11 characters from each record as the key we can say that the records are in no particular order. To be in ascending order the first record should be followed immediately by the third record because a0123456789 is the lowest key and a1234567890 is the second lowest key in the file.

If on the other hand we wished the records to be in descending order then the seventh record should be the first and the first record should be the last as defined by descending key order.

| Record | Characters |
| | 1 |
	12345678901
1:	a0123456789
2:	b1234567890
3:	a2345678901
4:	d3456789012
5:	e4567890123
6:	c5678901234
7:	z6789012345
8:	q7890123456
9:	m8901234567
10:	x9012345678

Figure 14.1 Ten unsorted records

In most cases it is not necessary to use all of the characters in a record as a key. Furthermore, a key does not have to start at the beginning of the record. We can see that if we needed the file in ascending order on the second character only then the records in Fig. 14.1 are correctly ordered.

Therefore a decision concerning whether or not a file is correctly ordered cannot be made without reference to at least one key that is expected to be either ascending or descending.

It is possible to order a file by more than one key. Imagine a set of library book extracts that contain fields for author, publication date and site location. It might be necessary to write a report which listed all of the authors in ascending alphabetical order and for each author to list their books in descending order by publication date. A third key might be the site location in ascending order so that alternative sources for the same book would always appear on the report in the same order within author and within publication date. The record description and some typical records for this problem are listed in Fig. 14.2. (Note the use of the prefix s to denote a sort-merge record description.)

```
01   s3-book.
     03   s3-shelf.
          05   s3-accession      pic 9(8).
          05   s3-subject        pic x(10).
          05   s3-site           pic xx.
     03   s3-author.
          05   s3-year           pic 9(6).
          05   s3-name           pic x(11).
          05   s3-title          pic x(31).
```

```
          1         2         3         4         5         6         7
1234567890123456789012345678901234567890123456789012345678901234567890123456
Accession          Site  Author
       Subject     Year                 Title

19234856001.5      A11984Balle,F        Nouveaux Medias
62931209001.53     B71969Porter,A       Cybernetics Simplified
23145678001.535    A21984Alexsander,I   Designing Intelligent Systems
23156789001.6      C41983Harrison,D     Data Processing
45123456001.61     A11982Krallmann,H    Sozio-Okonomische Anwendungen
26126789001.63     A11970Keys,W.J       Handbook of Modern Key Punch Operation
39102475001.64     C41982Day,C          Illustrating Computers
71345678001.64     A11976Weizenbaum,J   Computer Power and Human Reason
91728346001.6404   A11981Rouquerol,M    Micro-Ordinateurs
21823445001.6424   A11982Forsythe,R.S   Pascal at Work and Play
31023494001.6404   C51982Ruston,J       BBC Micro Revealed
30129345001.64042  B71982Zaks,R         Programming the Z80
81923445001.642    B71982Ben-Ari,M      Principles of Concurrent Programming
71029384001.642    A11982Darlington,J   Functional Programming and Its Applicat
39102344001.642    A11969Jackson,W.E    Local Gov't in England and Wales
21823445001.6424   A21982Forsythe,R.S   Pascal at Work and Play
51029345001.6425   A11985Marx,J.L       Clefs Pour Multiplan
21920345003        B71982Athey,T.H      Sytematic Systems Approach
51234567515.353    B71982Bathe,K.J      Finite Element Procedures In Engineerin
10123445621.38195  C41985Tocci,R.J      Digital Systems
43123456621.381957 C41963Ashley,J.R     Intro. to Analogue Computation
```

Figure 14.2 Unordered book extracts and sort record description (file extract1.dat)

The COBOL sort statement would allow us to order book records by ascending author, and within author by descending publication date, and within publication date by ascending site location.

14.1 SORT

The following simple format for the sort statement allows us to specify a sort by naming a sort-merge file (file-name-1), an input file (file-name-2), an output file (file-name-3) and one or more keys that define the ordering for the sort:

$$\text{sort file-name-1} \left\{ \begin{Bmatrix} \text{ascending} \\ \text{descending} \end{Bmatrix} \text{data-name-1} \ldots \right\} \ldots$$

```
using   {file-name-2}...
giving  {file-name-3}...
```

The format allows a list of keys to be specified for the sort. Any of the keys on the list can be either ascending or descending. (For example a first key based on ascending name would generate an output in alphabetical order. If the sort also specified a second key based on descending date this would force the dates to be in descending order within the name specified by the first field.) File-name-2 can be repeated. This allows many files of data to be input to the same sort. File-name-3 also can be repeated. This causes duplicate output files.

Program Sort1 in Fig. 14.3 uses this simple format for sorting a file of records. The input and output files for the sort are similar to files we have seen before. However, the sort-merge file is an internal file which has a restricted definition and restricted uses. Firstly, the select statement must use a literal to name the file and not a variable (line 10). (Some implementors may place an even greater restriction on the select statement and require the programmer to use certain predefined filenames such as sortwrk1.)

```
 1 identification division.
 2 program-id. sort1.
 3*Purpose: To demonstrate a simple sort using three keys.
 4
 5 environment division.
 6 input-output section.
 7 file-control.
 8     select i1-file assign w1-filename.
 9     select o2-file assign w2-filename.
10     select s3-file assign "anyname".
11
```

```cobol
12 data division.
13 file section.
14 fd  i1-file
15     record varying 37 to 80
16     value of id    w1-filename.
17 01  filler                  pic x(80).
18
19 fd  o2-file
20     record varying 37 to 80
21     value of id    w2-filename.
22 01  filler                  pic x(80).
23
24 sd  s3-file
25     record varying 37 to 80.
26 01  s3-rec.
27     03  s3-shelf.
28         05  s3-accession  pic 9(8).
29         05  s3-subject    pic x(10).
30         05  s3-site       pic xx.
31     03  s3-author.
32         05  s3-year       pic 9(4).
33         05  s3-name       pic x(13).
34         05  s3-title      pic x(43).
35
36 working-storage section.
37 01  w1-file.
38     03  w1-filename       pic x(20).
39
40 01  w2-file.
41     03  w2-filename       pic x(20).
42/
43 procedure division.
44 para1.
45     display "sort1 begins"
46
47     display "Enter name of  input file: " no advancing
48     accept w1-filename
49     display "Enter name of output file: " no advancing
50     accept w2-filename
51
52     sort s3-file
53        ascending   s3-name
54        descending  s3-year
55        ascending   s3-site
56        using       i1-file
57        giving      o2-file
58
59     display "sort1 ends"
60     stop run.
61
62 end program sort1
```

Figure 14.3 Program sort1

362 ESSENTIAL COBOL: A FIRST COURSE IN STRUCTURED COBOL

Secondly, the reserved word **sd** is used to identify the sort-merge file description (line 24). This description must define all of the keys that are used in the sort and the minimum record length must be long enough to include all of the keys that are used in the sort statement.

The sort statement at line 52 does all of the following:

1. Opens the input file and the internal sort-merge file.
2. Reads all of the input records into the sort-merge file and then closes the input file.
3. Sorts the sort-merge file.
4. Opens the output file and writes all of the sorted records from the sort-merge file into it.
5. Closes the sort-merge file and the output file.

In effect, the sort statement gives the programmer a high level of procedural abstraction as do other statements such as string, unstring, inspect, and search. As with the other statements there are a number of characteristics that must be well understood if the sort statement is to be used effectively.

The most common errors in using the sort statement are:

1. Attempting to open, read, write, or close any of the three files.
2. Using keys within the sort statement that are defined as part of the input fd. They must always be defined as part of the sd.

```
          1         2         3         4         5         6         7
1234567890123456789012345678901234567890123456789012345678901234567890123456
Accession       Site  Author
      Subject        Year         Title

23145678001.535     A21984Alexsander,I Designing Intelligent Systems
43123456621.381957C41963Ashley,J.R    Intro. to Analogue Computation
21920345003         B71982Athey,T.H   Sytematic Systems Approach
19234856001.5       A11984Balle,F     Nouveaux Medias
51234567515.353     B71982Bathe,K.J   Finite Element Procedures In Engineerin
81923445001.642     B71982Ben-Ari,M   Principles of Concurrent Programming
71029384001.642     A11982Darlington,J Functional Programming and Its Applicat
39102475001.64      C41982Day,C       Illustrating Computers
21823446001.6424    A11982Forsythe,R.S Pascal at Work and Play
21823445001.6424    A21982Forsythe,R.S Pascal at Work and Play
23156789001.6       C41983Harrison,D  Data Processing
39102344001.642     A11969Jackson,W.E Local Gov't in England and Wales
26126789001.63      A11970Keys,W.J    Handbook of Modern Key Punch Operation
45123456001.61      A11982Krallmann,H Sozio-Okonomische Anwendungen
51029345001.6425    A11985Marx,J.L    Clefs Pour Multiplan
62931209001.53      B71969Porter,A    Cybernetics Simplified
91728346001.6404    A11981Rouquerol,M Micro-Ordinateurs
31023494001.6404    C51982Ruston,J    BBC Micro Revealed
10123445621.38195   C41985Tocci,R.J   Digital Systems
71345678001.64      A11976Weizenbaum,J Computer Power and Human Reason
30129345001.64042   B71982Zaks,R      Programming the Z80
```

Figure 14.4 Book extracts in order by author, site and year (file extract2.dat)

When it executes program sort1 can take a file of book extract records that is in any order (file extract1.dat in Fig. 14.2) and create a new output file in the order that is specified by the sort statement and the related sort record. The contents of the output file are listed in Fig. 14.4.

14.1.1 Input procedures

There are times when only some of the data in an input file should be released into a sort. For these cases a programmer might decide to write one program to filter out unwanted records and then a second program to sort the result (see Fig. 14.5). For example, imagine that only those records that had an accession number in the inclusive range of 10 000 000 to 30 000 000 were required on the final report. In this case program filter could read the original input file (all.dat) and write the required records to a new intermediate file (wanted.dat). This file could then be sorted by program sort1 to produce the required sorted file (sorted.dat).

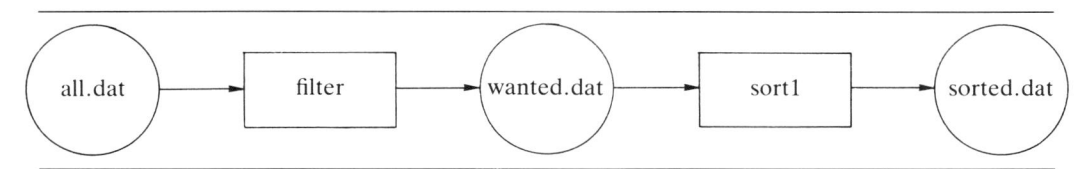

Figure 14.5 Using a filter program prior to a sort

This approach requires three files and two programs and is similar to the high-level approach that would be adopted when programming in other languages. However, the sort statement in COBOL allows us to include the filter within the sort program as an input procedure. As a result both the filter and the sort are in a single program and there is no need for an intermediate file.

$$\text{sort file-name-1} \left\{ \left\{ \begin{matrix} \text{ascending} \\ \text{descending} \end{matrix} \right\} \text{data-name-1} \ldots \right\} \ldots$$

$$\left\{ \begin{matrix} \text{using} & \{\text{file-name-2}\} \ldots \\ \text{input} & \text{procedure section-name-1} \end{matrix} \right\}$$

$$\text{giving } \{\text{file-name-3}\} \ldots$$

We can see that the **using** phrase and the **input procedure** phrase are mutually exclusive. If we choose the input procedure phrase then the filter which it names must be written as a COBOL section and it must contain all of the file operations necessary for the management of the input file. Therefore we are forced to choose between allowing the sort to manage the input completely as in program sort1 and managing the input ourselves as in program sort2 which contains an input filter (Fig. 14.6).

```cobol
 1 identification division.
 2 program-id. sort2.
 3*Purpose: To demonstrate a sort that uses an input procedure
 4
 5 environment division.
 6 input-output section.
 7 file-control.
 8     select i1-file assign w1-filename.
 9     select o2-file assign w2-filename.
10     select s3-file assign "anyname".
11
12 data division.
13 file section.
14 fd  i1-file
15     record varying 37 to 80
16     depending      w1-ctr
17     value of id    w1-filename.
18 01  filler                   pic x(80).
19
20 fd  o2-file
21     record varying 37 to 80
22     value of id    w2-filename.
23 01  filler                   pic x(80).
24
25 sd  s3-file
26     record varying 37 to 80
27     depending      w3-ctr.
28 01  s3-rec.
29     03  s3-shelf.
30         05   s3-accession  pic 9(8).
31         05   s3-subject    pic x(10).
32         05   s3-site       pic xx.
33     03  s3-author.
34         05   s3-year       pic 9(4).
35         05   s3-name       pic x(13).
36         05   s3-title      pic x(43).
37
38 working-storage section.
39 01  w1-file.
40     03  w1-ctr binary            pic 999.
41     03  w1-filename              pic x(20).
42     03  filler value "n"         pic x.
43         88  w1-eof               value 'y'.
44     03  w1-total value zero      pic 999.
45     03  w1-rec.
46         05  w1-accession         pic 9(8).
47             88  w1-chosenbooks   value 10000000 thru 30000000.
48         05  filler               pic x(72).
49
50 01  w2-file.
51     03  w2-filename              pic x(20).
52
53 01  w3-file.
54     03  w3-ctr binary            pic 999.
55     03  w3-total value zero      pic 999.
56/
57 procedure division.
58 a-main-program section.
59 a-para1.
60     display "sort2 begins"
61
```

```
 62      display "Enter name of  input file: " no advancing
 63      accept w1-filename
 64      display "Enter name of output file: " no advancing
 65      accept w2-filename
 66
 67      sort s3-file
 68         ascending      s3-name
 69         descending     s3-year
 70         ascending      s3-site
 71         input procedure b-filter-input
 72         giving          o2-file
 73
 74      display "Total records input to program  = " w1-total
 75      display "                input to sort    = " w3-total
 76      display "sort2 ends"
 77      stop run.
 78/
 79 b-filter-input section.
 80 b-para1.
 81      open input i1-file
 82
 83      read i1-file into w1-rec
 84         end     set w1-eof to true
 85         not end compute w1-total = w1-total + 1
 86      end-read
 87
 88      perform test before until w1-eof
 89         evaluate w1-chosenbooks
 90            when    true
 91               move    w1-ctr to    w3-ctr
 92               release s3-rec from w1-rec
 93               compute w3-total = w3-total + 1
 94         end-evaluate
 95
 96         read i1-file into w1-rec
 97            end     set w1-eof to true
 98            not end compute w1-total = w1-total + 1
 99         end-read
100
101      end-perform
102
103      close i1-file.
104
105 end program sort2
```

Figure 14.6 Program sort2

The input procedure must be a COBOL **section**. The section is a language feature that allows one or more paragraphs within a program to be grouped together and referenced by the section-name. (In practice, the section should now be considered as an outmoded language feature except that the sort and merge statements require them in order to maintain consistency with the previous COBOL standard.) Take a moment to look at lines 58, 59, 79 and 80 in program sort2.

When sections are used all paragraphs must be within a section and each section must contain at least one paragraph. Thus the fact that we need to create a section for the input filter forces us to write the main part of the program in a section as well. Therefore in sort2 the first line of the procedure division is a section header consisting of the section-name

366 ESSENTIAL COBOL: A FIRST COURSE IN STRUCTURED COBOL

`a-main-program` followed by the reserved word section. This is followed immediately by the paragraph `a-para1`. The filter is contained in the section `b-filter-input` and contains the paragraph `b-para1`.

As with paragraph-names, section-names can be any user-defined word. (In sort2 the names have been prefixed to show which paragraphs belong to which sections.) As with previous programs, execution begins with the first executable statement in the procedure division and continues until the stop run is encountered. The transfer of control from the sort statement to `b-filter-input` is analogous to a call. Control is returned to the sort statement once the last statement in `b-filter-input` has executed.

The sort statement at line 67 in program sort2 does all of the following:

1. Opens the sort file.
2. Transfers control to `b-filter-input` where:
   - the input file is opened,
   - all records are read and released as required to the sort file,
   - and the input file is closed.
3. Sorts the sort file in accordance with the defined keys.
4. Opens the output file and writes all of the sorted records into it.
5. Closes the sort file and the output file.

The most common error in writing an input procedure is to assume that the procedure is invoked for every record. This is not the case. It is invoked only once by the sort statement prior to the sort. When it is invoked it must provide all of the input to the sort. This implies that the input procedure must contain a loop that detects the end of the input stream as well as a statement to **release** selected records into the sort.

```
release record-name-1 [from identifier-1]
```

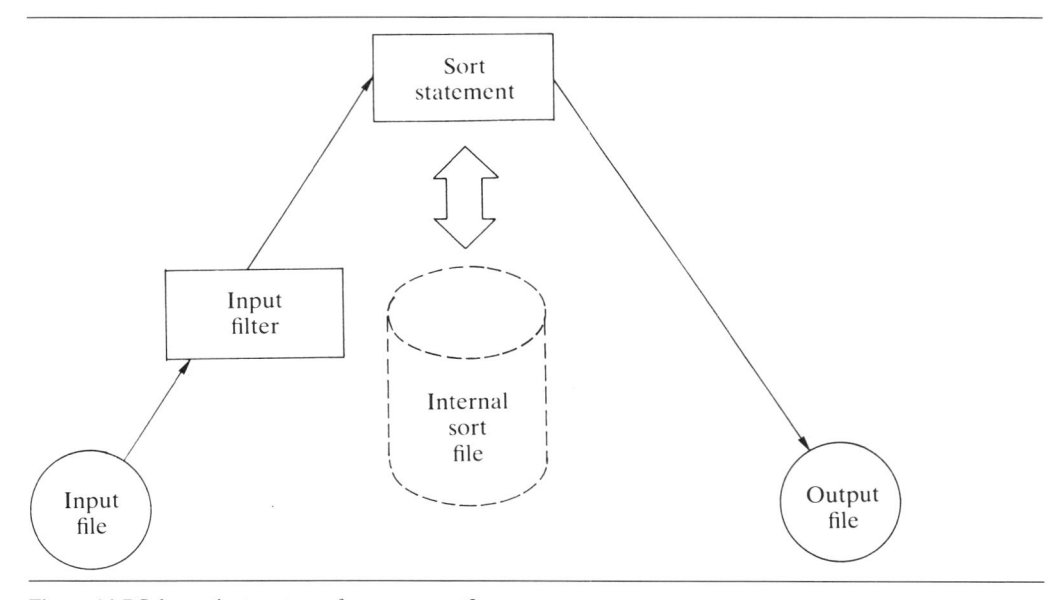

Figure 14.7 Schematic structure of program sort2

```
         1         2         3         4         5         6         7
1234567890123456789012345678901234567890123456789012345678901234567890123456
Accession          Site  Author
         Subject        Year          Title
```

```
23145678001.535    A21984Alexsander,I Designing Intelligent Systems
21920345003        B71982Athey,T.H   Sytematic Systems Approach
19234856001.5      A11984Balle,F     Nouveaux Medias
21823446001.6424   A11982Forsythe,R.S Pascal at Work and Play
21823445001.6424   A21982Forsythe,R.S Pascal at Work and Play
23156789001.6      C41983Harrison,D  Data Processing
26126789001.63     A11970Keys,W.J    Handbook of Modern Key Punch Operation
10123445621.38195  C41985Tocci,R.J   Digital Systems
```

Figure 14.8 Input filtered book extracts (file extract3.dat)

The release statement causes the transfer of a record into the sort file. It is most easily understood as a special form of write statement to be used when writing records into a sort file.

Figure 14.8 shows the records that will be written to the output file in program sort2 as a result of filtering out unwanted accession number records from extract1.dat.

14.1.2 Output procedures

An **output procedure** is constructed in a similar fashion to an input procedure and has a similar format within the sort statement.

$$\text{sort file-name-1} \left\{ \begin{Bmatrix} \text{ascending} \\ \text{descending} \end{Bmatrix} \text{data-name-1} \ldots \right\} \ldots$$

$$\begin{Bmatrix} \text{using} & \{\text{file-name-2}\} \ldots \\ \text{input} & \text{procedure section-name-1} \end{Bmatrix}$$

$$\begin{Bmatrix} \text{giving} & \{\text{file-name-3} \\ \text{output} & \text{procedure section-name-2} \end{Bmatrix}$$

It is perfectly legal to write a program with the using option for input and an output procedure to filter the output. However, in program sort3 both an input and output procedure have been incorporated in order to provide a sample program that incorporates all of the main features of the sort statement. The outline in Fig. 14.9 shows that the relationship between the sort statement and its two procedures is best conceptualized as a relationship between a root program and two called programs. (It is perfectly legal for the filters to contain calls to other programs and in this way filters of considerable complexity can be constructed. Unfortunately the whole of the filter cannot be put into a called program because statements such as the release and return which act upon the record in the sd must be in the same program as the sort.)

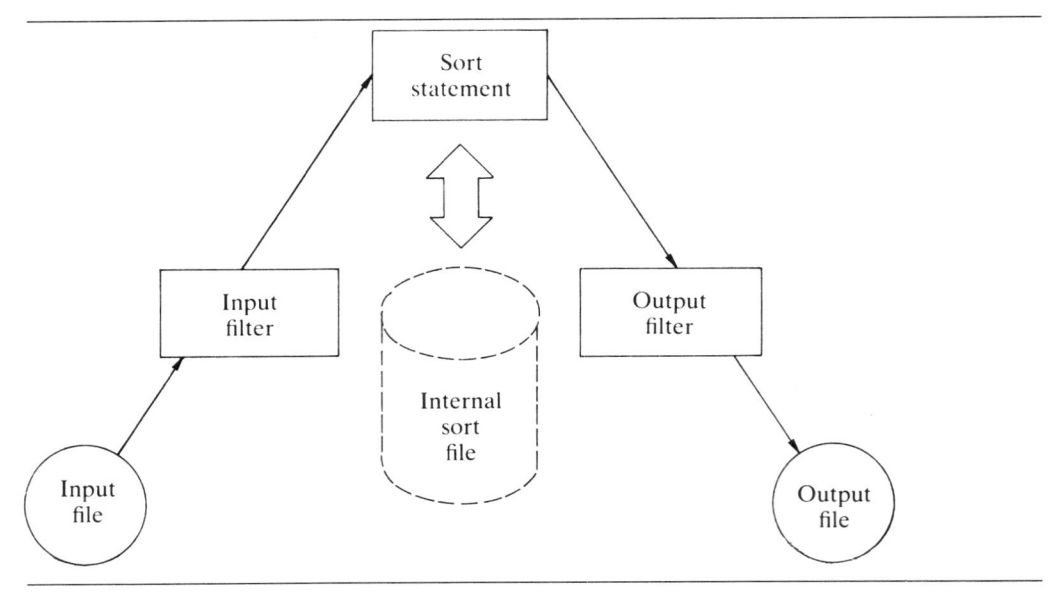

Figure 14.9 Schematic structure of program sort3

When program sort3 (Fig. 14.10) executes, the sort statement at line 77 does all of the following:

1. Opens the sort file.
2. Transfers control to `b-filter-input`, where:
   - the input file is opened,
   - all records are read and released as required to the sort file,
   - and the input file is closed.
3. Sorts the sort file in accordance with the defined keys.
4. Transfers control to `c-filter-output` where:
   - the output file is opened,
   - records are returned from the sort file and written as required to the output file,
   - and the output file is closed.
5. Closes the sort file.

The output filter uses a new statement to **return** records from the sort file into a target record in the program

```
return file-name-1 [into identifier-1]
    end     statement-1
  [not end statement-2]
end-return
```

File-name-1 must always be the sort file. Its return is most easily conceptualized as a special form of read statement that is only used to read records into a program from a sort file.

```
 1 identification division.
 2 program-id. sort3.
 3*Purpose: To demonstrate a sort that uses both input and output procedures
 4
 5 environment division.
 6 input-output section.
 7 file-control.
 8     select i1-file assign w1-filename.
 9     select o2-file assign w2-filename.
10     select s3-file assign "anyname".
11
12 data division.
13 file section.
14 fd  i1-file
15     record varying 37 to 80
16     depending       w1-ctr
17     value of id     w1-filename.
18 01  filler                  pic x(80).
19
20 fd  o2-file
21     record varying 37 to 80
22     depending       w2-ctr
23     value of id     w2-filename.
24 01  o2-rec                  pic x(80).
25
26 sd  s3-file
27     record varying 37 to 80
28     depending       w3-ctr.
29 01  s3-rec.
30     03  s3-shelf.
31         05  s3-accession    pic 9(8).
32         05  s3-subject      pic x(10).
33         05  s3-site         pic xx.
34     03  s3-author.
35         05  s3-year         pic 9(4).
36         05  s3-name         pic x(13).
37         05  s3-title        pic x(43).
38
39 working-storage section.
40 01  w1-file.
41     03  w1-ctr binary           pic 999.
42     03  w1-filename             pic x(20).
43     03  filler value "n"        pic x.
44         88  w1-eof              value 'y'.
45     03  w1-total value zero     pic 999.
46     03  w1-rec.
47         05  w1-accession        pic 9(8).
48             88  w1-chosenbooks  value 10000000 thru 30000000.
49         05  filler              pic x(72).
50
51 01  w2-file.
52     03  w2-ctr binary           pic 999.
53     03  w2-filename             pic x(20).
54     03  w2-rec.
55         05  filler              pic x(24).
56         05  w2-currname         pic x(13).
57         05  filler              pic x(43).
58     03  w2-prevname value low-value  pic x(13).
59     03  w2-total value zero     pic 999.
60
```

```
61 01  w3-file.
62     03  w3-ctr binary              pic 999.
63     03  filler value "n"           pic x.
64         88  w3-eof                 value "y".
65     03  w3-total value zero        pic 999.
66/
67 procedure division.
68 a-main-program section.
69 para1.
70     display "sort3 begins"
71
72     display "Enter name of  input file: " no advancing
73     accept w1-filename
74     display "Enter name of output file: " no advancing
75     accept w2-filename
76
77     sort s3-file
78       ascending       s3-name
79       descending      s3-year
80       ascending       s3-site
81       input procedure  b-filter-input
82       output procedure c-filter-output
83
84     display "Total records input to program  = " w1-total
85     display "                 input to sort     = " w3-total
86     display "                 output from program = " w2-total
87
88     display "sort3 ends"
89     stop run.
90/
91 b-filter-input section.
92 b-para1.
93     open input i1-file
94
95     read i1-file into w1-rec
96       end     set w1-eof to true
97       not end compute w1-total = w1-total + 1
98     end-read
99
100    perform test before until w1-eof
101      evaluate w1-chosenbooks
102        when    true
103          move    w1-ctr to    w3-ctr
104          release s3-rec from w1-rec
105          compute w3-total = w3-total + 1
106      end-evaluate
107
108      read i1-file into w1-rec
109        end     set w1-eof to true
110        not end compute w1-total = w1-total + 1
111      end-read
112
113    end-perform
114
115    close i1-file.
116/
117 c-filter-output section.
118 para1.
119    open output o2-file
120
```

```
121       return s3-file into w2-rec
122          end     set   w3-eof to true
123          not end move  w3-ctr to w2-ctr
124       end-return
125
126       perform test before until w3-eof
127          evaluate w2-currname not = w2-prevname
128             when    true
129                write o2-rec from w2-rec
130                compute w2-total = w2-total + 1
131                move w2-currname to w2-prevname
132          end-evaluate
133
134          return s3-file into w2-rec
135             end     set   w3-eof to true
136             not end move  w3-ctr to w2-ctr
137          end-return
138
139       end-perform
140
141       close o2-file.
142
143 end program sort3
```

Figure 14.10 Program sort3

```
          1         2         3         4         5         6         7
1234567890123456789012345678901234567890123456789012345678901234567890123456
Accession           Site  Author
        Subject          Year        Title

23145678001.535     A21984Alexsander,I Designing Intelligent Systems
21920345003         B71982Athey,T.H   Sytematic Systems Approach
19234856001.5       A11984Balle,F     Nouveaux Medias
21823446001.6424    A11982Forsythe,R.S Pascal at Work and Play
23156789001.6       C41983Harrison,D  Data Processing
26126789001.63      A11970Keys,W.J    Handbook of Modern Key Punch Operation
10123445621.38195   C41985Tocci,R.J   Digital Systems
```

Figure 14.11 Input and output filtered book extracts (file extract4.dat)

As a result of filtering both the input to the sort and the output from the sort, the output file will hold the records shown in Fig. 14.11.

14.2 MERGE

The merge statement is used to combine two or more files that are already in the same key order. It is usually used in close association with the sort in cases where a regular occurrence produces sorted files which then must be combined into a single ordered file prior to further processing. (Imagine a case where many different sites produce a sorted file of the day's transactions and send these to a central location where they are merged prior to a major update of the main files in the system.)

The full syntax for the merge statement is:

$$\text{merge file-name-1} \left\{ \begin{Bmatrix} \text{ascending} \\ \text{descending} \end{Bmatrix} \text{data-name-1} \ldots \right\} \ldots$$

$$\text{using file-name-2} \{\text{file-name-3}\} \ldots$$

$$\begin{Bmatrix} \text{giving } \{\text{file-name-4}\} \ldots \\ \text{output procedure section-name-1} \end{Bmatrix}$$

Program merge1 in Fig. 14.12 gives a simple example where two files of book extracts are being merged by accession number. The key for the merge is established at line 58.

If during the execution of a merge any of the input files is found to be out of order the result is undefined. (On many systems the program will fail with a run-time error but the COBOL standard does not guarantee that this will happen.)

Therefore it is always the case that merge operations are preceded by sorts in order to ensure that the records are indeed in order. It is a good defensive programming practice to assume that any file which is not positively known to be in sorted order must be sorted. In particular you should never require those who are preparing data with text editors to maintain records in sorted order.

In small applications where the files are on disk, the sorting is only a minor overhead for files that are already well ordered and that therefore need to have only a few records shuffled.

```
 1 identification division.
 2 program-id. merge1.
 3*Purpose: To demonstrate a simple merge of two files
 4
 5 environment division.
 6 input-output section.
 7 file-control.
 8     select i1-file assign w1-filename.
 9     select i4-file assign w4-filename.
10     select o2-file assign w2-filename.
11     select s3-file assign "anyname".
12
13 data division.
14 file section.
15 fd  i1-file
16     record varying 8 to 80
17     value of id    w1-filename.
18 01  filler                            pic x(80).
19
20 fd  i4-file
21     record varying 8 to 80
22     value of id    w4-filename.
23 01  filler                            pic x(80).
24
```

```
25 fd  o2-file
26     record varying 8 to 80
27     value of id    w2-filename.
28 01  filler                            pic x(80).
29
30 sd  s3-file
31     record varying 8 to 80.
32 01  s3-rec.
33     03  s3-accession                  pic 9(8).
34     03  filler                        pic x(72).
35
36 working-storage section.
37 01  w1-file.
38     03  w1-filename                   pic x(20).
39
40 01  w2-file.
41     03  w2-filename                   pic x(20).
42
43 01  w4-file.
44     03  w4-filename                   pic x(20).
45/
46 procedure division.
47 para1.
48     display "merge1 begins"
49
50     display "Enter name of  first input file: " no advancing
51     accept w1-filename
52     display "Enter name of second input file: " no advancing
53     accept w4-filename
54     display "Enter name of output file:       " no advancing
55     accept w2-filename
56
57     merge s3-file
58       ascending       s3-accession
59       using           i1-file
60                       i4-file
61       giving          o2-file
62
63     display "merge1 ends"
64     stop run.
65
66 end program merge1
```

Figure 14.12 Program merge1

14.2.1 Output procedures

An output procedure for the merge statement is constructed in a similar fashion to an output procedure for the sort. Once again the output file must be opened and closed and each record from the merge file must be returned into the filter until the end condition of the return statement becomes true.

Program merge2 checks for duplicate accession numbers in the merged stream of records and only writes the first of these records to the output file (Fig. 14.13).

```
 1  identification division.
 2  program-id. merge2.
 3 *Purpose: To demonstrate a merge with an output procedure
 4
 5  environment division.
 6  input-output section.
 7  file-control.
 8      select i1-file assign w1-filename.
 9      select i4-file assign w4-filename.
10      select o2-file assign w2-filename.
11      select s3-file assign "anyname".
12
13  data division.
14  file section.
15  fd  i1-file
16      record varying 8 to 80
17      value of id    w1-filename.
18  01  filler.
19      03  i1-accession                  pic 9(8).
20      03  filler                        pic x(72).
21
22  fd  i4-file
23      record varying 8 to 80
24      value of id    w4-filename.
25  01  filler                            pic x(80).
26
27  fd  o2-file
28      record varying 8 to 80
29      depending      w2-ctr
30      value of id    w2-filename.
31  01  o2-rec                            pic x(80).
32
33  sd  s3-file
34      record varying 8 to 80
35      depending      w3-ctr.
36  01  s3-rec.
37      03  s3-key.
38          05  s3-accession              pic 9(8).
39      03  filler                        pic x(72).
40
41  working-storage section.
42  01  w1-file.
43      03  w1-filename                   pic x(20).
44
45  01  w2-file.
46      03  w2-ctr binary                 pic 999.
47      03  w2-filename                   pic x(20).
48      03  w2-rec.
49          05  w2-curraccession          pic x(8).
50          05  filler                    pic x(72).
51      03  w2-prevaccession value low-value pic x(8).
52      03  w2-tot         value zero     pic 999.
53
```

```
54 01  w3-file.
55     03  w3-ctr    binary             pic 999.
56     03  filler value "n"             pic x.
57         88  w3-eof                   value "y".
58     03  w3-tot    value zero         pic 999.
59
60 01  w4-file.
61     03  w4-filename                  pic x(20).
62/
63 procedure division.
64 a-main-program section.
65 para1.
66     display "merge2 begins"
67
68     display "Enter name of  first input file: " no advancing
69     accept w1-filename
70     display "Enter name of second input file: " no advancing
71     accept w4-filename
72     display "Enter name of output file:       " no advancing
73     accept w2-filename
74
75     merge s3-file
76        ascending      s3-accession
77        using          i1-file
78                       i4-file
79        output procedure b-filter-output
80
81     display "Total records input to merge = " w3-tot
82     display "                 output to file  = " w2-tot
83     display "merge2 ends"
84     stop run.
85/
86 b-filter-output section.
87 para1.
88     open output o2-file
89
90     return s3-file into w2-rec
91        end     set    w3-eof to true
92        not end move w3-ctr to w2-ctr
93                compute w3-tot = w3-tot + 1
94     end-return
95
96     perform test before until w3-eof
97        evaluate w2-curraccession not = w2-prevaccession
98           when    true
99              write o2-rec from w2-rec
100             compute w2-tot = w2-tot + 1
101             move w2-curraccession to w2-prevaccession
102       end-evaluate
103
```

```
104        return s3-file into w2-rec
105          end     set  w3-eof to true
106          not end move w3-ctr to w2-ctr
107                  compute w3-tot = w3-tot + 1
108        end-return
109
110      end-perform
111
112      display "merge2 ends"
113      close o2-file.
114
115 end program merge2
```

Figure 14.13 Program merge2

The lack of input procedures can be considered a minor inconvenience when it is necessary to know which file was the source for particular duplicate records. In this case the merge should be preceded by sorts that have an output filter which adds a tag field to indicate the file from which it originated. These tagged records can then be merged. The output filter from the merge can use the tag to identify the source of the duplication. It can also write untagged records to its output file.

14.3 EXERCISES

1 Program sort1 will fail with a run-time error if it is not given correct file-names. Rewrite sort1 as sort1a so that the sort will not proceed unless it is given two file-names that are non-spaces.
2 Write poem1 which takes a file containing a short poem and sorts its lines of text by the first ten characters on each line.
3 The input and output for a sort does not have to be in files. Write program srtnum1 to sort strings of text from the keyboard and then display the results at the screen. A loop containing accept and release statements can be contained within the input procedure and another loop containing return and display statements can be contained within the output procedure.
4 Write concord1 to produce a concordance. A simple concordance takes lines of text and rotates the words on the line to produce a sorted output file that lists all of the rotated lines in first word order with a line number. Thus a first input line of:

   0∆say∆can∆you∆see

will be output as:

   1: ∆0∆say∆can∆you∆see
   1: ∆say∆can∆you∆see∆0
   1: ∆can∆you∆see∆0∆say
   1: ∆you∆see∆0∆say∆can
   1: ∆see∆0∆say∆can∆you

The sort is done on the first word in the line. Thus the lines of output will be interleaved with other lines to produce an alphabetical listing. (The rotation should be done in an input procedure. The sort key should be a string that is at least as long as the longest word in the file.)

5   Write program dups1 which takes two unsorted input files, sorts them separately with an input procedure that adds a tag, and then uses an output procedure that displays duplicates on the screen and deletes them. Once this is done a merge should merge the two files. Its output procedure should also check for duplicates. It should use the information in the tag to identify which file was the source of the duplicate and then allow the user to choose to delete one or the other from the output stream. As a result the output file should contain no duplicates even though there may have been any number of duplicates in an input file prior to sorting or two copies of record in each of the sorted but unmerged files.

6   Write tele3 which sorts the tele.dat file that you created for the exercises from the previous chapter.

7   Write tele4 which is a rewrite of tele2 from the exercises of the previous chapter. It should sort the records in the file prior to putting them as entries in the table. As a result even though the add, change and delete may have caused the table to become out of order on output, the sort will return it to sorted order on input.

8   Write program index1 which for a given text file will produce an index by line number. The words in the index should be those from the input that are five or more characters in length. The index should be in sorted alphabetical order and each entry in the index should give the line number on which the word appeared in the original. (Write separate index records when the same word appears on different lines. Your input procedure should build a record for each word consisting of the word and its line number and then sort on both of these fields.)

9   Rewrite index1 as index2 in which a word in the index is followed by all of its line references. This is most easily done by checking for duplicate words in an output procedure that builds new records for output.

15
WRITING REPORTS USING CONTROL BREAKS

This chapter introduces those issues associated with writing reports from input files that are in sorted order by a single key. There are many approaches available for designing programs that are capable of generating reports of this kind. The approach adopted in this chapter uses changes in key values as a means of determining the breaks in processing that are required by the application. In general the approach separates those aspects of a solution that are specific to an application from those aspects that are in general part of *control break* processing and therefore reusable. The next chapter on the problem of master file updating is treated as an extension of the control break problem discussed in this chapter.

Section 15.3 discusses the write statement and the linage clause as a means of printing reports with page numbers. By the end of the chapter you will be able to identify control breaks in an input stream of records and manage page breaks in an output stream that is intended for printing.

15.1 ALGORITHM DESIGN

This section introduces an algorithm for writing simple reports of information from a single file of input records where the file is ordered by a key field.

Figure 15.1 shows a record layout, a test file of seven records that conform to the record layout, and a sample output report that is to be produced from a single pass of the input file.

WRITING REPORTS USING CONTROL BREAKS   379

(a) Record layout for daily production

```
01   e1-daily-rec.
     03   e1-batch-id        pic xx.
     03   e1-batch-units     pic 999.
```

(b) Test input file containing seven records   *Comments*

```
B2020                                                   record 1
B2090                                                   record 2
D4015                                                   record 3
M1007                                                   record 4
P9023                                                   record 5
P9002                                                   record 5
R0073                                                   record 7
```

(c) Sample output report   *Comments*

```
Position batch units records         line 1    header
                                     line 2
       1    B2    110    2           line 3
       2    D4     15    1           line 4
       3    M1      7    1           line 5    batch lines
       4    P9     25                line 6
       5    R0     73    1           line 7
                                     line 8    trailer
Totals:           230    7           line 9
```

Figure 15.1 Control break example – daily production

Each of the input records is five characters long. The first field is the key by which the file is ordered. This field is a batch identifier on which the file has been previously sorted into ascending order. The second field is three characters long and holds a value for production units within a batch.

The sample output report shows that this input file should produce nine lines of output text. The report begins with a header consisting of a line of text followed by a blank line. This *header* appears only once at the beginning of processing. The next five lines each contain information for a single batch. Each line gives the batch identifier, the total number of units for that batch, and the total number of records in the file for that batch. In effect one of these lines summarizes information that appears on one or more records in the input file. The report ends with a *trailer* consisting of a blank line followed by a line of totals for all of the records in the file.

Within the report the processing of the records for each batch is to be preceded by a clearing of the batch totals and followed by writing the batch line to output.

The tree in Fig. 15.2 shows the order in which these operations should be undertaken in relation to the batch report.

The tree implies an order of execution for a program. It is read from top to bottom and left to right. The asterisk against 'process batch' and 'process record' is read as an operator meaning 'zero or more times'.

Thus the tree tells us that the program should write a header, process any number of

380 ESSENTIAL COBOL: A FIRST COURSE IN STRUCTURED COBOL

batches, and then write a trailer. It also tells us that the nested processing for a batch consists of clear totals, process any number of records, and write the batch.

```
write_header
perform test before until ____
   clear_totals
   perform test before until ____
      process_record
   end-perform
   write_batch
end-perform
write_trailer
```

The above pseudo-code is derived directly from the tree. It shows us that the report, the tree, and the pseudo-code all reflect the same structural characteristics for a program.

However, this view of the problem as derived from the order of the output operations disguises a number of important difficulties relevant to the design of a processing algorithm for the problem as a whole. These problems become more apparent when we look at the order of operations relative to the input.

Firstly, the break between batches is identified by a change in the batch identifier. For example, in the middle of file processing a change in value from batch "D4" to batch "M1" implies the following order of operations:

```
write batch "D4"        (5)
clear totals            (3)
process record "M1"     (4)
```

Secondly, this order of operations does not apply to batch "B2" which is the first batch in the file. It has no preceding batch and therefore only the following operations should be done:

```
clear totals            (3)
process record "B2"     (4)
```

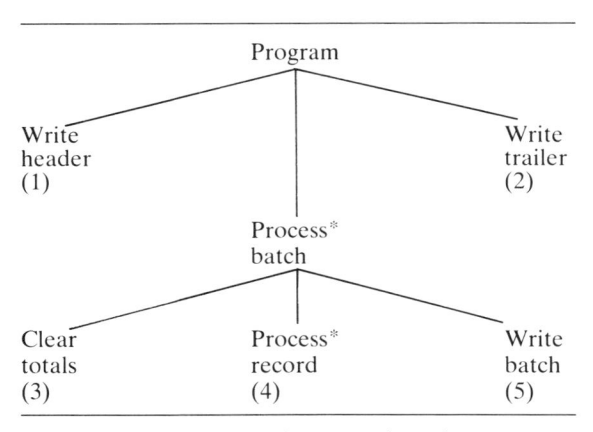

```
                    Program
        _____/   |   _____
       /               |               \
   Write           Process*            Write
   header          batch               trailer
   (1)               |                 (2)
          _____/|_____
         /           |           \
      Clear       Process*       Write
      totals      record         batch
      (3)         (4)            (5)
```

Figure 15.2 Tree to identify five processing points

Thirdly, the last batch in the file is not followed by a further batch. Therefore only the following operations should be done:

```
process record "R0"      (4)
write batch "R0"         (5)
```

All of the actions for writing the report are listed in Fig. 15.3. The read actions for the input file are listed to the right-hand side so that by reading both columns down the page it is possible to follow the execution history which any successful algorithm must be able to define.

One common method for reading input files uses a priming read before a main loop. Within the loop the statements at the top process the application. At the bottom of the loop a second read statement either refreshes the input (not end) or detects the end of file and sets the eof condition to terminate the loop.

	Report actions	*Input stream of records*
1.	Write header	
2.		Read "B2020"
3.	Clear totals	
4.	Process record "B2"	
5.		Read "B2090"
6.	Process record "B2"	
7.		Read "D4015"
8.	Write batch "B2"	
9.	Clear totals	
10.	Process record "D4"	
11.		Read "M1007"
12.	Write batch "D4"	
13.	Clear totals	
14.	Process record "M1"	
15.		Read "P9023"
16.	Write batch "M1"	
17.	Clear totals	
18.	Process record "P9"	
19.		Read "P9002"
20.	Process record "P9"	
21.		Read "R0073"
22.	Write batch "P9"	
23.	Clear totals	
24.	Process record "R0"	
25.		Respond to end of file detection
26.	Write batch "R0"	
27.	Write trailer	

Figure 15.3 Operation relationships between input and output streams

```
(1)
read input-file into ...
   end
      set eof to true
end-read
perform test before until eof
   (3,4) or (5,3,4) or (4,5)
   read input-file ...
      end
         set eof to true
   end-read
end-perform
(2)
```

The above pseudo-code shows such a processing loop for an input file. (The five operations for the control break report have been inserted at the appropriate points.) Clearly, it is necessary to distinguish the three sets of actions that are required within the loop.

The priming read has been used in COBOL because the former standard for the language did not include a not end phrase for the read. As a result the read prior to the loop could detect an empty file and set eof to true so that the loop did not execute. Clearly the priming read approach can now be replaced by a loop containing a single read statement that uses both the end and the not end phrases:

```
(1)
perform test before until eof
   read input-file into...
      end
         set eof to true
      not end
         (3,4) or (5,3,4) or (4,5)
   end-read
end-perform
(2)
```

For our purposes both of these loops will be considered equivalent because operations 1 and 2 are outside the loop and the other actions must be differentiated within the loop.

Most approaches to program design imply a loop of this kind together with guidelines for determining how to undertake the actions within the loop. One interesting approach used by M.A. Jackson takes advantage of the notion that the input and output orders imply different reading and writing programs. The method uses a set of rules for resolving an input program with an output program to produce a single program that combines the sequential characteristics of both.

The difficulty with most approaches including Jackson structured programming (JSP) is that the resulting program does not identify and collect together the application-specific statements in any coherent way. The result is that even though programs which solve similar problems will exhibit similar structures they do not contain clear boundaries between those statements that are general and reusable and those which are specific to the application.

Therefore in the following pages we shall identify those features that are common to control break processing in general and design a solution which isolates these features from those statements that vary with each application.

If we reconsider Fig. 15.3 we can see that actions 6 to 24 follow a regular pattern of operations. Provided that an algorithm can compare the key for the record just read to the key for the record that was previously processed it is possible to use the change in keys as a means of driving a program. The following pseudo-code expresses this idea:

```
evaluate current-key not = previous-key
   when    true
      write batch
      clear totals
      process record
   when    false
      process record
end-evaluate
```

Statements similar to the above are unexceptional. However, the source of many difficulties lies not with the processing in the middle of the file but with the first and last records and with empty files.

If all sets of actions involved in processing could be identified as changes in a single set of control keys then it would be possible to construct a single evaluate statement that could control actions depending on the values in the current and previous keys. The approach we will use exploits this idea and uses a main loop which contains a single evaluate statement. But before moving ahead to consider the features of the algorithm we need to consider the means by which all changes in the input stream can be represented as changes in key values.

The figurative constants **low-value** and **high-value** are commonly used in COBOL to provide keys values that are lower and higher than any character key that exists in an input file of records. They can be used to supply a continuous stream of input keys and records as shown in Fig. 15.4.

Thus the main part of the algorithm can make all of its decisions with reference to the input stream of key values without needing to resort to file conditions, special switches or other unintegrated features. The first key now identifies the start of the stream and the last key identifies the end of the stream.

Input stream supplying nine key values	Comments
\<lv\>	Both low-value and high-value
B2020	are unprintable characters. They
B2090	are shown here as \<lv\> and \<hv\>.
D4015	
M1007	
P9023	
P9002	
R0073	
\<hv\>	

Figure 15.4 Test input file (batch1.dat)

```
    evaluate true
      when    input-key-low
        open input input-file
        set  file-is-open to true
    end-evaluate

    evaluate true
      when    input-key-high
        continue
      when    other
        read input-file into linkage-record
          end set input-key-high to true
            close input-file
        end-read
    end-evaluate
    exit program.
```

Figure 15.5 Outline for input handler (program tinput)

The pseudo-code in Fig. 15.5 shows the main features that an input handler would need to contain in order to supply such an input stream to a calling program.

Processing starts with a key containing low-values. We can see that the first call will return the first input record, subsequent calls prior to the detection of the end of the file will supply in succession keys for the records that are in the file, and the call which detects the end of file will supply a key of high-values as will any subsequent calls. Therefore such an approach can produce a stream of keys as described in Fig. 15.4.

We can how turn our attention to the main algorithm. By comparing keys the algorithm must determine the appropriate set of actions to undertake in every possible circumstance (Fig. 15.6).

```
        move low-value to current-key previous-key
        perform test before until both_keys_are_high
Oper-
ations
            evaluate true
  (1)         when    both_keys_low                       do start-level-2
  (2)         when    current_high and previous_low       do empty-file
  (3)         when    previous_low                        do start-level-1
  (4)         when    current_high                        do finish-level-1; finish-level-2
  (5)         when    current > previous                  do finish-level-1; start-level-1
  (6)         when    current = previous                  do level-0
  (7)         when    current < previous                  do out-of-sequence
            end-evaluate

        move current-key to previous-key
        move input-key to current-key
        end-perform
        stop run.
```

Figure 15.6 Outline for the root program (program cbreak1)

It begins by setting the current and previous keys to low-values. The loop then begins and will continue until both of the keys have been transformed to high-values. At the top of the loop there is a single evaluate statement which contains the seven rules that cover all processing possibilities. All of these rules are expressed in terms of the current and previous keys. In every case one of the seven rules will be selected. (The sets of actions associated with the rules include calls to get input and calls to dispose of output.)

Once the relevant actions have been completed the current key that has just been processed is moved to the previous key and the next key from the input stream (input-key) is established as the current key for the next iteration of the loop.

The pseudo-code for the the main algorithm shows seven rules. Each rule gives the name of a list of actions to be undertaken when the key values tested by its condition are satisfied. Although the particular actions to be undertaken will differ from application to application, it is the case that these seven conditions are common to the control break problem in general.

The seven rules are most easily conceptualized as breaks in program control as dictated by changes in the stream of input keys. Rule 1 is a control break at the level of the whole of the input file. Rule 2 breaks control for an empty input file and rule 7 detects input files that are misordered.

The next three rules are control breaks for keys within the file. Rule 3 is for the first file key, rule 4 is for the last file key, and rule 5 for a break from one key value to another within the file.

Rule 6 is for the lowest level of processing at which no key break occurs.

The lowest level is commonly considered to be level-0. Breaks on the file key represent the next highest level of breaking at level-1. The input file is the next highest level of key break activity at level-2. The levels and the sets of actions can be represented as a tree which shows the order in which the actions must be undertaken. This is shown in Fig. 15.7 and looks similar to the original diagram we constructed (Fig. 15.2).

Level-2 (file break)	Program
	start-level-2 finish-level-2

Level-1 (key break)	Batch*
	start-level-1 finish-level-1

Level-0 (no key break)	Within* batch

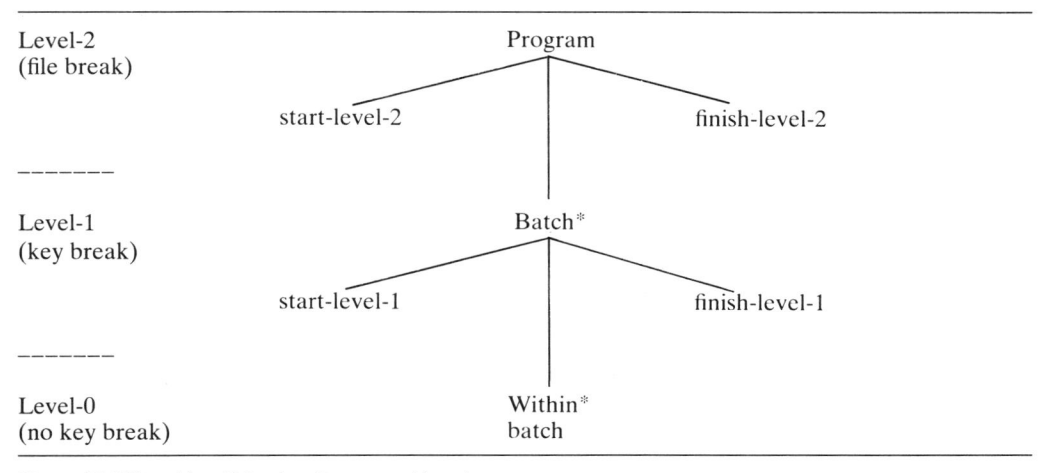

Figure 15.7 Tree identifying levels – control break

Current	Keys Previous	Key results	Actions
<lv>	<lv>	break on file	start-level-2
B2	lv	break on key	start-level-1
B2	B2	no break	level-0
D4	B2	break on key	finish-level-1; start-level-1
M1	D4	break on key	finish-level-1; start-level-1
P9	M1	break on key	finish-level-1; start-level-1
P9	P9	no break	level-0
R0	P9	break on key	finish-level-1; start-level-1
<hv>	R0	break on key	finish-level-1; finish-level-2
<hv>	<hv>	break on file	end-of-processing

Figure 15.8 Keys and actions – control break

It represents the order of events that the algorithm must enable for the benefit of the application-specific statements. The rules and the changing key values ensure that these events will occur in the correct sequence.

Figure 15.8 shows the values of the current and previous keys that will occur as each input becomes current. Listed against this are the actions that the algorithm will identify as being required.

```
evaluate true
   when    start-level-2
           move zero to trailer-count trailer-units
           open output report-file
           write a header line
           write a blank line

   when    finish-level-2
           write a trailer line
           write a blank line
           close report-file

   when    start-level-1
           move 1 to batch-count
           move input-units to batch-units

   when    finish-level-1
           write batch line
           compute trailer-count = record-count
           compute trailer-units = batch-units

   when    level-0
           compute batch-count = batch-count + 1
           compute batch-units = batch-units + input-units
end-evaluate
```

Figure 15.9 Outline for application (program batch1)

We can now specify a solution to the batch problem within the context of the control break algorithm. This is given in Fig. 15.9, which shows that the application has been reduced to a single evaluate statement, which specifies the output actions that are required to write the report.

15.2 PROGRAM DESIGN

Program cbreak1 in Fig. 15.10 implements a solution to the control break problem presented in the previous section.

It is always the case that when an algorithm is implemented it is necessary to insert additional statements to ensure that the programmed solution is truly general. In the case of the control break algorithm the majority of these additional statements relate to the name of the input file and the location and length of the record key. Provided that these are under general control it is possible to construct a program that is widely applicable.

This program is more complex than the simplest program capable of realizing the required output report. However, it has the advantage of separating general requirements from those that are specific to the application. It therefore indicates a basis for solving all control break problems.

```
 1 identification division.
 2 program-id. cbreak1.
 3*Purpose:
 4
 5 environment division.
 6
 7 data division.
 8
 9 working-storage section.
10 01   w1-inprec.
11      03   w1-ctr binary              pic 999.
12           88   w1-empty              value zero.
13      03   w1-filename                pic x(20).
14      03   w1-action                  pic xxx.
15           88   w1-start-level-2      value "sl2".
16           88   w1-finish-level-2     value "fl2".
17           88   w1-start-level-1      value "sl1".
18           88   w1-finish-level-1     value "fl1".
19           88   w1-process-level-0    value "l0 ".
20           88   w1-empty-file         value "emp".
21           88   w1-out-of-sequence    value "seq".
22      03   w1-keyarea.
23           05   w1-ref                pic 99.
24           05   w1-len                pic 99.
25           05   w1-key                pic x(20).
26                88   w1-eof           value high-value.
27                88   w1-sof           value low-value.
28      03   w1-rec                     pic x(255).
29
```

```
30 01  w4-controlarea.
31     03  w4-bothkeys value low-value pic x(40).
32         88  w4-start-level-2       value low-value.
33         88  w4-finish-level-2      value high-value.
34     03  filler redefines w4-bothkeys.
35         05  w4-current             pic x(20).
36             88  w4-finish-last-key value high-value.
37         05  w4-previous            pic x(20).
38             88  w4-start-first-key value low-value.
39/
40 procedure division.
41 para1.
42     display "cbreak1 begins"
43
44     perform test before until w4-finish-level-2
45
46       evaluate true
47         when    w4-start-level-2
48           set  w1-sof to true
49           set  w1-start-level-2 to true
50           call "batch1" using reference w1-inprec
51           call "tinput" using reference w1-inprec
52
53         when    w4-start-first-key and w4-finish-last-key
54           set  w1-empty-file to true
55           call "batch1" using content    w1-inprec
56
57         when    w4-start-first-key
58           set  w1-start-level-1 to true
59           call "batch1" using content    w1-inprec
60           call "tinput" using reference w1-inprec
61
62         when    w4-finish-last-key
63           set  w1-finish-level-1 to true
64           call "batch1" using content    w1-inprec
65           set  w1-finish-level-2 to true
66           call "batch1" using content    w1-inprec
67
68         when    w4-current > w4-previous
69           set  w1-finish-level-1 to true
70           call "batch1" using content w1-inprec
71           set  w1-start-level-1 to true
72           call "batch1" using content w1-inprec
73           call "tinput" using reference w1-inprec
74
75         when    w4-current = w4-previous
76           set  w1-process-level-0 to true
77           call "batch1" using content    w1-inprec
78           call "tinput" using reference w1-inprec
79
80         when    w4-current < w4-previous
81           set  w4-finish-last-key to true
82           set  w1-eof to true
83           set  w1-out-of-sequence to true
84           call "batch1" using content    w1-inprec
85       end-evaluate
86
```

```cobol
 87          move w4-current to w4-previous
 88          move w1-key     to w4-current
 89
 90      end-perform
 91
 92      display "cbreak1 ends"
 93      stop run.
 94/
 95  identification division.
 96  program-id. tinput.
 97
 98  environment division.
 99
100  input-output section.
101  file-control.
102      select i1-file   assign w1-filename.
103
104  data division.
105  file section.
106
107  fd  i1-file
108      record varying 1 to 255
109      depending       w1-ctr
110      value of id     w1-filename.
111  01  filler                          pic x(255).
112
113  working-storage section.
114  01  w1-inpfile.
115      03  w1-ctr binary               pic 999.
116      03  w1-filename                 pic x(20).
117
118  linkage section.
119  01  l1-file.
120      03  l1-ctr binary               pic 999.
121      03  l1-filename                 pic x(20).
122      03  filler                      pic xxx.
123      03  l1-keyarea.
124          05  l1-ref                  pic 99.
125          05  l1-len                  pic 99.
126          05  l1-key                  pic x(20).
127              88  l1-sof              value low-value.
128              88  l1-eof              value high-value.
129      03  l1-rec                      pic x(255).
130/
131  procedure division using l1-file.
132  para1.
133      evaluate true
134        when    l1-sof
135          move l1-filename to w1-filename
136          open input i1-file
137      end-evaluate
138
139      evaluate true
140        when    l1-eof
141          continue
142
```

```
143              when    other
144                 read i1-file into l1-rec
145                    end    set l1-eof to true
146                           close i1-file
147                    not end move w1-ctr to l1-ctr
148                            move l1-rec(l1-ref:l1-len) to l1-key
149                 end-read
150             end-evaluate
151
152             exit program.
153
154    end program tinput.
155
156    end program cbreak1
```

Figure 15.10 Program cbreak1

The contained program tinput (line 96) implements the input handler that was outlined in Fig. 15.5. At line 134 the test for l1-sof (start of file) is a test for low-values in the key that is associated with the input stream. At line 140 l1-eof tests for high-values in the same key. The read statement at line 144 is executed for all key values except high-values. The method of construction for program tinput ensures that it will open and read its input at the start of the file, read from the opened file, and finally respond to the end of the file by closing it and returning to the calling program a key of high-values.

The l1-file record (line 119) is a reference parameter that links the input handler to the root program. The file-name (line 121) is supplied to the handler by the root together with the characteristics of the input key (lines 123 to 128). L1-ref and l1-len are the start position and the length for the key. We can see that tinput is capable of reading any variable-length record up to 255 characters in length. In addition the key can be up to 20 characters in length (line 126) and may appear anywhere in the record. This is possible because the reference modification variables are passed to the program and are used by it as part of its definition of the input characteristics.

The root program contains the main loop at lines 46 to 90. Within its evaluate statement the set of actions that must be undertaken include setting an indicator, refreshing the input, and calling the application as necessary. For example, at line 68 the current and previous keys are found to be unequal. Therefore an indicator is set at line 69 to notify the application code of the condition that exists in the input stream and the application is called (line 70) so that it can process this condition. Immediately afterwards it is called a second time to start up level 1 for the incoming batch and once this is done tinput is called to supply the next input record.

Program batch1 (Fig. 15.11) is the separately compiled program that is specific to the batch production problem. It contains the name of the input file (line 19) as well as the start position of the key (line 78) and its length (line 79). In addition, it contains a complete definition for the output file which is under its control.

The input file is passed to it as the parameter l1-file (line 51). This record contains all of the information that is pertinent to the input as well as l1-action (line 54) which contains the conditions for the seven rules. The procedure division is a single evaluate statement that uses the l1-action values to drive the actions associated with the report.

The empty-file and out-of-sequence rules are made available to the program so that it can provide a suitable output message before the root program closes down the run.

The other five rules conform to the processing model given previously in the tree in Fig. 15.7. These five rules are the core of the application and provide the necessary *stubs* for writing the application. Other control break applications would require a change to the statements in these five rules but would not require changes to the other programs.

```
 1 identification division.
 2 program-id. batch1.
 3*Purpose:
 4
 5 environment division.
 6
 7 input-output section.
 8 file-control.
 9     select o2-file assign to w2-filename.
10
11 data division.
12 file section.
13 fd  o2-file
14     value of id w2-filename.
15 01  o2-line                          pic x(132).
16
17 working-storage section.
18 01  w1-file.
19     03  w1-filename value "batch1.dat" pic x(10).
20
21 01  w2-file.
22     03  w2-filename value "batch1.rpt" pic x(10).
23     03  w2-spacer   value space        pic x.
24
25     03  w2-head-line.
26         05  filler   value "Position Batch Units Records"
27                                        pic x(28).
28     03  w2-workers.
29         05  w2-batch-units            pic 999.
30         05  w2-batch-ctr              pic 999.
31         05  w2-trail-units            pic 9(5).
32         05  w2-trail-ctr              pic 9(5).
33
34     03  w2-batch-line.
35         05  filler value space        pic x(5).
36         05  w2-batch-num              pic zz9.
37         05  filler value space        pic x(4).
38         05  w2-batch-id               pic xx.
39         05  filler value space        pic xxx.
40         05  w2-batch-units-ed         pic zz9.
41         05  filler value space        pic x(5).
42         05  w2-batch-ctr-ed           pic zz9.
43
44     03  w2-trail-line.
45         05  filler value "Totals:"    pic x(15).
46         05  w2-trail-units-ed         pic z(4)9.
47         05  filler value space        pic xxx.
48         05  w2-trail-ctr-ed           pic z(4)9.
49
```

```cobol
50 linkage section.
51 01  l1-file.
52       03  l1-ctr binary            pic 999.
53       03  l1-filename              pic x(20).
54       03  l1-action                pic xxx.
55           88  l1-start-level-2     value "sl2".
56           88  l1-finish-level-2    value "fl2".
57           88  l1-start-level-1     value "sl1".
58           88  l1-finish-level-1    value "fl1".
59           88  l1-process-level-0   value "l0 ".
60           88  l1-empty-file        value "emp".
61           88  l1-out-of-sequence   value "seq".
62       03  l1-keyarea.
63           05  l1-ref               pic 99.
64           05  l1-len               pic 99.
65           05  l1-key               pic x(20).
66       03  l1-dailyrec.
67           05  l1-batch-id          pic xx.
68           05  l1-batch-units       pic 999.
69           05  filler               pic x(250).
70/
71 procedure division using l1-file.
72 para1.
73     display l1-action " key " l1-key
74
75     evaluate true
76       when   l1-start-level-2
77         move w1-filename to l1-filename
78         move 1 to l1-ref
79         move 2 to l1-len
80         move zero to w2-trail-units
81                      w2-trail-ctr
82         open output o2-file
83         write o2-line from w2-head-line
84         write o2-line from w2-spacer
85
86       when   l1-finish-level-2
87         write o2-line from w2-spacer
88         move w2-trail-units to w2-trail-units-ed
89         move w2-trail-ctr   to w2-trail-ctr-ed
90         write o2-line from w2-trail-line
91         close o2-file
92
93       when   l1-empty-file
94         display "Empty input file"
95
96       when   l1-start-level-1
97         compute w2-batch-ctr = 1
98         compute w2-batch-units = l1-batch-units
99         move    l1-batch-id to w2-batch-id
100
101      when   l1-finish-level-1
102        move w2-batch-ctr to w2-batch-ctr-ed
103        move w2-batch-units to w2-batch-units-ed
104        write o2-line from w2-batch-line
105        compute w2-trail-ctr = w2-trail-ctr + w2-batch-ctr
106        compute w2-trail-units = w2-trail-units + w2-batch-units
107
108      when   l1-process-level-0
109        compute w2-batch-ctr = w2-batch-ctr + 1
110        compute w2-batch-units = w2-batch-units + l1-batch-units
```

```
111
112         when    l1-out-of-sequence
113            display "Input out of sequence - FATAL"
114
115         end-evaluate
116         exit program.
117
118 end program batch1.
119
```

Figure 15.11 Program batch1

15.3 WRITING PRINTED REPORTS

Until now we have used small text files which we have either displayed on the screen or written to files from where they could be accessed using other programs such as text editors. However, it is often the case that output files are large and a copy of the output must be stored on printed paper for future reference. In these cases it is usual to format pages of printed output and to number the pages.

The **linage** clause allows you to specify the size of the page you want to use as well as the number of blank lines that should appear at the **top** and **bottom** of each page. Suppose that your page is to be 66 lines long with two blank lines at the top and four blank lines at the bottom. The following fd for a print file can be used to create this logical description of a page:

```
fd   o1-report
     linage   60
     footing  60
     top      2
     bottom   4
     value of id ....
01   o1-rec ...
```

The above fd constrains the output to be in logical pages of 66 lines in which only 60 lines can contain lines of text written by the program. The **footing** tells the compiler that you want to be notified when this line is written so that the end-of-page condition can be acted upon once this line is written. (If all 66 lines were to be used then the top and bottom could be omitted and a linage and footing of 66 specified.)

The write statement takes this information into account when writing lines to the file:

$$\text{write record-name-1 [from identifier-1]}$$
$$\left[\text{after}\begin{Bmatrix}\text{integer-1}\\\text{identifier-2}\end{Bmatrix}\right]$$
$$\left[\begin{Bmatrix}\text{eop} \quad\quad \text{statement-1}\\\text{not eop statement-2}\end{Bmatrix}\\\text{end-write}\right]$$

The **after** option allows you to specify how many lines are to be advanced by the printer. The integer can be a numeric literal in the range of 0 to n. If identifier-2 is used it must be a numeric item in the range of 0 to n. Therefore the following write statements will skip one line and two lines respectively:

```
write o1-rec from w1-rec after 2
write o1-rec from w1-rec after 3
```

If the value used is 1 no lines are skipped and the record appears on the next available line. (In this case the after option can be omitted altogether because the default is 1 line.) If the value is zero then the previous line is overprinted. Negative values are not allowed.

The **eop** phrases allow you to respond to the end-of-page condition. The compiled program automatically manages the linage counter for the report and when this reaches a value greater than the number of lines allowed on the page then eop becomes true. The linage counter for a report begins with a value of 1. In the above example the linage counter will move through the range of 1 to 60 and not eop will be true for every write statement. When it reaches a value greater than 60 then eop will become true.

Thus a program could begin by writing a header line followed by a line of spaces with the following write statements:

```
write o1-rec from w1-header
move spaces to o1-rec
write o1-rec
```

This will output two lines to the report on the first page as physical lines 3 and 4. (Remember that top specified that two lines will be skipped.)

In producing the main body of the report the following write statement could be used:

```
write o1-rec from w1-rec
   eop
      write o1-rec from w1-header
        not eop
           moves spaces to o1-rec
           write o1-rec
      end-write
end-write
```

When the 60th is written to the report the eop condition will become true. This will cause the statements associated with the eop phrase to be executed, thereby putting a header and a blank line on the next page in preparation for writing more lines. Thus the complete statement will either write a single line of text to lines 1 to 59 or a single line of text to line 60 followed by two lines on the next page.

The linage counter is available to the program in a special item created by the compiler which is called the **linage-counter**. It can be referenced by statements in the procedure division. If more than one report is being produced by the same program then any reference to the linage-counter item must be qualified, for example, `linage-counter of o1-report`.

The main reason for using the linage-counter item is to move to a new page immediately. In this example moving a value greater than 60 to the linage-counter will cause the next record that is written to be on the first available line of the next page:

```
move 61 to linage-counter
write o1-rec from w1-header
move spaces to o1-rec
write o1-rec
```

Our example shows a footing that is only one line long. It could have been longer, for example, two lines long by specifying that the footing began at line 59. This would be used if a write statement such as the following appeared in the program:

```
write o1-rec from w1-rec after 2
```

This statement implies that the footing could be two lines long. Line 59 would be blank and the line of text would appear on line 60 after which the eop condition would immediately become true. If you did not want this line to appear at line 60 but on line 1 of the next page then you would have to throw the page yourself and then write the line after 1.

The footing could also be used to hold totals. At any time you could move the footing line value to the linage-counter. All the intervening lines would be automatically skipped by the next write statement which would write out the the footing.

Once you have written a file that contains a report you will want to print it. To print a report that uses the linage clause on the VAX type:

```
$ PRINT file-name/NOFEED
```

The exercises at the end of this chapter suggest ways in which you might like to practise writing simple reports.

15.4 EXERCISES

15.4.1 General

Before doing these exercises check to find out the number of lines on the printer paper you intend to use. Also check the width, which may be up to 132 characters.

1 Write a program report1 to take any text file and write it as a simple report. The report should have a top and bottom margin which is never used for printing and a specified number of lines that are filled with lines from the text file. (Do not bother with a header.)
2 Rewrite report1 as report2 in which the last printable line on each page is shown as the footing so that you can test the eop condition. Produce the report with a header for each page.
3 Rewrite report2 as report3 in which the footing for each page contains a count of the

number of lines of reported text on the page. All pages should contain the same number of lines except the last one. Make sure that you are still reporting all of the lines from the text file.

The following three exercises can be written as separate programs or as called programs from cbreak1. (Try to write two such versions for one of the programs and compare the two to decide which is the less complex application.)

4 Write program concord2 to use the output concordance file from Exercise 4 in Chapter 14 as its input. Concord2 should print a header and trailer line for the whole of the file as well as a line of spaces when there is a major break in the alphabetic sequence. (In other words, treat all lines with a first word beginning with the same letter as a batch.)
5 Rewrite concord2 as concord3 in which each alphabetic group begins on a new page with a header line.
6 Rewrite concord3 as concord4. Adjust the header so that it contains the letter of the alphabet that appears on that page as well as a page number. Include a footing to show how many concordance lines have been printed in the alphabetic group.

15.4.2 Case study

7 Compile link and run programs cbreak1 and batch1.
8 Write a detailed systems specification for cbreak1. It should at a minimum include information concerning the limitations of the program concerning key positions and lengths as well as information concerning the seven rules that it implements.
9 Rewrite cbreak1 as cbreak2 so that it checks that:
   (a) it is given a non-blank file name by the application program;
   (b) the key characteristics conform with its processing requirements.
   Cbreak2 should display an appropriate fatal error message and come to a normal termination if the information provided by the application is outside its processing limits.
10 Rewrite batch1 as batch2 in which the name of the input file and the key position and length are taken as input from the keyboard.
11 Rewrite either batch1 or batch2 as batch3 in which all of the output is directed to the terminal screen.
12 Use your text editor to create an input file with a larger number of batches with more records per batch. Write program batch4 to produce a simple batch report in which each batch is printed on a new page under a standard header.
13 Rewrite batch4 as batch5 in which each header shows the batch identifer and a page counter. Add a footing line to show the number of records in the batch.
14 Design a new input file with a new key and different totalling requirements. For example, you might design a record for a bookshop. Each record could contain information concerning the title, author, and purchase price with a batch identifier of month. Write batch6 to write a report of these purchases with monthly totals for the number of books and the total cost per month. The report should end with grand totals for the number of books purchased and the cost for the year.

16
MASTER FILE UPDATE

This chapter not only introduces a generalized control break algorithm for updating a master file but also explains the range of possible transaction types that are associated with the master file update problem. It is closely related to the algorithm presented in the previous chapter.

A sequential master file is a set of records in which each record holds historical information that represents some individual or object in the real world. The file is maintained in order according to the key field on each record. The key is a field that is of the same length, in the same position within each record, and is unique to each record in the master file.

The SIMPLE bank will be used to illustrate the problem. The master file for the SIMPLE bank holds a record for each customer account. The account number is a seven-character numeric field that is always in positions one through seven of a master record. Each master record contains a unique value in this field. In other words there is only one master record for each possible bank account number. The other fields in a record contain information that is relevant to that particular account.

Figure 16.1 shows a record layout for the SIMPLE master record of 43 characters. It also lists the contents of a master file of three records that are consistent with the record layout. (Fields such as name and address have been shortened and other possible fields have been omitted so that the records are just large enough to assist the illustration.)

We can see that the three records are in ascending order by account number. Although this file contains only three master records, it is conceivable that if all possible numeric keys were allocated there would be 10 million records in the file in the range of 0 000 000 to 9 999 999 inclusive.

The purpose of a master file is to hold the relevant details for each and every object

Master record layout for accounts

```
01  mas-rec.
    03  mas-account              pic 9(7).
    03  customer-details.
        05  customer-name        pic x(10).
        05  customer-address     pic x(15).
    03  start-date               pic 9(6).
    03  balance                  pic 999v99.
```

Master file containing three records

```
         1         2         3         4
12345678901234567890123456789012345678901234

0000007John Doe   10 Oak St.     89010500000
0000010Alice Jay  5 Elm Lane     72020200000
0000231Ray Allen  12 Birch Ave.  80120100000
```

Figure 16.1 SIMPLE bank – master

that is being represented. What is relevant will of course depend on the particular application except for the general rules that:

- each record must identify the same key position and length,
- each record must have a unique key value,
- each master file must be maintained in either ascending or descending key order.

So far we have seen that the SIMPLE master could hold from 3 to 10 000 000 master records. By extension we can easily imagine that it might hold one or two master records at some stage. Could it hold no masters? In practice, we will find that the creation of the first master record in a new master file is essentially similar to the creation of subsequent master records. Let us look more closely at the ways in which possible keys might be allocated over time.

Imagine that customer B. Ben tried to open a new account with the number 10 against the above master file. Clearly this would be an error because this account number is at present allocated to Alice Jay. However, if we removed Alice's account from the file then account 10 could afterwards be allocated to a different person such as Mr Ben. Similarly, it would be an error to pay a sum of money into account 152 because this master key is not at present allocated to a customer as an account number. Therefore account 152 should not be credited or used in any way that would assume that it is allocated.

In general, we can see that there are always 10 000 000 possible accounts in the SIMPLE bank and at any time any number of them may be allocated or unallocated. Furthermore, any program that manages a master file must be able to distinguish clearly between:

- the allocation of unallocated masters,
- the de-allocation of allocated masters,
- the updating of allocated masters.

16.1 EXTERNAL TRANSACTIONS

Sequential transaction files are used as the main external source of new information for sequential master files. At a minimum they must provide the data needed to add new masters (allocate), change existing masters, and delete existing masters (de-allocate). The transactions to effect these alterations are usually termed add, change and delete transactions.

The transactions must be in the same key order as the master so that a program can write an updated version of the master as output while it is reading the old master and transaction files as input.

Figure 16.2 shows a record layout for some SIMPLE transactions and lists the contents of both a correctly ordered and a misordered transaction file. The key appears in

Record layout for three transaction types
```
01  trn-rec.
    03  trn-fixed.
        05  trn-type                    pic xx.
            88  add-account             value "AA".
            88  change-address          value "CA".
            88  delete-account          value "DD"
        05  trn-account                 pic 9(7).
    03  trn-aa.
        05  aa-customer-details.
            07  aa-customer-name        pic x(10).
            07  aa-customer-address     pic x(15).
        05  aa-start-date               pic 9(6).
    03  trn-ca redefines trn-aa.
        05  customer-address            pic x(15).
        05  filler                      pic x(16).
```

Ordered transaction file

```
         1         2         3         4
12345678901234567890123456789012345678901234

AA0000003Mary Jane 2 High St.    900102
CA000000101 5a Cool Sq.
AA0000017King Kong 5 Banana Row  891005
DD0000231
```

Misordered transaction file

```
         1         2         3         4
12345678901234567890123456789012345678901234

CA000000101 5a Cool Sq.
AA0000017King Kong 5 Banana Row  891005
AA0000003Mary Jane 2 High St.    900102
DD0000231
```

Figure 16.2 SIMPLE bank – record layout and transactions

Transaction + Old-master = New-master			Action
3		3	Master allocated
	7	7	No change
10	10	10	Master changed
17		17	Master allocated
231	231		Master de-allocated

Figure 16.3 Effect of processing a set of transactions on a master

positions 3 through 9 of each record. For the present we will assume that the data within each record is correct.

The record layout for the SIMPLE transaction file defines three transaction types. The first field in each transaction record contains two characters that identify the transaction type uniquely for this SIMPLE application. The next field contains the account number that uniquely identifies the master record which is the target for the transaction. These two fields are a fixed length of characters that must always exist for all transactions in the SIMPLE file.

The add-account transaction type contains three further fields for a total record length of 33 characters. The change-address type contains a single 15-character field for a total record length of 22 characters. The delete-account type contains only the fixed portion of 9 characters. Thus the transaction types are of variable length.

In the correctly ordered file we can see that it is possible to list the keys from the master file and the transaction file in their original order and from this to derive the correct key order for the new master in a single pass from the lowest to the highest keys (Fig. 16.3). Thus the four transaction records and three master records from the input files could cause the creation of an updated master file containing four records.

This cannot be done with the misordered file. Master 17 will already have been processed and written to output by the time that the request to allocate master 3 arrives on input. If master 3 were allocated and written to output at this point then the new master file would become misordered as a result. Therefore the correct action is to reject this transaction. (In practice, it is common to consider any key misorder to be fatal to the running of a master file update and therefore to stop the run with an appropriate error message. We will assume for the present that the input files are correctly ordered.)

Consider the transaction file in Fig. 16.4. We can see that the file is in order by account.

```
         1         2         3         4
1234567890123456789012345678901234

AA0000003Mary Jane 2 High St.    900102
CA000001015a Cool Sq.
CA00000172 Papaya Lane
AA0000017King Kong 5 Banana Row  891005
DD0000231
```

Figure 16.4 SIMPLE bank – transactions

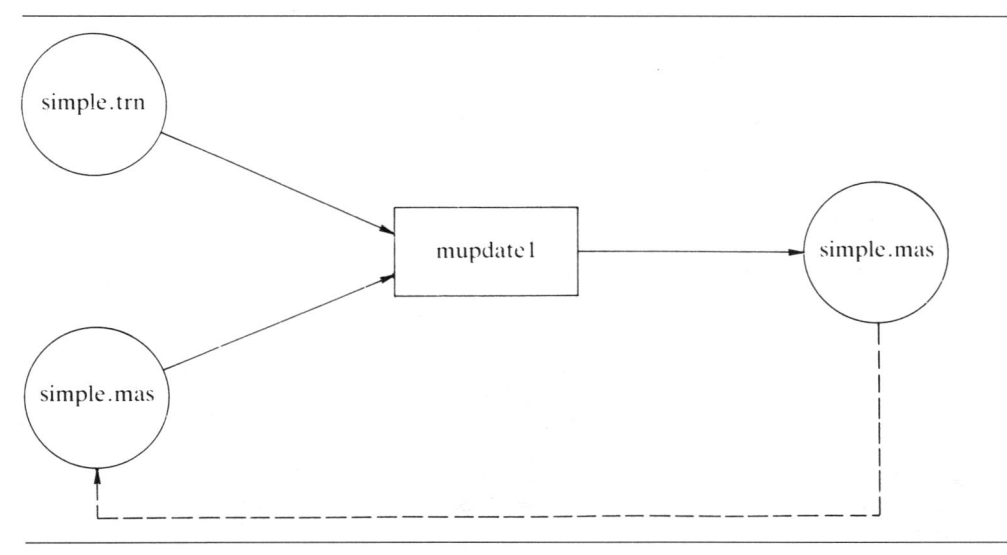

Figure 16.5 Run chart for the SIMPLE update

However, the change-address for account 17 appears in the file before the add-account. This is an error in the transaction input because it is not possible to change the address for an account prior to the account's allocation. However, it is not a fatal error because the application-specific aspects of the final program can reject the faulty change transaction and still produce an updated master file with its master accounts in the correct order.

Therefore the ordering of transactions is an issue that is specific to the application whereas the ordering of the master key is an issue that is of general importance to the success of all master file updates.

For the SIMPLE bank transaction file the correct file order should be ascending by account and within account ascending by transaction type. This will guarantee that an "AA" transaction is applied before a "CA" transaction for any particular account when the two transactions are in the same file.

Figure 16.5 shows the run chart for the SIMPLE master file update. We can see that a run requires both master and transaction input files and produces a master file. The dotted line shows that the output master from one run is the input master to the next run. (The first run is a special case in which only a transaction file is available on input.)

Figure 16.6 lists the required file contents for the first two test runs of the SIMPLE update. We can see that the first run uses the first transaction file and places three masters in the first master file.

This first master file is then input to the second run together with the second transaction file in order to produce the second master file. All of the records are correctly formed and all of the files are correctly ordered by master key.

The second transaction file contains three transactions that contain application errors. (The error for account 17 would not have occurred if the file had been fully ordered by transaction type within account number.)

Run 1	Comments
(simple.trn;1) AA0000007John Doe 10 Oak St. 890105 AA0000010Alice Jay 5 Elm Lane 720202 AA0000231Ray Allen 12 Birch Ave. 801201 (eof)	
(simple.mas;1) 0000007John Doe 10 Oak St. 89010500000 0000010Alice Jay 5 Elm Lane 72020200000 0000231Ray Allen 12 Birch Ave. 80120100000 (eof)	

Run 2	Comments
(simple.trn;2) AA0000003Mary Jane 2 High St. 900102 AA0000007John Doe 10 Oak St. 890105 CA000001015a Cool Sq. AA0000015S. Laurel 1 Hardy Place 870504 CA00000172 Papaya Lane AA0000017King Kong 5 Banana Row 891005 DD0000159 DD0000231 (eof)	application error-allocated application error-unallocated application error-unallocated
(simple.mas;2) 0000003Mary Jane 2 High St. 90010200000 0000007John Doe 10 Oak St. 89010500000 0000010Alice Jay 15a Cool Sq. 72020200000 0000015S. Laurel 1 Hardy Place 87050400000 0000017King Kong 5 Banana Row 89100500000 (eof)	

Figure 16.6 SIMPLE bank – files for the first two runs

16.2 ALGORITHM DESIGN

The basic requirement for the master file update algorithm is that the two input files must be presented to the application for processing in key order. It achieves the update by merging the two input keys into key order. When the master and transaction keys are unequal it always selects the lower of the two keys as its current key. When the master and transaction keys are equal it favours the master so that any master processing that must be done prior to transaction processing can be done.

The streams of key values from the two input files are merged in succession into the current key, appropriate processing is identified by comparing current and previous key values, and after processing the current key is moved to the previous key before selecting a new current key from one of the two input streams.

The input streams of keys are bounded by using low-value and high-value as in the single file control break algorithm presented in Chapter 15.

| | Keys | | | | |
Transaction	Master	Current	Previous	Key results	Actions
<lv>	<lv>	<lv>	<lv>	break on files	start-level-2
3	7	3	<lv>	break on transaction	start-level-1
7	7	7	3	break on master	finish-level-1; start-level-1
7	10	7	7	no break	level-0
10	10	10	7	break on master	finish-level-1; start-level-1
10	231	10	10	no break	level-0
15	231	15	10	break on transaction	finish-level-1; start-level-1
17	231	17	15	break on transaction	finish-level-1; start-level-1
17	231	17	17	no break	level-0
159	231	159	17	break on transaction	finish-level-1; start-level-1
231	231	231	159	break on master	finish-level-1; start-level-1
231	<hv>	231	231	no break	level-0
<hv>	<hv>	<hv>	231	break on master	finish-level-1
<hv>	<hv>	<hv>	<hv>	break on files	finish-level-2

Figure 16.7 Keys and actions – master file update

Figure 16.7 lists the successive key values from run 2 of the SIMPLE bank. The first two columns give the values of the input transaction and master streams.

The 'current' column shows the key value which is selected for processing and the 'previous' column shows the key value which was previously processed. The 'result' and 'action' columns are determined by the algorithm by comparing the current and previous keys as was done with the control break algorithm.

```
move low-value to current-key previous-key

perform test before until both_keys_are_high

    evaluate true
        when     both_keys_low                       do start-level-2
        when     both_keys_high                      do finish-level-2
        when     current_high and previous_low       do empty-file
        when     previous_low                        do start-level-1
        when     current_high                        do finish-level-1
        when     current > previous                  do finish-level-1, start-level-1
        when     current = previous                  do level-0
        when     current < previous                  do out-of-sequence
    end-evaluate

    move current-key to previous-key

    evaluate transaction-key < master-key
        when    true
          move transaction-key to current-key
        when    false
          move master-key to current-key
    end-evaluate

end-perform
stop run.
```

Figure 16.8 Outline for the root program (program mupdate1)

```
Level-2                        Program
(file break)                  /   |   \
              start-level-2  /    |    \  finish-level-2
                                  |
Level-1                        Master*
(key break)                   /   |   \
              start-level-1  /    |    \  finish-level-1
                                  |
Level-0                        Update*
(no key break)
```

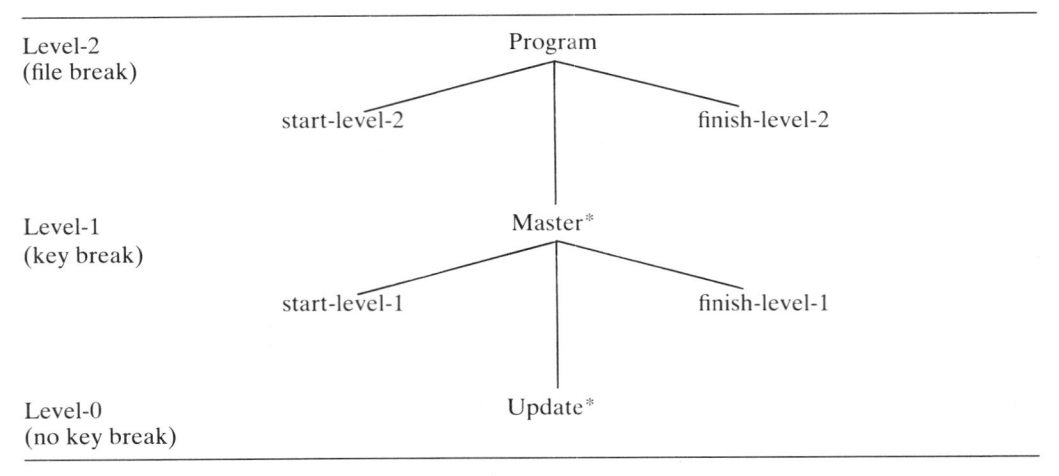

Figure 16.9 Tree identifying levels – master file update

16.3 INTERNAL TRANSACTIONS

Not all outputs from a master file update result from the processing of external transactions. At times the update must generate an output as a result of a particular set of circumstances that is found to exist on the master record. These sets of circumstances identify what is termed an internal transaction or internal *hit*.

The most common example in banking is the generation of a statement of account. Even when no deposits or withdrawals are made against an account a bank will usually send a statement from time to time. This can be generated by comparing a date on the master record to the run date. If the time for the statement has arrived then it can be produced.

A SIMPLE master record contains a start date. Let us suppose that all start days within the start date are in the range of 1 to 28, that is, that the SIMPLE bank never starts an account for the 29th, 30th, or 31st day of any month. Let us further suppose that the distribution of start dates to customers is random. Let us now suppose that the master file update program is run on most working days and that a run before a holiday always uses a run date that is just before the next working day. (Thus a run on Friday would use the date for Sunday except for long weekends when it would use the date for Monday.) This will give on average about 20 runs per month. The master file update could compare the run day against the start day for each account. If the start day and run day are equal then the monthly statement of account should be produced. If the start day is less than the run day then the account should also be produced because the system was not run on that start day.

There are many ways to use dates to force internal transactions but all methods try to balance the load across the master file so that an even number of internal hits occur in each run. The best method for balancing this load cannot be determined separately from a decision concerning which days in the year will normally be run days for the system.

It is possible for internal transactions to be processed both before and after external transactions. (The requirement for pre-internal transactions means that the master must be in memory and processed for these transactions prior to the processing of any external transactions.) A simple example of these concepts is that of the credit card company that calculates interest prior to crediting a payment. Let us imagine that you have sent away your monthly payment and it arrives as an external transaction on the very night you are to be billed. Firstly, your master comes into memory and the new balance is calculated. Secondly, the payment transaction is read in and the amount paid is put on the record. Thirdly, the monthly statement is produced at which time the balance is reduced by the amount paid which is then set to zero. The first and third transactions have been internally generated by comparing a date on your record against the run date. The second transaction is caused by you and is therefore optional on this particular day but when it occurs it must be sandwiched between the other two.

It might seem that the calculation of the balance and the production of the statement should both be done together. In this simple example it could be done this way but in more realistic cases the separation can be essential. Imagine an account that is calculated on a monthly basis but billed quarterly. In this case different information controls the two transactions.

A classic example from the life insurance industry of a pre-internal transaction is the maturation of an insurance policy. On the day it matures the system should pay out the face value and then refuse any further incoming premiums. Clearly, the pay-out must occur before the external transactions are processed on the maturation date.

Other common forms of internal transactions are annual statements of insurance, telephone and electricity bills, and medical reminders for check-ups. The SIMPLE bank does not include internal transactions so that the main illustration is not diverted by this secondary issue. Nevertheless the processing of internal transactions is important and a few exercises have been included at the end of the chapter should you wish to examine this topic further.

16.4 PROGRAM DESIGN

Program mupdate1 in Fig. 16.11 implements a solution to the master file update problem presented in this chapter. As with the control break program from the previous chapter it treats the names of files, the length of the key, and the position of the key within either the transaction or master record as data that is supplied for the run.

Figure 16.10 is a structure chart that outlines mupdate1 and its contained programs and shows its relationship to the application simple1. Mupdate1 has three contained programs for handling the input and output files. Ihandle4 and ohandle4 handle the master input and output files respectively. The input master is passed into the root program as parameter w1-inpmast and ihandle3 passes in the input transaction in w2-inptran. The root program uses the keys for comparison and constructs correct work masters in w3-wrkmast. (These may be either empty work masters when keys appear from the transaction file for which there is no matching master or copies of existing masters from the input master file.)

Every time the root identifies a control break it passes the input transaction and the work master to the application for processing. The transaction is shown as a content parameter because there is no reason for the application to change the transaction input

General solution

```
                                    R
                                 mupdate1

        r = w1-inpmast    r = w2-inptran    c = w3-wrkmast

    2                 2                              2
  ihandle4         ihandle3                      chandle4
```

Application

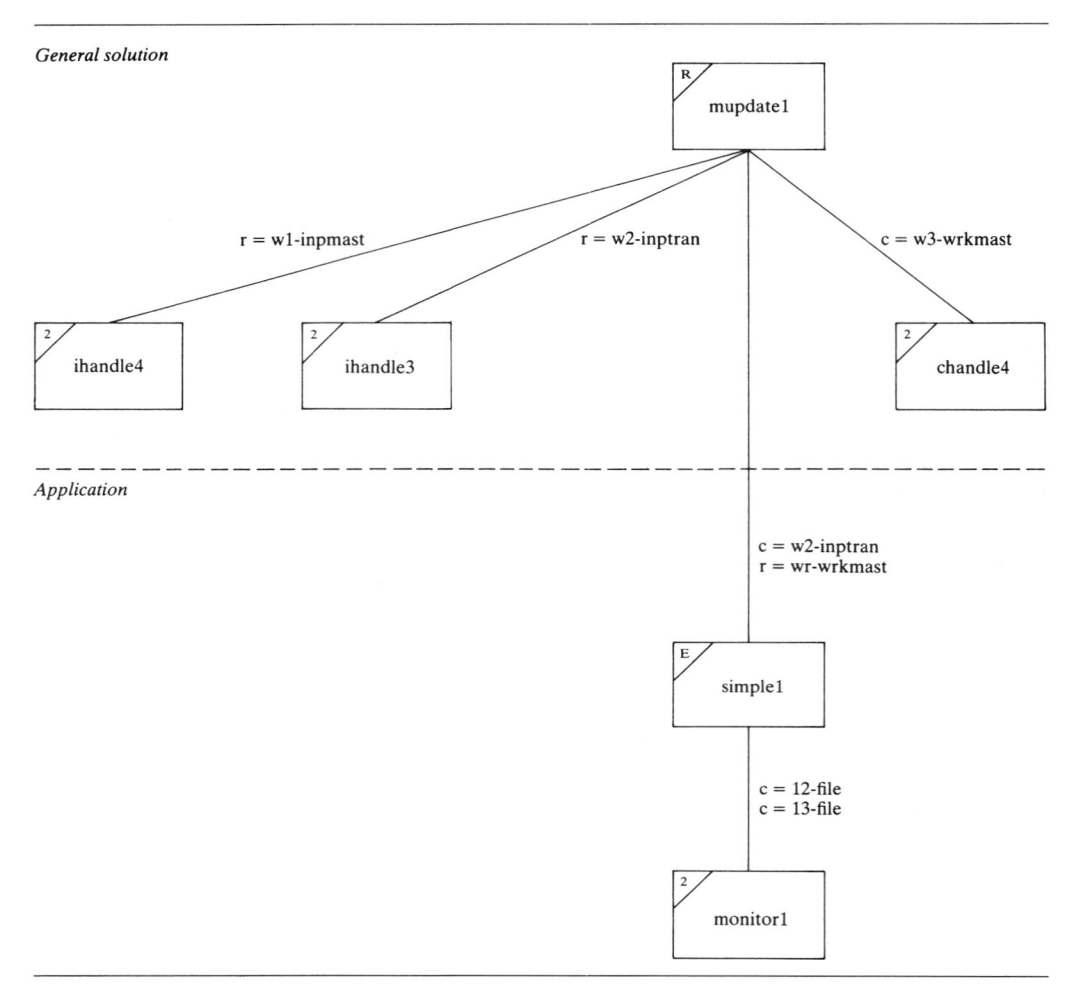

```
                                    c = w2-inptran
                                    r = wr-wrkmast

                                      E
                                   simple1

                                    c = l2-file
                                    c = l3-file

                                      2
                                   monitor1
```

Figure 16.10 Structure chart for mupdate1

stream. However, the work master is a reference parameter so that the application can alter the master as appropriate to the application and then pass the result back to the root for further processing. Once all processing for a master is complete the root calls the output handler and passes it the work master as a content parameter. (The output handler will not write out empty master records.)

The work master is the most important record for understanding the general solution to the problem. It appears at lines 31 to 50 in the root. $W3-ctr$ is the length of the master record in characters. When it is zero this means that there is no data in the master. The root sets the length to zero when it allocates a key for the first time for an external transaction. (The application must give the record a length if it is ever to be written to output. Thus a successful add transaction will give the master a length as dictated by the application and a successful delete will set the length to zero.)

The record length is followed by the names of the input and output masters as supplied by the application. The action then gives one of the seven possibilities to which the application must respond. Empty files and out of sequence input are errors that will stop the master file update. The other five actions are part of normal processing. The next item is the key. It consists of the reference and length items for use in reference modification followed by the actual value of the master key. The final item is the master record itself. Its internal definition is known by the application.

The root program is a single loop (lines 66 to 170) which checks the current and previous keys to determine which action is appropriate. Once an action is completed the current key is moved to the previous key (line 162). Then the lower of the two input keys is moved into the current key or the master key if the two input keys are equal. Thus the root merges the keys from the two input files and by checking the current against previous determines which breaks are appropriate. It is only concerned with keys and with making actions and records available to the application. For this reason it is general in its construction.

Program simple1 (Fig. 16.12) is a separately compiled program which holds the SIMPLE application. It knows of two parameters called l2-file and l3-file which are the transaction and the work master respectively. The main difference between these records and their definition in the root is that here they include the record details (lines 16 and 51) that are appropriate to the application. The procedure division of the program consists of a single evaluate statement that controls seven sets of statements to implement the seven application actions as a result of key breaks. (The call statement to program monitor (line 62) merely displays key information on the screen so that you can follow the progress of the update. Monitor1 is for demonstration purposes only and would not normally form part of a program run.)

The actions at the start of level 2 (lines 68 to 83) allow the application to give the names of the three files as well as the position and length of the transaction key and the master key. If the name of an input master is not supplied the root assumes that this is the first run and does not open an input master. The end of level 2 is empty in this program. This would be an appropriate point to include run totals and a final message to indicate a normal termination.

At line 88 the empty files action is shown. If this ever occurs the application will not be called again. Therefore this point could, for example, put an appropriate message to printed reports and then close the print files. The out of sequence action is similar at line 131 and could contain a message output to tell the user what has happened.

Line 91 shows a selection for start of level 1 and empty. In this case the key break must have arisen from the transaction file. Therefore there is a valid transaction but no master. The SIMPLE program expects that in this case the transaction should be an add. If it is it initializes the master and gives it a record length that is greater than zero.

The action at line 104 is for the start of level 1 when it is not empty. It is here that existing masters can be processed for pre-internal transactions. Line 107 gives a point for processing post-internal transactions.

Line 110 enables processing where there is no control break. It contains a nested evaluate that checks for all of the possible transactions. At line 112 the add transaction for an empty master is included. The reason for this is that an input stream might have two add transactions that come from different user sources. In this case the first one which caused the control break may have failed due to errors in the detail of the transaction. As a consequence the second add will not generate a control break even though the master is empty. However, if the master was successfully added by a previous add then the rule at line 119 will be used. Therefore in cases where there are multiple adds in the transaction input stream the first successful add will establish the master and all following adds will fail.

The other transactions follow at line 122. The only transaction of note is the delete which sets the record length to zero so that the output handler will not write a master record to the output file. In summary, we can see that for an unallocated master the following set of transactions in one run can be processed provided the application leaves adds that it rejects as empty masters and provided that it deletes records by setting the master to empty:

> Add   fail (validation error)
> Add   success
> Change success
> Change fail (validation error)
> Delete success
> Delete fail (master is now empty)

(In fact the add, change and delete transaction can be presented in any order any number of times in the one run.) It is the case that occurrences such as the one outlined above are unusual. Nevertheless a general solution should not be arbitrary in the restrictions that it places upon users. It is not for the master file update to determine that a sequence of external events such as this should not happen. In general a good program should allow the user or user application as much freedom as is consistent with a correct and efficient solution.

Let us end by imagining a case where the above set of transactions could occur. It is the end of the financial year in a life insurance company and it has been discovered that due to a past clerical error a payment from an annuity was too low during its final year which ended over 24 months ago. The master record is now deleted from the master file and the annuitant has written to claim the extra money due.

Because of other system constraints pertaining to accounting and auditing, money should always be paid against a master record. Therefore the solution is to add the master back in, generate the missing payments amount with a particular change transaction for this purpose, and then delete the master.

Clerk A has already completed these transactions successfully and sent them to be processed. As it happens the annuitant calls in the afternoon and demands payment. Clerk B, who is new to the department, handles the call on the telephone and discovers that the policy is deleted. He suggests that the annuitant wait until next year for the money and is told in no uncertain terms that the cheque is to be sent that evening. He therefore gets out a manual and proceeds to write a set of transactions that he thinks will solve the problem and then sends them for processing. Just as he finishes Clerk A returns from lunch and finds that the greenhorn has not followed procedures by checking first to see that the file was out to Clerk A and sitting on her desk. It is now too late to stop the transactions because they have left the department. However, Clerk A checks and realizes that the only transaction that B has coded correctly is the delete. Therefore A's good work will be unaffected because it does not matter which of their transactions deletes the master. Even if all of the transactions had been correct the worst that would have occurred is a double payment.

This scenario assumes that transactions are batched and sent for processing to a location that is remote from where clerical work takes place. Increasingly, master files are becoming available for direct update via terminals. In systems such as these the same sequence of events might occur for two clerks working at separate terminals. Although the programming approach for the update of direct files is different the behaviour seen by the clerks against the master file will be quite similar. Therefore there is even more reason to allow a similar flexibility in the programming of sequential master file updates as is supplied by direct systems.

```
 1 identification division.
 2 program-id. mupdate1.
 3*Purpose:
 4
 5 environment division.
 6
 7 data division.
 8 working-storage section.
 9 01  w1-inpmast.
10     03   w1-ctr binary            pic 999.
11     03   w1-filename              pic x(20).
12     03   w1-key.
13          05   w1-ref              pic 99.
14          05   w1-len              pic 99.
15          05   w1-mastkey          pic x(20).
16               88   w1-eof         value high-value.
17               88   w1-sof         value low-value.
18     03   w1-rec                   pic x(255).
19
20 01  w2-inptran.
21     03   w2-ctr binary            pic 999.
22     03   w2-filename              pic x(20).
23     03   w2-key.
24          05   w2-ref              pic 99.
25          05   w2-len              pic 99.
26          05   w2-trankey          pic x(20).
27               88   w2-eof         value high-value.
28               88   w2-sof         value low-value.
29     03   w2-rec                   pic x(255).
30
31 01  w3-wrkmast.
32     03   w3-ctr binary            pic 999.
33          88   w3-empty            value zero.
34     03   w3-imastname             pic x(20).
35     03   w3-omastname             pic x(20).
36     03   w3-action                pic xxx.
37          88   w3-start-level-2    value "sl2".
38          88   w3-finish-level-2   value "fl2".
39          88   w3-empty-file       value "emp".
40          88   w3-start-level-1    value "sl1".
41          88   w3-finish-level-1   value "fl1".
42          88   w3-process-level-0  value "l0 ".
43          88   w3-out-of-sequence  value "seq".
44     03   w3-key.
45          05   w3-ref              pic 99.
46          05   w3-len              pic 99.
47          05   w3-mastkey          pic x(20).
48               88   w3-sof         value low-value.
49               88   w3-eof         value high-value.
50     03   w3-rec                   pic x(255).
51
```

```
52 01  w4-controlarea.
53     03  w4-bothkeys value low-value pic x(40).
54         88  w4-start-level-2         value low-value.
55         88  w4-finish-level-2        value high-value.
56     03  filler redefines w4-bothkeys.
57         05  w4-current               pic x(20).
58             88  w4-finish-last-key   value high-value.
59         05  w4-previous              pic x(20).
60             88  w4-start-first-key   value low-value.
61/
62 procedure division.
63 para1.
64     display "mupdate1 begins"
65
66     perform test before until w4-finish-level-2
67        evaluate true
68          when    w4-start-level-2
69             set  w3-start-level-2 to true
70             set  w3-empty to true
71             set  w3-sof to true
72             set  w2-sof to true
73             set  w1-sof to true
74             call "simple1" using reference w2-inptran
75                                  reference w3-wrkmast
76             move w3-ref to w1-ref
77             move w3-len to w1-len
78             evaluate w3-imastname = spaces
79               when    true
80                  set w1-eof to true
81               when    false
82                  move w3-imastname to w1-filename
83             end-evaluate
84             call "ihandle4" using reference w1-inpmast
85             call "ihandle3" using reference w2-inptran
86             call "ohandle4" using content   w3-wrkmast
87
88          when    w4-start-first-key and w4-finish-last-key
89             set  w3-empty-file to true
90             call "simple1" using content   w2-inptran
91                                  content   w3-wrkmast
92
93          when    w4-start-first-key
94             set  w3-start-level-1 to true
95             evaluate w1-mastkey = w4-current
96               when    true
97                  move w1-ctr to w3-ctr
98                  move w1-mastkey to w3-mastkey
99                  move w1-rec to w3-rec
100                 call "simple1"  using content   w2-inptran
101                                       reference w3-wrkmast
102                 call "ihandle4" using reference w1-inpmast
103              when    false
104                 set  w3-empty to true
105                 move w2-trankey to w3-mastkey
106                 call "simple1"  using content   w2-inptran
107                                       reference w3-wrkmast
108                 call "ihandle3" using reference w2-inptran
109             end-evaluate
110
```

```
111        when    w4-finish-last-key
112          set   w3-finish-level-1 to true
113          call "simple1"   using content    w2-inptran
114                                 reference w3-wrkmast
115          call "ohandle4" using content    w3-wrkmast
116
117          set   w3-finish-level-2 to true
118          set   w3-empty to true
119          set   w3-eof to true
120          call "simple1"   using content    w2-inptran
121                                 content   w3-wrkmast
122          call "ohandle4" using content    w3-wrkmast
123
124        when    w4-current > w4-previous
125          set   w3-finish-level-1 to true
126          call "simple1"   using content    w2-inptran
127                                 reference w3-wrkmast
128          call "ohandle4" using content    w3-wrkmast
129
130          set   w3-start-level-1 to true
131          evaluate w1-mastkey = w4-current
132            when    true
133              move w1-ctr to w3-ctr
134              move w1-mastkey to w3-mastkey
135              move w1-rec to w3-rec
136              call "simple1 " using content    w2-inptran
137                                   reference w3-wrkmast
138              call "ihandle4" using reference w1-inpmast
139            when    false
140              set  w3-empty to true
141              move w2-trankey to w3-mastkey
142              call "simple1" using content    w2-inptran
143                                  reference w3-wrkmast
144              call "ihandle3" using reference w2-inptran
145          end-evaluate
146
147        when    w4-current = w4-previous
148          set   w3-process-level-0 to true
149          call "simple1" using content    w2-inptran
150                               reference w3-wrkmast
151          call "ihandle3" using reference w2-inptran
152
153        when    w4-current < w4-previous
154          set   w3-out-of-sequence to true
155          call "simple1" using content    w2-inptran
156                               content   w3-wrkmast
157          set   w4-finish-last-key to true
158          set   w1-eof to true
159          set   w2-eof to true
160      end-evaluate
161
162      move w4-current to w4-previous
163*     Get the lowest input key as the current but favour the master
164      evaluate w2-trankey < w1-mastkey
165        when    true
166          move w2-trankey to w4-current
167        when    false
168          move w1-mastkey to w4-current
169      end-evaluate
170    end-perform
171
```

```
172       display "mupdate1 ends"
173       stop run.
174/
175 identification division.
176 program-id. ihandle4.
177
178 environment division.
179 input-output section.
180 file-control.
181     select i1-file   assign w1-filename.
182
183 data division.
184 file section.
185 fd  i1-file
186     record varying 1 to 255
187     depending      w1-ctr
188     value of id    w1-filename.
189 01  filler                        pic x(255).
190
191 working-storage section.
192 01  w1-inpfile.
193     03  w1-ctr binary             pic 999.
194     03  w1-filename               pic x(20).
195
196 linkage section.
197 01  l1-file.
198     03  l1-ctr binary             pic 999.
199     03  l1-filename               pic x(20).
200     03  l1-keyarea.
201         05  l1-ref                pic 99.
202         05  l1-len                pic 99.
203         05  l1-key                pic x(20).
204             88  l1-sof            value low-value.
205             88  l1-eof            value high-value.
206     03  l1-rec                    pic x(255).
207/
208 procedure division using l1-file.
209 para1.
210     evaluate true
211       when    l1-sof
212         move l1-filename to w1-filename
213         open input i1-file
214     end-evaluate
215
216     evaluate true
217       when    l1-eof
218         continue
219
220       when    other
221         read i1-file into l1-rec
222            end      set l1-eof to true
223                     close i1-file
224            not end move w1-ctr to l1-ctr
225                    move l1-rec(l1-ref:l1-len) to l1-key
226         end-read
227     end-evaluate
228
229     exit program.
230 end program ihandle4.
231/
```

```
232 identification division.
233 program-id. ihandle3.
234
235 environment division.
236 input-output section.
237 file-control.
238     select i2-file   assign w2-filename.
239
240 data division.
241 file section.
242 fd  i2-file
243     record varying 1 to 255
244     depending       w2-ctr
245     value of id     w2-filename.
246 01  filler                          pic x(255).
247
248 working-storage section.
249 01  w2-file.
250     03  w2-ctr binary               pic 999.
251     03  w2-filename                 pic x(20).
252
253 linkage section.
254 01  l2-file.
255     03  l2-ctr binary               pic 999.
256     03  l2-filename                 pic x(20).
257     03  l2-keyarea.
258         05  l2-ref                  pic 99.
259         05  l2-len                  pic 99.
260         05  l2-key                  pic x(20).
261             88  l2-sof              value low-value.
262             88  l2-eof              value high-value.
263     03  l2-rec                      pic x(255).
264
265 procedure division using l2-file.
266 para1.
267     evaluate true
268       when    l2-sof
269         move l2-filename to w2-filename
270         open input i2-file
271     end-evaluate
272
273     evaluate true
274       when    l2-eof
275         continue
276
277       when    other
278         read i2-file into l2-rec
279           end     set l2-eof to true
280                   close i2-file
281           not end move w2-ctr to l2-ctr
282                   move l2-rec(l2-ref:l2-len) to l2-key
283         end-read
284     end-evaluate
285
286     exit program.
287 end program ihandle3.
288/
```

```
289 identification division.
290 program-id. ohandle4.
291
292 environment division.
293 input-output section.
294 file-control.
295     select o3-file   assign w3-filename.
296
297 data division.
298 file section.
299 fd  o3-file
300     record varying 1 to 255
301     depending      w3-ctr
302     value of id    w3-filename.
303 01  o3-rec                       pic x(255).
304
305 working-storage section.
306 01  w3-file.
307     03  w3-ctr binary            pic 999.
308     03  w3-filename              pic x(20).
309
310 linkage section.
311 01  l3-file.
312     03  l3-ctr binary            pic 999.
313         88  l3-empty             value zero.
314     03  filler                   pic x(20).
315     03  l3-omastname             pic x(20).
316     03  filler                   pic xxx.
317     03  l3-key.
318         05  filler               pic x(4).
319         05  l3-mastkey           pic x(20).
320             88  l3-sof           value low-value.
321             88  l3-eof           value high-value.
322     03  l3-rec                   pic x(255).
323
324 procedure division using l3-file.
325 para1.
326     evaluate true
327       when    l3-sof
328         move l3-omastname to w3-filename
329         open output o3-file
330
331       when    l3-eof
332         close o3-file
333
334       when    l3-empty
335         continue
336
337       when    other
338         move l3-ctr to w3-ctr
339         write o3-rec from l3-rec
340     end-evaluate
341
342     exit program.
343 end program ohandle4.
344 end program mupdate1
```

Figure 16.11 Program mupdate1

```
 1 identification division.
 2 program-id. simple1.
 3*Purpose:
 4
 5 environment division.
 6
 7 data division.
 8 linkage section.
 9 01  l2-file.
10     03  l2-ctr binary              pic 999.
11     03  l2-filename                pic x(20).
12     03  l2-keyarea.
13         05  l2-ref                 pic 99.
14         05  l2-len                 pic 99.
15         05  l2-trankey             pic x(20).
16     03  l2-trnrec.
17         05  l2-fixed.
18             07  l2-type            pic xx.
19                 88  l2-add-acct    value "AA".
20                 88  l2-chg-addr    value "CA".
21                 88  l2-del-acct    value "DD".
22             07  l2-account         pic x(7).
23         05  l2-aa.
24             07  l2-aa-cust-details.
25                 09  l2-aa-cust-name pic x(10).
26                 09  l2-aa-cust-addr pic x(15).
27             07  l2-start-date      pic 9(6).
28             07  filler             pic x(215).
29         05  l2-ca redefines l2-aa.
30             07  l2-ca-cust-addr    pic x(15).
31             07  filler             pic x(231).
32
33 01  l3-file.
34     03  l3-ctr binary              pic 999.
35         88  l3-empty               value zero.
36         88  l3-mast-exists         value 43.
37     03  l3-imastname               pic x(20).
38     03  l3-omastname               pic x(20).
39     03  l3-action                  pic xxx.
40         88  l3-start-level-2       value "sl2".
41         88  l3-finish-level-2      value "fl2".
42         88  l3-empty-file          value "emp".
43         88  l3-start-level-1       value "sl1".
44         88  l3-finish-level-1      value "fl1".
45         88  l3-process-level-0     value "l0 ".
46         88  l3-out-of-sequence     value "seq".
47     03  l3-keyarea.
48         05  l3-ref                 pic 99.
49         05  l3-len                 pic 99.
50         05  l3-mastkey             pic x(20).
```

```
51         03  l3-masrec.
52             05  l3-account           pic 9(7).
53             05  l3-cust-details.
54                 07  l3-cust-name     pic x(10).
55                 07  l3-cust-addr     pic x(15).
56             05  l3-start-date        pic 9(6).
57             05  l3-balance           pic 999v99.
58             05  filler               pic x(212).
59/
60 procedure division using l2-file l3-file.
61 para1.
62     call "monitor1" using content l2-file
63                           content l3-file
64
65     evaluate true
66       when    l3-start-level-2
67*       Start of run
68         display "Name of input master:    " no advancing
69         accept l3-imastname
70         evaluate l3-imastname = space
71           when    true
72             display "Name of output master:    " no advancing
73             accept l3-omastname
74           when    false
75             move l3-imastname to l3-omastname
76         end-evaluate
77         display "Name of transaction file: " no advancing
78         accept l2-filename
79
80         move 01 to l3-ref
81         move 03 to l2-ref
82         move 07 to l2-len
83                    l3-len
84
85       When    l3-finish-level-2
86         continue
87
88       when    l3-empty-file
89         continue
90/
91       when    l3-start-level-1 and l3-empty
92         evaluate true
93           when    l2-add-acct
94             set   l3-mast-exists   to true
95             move  l2-account       to l3-account
96             move  l2-aa-cust-addr  to l3-cust-addr
97             move  l2-aa-cust-name  to l3-cust-name
98             move  l2-start-date    to l3-start-date
99             move  zero             to l3-balance
100          when    other
101            display "First transaction must be an add"
102        end-evaluate
103
```

```
104         when    l3-start-level-1
105            continue
106
107         when    l3-finish-level-1
108            continue
109
110         when    l3-process-level-0
111            evaluate true
112               when    l2-add-acct and l3-empty
113                  set  l3-mast-exists  to true
114                  move l2-account       to l3-account
115                  move l2-aa-cust-addr  to l3-cust-addr
116                  move l2-aa-cust-name  to l3-cust-name
117                  move l2-start-date    to l3-start-date
118                  move zero             to l3-balance
119               when    l2-add-acct and l3-mast-exists
120                  display "Cannot add an existing master"
121
122*          Process a transaction for an existing master
123               when    l2-chg-addr
124                  move l2-ca-cust-addr to l3-cust-addr
125               when    l2-del-acct
126                  set  l3-empty to true
127               when    other
128                  display "Unknown transaction"
129            end-evaluate
130
131         when    l3-out-of-sequence
132            continue
133
134      end-evaluate
135
136      exit program.
137 end program simple1
```

Figure 16.12 Program simple1

```
1 identification division.
2 program-id. monitor1.
3*Purpose:
4
5 environment division.
6
7 data division.
8 working-storage section.
9 01  s4-ctr                            pic 999.
10
```

```
11 01  w5-table.
12     03  w5-values.
13         05  filler value "sl2start-level-2"    pic x(18).
14         05  filler value "fl2finish-level-2"   pic x(18).
15         05  filler value "empempty-files"      pic x(18).
16         05  filler value "sl1start-level-1"    pic x(18).
17         05  filler value "fl1finish-level-1"   pic x(18).
18         05  filler value "l0 process-level-0"  pic x(18).
19         05  filler value "seqout-of-sequence"  pic x(18).
20     03  w5-entries redefines w5-values.
21         05  w5-entry occurs 7
22                     indexed w5-ind.
23             07  w5-action                      pic xxx.
24             07  w5-message                     pic x(15).
25
26 linkage section.
27 01  l2-file.
28     03  l2-ctr binary              pic 999.
29     03  l2-filename                pic x(20).
30     03  l2-keyarea.
31         05  l2-ref                 pic 99.
32         05  l2-len                 pic 99.
33         05  l2-trankey             pic x(20).
34
35 01  l3-file.
36     03  l3-ctr binary              pic 999.
37     03  l3-inpfilename             pic x(20).
38     03  l3-outfilename             pic x(20).
39     03  l3-action                  pic xxx.
40     03  l3-keyarea.
41         05  l3-ref                 pic 99.
42         05  l3-len                 pic 99.
43         05  l3-mastkey             pic x(20).
44
45/
46 procedure division using l2-file l3-file.
47 para1.
48     display "---------------------------"
49     set w5-ind to 1
50     search w5-entry
51       end
52         display "unknown action"
53       when w5-action(w5-ind) = l3-action
54         display w5-message(w5-ind)
55     end-search
56
```

```
57      move l3-ctr to s4-ctr
58      display "omast len = " s4-ctr
59
60      display "wmast key = " no advancing
61      evaluate true
62        when    l3-mastkey = low-value
63          display "low-value"
64        when    l3-mastkey = high-value
65          display "high-value"
66        when    other
67          display l3-mastkey
68      end-evaluate
69
70      display "itran key = " no advancing
71      evaluate true
72        when    l2-trankey = low-value
73          display "low-value"
74        when    l2-trankey = high-value
75          display "high-value"
76        when    other
77          display l2-trankey
78      end-evaluate
79
80      exit program.
81
82  end program monitor1
```

Figure 16.13 Program monitor1

16.5 CASE STUDY EXERCISES

1 Compile mupdate1, simple1 and monitor1. Link them into simple1 and run the program through runs 1 and 2 with the transactions that are in files simple.trn;1 and simple.trn;2 (Fig. 16.6). The monitor1 program (Fig. 16.13) will assist you in following the progress of the two updates.

2 Devise a larger transaction file (simple.trn;3) and do a third run of mupdate1.
   (Programs simple2 and simple3 are introduced in the next chapter.)

3 Rewrite simple1 as simple4 in which a transaction report is produced that prints a run header and trailer as well as a line for every master, followed by lines for any transactions for the master, followed by a line for the new master if it has been changed by transactions.

4 Design a new external transaction for the SIMPLE bank such as a credit to an account. Rewrite simple4 as simple5 to process this transaction and process run 4 with a new transaction file (simple.trn;4) that contains this new transaction.

5 Design a new internal transaction such as monthly billing. Rewrite simple5 as simple6 to process this transaction. The bills should be printed in a new output report and at the start of level 2 simple6 should be modified to take a run date from the keyboard.

6 Mupdate1 always requires the name of the input and output master for subsequent runs. Rewrite mupdate1 as mupdate2 so that if the name of an output master is not supplied then it will default to be the same name as the input master.

7   Write a detailed system specification for mupdate2.
8   Mupdate1 currently passes the input transaction and work master as parameters. Rewrite mupdate1 or mupdate2 as mupdate3 to use external records. This will allow the calling program and the called programs to omit the using phrases for the parameters.
9   The reason that the simple1 program or any subsequent versions you have written require a large case statement is that mupdate1 does not have the names of seven application programs that it can call in order to service the seven actions. Rewrite mupdate3 as mupdate4 so that the seven calls are to particular programs the names of which can be devised from the condition-names at lines 37 to 43 of mupdate1. Then rewrite the latest version of an application so that it is seven separately compiled programs internal to the same text file. They should have the same names as the names chosen in the root and each of these programs should define the records it requires from the root as external records. Any records that these programs share with each other should also be defined as external. The result will be a root that calls seven application programs by a set of names that are predefined in the root. When you have finished write a detailed system specification for mupdate4 which explains how an application should be written for the seven action calls.
10 Add screen2 to an application so that the screen is directly managed for all terminal inputs and outputs. (Remove the monitor1 program first.)

17
INDEXED FILES

Indexed files provide a means to manage a file of records that are indexed by key. Unlike sequential files where access to records is determined by the order in which they were originally written to the file, an indexed file allows records to be read in orders that are established by a key value that is set at the time a record is read from the indexed file. The mechanism for achieving this is an index to the physical location of the data within the file. The index and its management is not directly visible to the COBOL program, nor is information concerning the physical location of records within the file.

Indexed files can be accessed in three different modes. The **random** access mode allows the program to add, change, and delete records within an existing file in any order provided that the program supplies values for the record keys.

Indexed files can also be processed in ascending key order when the access mode is **sequential**. This is usually the mode in which files are opened when they are created although some systems may be more flexible than this.

The third access mode is **dynamic**. It is inclusive and supports all of the features of the sequential and random access modes.

The access mode for a given indexed file is established when the file is opened. Thus a file might be opened sequentially when it is first created. At other times it might be opened sequentially to process a master file update for a transaction file that is sorted into ascending key order. Companies often do processing of this kind overnight when large numbers of records need to be processed for external transactions that are in large volumes such as account payments and for internal transactions such as monthly billings.

At other times the file might be opened in random access mode so that particular records can be added, changed, or deleted. Individual transaction processing of this kind commonly occurs during the daytime in response to particular low volume transactions originating from terminals such as an approval for spending a large amount for a single purchase on a credit card.

17.1 SEQUENTIAL ACCESS

Figure 17.1 lists program simple2. It takes as input the master file of the SIMPLE bank and writes it as an indexed file with fixed length records.

Line 11 defines the file as having an indexed organization and line 13 gives the name of the key as o2-key which is a reference to the file description record for o2-file (line 23).

The key which is given in the select statement must always identify a data item in the selected file description. This is the *primary key* for the file and is subject to the following rules:

1. It can be of any length (subject to a maximum given by a particular implementation).
2. It can appear as a data item at any point in the record provided that it is part of the fixed portion of the record. (In this respect it is similar to a sort key.)
3. It must be a character string. If it is numeric it must be unsigned.
4. Every record in a file must have a unique key value.
5. Items in the record other than the key can have a usage other than display.

```
 1 identification division.
 2 program-id. simple2.
 3*Purpose: Copy the existing variable length master file for
 4*          the SIMPLE bank to a new fixed-length indexed file.
 5
 6 environment division.
 7 input-output section.
 8 file-control.
 9     select i1-file   assign w1-filename.
10     select o2-file   assign w2-filename
11        organization  indexed
12        access        sequential
13        record        o2-key.
14
15 data division.
16 file section.
17 fd   i1-file
18      record varying 1 to 43
19      depending w1-ctr
20      value of id    w1-filename.
21 01   filler                       pic x(43).
22
23 fd   o2-file
24      value of id    w2-filename.
25 01   o2-rec.
26      03  o2-key                   pic x(7).
27      03  filler                   pic x(36).
28
29 working-storage section.
30 01   w1-file.
31      03  w1-ctr binary            pic 999.
32      03  w1-filename              pic x(20).
33      03  filler value "n"         pic x.
34          88  w1-eof               value "y".
35
```

```
36 01  w2-file.
37     03  w2-filename             pic x(20).
38     03  w2-rec.
39         05  w2-key              pic x(7).
40         05  filler              pic x(36).
41
42 procedure division.
43 para1.
44     display "simple2 begins"
45     display space
46
47     display "Enter name of sequential file: " no advancing
48     accept w1-filename
49     open input   i1-file
50
51     display "Enter name of new indexed file: " no advancing
52     accept w2-filename
53     open  output o2-file
54
55     perform until w1-eof
56       read i1-file into w2-rec
57         end
58           set w1-eof to true
59         not end
60           evaluate w1-ctr not = 43
61             when true
62               display "Faulty length. Key: " w2-key " skipped"
63             when false
64               write o2-rec from w2-rec
65                 invalid
66                   display "Input file is out of sequence"
67                   set w1-eof to true
68               end-write
69           end-evaluate
70       end-read
71     end-perform
72
73     close i1-file
74           o2-file
75
76     display "simple2 ends"
77     stop run.
78
79 end program simple2
```

Figure 17.1 Program simple2

The input file (line 17) is a text file of variable-length records. The output file (line 23) does not contain either a record varying or a depending clause. The omission of these two clauses causes the records in the file to be fixed length by default. In order to determine the record length the compiler checks the definition of the record, which in this case gives a length of 43 characters. Therefore the records written to the indexed file will each be 43 characters long. Unused character positions at the end of records that were shorter than this will be space filled.

424 ESSENTIAL COBOL: A FIRST COURSE IN STRUCTURED COBOL

The indexed file is opened for output at line 53. The fact that its access mode is sequential (line 12) restricts the file operations that can be used to those that are compatible with sequential files.

The loop of the program is at lines 55 to 71. As each record is read from the input file it is written to the indexed file by the write statement at line 64. This write statement introduces the **invalid** phrase:

```
write record-name-1 [from identifier-1]
   invalid     statement-1
 [not invalid statement-2]
end-write
```

When a write operation is attempted by the system the result may be valid or invalid. For indexed files that are open in sequential access mode the invalid condition will occur if a key for a record is found not to be higher in value than the previous key that was written to the file. In other words, you should only create an indexed file from a sequential file when you know that it is already in ascending key order. This may have been achieved by a prior sort or it may be a known characteristic of the existing file, as is the case with a sequential master file.

Therefore the invalid phrase at line 65 is there to trap a fatal error for the program and after displaying a message the switch that controls the input file is set to eof so that the loop will terminate immediately.

17.2 RANDOM ACCESS

Once an indexed file exists it can be opened in random access mode. In this mode the program can use a key value so that certain file operations such as reading are done for the record that has that key.

Program simple3 in Fig. 17.2 is a simple query program that allows read access to records in the indexed file that was created by simple2. Line 11 defines the access mode as indexed and line 12 states the key by which the file is organized.

At line 36 the file is opened as i-o which stands for input-output. This is the most flexible way to open an indexed file with an access mode that is random because it allows the maximum range of file operations which includes operations such as writing and rewriting. (These will be considered in the next section.)

The loop for the program is at lines 40 to 49. The user is asked for the key of a record. This key is then used to attempt to read the record from the file at line 43.

```
read record-name-1 into identifier-1
   invalid     statement-1
 [not invalid statement-2]
end-read
```

```cobol
 1 identification division.
 2 program-id. simple3.
 3*Purpose: Demonstrate a simple query
 4*         for the SIMPLE bank indexed master file.
 5
 6 environment division.
 7 input-output section.
 8 file-control.
 9     select i1-file  assign w1-filename
10        organization    indexed
11        access          random
12        record          i1-key.
13
14 data division.
15 file section.
16 fd  i1-file
17     value of id w1-filename.
18 01  i1-rec.
19     03  i1-key              pic x(7).
20     03  filler              pic x(36).
21
22 working-storage section.
23 01  w1-file.
24     03  w1-filename         pic x(20).
25     03  w1-user             pic x.
26         88  w1-eok      value "Q" "q".
27     03  w1-rec              pic x(41).
28
29 procedure division.
30 para1.
31     display "simple3 begins"
32     display space
33
34     display "Enter the name of the indexed file: " no advancing
35     accept w1-filename
36     open i-o i1-file
37
38     display "Type RET or 'Q' to quit"
39     accept w1-user
40     perform until w1-eok
41       display "Enter a simple key = " no advancing
42       accept w1-key
43       read i1-file into w1-rec
44         invalid     display "no-such-record"
45         not invalid display "record = " w1-rec
46       end-read
47       display "Type RET or 'Q' to quit"
48       accept w1-user
49     end-perform
50
51     close i1-file
52     display "simple3 ends"
53     stop run.
54
55  end program simple3.
```

Figure 17.2 Program simple3

This form of the read statement is used when reading records from an indexed file. Prior to the read statement the program must always move a value to the key (line 42). When the read is attempted either the record will be in the file or it will not. The invalid phrases allow the program to respond to these two possibilities. Simple3 responds either by displaying a message to say that the record was not in the file or by displaying the record.

There is no end of file condition for this form of the read statement because the operation is done on a per record basis. A record for the SIMPLE bank can take a value in the range of "0000000" to "9999999". Therefore the key can be set to any value in this range and the program will respond appropriately.

The SIMPLE bank problem was defined to have a numeric string as a key. However, the definition of the key at line 19 shows that it is alphanumeric. Therefore for this program it is valid to use other printable characters in the key such as "A000001". If you check the ASCII table in Appendix D you will see that the character "A" has a higher value than the characters for the digits. Therefore this key is higher than "9999999". Thus it is possible to write more than eight million records to this file.

Normally an application program will use numeric values for the records that are directly available to users. Records with alphabetic characters in the key could be used to provide additional records for other purposes such as trailer records that held information such as the total number of records in the file. Such a record would be read into working storage at the beginning of the run and the total would be maintained by the running program. At the end of the run the record could be rewritten to file with the new total.

17.3 DYNAMIC ACCESS

COBOL allows a third file access mode which is the dynamic mode. It allows all of the possible operations when the file is open in i-o mode. The relationship between the three file access modes, the four open modes, and the available file operations are given in Fig. 17.3.

By choosing the right modes for a particular program it is possible to restrict a program to exactly the file operations that it requires for its particular purpose. (This is very important in multi-user systems where, for example, many users running copies of the same or different programs may be accessing the same file of data. A discussion of multiple concurrent access to the same file is beyond the scope of this book.) Therefore once you have created an indexed file you should use the dynamic file access mode with the file open in i-o mode so that your program can take advantage of any of the possible file operations without your needing to worry about the relationships between operations and modes.

When the file access is sequential it is possible to read the file sequentially. The read statement has the same form that we have used for sequential reads in the past:

```
read file-name-1 [into identifier-1]
   end     statement-1
 [not end  statement-2]
 end-read
```

File-access mode	Statement	Open mode			
		Input	Output	Input–output	Extend
Sequential	Read	Y		Y	
	Write		Y		Y
	Rewrite			Y	
	Start	Y		Y	
	Delete			Y	
Random	Read	Y		Y	
	Write		Y	Y	
	Rewrite			Y	
	Start				
	Delete			Y	
Dynamic	Read	Y		Y	
	Write		Y	Y	
	Rewrite			Y	
	Start	Y		Y	
	Delete			Y	

Figure 17.3 Relationship between operations and modes

However, it takes account of the index for the file and therefore presents the records to the program in their ascending key order from the very first to the last. Therefore a program with sequential file access can read the file like any other sequential file. The last record read in the file will be the record with the highest key value and the next read after this will cause the end of file condition to become true.

When the file access is dynamic it is also possible to read the file sequentially. In this case there is no certain rule concerning what record will be next to be read because the program may also have been reading records at random with the other form of the read statement. Therefore the **start** statement is available to start the key with a certain value:

$$\text{start file-name-1} \begin{Bmatrix} = \\ > \\ \text{not} < \\ >= \end{Bmatrix} \text{data-name-1}$$

```
    invalid      statement-1
    [not invalid statement-2]
    end-start
```

The data-name that is used is the key for the record. It is preceded by one of the four operators. For example:

```
move zero to i1-key
start i1-file = i1-key
    invalid     display "no such key in the file"
    not invalid display "key is now started"
end-start
```

Provided that the key is correctly started the next sequential read in the program will be for this record. There are times when you do not know what the first key in the file is going to be but you may know as in the case of the SIMPLE bank that the valid key range is "0000000" to "9999999". In this case the key can be set to zero and the >= operator will get the first key in the file that is either zero or higher. The start statement only looks at the index for the file and not at the actual records. Therefore it is very efficient in its operation and can be used to browse around a file to see if records actually exist without committing the program to reading them. This could be useful, for example, if you merely wanted to count the number of records in a file or check for the existence of certain keys that might fulfil other criteria that can be expressed in terms of key values.

The delete and rewrite statements are straightforward to use. The delete statement logically deletes a record from the file so that the program can no longer access that record. The rewrite statement writes an existing record back to a file. In both cases the delete or rewrite must be immediately preceded by a read statement for the record with the same key. For example, imagine that a program has a file access that is dynamic with the file open in i–o mode. The operations shown in Fig. 17.4 are legal for key "1234567", which we know not to be in the file at the beginning of this sequence of statements.

The ellipsis ". . ." suggests that other statements may have intervened in the running program. Where the message "impossible" is used it does not imply that this condition could never occur. For example, a system error might generate an invalid condition for an attempt to write to a file that was physically full of data and could not hold another record. "Impossible" in this context means that this condition will not arise in a normal running program for the record with key "1234567" if the record did not exist in the first place and if the file operations for this record take place in this order.

The first group checks to see that the record is not in the file and then writes the record to the file. It is illegal to try to write a record to a file when a record with that key is already in the file. The second group occurs later perhaps after other records have been dealt with. This group reads the record from the file. The third group exists to delete the record. It has a prior read so that the delete operation will be successful for the record with that key. Once the record is deleted this key can be used again by another write operation.

The general rules that are implied by these operations are as follows:

1. Never attempt to write a record unless you are sure that it does not exist.
2. Never attempt to delete or rewrite a record unless you know the last file operation was a read for a record with that key.
3. Use the start statement to check to see if records exist or to initialize prior to sequential reading operations.
4. The invalid condition can be raised for system errors, the most common of which is a full file for an attempted write. System errors will not normally occur when running the programs in this chapter. (Although COBOL has additional features for handling errors found by the system this topic is outside the scope of this book.)

The case-study program at the end of the chapter includes a file handler for an indexed file. You should experiment with this program extensively so that you get a good grasp of the ways in which an indexed file can be used. This practice is more valuable than any number of additional rules outlining further minor details.

```
...
move "1234567" to i1-key
start i1-file = i1-key
  invalid
    display "We knew it wasn't in the file"
    write i1-rec from w1-rec
      invalid
        display "impossible"
      not invalid
        display "record written to the file"
    end-write
  not invalid
    display "impossible"
end-start
...
move "1234567" to i1-key
read i1-file into w1-rec
  invalid
    display "impossible"
  not invalid
    display "record is " w1-rec
end-read
...
move "1234567" to i1-key
read i1-file into w1-rec
  invalid
    display "impossible"
  not invalid
    display "record found"
    delete i1-file
      invalid
        display "impossible"
      not invalid
        display "record now deleted"
    end-delete
end-read
...
```

Figure 17.4 Ordered set of operations for an indexed file

17.4 CASE STUDY: INDTUT1 (HANDLING INDEXED FILES)

Program indtut1 (Fig. 17.6) is an indexed file program exerciser to give you practical experience with seeing an indexed file in operation prior to writing your own programs that use them. The structure chart in Fig. 17.5 shows how this program relates to indfh1 which is the indexed file handler itself for the indexed file.

Indtut1 contains program menu1 which is called to put a menu on the screen. It then calls indfh1 (Fig. 17.7) which manages the indexed file. I1-file is the file when it is open in dynamic access mode. I2-file is the same file when it is open in sequential access

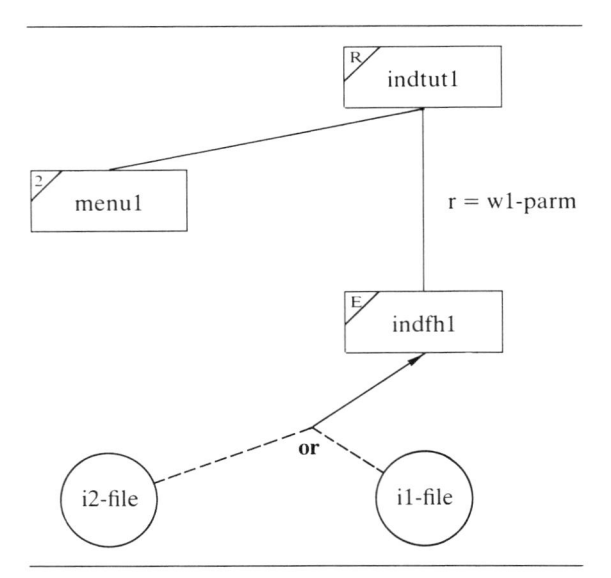

430 ESSENTIAL COBOL: A FIRST COURSE IN STRUCTURED COBOL

Figure 17.5 Structure chart for indtut1

```
 1 identification division.
 2 program-id. indtut1.
 3*Purpose: Demonstrate the use of the indexed file handler 'indfh1'.
 4
 5 environment division.
 6
 7 data division.
 8 working-storage section.
 9 01  w1-parm.
10     03  w1-filename      pic x(20).
11     03  w1-currfunc      pic xxx.
12         88  w1-create        value "cre".
13         88  w1-open          value "ops" "opd".
14         88  w1-open-seq      value "ops".
15         88  w1-open-dyn      value "opd".
16         88  w1-startequal    value "s= ".
17         88  w1-startgreater  value "s> ".
18         88  w1-startnotless  value "sn<".
19         88  w1-read          value "rea".
20         88  w1-readnext      value "ren".
21         88  w1-write         value "wri".
22         88  w1-rewrite       value "rew".
23         88  w1-delete        value "del".
24         88  w1-close         value "clo".
25*        values used to control tutorial
26         88  w1-eok           value "q  ".
27         88  w1-inp-data      value "wri" "rew".
28         88  w1-out-data      value "rea" "ren" "rew" "wri".
29         88  w1-inkey         value "s= " "s> " "sn<" "rea"
30                                    "wri" "rew" "del".
31
32     03  w1-retcode       pic 99.
33         88  w1-success       value 00 10 22 23.
34         88  w1-fatal         value 99.
35
```

```
36        03  w1-rec.
37            05  w1-key            pic x(5).
38            05  w1-data           pic x(20).
39
40   01  s2-foundline.
41        03  filler value "found key="  pic x(10).
42        03  s2-key                     pic x(5).
43        03  filler value "; data="     pic x(7).
44        03  s2-data                    pic x(25).
45        03  filler value "; retcode="  pic x(10).
46        03  s2-retcode                 pic 99.
47        03  filler value space         pic x.
48        03  s2-retran                  pic x(18).
49
50   01  w3-errortable.
51        03  w3-values.
52            05  filler value "00success"          pic x(20).
53            05  filler value "01end of file"      pic x(20).
54            05  filler value "02record exists"    pic x(20).
55            05  filler value "03no such record"   pic x(20).
56            05  filler value "04file is closed"   pic x(20).
57            05  filler value "05file is open"     pic x(20).
58            05  filler value "06wrong access mode" pic x(20).
59            05  filler value "07out of sequence"  pic x(20).
60            05  filler value "08no such key"      pic x(20).
61            05  filler value "09no key set"       pic x(20).
62            05  filler value "99unknown request"  pic x(20).
63        03  w3-table redefines w3-values.
64            05  w3-entries occurs 11
65                        ascending w3-retcode
66                        indexed by w3-ind.
67                07  w3-retcode                 pic 99.
68                07  w3-retran                  pic x(18).
69
70   01  w4-convert.
71        03  w4-upper value "ABCDEFGHIJKLMNOPQRSTUVWXYZ" pic x(26).
72        03  w4-lower value "abcdefghijklmnopqrstuvwxyz" pic x(26).
73/
74   procedure division.
75   para1.
76        display "Enter name of file: " no advancing
77        accept w1-filename
78
79*       PROCESS requests
80        call "menu1"
81        display "function: " with no advancing
82        accept w1-currfunc
83        inspect w1-currfunc
84          converting w4-upper to w4-lower
85
86        perform until w1-eok
87*         Prompt for a key when the function requires one
88          evaluate w1-inkey
89            when    true
90              display "key: " with no advancing
91              accept w1-key
92          end-evaluate
93*         Prompt for data when the function requires it
94          evaluate w1-inp-data
95            when    true
96              display "data: " with no advancing
97              accept w1-data
98          end-evaluate
99
```

```
100        call "indfh1" using reference w1-parm
101
102*       Prepare to display output when the function requires it
103        evaluate w1-out-data
104          when    true
105            move w1-key  to s2-key
106            move w1-data to s2-data
107          when    false
108            move spaces  to s2-key
109            move spaces  to s2-data
110        end-evaluate
111
112        move w1-retcode to s2-retcode
113
114*       Translate the return code into a message for the user
115        search all w3-entries
116          end
117            move "not in error table" to s2-retran
118          when w3-retcode(w3-ind) = w1-retcode
119            move w3-retran(w3-ind) to s2-retran
120        end-search
121
122        display s2-foundline
123
124        call "menu1"
125        display space
126        display "function: " with no advancing
127        accept w1-currfunc
128        inspect w1-currfunc
129          converting w4-upper to w4-lower
130      end-perform
131*     END-PROCESS
132
133      stop run.
134/
135 identification division.
136 program-id. menu1.
137
138 environment division.
139
140 data division.
141 working-storage section.
142 01   w4-menu.
143      03   w4-size binary value 16          pic 99.
144      03   w4-menulines.
145        05   filler value "indexed file driver " pic x(20).
146        05   filler value "key-x(5); data-x(20)" pic x(20).
147        05   filler value "********************" pic x(20).
148        05   filler value "CREATE          - cre" pic x(20).
149        05   filler value "open sequential- ops" pic x(20).
150        05   filler value "open dynamic    - opd" pic x(20).
151        05   filler value "start =         - s=" pic x(20).
152        05   filler value "start >         - s>" pic x(20).
153        05   filler value "start not <     - sn<" pic x(20).
154        05   filler value "read            - rea" pic x(20).
155        05   filler value "read next       - ren" pic x(20).
156        05   filler value "write           - wri" pic x(20).
157        05   filler value "rewrite         - rew" pic x(20).
158        05   filler value "delete          - del" pic x(20).
159        05   filler value "close           - clo" pic x(20).
160        05   filler value "QUIT            - q " pic x(20).
161      03   filler redefines w4-menulines.
162        05   w4-menuline  occurs 16
163                          indexed by w4-ind   pic x(20).
164
```

```
165 procedure division.
166 para1.
167     display space
168     set w4-ind to 1
169     perform test before until w4-ind > w4-size
170       display w4-menuline(w4-ind)
171       set w4-ind up by 1
172     end-perform
173     display space
174
175     exit program.
176
177 end program menu1.
178 end program indtut1.
```

Figure 17.6 Program indtut1

```
 1 identification division.
 2 program-id. indfh1.
 3*Purpose: To manage an indexed file for a calling program.
 4
 5 environment division.
 6 input-output section.
 7 file-control.
 8 select i1-file
 9     organization indexed
10     assign       w1-filename
11     access       dynamic
12     record       i1-key.
13
14 select i2-file
15     organization indexed
16     assign       w1-filename
17     access       sequential
18     record       i2-key.
19
20 data division.
21 file section.
22 fd  i1-file
23     value of id w1-filename.
24 01  i1-rec.
25     03  i1-key              pic x(5).
26     03  filler              pic x(20).
27
28 fd  i2-file
29     value of id w1-filename.
30 01  i2-rec.
31     03  i2-key              pic x(5).
32     03  filler              pic x(20).
33
34 working-storage section.
35 01  w1-file.
36     03  w1-filename         pic x(20).
37     03  w1-prevfunc value "clo" pic xxx.
38         88  w1-start        value "s= " "s> " "sn<".
39         88  w1-read         value "rea".
40         88  w1-readnext     value "ren".
41         88  w1-rnok         value "s= " "s> " "sn<"
42                                   "ren" "rea".
43         88  w1-rwdelok      value "rea" "ren".
44
```

```
 45       03  filler       value "clo" pic xxx.
 46           88  w1-closed            value "clo".
 47           88  w1-open              value "ops", "opd".
 48           88  w1-open-seq          value "ops".
 49           88  w1-open-dyn          value "dyn".
 50
 51       03  filler                   pic xxx.
 52           88  w1-eof               value "eof".
 53           88  w1-noteof            value "nof".
 54/
 55 linkage section.
 56 01  l1-parm.
 57       03  l1-filename              pic x(20).
 58       03  l1-currfunc              pic xxx.
 59           88  l1-create            value "cre".
 60           88  l1-open              value "ops", "opd".
 61           88  l1-open-seq          value "ops".
 62           88  l1-open-dyn          value "opd".
 63           88  l1-startequal        value "s= ".
 64           88  l1-startgreater      value "s> ".
 65           88  l1-startnotless      value "sn<".
 66           88  l1-read              value "rea".
 67           88  l1-readnext          value "ren".
 68           88  l1-write             value "wri".
 69           88  l1-rewrite           value "rew".
 70           88  l1-delete            value "del".
 71           88  l1-close             value "clo".
 72       03  l1-retcode               pic 99.
 73           88  l1-success           value 00.
 74           88  l1-eof               value 01.
 75           88  l1-record-exists     value 02.
 76           88  l1-no-such-record    value 03.
 77           88  l1-file-is-closed    value 04.
 78           88  l1-file-is-open      value 05.
 79           88  l1-wrong-access      value 06.
 80           88  l1-out-of-sequence   value 07.
 81           88  l1-no-such-key       value 08.
 82           88  l1-no-key-set        value 09.
 83           88  l1-unknown           value 99.
 84       03  l1-rec.
 85           05  l1-key               pic x(5).
 86           05  l1-data              pic x(20).
 87/
 88 procedure division using l1-parm.
 89 para1.
 90      set l1-success to true
 91
 92*     MODE check
 93      evaluate true
 94         when   l1-open
 95            evaluate true
 96               when   w1-open
 97                  set l1-file-is-open to true
 98               when   l1-open-dyn
 99                  move l1-filename to w1-filename
100                  open i-o i1-file
101                  set w1-open-dyn to true
102                  set w1-noteof to true
103               when   l1-open-seq
104                  move l1-filename to w1-filename
105                  open output i2-file
106                  set w1-open-seq to true
107            end-evaluate
108            go to para-exit
109
```

```
110          when    l1-close
111            evaluate true
112              when    w1-closed
113                set l1-file-is-closed to true
114              when    w1-open-dyn
115                close i1-file
116                set w1-closed to true
117              when    w1-open-seq
118                close i2-file
119                set w1-closed to true
120            end-evaluate
121            go to para-exit
122        end-evaluate
123*      END-MODE
124/
125*      SEQUENTIAL mode processing
126        evaluate true
127          when    l1-create
128            evaluate w1-closed
129              when    true
130                move l1-filename to w1-filename
131                open output i2-file
132                close i2-file
133              when false
134                set l1-file-is-open to true
135            end-evaluate
136            go to para-exit
137
138          when   w1-open-seq
139            evaluate l1-write
140              when    true
141                write i2-rec from l1-rec
142                  invalid
143                    set l1-out-of-sequence to true
144                end-write
145              when    false
146                set l1-wrong-access to true
147            end-evaluate
148            go to para-exit
149        end-evaluate
150*      END-SEQUENTIAL
151
152/
153*      DYNAMIC mode processing
154        evaluate w1-open-dyn
155          when    false
156            set l1-file-is-closed to true
157            go to para-exit
158        end-evaluate
159
160*      FILE IS OPEN ONLY IN DYNAMIC MODE WHEN THIS POINT IS REACHED
161
162        evaluate true
163          when    l1-write
164            write i1-rec from l1-rec
165              invalid
166                set l1-record-exists to true
167            end-write
168
```

```
169         when    l1-readnext
170            evaluate true
171               when w1-readnext and w1-eof
172                  set l1-eof to true
173               when w1-rnok
174                  read i1-file next into l1-rec
175                     end
176                        set w1-eof to true
177                        set l1-eof to true
178                     not end
179                        set w1-noteof to true
180                  end-read
181               when other
182                  set l1-no-key-set to true
183            end-evaluate
184
185         when    l1-read
186            move l1-key to i1-key
187            move spaces to l1-data
188            read i1-file record into l1-rec
189               invalid
190                  set l1-no-such-record to true
191            end-read
192
193         when    l1-rewrite
194            evaluate w1-rwdelok and l1-key = i1-key
195               when    true
196                  rewrite i1-rec from l1-rec
197                     invalid
198                        set l1-unknown to true
199                  end-rewrite
200               when    false
201                  move l1-key to i1-key
202                  read i1-file record
203                     invalid
204                        set l1-no-such-record to true
205                     not invalid
206                        rewrite i1-rec from l1-rec
207                           invalid
208                              set l1-unknown to true
209                        end-rewrite
210                  end-read
211            end-evaluate
212
```

```
213          when    l1-delete
214            evaluate w1-rwdelok and l1-key = i1-key
215              when    true
216                delete i1-file record
217                  invalid
218                    set l1-unknown to true
219                  not invalid
220                    move spaces to l1-rec
221                end-delete
222              when    false
223                move l1-key to i1-key
224                read i1-file record
225                  invalid
226                    set l1-no-such-record to true
227                  not invalid
228                    delete i1-file record
229                      invalid
230                        set l1-unknown to true
231                      not invalid
232                        move spaces to l1-rec
233                    end-delete
234                end-read
235            end-evaluate
236
237          when    l1-startequal
238            move l1-key to i1-key
239            start i1-file key = i1-key
240              invalid
241                set l1-no-such-key to true
242            end-start
243
244          when    l1-startgreater
245            move l1-key to i1-key
246            start i1-file key > i1-key
247              invalid
248                set l1-no-such-key to true
249            end-start
250
251          when    l1-startnotless
252            move l1-key to i1-key
253            start i1-file key not < i1-key
254              invalid
255                set l1-no-such-key to true
256            end-start
257          when    other
258            set l1-unknown to true
259
260        end-evaluate.
261*       END-DYNAMIC
262
263 para-exit.
264        evaluate true
265          when    l1-success
266            move l1-currfunc to w1-prevfunc
267        end-evaluate
268
269        exit program.
270
271 end program indfh1.
```

Figure 17.7 Program indfh1

mode. This arrangement allows the indexed file to be created with values from the keyboard (i2-file) and then reopened in dynamic access mode (i1-file) for other file operations. (It is possible to open the file sequentially, close it without having written data to the file, and then to reopen it dynamically directly afterwards by requesting a 'create'.) The reason that both modes are allowed is not only to give you practice with using both file access modes. It is also done this way because most compilers will not allow you to open a file in dynamic access mode if it does not already exist.

Indtut1 allows you to select one of 13 options from the menu. Once you have selected an option it will then prompt you for any further data that is required for that option. It will then call the file handler which will attempt the file operations that are implied by the option. The file handler returns a return code which is either success or an error. This is translated back to the screen so that you can assess the effect of your attempted file operation. For example, an attempt to read a file that you have not previously opened will give the message 'file is closed'. The file it implements is for demonstration purposes only. Its key is any five characters and the data portion is 20 characters long in which you can put a text message to help you keep track of your progress through the exercise.

Infh1 begins at line 90 with the assumption that the request made of it will be successful. It then sets out either to fulfil the request or to prove that it is invalid. At any point where it finds that the request is illegal it sets the appropriate return code and escapes forward to the end of the program.

Lines 92 to 123 implement the open and close options and ensure that the option you have selected does not conflict with the current status of the file. For example, an attempt to open a file that is already open will fail at this point.

At line 125 the program begins to check the operations associated with sequential processing. The only two that are implemented are create and write. A create will succeed if the file is closed and a write will succeed if the file is open and the key for the record that you want to write is higher in value than the key for any previous write you have done in this run. These two options allow you to create a file from scratch without the need to run another program.

By line 153 not only the options for opening and closing files have been processed but also the options associated with sequential files. From this point on the only options left are for an open dynamic file. Therefore the program now checks to ensure that the file is in this state. If it is, the processing can continue.

Lines 162 to the end implement the various operations associated with a file that is open in dynamic mode with the exception of the close which was handled at the top of the program. The program keeps track of the previous key and whether or not the previous operation was a read. Therefore for the delete and rewrite operations it reads the record if it has to. This approach means that the need to do a read before deletes and rewrites is transparent to the calling program.

17.5 EXERCISES

17.5.1 General

1 Rewrite simple2 as simple10 so that it can write the SIMPLE master file into an indexed file.

2   Rewrite simple3 as simple11 so that it can read records from the new SIMPLE indexed master file.
3   Rewrite an earlier version of the telephone directory program (tele2 from Chapter 13 or tele4 from Chapter 14) as tele5. It should use an indexed file rather than a sequential file with a table. Each entry in the table can be a record in the indexed file.

17.5.2 Case study

4   Compile indtut1 and indfh1. Link indfh1 into intut1. Run indtut1 a number of times until you are sure that you understand the file operations associated with indexed files. (List your test cases in their input order as you present them to the program.)
5   Write a detailed system specification for indfh1.
6   Rewrite indfh1 as indfh2 so that it can manage the SIMPLE bank indexed master file. (The only change that you need to make is to the record descriptions and the associated items.) Rewrite simple11 as simple12 so that it calls indfh2 to read its records for it. (Simple12 will not need to describe the file itself.)
7   All of the operations in indfh1 and indfh2 are dependent on the state of the file at any time. These can be described by a character string that can be constructed from previous operations.

```
01   e1-state.
     03   e1-file-mode         pic x.
          88   no-mode         value space.
          88   s-mode          value "s".
          88   r-mode          value "r".
          88   d-mode          value "d".
     03   e1-open-mode         pic x.
          88   closed          value space.
          88   i-open          value "i".
          88   o-open          value "o".
          88   io-open         value "b".
          88   e-open          value "e".
     03   e1-current-op        pic xx.
          88   op-read         value "re".
          88   op-write        value "wr".
          88   op-rewrite      value "rx".
          88   op-start        value "st".
          88   op-delete       value "de".
          88   op-create       value "ce".
     03   e1-previous-op       pic xx.
```

The only essential piece of data not contained in the above record is the last key that was used for a successful file operation. This can be maintained separately.

Figure 17.3 shows all of the possible combinations that are allowed for a given operation with a given file state. Each of these possibilities can be rewritten as an entry in a table. Each entry should be a string of characters that conforms to the above record.

Rewrite indfh1 or indfh2 as indfh3 in which the file handler constructs an argument based on the operations that have gone before and the current option. It should then do a look-up in the table for a matching entry. If there is one in the table then the operation is allowed and can be done. The main body of the program should be a single evaluate statement.

18
ADDITIONAL COBOL FEATURES

The purpose of this chapter is to mention those additional features of COBOL that have not been covered fully in the book. Many students have the mistaken impression that COBOL consists of only those features that are presented in the study text that they have used to learn the language. The brief notes in this chapter may help to dispel this notion and perhaps will suggest further topics which you may wish to explore with the assistance of manuals or a copy of the COBOL standard.

The case-study program in Section 18.5 gives you an opportunity to consider an unstructured program that is written in COBOL-74.

By the end of the chapter you will not only have identified those features that are not covered in this text but also will have had an opportunity to consider many aspects of the language that in spite of being included in the latest standard are best avoided.

18.1 MODULES

Of the 11 functional modules in the language, this text presents only some of the features that are in six of the required modules. The required module that has been omitted entirely is the relative input–output module. This contains features for accessing records at random and sequentially in relative files. Each record in a relative file is uniquely addressable by an integer value in the range of 1 to n. From a conceptual point of view one can imagine a relative file to be a large table, the entries for which are stored as records in the file. The record key is similar in concept to an index for a table. Not only can a relative file be used for storing tables that are too large to keep in memory, they can also be used to store any records for which the application constructs a record key by using hashing techniques. The program must also manage instances where the hashing technique causes more than one application key to resolve to the same file key. Although a relative file is very efficient in its use of system resources it is more primitive than an indexed file which not only includes an index to the records in the file but also the management of the file and its index as part of the file operations.

The report writer, communication, debug and segmentation modules have not been covered. The report writer is useful for applications where many reports have to be written that include headings, footings and summed totals which are associated with particular data items in the stream of input records. It is included in most compilers. The communication module provides features for enabling a program to communicate with the message control system that is provided by the operating system. It is often not included by suppliers who provide more sophisticated facilities by other means such as system libraries that contain programs that can be called by applications. The debug module is often used for testing very large programs that are known or suspected to be difficult to comprehend owing to their poor structure. The module essentially provides features for embedding debug statements in a program which can then be used in tracing the flow of execution and the changes in data values as the program runs. The segmentation module provides features for dividing large programs into segments when the memory in a computer is not large enough to hold the whole of the program in memory at one time. Both the debug and segmentation modules are now obsolete and therefore will be deleted by the next COBOL standard.

18.2 STATEMENTS

Many statements have been omitted or included in a shortened form. This has been done for one or more of the following reasons:

1. An omitted alternative merely duplicates the functionality of an included form (e.g. write with the before option).
2. An alternative conflicts with the forms that are used in the text. New practice should move away from the use of these alternatives because the language now provides improved means for accomplishing the same requirement (e.g. the next sentence phrase or perform procedure-name).
3. A feature is now obsolete and will be deleted in the next standard. Therefore new programs should not be written to use it (e.g. the alter statement).
4. A feature incorporates system-dependent aspects that are not strictly required to cover the language adequately (e.g. format 2 of the accept statement).

The following notes cover those main statements and phrases that have been omitted.

The **accept** statement contains options to allow a program to accept variables such as the current date from the operating system. The form in which these variables are presented to the program is system dependent.

The **alter** statement allows a program to change the destination of a go to in a running program. It is now an obsolete statement and will be deleted by the next standard.

The **cancel** statement allows a calling program to cancel a called program so that the next time it is called it will be in its initial state. This is often used in microcomputer applications where called programs are held in separate files at run time. In response to a cancel statement the system then deletes the program from memory such that any future call will cause the program to be loaded once again from the file. This feature can be used to write a program that is larger than the available memory in a more structured way than is allowed by the segmentation module.

The **copy** statement has a **replacing** option that allows for limited forms of textual substitution when text is copied into the program. It is mainly useful in program maintenance where the name of a data item needs to be changed. Many suppliers have extended this option so that prefixes can be changed at the time of copying.

The **go to** statement contains a **depending** option that allows multi-way branching to paragraphs in a program. It can be used to construct jump tables where run-time efficiency is an important requirement.

The most obvious omission is the **if** statement. It is used when a selection needs to be made on a condition that is either true or false. Many COBOL texts devote a complete chapter to the if statement and the complications that arise from nesting if statements in order to control selection on more than one condition. This book has presented the evaluate statement in preference to the if statement which is more primitive and therefore more difficult to use in all but the most simple cases. (The case-study program at the end of this chapter uses if statements.)

The **move** statement and some of the arithmetic statements have a **corresponding** option that allows lists of data items to be processed. The option is of limited use and requires a source and target record to contain the same data-names, which for other program references then need to be qualified by their record-names.

The **perform** statement has a **test after** option so that the termination test takes place at the bottom of the loop instead of at the top. It also contains an *n* **times** option so that a loop will be iterated a specific number of times. The first option creates what in general terms is called a *repeat* loop and the second option creates a primitive version of a *for* loop. The **varying** option for the perform statement provides a means for specifying the counter that controls a loop as well as the value by which it should be incremented. The 'procedure-name' option allows a perform statement to execute the statements in a paragraph or section that appears elsewhere in the program and the **thru** option allows the execution of a range of paragraphs or sections. None of these different options are essential for writing well-structured programs and the two options that allow the execution of paragraphs and sections should be avoided in general.

The **search** statement has a **varying** option for sequential searches that allows other indexes to be given the same values as the index for a table during a search. This can be useful when a program is using additional tables with matching entries so that when an entry is extracted from one table the other indexes that have been varied can then be used to extract the entries from the other tables.

The **write** statement includes a **page** option which will cause a program to generate a form feed for a report. The page option and the eop conditions are mutually exclusive.

Lastly, the **next sentence** phrase transfers control from the current sentence to the next sentence in the program. Sentences are terminated by the period character. Most of the programs in this text are only one sentence long. Therefore the effect of using a next sentence in most of these programs is to transfer control to the end of the program and not to the next statement. The **continue** statement should be used when a null statement is required and the next sentence phrase should be avoided.

18.3 FILES

The file-processing capabilites of COBOL are extensive and many features are usually considered to be beyond the scope of an introductory text. The most important of these is the use of **declaratives**. This feature allows one or more sections that are associated with one or more files to be written at the very beginning of the procedure division. When declaratives are used for a file the file statements such as read and write are written without their conditional phrases or the end of scope delimiters. For example, the read statement for a sequential file would simply be written as

```
read e1-file into w1-record
```

After a file statement such as open, close, read, or write is executed control is first passed back to the appropriate declaratives section for the file. Statements can be included within it to interrogate a return code from the operating system and to take any necessary action such as terminating the program or mapping the return code from the operating system into a local variable which may be more suited to the program's condition-testing strategy. Control is then passed back to the main program to the next statement after the one that initiated the file operation. This might be an evaluate statement that does selective processing depending on the state of the file. The advantage of this approach is that a correctly written program will never fail with a run-time error generated by the system. For example, an attempt to open a non-existent file will be reported back to the program thereby allowing the program to tell the user that the file does not exist and allowing the input of another file-name. Programs that need to be completely user friendly so that they never fail due to a file error are written using declaratives. If you intend other people to use your programs you should spend some time learning how to use declaratives.

It is possible to use **alternate keys** for an indexed file. The primary key must always be unique but the alternate keys can be duplicated. For example, one could create a file for a telephone directory in which the telephone number is used as the primary key and the name and postcode of the subscriber were each alternate keys. Such a file could be read by any of the keys thereby allowing a program to produce lists by name or lists by postcode without the need to sort records. These additional keys are supported by further indexes to the records in the file. Thus there may be many indexes but in every case only one set of records. An action such as deleting a record by its primary key value causes all of the indexes to be updated automatically.

COBOL also provides the means to control the *physical blocking* characteristics of data in files. Thus a program such as a master file update for a file of millions of records can be tuned to ensure that the records in the file are physically read in blocks that are optimum in size for the storage device and medium that is being used. In large applications this may result in a significant reduction in run time.

In applications where many users are accessing the same files at the same time it is possible to incorporate *record-locking* into programs by using language extensions that are provided by most of the major suppliers. They also often provide facilities for accessing databases from COBOL programs. None of these features are included in the standard.

18.4 OTHER

Many COBOL compilers are extended to allow additional usages for floating point numbers. (These usages closely correspond to the real types in FORTRAN and in Pascal.)

Furthermore, many compilers for other languages produce object code that is compatible with that which is produced for COBOL. The result is that external programs can be written in more than one language and then linked together to produce an executable program. In order to do this you need to determine how data is physically represented in the other language and then ensure that the same physical representation and parameter passing mechanism is chosen for parameters at the call interface. On systems such as the VAX signed binary numbers that take four bytes and strings of characters that are in multiples of four bytes are easily passed to programs in Pascal and FORTRAN. The reference and content mechanisms in COBOL correspond to the variable and value mechanisms in Pascal.

Finally, most systems are supplied with libraries of programs that can be called from COBOL as well as other high-level languages. These libraries are filled with programs that may assist you to create a new feature that is difficult or impossible to do in COBOL. For example, it is possible to discover with the help of system routines how many characters were typed at the keyboard for an input string. These could then be incorporated into a program such as accept3 thereby allowing applications to have this additional information. Calls to such programs should always be contained within a single external COBOL program that is made generally available to all application systems within an organization so that the portability of applications is not reduced.

18.5 CASE STUDY: TRANS1 (A STRING TRANSLATOR WRITTEN IN COBOL-74)

Program trans1 in Fig. 18.1 has been adapted from a sample program in a popular teaching text for COBOL-74. It reads a stream of 80 character card images as input and writes 160

```
 1 IDENTIFICATION DIVISION.
 2 PROGRAM-ID. TRANS1.
 3 ENVIRONMENT DIVISION.
 4 INPUT-OUTPUT SECTION.
 5 FILE-CONTROL.
 6 SELECT CARDFILE  ASSIGN TO "CARD.DAT".
 7 SELECT REPORTFILE ASSIGN TO "REPORT.DAT".
 8 DATA DIVISION.
 9 FILE SECTION.
10 FD CARDFILE LABEL RECORDS STANDARD
11             DATA RECORD INP-REC.
```

```
12 01  INP-REC.
13     02  INP-CHR PICTURE X OCCURS 80 TIMES.
14 FD REPORTFILE LABEL RECORDS STANDARD
15              DATA RECORD OUT-REC.
16 01  OUT-REC.
17     02  OUT-CHR PICTURE X OCCURS 160 TIMES.
18 WORKING-STORAGE SECTION.
19 77  SUBINPREC  PICTURE 99.
20 77  SUBOUTREC  PICTURE 999.
21 77  SUBTABLE   PICTURE 99.
22 01  TABLES.
23     02  TAB-SOURCE PICTURE X(20) VALUE "ABCDEFGHIJ0123456789".
24     02  FILLER REDEFINES TAB-SOURCE.
25         03  CHR-SOURCE PICTURE X OCCURS 20 TIMES.
26     02  TAB-TARGET PICTURE X(20) VALUE "0123456789ABCDEFGHIJ".
27     02  FILLER REDEFINES TAB-TARGET.
28         03  CHR-TARGET PICTURE X OCCURS 20 TIMES.
29 PROCEDURE DIVISION.
30 P0-INITIALIZE.
31     OPEN INPUT CARDFILE OUTPUT REPORTFILE.
32 P1-READ-REC.
33     READ CARDFILE AT END GO TO P2-CLOSE.
34     PERFORM P101-TRANSLATE-REC
35     WRITE OUT-REC.
36     GO TO P1-READ-REC.
37 P101-TRANSLATE-REC.
38     MOVE SPACES TO OUT-REC.
39     MOVE 1 TO SUBOUTREC.
40     PERFORM P102-TRANSLATE THRU P105-EXIT VARYING SUBINPREC
41        FROM 1 BY 1 UNTIL SUBINPREC = 81.
42 P102-TRANSLATE.
43     IF INP-CHR (SUBINPREC) = "]"
44         PERFORM P104-MOVE-ZERO 2 TIMES
45         GO TO P105-EXIT.
46     MOVE 1 TO SUBTABLE.
47 P103-LOOKUP.
48     IF INP-CHR (SUBINPREC) = CHR-SOURCE (SUBTABLE)
49         MOVE CHR-TARGET (SUBTABLE) TO OUT-CHR (SUBOUTREC)
50         ADD 1 TO SUBOUTREC
51         GO TO P105-EXIT.
52     IF SUBTABLE NOT = 20
53         ADD 1 TO SUBTABLE
54         GO TO P103-LOOKUP
55     ELSE
56         MOVE INP-CHR (SUBINPREC) TO OUT-CHR (SUBOUTREC)
57         ADD 1 TO SUBOUTREC
58         GO TO P105-EXIT.
59 P104-MOVE-ZERO. MOVE ZERO TO OUT-CHR (SUBOUTREC).
60                 ADD 1 TO SUBOUTREC.
61 P105-EXIT. EXIT.
62 P2-CLOSE.
63     CLOSE CARDFILE REPORTFILE
64     STOP RUN.
```

Figure 18.1 Program trans1

Main flowchart
(Level 1)

Controlled by line 34
(Level 2)

P0-INITIALIZE

| 31 | OPEN |

P1-READ-REC

| 33 | READ |

33 END — T

F

| 34 | PERFORM |

P101-TRANSLATE-REC

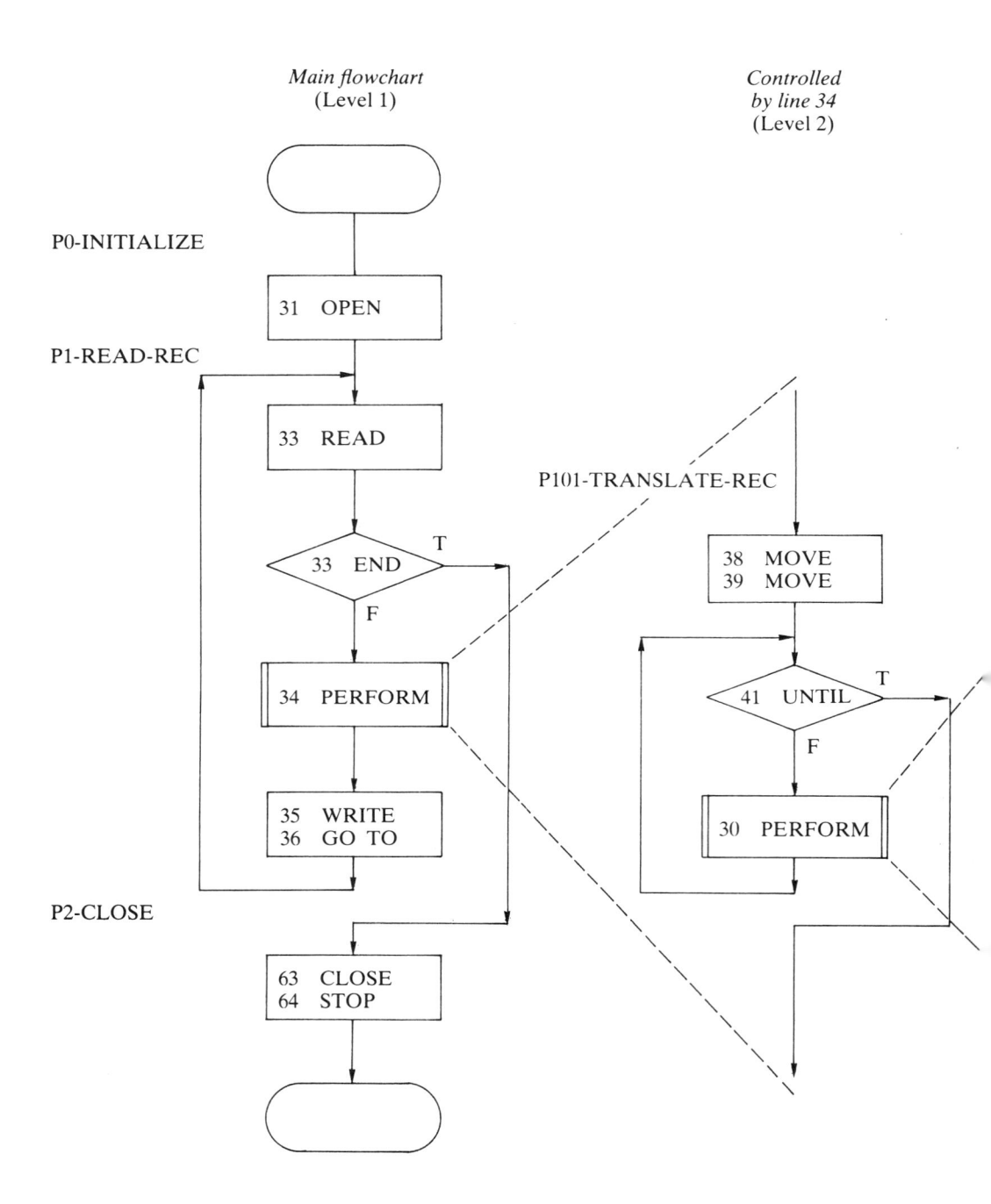

| 38 | MOVE |
| 39 | MOVE |

41 UNTIL — T

F

| 30 | PERFORM |

| 35 | WRITE |
| 36 | GO TO |

P2-CLOSE

| 63 | CLOSE |
| 64 | STOP |

Figure 18.2 Flowchart of program trans1

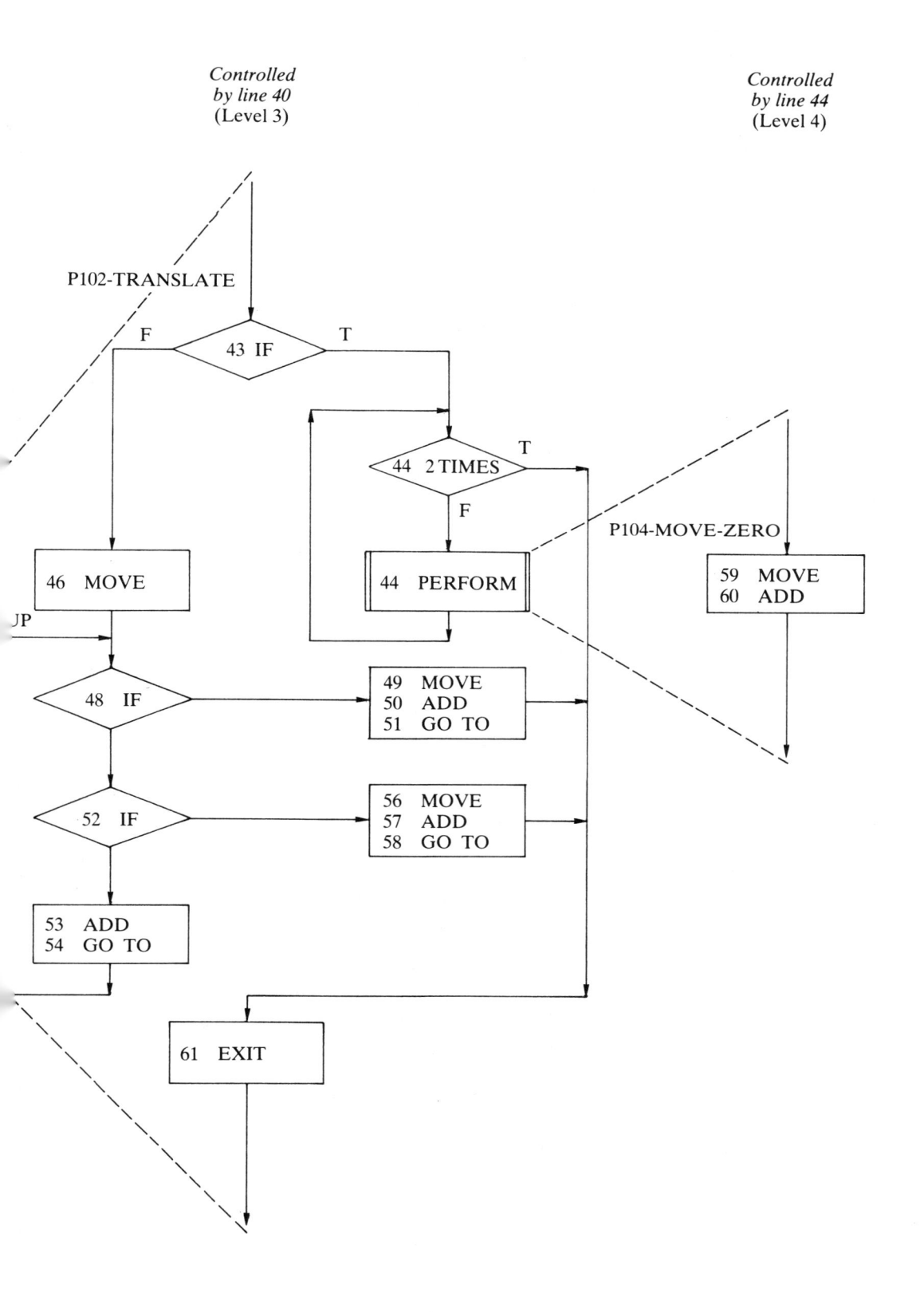

Controlled by line 40 (Level 3)   *Controlled by line 44* (Level 4)

character records as output. The purpose of the program is to do the following translations to output for each character of input:

1. The digits "0" . . "9" become "A" . . "J".
2. The alphabetics "A" . . "J" become "0" . . "9".
3. The character "]" becomes the two digits "00".
4. Any other character becomes a space.

Both files are defined as fixed-length record files. Under VAX/VMS COBOL automatically creates a fixed-length record when files are opened as output. However, the default file format is variable-length records. Therefore if you want to test trans1, write your own program to read in lines of text and output them as fixed-length card images. (You can convert text files using VAX/VMS utilities but this is a more complicated way to go about the task.)

Like many programs written prior to the latest standard it exhibits a number of structural weaknesses. Some of these can be directly attributed to failings in the language while others result from poor design practice. Nevertheless trans1 is a typical program of the past and by no means represents the worst possible case.

It should be a matter of concern for any COBOL programmer who wishes to write good programs in a clear style that trans1 is written in standard COBOL. (Remember that most of the features of COBOL-74 have been included in the third standard.) This means that statements of this kind could be combined with statements that have been more recently added to the language in order to produce programs of high complexity but low design quality.

Figure 18.2 contains a flowchart for program trans1. It is not intended as an exercise in flowcharting but rather as an aid in trying to comprehend the flow of control that is implemented by the program. Take a few minutes to try to acquaint yourself with the overall structure of trans1.

The main flowchart describes all of the statements that are executed by the program as it moves from the first to the last statement but excluding those that are performed. This is analogous to level 1 of the program. The next level contains those statements that are controlled by the perform at line 34. These statements are at level 2 and contained within paragraph P101-TRANSLATE-REC. This paragraph also contains a perform that uses the thru option as a means of controlling a set of paragraphs at level 3. Within level 3 a perform statement uses the times option to execute a paragraph at level 4.

Both levels 1 and 3 use go to statements for iteration and as a means of reaching the end of the level. These statements have the effect of coupling many statements together in ways which are difficult to understand and to test. It is possible to measure coupling in formal ways. For our purposes it is enough to realize that it is difficult to contemplate a change to the program without either studying its flowchart or having a deep understanding that is more or less an equivalent to its flowchart.

Program trans2 in Fig. 18.3 is a rewritten version that attempts to produce an improved quality program within the limitations of COBOL-74. The main changes involve the controlled use of go to statements and the use of sections.

```cobol
 1 IDENTIFICATION DIVISION.
 2 PROGRAM-ID. TRANS2.
 3 ENVIRONMENT DIVISION.
 4 INPUT-OUTPUT SECTION.
 5 FILE-CONTROL.
 6 SELECT CARDFILE   ASSIGN TO "CARD.DAT".
 7 SELECT REPORTFILE ASSIGN TO "REPORT.DAT".
 8 DATA DIVISION.
 9 FILE SECTION.
10 FD CARDFILE LABEL RECORDS STANDARD
11             DATA RECORD INP-REC.
12 01  INP-REC.
13     02  INP-CHR PICTURE X OCCURS 80 TIMES.
14 FD REPORTFILE LABEL RECORDS STANDARD
15             DATA RECORD OUT-REC.
16 01  OUT-REC.
17     02  OUT-CHR PICTURE X OCCURS 160 TIMES.
18 WORKING-STORAGE SECTION.
19 77  SUBINPREC   PICTURE 99.
20 77  SUBOUTREC   PICTURE 999.
21 77  SUBTABLE    PICTURE 99.
22 01  TABLES.
23     02  TAB-SOURCE PICTURE X(20) VALUE "ABCDEFGHIJ0123456789".
24     02  FILLER REDEFINES TAB-SOURCE.
25         03  CHR-SOURCE PICTURE X OCCURS 20 TIMES.
26     02  TAB-TARGET PICTURE X(20) VALUE "0123456789ABCDEFGHIJ".
27     02  FILLER REDEFINES TAB-TARGET.
28         03  CHR-TARGET PICTURE X OCCURS 20 TIMES.
29 PROCEDURE DIVISION.
30 A-START-END SECTION
31 P0-INITIALIZE.
32     OPEN INPUT CARDFILE OUTPUT REPORTFILE.
33 P1-READ-REC.
34     READ CARDFILE AT END GO TO P2-CLOSE.
35     MOVE SPACES TO OUT-REC.
36     MOVE 1 TO SUBOUTREC.
37
38     PERFORM B-TRANSLATE VARYING SUBINPREC
39        FROM 1 BY 1 UNTIL SUBINPREC = 81.
40
41     WRITE OUT-REC.
42     GO TO P1-READ-REC.
43 P2-CLOSE
44     CLOSE CARDFILE REPORTFILE
45     STOP RUN.
```

```
46
47 B-TRANSLATE SECTION.
48 P102-TRANSLATE.
49     IF  INP-CHR (SUBINPREC) = "]"
50         PERFORM P104-MOVE-ZERO 2 TIMES
51         GO TO P105-EXIT.
52     MOVE 1 TO SUBTABLE.
53 P103-LOOKUP.
54     IF  INP-CHR (SUBINPREC) = CHR-SOURCE (SUBTABLE)
55         MOVE CHR-TARGET (SUBTABLE) TO OUT-CHR (SUBOUTREC)
56         ADD 1 TO SUBOUTREC
57         GO TO P105-EXIT.
58     IF  SUBTABLE NOT = 20
59         ADD 1 TO SUBTABLE
60         GO TO P103-LOOKUP
61     ELSE
62         MOVE INP-CHR (SUBINPREC) TO OUT-CHR (SUBOUTREC)
63         ADD 1 TO SUBOUTREC
64         GO TO P105-EXIT.
65 P104-MOVE-ZERO
66         MOVE ZERO TO OUT-CHR (SUBOUTREC).
67             ADD 1 TO SUBOUTREC.
68 P105-EXIT
69     EXIT.
```

Figure 18.3 Program trans2

Program trans3 in Fig. 18.4 is a rewritten version of trans1. It attempts to translate the structure of the original program directly into statements that use scope delimiters. It demonstrates that once the flow of control of the original program has been improved, other defects in program design become more obvious.

```
 1 IDENTIFICATION DIVISION.
 2 PROGRAM-ID. TRANS3.
 3 ENVIRONMENT DIVISION.
 4 INPUT-OUTPUT SECTION.
 5 FILE-CONTROL.
 6 SELECT CARDFILE   ASSIGN TO "CARD.DAT".
 7 SELECT REPORTFILE ASSIGN TO "REPORT.DAT".
 8 DATA DIVISION.
 9 FILE SECTION.
10 FD   CARDFILE.
11 01   INP-REC.
12      02  INP-CHR  PICTURE X OCCURS 80 TIMES.
13 FD REPORTFILE.
14 01   OUT-REC.
15      02  OUT-CHR PICTURE X OCCURS 160 TIMES.
16 WORKING-STORAGE SECTION.
17 77  INP-SWX     PICTURE X VALUE "N".
18      88  INP-EOF         VALUE "Y".
19 77  SUBINPREC   PICTURE 99.
20 77  SUBOUTREC   PICTURE 999.
21 77  SUBTABLE    PIC 99.
22 01  TABLES.
23      02  TAB-SOURCE    PICTURE X(20) VALUE "ABCDEFGHIJ0123456789".
```

```
24      02  FILLER REDEFINES TAB-SOURCE.
25          03  CHR-SOURCE PICTURE X OCCURS 20 TIMES.
26      02  TAB-TARGET      PICTURE X(20) VALUE "0123456789ABCDEFGHIJ".
27      02  FILLER REDEFINES TAB-TARGET.
28          03  CHR-TARGET PICTURE X OCCURS 20 TIMES.
29  PROCEDURE DIVISION.
30  P0-INITIALIZE.
31      OPEN INPUT CARDFILE OUTPUT REPORTFILE
32      PERFORM TEST BEFORE UNTIL INP-EOF
33        READ CARDFILE
34          END
35            SET INP-EOF TO TRUE
36          NOT END
37            MOVE SPACES TO OUT-REC
38            MOVE 1 TO SUBOUTREC
39            PERFORM VARYING SUBINPREC FROM 1 BY 1 UNTIL SUBINPREC = 81
40              IF INP-CHR (SUBINPREC) = "]"
41                THEN
42                  PERFORM 2 TIMES
43                    MOVE ZERO TO OUT-CHR (SUBOUTREC)
44                    ADD 1 TO SUBOUTREC
45                  END-PERFORM
46                ELSE
47                  MOVE 1 TO SUBTABLE
48                  PERFORM TEST BEFORE UNTIL SUBTABLE = 20
49                    IF INP-CHR (SUBINPREC) = CHR-SOURCE (SUBTABLE)
50                      THEN
51                        MOVE CHR-TARGET (SUBTABLE) TO OUT-CHR (SUBOUTREC)
52                        MOVE 20 TO SUBTABLE
53                        ADD 1 TO SUBOUTREC
54                      ELSE
55                        IF SUBTABLE NOT = 20
56                          THEN
57                            ADD 1 TO SUBTABLE
58                          ELSE
59                            MOVE INP-CHR (SUBINPREC) TO OUT-CHR (SUBOUTREC)
60                            MOVE 20 TO SUBTABLE
61                            ADD 1 TO SUBOUTREC
62                        END-IF
63                    END-IF
64                  END-PERFORM
65              END-IF
66            END-PERFORM
67            WRITE OUT-REC
68        END-READ
69      END-PERFORM
70
71      CLOSE CARDFILE REPORTFILE
72      STOP RUN.
```

Figure 18.4 Program trans3

Program trans4 in Fig. 18.5 is a complete redesign of the program in the style of COBOL recommended in this text. It uses fixed-length records files. Program trans5 in Fig. 18.6 uses variable-length record files. It differs from trans4 in its file descriptions (lines, 13, 16, 17), its character counter for the output file (lines 31 to 33), and its routine for calculating the length of output records (lines 79 to 82).

```cobol
     1  identification division.
     2  program-id. trans4.
     3
     4  environment division.
     5  input-output section.
     6  file-control.
     7  select i1-file assign to "card.dat".
     8  select o2-file assign to "report.dat".
     9
    10  data division.
    11  file section.
    12  fd  i1-file.
    13  01  filler      pic x(80).
    14  fd  o2-file.
    15  01  o2-rec      pic x(160).
    16
    17  working-storage section.
    18  01  w1-file.
    19      03  filler              pic x       value "n".
    20          88  w1-eof                      value "y".
    21      03  w1-ref              pic 99.
    22          88  w1-start                    value 01.
    23          88  w1-converted                value 81.
    24      03  w1-rec              pic x(80).
    25      03  w1-filter           pic x(80).
    26
    27  01  w2-file.
    28      03  w2-ref              pic 999.
    29          88  w2-start                    value 001.
    30      03  w2-rec              pic x(160).
    31
    32  01  w3-tables.
    33      02  w3-old              pic x(20) value "ABCDEFGHIJ0123456789".
    34      02  w3-new              pic x(20) value "0123456789ABCDEFGHIJ".
    35      02  w3-space            pic x(20) value space.
    36
    37  procedure division.
    38  para1.
    39      open input   i1-file
    40           output  o2-file
    41
    42      perform test before until w1-eof
    43        read i1-file into w1-rec
    44          end
    45            set w1-eof to true
    46          not end
    47            move w1-rec to w1-filter
    48            inspect w1-rec    converting w3-old to w3-new
    49            inspect w1-filter converting w3-old to w3-new
    50            inspect w1-filter converting w3-new to w3-space
    51*           w1-rec now holds converted string except that:
    52*            - the "]" has not been expanded
    53*            - a non-space character in w1-filter marks the corresponding
    54*              character in w1-rec as illegal so that it can be
    55*              converted to a space.
    56
```

```
57             set w1-start to true
58             set w2-start to true
59             move spaces   to w2-rec
60             perform test before until w1-converted
61               evaluate true
62                 when   w1-rec(w1-ref:1) = "]"
63                   move "00" to w2-rec(w2-ref:2)
64                   add 2 to w2-ref
65                 when w1-filter(w1-ref:1) not = space
66                   add 1 to w2-ref
67                 when    other
68                   move w1-rec(w1-ref:1) to w2-rec(w2-ref:1)
69                   add 1 to w2-ref
70               end-evaluate
71               add 1 to w1-ref
72             end-perform
73             write o2-rec from w2-rec
74         end-read
75      end-perform
76
77      close i1-file o2-file
78      stop run.
79  end program trans4.
```

Figure 18.5 Program trans4

```
 1  identification division.
 2  program-id. trans5.
 3
 4  environment division.
 5  input-output section.
 6  file-control.
 7  select i1-file assign to "card.dat".
 8  select o2-file assign to "report.dat".
 9
10  data division.
11  file section.
12  fd  i1-file
13      record varying 1 to 80.
14  01  filler     pic x(80).
15  fd  o2-file
16      record varying 1 to 160
17      depending w2-ctr.
18  01  o2-rec     pic x(160).
19
20  working-storage section.
21  01  w1-file.
22      03  filler              pic x       value "n".
23          88  w1-eof                      value "y".
24      03  w1-ref              pic 99.
25          88  w1-start                    value 01.
26          88  w1-converted                value 81.
27      03  w1-rec              pic x(80).
28      03  w1-filter           pic x(80).
29
```

```cobol
30 01  w2-file.
31     03  w2-ctr    binary      pic 999  value 160.
32         88  w2-maxlen                  value 160.
33         88  w2-minlen                  value 001.
34     03  w2-ref                pic 999.
35         88  w2-start                   value 001.
36     03  w2-rec                pic x(160).
37
38 01  w3-tables.
39     03  w3-old                pic x(20) value "ABCDEFGHIJ0123456789".
40     03  w3-new                pic x(20) value "0123456789ABCDEFGHIJ".
41     03  w3-space              pic x(20) value space.
42
43 procedure division.
44 para1.
45     open input  i1-file
46          output o2-file
47
48     perform test before until w1-eof
49       read i1-file into w1-rec
50         end
51           set w1-eof to true
52         not end
53           move w1-rec to w1-filter
54           inspect w1-rec    converting w3-old to w3-new
55           inspect w1-filter converting w3-old to w3-new
56           inspect w1-filter converting w3-new to w3-space
57*          w1-rec now holds converted string except that:
58*            - the "]" has not been expanded
59*            - a non-space character in w1-filter marks the corresponding
60*              character in w1-rec as illegal so that it can be
61*              converted to a space.
62
63           set w1-start to true
64           set w2-start to true
65           move spaces  to w2-rec
66           perform test before until w1-converted
67             evaluate true
68               when   w1-rec(w1-ref:1) = "]"
69                 move "00" to w2-rec(w2-ref:2)
70                 add 2 to w2-ref
71               when w1-filter(w1-ref:1) not = space
72                 add 1 to w2-ref
73               when  other
74                 move w1-rec(w1-ref:1) to w2-rec(w2-ref:1)
75                 add 1 to w2-ref
77             end-evaluate
77             add 1 to w1-ref
78           end-perform
79           set w2-maxlen to true
80           perform test before until w2-minlen or w2rec(w2-ctr:1) not = space
81             subtract 1 from w2-ctr
82           end-perform
83           write o2-rec from w2-rec
84       end-read
85     end-perform
86
87     close i1-file o2-file
88     stop run.
89 end program trans5.
```

Figure 18.6 Program trans5

18.6 EXERCISES

18.6.1 General

1. Rewrite angle1 or angle2 from Chapter 8 as angle3. Remove all evaluate statements and use only if statements.
2. Rewrite trans5 as trans6 using a declaratives section. (You will need to refer to the *Language Reference Manual* and *User Guide* for your COBOL compiler. In particular, note that the read statement will have to become unconditional, that is, the end and not end phrases must be replaced by file status tests.)

18.6.2 Case study

3. Draw a flowchart for program trans5 and compare it to trans1. (Consider each scoped statement, e.g. perform . . . end-perform to be a predefined routine.)
4. Rewrite trans1 as trans1a so that the input pattern of "AA" is changed on output to "/".
5. Rewrite trans5 as trans5a with the same amendment as for Exercise 4.
6. Compare the programs trans1a and trans5a. Which was the easier to rewrite and why?
7. Rewrite trans5 and trans5b in which a called program translates the input pattern to the output pattern. All of the file handling should remain in the main program.
8. Rewrite trans1 as trans1b with a main program and a called program as described in Exercise 7. Do not use any features of the language that are not part of COBOL-74. Try to maintain the organization of the original as much as possible. (The called program must be an external program that is linked into the main program at link time.)
9. Compare the programs trans1b and trans5b. Which was the easier to rewrite?

Appendices

A
LISTS OF RESERVED WORDS

A.1 FULL LIST

The following list of reserved words contains less than 200 unique entries. It includes all of the COBOL words that are included in the programs in this text and that are considered essential.

accept	character(s)	down
access	close	dynamic
add, end-add	common	else
after	comp, computational	end
all	compute, end-compute	environment
alphabet	configuration	eop
alphabetic	content	error
alphabetic-lower	continue	evaluate, end-evaluate
alphabetic-upper	converting	exception
also	copy	exit
and	count	extend
any	data	external
ascending	delete	false
assign	delimited	fd
at	delimiter	file
before	depending	file-control
binary	descending	filler
bottom	display	first
by	divide, end-divide	footer
call	division	for

LISTS OF RESERVED WORDS

from
giving
global
go
high-value(s)
i–o
i–o-control
identification
if, end-if
in
index
indexed
initial
input
input–output
inspect
into
invalid
is
just, justified
key
last
leading
left
length
limit(s)
linage
linage-counter
line(s)
linkage
low-value(s)
merge
move
multiply, end-multiply
no
not
number
numeric
occurs
of
off
on
open
or
order

organization
other
output
overflow
packed-decimal
perform, end-perform
pic, picture
plus
pointer
position
procedure(s)
program
program-id
random
read, end-read
record(s)
redefines
reference(s)
relative
release
remainder
replacing
return, end-return
rewrite
right
rounded
run
sd
search, end-search
section
select
separate
sequential
set
sign
size
sort
sort-merge
space(s)
special-names
start
stop
string, end-string
subtract, end-subtract
symbolic

sync, synchronized
tallying
test
than
then
through, thru
time
times
to
top
trailing
true
unstring, end-unstring
until
up
usage
use
using
value(s)
varying
when

with
working-storage
write, end-write
zero(s), zeroes

ARITHMETIC
  OPERATORS
+
−
*
/
**

RELATION
  OPERATORS
=
>
<
>=
<=
not >
not <
not =

A.2 GENERAL LIST – X3.23

COBOL contains the following 357 reserved words. A valid compiler should recognize the complete list even though it may not implement the higher level features that require certain words:

accept	clock-units	debugging	end-subtract
access	close	decimal-point	end-unstring
add	cobol	declaratives	end-write
advancing	code	delete	enter
after	code-set	delimited	environment
all	collating	delimiter	eop
alphabet	column	depending	equal
alphabetic	comma	descending	error
alphabetic-lower	common	destination	esi
alphabetic-upper	communication	detail	evaluate
alphanumeric	comp	disable	every
alphanumeric-edited	computational	display	exception
also	compute	divide	exit
alter	configuration	division	extend
alternate	contains	down	external
and	content	duplicates	
any	continue	dynamic	false
are	control		fd
area	controls	egi	file
areas	converting	else	file-control
ascending	copy	emi	filler
assign	corr	enable	final
at	corresponding	end	first
author	count	end-add	footing
	currency	end-call	for
before		end-compute	from
binary	data	end-delete	
blank	date	end-divide	generate
block	date-compiled	end-evaluate	giving
bottom	date-written	end-if	global
by	day	end-multiply	go
	day-of-week	end-of-page	greater
call	de	end-perform	group
cancel	debug-contents	end-read	
cd	debug-item	end-receive	heading
cf	debug-line	end-return	high-value
ch	debug-name	end-rewrite	high-values
character	debug-sub-1	end-search	
characters	debug-sub-2	end-start	i–o
class	debug-sub-3	end-string	i–o-control

LISTS OF RESERVED WORDS

identification	multiple	program-id	segment-limit
if	multiply	purge	select
in			send
index	native	queue	sentence
indexed	negative	quote	separate
indicate	next	quotes	sequence
initial	no		sequential
initialize	not	random	set
initiate	number	rd	sign
input	numeric	read	size
input–output	numeric-edited	receive	sort
inspect		record	sort-merge
installation		records	source
into	object-computer	redefines	source-computer
invalid	occurs	reel	space
is	of	reference	spaces
	off	references	special-names
just	omitted	relative	standard
justified	on	release	standard-1
	open	remainder	standard-2
key	optional	removal	start
	or	renames	status
label	order	replace	stop
last	organization	replacing	string
leading	other	report	sub-queue-1
left	output	reporting	sub-queue-2
length	overflow	reports	sub-queue-3
less		rerun	subtract
limit	packed-decimal	reserve	sum
limits	padding	reset	suppress
linage	page	return	symbolic
linage-counter	page-counter	reversed	sync
line	perform	rewind	synchronized
line-counter	pf	rewrite	
lines	ph	rf	table
linkage	pic	rh	tallying
lock	picture	right	tape
low-value	plus	rounded	terminal
low-values	pointer	run	terminate
	position		test
memory	positive	same	text
merge	printing	sd	than
message	procedure	search	then
mode	procedures	section	through
modules	proceed	security	thru
move	program	segment	time

times	up	when	+
to	upon	with	−
top	usage	words	*
trailing	use	working-storage	/
true	using	write	**
type			>
	value	zero	<
unit	values	zeroes	=
unstring	varying	zeros	>=
until			<=

B
GLOSSARY

Entries that begin with an asterisk are general terms within computing that are not part of the COBOL jargon, e.g. tree. Other entries are COBOL terms.

abbreviated combined relation condition A relation condition in which successive subjects or subjects and operators are omitted. For example,

$((a > b)$ and $(a$ not $< c))$ or $(a$ not $< d)$

can be abbreviated in the following way:

$a > b$ and not $< c$ or d

*abstraction Concentration on aspects of a subject that are relevant to the purpose at hand to the exclusion of other things. See data abstraction and procedural abstraction.
access mode The manner in which records are to be operated upon within a file. The access modes that are available are established when a file is created. The select statement further restricts the modes available when a file is selected. Further restriction occurs as the result of an open statement. See mode, i-o mode, input mode, output mode.
*action An activity undertaken when a set of conditions is satisfied. See decision table.
actual decimal point The physical representation of the decimal point position in an edited numeric data item. The characters "." or "," can be used to do this. See assumed decimal point.
*actual parameter 1. The data that is passed at the time a call is made to a program.
  2. Sometimes the parameter identifier that is written as part of a call statement instead of its value at the time of the call. See formal parameter.
*algorithm A set of well-defined instructions for the solution of a problem in a finite number of steps. Many of the things that are true of algorithms are also true of programs.

In particular, it is difficult to prove that any but the simplest of algorithms or programs is correct. The validation of an algorithm or program is usually undertaken by verifying that it produces the correct output for known test cases of input. The greater the coverage of test cases the more likely it is that the algorithm or program can be used with confidence. In most cases algorithms are not directly compiled but are rewritten in languages such as COBOL. At this stage certain maxima are often introduced such as the size of the largest integer that can be processed. See program.

alphabetic character   A letter or a space character.

alphanumeric character   Any character in the computer's character set.

alternate record key   A key other than the prime record key that identifies a record in an indexed file.

area A   COBOL columns 8 to 11 inclusive. This area is used to begin certain important statements and elements.

area B   COBOL column 12 and beyond. The size of area B is defined by the implementor. Many implementations extend only to column 72 inclusive because this was the extent of the area in COBOL-74.

arithmetic expression   Any of the following is an arithmetic expression:

1. Identifier of a numeric elementary item.
2. Numeric literal.
3. Any combination of 1 or 2 separated by arithmetic operators or parentheses according to the standard rules of arithmetic.

arithmetic operator   A single character or fixed two-character combination belonging to the following set:

    +   addition
    −   subtraction
    *   multiplication
    /   division
    **   exponentiation

arithmetic statement   A statement that causes an arithmetic operation to be executed. The arithmetic statements are add, compute, divide, multiply and subtract.

*****array**   An ordered collection of elements of the same type for which particular elements can be referenced by means of a subscript or index. In COBOL arrays are written by using the occurs clause in conjunction with the definition of the element. The resulting collection is known as a table. COBOL uses subscripts or indexes against the element identifier whereas other languages such as Pascal give a name to the array which is then subscripted or indexed. See table.

ascending key   A key upon which the data in a table is ordered starting with the lowest key and ending with the highest key.

assign   A clause of the file-control entry that in conjunction with the select clause gives information for resolving the external name of a file to its internal name.

*****assignment**   The action of causing a data item to take a new value. COBOL does not have an assignment operator such as the := operator of Pascal. In COBOL the arithmetic statements and the move statement imply assignment to one or more data items.

*****assignment compatibility**   A characteristic of operands that ensures that given the value of the subject operand(s), the value of the object operand(s) can be defined by the operation. Languages that contain well-defined types, e.g. Pascal, tend to have clear rules concerning assignment compatibility and hence incompatibility. COBOL does not contain strongly defined data types and therefore it is possible to make assignments which have undefined results and which do not necessarily generate a run-time error that halts execution. It is always the responsibility of the COBOL programmer to ensure that a data item is never used in a way that is incompatible with its implied type and value. See class and category.

assumed decimal point   A decimal point which does not involve the existence of an actual character in a data item. It has logical meaning but no physical representation. See actual decimal point.

at end condition   See end condition.

*****binary**   A number system using base 2. Binary numbers can be represented in computers as strings of bits in which the string lengths are usually implemented as powers of two. Thus binary numbers stored as 8, 16, 32 and 64 bits are commonly available.

*****binary decision**   A decision that can be represented as two states. The two states are often interpreted as exclusive pairs such as false and true, no and yes, or off and on.

*****binary search**   A searching strategy in which the keys are ordered prior to the start of the search and in which the set of keys containing a possible match is successively halved.

*****binding**   The resolution of a name to a particular instance. For example, the formal parameters in a program are bound to particular actual parameter values when a call is made. Binding may occur at the earliest stage of compilation or at later stages until the moment of execution. For example, a call statement that uses the literal option will have the name of the called program bound at the time of compilation whereas a call using an identifier is not bound until the call is made during program execution.

*****binding power**   See precedence.

block   A physical unit of storage that is normally composed of one or more logical records. For mass storage files, a block may contain a portion of a logical record. The size of a block has no direct relationship to the logical size of a file. The term is a synonym for physical record.

*****box diagram**   A set of nested boxes that is used to visualize the nested structure of programs.

*****buffer**   A temporary storage area for physical records that are being read into or written from a program. The buffer sits logically between the program and the external structure which might be a file, the keyboard or the screen.

*****byte**   A group of bits that can be used to represent a unit at a higher level of abstraction, e.g. a character. Nowadays a byte usually consists of 8 bits but in some fields such as communications there may be a need to use bytes with greater or fewer bits.

*****call**   A statement that transfers control to another program with the provision for a resumption of control at the statement after the call.

called program   A program which is the object of a call statement. The called program upon completion returns control to its calling program.

calling program   A program that executes a CALL to another program.

cancel   A statement that references the name of a program and ensures that the next time the program is called it will be in its initial state.

*****carriage return**   See RETURN.

category A data concept that attempts to formalize the rules for determining the correctness of a data item with reference to its picture clause. There are five categories: alphabetic, numeric, numeric edited, alphanumeric edited and alphanumeric. It is possible through group moves or moves to redefined items to cause the contents of a data item to be incompatible with its category.

character The basic indivisible unit of the COBOL language. In a byte-oriented computer a character will be stored in a single byte.

character position A character position is the amount of physical storage required to store a single standard data format character whose usage is display. Further characteristics of the physical storage are defined by the implementor.

character set The complete COBOL character set consists of the characters listed below:

Character	Meaning
0, 1 . . 9	digit
A . . Z	upper-case letter
a . . z	lower-case letter
	space
+	plus sign; addition
−	minus sign; subtraction; hyphen
*	asterisk; multiplication
/	slant; division
=	equal sign
$	currency sign
,	comma (decimal point)
;	semicolon
.	period or full-stop (decimal point)
"	quotation mark
(	left parenthesis
)	right parenthesis
>	greater than
<	less than
:	colon

See collating sequence.

character-string 1. A sequence of contiguous characters.

2. A sequence of contiguous characters which form a word, a literal, a picture character-string or a comment-entry.

*****child** See tree.

class condition The truth proposition that the content of a data item is exclusively alphabetic, alphabetic-upper, alphabetic-lower, numeric, or exclusively consists of the characters listed in a class-name definition.

class-name A user-defined word in the special-names paragraph that supports user-defined class tests in program statements. It assigns a name to the truth proposition that the content of a data item consists exclusively of the characters listed in its definition. Class-name tests can only be made against items that are defined with the symbol 'x' or 'a', that is, items that are in class alphanumeric or alphabetic. As such it provides a means for defining subsets of these two classes.

class test See class condition.

clause A word or words that specify an attribute of an entry. Thus select is a clause and not a statement.

*****cohesion** A characteristic of statements within a program that considers their relationship towards a common task. A set of statements may be referred to as exhibiting high cohesion or low cohesion according to some means of measurement which is either formal or informal. See coupling.

collating sequence The sequence in which the characters that are acceptable to a computer are ordered for purposes such as sorting and comparing. All COBOL implementations have a default collating sequence such as ASCII. COBOL provides facilities for programs to use collating sequences other than the default.

combined relation condition See abbreviated combined relation condition.

comment A line in a program with an asterisk '*' in the indicator area.

common program A program which, despite being directly contained within another program, may be called from any program directly or indirectly contained in that other program.

*****compatibility** A characteristic of operands or other elements that are used together to achieve a result. For example, a divisor of 0 is incompatible with the / operator, the number nine and the ASCII character "9" are incompatible in the condition 9 = "9", and a subject of false is incompatible with a literal such as "xx" as an object.

*****compilation unit** A unit of object code produced by a compiler. In COBOL a compilation unit may contain nested programs. It may also contain references to statements that were copied into the compiler's input stream as the result of processing a copy statement. See object file, run unit.

compile time The time at which a source program is translated by a compiler to an object program.

*****compiler** A program that translates high-level code such as COBOL source program into a lower-level code such as the object code of a computer. A compiler translates the whole of the program during a single execution. Some compilers may also produce an intermediate code which is then interpreted by a run-time system. See interpreter.

compiler directing statement A statement beginning with a compiler-directing verb (copy, enter, replace, use) that causes the compiler to take a specific action during compilation.

complex condition A condition in which one or more logical operators act upon one or more conditions.

compound condition See complex condition.

*****computer → digital computer** An electronic machine or system made up of such machines that processes discrete units of data. Processing is defined by instructions that implement logical, arithmetical and branching operations for a particular computer. Both instructions and data are stored in memory. A program is a set of instructions that can be executed. All computation is carried out within a finite number system which is usually binary.

computer-name A system-name that identifies the computer upon which the program is to be compiled or executed.

*****computer system** 1. A computer together with its operating system, hardware devices such as disk drives, and software such as text editors and compilers.

2. A system made up of computers.

*concatenation   A function that forms a single string of characters from two given strings by placing the second after the first.
condition   A truth proposition in a program which can be determined at run time.
condition-name   A user-defined word that names a subset of values that a conditional variable may assume. Its uniqueness of reference rules are the same as those for a data name. Its level number is 88.
condition-name condition   The truth proposition that the value of a conditional variable is a member of the set of values. The condition is attributed to a condition-name which is associated with the conditional variable.
conditional expression   A simple or complex condition specified in an evaluate if, perform, or search statement. See also simple condition, complex condition, and abbreviated combined relation condition.
conditional statement   A conditional statement specifies that the truth value of a condition is to be determined and that the subsequent action of the program at run time is dependent on this truth value.
conditional test   A test that when made yields a result of true or false.
conditional variable   A data item which has condition names associated with it.
configuration section   A section of the environment division that specifies certain characteristics of the computer for which the program is intended. Its most important entry is the special-names entry. See special-names.
contained program   A program that exists within the source of another program. A directly contained program exists at the next level of nesting whereas an indirectly contained program is contained at a lower level of nesting. A synonym for nested program.
*context dependent   A characteristic such that the meaning or interpretation of an element cannot be known completely without considering the particular instances of its use. For example, the element thru is used in a number of entries and statements and its meaning is dependent on the particular entry or statement that uses it.
*contiguous characters   Characters that appear consecutively.
*contiguous items   Items that are described by consecutive entries in the data division and that bear a definite hierarchical relationship to each other.
*contiguous words   Words in memory that are at consecutive addresses.
*control break   A change in the pattern of processing that comes about by recognizing a change between something that has just been processed when compared with something that is about to be processed. A common control break to occur in data processing concerns sorted files of transactions where a break occurs between each set of transactions for the different unique keys as identified by a particular field on each record.
*control line   See structure chart.
*counter   A data item used for storing a number in a manner that permits the number to be increased or decreased by a specified value. A counter is usually initialized to an arbitrary value such as zero prior to the execution of a set of statements that are being counted.
*coupling   A characteristic of statements or programs when compared with one another such that a change in one causes a change in the other. For example, a reference parameter is likely to couple the behaviour between a calling program and its called program. See cohesion.

currency sign   The character $ in the character set. The special-names entry can be used to change this character to another from the available set.

currency symbol   The character defined by the currency sign clause in the special-names paragraph. If no currency sign clause is written the currency symbol is identical to the currency sign.

*****cursor control**   The ability to manipulate the cursor under the control of a program. The COBOL standard does not define cursor control statements. Some COBOL compilers have extensions that do this. It is possible to write a small program to implement cursor control provided that the characters needed for a particular screen are known.

*****data abstraction**   A principle that constrains the manipulation of data objects to the operations that are defined by its data type. COBOL does not have a high degree data abstraction. See abstraction and type.

data clause   A clause in a data description entry that provides information describing a particular attribute of a data item.

data description entry   An entry in the data division that is composed of a level number followed by a data-name, if required, and then followed by a set of data clauses as required.

data division   The division that describes the data that is to be processed by the program. It is optional.

data entry   See data description entry.

data item   A unit of data (excluding literals) defined by a program. See variable.

data-name   A user-defined word that names a data item described in a data description entry. When used in the general formats, data-name represents a word which must not be reference-modified, subscripted, or qualified unless specifically permitted by the rules of the format. See identifier.

*****data processing**   Operations routinely applied with machine assistance to data in order to convert it into information for particular human purposes. Usually the term is reserved for cases where specialists are dedicated to the task.

*****data stream**   A term which implies an input or output order for data without implying that it is physically stored in a sequential file. Thus a particular program will introduce or generate a stream of data as the result of executing successive input or output statements.

*****database**   A collection of inter-related values and the means of relating one set of values to other matching sets. Normally databases contain sets of records within one or more physical files, and key values that occur in one set of records can be used to select records from other sets. It is not normal practice to refer to data in sequential files as a database. It is now uncommon in computing to refer to a database outside the context of a database management system.

*****database management system**   The software interface that manages a database as well as the database itself. Most systems provide an interactive interface so that queries can be made directly from the keyboard. The same queries can be made under program control by direct calls to the software.

date   A conceptual data item that can be accessed from the system by the accept statement. Day, day-of-week and time are also available from the system. The logical contents of all of these items is defined by COBOL but there is some discretion allowed in this implementation. In consequence, their use is not fully portable.

day-of-week   See date.

*****DBMS**   See database management system.

*****debug**   1.   A loose term meaning the act of attempting to remove semantic errors from a program. Such errors are nearly always human in origin and arise from an inability to construct a program to meet the user's specification.

2.   Use of debug statements defined by the now obsolete COBOL debug module.

declarative sentence   A compiler-directing sentence consisting of a single use statement terminated by a separator period.

declaratives   A set of one or more special purpose sections written at the beginning of the procedure division. Declaratives are used to specify procedures for trapping file-handling exceptions. As a result the program must use imperative formats for its file-operation statements.

*****decision table**   A table that relates sets of conditions to actions that should be undertaken. Usually a decision table contains a row for each input to a decision (condition stub) and a column for each set of input values that results in an output (condition entry). Below the condition stub additional rows list all of the possible actions (action stub). Below the condition entry an indication is given in the action entry for those actions which should be undertaken. Thus the two stubs list all of the conditions and actions and the two entries list all of the rules as columns. Each rule maps a set of input values to a set of output actions. Limited-entry tables restrict conditions to the values true and false. Extended-entry tables allow multi-value conditions. Both forms of tables can be implemented in COBOL with the evaluate statement.

de-edit   The logical removal of all editing characters from a numeric edited data item in order to determine the item's unedited numeric value.

delimited scope statement   Any statement which includes its explicit scope terminator.

delimiter   A character or sequence of characters that identifies the beginning or end of a string of characters.

*****delimiter-list**   A list of delimiters used by the simple syntax for the inspect statement.

*****denary**   A number system using base 10. It is also referred to as the decimal system.

descending key   A key upon which the data in a table is ordered starting with the highest key and ending with the lowest key.

*****detail line**   A line of information in a report that corresponds to a record from a file. For example, a sales record in a file might be reported as a sales detail line. See also header, trailer and footer.

*****dialect**   A version of a language such as COBOL that has been extended to incorporate other features that are non-standard COBOL. Some dialects of COBOL omit standard features when their own extensions provide a different implementation of the same or a similar functionality. Such dialects are inferior in that they encourage the writing of non-portable programs.

digit position   The amount of physical storage required to store a single digit. This amount may vary depending on the usage specified. If the usage is display then a digit position is synonymous with a character position. For other type of usage the physical storage is defined by the implementor.

*****directly contained**   See contained.

*****doubleword**   See word.

*****dynamic**   The opposite of static.

dynamic access An access mode in which specific logical records can be obtained from or placed into a mass storage file in a non-sequential manner and obtained from a file in a sequential manner during the scope of the same open statement.

editing character A single character or a fixed two-character combination belonging to the following set:

Character	Meaning
b	space
0	zero
+	plus
−	minus
cr	credit
db	debit
z	zero suppress
*	cheque protect
$	currency sign
,	comma (decimal-point)
.	period (decimal-point)
/	slant, slash, solidus

These characters are used to construct picture clauses that implement editing masks.

*****element** See language element and table element.

elementary item A data item that is not further subdivided.

end condition A condition caused during the execution of a read, return or search statement. When it becomes true as the result of a read or return statement no next record exists. When it becomes true as the result of a search statement the search terminates without satisfying any of the when phrases.

end program header Three words followed by a period and taking the form:

    end program program-name.

The end program header is optional for the program at nesting level 1 in order to maintain conformity with the COBOL-74 standard.

entry 1. Any set of consecutive clauses terminated by a period and written in the first three divisions of a program. See statement and sentence.

    2. See decision table.

environment division The second division of a COBOL program. It specifies those aspects that are dependent on the physical characteristics of a specific computer. It is optional.

*****escape** 1. A non-printable control character that changes the meaning of one or more characters that follow it. In the ASCII collating sequence the escape character has the value 27d.

    2. A programming structure in which control is passed immediately to the end of the structure by means of a forward phrase when no further statements within the structure can be executed. This structure is not directly supported by the syntax of COBOL. Therefore it must be programmed, most commonly by using a go to statement for each forward and a single paragraph for the end-escape.

*evaluation   See order of evaluation.

*execution history   All of the information that is needed to describe how a program is executed. In theory, this includes the initial data state of the program together with the data states produced after the execution of each statement in the program. See also debug and trace.

execution time   See run time.

explicit scope terminator   A reserved word which terminates the scope of a particular statement in the procedure division, e.g. end-perform.

exponentiation   The arithmetic operation of raising a number to a power. COBOL allows numbers to be raised to a fractional power. Therefore a square root can be derived by raising a number to the power of 0.5. The exponentiation operator is **.

expression   An arithmetic or conditional expression.

extended entry decision table   See decision table.

external attribute   An attribute given to a record or a file so that every program in the run unit that describes the record or file can use it.

*external program   A term to denote a called program that is available to the run unit but which was separately compiled from the calling program. It may contain nested programs.

*facility   A property of a language or system that enables efficient solutions for a class of problem. For example, the sort statement provides a facility for sorting records. In most cases it provides a standard interface to the sorting facilities provided by the operating system. See feature.

*fan-in   The visual appearance of control lines on a structure chart when a program is called by more than one calling program. In data processing fan-in usually occurs when a called program is required to provide an enhanced facility for the benefit of other programs, e.g. data validation, screen management.

*fan-out   The visual appearance of control lines on a structure chart when a program calls more than one called program. In data processing fan-out usually occurs when the root program calls programs that are designed to handle certain transactions or other inputs.

*feature   A characteristic that distinguishes a language from others. For example, reference modification, the evaluate statement, and file handling are all features of COBOL. See facility.

*field   A somewhat vague term that is used to denote a contiguous area of data that is to be treated as a unit. Thus the referencing of a field is dependent on the context in which it is referenced.

figurative constant   Certain reserved words are used to reference specific constant values which are generated by the compiler. These words are never bounded by quotation marks. The singular and plural forms may be used interchangeably. The figurative constants are:

[all] zero,	[all] zeros,	[all] zeroes
[all] space,	[all] spaces	
[all] high-value,	[all] high-values	
[all] low-value,	[all] low-values	
[all] quote,	[all] quotes	

In addition, a literal, a display data item or symbolic-character can be used with the reserved word all to generate a figurative constant. The literal cannot be numeric if it is more than one character long:

[all] literal
[all] symbolic-character

When the figurative constant represents a string of one or more characters, the length of the string is determined by the compiler.

file A collection of logical records. See file control entry.

file clause A clause that appears as part of a file description entry (fd) or sort-merge file description entry (sd).

file connector A storage area which contains information about a file and is used as the link between a file-name and a physical file and between a file-name and its associated record area.

file control entry A select clause and all its subordinate clauses which declare the relevant physical attributes of a file.

file description entry An entry that is composed of the indicator (fd) followed by a file-name and then followed by a set of file clauses.

file-name A user-defined word that names a file connector.

file organization The permanent logical file structure established at the time that a file is created.

file position indicator A conceptual item that contains the value of the current key within the key of reference for an indexed file, or the record number of the current record for a sequential file, or the relative record number of the current record for a relative file, or indicates that no next logical record exists or can be established. The indicator is not directly referenced by a COBOL program.

*__file processing__ Usually the activity of reading the contents of one or more files in order to produce one or more files. Any processing where the management of files is the predominant activity. See data processing.

filler This keyword is used to specify a data-name which is not referenced explicitly. It may be used to name a conditional variable because such use does not require explicit reference to the data item itself but only to the value therein by using condition-names.

*__filter__ A program that transforms one input stream into another according to a clear and generally small set of well-defined rules.

fixed file attributes Information about a file that is established when a file is created and that cannot be changed subsequently. These attributes include the organization of a file (sequential, relative, indexed), the prime record key, the alternate record keys, the code set, the minimum and maximum record size, the record type (fixed, variable), the collating sequence of keys, and other factors relating to physical storage.

fixed-length record A record associated with a file whose file description or sort-merge description entry requires that all records contain the same number of character positions.

*__flow of control__ The path a program follows through its statements when it executes. Typically the pattern of flow changes in response to changes in input. See trace.

*__flowchart__ A diagrammatic means of showing the low-level structure of a program. Flowcharts use boxes (sequence), diamonds (decisions), and directed arcs (flow of control). They do not lend themselves to illustrating the structure of a program using nested structured statements and provide no information concerning data. See flowgraph.

*__flowgraph__ A diagrammatic means of showing flow of control in a program. Flowgraphs often use circles (points of decision) and directed arcs (flow of control). Flowgraphs are easily represented as tables and therefore are often the basis for specifying input-driven solutions where the input is a command language.

***footer**   A line that appears at the bottom of a page. It often contains totals, page numbers, or other summary information. See header, trailer and detail line.

***formal parameter**   The information given in the using phrase of a called program. (It is formal in the sense that it merely states the type of data that the called program expects to receive.) See actual parameter.

format   The convention used for specifying the syntax of COBOL. Sometimes referred to as the reference format or instruction format. The formats fulfil the same purpose for COBOL as other techniques such as syntax diagrams do for Pascal. See full format, simple format and general format.

***forward**   See escape.

***full format**   The instruction format used in this text. A full format does not include the many alternatives provided by a general format. It also omits optional reserved words. See format.

***function**   1. A called program that maps one set of values to another. Some languages such as Pascal implement functions such that the function call stands in the place of a value, e.g. succ(x) returns the value that is the successor to x. In COBOL functions of this type are not supported and would have to be simulated by a call statement, e.g. `call "succ" using content x reference y` in which y would hold the returned successor value.

2. Human purpose or goal that is required of a program or system.

***functional behaviour**   Correct behaviour relative to a purpose or goal as opposed to dysfunctional behaviour.

***functional decomposition**   A design process whereby the overall purpose of a program is stated in terms of called programs in which each called program achieves some purpose for the benefit of the calling program or programs.

***garbage**   Data in memory for which initial values have not been established or which has been corrupted during program execution.

general format   The reference format as published in the X3.23 standard. See format.

global name   A name that is declared in only one program but which may be referenced from that program or from any program contained within it.

group item   A data item that contains elementary items.

***half-word**   See word.

***hashing**   Any technique for mapping a set of unique values into a smaller set of values by means of a hash function. A good hash function distributes the keys fairly across the smaller set. Mapping a large set into a smaller set means that two or more keys from the large set may map to the same key in the smaller set. Therefore any algorithm for storing and retrieving data by means of hashing must also deal with this problem of 'collision'. Hashing is most commonly used in data processing with relative files and by compilers for tables of symbols that are required during compilation.

***header**   1. A line or group of lines in a report that are at the beginning of the report (report header). Also a similar group at the beginning of a page (page header). See also trailer, footer, and detail line.

2. The first record in a file of records and holding summary information concerning the records that follow.

hexadecimal   A number system using base 16.
hierarchy   In computing a top-down arrangement of data or programs that can be visualized as a tree.
hit   See transaction.
identification division   The first division of a COBOL program in which the program name as well as the initial and/or common attributes are specified.
identifier   A syntactically correct combination of a data-name, with its qualifiers, subscripts, and reference modifiers, as required for uniqueness of reference, that names a data item. The rules for identifiers associated with the general formats may in some instances specifically prohibit qualification, subscripting or reference modification. See data-name.
imperative statement   A statement observing the following rules:

1. A statement that specifies an unconditional action, e.g. move, compute without an overflow clause.
2. A conditional statement that is delimited by its explicit scope delimiter, e.g. end-compute, end-perform.
3. Any sequence of statements obeying the above two rules.

implementation   1. A COBOL compiler on a particular computer system.
    2. The running of a program in its final required form as opposed to its specification or its test runs.
implementor   The person or people who write:

1. A COBOL compiler for a particular computer system.
2. A data processing application system.

implementor-name   A system-name that refers to a particular feature available to the COBOL program from the virtual environment.
implicit scope terminator   A separator period which terminates the scope of all preceding unterminated statements or a phrase which by its appearance indicates the end of scope of all preceding phrases.
implied decimal point   See assumed decimal point.
index   A special register that holds values for an index data item.
index data item   An item that stores values that are associated with an index-name. The form of storage is specified by the implementor. As a result an index data item does not have a picture clause. See subscript.
indexed file   A file with indexed organization.
indexed organization   The permanent logical file structure in which each record is identified by the value of one or more keys within that record.
indicator area   COBOL column 7. This column may contain one of the following:

* *   indicating that the rest of the line is a comment.
* /   indicating that the compiler listing should generate a form feed.
* -   indicating a continuation of an element from the previous line.

indirectly contained   See contained program.
initial program   A program that is placed into an initial state every time the program is called in a run unit.
initial state   The state of a program when it is first called in a run unit.

initialization   See also standard initialization.
*__inline__   A characteristic of statements which are contained within the scope of other statements. For example, statements held within a perform . . . end-perform scope.
input mode   The state of a file after execution of an open statement with the input phrase specified for that file and before the execution of its close statement.
input procedure   A section in the procedure division to which control is given by a sort statement prior to the beginning of the sort and before there are records in the sort file. Release statements in the procedure cause records to be written sequentially into the sort file.
*__input stream__   A flow of input characters, data items or records. See data stream.
instruction format   See format.
integer   1. In COBOL a numeric literal or numeric data item that is a whole number. When the word integer appears in the formats it must be an unsigned whole number greater than zero unless otherwise specified.
  2. A signed whole number.
*__interface__   A junction between two programs where control can be passed from one to the other.
*__internal file__   A file that exists for use by a program only during its execution. In COBOL a sort file is an example of an internal file.
*__internal program__   See nested program.
*__internal representation__   A collective term for any form of numeric representation in memory that does not represent the digits as characters. For example, the usage binary implies an internal representation.
*__interpreter__   A language processor that analyses statements and then carries out the required actions directly. Languages such as BASIC are often interpreted. See compiler.
i–o mode   The state of a file after execution of an open statement with the i-o phrase specified for that file and before the execution of its close statement.
item   A common synonym for data item.
*__iteration__   The repetition of a process from an initial condition that is established prior to the repetition and until a final condition is achieved. The process itself usually contributes towards reaching the final condition.
justification   See left justification; right justification.
key   A data item used to identify the ordering of data.
key of reference   A primary or alternate key currently being used to access records within an indexed file.
*__keyword__   See reserved word.
*__language__   A precise notation for describing programs. All programming languages are artificial in that they have syntax and semantic restrictions placed upon them to remove ambiguity and thus make their use mechanistic. As a result it is possible to execute programs on computers.
language element   An indivisible unit of functionality within the COBOL language. For example, a string of spaces and/or carriage returns is a single element as are reserved words and relational operators. Therefore the line:

```
    evaluate      e1 numeric and e1 > 9
```

consists of 15 elements. See also table element.

*language translator   A program that is capable of mapping one computing language into another. The term covers both compilers and interpreters for high-level languages such as COBOL and Pascal as well as command interpreters used in operating systems or other programmed systems such as text editors and spreadsheets where a language is implemented.

left justification   The alignment of a source string of characters from the left to the right of a target data item. When the source is shorter than the target, the target is padded with spaces. When the source is longer than the target, the target is truncated. See right justification.

level   See nesting and hierarchy.

level indicator   A peculiar COBOL term for the two alphabetic characters that identify a specific type of file or a position in a hierarchy. The level indicators in the data division are cd, fd, rd, sd.

level number   A user-defined word expressed as a number. It indicates the hierarchical position of a data item (01 to 49) or special properties such as a condition-name (88). The level number for a record is 01.

level-88 item   A synonym for condition-name.

*limited entry decision table   See decision table.

*limit-test   A test defined as part of the full syntax of the unstring statement.

linage-counter   A special register whose value points to the current position within the page body.

*line feed   See Return.

linkage section   The section in the data division of a called program that describes data items available from the calling program as a result of a call.

*linker   A program that combines separately compiled programs and produces a single executable image that resolves references between them.

*list   A finite ordered sequence of items, objects or elements.

literal   A character string whose value is implied by an ordered set of characters of which the literal is composed or by specification or a reserved word which references a figurative constant. Every literal belongs to one of two types: nonnumeric or numeric.

*local   A term usually applied to data to denote that the usage of the data is restricted to the program that defines it and allocates storage to it. See global name.

*logarithmic search   A synonym for binary search.

logical operator   One of the reserved words: not, and, or.

logical page   A conceptual entity consisting of the top margin, the page body, and the bottom margin.

logical record   The most inclusive data item. The level-number for a record is 01. A record may be either an elementary item or a group item. The term is synonymous with record.

*loop   A general term for any statement or set of statements that causes iteration. See iteration.

*machine-independence   See portability.

*main program   The root program in an executable program.

*mask   See editing character and picture clause.

mass storage   A medium in which files may be organized and maintained in both a sequential and non-sequential manner. An example is a magnetic disk.

mnemonic-name A user-defined word that is associated with a specific implementor-name.
mode A term that relates a file to its logical file operations. See access mode, i-o mode, input mode and output mode.
module 1. A program that has a well-defined function and interface and which works in co-operation with other modules to produce an overall result.
  2. One of the functional modules used to define the COBOL standard.
nested program A program that is written as text within the source statements of another program.
*****nesting** A term that denotes embedded instances of similar objects, e.g. nested programs or nested loops. See also contained program and scope.
nesting level 1 The highest level of a nest of programs or statements.
*****nibble** The first or last four bits of a byte.
nonnumeric literal A character-string delimited by quotation marks. They can be from 1 to 160 characters in length. The characters in a literal can be any of the printable characters in the computer character set. Two contiguous quotation marks '""' can be used to represent one quotation mark within a nonnumeric literal. All nonnumeric literals are alphanumeric. See literal.
numeric character One of the characters "0" . . "9".
numeric literal A character-string constructed from the characters "+" or "−", "0" . . "9" and the ".". They can be from 1 to 18 digits in length, can be preceded by a sign if it is required, and can contain one decimal point which must appear after the sign and before the last digit. They are not enclosed in quotation marks. See literal.
object file The file to which a compiler writes the object program from a compilation.
object list A list of one or more selection objects separated by the reserved word also. All selection objects must match with all selection subjects for the rule to be followed.
object program The program output from a compiler that corresponds to the source program that was input.
*****octet** See byte.
*****operand** 1. The general definition is 'that component which is operated upon.
  2. In COBOL an operand is any word in a format that is or implies a reference to data.
*****operating environment** A collection of computing resources used by an individual, group or organization.
*****operating system** The programs and other software resources that control the processes on a computer system.
*****order** See successor.
order of evaluation All conditional expressions in COBOL are evaluated from left to right in conformity with the binding precedence: not, and, or. Sub-expressions nested in parentheses are solved first as they are encountered. Evaluation stops at the earliest opportunity that the overall truth value of an expression is known. For example:

  a number and (a > 3 and < 8)

  a > b and q = y

In both of these expressions the second sub-expression will not be evaluated if the first is found to be false. Equally, for example:

a > b or q = y

In this expression the second sub-expression will not be evaluated if the first is found to be true. This technique of stopping evaluation at the first opportunity that the overall truth value can be known is sometimes called short-circuit evaluation.

output mode   The state of a file after execution of an open statement with the output phrase specified for that file and before the execution of its close statement.

output procedure   A section in the procedure division to which control is given by a sort statement after the sort is completed but while the sorted records are still in the sort file. Return statements in the procedure cause records to be read sequentially from the sort file.

*****output stream**   A flow of output characters, data items or records. See data stream.

overflow   A condition that occurs when an attempt is made to access beyond the bounds of a data item. Overflow can occur during arithmetic as well as during the processing strings of characters. Arithmetic overflow is the result of a semantic error in the program and it is notified to the program by the size error phrase. Character string overflow may be intended by the program and it is notified to the program by the overflow phrase. If overflow occurs when these phrases are not specified then the result is undefined.

paragraph   See subroutine.

*****para1**   A user-defined word used as a paragraph name in this text. This word has no meaning in COBOL.

*****parameter**   Information that is passed to a program when it is called.

*****parameter list**   A list of one or more parameters.

*****parameter list compatibility**   The parameter lists in both the calling and the called programs must be managed in such a way that they do not conflict with each other. Generally a parameter in the called program can be considered as a redefinition of the matching parameter in the calling program. Therefore it can define a shorter length but not a longer one and can use a different picture definition provided that the picture is in conformity with the data that is passed.

*****parent**   See tree.

phrase   A portion of a statement or a clause that has a particular purpose. Thus the read statement has an 'end' phrase.

physical record   The term is synonymous with block.

picture clause   The means for defining the general characteristics and editing requirements of an elementary item. Elementary items with usage of index do not have picture clauses.

*****portability**   A quality of programs that allows them to be transferred between systems and reused. The most important form of portability is source code portability where the source is transferred between systems and then recompiled to produce programs with the same functional behaviour. Portability in this context is a synonym for machine-independence.

*****power**   See exponentiation.

*****precedence**   A concept that determines the ordering of operands. For example,

not a and b

x ∗ y + 1

In the first expression the not operator is evaluated for a and then the result is anded with b.

This is because not has a higher precedence than and. In the second expression the multiplication occurs first and then 1 is added to the result. See order of evaluation.

prime record key   A key whose contents uniquely identify a record within an indexed file.

*__priming read__   A read that is executed immediately before entering a loop which will process an input file until the end of the file is detected.

*__primitive__   A simpler statement that can be used to construct simulations of more complex statements. Thus the if and the go to statements are primitive statements that could be used to construct loops with the same behaviour as loops written with the perform statement.

procedural abstraction   A quality of certain statements in a high-level language whereby the details of a processing algorithm are hidden but the goal of the algorithm and its data requirements are defined as part of the statement. Statements such as string, unstring and sort exhibit a high degree of procedural abstraction.

procedure   In general computing use it is a synonym for a called program. Unfortunately the COBOL standard defines paragraphs and sections in the procedure division to be procedures when in fact they should be more correctly classed as subroutines.

procedure division   The division of a COBOL program which holds executable statements. It is optional.

*__program__   A set of instructions that enable a computer to perform operations upon data. See algorithm.

*__programming style__   An attribute of programs that is recognized by experienced programmers. Attempts have been made to quantify style but these attempts have provided few general conclusions. In spite of this there are many rules concerning style that are generally accepted, e.g. the importance of sensible data-naming conventions.

*__pseudo-code__   A language for specifying the nature of a programmable solution without all of the syntactic detail that would be required by the program itself. For example, a published or known algorithm might be cast in a pseudo-code that approximated to COBOL as a means of evaluating the solution and then programmed in COBOL from this specification. There are no agreed standards for pseudo-codes. Typically programmers use fragments of COBOL and pseudo-code statements in combination as a means of refining a solution.

qualified data-name   An identifier that is composed of a data-name followed by one or more sets of the connective **in** and a data-name qualifier. For example,

```
01   e1.
     03   e2   pic x
01   e3.
     03   e2   pic x
     display e2 in e1
```

The display statement uses a qualified data-name in order to construct a unique identifier. The reserved word **of** is a synonym for **in**.

random access   An access mode in which the program-specified value of a key data item identifies the logical record that is obtained from, deleted from, or placed into a relative or index file. The term is a misnomer in that it is intended to mean that records from the file can be processed in any key order. It does not mean that keys are processed at random as if the keys were generated by a random number generator.

real number In computing the type real is used for those numbers that can be expressed as the ratio of two integers, e.g. 0.3 repeating is the ratio 1/3. Pascal is a language that includes the type REAL for these numbers. Standard COBOL does not include this type of approximation although the ability to specify decimal points allows the use of scaled integers. Many implementations of COBOL are extended to allow the equivalent of Pascal reals by using the usages COMP-1 and COMP-2. They are useful when approximations of values that are too large or too small to be held in 18 digits are needed. (In mathematics the term real number also includes irrational numbers such as the square root of 2.)
record See logical record and physical record. Also variable-length record and fixed-length record.
record area The storage area allocated for processing records as defined by an fd.
record key A key whose contents identifies a record within an indexed file. The key may be either a prime key or an alternate key.
*__record locking__ A facility for denying access to a record by other programs when a record is being processed in a multi-user environment. Many COBOL implementations have been extended to support record locking.
*__recursion__ A process whereby a function is defined in terms of itself. Within the context of COBOL the point at issue is recursive program calls, that is, a situation where a program attempts to call itself or where a calling path through a set of programs results in a call to the program that initiated the calling path (e.g. A calls B calls C calls A). COBOL does not define recursion and therefore it should not be used in COBOL programs. Some compilers might succeed in some recursive calls as a consequence of providing a common environment that includes recursive languages (e.g. the VAX/VMS implementation of Pascal and COBOL).
redefinition The use of the redefines clause to allow data in memory to be accessed with different data descriptions. The use of more than one record within an fd to achieve the same purpose. This COBOL feature allows a program to over-ride the typing of one definition by its redefinition.
reference format See format.
reference modification A means of defining a substring by specifying a left-most character position and a length. See reference modifier.
reference modifier An expression in parentheses consisting of two parts separated by a colon. The first part specifies a left-most character position. The second part specifies a length when present or the balance of the string when absent.
relation condition A condition that relates two or more operands by using relational operators.
relational operator An operator such as > which is used in constructing a relation condition.
relative file A file with relative organization.
relative key A key whose contents identify a logical record in a relative file.
relative organization The permanent logical file structure in which each record is uniquely identified by an integer value greater than zero. The integer value specifies the record's logical ordinal position in the file.
relative record number The ordinal number of a record in a file whose organization is relative. This number is treated as a numeric literal which is an integer.
*__repeat loop__ See test after loop.

replace-list   A paired list of strings with their replacements that is used by the full syntax of the inspect statement.

reserved word   A COBOL word specified in the list of words which may be used in a COBOL source program but which must not appear in the program as a user-defined word or system-name.

resolution   See linker.

return   The action of passing control back to a calling program such that execution continues in the calling program at the next statement after the call.

Return   An ASCII character that causes a device to reposition to the beginning of a line. In many instances the use of a Return key also causes the device to reposition to the beginning of the next line. This may be because the Return character for that device also causes a reposition to the next line. However, it may occur because the key generates two characters: a Return and a Line-feed. These characters cannot be detected by the COBOL accept statement where the Return key merely returns the input string excluding any control characters.

right justification   The alignment of a source string of characters from the right to the left of a target data item. When the source is shorter than the target, the target is padded with spaces. When the source is longer than the target, the target is truncated. When the target item is a number then the alignment is on the decimal point and either truncation or padding with leading and/or trailing zeros will occur. See left justification.

root   See tree.

routine   See subroutine.

rule   The reserved word when followed by an object list and a set of statements to be executed when the object list matches the subject list. Rules are used within evaluate statements and can be specified in decision tables.

run chart   A diagram that shows data streams, programs, and the inter-relations between them.

run time   The time when a program is run or executed as opposed to when it was compiled or linked. The term is synonymous with execution time.

run-time error   An error that occurs during the execution of a program. Not all run-time errors cause a program to fail. The action that is taken when a run-time error happens depends upon the COBOL implementation.

run unit   One or more object programs which interact with one another and which function at run time as an entity.

scale   The most common method of giving scale to COBOL numbers is by using the symbol 'v' to denote an assumed decimal point. COBOL also uses the symbol 'p' to denote leading or trailing zeros that represent a scale factor. Thus the numbers 0.00 to 0.09 could be stored in an item that used a picture clause of 'pic p9'. The 'v' and 'p' symbols cannot appear in the same picture clause.

scanner   A program or part of a program that can manipulate strings and substrings according to a set of rules for sequential processing. The string, unstring, and inspect statements in COBOL can be used to implement simple scanners.

scope → scope of control   A property of statements such that they control the access during execution of statements that are nested within them. Typically such a statement opens its scope with a reserved word and then closes with its paired reserved word, e.g. evaluate . . . end-evaluate. See nesting.

scope terminator See implicit scope terminator and explicit scope terminator.
*****screen protection** The ability to deny access to certain fields on a terminal screen when the screen is being manipulated from the keyboard under cursor control. The terminal must possess screen protection characteristics which are then driven by a program using the required control character sequences.
section header A combination of words and a period that indicates a section, e.g.

> **file section**.
> **OR**
> section-name **section**.

section-name A user-defined word which names a set of paragraphs that can be performed by name.
*****selection** The choosing of one of several paths at a particular point in the execution of a program. The evaluate and if statements are examples of two COBOL statements that implement selection. See sequence and iteration.
selection object An expression appearing immediately after the reserved word when in an evaluate statement. If this expression is the only selection object and matches the selection subject then the actions specified immediately after this expression will be executed and then control will pass to the next statement after the end-evaluate. See selection subject and object list.
selection subject An expression appearing immediately after the reserved word evaluate. See selection object and subject list.
*****semantics** 1. That part of a definition of a language that is concerned with the meaning of entries and statements as opposed to their syntax.
  2. The run-time behaviour of a program.
sentence A sequence of one or more statements terminated by a separator period. See entry.
separately compiled program See external program.
separator A character such as the space which is used to delimit words and other strings.
*****sequence** A set of one or more statements that contain neither selection nor iteration and therefore can only be executed in the order in which they are written.
sequence number area The first six columns of the COBOL source line. These columns can be omitted with some compilers.
sequential See sequential access and successor.
sequential access An access mode in which logical records are obtained from or placed into a file in a consecutive predecessor-to-successor logical record sequence determined by the order of the records in the file.
sequential file A file with sequential organization.
sequential organization The permanent logical file structure in which a record is identified by a predecessor–successor relationship established when the record is placed into the file.
serial A term used in expressions such as serial access and serial order which implies that the physical order of elements is the processing order. For example, the elements might be records in a sequential file or characters in a string of text.
*****set** A collection of distinct objects of any sort. The idea of order is also important in

computing. Thus a program may be considered as an ordered set of statements or the items on a list as an ordered set of items.

*short circuit evaluation   See order of evaluation.

*sibling   See tree.

*side effect   A change in data and therefore possibly behaviour that is observed in one program as a result of changes to the data by another program. All reference parameters can be thought of as a potential source of side effects. Usually the term is only used to denote unintended side effects.

*simple format   Those formats used in the main text for illustration. They are always subsets of the full formats. See format.

*simulation   Imitation of the behaviour of one system or subsystem by another.

size error   See overflow.

*slack byte   A byte that is generated by a compiler in order to force necessary alignments in memory. Slack bytes should be avoided by inserting filler items in the program as required.

*source program   A program written as text and in conformity with a language definition such as COBOL.

special names   A paragraph in the environment division in which implementor names and values are related to user-specified names.

special registers   Certain compiler-generated storage areas that are used in conjunction with certain COBOL special features such as the linage-counter. These are not in any way associated with machine registers.

*standard   A document which defines the syntax and semantics of a language.

standard COBOL   That standard which is published by ANSI and the ISO.

*standard initialization   Initialization that occurs as defined by the COBOL standard. See also initialization.

statement   A syntactically valid combination of words, literals, and separators that begins with a verb. At times the term is also used to mean both statements and entries in general. See imperative statement.

*static   The opposite of dynamic. When referring to data:
1. A referenced area in memory which does not change in size during the execution of a program.
2. A reference to data that is not altered during execution by changes in value to indexes, subscripts or reference modifiers.

*string   A one-dimensional array of characters. Some languages such as Turing incorporate a string length variable as part of the string data type. Thus a concatenation of two strings will result in a longer string for which the length is automatically updated. COBOL does not contain this feature.

*structure chart   (Compare with run chart.)

*stub   1. A called program that is used during program development prior to the inclusion of all of its application-specific statements. Stubs are used in top-down development.
2. See decision table.

*style   See programming style.

subject list   A list of one or more selection subjects separated by the reserved word also. See object list.

***subprogram**   A called program.

***subroutine**   A set of statements that is used out-of-line with the main program. Performed paragraphs in COBOL are examples of subroutines. They are to be avoided because they have access to the same data as the rest of the program.

***subscript**   An integer or an expression that equates to an integer that is used to refer to an element in a table. An index can be used as a subscript. Only the arithmetic operators + and − can be used to construct subscript expressions.

***successive**   See successor.

***successor**   The next in sequence. Thus successor statement, successor character, successor record, etc.

***switch**   A data item that stores a state to indicate an exclusive action that may be taken by a program. Most switches are binary and record the states of true or false for a major condition such as the end of a file. However, there is no reason why a switch cannot be used to record more than two states provided that they are mutually exclusive.

symbolic-character   A user-defined word that is specified in the special-names paragraph and defines a figurative constant. Symbolic-characters are commonly specified for characters that cannot be printed, such as the escape character.

***syntax**   The deterministic rules governing the formation of correct sentences in a language. The term excludes questions of meaning. See semantics.

***system**   Anything we choose to consider as a whole with interconnecting parts. The term in computing is also closely associated with the concept of layering and with the implication of complexity. There is no satisfactory means for differentiating a complex program from a system.

system-name   A COBOL word which is used to communicate with the operating environment.

table   A set of logically consecutive items of data that are defined in the data division of a COBOL program by means of the occurs clause.

table element   One of the items in a table against which the occurs phrase has been specified.

tally-list   A list consisting of a definition of which characters to tally including a delimiter-list. It is used by the full syntax for the inspect statement.

***template**   A pattern serving to show the outline structure for a programmed solution.

test after loop   A loop in which the condition that terminates it is tested at the bottom of the loop. Also called a repeat loop and sometimes a repeat-until loop.

test before loop   A loop in which the condition that terminates it is tested at the top of the loop. It is the most commonly required looping construct in data processing. Also called a while loop.

***test case**   A set of one or more data items treated as a single input that stimulates a predictable response from a system or program. Test cases typically cover boundary conditions such as those that govern the initialization and termination of a loop.

***text**   Strings of characters. Text characters are not necessarily printable.

***text editor**   A program that can manipulate lines and substrings within a text file. Text editors and word processors overlap considerably in their functionality.

***text file**   A file containing strings of characters representing lines. In COBOL lines of text are read and written as variable length records.

time   See date.

*trace   A report of the flow of control during a particular program run. It usually contains lists of line numbers relating to the source text of the program as well as the values of selected variables.

*trailer   1.   A line or group of lines in a report that are at the end of the report (report trailer). See also trailer, footer, and detail line.

2.   The last record in a file of records and holding information pertinent to the records that were processed as well as any information concerning additional similar files that may be part of the same input set.

*transitive   A logical term stating the property that if one object bears a relationship to a second object and if the second object bears the same relationship to a third object then the first and third object also have this relationship.

*translator   See language translator.

*trap   See validation trap.

*tree → rooted tree   A set of one or more nodes for which the following is true:

1.   Only one node is the root.
2.   All other nodes are partitioned into disjoint sets where each set is also a tree.

Except for the root each node has only one parent but a parent may have many children. Children of the same parent are siblings.

*truth table   A tabular description of a logical operand such as and. It lists all possible truth values for the operands as well as the truth outcome for each combination of operand values.

truth value   One of the values false or true. All conditional expressions in programs can be reduced to one of these two values.

*type → data type   A definition of the structure of a data object, the values it may take, and the operations that may be performed upon it. Langauges such as Pascal are strongly typed and in consequence many errors in the use of data can be found by the compiler. COBOL is weakly typed. This is useful for data validation but it does mean that inexperienced programmers often make data typing errors in their programs which then appear as semantic errors during program execution. See category.

*unreachable   A characteristic of statements that cannot be executed. This is usually due to an error in the design of a program, e.g. an evaluate statement immediately within a test before loop where both statements test the same condition to be true. Although such an error is technically a semantic error it can be discovered through an analysis of the program text. Therefore some compilers may spot such an error even though the COBOL standard does not oblige them to do so.

usage   A clause that specifies the format in which data is to be stored. The most common COBOL usage is display in which data is stored as character strings according to the character set that is specified as the collating sequence. Other forms of usage such as binary imply other internal representations.

user-defined word   A COBOL word that must be supplied to satisfy the format of a clause or statement.

*validation   The act of determining whether or not an input to a program is within the expected specification. Typically validation is done in two stages. The first determines that an input is inherently correct, e.g. that it is numeric and within an expected range. The second stage will check to ensure that the value of an input is within the range determined by other items of data with which it is associated.

*validation trap   1.   A paired accept statement and a test before loop within an interactive program to ensure that incorrect inputs are identified and re-entered at the point of input.

2.   Any similar scheme for trapping errors at a data source.

variable   A data item whose value may be changed during execution of the program. (A variable in an arithmetic expression must be a numeric elementary item.) See data-item.

*variable declaration   See data description entry.

variable-length record   A record associated with a file whose file description or sort-merge description entry permits records to contain a varying number of character positions. The characters can be any values from the character set. In consequence, variable-length records can contain items with usages other than display.

*vector   A one-dimensional array of elements such as the bits of a word or the words of memory in a computer.

*Venn diagram   A form of diagram for representing set relations named for the 19th-century English logician, John Venn.

verb   A word that expresses an action to be taken by a compiler or the object program. All statements in COBOL begin with a verb. Copy is an example of a verb which requires a compiler action. Display is an example of a verb which requires an object program action.

virtual environment   A layer within an operating environment that offers a collection of resources which when considered as a whole provide an integrated work environment. The term is biased towards software and its visual representations at interactive devices. For example, for a programmer the virtual environment would largely consist of that software used to support program development. See system, computer system, operating environment, operating system.

when phrase   See rule.

*while loop   See test before loop

*word   1.   A vector of bits in memory that is addressed by a computer as a single unit. A doubleword is two consecutive words. A half-word is the top or bottom half of a word.

2.   In COBOL a string of not more than 30 characters which forms a user-defined word, a system-name, or a reserved word.

working-storage section   The section of the data division that describes data items that by default are local to the program.

C
INSTRUCTION FORMATS

C.1 FULL FORMATS

Identification division

```
identification division.

program-id. program-name [common] [initial].
```

Environment division

$$\begin{bmatrix} \text{environment division.} \\ \begin{bmatrix} \text{special-names.} \\ \quad \text{[symbolic symbolic-character-list is integer-value-list]} \\ \quad \text{[class class-name-1 literal-1 [thru literal-2]]...} \\ \quad \text{[currency} \qquad \text{literal-3]} \\ \quad \text{[decimal-point} \quad \text{literal-4].} \end{bmatrix} \\ \begin{bmatrix} \text{input-output section.} \\ \begin{bmatrix} \text{file-control.} \\ \quad \{\text{file-control-entry}\}... \end{bmatrix} \end{bmatrix} \end{bmatrix}$$

Data division

$$\begin{bmatrix} \text{data division.} \\ \begin{bmatrix} \text{file section.} \\ \begin{bmatrix} \text{file-description-entry \{record-description-entry\}...} \\ \text{sort-merge-file-description-entry \{record-description-entry\}...} \end{bmatrix}... \end{bmatrix} \\ \begin{bmatrix} \text{working-storage section.} \\ \text{[record-description-entry]...} \end{bmatrix} \\ \begin{bmatrix} \text{linkage section.} \\ \text{[record-description-entry]...} \end{bmatrix} \end{bmatrix}$$

Procedure division

(a) Programs in paragraphs only

$$\left[\begin{array}{l}\texttt{procedure division [using \{data-name-1\}...].}\\ \texttt{\{paragraph-name. [sentence]... \}...}\end{array}\right]$$

(b) Programs in both sections and paragraphs

$$\left[\begin{array}{l}\texttt{procedure division [using \{data-name-1\}...].}\\ \texttt{\{section-name section.}\\ \texttt{[paragraph-name. [sentence]...]... \}...}\end{array}\right]$$

File control entries

(a) Sequential, sort or merge files

```
select  file-name-1   assign
```
$\left\{\begin{array}{l}\texttt{implementor-name-1}\\ \texttt{literal-1}\end{array}\right\}.$

(b) Indexed files

```
select  file-name-1   assign
```
$\left\{\begin{array}{l}\texttt{implementor-name-1}\\ \texttt{literal-1}\end{array}\right\}.$

```
    organization   indexed

access
```
$\left\{\begin{array}{l}\texttt{sequential}\\ \texttt{random}\\ \texttt{dynamic}\end{array}\right\}$

```
    record   data-name-1.
```

File description entries

(a) Sequential files

```
fd   file-name-1
   [external]
   [global]
   [record varying integer-1 to integer-2
   [depending data-name-1]
```
$\left[\texttt{value of implementor-name-1 is }\left\{\begin{array}{l}\texttt{data-name-2}\\ \texttt{literal-2}\end{array}\right\}\right].$

(b) Sort or merge files

```
sd   file-name-1
   [record varying integer-1 to integer-2]
   [depending data-name-1]
```
$\left[\texttt{value of implementor-name-1 is }\left\{\begin{array}{l}\texttt{data-name-2}\\ \texttt{literal-2}\end{array}\right\}\right].$

(c) Indexed

```
fd  file-name-1
    [external]
    [global]
```
$$\left[\text{value of implementor-name-1 is } \begin{Bmatrix} \text{data-name-2} \\ \text{literal-2} \end{Bmatrix}\right].$$

(d) Files for use in reports with the linage clause

```
fd  filename-1
```
$$\left[\text{linage} \begin{Bmatrix} \text{data-name-1} \\ \text{integer-1} \end{Bmatrix}\right]$$

$$\left[\text{footing} \begin{Bmatrix} \text{data-name-2} \\ \text{integer-2} \end{Bmatrix}\right]$$

$$\left[\text{top} \begin{Bmatrix} \text{data-name-3} \\ \text{integer-3} \end{Bmatrix}\right]$$

$$\left[\text{bottom} \begin{Bmatrix} \text{data-name-4} \\ \text{integer-4} \end{Bmatrix}\right]$$

$$\left[\text{value of implementor-name-1} \begin{Bmatrix} \text{data-name-5} \\ \text{integer-5} \end{Bmatrix}\right]$$

Data description entries

(a) Levels 01 to 49

$$\text{level-number } \begin{Bmatrix} \text{data-name-1} \\ \text{filler} \end{Bmatrix}$$

```
    [redefines  data-name-2]

    [external]

    [global]

    [pic character-string]
```

$$\left[\text{usage} \begin{Bmatrix} \text{binary} \\ \text{display} \\ \text{index} \\ \text{packed-decimal} \end{Bmatrix}\right]$$

$$\left[\text{sign} \begin{Bmatrix} \text{leading} \\ \text{trailing} \end{Bmatrix} \text{ [separate]}\right]$$

$$\left[\text{occurs integer-1} \left[\begin{Bmatrix} \text{ascending} \\ \text{descending} \end{Bmatrix} \text{ data-name-3 [indexed index-name-1]}\right]\right]$$

```
    [just]

    [value literal-1].
```

(b) Level 88

```
88 condition-name-1  { value literal-1 [thru literal-2]...}...  .
```

Verbs

```
accept identifier-1


add  {identifier-1}  ... to  {{identifier-2 [rounded]}...                                    }
     {literal-1    }         {{identifier-3} giving {identifier-4 [rounded]}...}
                             {{literal-2   }                                   }
[{|size error      statement-1|}]
[{|not size error  statement-2|}]
[end-add                        ]


call {literal-1   } [using {[{reference}]}  identifier-1} ...]
     {identifier-1}        [ {content  } ]
[ exception      statement-1 ]
[[not exception  statement-2]]
[end-call                    ]


close {file-name-1}...


compute {identifier-1 [rounded]}... = arithmetic-expression-1
[{|size error      statement-1|}]
[{|not size error  statement-2|}]
[end-compute                    ]


continue


copy file-name-1


delete file-name-1
   invalid       statement-1
  [not invalid  statement-2]
end-delete


display {identifier-1} ... [no advancing]
        {literal-1   }
```

```
divide
    {identifier-1} into {identifier-2 [rounded]} ...
    {literal-1   }

    {identifier-1} into {identifier-2} giving {identifier-3 [rounded] ...                        }
    {literal-1   } by   {literal-2   }        {identifier-4 [rounded] [remainder identifier-4]}

    [{|size error     statement-1|}]
    [{|not size error statement-2|}]
    end-divide


evaluate subject [also subject]...

    {when  object [also object]... statement-1} ...
    [when  other                   statement-2]
    end-evaluate
```

Evaluate notes

1. A subject has the following format:

    $$\begin{Bmatrix} \text{identifier-1} \\ \text{literal-1} \\ \text{expression-1} \\ \text{true} \\ \text{false} \end{Bmatrix}$$

2. An object has the following format:

    $$\begin{Bmatrix} \text{any} \\ \text{condition-1} \\ \text{true} \\ \text{false} \\ \text{test} \end{Bmatrix}$$

3. A test has the following format:

    $$[\text{not}] \begin{Bmatrix} \text{identifier-3} \\ \text{literal-3} \\ \text{arithmetic-expression-3} \end{Bmatrix} \text{thru} \begin{Bmatrix} \text{identifier-4} \\ \text{literal-4} \\ \text{arithmetic-expression-4} \end{Bmatrix}$$

```
exit


exit program


go to procedure-name-1


if condition-1
   then   statement-1
  {else   statement-2}
end-if
```

```
inspect identifier-1
        ⎧ tallying    {identifier-4 for tally-list}...                                    ⎫
        ⎪ replacing   {replace-list}...                                                   ⎪
        ⎨ tallying    {identifier-4 for tally-list}... replacing {replace-list}...        ⎬
        ⎪ converting  ⎧identifier-2⎫  to  ⎧identifier-3⎫  [delimiter-list]...             ⎪
        ⎩             ⎩literal-1   ⎭     ⎩literal-2   ⎭                                   ⎭
```

Inspect notes

1. A delimiter-list has the following format:
```
        ⎧before⎫  ⎧identifier-5⎫
        ⎩after ⎭  ⎩literal-3   ⎭
```

2. A tally-list has the following format:
```
        ⎧ characters                        ⎫
        ⎨ ⎧all    ⎫  ⎧identifier-6⎫         ⎬  [delimiter-list]...
        ⎩ ⎩leading⎭  ⎩literal-4   ⎭         ⎭
```

3. A replace-list has the following format:
```
        ⎧ characters by  ⎧identifier-7⎫                                ⎫
        ⎪                ⎩literal-5   ⎭                                ⎪
        ⎨ ⎧all    ⎫      ⎧identifier-8⎫  by  ⎧identifier-9⎫            ⎬  [delimiter-list]...
        ⎪ ⎨leading⎬      ⎩literal-6   ⎭      ⎩literal-7   ⎭            ⎪
        ⎩ ⎩first  ⎭                                                    ⎭
```

```
merge file-name-1  {⎧ascending ⎫  data-name-1 ...}...
                    ⎩descending⎭

        using  file-name-2  {file-name-3}...

        ⎧output procedure section-name-1⎫
        ⎩giving {file-name-4}...        ⎭

move  ⎧identifier-1⎫  to  {identifier-2}...
      ⎩literal-1   ⎭

multiply  ⎧identifier-1⎫  by  ⎧{identifier-2 [rounded]}...                                   ⎫
          ⎩literal-1   ⎭      ⎨⎧identifier-3⎫                                                ⎬
                              ⎩⎩literal-2   ⎭  giving {identifier-4 [rounded]}...           ⎭

        ⎡⎧⎧size error     statement-1⎫⎫⎤
        ⎣⎩⎩not size error statement-2⎭⎭⎦
end-multiply

open  ⎧input   {file-name-1}...⎫
      ⎨output  {file-name-2}...⎬  ...
      ⎪i-o     {file-name-3}...⎪
      ⎩extend  {file-name-4}...⎭
```

```
perform test {before/after} until condition-1
    statement-1
end-perform


perform {identifier-1/integer-1} times
    statement-1
end-perform


read file-name-1 [into identifier-1]
    end           statement-1
  [not end        statement-2]
end-read


read file-name-1 [into identifier-1]
    invalid       statement-1
  [not invalid    statement-2]
end-read


release record-name-1 [from identifier-1]


return file-name-1 [into identifier-1]
    end           statement-1
  [not end        statement-2]
end-return


rewrite record-name-1 [from identifier-1]
    invalid       statement-1
  [not invalid    statement-2]
end-rewrite


search identifier-1
  [end                    statement-1]
  {when condition-1 statement-2}...
end-search
```

```
search all identifier-1

   [end                    statement-1]
     when     test-list statement-2
   end-search
```

> *Search all notes*
>
> 1. A test-list has the following format:
>
>   test-1 [and test-2]...
>
> 2. A test has the following format:
>
> $$\left\{ identifier\text{-}2 = \begin{Bmatrix} identifier\text{-}3 \\ literal\text{-}1 \\ arithmetic\text{-}expression\text{-}1 \end{Bmatrix} \right\}$$
>
> 3. Identifier-2 must be an indexed data-name that is associated with identifier-1.

$$\text{set } \begin{Bmatrix} \text{index-name-1} \\ \text{identifier-1} \end{Bmatrix} \ldots \text{ to } \begin{Bmatrix} \text{index-name-2} \\ \text{identifier-2} \\ \text{integer-1} \end{Bmatrix}$$

$$\text{set } \{\text{index-name-1}\}\ldots \begin{Bmatrix} \text{up by} \\ \text{down by} \end{Bmatrix} \begin{Bmatrix} \text{identifier-1} \\ \text{integer-1} \end{Bmatrix}$$

set {condition-name-1}... to true

$$\text{sort file-name-1} \left\{ \begin{Bmatrix} \text{ascending} \\ \text{descending} \end{Bmatrix} \text{data-name-1} \ldots \right\} \ldots$$

$$\begin{Bmatrix} \text{input procedure section-name-1} \\ \text{using \{file-name-2\}}\ldots \end{Bmatrix}$$

$$\begin{Bmatrix} \text{output procedure section-name-2} \\ \text{giving \{file-name-3\}}\ldots \end{Bmatrix}$$

$$\text{start file-name-1} \begin{Bmatrix} = \\ > \\ \text{not } < \\ >= \end{Bmatrix} \text{data-name-1}$$

```
      invalid      statement-1
     [not invalid statement-2]
   end-start


   stop run
```

$$\text{string } \begin{Bmatrix} \text{identifier-1} \\ \text{literal-1} \end{Bmatrix} \ldots \text{ delimited } \begin{Bmatrix} \text{identifier-2} \\ \text{literal-2} \\ \text{size} \end{Bmatrix} \ldots$$

into identifier-3

[pointer identifier-4]

$$\begin{bmatrix} \left\{ \begin{vmatrix} \text{overflow} & \text{statement-1} \\ \text{not overflow} & \text{statement-2} \end{vmatrix} \right\} \\ \text{end-string} \end{bmatrix}$$

$$\text{subtract } \begin{Bmatrix} \text{identifier-1} \\ \text{literal-1} \end{Bmatrix} \ldots \text{ from } \begin{Bmatrix} \{\text{identifier-2 [rounded]}\} \ldots \\ \begin{Bmatrix} \text{identifier-3} \\ \text{literal-2} \end{Bmatrix} \text{giving } \{\text{identifier-4 [rounded]}\} \ldots \end{Bmatrix}$$

$$\begin{bmatrix} \left\{ \begin{vmatrix} \text{size error} & \text{statement-1} \\ \text{not size error} & \text{statement-2} \end{vmatrix} \right\} \\ \text{end-subtract} \end{bmatrix}$$

unstring identifier-1 [delimited limit-test [or limit-test]...]

  into {identifier-2 [delimiter identifier-3] [count identifier-4]}...

[pointer identifier-5]
[tallying identifier-6]

$$\begin{bmatrix} \left\{ \begin{vmatrix} \text{overflow} & \text{statement-1} \\ \text{not overflow} & \text{statement-2} \end{vmatrix} \right\} \\ \text{end-unstring} \end{bmatrix}$$

Unstring note

1. The limit test format is: [all] $\begin{Bmatrix} \text{identifier-7} \\ \text{literal-1} \end{Bmatrix}$

---

write record-name-1 [from identifier-1]
   invalid   statement-1
 [not invalid statement-2]
end-write

write record-name-1 [from identifier-1]

$$\left[\text{after } \begin{Bmatrix} \text{integer-1} \\ \text{identifier-1} \end{Bmatrix} \right]$$

$$\begin{bmatrix} \left\{ \begin{vmatrix} \text{eop} & \text{statement-1} \\ \text{not eop} & \text{statement-2} \end{vmatrix} \right\} \\ \text{end-write} \end{bmatrix}$$

Relation condition

$$\begin{Bmatrix} \text{identifier-1} \\ \text{literal-1} \\ \text{arithmetic expression-1} \\ \text{index-name-1} \end{Bmatrix} \begin{Bmatrix} \text{[not]} > \\ \text{[not]} < \\ \text{[not]} = \\ >= \\ <= \end{Bmatrix} \begin{Bmatrix} \text{identifier-2} \\ \text{literal-2} \\ \text{arithmetic-expression-2} \\ \text{index-name-2} \end{Bmatrix}$$

Class condition

$$\text{identifier-1 [not]} \begin{Bmatrix} \text{numeric} \\ \text{alphabetic} \\ \text{alphabetic-lower} \\ \text{alphabetic-upper} \\ \text{class-name-1} \end{Bmatrix}$$

Condition-name condition

```
condition-name-1
```

Sign condition

$$\text{arithmetic-expression-1 [not]} \begin{Bmatrix} \text{positive} \\ \text{negative} \\ \text{zero} \end{Bmatrix}$$

Qualification for data-names or condition-names

```
[in data-name-2]... [in file-name-1]
```

Subscript for data-names or condition-names

$$\begin{Bmatrix} \text{integer-1} \\ \text{data-name-1} \quad \left[\begin{Bmatrix} + \\ - \end{Bmatrix} \text{integer-2} \right] \\ \text{index-name-1} \quad \left[\begin{Bmatrix} + \\ - \end{Bmatrix} \text{integer-3} \right] \end{Bmatrix}$$

Reference modifier for data-names

```
leftmost-character-position: [length]
```

Construction of identifiers

```
data-name-1  [in data-name-2]... [in file-name-1]
             [(subscript-1 [,subscript-2]...)]
             [(reference-modifier)]
```

C.2 GENERAL FORMATS – X3.23

<u>GENERAL FORMAT FOR IDENTIFICATION DIVISION</u>

<u>IDENTIFICATION</u> <u>DIVISION</u>.

<u>PROGRAM-ID</u>. program-name $\left[\text{IS} \left\{ \left| \begin{array}{c} \underline{\text{COMMON}} \\ \underline{\text{INITIAL}} \end{array} \right| \right\} \text{PROGRAM} \right]$.

[<u>AUTHOR</u>. [comment-entry] ...]

[<u>INSTALLATION</u>. [comment-entry] ...]

[<u>DATE-WRITTEN</u>. [comment-entry] ...]

[<u>DATE-COMPILED</u>. [comment-entry] ...]

[<u>SECURITY</u>. [comment-entry] ...]

GENERAL FORMAT FOR ENVIRONMENT DIVISION

[ENVIRONMENT DIVISION.

[CONFIGURATION SECTION.

[SOURCE-COMPUTER. [computer-name [WITH DEBUGGING MODE].]]

[OBJECT-COMPUTER. [computer-name

    $\left[\text{MEMORY SIZE integer-1} \begin{Bmatrix} \underline{\text{WORDS}} \\ \underline{\text{CHARACTERS}} \\ \underline{\text{MODULES}} \end{Bmatrix} \right]$

    [PROGRAM COLLATING SEQUENCE IS alphabet-name-1]

    [SEGMENT-LIMIT IS segment-number].]]

[SPECIAL-NAMES. [[implementor-name-1

$\begin{Bmatrix} \text{IS mnemonic-name-1 [\underline{ON} STATUS IS condition-name-1 [\underline{OFF} STATUS IS condition-name-2]]} \\ \text{IS mnemonic-name-2 [\underline{OFF} STATUS IS condition-name-2 [\underline{ON} STATUS IS condition-name-1]]} \\ \underline{\text{ON}} \text{ STATUS IS condition-name-1 [\underline{OFF} STATUS IS condition-name-2]} \\ \underline{\text{OFF}} \text{ STATUS IS condition-name-2 [\underline{ON} STATUS IS condition-name-1]} \end{Bmatrix}$ ...

[ALPHABET alphabet-name-1 IS

$\begin{Bmatrix} \begin{Bmatrix} \underline{\text{STANDARD-1}} \\ \underline{\text{STANDARD-2}} \\ \underline{\text{NATIVE}} \\ \text{implementor-name-2} \end{Bmatrix} \\ \begin{Bmatrix} \text{literal-1} \left[\begin{Bmatrix} \underline{\text{THROUGH}} \\ \underline{\text{THRU}} \end{Bmatrix} \text{literal-2} \\ \{\underline{\text{ALSO}} \text{ literal-3}\} \dots \end{Bmatrix} \right] \end{Bmatrix}$ ...

$\left[\underline{\text{SYMBOLIC}} \text{ CHARACTERS} \left\{ \{\text{symbolic-character-1}\} \dots \begin{Bmatrix} \text{IS} \\ \text{ARE} \end{Bmatrix} \{\text{integer-1}\} \dots \right\} \dots \right.$
$\left. [\underline{\text{IN}} \text{ alphabet-name-2}] \right\} \dots \right]$

$\left[\underline{\text{CLASS}} \text{ class-name-1 IS} \left\{ \text{literal-4} \left[\begin{Bmatrix} \underline{\text{THROUGH}} \\ \underline{\text{THRU}} \end{Bmatrix} \text{literal-5} \right] \right\} \dots \right] \dots$

[CURRENCY SIGN IS literal-6]

[DECIMAL-POINT IS COMMA].]]]

GENERAL FORMAT FOR ENVIRONMENT DIVISION

[INPUT-OUTPUT SECTION.

FILE-CONTROL.

    {file-control-entry} ...

[I-O-CONTROL.

$$\left[\left[\underline{\text{RERUN}} \left[\underline{\text{ON}} \begin{Bmatrix} \text{file-name-1} \\ \text{implementor-name-1} \end{Bmatrix}\right]\right. \text{EVERY} \begin{Bmatrix} \begin{Bmatrix} [\underline{\text{END}} \text{ OF}] \begin{Bmatrix} \underline{\text{REEL}} \\ \underline{\text{UNIT}} \end{Bmatrix} \end{Bmatrix} \text{OF file-name-2} \\ \text{integer-1 } \underline{\text{RECORDS}} \\ \text{integer-2 } \underline{\text{CLOCK-UNITS}} \\ \text{condition-name-1} \end{Bmatrix} \right] ...$$

$$\left[\underline{\text{SAME}} \begin{bmatrix} \underline{\text{RECORD}} \\ \underline{\text{SORT}} \\ \underline{\text{SORT-MERGE}} \end{bmatrix} \text{AREA FOR file-name-3 } \{\text{file-name-4}\} ... \right] ...$$

[MULTIPLE FILE TAPE CONTAINS {file-name-5 [POSITION integer-3]} ...] ... .]]]

GENERAL FORMATS — X3.23 **501**

GENERAL FORMAT FOR FILE CONTROL ENTRY

SEQUENTIAL FILE:

SELECT [OPTIONAL] file-name-1

　　ASSIGN TO $\begin{Bmatrix} \text{implementor-name-1} \\ \text{literal-1} \end{Bmatrix}$ ...

　　$\left[\underline{\text{RESERVE}}\ \text{integer-1}\ \begin{bmatrix} \text{AREA} \\ \text{AREAS} \end{bmatrix} \right]$

　　[[ORGANIZATION IS] SEQUENTIAL]

　　$\left[\underline{\text{PADDING}}\ \text{CHARACTER IS}\ \begin{Bmatrix} \text{data-name-1} \\ \text{literal-2} \end{Bmatrix} \right]$

　　$\left[\underline{\text{RECORD}}\ \underline{\text{DELIMITER}}\ \text{IS}\ \begin{Bmatrix} \underline{\text{STANDARD-1}} \\ \text{implementor-name-2} \end{Bmatrix} \right]$

　　[ACCESS MODE IS SEQUENTIAL]

　　[FILE STATUS IS data-name-2].

RELATIVE FILE:

SELECT [OPTIONAL] file-name-1

　　ASSIGN TO $\begin{Bmatrix} \text{implementor-name-1} \\ \text{literal-1} \end{Bmatrix}$ ...

　　$\left[\underline{\text{RESERVE}}\ \text{integer-1}\ \begin{bmatrix} \text{AREA} \\ \text{AREAS} \end{bmatrix} \right]$

　　[ORGANIZATION IS] RELATIVE

　　$\left[\underline{\text{ACCESS}}\ \text{MODE IS}\ \begin{Bmatrix} \underline{\text{SEQUENTIAL}}\ [\underline{\text{RELATIVE}}\ \text{KEY IS data-name-1}] \\ \begin{Bmatrix} \underline{\text{RANDOM}} \\ \underline{\text{DYNAMIC}} \end{Bmatrix} \underline{\text{RELATIVE}}\ \text{KEY IS data-name-1} \end{Bmatrix} \right].$

　　[FILE STATUS IS data-name-2].

GENERAL FORMAT FOR FILE CONTROL ENTRY

INDEXED FILE:

SELECT [OPTIONAL] file-name-1

    ASSIGN TO $\begin{Bmatrix} \text{implementor-name-1} \\ \text{literal-1} \end{Bmatrix}$ ...

    $\left[\text{RESERVE integer-1} \begin{bmatrix} \text{AREA} \\ \text{AREAS} \end{bmatrix} \right]$

    [ORGANIZATION IS] INDEXED

    $\left[\text{ACCESS MODE IS} \begin{Bmatrix} \text{SEQUENTIAL} \\ \text{RANDOM} \\ \text{DYNAMIC} \end{Bmatrix} \right]$

    RECORD KEY IS data-name-1

    [ALTERNATE RECORD KEY IS data-name-2 [WITH DUPLICATES]] ...

    [FILE STATUS IS data-name-3].

SORT OR MERGE FILE:

    SELECT file-name-1 ASSIGN TO $\begin{Bmatrix} \text{implementor-name-1} \\ \text{literal-1} \end{Bmatrix}$ ... .

GENERAL FORMAT FOR FILE CONTROL ENTRY

REPORT FILE:

SELECT [OPTIONAL] file-name-1

$\quad$ ASSIGN TO $\begin{Bmatrix} \text{implementor-name-1} \\ \text{literal-1} \end{Bmatrix}$ ...

$\quad \left[\text{RESERVE integer-1} \begin{bmatrix} \text{AREA} \\ \text{AREAS} \end{bmatrix} \right]$

$\quad$ [[ORGANIZATION IS] SEQUENTIAL]]

$\quad \left[\text{PADDING CHARACTER IS} \begin{Bmatrix} \text{data-name-1} \\ \text{literal-2} \end{Bmatrix} \right]$

$\quad \left[\text{RECORD DELIMITER IS} \begin{Bmatrix} \text{STANDARD-1} \\ \text{implementor-name-2} \end{Bmatrix} \right]$

$\quad$ [ACCESS MODE IS SEQUENTIAL]

$\quad$ [FILE STATUS IS data-name-2].

GENERAL FORMAT FOR DATA DIVISION

[<u>DATA</u> <u>DIVISION</u>.

[<u>FILE</u> <u>SECTION</u>.

$$\left[\begin{array}{l} \text{file-description-entry \{record-description-entry\} ...} \\ \text{sort-merge-file-description-entry \{record-description-entry\} ...} \\ \text{report-file-description-entry} \end{array} \right] ... \right]$$

[<u>WORKING-STORAGE</u> <u>SECTION</u>.

$$\left[\begin{array}{l} \text{77-level-description-entry} \\ \text{record-description-entry} \end{array} \right] ... \right]$$

[<u>LINKAGE</u> <u>SECTION</u>.

$$\left[\begin{array}{l} \text{77-level-description-entry} \\ \text{record-description-entry} \end{array} \right] ... \right]$$

[<u>COMMUNICATION</u> <u>SECTION</u>.

[communication-description-entry [record-description-entry] ...] ...]

[<u>REPORT</u> <u>SECTION</u>.

[report-description-entry {report-group-description-entry} ...] ...]]

GENERAL FORMATS — X3.23 **505**

GENERAL FORMAT FOR FILE DESCRIPTION ENTRY

SEQUENTIAL FILE:

<u>FD</u> file-name-1

  [IS <u>EXTERNAL</u>]

  [IS <u>GLOBAL</u>]

$$\left[\underline{\text{BLOCK}} \text{ CONTAINS } [\text{integer-1 } \underline{\text{TO}}] \text{ integer-2 } \left\{\begin{array}{l}\underline{\text{RECORDS}}\\ \text{CHARACTERS}\end{array}\right\}\right]$$

$$\left[\underline{\text{RECORD}} \left\{\begin{array}{l}\text{CONTAINS integer-3 CHARACTERS}\\ \text{IS } \underline{\text{VARYING}} \text{ IN SIZE } [[\text{FROM integer-4}] \text{ } [\underline{\text{TO}} \text{ integer-5}] \text{ CHARACTERS}]\\ \quad [\underline{\text{DEPENDING}} \text{ ON data-name-1}]\\ \text{CONTAINS integer-6 } \underline{\text{TO}} \text{ integer-7 CHARACTERS}\end{array}\right\}\right]$$

$$\left[\underline{\text{LABEL}} \left\{\begin{array}{l}\underline{\text{RECORD}} \text{ IS}\\ \underline{\text{RECORDS}} \text{ ARE}\end{array}\right\} \left\{\begin{array}{l}\underline{\text{STANDARD}}\\ \underline{\text{OMITTED}}\end{array}\right\}\right]$$

$$\left[\underline{\text{VALUE}} \text{ } \underline{\text{OF}} \text{ } \left\{\text{implementor-name-1 IS } \left\{\begin{array}{l}\text{data-name-2}\\ \text{literal-1}\end{array}\right\}\right\} \dots \right]$$

$$\left[\underline{\text{DATA}} \left\{\begin{array}{l}\underline{\text{RECORD}} \text{ IS}\\ \underline{\text{RECORDS}} \text{ ARE}\end{array}\right\} \{\text{data-name-3}\} \dots \right]$$

$$\left[\underline{\text{LINAGE}} \text{ IS } \left\{\begin{array}{l}\text{data-name-4}\\ \text{integer-8}\end{array}\right\} \text{ LINES } \left[\text{WITH } \underline{\text{FOOTING}} \text{ AT } \left\{\begin{array}{l}\text{data-name-5}\\ \text{integer-9}\end{array}\right\}\right]\right.$$

$$\left.\left[\text{LINES AT } \underline{\text{TOP}} \left\{\begin{array}{l}\text{data-name-6}\\ \text{integer-10}\end{array}\right\}\right] \left[\text{LINES AT } \underline{\text{BOTTOM}} \left\{\begin{array}{l}\text{data-name-7}\\ \text{integer-11}\end{array}\right\}\right]\right]$$

[<u>CODE-SET</u> IS alphabet-name-1].

GENERAL FORMAT FOR FILE DESCRIPTION ENTRY

RELATIVE FILE:

<u>FD</u> file-name-1

    [IS <u>EXTERNAL</u>]

    [IS <u>GLOBAL</u>]

$$\left[\underline{\text{BLOCK}} \text{ CONTAINS [integer-1 } \underline{\text{TO}}\text{] integer-2} \begin{Bmatrix} \underline{\text{RECORDS}} \\ \text{CHARACTERS} \end{Bmatrix}\right]$$

$$\left[\underline{\text{RECORD}} \begin{Bmatrix} \text{CONTAINS integer-3 CHARACTERS} \\ \text{IS } \underline{\text{VARYING}} \text{ IN SIZE [[FROM integer-4] [}\underline{\text{TO}}\text{ integer-5] CHARACTERS]} \\ \text{[}\underline{\text{DEPENDING}}\text{ ON data-name-1]} \\ \text{CONTAINS integer-6 } \underline{\text{TO}} \text{ integer-7 CHARACTERS} \end{Bmatrix}\right]$$

$$\left[\underline{\text{LABEL}} \begin{Bmatrix} \underline{\text{RECORD}} \text{ IS} \\ \underline{\text{RECORDS}} \text{ ARE} \end{Bmatrix} \begin{Bmatrix} \underline{\text{STANDARD}} \\ \underline{\text{OMITTED}} \end{Bmatrix}\right]$$

$$\left[\underline{\text{VALUE OF}} \left\{\text{implementor-name-1 IS} \begin{Bmatrix} \text{data-name-2} \\ \text{literal-1} \end{Bmatrix}\right\} \dots \right]$$

$$\left[\underline{\text{DATA}} \begin{Bmatrix} \underline{\text{RECORD}} \text{ IS} \\ \underline{\text{RECORDS}} \text{ ARE} \end{Bmatrix} \{\text{data-name-3}\} \dots \right].$$

GENERAL FORMAT FOR FILE DESCRIPTION ENTRY

INDEXED FILE:

FD file-name-1

  [IS EXTERNAL]

  [IS GLOBAL]

$$\left[\text{BLOCK CONTAINS [integer-1 TO] integer-2} \begin{Bmatrix}\text{RECORDS}\\\text{CHARACTERS}\end{Bmatrix}\right]$$

$$\left[\text{RECORD} \begin{Bmatrix}\text{CONTAINS integer-3 CHARACTERS}\\\text{IS VARYING IN SIZE [[FROM integer-4] [TO integer-5] CHARACTERS]}\\\quad\text{[DEPENDING ON data-name-1]}\\\text{CONTAINS integer-6 TO integer-7 CHARACTERS}\end{Bmatrix}\right]$$

$$\left[\text{LABEL} \begin{Bmatrix}\text{RECORD IS}\\\text{RECORDS ARE}\end{Bmatrix} \begin{Bmatrix}\text{STANDARD}\\\text{OMITTED}\end{Bmatrix}\right]$$

$$\left[\text{VALUE OF} \left\{\text{implementor-name-1 IS} \begin{Bmatrix}\text{data-name-2}\\\text{literal-1}\end{Bmatrix}\right\} \ldots\right]$$

$$\left[\text{DATA} \begin{Bmatrix}\text{RECORD IS}\\\text{RECORDS ARE}\end{Bmatrix} \{\text{data-name-3}\} \ldots\right] .$$

GENERAL FORMAT FOR FILE DESCRIPTION ENTRY

SORT-MERGE FILE:

SD file-name-1

$$\left[\underline{\text{RECORD}} \begin{cases} \text{CONTAINS integer-1 CHARACTERS} \\ \text{IS } \underline{\text{VARYING}} \text{ IN SIZE [[FROM integer-2] [\underline{TO} integer-3] CHARACTERS]} \\ \quad [\underline{\text{DEPENDING}} \text{ ON data-name-1}] \\ \text{CONTAINS integer-4 } \underline{\text{TO}} \text{ integer-5 CHARACTERS} \end{cases}\right]$$

$$\left[\underline{\text{DATA}} \begin{Bmatrix} \underline{\text{RECORD}} \text{ IS} \\ \underline{\text{RECORDS}} \text{ ARE} \end{Bmatrix} \{\text{data-name-2}\} \ldots \right] .$$

REPORT FILE:

FD file-name-1

[IS EXTERNAL]

[IS GLOBAL]

$$\left[\underline{\text{BLOCK}} \text{ CONTAINS [integer-1 } \underline{\text{TO}}] \text{ integer-2} \begin{Bmatrix} \underline{\text{RECORDS}} \\ \underline{\text{CHARACTERS}} \end{Bmatrix}\right]$$

$$\left[\underline{\text{RECORD}} \begin{Bmatrix} \text{CONTAINS integer-3 CHARACTERS} \\ \text{CONTAINS integer-4 } \underline{\text{TO}} \text{ integer-5 CHARACTERS} \end{Bmatrix}\right]$$

$$\left[\underline{\text{LABEL}} \begin{Bmatrix} \underline{\text{RECORD}} \text{ IS} \\ \underline{\text{RECORDS}} \text{ ARE} \end{Bmatrix} \begin{Bmatrix} \underline{\text{STANDARD}} \\ \underline{\text{OMITTED}} \end{Bmatrix}\right]$$

$$\left[\underline{\text{VALUE}} \underline{\text{ OF}} \begin{Bmatrix} \text{implementor-name-1 IS} \begin{Bmatrix} \text{data-name-1} \\ \text{literal-1} \end{Bmatrix} \end{Bmatrix} \ldots \right]$$

[CODE-SET IS alphabet-name-1]

$$\begin{Bmatrix} \underline{\text{REPORT}} \text{ IS} \\ \underline{\text{REPORTS}} \text{ ARE} \end{Bmatrix} \{\text{report-name-1}\} \ldots \quad .$$

GENERAL FORMAT FOR DATA DESCRIPTION ENTRY

FORMAT 1:

level-number $\begin{bmatrix} \text{data-name-1} \\ \text{FILLER} \end{bmatrix}$

   [REDEFINES data-name-2]

   [IS EXTERNAL]

   [IS GLOBAL]

   $\left[\left\{ \dfrac{\text{PICTURE}}{\text{PIC}} \right\} \text{IS character-string} \right]$

   $\left[\text{USAGE IS} \right] \left\{ \begin{matrix} \text{BINARY} \\ \text{COMPUTATIONAL} \\ \text{COMP} \\ \text{DISPLAY} \\ \text{INDEX} \\ \text{PACKED-DECIMAL} \end{matrix} \right\}$

   $\left[\text{SIGN IS} \right] \left\{ \dfrac{\text{LEADING}}{\text{TRAILING}} \right\} \text{[SEPARATE CHARACTER]}$

   $\begin{bmatrix} \text{OCCURS integer-2 TIMES} \\ \quad \left[\left\{ \dfrac{\text{ASCENDING}}{\text{DESCENDING}} \right\} \text{KEY IS \{data-name-3\} ...} \right] \text{...} \\ \quad \text{[INDEXED BY \{index-name-1\} ...]} \\ \text{OCCURS integer-1 TO integer-2 TIMES DEPENDING ON data-name-4} \\ \quad \left[\left\{ \dfrac{\text{ASCENDING}}{\text{DESCENDING}} \right\} \text{KEY IS \{data-name-3\} ...} \right] \text{...} \\ \quad \text{[INDEXED BY \{index-name-1\} ...]} \end{bmatrix}$

   $\left[\left\{ \dfrac{\text{SYNCHRONIZED}}{\text{SYNC}} \right\} \left[\dfrac{\text{LEFT}}{\text{RIGHT}} \right] \right]$

   $\left[\left\{ \dfrac{\text{JUSTIFIED}}{\text{JUST}} \right\} \text{RIGHT} \right]$

   [BLANK WHEN ZERO]

   [VALUE IS literal-1].

GENERAL FORMAT FOR DATA DESCRIPTION ENTRY

FORMAT 2:

66 data-name-1 <u>RENAMES</u> data-name-2 $\left[\left\{ \begin{array}{c} \underline{\text{THROUGH}} \\ \underline{\text{THRU}} \end{array} \right\} \text{data-name-3} \right]$.

FORMAT 3:

88 condition-name-1 $\left\{ \begin{array}{c} \underline{\text{VALUE}} \text{ IS} \\ \underline{\text{VALUES}} \text{ ARE} \end{array} \right\}$ $\left\{ \text{literal-1} \left[\left\{ \begin{array}{c} \underline{\text{THROUGH}} \\ \underline{\text{THRU}} \end{array} \right\} \text{literal-2} \right] \right\}$ ...

GENERAL FORMATS — X3.23   **511**

GENERAL FORMAT FOR COMMUNICATION DESCRIPTION ENTRY

FORMAT 1:

<u>CD</u> cd-name-1

FOR [<u>INITIAL</u>] <u>INPUT</u>
⎡ [[SYMBOLIC <u>QUEUE</u> IS data-name-1]
     [SYMBOLIC <u>SUB-QUEUE-1</u> IS data-name-2]
     [SYMBOLIC <u>SUB-QUEUE-2</u> IS data-name-3]
     [SYMBOLIC <u>SUB-QUEUE-3</u> IS data-name-4]
     [<u>MESSAGE</u> <u>DATE</u> IS data-name-5]
     [<u>MESSAGE</u> <u>TIME</u> IS data-name-6]
     [SYMBOLIC <u>SOURCE</u> IS data-name-7]
     [<u>TEXT</u> <u>LENGTH</u> IS data-name-8]
     [<u>END</u> <u>KEY</u> IS data-name-9]
     [<u>STATUS</u> <u>KEY</u> IS data-name-10]
     [<u>MESSAGE</u> <u>COUNT</u> IS data-name-11]]
 [data-name-1, data-name-2, data-name-3,
     data-name-4, data-name-5, data-name-6,
     data-name-7, data-name-8, data-name-9,
     data-name-10, data-name-11] ⎦

GENERAL FORMAT FOR COMMUNICATION DESCRIPTION ENTRY

FORMAT 2:

CD cd-name-1 FOR OUTPUT

    [DESTINATION COUNT IS data-name-1]

    [TEXT LENGTH IS data-name-2]

    [STATUS KEY IS data-name-3]

    [DESTINATION TABLE OCCURS integer-1 TIMES

        [INDEXED BY {index-name-1} ...]]

    [ERROR KEY IS data-name-4]

    [SYMBOLIC DESTINATION IS data-name-5].

FORMAT 3:

CD cd-name-1

    FOR [INITIAL] I-O
$\begin{bmatrix} [[\text{MESSAGE DATE IS data-name-1}] \\ \quad [\text{MESSAGE TIME IS data-name-2}] \\ \quad [\text{SYMBOLIC TERMINAL IS data-name-3}] \\ \quad [\text{TEXT LENGTH IS data-name-4}] \\ \quad [\text{END KEY IS data-name-5}] \\ \quad [\text{STATUS KEY IS data-name-6}]] \\ [\text{data-name-1, data-name-2, data-name-3,} \\ \quad \text{data-name-4, data-name-5, data-name-6}] \end{bmatrix}$

GENERAL FORMATS — X3.23 **513**

GENERAL FORMAT FOR REPORT DESCRIPTION ENTRY

<u>RD</u> report-name-1

  [IS <u>GLOBAL</u>]

  [<u>CODE</u> literal-1]

  $\left[\begin{Bmatrix} \underline{\text{CONTROL IS}} \\ \underline{\text{CONTROLS}} \text{ ARE} \end{Bmatrix} \begin{Bmatrix} \{\text{data-name-1}\} \ldots \\ \underline{\text{FINAL}} \text{ [data-name-1]} \ldots \end{Bmatrix} \right]$

  $\left[\underline{\text{PAGE}} \begin{bmatrix} \text{LIMIT IS} \\ \text{LIMITS ARE} \end{bmatrix} \text{integer-1} \begin{bmatrix} \text{LINE} \\ \text{LINES} \end{bmatrix} [\underline{\text{HEADING}} \text{ integer-2}] \right.$

  $\quad [\underline{\text{FIRST}}\ \underline{\text{DETAIL}}\ \text{integer-3}]\ [\underline{\text{LAST}}\ \underline{\text{DETAIL}}\ \text{integer-4}]$

  $\left. [\underline{\text{FOOTING}}\ \text{integer-5}] \right] .$

GENERAL FORMAT FOR REPORT GROUP DESCRIPTION ENTRY

<u>FORMAT 1</u>:

01 [data-name-1]

  $\left[\underline{\text{LINE}} \text{ NUMBER IS} \begin{Bmatrix} \text{integer-1 [ON } \underline{\text{NEXT}} \underline{\text{PAGE}}] \\ \underline{\text{PLUS}} \text{ integer-2} \end{Bmatrix} \right]$

  $\left[\underline{\text{NEXT}}\ \underline{\text{GROUP}} \text{ IS} \begin{Bmatrix} \text{integer-3} \\ \underline{\text{PLUS}} \text{ integer-4} \\ \underline{\text{NEXT}}\ \underline{\text{PAGE}} \end{Bmatrix} \right]$

  $\underline{\text{TYPE}} \text{ IS} \begin{Bmatrix} \begin{Bmatrix} \underline{\text{REPORT}}\ \underline{\text{HEADING}} \\ \underline{\text{RH}} \end{Bmatrix} \\ \begin{Bmatrix} \underline{\text{PAGE}}\ \underline{\text{HEADING}} \\ \underline{\text{PH}} \end{Bmatrix} \\ \begin{Bmatrix} \underline{\text{CONTROL}}\ \underline{\text{HEADING}} \\ \underline{\text{CH}} \end{Bmatrix} \begin{Bmatrix} \text{data-name-2} \\ \underline{\text{FINAL}} \end{Bmatrix} \\ \begin{Bmatrix} \underline{\text{DETAIL}} \\ \underline{\text{DE}} \end{Bmatrix} \\ \begin{Bmatrix} \underline{\text{CONTROL}}\ \underline{\text{FOOTING}} \\ \underline{\text{CF}} \end{Bmatrix} \begin{Bmatrix} \text{data-name-3} \\ \underline{\text{FINAL}} \end{Bmatrix} \\ \begin{Bmatrix} \underline{\text{PAGE}}\ \underline{\text{FOOTING}} \\ \underline{\text{PF}} \end{Bmatrix} \\ \begin{Bmatrix} \underline{\text{REPORT}}\ \underline{\text{FOOTING}} \\ \underline{\text{RF}} \end{Bmatrix} \end{Bmatrix}$

  [[<u>USAGE</u> IS] <u>DISPLAY</u>].

GENERAL FORMAT FOR REPORT GROUP DESCRIPTION ENTRY

FORMAT 2:

level-number [data-name-1]

$$\left[\underline{\text{LINE}} \text{ NUMBER IS } \begin{Bmatrix} \text{integer-1 } [\text{ON } \underline{\text{NEXT}} \text{ } \underline{\text{PAGE}}] \\ \underline{\text{PLUS}} \text{ Integer-2} \end{Bmatrix} \right]$$

[[USAGE IS] DISPLAY].

FORMAT 3:

level-number [data-name-1]

$$\begin{Bmatrix} \underline{\text{PICTURE}} \\ \underline{\text{PIC}} \end{Bmatrix} \text{ IS character-string}$$

[[USAGE IS] DISPLAY]

$$\left[[\underline{\text{SIGN}} \text{ IS}] \begin{Bmatrix} \underline{\text{LEADING}} \\ \underline{\text{TRAILING}} \end{Bmatrix} \text{ SEPARATE CHARACTER} \right]$$

$$\left[\begin{Bmatrix} \underline{\text{JUSTIFIED}} \\ \underline{\text{JUST}} \end{Bmatrix} \text{ RIGHT} \right]$$

[BLANK WHEN ZERO]

$$\left[\underline{\text{LINE}} \text{ NUMBER IS } \begin{Bmatrix} \text{integer-1 } [\text{ON } \underline{\text{NEXT}} \text{ } \underline{\text{PAGE}}] \\ \underline{\text{PLUS}} \text{ integer-2} \end{Bmatrix} \right]$$

[COLUMN NUMBER IS integer-3]

$$\begin{Bmatrix} \underline{\text{SOURCE}} \text{ IS identifier-1} \\ \underline{\text{VALUE}} \text{ IS literal-1} \\ \{\underline{\text{SUM}} \text{ } \{\text{identifier-2}\} \text{ ... } [\underline{\text{UPON}} \text{ } \{\text{data-name-2}\} \text{ ... }] \} \text{ ...} \\ \left[\underline{\text{RESET}} \text{ ON } \begin{Bmatrix} \text{data-name-3} \\ \underline{\text{FINAL}} \end{Bmatrix} \right] \end{Bmatrix}$$

[GROUP INDICATE].

GENERAL FORMATS — X3.23 **515**

GENERAL FORMAT FOR PROCEDURE DIVISION

FORMAT 1:

[PROCEDURE DIVISION   [USING   {data-name-1} ...].

[DECLARATIVES.

{section-name SECTION [segment-number].

    USE statement.

[paragraph-name.

    [sentence] ...] ... } ...

END DECLARATIVES.]

{section-name SECTION [segment-number].

[paragraph-name.

    [sentence] ...] ... } ...]

FORMAT 2:

[PROCEDURE DIVISION   [USING   {data-name-1} ...].

{paragraph-name.

    [sentence] ... } ...]

GENERAL FORMAT FOR COBOL VERBS

<u>ACCEPT</u> identifier-1 [<u>FROM</u> mnemonic-name-1]

<u>ACCEPT</u> identifier-2 <u>FROM</u> $\begin{Bmatrix} \underline{DATE} \\ \underline{DAY} \\ \underline{DAY\text{-}OF\text{-}WEEK} \\ \underline{TIME} \end{Bmatrix}$

<u>ACCEPT</u> cd-name-1 MESSAGE <u>COUNT</u>

<u>ADD</u> $\begin{Bmatrix} \text{identifier-1} \\ \text{literal-1} \end{Bmatrix}$ ... <u>TO</u> {identifier-2 [<u>ROUNDED</u>]} ...

   [ON <u>SIZE</u> <u>ERROR</u> imperative-statement-1]

   [<u>NOT</u> ON <u>SIZE</u> <u>ERROR</u> imperative-statement-2]

   [<u>END-ADD</u>]

<u>ADD</u> $\begin{Bmatrix} \text{identifier-1} \\ \text{literal-1} \end{Bmatrix}$ ... <u>TO</u> $\begin{Bmatrix} \text{identifier-2} \\ \text{literal-2} \end{Bmatrix}$

   <u>GIVING</u> {identifier-3 [<u>ROUNDED</u>]} ...

   [ON <u>SIZE</u> <u>ERROR</u> imperative-statement-1]

   [<u>NOT</u> ON <u>SIZE</u> <u>ERROR</u> imperative-statement-2]

   [<u>END-ADD</u>]

<u>ADD</u> $\begin{Bmatrix} \underline{CORRESPONDING} \\ \underline{CORR} \end{Bmatrix}$ identifier-1 <u>TO</u> identifier-2 [<u>ROUNDED</u>]

   [ON <u>SIZE</u> <u>ERROR</u> imperative-statement-1]

   [<u>NOT</u> ON <u>SIZE</u> <u>ERROR</u> imperative-statement-2]

   [<u>END-ADD</u>]

<u>ALTER</u> {procedure-name-1 <u>TO</u> [<u>PROCEED</u> <u>TO</u>] procedure-name-2} ...

<u>CALL</u> $\begin{Bmatrix} \text{identifier-1} \\ \text{literal-1} \end{Bmatrix}$ $\left[\underline{USING} \begin{Bmatrix} [BY \underline{REFERENCE}] \ \{\text{identifier-2}\} \ ... \\ BY \underline{CONTENT} \ \{\text{identifier-2}\} \ ... \end{Bmatrix} ... \right]$

   [ON <u>OVERFLOW</u> imperative-statement-1]

   [<u>END-CALL</u>]

GENERAL FORMATS — X3.23   **517**

GENERAL FORMAT FOR COBOL VERBS

<u>CALL</u> $\begin{Bmatrix} \text{identifier-1} \\ \text{literal-1} \end{Bmatrix}$ $\left[\underline{\text{USING}} \begin{Bmatrix} [\text{BY } \underline{\text{REFERENCE}}] & \{\text{identifier-2}\} \ldots \\ \text{BY } \underline{\text{CONTENT}} & \{\text{identifier-2}\} \ldots \end{Bmatrix} \ldots \right]$

    [ON <u>EXCEPTION</u> imperative-statement-1]

    [<u>NOT</u> ON <u>EXCEPTION</u> imperative-statement-2]

    [<u>END-CALL</u>]

<u>CANCEL</u> $\begin{Bmatrix} \text{identifier-1} \\ \text{literal-1} \end{Bmatrix}$ ...

SW <u>CLOSE</u> $\left\{ \text{file-name-1} \left[\begin{Bmatrix} \underline{\text{REEL}} \\ \underline{\text{UNIT}} \end{Bmatrix} \begin{bmatrix} \text{FOR } \underline{\text{REMOVAL}} \end{bmatrix} \\ \text{WITH} \begin{Bmatrix} \underline{\text{NO REWIND}} \\ \underline{\text{LOCK}} \end{Bmatrix} \right] \right\} \ldots$

RI <u>CLOSE</u> {file-name-1 [WITH <u>LOCK</u>]} ...

<u>COMPUTE</u> {identifier-1 [<u>ROUNDED</u>]} ... = arithmetic-expression-1

    [ON <u>SIZE</u> <u>ERROR</u> imperative-statement-1]

    [<u>NOT</u> ON <u>SIZE</u> <u>ERROR</u> imperative-statement-2]

    [<u>END-COMPUTE</u>]

CONTINUE

<u>DELETE</u> file-name-1 RECORD

    [<u>INVALID</u> KEY imperative-statement-1]

    [<u>NOT</u> <u>INVALID</u> KEY imperative-statement-2]

    [<u>END-DELETE</u>]

<u>DISABLE</u> $\begin{Bmatrix} \underline{\text{INPUT}} \ [\underline{\text{TERMINAL}}] \\ \underline{\text{I-O}} \ \underline{\text{TERMINAL}} \\ \underline{\text{OUTPUT}} \end{Bmatrix}$ cd-name-1 $\left[\text{WITH } \underline{\text{KEY}} \begin{Bmatrix} \text{identifier-1} \\ \text{literal-1} \end{Bmatrix} \right]$

GENERAL FORMAT FOR COBOL VERBS

<u>DISPLAY</u> {identifier-1 / literal-1} ... [<u>UPON</u> mnemonic-name-1] [WITH <u>NO</u> <u>ADVANCING</u>]

<u>DIVIDE</u> {identifier-1 / literal-1} <u>INTO</u> {identifier-2 [<u>ROUNDED</u>]} ...

  [ON <u>SIZE</u> <u>ERROR</u> imperative-statement-1]

  [<u>NOT</u> ON <u>SIZE</u> <u>ERROR</u> imperative-statement-2]

  [<u>END-DIVIDE</u>]

<u>DIVIDE</u> {identifier-1 / literal-1} <u>INTO</u> {identifier-2 / literal-2}

  <u>GIVING</u> {identifier-3 [<u>ROUNDED</u>]} ...

  [ON <u>SIZE</u> <u>ERROR</u> imperative-statement-1]

  [<u>NOT</u> ON <u>SIZE</u> <u>ERROR</u> imperative-statement-2]

  [<u>END-DIVIDE</u>]

<u>DIVIDE</u> {identifier-1 / literal-1} <u>BY</u> {identifier-2 / literal-2}

  <u>GIVING</u> {identifier-3 [<u>ROUNDED</u>]} ...

  [ON <u>SIZE</u> <u>ERROR</u> imperative-statement-1]

  [<u>NOT</u> ON <u>SIZE</u> <u>ERROR</u> imperative-statement-2]

  [<u>END-DIVIDE</u>]

<u>DIVIDE</u> {identifier-1 / literal-1} <u>INTO</u> {identifier-2 / literal-2} <u>GIVING</u> identifier-3 [<u>ROUNDED</u>]

  <u>REMAINDER</u> identifier-4

  [ON <u>SIZE</u> <u>ERROR</u> imperative-statement-1]

  [<u>NOT</u> ON <u>SIZE</u> <u>ERROR</u> imperative-statement-2]

  [<u>END-DIVIDE</u>]

GENERAL FORMAT FOR COBOL VERBS

$\underline{\text{DIVIDE}} \begin{Bmatrix} \text{identifier-1} \\ \text{literal-1} \end{Bmatrix} \underline{\text{BY}} \begin{Bmatrix} \text{identifier-2} \\ \text{literal-2} \end{Bmatrix} \underline{\text{GIVING}}$ identifier-3 [$\underline{\text{ROUNDED}}$]

    $\underline{\text{REMAINDER}}$ identifier-4

    [ON $\underline{\text{SIZE}}$ $\underline{\text{ERROR}}$ imperative-statement-1]

    [$\underline{\text{NOT}}$ ON $\underline{\text{SIZE}}$ $\underline{\text{ERROR}}$ imperative-statement-2]

    [$\underline{\text{END-DIVIDE}}$]

$\underline{\text{ENABLE}} \begin{Bmatrix} \underline{\text{INPUT}} \text{ [}\underline{\text{TERMINAL}}\text{]} \\ \underline{\text{I-O}} \text{ } \underline{\text{TERMINAL}} \\ \underline{\text{OUTPUT}} \end{Bmatrix}$ cd-name-1 $\left[\text{WITH } \underline{\text{KEY}} \begin{Bmatrix} \text{identifier-1} \\ \text{literal-1} \end{Bmatrix} \right]$

$\underline{\text{ENTER}}$ language-name-1 [routine-name-1].

$\underline{\text{EVALUATE}} \begin{Bmatrix} \text{identifier-1} \\ \text{literal-1} \\ \text{expression-1} \\ \underline{\text{TRUE}} \\ \underline{\text{FALSE}} \end{Bmatrix} \left[\underline{\text{ALSO}} \begin{Bmatrix} \text{identifier-2} \\ \text{literal-2} \\ \text{expression-2} \\ \underline{\text{TRUE}} \\ \underline{\text{FALSE}} \end{Bmatrix} \right] \ldots$

  {{$\underline{\text{WHEN}}$

$\begin{Bmatrix} \underline{\text{ANY}} \\ \text{condition-1} \\ \underline{\text{TRUE}} \\ \underline{\text{FALSE}} \\ [\underline{\text{NOT}}] \begin{Bmatrix} \text{identifier-3} \\ \text{literal-3} \\ \text{arithmetic-expression-1} \end{Bmatrix} \left[\begin{Bmatrix} \underline{\text{THROUGH}} \\ \underline{\text{THRU}} \end{Bmatrix} \begin{Bmatrix} \text{identifier-4} \\ \text{literal-4} \\ \text{arithmetic-expression-2} \end{Bmatrix} \right] \end{Bmatrix}$}

  [$\underline{\text{ALSO}}$

$\begin{Bmatrix} \underline{\text{ANY}} \\ \text{condition-2} \\ \underline{\text{TRUE}} \\ \underline{\text{FALSE}} \\ [\underline{\text{NOT}}] \begin{Bmatrix} \text{identifier-5} \\ \text{literal-5} \\ \text{arithmetic-expression-3} \end{Bmatrix} \left[\begin{Bmatrix} \underline{\text{THROUGH}} \\ \underline{\text{THRU}} \end{Bmatrix} \begin{Bmatrix} \text{identifier-6} \\ \text{literal-6} \\ \text{arithmetic-expression-4} \end{Bmatrix} \right] \end{Bmatrix}$] $\ldots$}

  imperative-statement-1} $\ldots$

  [$\underline{\text{WHEN}}$ $\underline{\text{OTHER}}$ imperative-statement-2]

  [$\underline{\text{END-EVALUATE}}$]

GENERAL FORMAT FOR COBOL VERBS

<u>EXIT</u>

<u>EXIT</u> <u>PROGRAM</u>

<u>GENERATE</u> {data-name-1 / report-name-1}

<u>GO</u> TO [procedure-name-1]

<u>GO</u> TO {procedure-name-1} ... <u>DEPENDING</u> ON identifier-1

<u>IF</u> condition-1 THEN {{statement-1} ... / <u>NEXT</u> <u>SENTENCE</u>} {<u>ELSE</u> {statement-2} ... [<u>END-IF</u>] / <u>ELSE</u> <u>NEXT</u> <u>SENTENCE</u> / <u>END-IF</u>}

<u>INITIALIZE</u> {identifier-1} ...

[<u>REPLACING</u> { <u>ALPHABETIC</u> / <u>ALPHANUMERIC</u> / <u>NUMERIC</u> / <u>ALPHANUMERIC-EDITED</u> / <u>NUMERIC-EDITED</u> } DATA <u>BY</u> {identifier-2 / literal-1} ...]

<u>INITIATE</u> {report-name-1} ...

<u>INSPECT</u> identifier-1 <u>TALLYING</u>

{ {identifier-2 <u>FOR</u> { <u>CHARACTERS</u> [{<u>BEFORE</u>/<u>AFTER</u>} INITIAL {identifier-4/literal-2}] ... / {<u>ALL</u>/<u>LEADING</u>} {identifier-3/literal-1} [{<u>BEFORE</u>/<u>AFTER</u>} INITIAL {identifier-4/literal-2}] ... } ... } ... } ...

<u>INSPECT</u> identifier-1 <u>REPLACING</u>

{ <u>CHARACTERS</u> <u>BY</u> {identifier-5/literal-3} [{<u>BEFORE</u>/<u>AFTER</u>} INITIAL {identifier-4/literal-2}] ... / {<u>ALL</u>/<u>LEADING</u>/<u>FIRST</u>} {identifier-3/literal-1} <u>BY</u> {identifier-5/literal-3} [{<u>BEFORE</u>/<u>AFTER</u>} INITIAL {identifier-4/literal-2}] ... } ...

GENERAL FORMAT FOR COBOL VERBS

$$\underline{\text{INSPECT}} \text{ identifier-1 } \underline{\text{TALLYING}}$$

$$\left\{ \text{identifier-2 } \underline{\text{FOR}} \left\{ \begin{matrix} \underline{\text{CHARACTERS}} \left[\left\{ \begin{matrix} \underline{\text{BEFORE}} \\ \underline{\text{AFTER}} \end{matrix} \right\} \text{INITIAL} \left\{ \begin{matrix} \text{identifier-4} \\ \text{literal-2} \end{matrix} \right\} \right] \dots \\ \left\{ \begin{matrix} \underline{\text{ALL}} \\ \underline{\text{LEADING}} \end{matrix} \right\} \left\{ \begin{matrix} \text{identifier-3} \\ \text{literal-1} \end{matrix} \right\} \left[\left\{ \begin{matrix} \underline{\text{BEFORE}} \\ \underline{\text{AFTER}} \end{matrix} \right\} \text{INITIAL} \left\{ \begin{matrix} \text{identifier-4} \\ \text{literal-2} \end{matrix} \right\} \right] \dots \right\} \dots \right\} \dots$$

$$\underline{\text{REPLACING}}$$

$$\left\{ \begin{matrix} \underline{\text{CHARACTERS}} \text{ } \underline{\text{BY}} \left\{ \begin{matrix} \text{identifier-5} \\ \text{literal-3} \end{matrix} \right\} \left[\left\{ \begin{matrix} \underline{\text{BEFORE}} \\ \underline{\text{AFTER}} \end{matrix} \right\} \text{INITIAL} \left\{ \begin{matrix} \text{identifier-4} \\ \text{literal-2} \end{matrix} \right\} \right] \dots \\ \left\{ \begin{matrix} \underline{\text{ALL}} \\ \underline{\text{LEADING}} \\ \underline{\text{FIRST}} \end{matrix} \right\} \left\{ \begin{matrix} \text{identifier-3} \\ \text{literal-1} \end{matrix} \right\} \underline{\text{BY}} \left\{ \begin{matrix} \text{identifier-5} \\ \text{literal-3} \end{matrix} \right\} \left[\left\{ \begin{matrix} \underline{\text{BEFORE}} \\ \underline{\text{AFTER}} \end{matrix} \right\} \text{INITIAL} \left\{ \begin{matrix} \text{identifier-4} \\ \text{literal-2} \end{matrix} \right\} \right] \dots \right\} \dots$$

$$\underline{\text{INSPECT}} \text{ identifier-1 } \underline{\text{CONVERTING}} \left\{ \begin{matrix} \text{identifier-6} \\ \text{literal-4} \end{matrix} \right\} \underline{\text{TO}} \left\{ \begin{matrix} \text{identifier-7} \\ \text{literal-5} \end{matrix} \right\}$$

$$\left[\left\{ \begin{matrix} \underline{\text{BEFORE}} \\ \underline{\text{AFTER}} \end{matrix} \right\} \text{INITIAL} \left\{ \begin{matrix} \text{identifier-4} \\ \text{literal-2} \end{matrix} \right\} \right] \dots$$

$$\underline{\text{MERGE}} \text{ file-name-1 } \left\{ \text{ON} \left\{ \begin{matrix} \underline{\text{ASCENDING}} \\ \underline{\text{DESCENDING}} \end{matrix} \right\} \text{KEY } \{\text{data-name-1}\} \dots \right\} \dots$$

[COLLATING $\underline{\text{SEQUENCE}}$ IS alphabet-name-1]

$\underline{\text{USING}}$ file-name-2 {file-name-3} ...

$$\left\{ \begin{matrix} \underline{\text{OUTPUT}} \text{ } \underline{\text{PROCEDURE}} \text{ IS procedure-name-1 } \left[\left\{ \begin{matrix} \underline{\text{THROUGH}} \\ \underline{\text{THRU}} \end{matrix} \right\} \text{ procedure-name-2} \right] \\ \underline{\text{GIVING}} \text{ {file-name-4} } \dots \end{matrix} \right\}$$

$\underline{\text{MOVE}} \left\{ \begin{matrix} \text{identifier-1} \\ \text{literal-1} \end{matrix} \right\} \underline{\text{TO}}$ {identifier-2} ...

$\underline{\text{MOVE}} \left\{ \begin{matrix} \underline{\text{CORRESPONDING}} \\ \underline{\text{CORR}} \end{matrix} \right\}$ identifier-1 $\underline{\text{TO}}$ identifier-2

$\underline{\text{MULTIPLY}} \left\{ \begin{matrix} \text{identifier-1} \\ \text{literal-1} \end{matrix} \right\} \underline{\text{BY}}$ {identifier-2 [$\underline{\text{ROUNDED}}$]} ...

[ON $\underline{\text{SIZE}}$ $\underline{\text{ERROR}}$ imperative-statement-1]

[$\underline{\text{NOT}}$ ON $\underline{\text{SIZE}}$ $\underline{\text{ERROR}}$ imperative-statement-2]

[$\underline{\text{END-MULTIPLY}}$]

GENERAL FORMAT FOR COBOL VERBS

MULTIPLY {identifier-1 / literal-1} BY {identifier-2 / literal-2}

    GIVING {identifier-3 [ROUNDED]} ...

    [ON SIZE ERROR imperative-statement-1]

    [NOT ON SIZE ERROR imperative-statement-2]

    [END-MULTIPLY]

S OPEN {INPUT {file-name-1 [REVERSED / WITH NO REWIND]} ... / OUTPUT {file-name-2 [WITH NO REWIND]} ... / I-O {file-name-3} ... / EXTEND {file-name-4} ...} ...

RI OPEN {INPUT {file-name-1} ... / OUTPUT {file-name-2} ... / I-O {file-name-3} ... / EXTEND {file-name-4} ...} ...

W OPEN {OUTPUT {file-name-1 [WITH NO REWIND]} ... / EXTEND {file-name-2} ...} ...

PERFORM [procedure-name-1 [{THROUGH / THRU} procedure-name-2]]

    [imperative-statement-1 END-PERFORM]

PERFORM [procedure-name-1 [{THROUGH / THRU} procedure-name-2]]

    {identifier-1 / integer-1} TIMES [imperative-statement-1 END-PERFORM]

PERFORM [procedure-name-1 [{THROUGH / THRU} procedure-name-2]]

    [WITH TEST {BEFORE / AFTER}] UNTIL condition-1

    [imperative-statement-1 END-PERFORM]

GENERAL FORMATS — X3.23 **523**

GENERAL FORMAT FOR COBOL VERBS

$\underline{\text{PERFORM}} \left[\text{procedure-name-1} \left[\left\{ \begin{array}{l} \underline{\text{THROUGH}} \\ \underline{\text{THRU}} \end{array} \right\} \text{procedure-name-2} \right] \right]$

$\left[\text{WITH } \underline{\text{TEST}} \left\{ \begin{array}{l} \underline{\text{BEFORE}} \\ \underline{\text{AFTER}} \end{array} \right\} \right]$

$\underline{\text{VARYING}} \left\{ \begin{array}{l} \text{identifier-2} \\ \text{index-name-1} \end{array} \right\} \underline{\text{FROM}} \left\{ \begin{array}{l} \text{identifier-3} \\ \text{index-name-2} \\ \text{literal-1} \end{array} \right\}$

$\underline{\text{BY}} \left\{ \begin{array}{l} \text{identifier-4} \\ \text{literal-2} \end{array} \right\} \underline{\text{UNTIL}} \text{ condition-1}$

$\left[\underline{\text{AFTER}} \left\{ \begin{array}{l} \text{identifier-5} \\ \text{literal-3} \end{array} \right\} \underline{\text{FROM}} \left\{ \begin{array}{l} \text{identifier-6} \\ \text{index-name-4} \\ \text{literal-3} \end{array} \right\} \right.$

$\left. \underline{\text{BY}} \left\{ \begin{array}{l} \text{identifier-7} \\ \text{literal-4} \end{array} \right\} \underline{\text{UNTIL}} \text{ condition-2} \right] \ldots$

[imperative-statement-1 <u>END-PERFORM</u>]

<u>PURGE</u> cd-name-1

SRI <u>READ</u> file-name-1 [<u>NEXT</u>] RECORD [<u>INTO</u> identifier-1]

    [AT <u>END</u> imperative-statement-1]

    [<u>NOT</u> AT <u>END</u> imperative-statement-2]

    [<u>END-READ</u>]

R <u>READ</u> file-name-1 RECORD [<u>INTO</u> identifier-1]

    [<u>INVALID</u> KEY imperative-statement-3]

    [<u>NOT</u> <u>INVALID</u> KEY imperative-statement-4]

    [<u>END-READ</u>]

GENERAL FORMAT FOR COBOL VERBS

I <u>READ</u> file-name-1 RECORD [<u>INTO</u> identifier-1]

    [<u>KEY</u> IS data-name-1]

    [<u>INVALID</u> KEY imperative-statement-3]

    [<u>NOT</u> <u>INVALID</u> KEY imperative-statement-4]

    [<u>END-READ</u>]

<u>RECEIVE</u> cd-name-1 $\begin{Bmatrix} \underline{MESSAGE} \\ \underline{SEGMENT} \end{Bmatrix}$ <u>INTO</u> identifier-1

    [<u>NO</u> <u>DATA</u> imperative-statement-1]

    [WITH <u>DATA</u> imperative-statement-2]

    [<u>END-RECEIVE</u>]

<u>RELEASE</u> record-name-1 [<u>FROM</u> identifier-1]

<u>RETURN</u> file-name-1 RECORD [<u>INTO</u> identifier-1]

    AT <u>END</u> imperative-statement-1

    [<u>NOT</u> AT <u>END</u> imperative-statement-2]

    [<u>END-RETURN</u>]

S <u>REWRITE</u> record-name-1 [<u>FROM</u> identifier-1]

RI <u>REWRITE</u> record-name-1 [<u>FROM</u> identifier-1]

    [<u>INVALID</u> KEY imperative-statement-1]

    [<u>NOT</u> <u>INVALID</u> KEY imperative-statement-2]

    [<u>END-REWRITE</u>]

GENERAL FORMATS - X3.23 **525**

GENERAL FORMAT FOR COBOL VERBS

<u>SEARCH</u> identifier-1 $\left[\underline{\text{VARYING}} \begin{Bmatrix} \text{identifier-2} \\ \text{index-name-1} \end{Bmatrix}\right]$

   [AT <u>END</u> imperative-statement-1]

   $\begin{Bmatrix} \underline{\text{WHEN}} \text{ condition-1} \begin{Bmatrix} \text{imperative-statement-2} \\ \underline{\text{NEXT}} \ \underline{\text{SENTENCE}} \end{Bmatrix} \end{Bmatrix} \ldots$

   [<u>END-SEARCH</u>]

<u>SEARCH</u> <u>ALL</u> identifier-1 [AT <u>END</u> imperative-statement-1]

  <u>WHEN</u> $\begin{Bmatrix} \text{data-name-1} \begin{Bmatrix} \text{IS } \underline{\text{EQUAL}} \text{ TO} \\ \text{IS } = \end{Bmatrix} \begin{Bmatrix} \text{identifier-3} \\ \text{literal-1} \\ \text{arithmetic-expression-1} \end{Bmatrix} \\ \text{condition-name-1} \end{Bmatrix}$

  $\left[\underline{\text{AND}} \begin{Bmatrix} \text{data-name-2} \begin{Bmatrix} \text{IS } \underline{\text{EQUAL}} \text{ TO} \\ \text{IS } = \end{Bmatrix} \begin{Bmatrix} \text{identifier-4} \\ \text{literal-2} \\ \text{arithmetic-expression-2} \end{Bmatrix} \\ \text{condition-name-2} \end{Bmatrix}\right] \ldots$

  $\begin{Bmatrix} \text{imperative-statement-2} \\ \underline{\text{NEXT}} \ \underline{\text{SENTENCE}} \end{Bmatrix}$

  [<u>END-SEARCH</u>]

<u>SEND</u> cd-name-1 <u>FROM</u> identifier-1

<u>SEND</u> cd-name-1 [<u>FROM</u> identifier-1] $\begin{Bmatrix} \text{WITH identifier-2} \\ \text{WITH } \underline{\text{ESI}} \\ \text{WITH } \underline{\text{EMI}} \\ \text{WITH } \underline{\text{EGI}} \end{Bmatrix}$

  $\left[\begin{Bmatrix} \underline{\text{BEFORE}} \\ \underline{\text{AFTER}} \end{Bmatrix} \text{ADVANCING} \begin{Bmatrix} \begin{Bmatrix} \text{identifier-3} \\ \text{integer-1} \end{Bmatrix} \begin{bmatrix} \text{LINE} \\ \text{LINES} \end{bmatrix} \\ \begin{Bmatrix} \text{mnemonic-name-1} \\ \underline{\text{PAGE}} \end{Bmatrix} \end{Bmatrix}\right]$

  [<u>REPLACING</u> LINE]

<u>SET</u> $\begin{Bmatrix} \text{index-name-1} \\ \text{identifier-1} \end{Bmatrix} \ldots \underline{\text{TO}} \begin{Bmatrix} \text{index-name-2} \\ \text{identifier-2} \\ \text{integer-1} \end{Bmatrix}$

GENERAL FORMAT FOR COBOL VERBS

SET {index-name-3} ... {UP BY / DOWN BY} {identifier-3 / integer-2}

SET {{mnemonic-name-1} ... TO {ON / OFF}} ...

SET {condition-name-1} ... TO TRUE

SORT file-name-1 {ON {ASCENDING / DESCENDING} KEY {data-name-1} ...} ...

   [WITH DUPLICATES IN ORDER]

   [COLLATING SEQUENCE IS alphabet-name-1]

   {INPUT PROCEDURE IS procedure-name-1 [{THROUGH / THRU} procedure-name-2] / USING {file-name-2} ...}

   {OUTPUT PROCEDURE IS procedure-name-3 [{THROUGH / THRU} procedure-name-4] / GIVING {file-name-3} ...}

START file-name-1 [KEY {IS EQUAL TO / IS = / IS GREATER THAN / IS > / IS NOT LESS THAN / IS NOT < / IS GREATER THAN OR EQUAL TO / IS >=} data-name-1]

   [INVALID KEY imperative-statement-1]

   [NOT INVALID KEY imperative-statement-2]

   [END-START]

STOP {RUN / literal-1}

GENERAL FORMAT FOR COBOL VERBS

<u>STRING</u> $\begin{Bmatrix}\text{identifier-1}\\ \text{literal-1}\end{Bmatrix}$ ... <u>DELIMITED</u> BY $\begin{Bmatrix}\text{identifier-2}\\ \text{literal-2}\\ \underline{\text{SIZE}}\end{Bmatrix}$ ...

  <u>INTO</u> identifier-3

  [WITH <u>POINTER</u> identifier-4]

  [ON <u>OVERFLOW</u> imperative-statement-1]

  [<u>NOT</u> ON <u>OVERFLOW</u> imperative-statement-2]

  [<u>END-STRING</u>]

<u>SUBTRACT</u> $\begin{Bmatrix}\text{identifier-1}\\ \text{literal-1}\end{Bmatrix}$ ... <u>FROM</u> {identifier-3 [<u>ROUNDED</u>]} ...

  [ON <u>SIZE</u> <u>ERROR</u> imperative-statement-1]

  [<u>NOT</u> ON <u>SIZE</u> <u>ERROR</u> imperative-statement-2]

  [<u>END-SUBTRACT</u>]

<u>SUBTRACT</u> $\begin{Bmatrix}\text{identifier-1}\\ \text{literal-1}\end{Bmatrix}$ ... <u>FROM</u> $\begin{Bmatrix}\text{identifier-2}\\ \text{literal-2}\end{Bmatrix}$

  <u>GIVING</u> {identifier-3 [<u>ROUNDED</u>]} ...

  [ON <u>SIZE</u> <u>ERROR</u> imperative-statement-1]

  [<u>NOT</u> ON <u>SIZE</u> <u>ERROR</u> imperative-statement-2]

  [<u>END-SUBTRACT</u>]

<u>SUBTRACT</u> $\begin{Bmatrix}\underline{\text{CORRESPONDING}}\\ \underline{\text{CORR}}\end{Bmatrix}$ identifier-1 <u>FROM</u> identifier-2 [<u>ROUNDED</u>]

  [ON <u>SIZE</u> <u>ERROR</u> imperative-statement-1]

  [<u>NOT</u> ON <u>SIZE</u> <u>ERROR</u> imperative-statement-2]

  [<u>END-SUBTRACT</u>]

<u>SUPPRESS</u> PRINTING

<u>TERMINATE</u> {report-name-1} ...

GENERAL FORMAT FOR COBOL VERBS

UNSTRING identifier-1

$$\left[\underline{\text{DELIMITED}} \text{ BY } [\underline{\text{ALL}}] \begin{Bmatrix} \text{identifier-2} \\ \text{literal-1} \end{Bmatrix} \left[\underline{\text{OR}} \text{ } [\underline{\text{ALL}}] \begin{Bmatrix} \text{identifier-3} \\ \text{literal-2} \end{Bmatrix} \right] \dots \right]$$

INTO {identifier-4 [DELIMITER IN identifier-5] [COUNT IN identifier-6]} ...

[WITH POINTER identifier-7]

[TALLYING IN identifier-8]

[ON OVERFLOW imperative-statement-1]

[NOT ON OVERFLOW imperative-statement-2]

[END-UNSTRING]

$$SRI \text{ } \underline{\text{USE}} \text{ } [\underline{\text{GLOBAL}}] \text{ } \underline{\text{AFTER}} \text{ STANDARD } \begin{Bmatrix} \underline{\text{EXCEPTION}} \\ \underline{\text{ERROR}} \end{Bmatrix} \underline{\text{PROCEDURE}} \text{ ON } \begin{Bmatrix} \{\text{file-name-1}\} \dots \\ \underline{\text{INPUT}} \\ \underline{\text{OUTPUT}} \\ \underline{\text{I-O}} \\ \underline{\text{EXTEND}} \end{Bmatrix}$$

$$W \text{ } \underline{\text{USE}} \text{ } \underline{\text{AFTER}} \text{ STANDARD } \begin{Bmatrix} \underline{\text{EXCEPTION}} \\ \underline{\text{ERROR}} \end{Bmatrix} \underline{\text{PROCEDURE}} \text{ ON } \begin{Bmatrix} \{\text{file-name-1}\} \dots \\ \underline{\text{OUTPUT}} \\ \underline{\text{EXTEND}} \end{Bmatrix}$$

USE [GLOBAL] BEFORE REPORTING identifier-1

$$\underline{\text{USE}} \text{ FOR } \underline{\text{DEBUGGING}} \text{ ON } \begin{Bmatrix} \text{cd-name-1} \\ [\underline{\text{ALL}} \text{ REFERENCES OF}] \text{ identifier-1} \\ \text{file-name-1} \\ \text{procedure-name-1} \\ \underline{\text{ALL}} \text{ PROCEDURES} \end{Bmatrix} \dots$$

GENERAL FORMATS — X3.23 **529**

<u>GENERAL FORMAT FOR COBOL VERBS</u>

S <u>WRITE</u> record-name-1 [<u>FROM</u> identifier-1]

$$\left[\left\{\begin{matrix}\underline{BEFORE}\\\underline{AFTER}\end{matrix}\right\} \text{ADVANCING} \left\{\begin{matrix}\left\{\begin{matrix}\text{identifier-2}\\\text{integer-1}\end{matrix}\right\} \left[\begin{matrix}\text{LINE}\\\text{LINES}\end{matrix}\right]\\\left\{\begin{matrix}\text{mnemonic-name-1}\\\underline{PAGE}\end{matrix}\right\}\end{matrix}\right\}\right]$$

$$\left[\text{AT} \left\{\begin{matrix}\underline{END\text{-}OF\text{-}PAGE}\\\underline{EOP}\end{matrix}\right\} \text{imperative-statement-1}\right]$$

$$\left[\underline{NOT} \text{ AT} \left\{\begin{matrix}\underline{END\text{-}OF\text{-}PAGE}\\\underline{EOP}\end{matrix}\right\} \text{imperative-statement-2}\right]$$

[<u>END-WRITE</u>]

RI <u>WRITE</u> record-name-1 [<u>FROM</u> identifier-1]

    [<u>INVALID</u> KEY imperative-statement-1]

    [<u>NOT</u> <u>INVALID</u> KEY imperative-statement-2]

    [<u>END-WRITE</u>]

<u>GENERAL FORMAT FOR COPY AND REPLACE STATEMENTS</u>

<u>COPY</u> text-name-1 $\left[\left\{\begin{matrix}\underline{OF}\\\underline{IN}\end{matrix}\right\}\text{ library-name-1}\right]$

$$\left[\underline{REPLACING} \left\{\left\{\begin{matrix}\text{==pseudo-text-1==}\\\text{identifier-1}\\\text{literal-1}\\\text{word-1}\end{matrix}\right\} \underline{BY} \left\{\begin{matrix}\text{==pseudo-text-2==}\\\text{identifier-2}\\\text{literal-2}\\\text{word-2}\end{matrix}\right\}\right\} \ldots\right]$$

<u>REPLACE</u> {==pseudo-text-1== <u>BY</u> ==pseudo-text-2==} ...

<u>REPLACE</u> <u>OFF</u>

GENERAL FORMAT FOR CONDITIONS

RELATION CONDITION:

$$\begin{Bmatrix} \text{identifier-1} \\ \text{literal-1} \\ \text{arithmetic-expression-1} \\ \text{index-name-1} \end{Bmatrix} \begin{Bmatrix} \text{IS [\underline{NOT}] \underline{GREATER} THAN} \\ \text{IS [\underline{NOT}] >} \\ \text{IS [\underline{NOT}] \underline{LESS} THAN} \\ \text{IS [\underline{NOT}] <} \\ \text{IS [\underline{NOT}] \underline{EQUAL} TO} \\ \text{IS [\underline{NOT}] =} \\ \text{IS \underline{GREATER} THAN \underline{OR} \underline{EQUAL} TO} \\ \text{IS >=} \\ \text{IS \underline{LESS} THAN \underline{OR} \underline{EQUAL} TO} \\ \text{IS <=} \end{Bmatrix} \begin{Bmatrix} \text{identifier-2} \\ \text{literal-2} \\ \text{arithmetic-expression-2} \\ \text{index-name-2} \end{Bmatrix}$$

CLASS CONDITION:

$$\text{identifier-1 IS [\underline{NOT}]} \begin{Bmatrix} \underline{\text{NUMERIC}} \\ \underline{\text{ALPHABETIC}} \\ \underline{\text{ALPHABETIC-LOWER}} \\ \underline{\text{ALPHABETIC-UPPER}} \\ \text{class-name-1} \end{Bmatrix}$$

CONDITION-NAME CONDITION:

condition-name-1

SWITCH-STATUS CONDITION:

condition-name-1

SIGN CONDITION:

$$\text{arithmetic-expression-1 IS [\underline{NOT}]} \begin{Bmatrix} \underline{\text{POSITIVE}} \\ \underline{\text{NEGATIVE}} \\ \underline{\text{ZERO}} \end{Bmatrix}$$

NEGATED CONDITION:

<u>NOT</u> condition-1

GENERAL FORMAT FOR CONDITIONS

<u>COMBINED CONDITION</u>:

condition-1 $\left\{\left\{\begin{matrix}\text{AND}\\\text{OR}\end{matrix}\right\}\text{ condition-2}\right\}$ ...

<u>ABBREVIATED COMBINED RELATION CONDITION</u>:

relation-condition $\left\{\left\{\begin{matrix}\text{AND}\\\text{OR}\end{matrix}\right\}\text{ [NOT] [relational-operator] object}\right\}$ ...

GENERAL FORMAT FOR QUALIFICATION

FORMAT 1:

$$\begin{Bmatrix} \text{data-name-1} \\ \text{condition-name-1} \end{Bmatrix} \begin{Bmatrix} \left\{ \begin{Bmatrix} \underline{\text{IN}} \\ \underline{\text{OF}} \end{Bmatrix} \text{data-name-2} \right\} \dots \left[\begin{Bmatrix} \underline{\text{IN}} \\ \underline{\text{OF}} \end{Bmatrix} \begin{Bmatrix} \text{file-name-1} \\ \text{cd-name-1} \end{Bmatrix} \right] \\ \begin{Bmatrix} \underline{\text{IN}} \\ \underline{\text{OF}} \end{Bmatrix} \begin{Bmatrix} \text{file-name-1} \\ \text{cd-name-1} \end{Bmatrix} \end{Bmatrix}$$

FORMAT 2:

$$\text{paragraph-name-1} \begin{Bmatrix} \underline{\text{IN}} \\ \underline{\text{OF}} \end{Bmatrix} \text{section-name-1}$$

FORMAT 3:

$$\text{text-name-1} \begin{Bmatrix} \underline{\text{IN}} \\ \underline{\text{OF}} \end{Bmatrix} \text{library-name-1}$$

FORMAT 4:

$$\underline{\text{LINAGE-COUNTER}} \begin{Bmatrix} \underline{\text{IN}} \\ \underline{\text{OF}} \end{Bmatrix} \text{file-name-2}$$

FORMAT 5:

$$\begin{Bmatrix} \underline{\text{PAGE-COUNTER}} \\ \underline{\text{LINE-COUNTER}} \end{Bmatrix} \begin{Bmatrix} \underline{\text{IN}} \\ \underline{\text{OF}} \end{Bmatrix} \text{report-name-1}$$

FORMAT 6:

$$\text{data-name-3} \begin{Bmatrix} \begin{Bmatrix} \underline{\text{IN}} \\ \underline{\text{OF}} \end{Bmatrix} \text{data-name-4} \left[\begin{Bmatrix} \underline{\text{IN}} \\ \underline{\text{OF}} \end{Bmatrix} \text{report-name-2} \right] \\ \begin{Bmatrix} \underline{\text{IN}} \\ \underline{\text{OF}} \end{Bmatrix} \text{report-name-2} \end{Bmatrix}$$

MISCELLANEOUS FORMATS

SUBSCRIPTING:

$$\begin{Bmatrix} \text{condition-name-1} \\ \text{data-name-1} \end{Bmatrix} \quad (\begin{Bmatrix} \text{integer-1} \\ \text{data-name-2 } [\{\pm\} \text{ integer-2}] \\ \text{index-name-1 } [\{\pm\} \text{ integer-3}] \end{Bmatrix} \ldots)$$

REFERENCE MODIFICATION:

data-name-1 (leftmost-character-position: [length])

IDENTIFIER:

$$\text{data-name-1} \left[\begin{Bmatrix} \underline{\text{IN}} \\ \underline{\text{OF}} \end{Bmatrix} \text{data-name-2} \right] \ldots \left[\begin{Bmatrix} \underline{\text{IN}} \\ \underline{\text{OF}} \end{Bmatrix} \begin{Bmatrix} \text{cd-name-1} \\ \text{file-name-1} \\ \text{report-name-1} \end{Bmatrix} \right]$$

[({subscript} ...)]   [(leftmost-character-position: [length])]

GENERAL FORMAT FOR NESTED SOURCE PROGRAMS

IDENTIFICATION DIVISION.

PROGRAM-ID. program-name-1 [IS INITIAL PROGRAM].

[ENVIRONMENT DIVISION. environment-division-content]

[DATA DIVISION. data-division-content]

[PROCEDURE DIVISION. procedure-division-content]

[[nested-source-program] ...

END PROGRAM program-name-1.]

GENERAL FORMAT FOR NESTED-SOURCE-PROGRAM

IDENTIFICATION DIVISION.

PROGRAM-ID. program-name-2 $\left[IS \left\{ \begin{array}{c} \underline{COMMON} \\ \underline{INITIAL} \end{array} \right\} PROGRAM \right]$.

[ENVIRONMENT DIVISION. environment-division-content]

[DATA DIVISION. data-division-content]

[PROCEDURE DIVISION. procedure-division-content]

[nested-source-program] ...

END PROGRAM program-name-2.

GENERAL FORMAT FOR A SEQUENCE OF SOURCE PROGRAMS

{ IDENTIFICATION DIVISION.

  PROGRAM-ID. program-name-3 [IS INITIAL PROGRAM].

  [ENVIRONMENT DIVISION. environment-division-content]

  [DATA DIVISION. data-division-content]

  [PROCEDURE DIVISION. procedure-division-content]

  [nested-source-program] ...

  END PROGRAM program-name-3.} ...

  IDENTIFICATION DIVISION.

  PROGRAM-ID. program-name-4 [IS INITIAL PROGRAM].

[ENVIRONMENT DIVISION. environment-division-content]

[DATA DIVISION. data-division-content]

[PROCEDURE DIVISION. procedure-division-content]

[[nested-source-program] ...

  END PROGRAM program-name-4.]

D

ASCII CODES

Table D.1 7-bit ASCII codes and characters

	DEN	HEX	BIN	HIGH NIBBLE							
				0	16	32	48	64	80	96	112
				0	1	2	3	4	5	6	7
				000	001	010	011	100	101	110	111
	00	00	0000	NUL	DLE	Δ	0	@	P	`	p
	01	01	0001	SOH	DC1	!	1	A	Q	a	q
	02	02	0010	STX	DC2	"	2	B	R	b	r
L	03	03	0011	EXT	DC3	#	3	C	S	c	s
O	04	04	0100	EOT	DC4	$	4	D	T	d	t
W	05	05	0101	ENQ	NAK	%	5	E	U	e	u
	06	06	0110	ACK	SYN	&	6	F	V	f	v
N	07	07	0111	BEL	ETB	'	7	G	W	g	w
I	08	08	1000	BS	CAN	(	8	H	X	h	x
B	09	09	1001	HT	EM	)	9	I	Y	i	y
B	10	0A	1010	LF	SUB	*	:	J	Z	j	z
L	11	0B	1011	VT	ESC	+	;	K	[	k	{
E	12	0C	1100	FF	FS	,	<	L	\	l	|
	13	0D	1101	CR	GS	-	=	M	]	m	}
	14	0E	1110	SO	RS	.	>	N	^	n	~
	15	0F	1111	SI	US	/	?	O	_	o	DEL

Note: The binary and hexadecimal nibble values can be read directly from the table.
To find a denary value for a byte read a value from the top and then add the value to the left.

Table D.2 Non-printing characters – ASCII meanings

DEN	HEX	CODE	INPUT	ECHO	ASCII Definition
0	0	NUL	⟨CTRL⟩@	Null	
1	1	SOH	⟨CTRL⟩A	ΔA	Start of heading
2	2	STX	⟨CTRL⟩B	ΔB	Start of text
3	3	ETX	⟨CTRL⟩C	ΔC	End of text
4	4	EOT	⟨CTRL⟩D	ΔD	End of transmission
5	5	ENQ	⟨CTRL⟩E	ΔE	Enquiry
6	6	ACK	⟨CTRL⟩F	ΔF	Acknowledge
7	7	BEL	⟨CTRL⟩G	bell	Bell
8	8	BS	⟨CTRL⟩H	backspace	Backspace
9	9	HT	⟨CTRL⟩I	tab	Horizontal tab
10	A	LF	⟨CTRL⟩J	LF	Line feed
11	B	VT	⟨CTRL⟩K	4 LFs	Vertical tab
12	C	FF	⟨CTRL⟩L	8 LFs	Form feed
13	D	CR	⟨CTRL⟩M	CR LF	Carriage return
14	E	SO	⟨CTRL⟩M	ΔN	Shift out
15	F	SI	⟨CTRL⟩O	ΔO	Shift in
16	10	DLE	⟨CTRL⟩P	ΔP	Data link escape
17	11	DC1	⟨CTRL⟩Q	ΔQ	Device control 1
18	12	DC2	⟨CTRL⟩R		Device control 2
19	13	DC3	⟨CTRL⟩S		Device control 3
20	14	DC4	⟨CTRL⟩T		Device control 4
21	15	NAK	⟨CTRL⟩U	ΔU	Negative acknowledge
22	16	SYN	⟨CTRL⟩V	ΔV	Synchronous idle
23	17	ETB	⟨CTRL⟩W		End of transmission block
24	18	CAN	⟨CTRL⟩X	ΔX	Cancel
25	19	EM	⟨CTRL⟩Y	ΔY	End of medium
26	1A	SUB	⟨CTRL⟩Z	ΔZ	Substitute
27	1B	ESC	⟨CTRL⟩[	$	Escape
28	1C	FS	⟨CTRL⟩\	Δ\	File separator
29	1D	GS	⟨CTRL⟩]	Δ]	Group separator
30	1E	RS	⟨CTRL⟩Δ	$\Delta\Delta$	Record separator
31	1F	US	⟨CTRL⟩	Δ	Unit separator

E
VT TERMINALS

Function	Escape sequence
Cursor positioning:	
Move CURSOR UP Pn LINES	⟨ESC⟩[PnA
Move CURSOR DOWN Pn LINES	⟨ESC⟩[PnB
Move CURSOR RIGHT Pn COLUMNS	⟨ESC⟩[PnC
Move CURSOR LEFT Pn COLUMNS	⟨ESC⟩[PnD
Move CURSOR TO LINE Pl, COLUMN Pc	⟨ESC⟩[Pl;PcH
Move CURSOR DOWN ONE LINE	⟨ESC⟩D
Move CURSOR UP ONE LINE	⟨ESC⟩M
Move CURSOR to COLUMN ONE on NEXT LINE	⟨ESC⟩E
Editing:	
INSERT Pn LINES at cursor	⟨ESC⟩[PnL
DELETE Pn LINES from cursor	⟨ESC⟩[PnM
INSERT Pn BLANK CHARACTERS from cursor	⟨ESC⟩[Pn@
DELETE Pn CHARACTERS from CURSOR	⟨ESC⟩[PnP
Erasing control:	
ERASE cursor character and Pn-1 next chars	⟨ESC⟩[PnX
ERASE cursor character and to END OF LINE	⟨ESC⟩[K
ERASE from cursor to START OF LINE	⟨ESC⟩[1K
ERASE complete LINE	⟨ESC⟩[2K
ERASE from CURSOR to END OF SCREEN	⟨ESC⟩[J
ERASE from CURSOR to START OF SCREEN	⟨ESC⟩[1J
ERASE complete SCREEN	⟨ESC⟩[2J
Text display attributes:	
MAKE LINE with cursor TOP HALF of DOUBLE HEIGHT, DOUBLE WIDTH	⟨ESC⟩#3
Make LINE with cursor BOTTOM HALF of DOUBLE HEIGHT, DOUBLE WIDTH	⟨ESC⟩#4
Make CURSOR SINGLE HEIGHT, SINGLE WIDTH	⟨ESC⟩#5
Make CURSOR DOUBLE HEIGHT, DOUBLE WIDTH	⟨ESC⟩#6
Reset:	
Soft RESET the terminal	⟨ESC⟩[6h
Hard RESET the terminal	⟨ESC⟩c
Terminal modes:	
Select 132 COLUMN mode	⟨ESC⟩[3h
Select 80 COLUMN mode	⟨ESC⟩[3l
SHOW CURSOR	⟨ESC⟩[?25h
HIDE CURSOR	⟨ESC⟩[?25l
Select INVERSE VIDEO	⟨ESC⟩[?5h
Select NORMAL VIDEO	⟨ESC⟩[?5l

Notes:
1. Pn, Pl and Pc are all 1 to 3 ASCII digits.
2. ⟨ESC⟩ is the escape character. It is a byte with a value of 27. It is the 28th character in the ASCII collating sequence.

INDEX TO PROGRAMS AND FILES

Programs

accept1a, 247–248
accept1b, 251–253
accept2, 256–259
accept3, 261–266

batch1 for cbreak1, 391–393
bike1, 338–339
bike2, 340–341
bike3, 344

calc-resist in resist1, 352–355
cbreak1, 387–390
check1 in post4, 100–101
concat1 in string1, 97
copy1, 192–193
copy2, 195–197
copy3, 200–201
copy4 in renum1, 203–207

draw1, 26
driver1, 279–280
driver2, 299–300

echo1, 18
echo2, 24
echo3, 36
enter-play in lim1, 131–133

get-input in resist1, 351–352

get-lim in lim1, 172–173
getnum1, 243
getnum2, 245
getnum3, 245

ihandle2 in renum1, 205–206
ihandle3 in mupdate1, 413
ihandle4 in mupdate1, 412
indfhl, 433–437
indtut1, 430–433

lim1, 172–176
look-up1, 108–109
look-up2, 347

main1, 82
main2, 84
main3, 88–89
main4, 92
mencken1 in look-up1, 108–109
mencken2, 347–348
menu1 in indtut1, 432–433
merge1, 372–373
merge2, 374–376
monitor1 for simple1, 417–419
mupdate1, 409–414

nest1 in main1, 82
nest2 in main2, 84
nest3 in main3, 89
noddy1, 15

539

540 INDEX TO PROGRAMS AND FILES

ohandle1 in copy2, 196–197
ohandle2 in renum1, 206–207
ohandle4 in mupdate1, 414

post1, 45
post2, 56–57
post3, 74–75
post4, 100–101

read1, 188
refmod1, 69
renum1, 202–207
resist1, 350–355
rewrite1, 198–199
risk1, 213

screen1, 272–273
screen2, 300–301
show-board in tic1, 133–135
simple1 for mupdate1, 415–417
simple2, 422–423
simple3, 425
sort1, 360–361
sort2, 364–365
sort3, 369–371
stock1, 316–318
string1, 96–97
study-game in tic1, 135–136
study-lim in lim1, 173–176

tic1, 130–136
tinput in cbreak1, 389–390

trans1, 444–445
trans2, 449–450
trans3, 450–451
trans4, 452–453
trans5, 453–454

usage1, 308

write1, 191

Data files

batch1.dat, 383

extract1.dat, 359
extract2.dat, 362
extract3.dat, 367
extract4.dat, 371

idriver2.dat, 298
imencken.dat, 346

simple.mas;1, 402
simple.mas;2, 402
simple.trn;1, 402
simple.trn;1, 402

Copy files

rec001.cop, 288
rec002.cop, 297

INDEX TO FIGURES

1.1	COBOL's functional modules, 4	2.17	Truth table for the logical operator **or**, 38
1.2	Conforming COBOL implementations, 5	2.18	Truth table for the logical operator **not**, 39
1.3	Advantages and disadvantages of COBOL, 6	2.19	Truth value combinations for two conditions, 39
1.4	Virtual environments, 7	2.20	Result of applying the logical operator **not**, 40
1.5	Rules for forming user-defined words, 10	2.21	Result of expression-1, 40
2.1	Program noddy1, 15	2.22	Truth table proving that expression-1 and expression-2 are unequal, 40
2.2	Reference format for source code lines, 16	2.23	Truth table for the logical operator xor, 41
2.3	Program echo1, 18		
2.4	Default rules governing **accept** with alphanumeric strings, 20	2.24	Truth table proving one of De Morgan's rules, 41
2.5	Effect of **accept** on alphanumeric data items, 21	2.25	Effect of **move** on group items, 43
		2.26	Effect of **value** clause and **filler** items, 43
2.6	Program echo2, 24	2.27	Program post1, 45
2.7	Flowchart of program echo2, 25		
2.8	Program draw1, 26	3.1	Relationship between types of character strings, 51
2.9	Order of statement execution in program draw1, 27	3.2	Item levels and data classes, 52
2.10	A simple flowgraph, 28	3.3	Basic rules for making class condition tests, 52
2.11	Flowgraph with a return link, 28		
2.12	Default rules governing the use of **move** with numeric data items, 30	3.4	Program post2, 56–57
		3.5	Flowchart of program post2, 58
2.13	Effect of moving data to numeric data items, 30	3.6	Pseudo-code and flowchart for selection, 59
2.14	Relational operators, 34	3.7	Flowgraph expansion showing statement nesting, 59
2.15	Program echo3, 36		
2.16	Truth table for the logical operator **and**, 38	3.8	Truth table for the **evaluate** statement, 61

541

3.9 Valid references using reference modification, 65
3.10 Rules for using reference modification, 65
3.11 Test data for program refmod1, 66
3.12 Program refmod1, 69
3.13 Test cases for two runs of program refmod1, 70
3.14 Rules for constructing certain international postcodes, 71
3.15 Some valid postcodes, 72
3.16 Postcode patterns, 72
3.17 Program post3, 74–75
3.18 Full set of tests for postcodes in original form, 77

4.1 Structure chart for program main1, 81
4.2 Program main1 containing nested program main1, 82
4.3 Programs main2 and nest2 with two parameters, 84
4.4 Structure chart for program P, 86
4.5 Structure chart for program main2, 86
4.6 Structure chart for program main3, 86
4.7 Program main3, 88–89
4.8 Structure chart for program main4, 90
4.9 Alternative forms of representing structure for program main4, 91
4.10 Textual structure for program main4, 92
4.11 Nested calling scope for program main4, 93
4.12 Box diagram for program A, 94
4.13 Structure chart for program string1, 95
4.14 Sample test data for concatenation, 95
4.15 Program string1, 96–97
4.16 Program post4, 100–101

5.1 Common examples of table problems, 103
5.2 Some American expressions and their British counterparts, 104
5.3 Some valid statements using tables, 106
5.4 Main rules governing the use of the **redefines** clause, 107
5.5 Program look-up1 containing the nested program mencken1, 108–109
5.6 More American expressions and their British counterparts, 111
5.7 Record containing a two-level table, 112
5.8 Playing board for tic1, 116
5.9 Initial pseudo-code for program tic1, 117
5.10 Structure chart for tic1 showing input streams, 120
5.11 Data for root program tic1; flowgraph model of `w2-result`, 121
5.12 Final pseudo-code for program tic1, 122
5.13 Guidelines for writing programs, 124
5.14 Outline for program enter-play, 125
5.15 Outline for program show-board, 126
5.16 Outline for program study-game, 127
5.17 Implementation sequence for program tic1, 128
5.18 Program tic1, 130–136
5.19 Parameters used for board, 139

6.1 Three simple **string** statements, 141
6.2 Simulation outline for a **string** statement, 145
6.3 Full format and rules governing the **string** statement, 146
6.4 Using alphanumeric edit masks–space character insertions, 167
6.5 Using alphanumeric edit masks–other character insertions, 167
6.6 Using numeric edit masks–space character insertions, 168
6.7 Input layout for lim1, 168
6.8 Layout for error messages for lim1, 169
6.9 Output layout for lim1, 169
6.10 Structure chart for lim1, 171
6.11 Program lim1, 172–176

7.1 Legal **open** statements, 185
7.2 Order of execution of file operations, 186
7.3 Program read1, 188
7.4 Program write1, 191
7.5 Program copy1, 192–193
7.6 Relationship between loop and files in program copy1, 194
7.7 Structure chart for copy2, 194
7.8 Program copy2, 195–197
7.9 Program rewrite1, 198–199
7.10 Program copy3, 200–201
7.11 Decision tree for program renum1, 201
7.12 Structure chart for renum1, 202
7.13 Program renum1, 202–207

8.1 Four quadrants of a decision table, 209
8.2 Decision table with one condition–two rules, 210
8.3 Decision table with two conditions–four rules, 210
8.4 Decision table with three conditions–eight rules, 212
8.5 Program risk1, 213
8.6 Decision table for three risk conditions–seven rules, 214

INDEX TO FIGURES 543

8.7	Decision table using abbreviated rules, 214	9.17	Program accept1a, 247–248
8.8	Mutually exclusive rules for six conditions, 216	9.18	Comparative outlines for programs accept1a and accept1b, 250
8.9	Version of Fig. 8.8 but with rules rotated, 216	9.19	Program accept1b, 251–253
8.10	Possible priority conditions for a text file, 217	9.20	Valid test cases for signed number input, 254
8.11	Two binary decision trees for three conditions, 218	9.21	Strategy for signed numbers, 255
		9.22	Program accept2, 256–259
8.12	Decision table with ambiguous rules, 220	9.23	Strategy for signed numbers with decimal points, 260
8.13	Binary decision tree demonstrating ambiguity, 220	9.24	Program accept3, 261–266
		9.25	Detailed system specification for program accept3, 267–268
8.14	Incomplete and ambiguous decision table, 221	9.26	Program accept3 viewed as a filter, 269
8.15	Incomplete decision table without ambiguity, 221	9.27	Some examples of VT control codes, 271
8.16	Full format–**evaluate** statement, 222	9.28	Effect of using a symbolic character within a COBOL program, 272
8.17	**Evaluate**–compatible subject and object lists, 223	9.29	Program screen1, 272–273
		9.30	Screen image for program busy1, 275
8.18	Myers' checklist for test data for the 'triangle problem', 225	10.1	Program classification–four main ways, 278
8.19	Comparing the length of the three sides, 226	10.2	Relationship between separately compiled and nested programs, 279
8.20	Right-angled triangle, 226		
8.21	Steps in solving the triangle problem, 227	10.3	Program driver1–a driver to test program accept3, 279–280
8.22	Structure chart for angle1, 229	10.4	Developing a main program and an external called program, 282
9.1	Decoding a Roman numeral into modern denary notation, 234	10.5	Program driver1 linked to three programs, 284
9.2	Number line in denary, 234	10.6	Main6–resolution of program-names, 285
9.3	Denary, hexadecimal and binary compared, 235	10.7	Main6–structure chart, 286
		10.8	Using the **copy** statement, 288
9.4	Comparing binary to hexadecimal, 236	10.9	Calling relationships using the **common** attribute, 290
9.5	Converting a nibble from binary to hexadecimal by adding powers of 2, 237	10.10	Outline for main7 with a common program, 291
9.6	Converting a nibble from hexadecimal to binary by subtracting powers of 2, 237	10.11	Structure chart–main7, 292
		10.12	Alternative structure for Fig. 10.9, 293
9.7	Different contexts for the "–" character, 238	10.13	Outline for program main8–**global** names, 294
9.8	7-bit ASCII codes and characters, 239	10.14	Main8–structure chart notation for **global** data, 295
9.9	Creating a text file to dump, 241		
9.10	Dump of a text file, 242	10.15	Parameter record in text file rec002.cop, 297
9.11	Program getnum1, 243		
9.12	Test cases for program getnum1, 243	10.16	Structure chart for driver2 calling screen2, 297
9.13	Some different COBOL compiler implementations for accepting numbers, 244	10.17	File idriver2.dat–test cases for program driver2, 298
		10.18	Program driver2, 299–300
9.14	Program getnum2, 245	10.19	Program screen2, 300–301
9.15	Program getnum3, 245		
9.16	Strategy for unsigned numbers, 246	11.1	Categories and pictures, 304

544 INDEX TO FIGURES

11.2 Relationship between level type, class, and category, 306
11.3 Three different ways to define display usage, 307
11.4 Program usage1, 308
11.5 Typical storage strategy for binary numbers, 309
11.6 Six valid record definitions to illustrate the usage **binary**, 310
11.7 Typical storage strategy for usage **packed–decimal**, 311
11.8 Effect of **move** statement by category of source and target, 312
11.9 Data requirements and choice of representation, 313
11.10 Usage in COBOL, 313
11.11 Program stock1, 316–318

12.1 Arithmetic rules and operators, 326

13.1 Program bike1, 338–339
13.2 Program bike2, 340–341
13.3 Search space reductions for a table of 64 elements, 343
13.4 Program bike3, 344
13.5 File imencken.dat containing data for a table, 346
13.6 Program look-up2, 347
13.7 Program mencken2, 347–348
13.8 Resistor colour codes, 349
13.9 Program resist1, 350–355

14.1 Ten unsorted records, 358
14.2 Unordered book extracts and sort record description (file extract1.dat), 359
14.3 Program sort1, 360–361
14.4 Book extracts in order by author, site, and year (file extract2.dat), 362
14.5 Using a filter program prior to a sort, 363
14.6 Program sort2, 364–365
14.7 Schematic structure of program sort2, 366
14.8 Input filtered book extracts (file extract3.dat), 367
14.9 Schematic structure of program sort3, 368
14.10 Program sort3, 369–371
14.11 Input and output filtered book extracts (file extract4.dat), 371
14.12 Program merge1, 372–373
14.13 Program merge2, 374–376

15.1 Control break example–daily production, 379
15.2 Tree to identify five processing points, 380
15.3 Operation relationships between input and output streams, 381
15.4 Test input file (batch1.dat), 383
15.5 Outline for input handler (program tinput), 384
15.6 Outline for the root program (program cbreak1), 384
15.7 Tree identifying levels–control break, 385
15.8 Keys and actions–control break, 386
15.9 Outline for application (program batch1), 386
15.10 Program cbreak1, 387–390
15.11 Program batch1, 391–393

16.1 SIMPLE bank–master, 398
16.2 SIMPLE bank–record layout and transactions, 399
16.3 Effect of processing a set of transactions on a master, 400
16.4 SIMPLE bank–transactions, 400
16.5 Run chart for the SIMPLE update, 401
16.6 SIMPLE bank–files for the first two runs, 402
16.7 Keys and actions–master file update, 403
16.8 Outline for the root (program mupdate1), 403
16.9 Tree identifying levels–master file update, 404
16.10 Structure chart for mupdate1, 406
16.11 Program mupdate1, 409–414
16.12 Program simple1, 415–417
16.13 Program monitor1, 417–419

17.1 Program simple2, 422–423
17.2 Program simple3, 425
17.3 Relationship between operations and modes, 427
17.4 Ordered set of operations for an indexed file, 429
17.5 Structure chart for indtut1, 430
17.6 Program indtut1, 430–433
17.7 Program indfh1, 433–437

18.1 Program trans1, 444–445
18.2 Flowchart of program trans1, 446–447
18.3 Program trans2, 449–450
18.4 Program trans3, 450–451
18.5 Program trans4, 452–453
18.6 Program trans5, 453–454

SUBJECT INDEX

A margin, *See* **Margin**
'a' **picture** symbol, 50, 306
Abbreviated combined relation condition, *See* **Condition**
Abstraction, 463
    data, 469
    procedural, 61, 343, 362, 480
Accept statement, 190–192, 441
    alphanumeric, 20–21
    numeric data, 242–249
Access clause:
    dynamic, 421, 426–429
    random, 421, 424–426
    sequential, 421–424
Action entry, 209
Action stub, 209
Actual decimal point, *See* **Decimal point**
Add statement, 329
Adding a file record, 190–192, 401
Address in memory, 310
Advancing phrase, *See* **Write**
After phrase, *See* **Inspect**; **Write**
Algorithm design, 378–387, 402–404
Alignment boundaries for data, 20, 30, 166, 310
All:
    with figurative constant, *See* **Figurative constant**
    with literal, *See* **Figurative constant**
    See also **Inspect**; **Search all**

Alphabetic:
    category, 303–306
    data item, 50–51, 306
Alphabetic class tests, 51–54
Alphanumeric:
    category, 303–306
    character, 18
    class, 51–52
    data item, 18, 304–306
    edited data item, 304–306
Also phrase, *See* **Evaluate**
Alter statement, 441
Alternate key, *See* **Key**
Ambiguity, 220
And logic, 38–40
Any, *See* **Evaluate**
ANSI, 4
Application programmer, 8–9
Areas A and B, 16
Argument, *See* Searching; Table-handling
Arithmetic:
    expression, 326–327
    operator, 326
    statement, 323–332
Ascending phrase, *See* **Merge**; **Occurs**; **Search all**; **Sort**
ASCII, 238–242
Assign clause, 181–182
Assumed decimal point, *See* **Decimal point**
Asterisk '*':

545

546 SUBJECT INDEX

comment line, 16
picture symbol, 167
At end–of–page phrase, *See* **Eop** phrase
At end phrase, *See* **End** phrase
At eop phrase, *See* **Eop** phrase

B margin, *See* Margin
'b' **picture** symbol, 167
Base numbers, *See* Number
Batch processing, 379–393
Before phrase, *See* **Inspect**; **Perform**; **Write**
Binary usage, *See* **Usage** clause
Binary:
   condition, *See* Condition
   numbers, *See* Number
   search, *See* Searching
Bit, 235
Bottom, *See* **Linage**
Bottom-up, 128–129
Boundary alignment, *See* Alignment boundaries for data
Box diagram, 92
Braces, 11
Brackets, 11
Buffer, 70, 186–187
By, *See* **Divide**; **Inspect**; **Multiply**; **Perform**
By Content phrase, *See* Parameters
By Reference phrase, *See* Parameters
Byte, 235, *See also* Slack byte

Calculations, 323–336
Call resolution, 284–285
Call statement, 81, 282–283
Called program, *See* Program
Calling program, *See* Program
Cancel statement, 441–442
Carriage control for printer, 393–395
Case structure, *See* **Evaluate**
Category of data, 303–306
Cathode ray tube, *See* Terminal
Central processing unit, *See* CPU
Character, *See* Character set and ASCII
Character set, 51–53
Character-string, 20, 30, 140
Characters by clause, *See* **Inspect**
Choice indicators, 11
Class condition, *See* Condition
Class-name, 52
Class of data, 51–53, 303–306
Class test, 51–55
Close statement, 185
COBOL:
   1974 standard, 3–4, 444–455
   acronym, 3

advantages and disadvantages, 5–6
coding format, 16
dialects, 6–7
element, 16
formats, *See* General formats
history, 3–5
machine independence, 6
module, 4–5
reference format, 16
reserved word, 9, 458–462
sentence, 16
standard, xiii–xiv, 3–4, 244–245, 448
statement, 16
word, 16
CODASYL, 3
Column alignment, 16
Comment, 16–17
Common attribute, 289
Common program, *See* Program
Communication module, 4, 441
Compute statement, 11, 29, 32–33, 323–329
Computational usage, *See* **Usage** clause
Comp usage, *See* **Usage** clause
Comp–3 usage, *See* **Usage** clause
Comparison of operands, *See* Condition
Compatibility:
   operands, 34, *See also* Condition
   subject and object, *See* **Evaluate**
Compilation unit, 278–282
Compiler-directing statement, *See* **Copy** statement
Completeness, 214
Complex condition, *See* Condition
Compound condition, *See* Condition
Concatenation, 95
Concordance, 376–377
Condition, 33
   abbreviated combined relation condition, 463
   binary condition, 212
   class condition, 53
   combined condition, *See* complex condition
   complex condition, 37–40, 467
   compound condition, *See* complex condition
   condition entry, 34–35, 209
   condition stub, 209
   conditional tests, 23
   condition-name, 34–35
   condition-name condition, 34–37
   list of conditions, *See* **Evaluate**
   order of evaluation, 38, 319
   nonnumeric operands, 23–26, 37–40
   numeric operands, 37–40
   simple condition, 33–37
   subject and object, *See* **Evaluate**

SUBJECT INDEX

with figurative constant, 31–33, 383–384
   See also File; Searching
Configuration section, 271
Constant, *See* Figurative constant
Constructing edit masks, *See* Editing
Contained program, *See* Program
Content phrase, *See* Parameter
Continue statement, 73, 443
Control breaks, 378–419
   control keys, 379, 383–384, 403
   initializing control values, 383–384, 402–403
Control codes, *See* VT Control codes
Control line, 81
Conversion:
   between number bases, *See* Number
   between usages, 309–316
Converting phrase, *See* **Inspect**
Copy statement, 287–289, 442
   replacing option, 442
Copying files, 192–194
   blank lines, 193
Corresponding option, *See* **Move**
Count phrase, 154
Counter, 27, 29
Coupling, 249, 448, 468
CPU efficiency and usages, 309–316
CRT (Cathode ray tube), *See* Terminal
CTL key, 240–241
Current key, *See* Control breaks
Cursor control, 271–275

Data:
   abstraction, *See* Abstraction
   description entry, *See* entry
   entry, 18
   item, *See* Elementary data; Group data
   validation, 50, 152–156, 269–270, 314–316
Databases, 180
Data division, 15
Data-name, 18
   conventions, 26
   identifier, 9, 19
   qualified, 9
Date, **Day** and **Day-of-week** options, 441–516
DCL, *See* VAX
Debug module
Decimal point, 260–266
   actual, 304, 315
   assumed, *See* implied
   implied, 304, 315
Decision:
   symbol, 25
   table, 209
Decomposition, 60

Declaratives, 443
Delete statement, 491
Deleting a file record, 198–199, 428
Delimited phrase, *See* **String**; **Unstring**
Delimiter phrase, 154
Delimiters, 14, 142
De Morgan's laws, 41–42
Denary, *See* Numbers
Depending clause:
   tables, *See* Table-handling
   files, *See* Files
Depending phrase, *See* Go to
Descending clause, *See* **Occurs**; **Merge**; **Sort**
Description of a file, *See* **FD**; **SD**
Designing structured programs, *See* Program
Desk-checking COBOL programs, *See* Program
Detailed system specification, 267–268
Digital Command Language (DCL), *See* VAX
Display:
   statement, 15, 21–23
   usage, *See* Usage clause
Divide statement, 331–332
Division by zero, 324
Divisions in COBOL program, *See* Program
Documentation, 37, 79, 86, 102, 219, 266–268, 270, 295, 302
Dollar sign, *See* Editing
Down by phrase, 338–339
Driver, *See* Program
Dump, 241–242
Duplicates phrase
   alternate keys, 502
   sorting, *See* **Sort**
Duplicate:
   input keys, *See* **Sort**
   output files, *See* Sorting
   output keys, *See* Merging
Dynamic access, *See* **Access** clause

Editing:
   alphabetic fields, 306
   alphanumeric fields, 306
   edit masks, 167–168
   floating dollar sign, 316
   numeric fields, 168, 315–316, 306
   slant insertion, 167
   space insertion, 167
   zero insertion, 167
Element, *See* COBOL; Table-handling
Elementary item, 17–18
Ellipsis, 11
Else phrase, *See* **If** statement
Embedded spaces, 76
End of data, 242

SUBJECT INDEX

End of file, *See* File
End–of–page phrase, *See* **Eop** phrase
END phrase, *See* **Read**; **Return**; **Search all**; **Search**; **String**
End program header, 15
END-statement delimiter, *See* Scope termination
Eof condition, *See* File
Eop phrase, 393–394
Environment, *See* Virtual environment
Environment division, 15, 181, 271
Equality, *See* Relational operators
Equivalence, 63
ESC, 240–241, 271
Escape statement, 251
Evaluate statement, 53–64, 222–224
   also phrase, 222–223
   any phrase, 215
   list of conditions, 222
   object, 223
   other, 60, 64, 247
   subject, 223
   when phrase, 54, 60
Evaluation, *See* Condition
Execution, *See* Program
Exit program statement, 81
Explicit scope termination, *See* Scope termination
Exponentiation, 326
Extend phrase, *See* **Open**
Extensions to COBOL compiler, *See* COBOL – standard
External:
   name, 181, 186
   program, *See* Program
   transaction, 399–402
External attribute, 293–296

False, 27, 34, 55
Fanning, 287
FD (File description entry), *See* File
Field, 472
   See also Variable; Data item
Figurative constant, 31–32, 143–144, 157
   all, 156–157
   high–value, 383, 403
   low–value, 383, 403
   space, 31–32
   zero, 31–32
File, 179–208, 443–444
   connector, 186
   depending clause, 182
   description entry, *See* **FD**
   end of file condition, 381–383
   entry, *See* **FD**

eof, *See* end of file condition
FD, 182
file-name, 181, 293, 363, 368
fixed-length record, 182, 444–478, 473
indexed file, 180, 421–439
merge, *See* **Merge** statement
mode, 181, 185–186, 427
operations, 179, 186, 427
sequential file, 180–207, 378–419
sort file, *See* Sorting
variable-length record, 180–182, 184, 193
File–control paragraph, 181
File section, 182
Filler reserved word, 42–43
Filtering, 269–270, 363
Fixed-length records, *See* File
Flow of control, 24
Flowchart, 25
Flowgraph, 28
Footing, 393
Formats, 10–11, 488–535
   full, 488–497
   general, 498–435
   simple, 10–11
   See also Reference format
FORTRAN, 6, 444
Forward, *See* Escape statement
From phrase, *See* **Release**; **Rewrite**; **Subtract**; **Write**
Full formats, *See* Formats
Function mapping, *See* Filters
Functionality, 4

General formats, *See* Formats
Giving phrase, *See* **Add**; **Divide**; **Merge**; **Multiply**; **Sort**; **Subtract**
Global attribute, 293–296
Go to:
   depending phrase, 442
   statement, 249–253, 442, 448
   used to implement Escape, *See* Escape
Group item, 42–43
Guidelines for writing programs, *See* Program

Hard-coding table values, *See* Table-handling
Header, 379
Hexadecimal, *See* Number
High-order truncation or padding, *See* Justification
High–value, *See* Figurative constant
Hopper, Grace, 3
Hyphen:
   different contexts, 238
   '-' continuation line, 16
   '-' operator, *See* Arithmetic operator

Identification division, 15
Identifier:
  general, 9, 18, 105
  qualification, *See* Qualification
  See also Scope
If statement, 442
Imperative statement, 475
Implementation sequence, 128
Implementor, 8, 475
Implementor-name, 475
Implied decimal point, *See* Decimal point
In, *See* Qualification
Index usage, *See* **Usage** clause
Indexed file, *See* File
Indexes, *See* Table-handling
Indicator area, 16
Indirectly contained program, *See* Program
Information:
  codes, 237–242
  hiding, 95
Initial attribute, 289
Initial phrase, 521
Initial state of program, 24–29, 289
Initialize statement, 520
Initializing:
  counter, 27–29
  field, 20, 29
  table, *See* Table-handling
  with **VALUE** clause, 42–44
  See also Initial state of program
In-line **perform** statement, 23–29
Input:
  data validation, *See* Data validation
  file, *See* File
  stream, 120
Input handler, *See* Program
Input–output section, 181
Input phrase, *See* **Open**
Input procedure, *See* **Sort**
Inspect statement, 160–166, 493
  after phrase, 162, 493
  all, 162–163, 493
  before phrase, 493
  characters by, 493
  converting phrase, 161–163
  delimiter-list, 493
  leading, 161, 493
  replace-list, 162–164, 493
  tally-list, 161–162, 164, 493
Instruction formats, *See* Formats
Interactive terminal, *See* Terminal
Interface, 8
  See also Parameters
Intermediate results, 327

Internal:
  data representation, 312
  name, 181, 186
  program, *See* Program
  transaction, 404–405
Inter-program communication, 80
Into phrase, *See* **Divide**; **Read**; **Return**; **String**; **Unstring**
Invalid phrase, *See* **Delete**; **Read**; **Rewrite**; **Start**; **Write**
I–O phrase, *See* **Open**
Item, *See* Elementary item; Group item
Iteration, 23

Jackson's Structured Method (JSP), 382
Justification:
  just right clause, 166–167, 247–249
  justify right clause, *See* **just right** clause
  left, 20
  right, 30
  See also **just right** clause

Keys:
  alternate key, 443
  primary key, 422, 426–428
  See also Control breaks; **Merge**; **Sort**; Table-handling
Keywords, 11

Language:
  formats, *See* Formats
  reference format, *See* Reference format
Leading, *See* **Inspect**; **Sign separate**
Leap year, 332
Left-justify, *See* Justification
Level:
  COBOL language modules, 5
  concept relating to records, 303–306
  control breaks, *See* Control breaks
  nested programs, *See* Program
  numbers, *See* 01-level number, etc.
Level-88 item, *See* Condition-name
Linage clause, 393–394
Linage–counter, *See* **Linage** clause
Link in flowgraph, 28
Linkage editor, *See* Linker
Linkage section, 83
Linker, 81, 281, 284–285
List of conditions, *See* **Evaluate** statement
Literal:
  all, *See* Figurative constant
  nonnumeric, 14–15, 21–23
  numeric, 30
Local names, 81

550 SUBJECT INDEX

Logarithmic search, *See* Search – binary
Logical:
    operator, 37
    record, 186, 393
Looping, *See* Iteration
Low-order truncation or padding, *See*
        Justification
Low–value, *See* Figurative constant
Lowercase letters, 10, 239

Machine independence, *See* COBOL
Mapping, *See* Filter
Margins, *See* Reference format
Masks, *See* Editing
Master file, 397–398, 402
Master file update, 397–420
Memory, *See* CPU efficiency and usage
Merge statement, 372
    ascending phrase
    descending phrase
    output procedure, 373
Merging, 371–376
    records with duplicate keys, 373–376
    merge file, 372
Mode, *See* File mode; **Access** clause
Module:
    COBOL language module, 4–5, 440–441
    program module, *See* Program
Move statement:
    alphanumeric, 17
    corresponding option, 442
    data conversion, 312
    figurative constants, 31–32
    group items, 43
    numeric, 27, 30–31
    rules governing alphanumeric moves, 21–23
Multi-level:
    control breaks, *See* Control breaks
    table, *See* Table-handling
Multiply statement, 330–331.
Myers, Glenford J., 225

Name:
    condition, *See* Condition-name
    data, *See* Data-name
    file, *See* File-name
    implementor, *See* Implementor-name
    index, *See* index-name
    program, *See* Program
    qualification, *See* Qualification
Natural number, *See* Number
Nested:
    program, *See* Program
    statement, *See* Statement
    table, *See* Table-handling

Next phrase, *See* **Read**
Next sentence phrase, 442–443
Nibble, 235–237, 239
Nim, 335–336
Nonnumeric literal, *See* Literal
Not:
    logical operator, 38–39
    with relational operators, 34
    See also **Evaluate**
Not end phrase, *See* **End** phrase
Not eop phrase, *See* **Eop** phrase
Not invalid key phrase, *See* **Invalid key** phrase
Not overflow phrase, *See* **Overflow** phrase
Not size error phrase, *See* **Size error** phrase
Nucleus module, 4
Number:
    bases, 235
    binary, 235–240, 309
    conversion between bases, 237, 355–356
    denary, 234
    efficiency and usage, 308–316
    hexadecimal, 235–242
    natural, 233–235
    other languages, 444
    Roman numerals, 233–234
    scaled input, 260–266
    signed input, 253–259
    unsigned input, 242–249
Numeric:
    data item, 26, 30
    edited data item, 306, 315–316
    field, 30
    input data, 138–139, *See also* Number
    literal, *See* Literal
    unedited data, 138–139
Numeric class test, 51–55, 246

Object, *See* **Evaluate** statement
Object:
    code, 277
    file, 81
    list, 223
    module, 81
Obsolete language elements, 441–444
Occurrence operator, *See* **Picture**
Occurs clause, 104
    See also **Move**; **Redefines**; **Search**; **Set**; **Value**
Of, *See* Qualification
Ohms, 349
Open statement:
    extend phrase, 197
    input phrase, 184–187
    I–O phrase, 197, 424–428
    output phrase, 184–187, 422–424
Operand, 33–34, 40, 46, 327, 332, 478

SUBJECT INDEX

Operating system, 7–8
Operator:
  arithmetic, 326
  logical, 37
  occurrence operator, *See* **Picture**
  relational, 34
Or logic, 38
Order of evaluation, *See* Condition
Ordinal position, 271
  See also Number
Other, 60, 64
Out-of-line perform statement, 444–447
Output:
  file, *See* File
  handler, *See* Program
Output phrase, *See* Open
Output procedure, *See* **Sort** statement; **Merge** statement
Overflow phrase, *See* **Call**; **String**; **Unstring**

'p' **picture** symbol, 482
Packed-decimal usage, *See* **Usage**
Padding, *See* Justification
Page control for reports, *See* **Write**; Reports
Page option, *See* **Write**
Palindrome, 79, 334
Paragraph, 15, 22, 181, 187, 249–251, 271, 274, 365–366, 442, 448, 449
Parameters, 83
  content, 83
  design, 246–248
  reference, 83
Parentheses:
  arithmetic expression, 326
  occurrence operator, *See* **Picture**
  reference modification, 64
  subscripting, 105
Pascal language, 6, 180, 444
Pascal's triangle, 334–335
Path, 81
Perform statement, 23–26
  test after phrase, 442
  test before phrase
  times phrase, 442
  thru option, 442
  varying phrase, 442
Physical record-blocking, 443
Picture clause, 18
  character-string, 19
  currency sign, 469
  occurrence operator, 19
  sign separate clause, 253–254
  synchronized clause, 311
  usage clause, *See* **Usage** clause

Pointer phrase:
  string statement, 144–145
  unstring statement, 157
Postcodes, 71–77
Powers, *See* Number; Exponentiation
Precedence, 38
Prefix conventions, 18, 27, 139, 359, 366, 442
Previous key, *See* Control breaks
Primary key, *See* Key
Procedural abstraction, *See* Abstraction
Procedure, 480
  See also Subroutine; Program
Procedure division, 15
Process symbol, 25
Program:
  called program, 81, 278
  calling program, 81, 278
  common program, 289–293
  design, 124, 387–393, 405–419
  directly contained program, 80–93, 284–285
  drivers, 279–281, 297–301
  external, 278
  guidelines for writing, 124–126
  implementation sequence, 127–128
  indirectly contained program, 93, 284–285
  input handler, 205–206, 412, 413
  internal, 278
  module, *See* called program; calling program
  nesting, 80–93, 278–279
  output handler, 196–197, 206–207, 414
  run unit organization, 279–287
  structured, 444–455
  traditional, *See* unstructured
  unstructured, 444–455
Program–id paragraph, 15, 291
Programming, *See* Program
Program-name, *See* **Program–id**
Pseudo-code, 29, 124

Qualification, 9, 480, 497
Quotation mark, 14

Random access, *See* **Access** clause
Read statement, 444
  indexed I-O, 424
  next phrase, 436, 523
  sequential I-O, 186
Record:
  concepts, 17, 42, 293–296
  description, 42–47, 51
  fixed-length records, *See* File
  linkage records, *See* **Linkage**
  locking, 443–444
  logical, 17, 42
  physical, 479

Record—*cont.*
   variable-length record, *See* File
   working-storage record, 17, 42
Record clause, 182
Recursion, 285, 481
Redefines clause, 106–107, 114–115, 190, 254, 295–296, 303, 305, 315, 320, 356, 399
   synchronized clause
   value clause, 106
Reference format, 16
Reference modification, 64–71
   tables, *See* Table-handling
Reference phrase, *See* Parameter
Relation condition, *See* Condition
Relational operators, 34
Relative:
   file, 180
   I-O module, 4, 440
Release statement, 366–367
Remainder clause, *See* **Divide**
Replacing:
   phrase, *See* **Inspect**
   option, *See* **Copy**
Report writer module, 4, 441
Reports, 379–396
Reserved words, 10, 458–462
Resistance, 349
Resolution, *See* **Call** statement
Return:
   key, 20–21, 241
   link in flowgraph, 28
   of control, 81
Return statement, 366–368
Rewrite statement, 428
   indexed I-O, 428
   sequential I-O, 197
Right-justify, 30, 166
   See Justification
Roman numeral, *See* Number
Root, 81, 278
Rotated rules, 216
Rounded phrase, 323
Rules, 384–385
   See also **Evaluate** statement
Run unit, 284–285

's' picture symbol, 253–254, 304
Scaled numbers, *See* Number
Scanner, 482
Scanning, *See* **Inspect**; **String**; **Unstring**
Scope:
   delimiters, *See* Scope termination or delimitation
   local scope, 83, 477
   of calls, 92–93
   of control, 23–24, 287
   of names, 83, 90–94, 293
   of statements, 54, 54
Scope termination or delimitation:
   explicit, 141, 159, 326, 443, 450, 455, 470, 472
   implicit, 475
   See also Imperative statement
Screen management, 270–275
SD, *See* Sorting
Search all statement, 342–346
   ascending clause, 343
   conditions, *See* **end** and **when** phrases
   descending clause, 343
   end phrase, 345
   when phrase, 345
Search statement, 339–342
   conditions, *See* **end** phrase; **when** phrase
   end phrase, 340, 342
   varying phrase, 442
   when phrase, 339–340, 342
Searching:
   binary search, 342
   search argument, 339
   sequential search, 339
Secondary key, *See* Alternate key
Section, 15, 363–366
   procedure division, 365, 448
   sort procedures, 363, 365
Segmentation module, 4, 441
Select clause:
   indexed I-O, 422–428
   sequential I-O, 181
Selection, 54, 59
Semantics, 68, 113, 146
Sentence, 483
   See also Imperative statement
Separately compiled program, 93–94, 277–283, 390
Sequence, 23, 483
Sequence number area, 16
Sequential:
   access, *See* **Access** clause
   file, *See* File
   I-O module, 4
   organization, 483
   search, *See* **Search** statement
Set statement, 55, 61, 337–338
SHIFT key, 240–241
Short circuit evaluation, 319
Sign separate clause, *See* **Picture**
Signed number, *See* Number
Signed numeric field, 304
Simple:
   bank, 397–420

conditions, *See* Condition
formats, *See* Formats
Single-level:
    control break, *See* Control breaks
    table, *See* Table-handling
Size error phrase, 323–325
    See also **Add**; **Computer**; **Divide**; **Multiply**; **Subtract**
Slack byte, 311
Slant, 16
    '/' comment line, 16
    '/' **picture** symbol, 167
Slash, *See* Slant
Solidus, *See* Slant
Sort statement, 360
    ascending phrase, 363
    descending phrase, 363
    duplicates phrase, 526
    input procedure, 363–366
    key, 358–360
    output procedure, 367–371
Sorting, 358–371
    duplicate input records, 526
    duplicate output files, 360
    SD, 362
    sort file, 362–368
    sort-merge description entry, *See* SD
    sort-merge entry, *See* SD
    sort-merge module, 4, 358–371
Space, *See* Figurative constant
Space insertion editing, *See* Editing
Special–names paragraph, 271
Special:
    character, 239, 270–272
    registers, 484
Standard:
    COBOL, *See* COBOL
    deviation, 334
Start statement, 427
Statement, 16, 441–443, 484
    nesting, 59–60, 251
    See also Imperative statement
Stop run statement, 15, 81
String, *See* character-string
String statement, 140–151
Structure chart, 80–81
Structured:
    programming, *See* Program
    testing, *See* Top-down
Subject, *See* **Evaluate** statement
Subprogram, *See* Called program
Subroutine:
    paragraph, *See* Paragraph
    section, *See* Section
Subscripting, 105, 337–338

Subtract statement, 330
Symbolic–character, *See* **Symbolic** clause
Symbolic clause, 271
Synchronized clause, *See* **Picture**
Syntax, 10–13

Table-handling, 103–139, 337–359
    argument, 103, 339
    ascending phrase, 343
    binary search, *See* **Search**
    calculating table size, 110–112, 114–115
    conditions, *See* **end** and **when**
    decision table, *See* Decision table
    depending clause, 346–349
    descending phrase, 343
    efficiency, 343
    elements, 104
    end phrase, 340, 342
    entries, *See* **occurs**
    hard-coding table values, 106, 338
    index clause, 337–338
    initializing, 106, 333, 346–349, 345
    logarithmic relationship, 343
    matching correct entry, 110, 339
    multiple-level (nested tables), 111–116
    occurs clause, 104
    reading in values, 346–349
    redefines clause, 106–107
    reference modification and subscripting, 115
    search all statement, 339, 342–349
    search statement, 339–342
    serial search, 103–139
    See also **search**
    single-level, 106
    subscript, 105, 112–114, 337–338
    value clause, 106, 338
    variable-length, 346–349
    when phrase, 339, 342
Tagged records, 376
Tallying phrase:
    inspect statement, 161
    unstring statement, 154
Tasks, 81
Terminal, 405, 270–272
Terminal symbol, 25
Terminology, 25
Test:
    class, *See* Class test
    condition-name, *See* Condition
    relational, *See* Condition
Test after loop, *See* **Perform**
Test before loop, *See* **Perform**
Test cases, 70, 243, 254, 298
Test driver, *See* Program

Test for errors, 51, 68–70, 98, 128–129, 136–137, 243, 254, 269, 298
Text:
  editor
  file, 179
  string, *See* Character-string
Three-level table, *See* Table-handling
Through phrase, *See* **Thru** phrase
Thru phrase:
  value clause, 36
  See also **Evaluate**; **Merge**; **Perform**; **Sort**
Time option, 516
Times phrase, 442
Top, *See* **Linage**
Top-down:
  coding and testing, 128–129
  design, 116–128
Tracing, 27–28
Traditional programming, *See* Program
Trailer, 379
Trailing, *See* **Sign separate**
Trailing spaces, 20, 189
Transaction:
  file, 399–402
  type, 398, 400–401
Transfer of control, *See* Flow of control
Trap, *See* Validation trap
Tree, 81, 379–380
Triangle problem, 224–227
True, 27, 34, 55, 61
Truncation, *See* Justification
Truth tables, 37–42, 61
Two-level table, *See* Table-handling

Unreachable statements, 19
Unsigned number, *See* Number
Unstring statement, 151–160
Unstructured programming, *See* Program
Until phrase, *See* **Perform**
Up by phrase, 338–339
Uppercase letters, 10, 239
Usage clause, 307–314
  binary (**comp**; **computational**), 314
  display, 307
  index, 313–314
  packed-decimal (**comp-3**), 311–313
User-defined words, 10
Using phrase:
  call statement
  merge statement
  procedure division header, 84
  sort statement, 360

'v' **picture** symbol, 304, 482
Validation:
  of data, *See* Data validation
  trap, 129
Value clause, 35, 44
Value of id clause, 183
Variable, 66, 70, 107, 209, 303–305, 312, 487
  See also Field item; Data item
Variable length:
  record, *See* File
  table, *See* Table-handling
Variety:
  decision tables, 212
  reduction, 76
Varying, *See* Record clause
Varying phrase, *See* **Perform**; **Search**
VAX and VAX/VMS, 240–241, 282, 395, 448
VDU (Visual Display Unit), *See* Terminal
Venn diagram, 91
Verb, 487
Virtual environment, 7–8
Visual Display Unit, *See* Terminal
VT control codes, 271

When phrase, *See* **Evaluate**; **Search**; **Search all**
With duplicates phrase, *See* **Duplicates** phrase
With no advancing phrase, *See* **Write**
With Pointer phrase, *See* **Pointer** phrase
With test phrase, *See* **Perform**
Word, 10, 16, 307
Working-storage section, 17
Write statement:
  after phrase, 393–394
  before phrase, 529
  indexed I-O, 424
  page option, 442
  reports, 393
  sequential I-O, 187

'x' **picture** symbol, 19
Xor logic, 41

'z' **picture** symbol, 168
Zero, *See* Figurative constant
Zero:
  divisor, 324
  suppression editing, 167

01-level number, 17, 42, 83, 183, 296
02-49 level numbers, 42
88-level number, *See* condition-name

>, <, =, Relations, *See* Relational operators
+, –, *, /, **, Operators, *See* Arithmetic operators
– continuation line, 16
* comment line, 16
/ page throw, 16
'/' **picture** symbol, 167